PHOTOGRAPH LIKE A THIEF

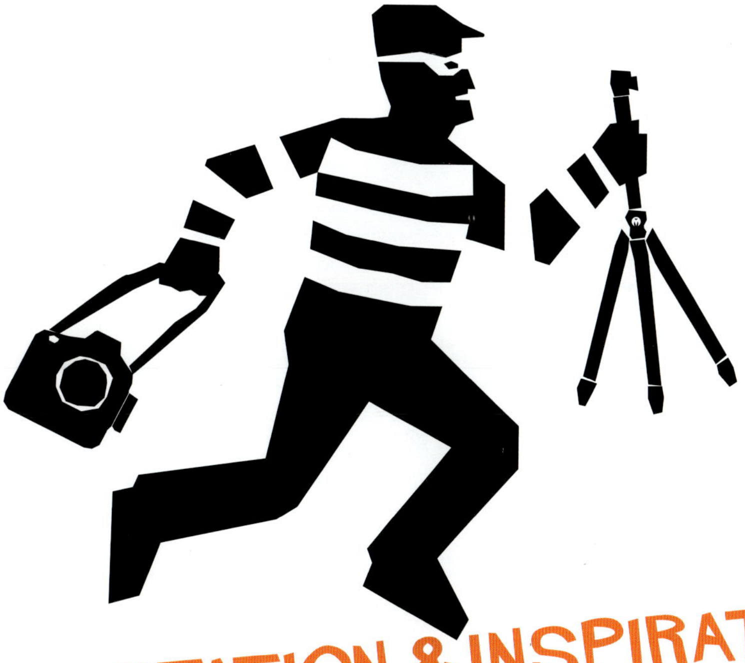

USING IMITATION & INSPIRATION TO CREATE GREAT IMAGES

GLYN DEWIS

rockynook

PHOTOGRAPH LIKE A THIEF

Glyn Dewis

www.glyndewis.com

Editor: Jocelyn Howell
Project manager: Lisa Brazieal
Marketing coordinator: Mercedes Murray
Interior design, layout, and type: WolfsonDesign
Cover graphics, interior graphics, and title font: Dave Clayton
Cover design: Dave Clayton
Lighting diagrams throughout the book created with Sylights software

ISBN: 978-1-68198-182-6
1st Edition (1st printing, April 2017)
© 2017 Glyn Dewis

Rocky Nook Inc.
1010 B Street, Suite 350
San Rafael, CA 94901
USA

www.rockynook.com

Distributed in the U.S. by Ingram Publisher Services
Distributed in the UK and Europe by Publishers Group UK

Library of Congress Control Number: 2016941045

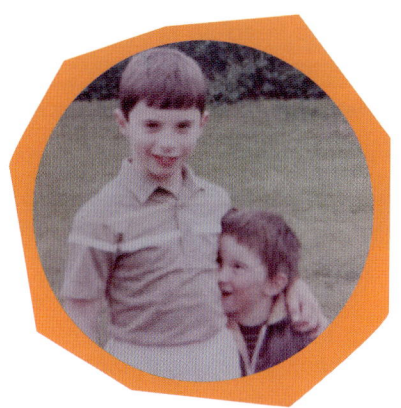

This book is dedicated to my wonderful brother, Liam.

Being back in each other's lives after such a terribly long time has shown how big of a hole we both had in our hearts, a hole that has now well and truly been filled.

I'm so incredibly proud to see the man, husband, and father you've become.

I love you.

ACKNOWLEDGMENTS

Anne: You give me reason to keep on keeping on, and having you beside me on this journey makes me feel like the luckiest man alive. You're my world and I love you more than I can possibly explain! xxx

Liam and Bev: We've missed so many years with each other, but thankfully that has now changed. Every day I feel truly blessed that we are all back in each other's lives.

Shannon, Will, and Ben: To be your uncle is the gift that keeps on giving. We love you all so very much and are always here for you. Raising a glass to the future, Uncle Glyn and Aunty Anne xxx

Will: I'll never be able to thank you enough for bringing our family back together. What you did was so incredibly brave. You stepped into the unknown and I'm so glad you did. Uncle Glyn xxx

Dave Clayton: It's hard to believe how many great times we've had and how much has happened in such a short span of time. Thanks for everything, buddy. You're one in a million and I'll be forever thankful that Scott had a hunch we'd get on and should meet. How right was he?!?! Looking forward to what's ahead.

Scott Kelby: Guv'nor, what can I say that I haven't found myself saying so many times over the past years? Friendship, advice, guidance, support, and trust. To say thank you just doesn't come close, but I think you know what I mean and how much.

Alan Hess: You are, without a doubt, one of life's great people! I just wish we could hang out more often. Always good times, always a laugh. I'm proud to have you as a friend.

Joel Grimes: You'll never know how much you have and continue to inspire, educate, and motivate me to be the best "me" I can be. You set the standard and to have both Amy and you as friends is the icing on the cake.

Scott Cowlin & Ted Waitt, a.k.a. the Dynamic Duo (Rocky Nook): Thank you for hearing me out and helping to bring the pages we have in our hands to reality. Your professionalism and creativity is second to none. I'll be forever grateful.

Jocelyn Howell (Rocky Nook): You've made writing this book a dream, thanks to your keen eye and pride in the end product. The pleasure has most definitely been mine. Thank you.

Jessica Tiernan (Rocky Nook): Thank you so much for all the support and promotion along the way. Writing this book really has been a fun journey.

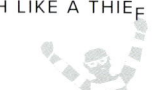

Barry Payne: You epitomise what being a friend is all about and if everyone had you in their life, theirs would be so much better for it.

Aaron Blaise: Damn, I wish we lived closer! Our "brother from another mother." I feel blessed that this industry has brought us together.

Brian Worley: If anyone can, Brian can. Thank you so much, mate, for your constant support and friendship.

Moose Peterson: I could sit and talk with you for literally hours! From your closing presentations at Photoshop World to your personal projects, I'm constantly moved by the emotion you are able to bring to your work.

Steven Cook: Dedicated, talented, professional, and loyal are just some of the many words I use to describe you. It's a pleasure to know you and to be your friend.

Jesús Ramirez: You have talent in abundance and you're a bloomin' nice guy, too. Welcome to the gang, brother.

The Flash Centre / Elinchrom: Thank you so much for the constant ongoing support. Working with you and your kick a$$ gear makes my creative life so much easier.

Loxley Colour (Ian, Calum, Ashley, and all...): You folks ROCK! 'nuff said!

Adobe, 3Legged Thing, CRU & CHNO Technology, Phottix, Wacom, TetherTools, Rogue, Benq, Topaz, and all: Your vision and drive to create the very best "tool" leaves me forever in your debt.

Mark "The Markster" Armstrong: You truly are a top fella! Thanks as always for looking in.

Austin Kleon: You don't know me from Adam, but should you, in a bizarre twist of fate, ever happen to read this, thank you! Your books are AWESOME and have had a huge impact on me and how I work.

And finally, a HUGE thanks to everyone who has stood in front of my camera and put their trust in me, without which I wouldn't be typing the words for the pages in this book.

CONTENTS

4 MY COMMONLY USED TECHNIQUES   49

5 ANNIE LEIBOVITZ INSPIRED   97

6 INTERNET INSPIRED   125

FOREWORD

Glyn and I have a lot in common, and it has nothing to do with our hairstyles. We have discovered the secret to success. It comes down to one major thing: we understand the value of hard work and putting in the time. The more hours you put into practicing something, the more proficient you become.

Often when you meet someone, they radiate an air of arrogance or an air of confidence. Arrogance comes from someone trying to hide the truth and attempting to portray more than who they are. Confidence comes from knowing you have done the hard work and there is still room for improvement. Glyn is a man who exhibits confidence with a touch of humility. Much of this comes from his days competing as a bodybuilder. When you stand on stage in front of the judges and spectators, you bare it all. There is no place to hide. Either you have done the best you can building up to that moment, or you have not.

Being an artist is very similar. When you present your work, you have to lay it on the line. No matter how brilliant you are, there will always be a group of people who love or hate what you do. This is life. The best you can hope for is to build an audience who loves what you do. This takes building a recognizable brand and beating it into the marketplace until it takes root. Again, it takes a lot of work.

One of the things I love about Glyn as an educator is that he takes his audience beyond just the technical nuts and bolts of photography and emphasizes the creative side of building an image. Too often we get stuck on f-stops and shutter speeds and forget that there is more to creating a successful photograph. In a way, Glyn is a coach, but instead of building muscles, he is motivating you to build a body of images that represent you as an artist. A good coach will always nurture you along to get the best out of you. Glyn has this gift.

—Joel Grimes

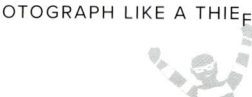

INTRODUCTION

Before you dive into the following pages, I want take a moment to thank you for purchasing this book. I've always been someone who gains tremendous pleasure from sharing what I do and seeing others progress, so my hope is that the content in this book not only teaches you some tips, tricks, and techniques, but also serves to inspire and motivate you.

If you've been following any of the work I share online through my blog, YouTube channel, presentations, and social media platforms, then you're no doubt aware of how much importance I place on having personal projects. Without question, my personal projects have been instrumental in helping me to define who I am as a photographer and digital artist.

This creative industry—photography, in particular—involves gear and lots of it. I have spent, or rather wasted, so much money on gear that I thought was going to be the answer to developing my portfolio, when in reality, it probably hindered it. The moment I truly acknowledged the importance of projects and using what I had, everything began to click into place, especially when I started creating what I wanted rather than what others wanted. This alone brought the fun back, and now I have more projects and pictures I want to create than I have time for, and that is exciting.

HOW TO USE THIS BOOK

Well, this is your book so you can dive in and out wherever you like, but if you want to really get the most out of it, I'd suggest you go through chapters 1 through 4 before getting started on the individual projects in chapters 5 through 14.

Chapter 1 explains how and why everything clicked into place for me and got me out of a creative rut—a rut that you may be going through right now.

In chapter 2 I explain reverse engineering, which is how I look at a picture and examine the shadows, highlights, and catch lights to figure out how the picture was lit and what gear could have been used. I really do believe that knowing how to do this is an essential skill for developing your own lighting style and, ultimately, building your own unique portfolio.

I'm frequently asked what gear I use, so in chapter 3 I cover the lot. However, I will add that the gear I use is what I find works best for me and how I work. I'm certainly not someone who is loyal to a brand no matter what, but I will stick to a piece of equipment that works well and never lets me down.

In chapter 4 I take you step-by-step through a photography technique and some Photoshop retouching techniques I use frequently. You'll see that I refer back to this chapter throughout the book to avoid repeating the same instructions over and over.

Chapters 5 through 14 cover individual photo projects. In each chapter, I take you through the entire process of creating the photograph. I start by explaining the inspiration for the picture, be it another photographer's work, a movie poster, a book cover, or something else. Then I move into the reverse engineering, examining the picture I used for inspiration to figure out how it was put together, including how many lights were used and where they were likely positioned. We can use this information to recreate our own version of the image, which allows us to learn from the work that inspires us and gives us an opportunity to create something completely new.

I share the lighting setup, gear, and camera settings I used for each photo shoot, and I also cover gear that could be used to achieve a similar style if you're using small, battery-powered flashes rather than big, powerful studio lights. Finally, together we go through the post-production step-by-step, starting with the out-of-the-camera picture and working our way through the retouching process until we end up with a print-ready picture.

You can work through chapters 5 through 14 in any order you choose because each chapter is one individual project.

DOWNLOAD THE IMAGE FILES

I've made the working image files for each chapter available for you to download so that you can follow along step-by-step.

You can access them at: http://www.rockynook.com/photograph-like-a-thief-reference/

Please be aware that I've made these files available to you so that you can follow along with the book because I feel that's the best way to learn. Feel free to use them to practice post-production techniques. However, these are my original image files and they are not for commercial or public use.

Again, thank you so much for purchasing this book. Please keep me posted on your progress by sharing pictures online. I'd love to see anything that you go on to make after reading what is contained in the pages ahead.

Keep creating, and most of all, keep enjoying!

Best wishes,
Glyn

Website www.glyndewis.com

YouTube www.youtube.com/glyndewis

Instagram www.instagram.com/glyndewis

Facebook www.facebook.com/glyndewis

Twitter www.twitter.com/glyndewis

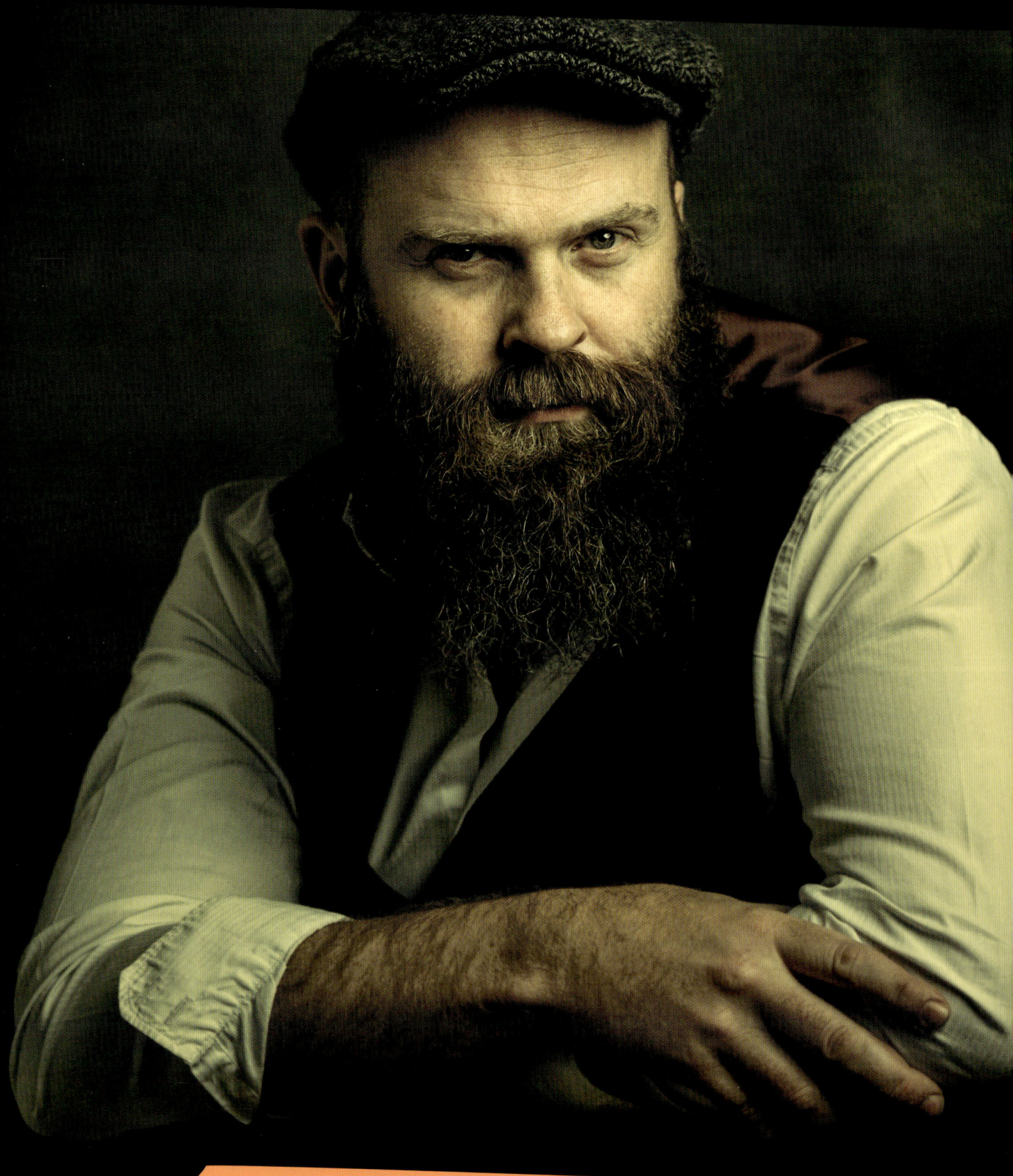

1 PHOTOGRAPH LIKE A THIEF

"I invented nothing new. I simply assembled the discoveries of other men behind whom were centuries of work. Had I worked fifty or ten or even five years before, I would have failed. So it is with every new thing." —Sir Henry Ford

Before I jump into explaining why I decided to call this book *Photograph Like a Thief*, let me give you a quick summary of how I came to be here in the first place.

At the time of writing I've been involved in the photography industry for around 10 years. I was first introduced to Photoshop by an uncle who had always been the family photographer, turning up at every family gathering armed with a camera. He knew I was interested in computers and on one visit he brought along his (not so laptop) laptop and showed me how he could literally perform magic with one click of the mouse and remove red eye from one of his pictures. And well, from that moment on I was hooked.

AS SOON AS I COULD I got a copy of Photoshop and loaded it onto my Gateway computer, with its 19-inch monitor and 38-inch depth, but the excitement quickly turned into confusion because I didn't know where to begin. I went online and searched for free Photoshop tutorials, and on the first page of Yahoo results I found an organization called the N.A.P.P. (now KelbyOne) hosted by three main guys—Scott Kelby, Matt Kloskowski, and Dave Cross. I was completely fascinated by their tutorials so I paid my membership fee and not too long after, I found myself on a plane heading to Las Vegas (my first time ever in the United States) for a four-day conference and expo called Photoshop World.

Photoshop World completely blew my mind and after four days packed full of learning, I headed back to the UK with newfound motivation. I went on to take the Adobe ACE exam (purely for my own sense of achievement), and then things seemed to just happen from there as friends got to know I used Photoshop and could swap heads in photos and create funny posters. This progressed to other photographers contacting me and paying me to retouch their wedding and portrait photographs. But, if I said the phrase "you can't make a silk purse out of a sow's ear," would you know what I mean?

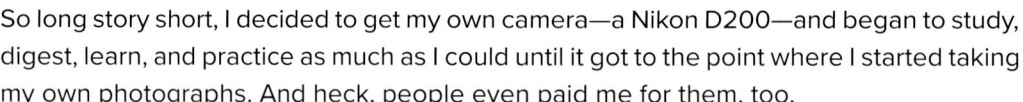

Now don't get me wrong, I don't say this referring to all the photographers, but there were a few for sure who had the opinion that because I knew how to use Photoshop I could make any picture a good one; but we photographers know better, right? I mean, no matter how good Photoshop becomes with all its regular enhancements, it is and always will be a case of "garbage in, garbage out."

So long story short, I decided to get my own camera—a Nikon D200—and began to study, digest, learn, and practice as much as I could until it got to the point where I started taking my own photographs. And heck, people even paid me for them, too.

Seeing as how people were prepared to hand over their hard-earned cash, I thought it wise to set myself up in business and keep everything above board—which, when I look back, maybe wasn't the best thing to do. At this time I still didn't have a clue what I wanted to specialize in, and I certainly didn't have a recognizable style. Geez, when I look back at my earlier work I can see that there's definitely no consistency. Every photo shoot looks like it could have been from a completely different photographer.

Almost from day one I remember people saying to me that: 1) You MUST specialize, and 2) You MUST have a unique and recognizable style.

Both points made complete sense, but how on earth do you get to that point?

Well, in terms of specializing, I honestly just went out and tried everything. Have you ever heard the phrase "spinning too many plates"? That was me. I tried weddings, family portraits, baby photos, food photography, architectural photography, and so on. By doing so I very quickly realized what I didn't like to do, which by default left me with what I did like to do—portraits. Developing a recognizable style, however, was a completely different ball game.

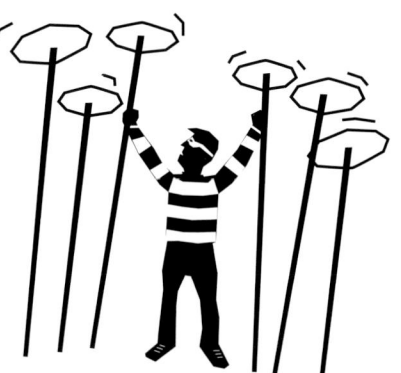

DEVELOPING A PERSONAL STYLE

One thing I did when I first started out was to set up a blog; not with the intention of gaining masses of followers or anything like that, but rather as something to motivate me to get out there and produce content. You see, committing myself to writing one post per week meant now I **had** to go out with my camera and create a new picture every week that I could write about. As the blog grew and gained more followers than just my wife, I introduced a "Monthly Interview" section. Each month I would interview a photographer whose work I liked or who was well known in the industry and ask them a set list of questions, one of which was about style, and in particular, how to develop a personal style.

Ninety-nine percent of the photographers I interviewed basically said that you can't force your own style; it just develops after lots and lots of time behind the camera and in front of the computer screen. One photographer said that he believed your style is heavily influenced by your life experiences from childhood to adulthood and your likes and dislikes. This definitely rang true for me. In my portfolio you'll never see pictures of white backgrounds, balloons, or people jumping in the air clapping their hands. Not to say there's anything wrong with that, but it's just not for me. That's not a conscious decision I made; it's just a style I was never interested in.

So if style comes from your life experiences, likes, and dislikes, where do you start? Surely you have to have a starting point from where you can move on, and this would likely mean copying, right?

COPYING OTHERS

It's at this moment when you mention copying that there's a sharp intake of breath across the photography world: "Copy? You can't copy! You MUST have your own unique and identifiable style." Well that's all well and good, and I get the whole unique thing, but what I'm talking about here is using copying as a way to develop yourself, not plagiarizing the work of others. When I say copying I mean it in the loosest use of the term. We're not talking about trying to recreate an exact copy of another piece of work, but instead about being inspired by the work of others. Yes, *inspired* is a good word for it.

The best way I can explain this is by going off topic for a moment, so let's look at the music industry as a perfect example. You may be someone who plays a musical instrument; you may even be someone who plays the guitar, for instance. Now, do you think it's reasonable to say that if you were someone who plays guitar (or maybe you know someone who does), when you started learning how to play you would listen to music you liked and try to copy the guitar tracks as a way of practicing? Of course!

Copying is widely accepted within the music industry. Every day you can listen to the radio and almost every other track you listen to is either a cover version or has parts of one song mixed in to create a completely different track, and this is just the norm. But if you mention copying in photography, lightning bolts will strike.

Back when The Beatles started out, they would tour all the working men's clubs and perform at the Cavern Club and other similar places playing cover versions of songs by artists such as Elvis, Buddy Holly, and Jerry Lee Lewis. In fact, it was Paul McCartney who said they only started writing their own music so they could perform their own unique-sounding gigs. And you see, that's the point here—they copied other artists' work until eventually they developed their own style and sound that became instantly recognizable as them.

One of my favorite tracks of all time is "Every Breath You Take" by The Police, with its famous guitar riff. You hear just a few seconds of it and instantly you recognize the track. American rapper Puff Daddy used the same guitar riff in his song "I'll Be Missing You," which he released following the death of his friend and fellow rapper The Notorious B.I.G. So,

same guitar riff, completely different song, and this goes on all the time and is widely accepted. Granted, this may not be the very best example since this led to a lawsuit because permission to use the guitar riff was not granted, but you get my point, right?

Moving away from the music industry, but still focusing on the subject of copying, let's take a quick look at the movie industry; in particular, movie posters and artwork.

Figure 1.1 shows some examples in which copying has been used to create a multitude of movie posters. I first became aware of this pose with a man and woman leaning against each

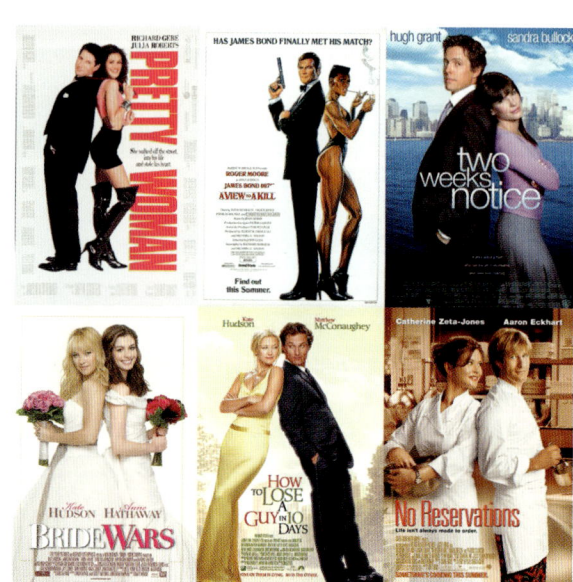

FIGURE 1.1

other when the film *Pretty Woman* was released, but just take a look at all the similar examples here. I don't know when or where this pose was used first, and I'm not suggesting that the pose is copyrighted in any particular way, but this is a prime example of how something from one piece of work can be used in another to create something new. To reinforce this point, check out the examples in **Figure 1.2**, all of which use a similar concept of a person running.

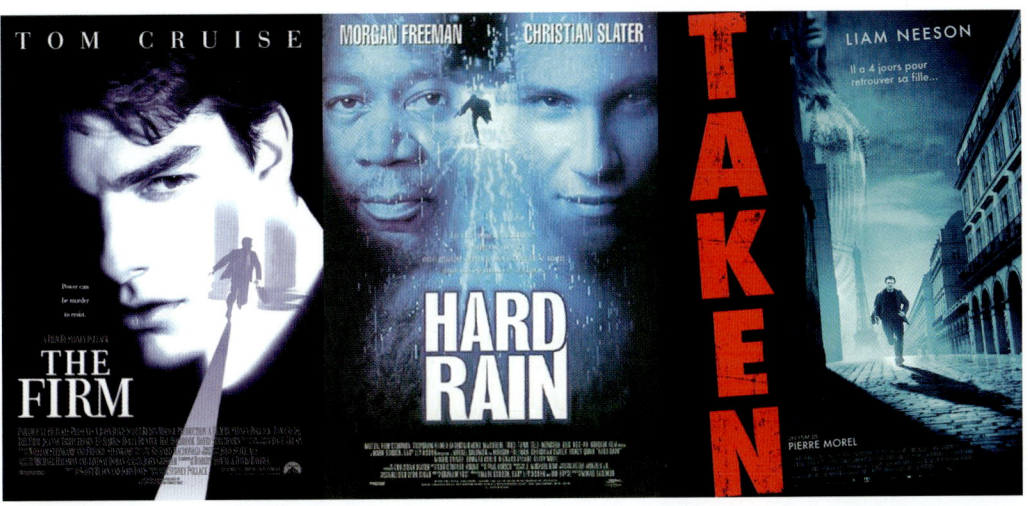

FIGURE 1.2

Occasionally I run workshops on photography and retouching in which each attendee has their own computer to work on and I give each of them the same RAW file to install. I then guide them through the retouching process step by step, and from time to time I'll stop what I'm doing and wander around to see how everyone is getting on. The interesting thing here is that without fail, even though I've shown them the exact steps to do, every one of the attendees will produce something that looks a little different. This isn't because they've done something wrong, but is because they may have altered some of the settings I suggested to suit their own taste.

WE WANT YOU TO TAKE FROM US. *We want you, at first, to steal from us, because you can't steal. You will take what we give you and you will put it in your own voice and that's how you will find your voice. And that's how you begin. And then one day someone will steal from you.*

— Francis Ford Coppola, Screenwriter, Film Director & Producer

FINDING INSPIRATION

I became interested in bodybuilding when I was around 14 years old, and I competed in the sport up until I reached about 35 years of age (**Figure 1.3**).

I remember after one competition having a photo shoot with a photographer who had never photographed a physique before. Unfortunately, this showed in the results. There were no obvious shadows and highlights to complement my physique, so despite weeks of training and dieting, I looked more like Casper the Ghost than Arnold Schwarzenegger.

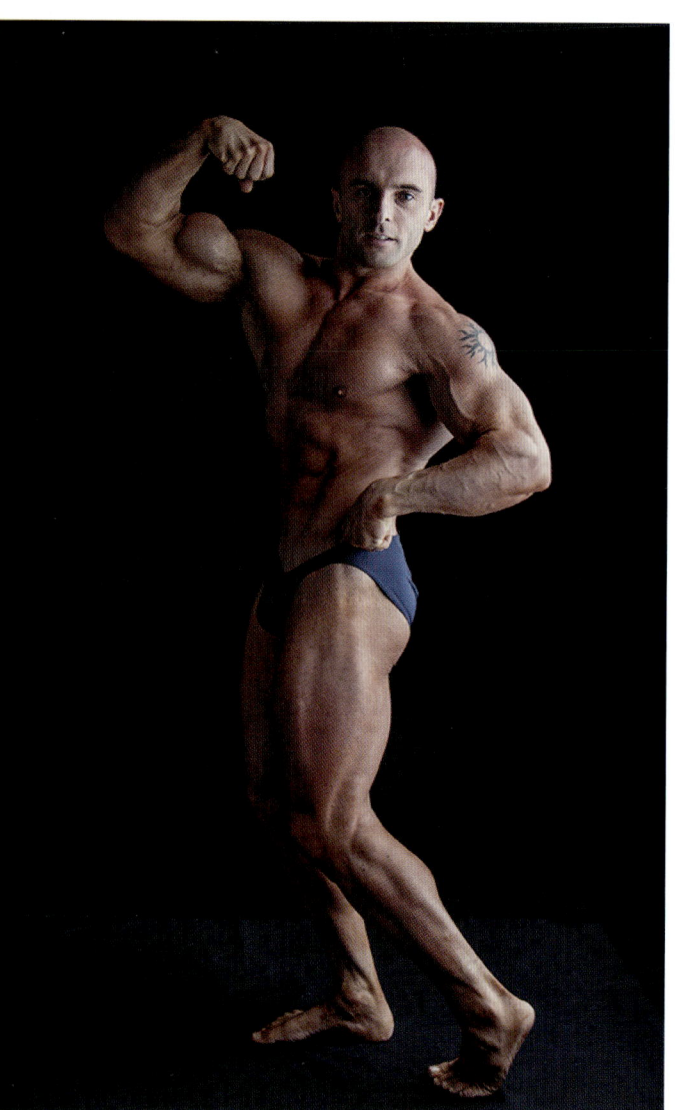

FIGURE 1.3 Me at 33 years old (or thereabouts)

So later when I became interested in photography, I was naturally drawn to photographing physiques, but in a way that I would have liked to have been photographed, treating the body, as Arnold Schwarzenegger says in *Pumping Iron*, as a sculpture (**Figures 1.4** and **Figure 1.5**).

I used to love looking through all the old bodybuilding magazines and seeing photographs by Jimmy Caruso, who was the go-to guy back in the day and photographed the likes of Arnold Schwarzenegger, Reg Park, Dave Draper, and other well-known bodybuilders. His style of lighting fascinated me, so I would try to deconstruct it and attempt my own version of the Caruso look, as you can see in this photograph I made of my friend Steve Lewington (**Figure 1.6**).

The Internet is a great place to start when you're looking for ideas and inspiration to copy from. I'm forever trawling around and coming across pictures I like, and I look to see how I can use an element of each picture, such as the lighting style, in my own work. One such example is a picture I saw by New York–based photographer Joey Lawrence (Joey L) that he made for a National Geographic Channel program called *Killing Lincoln*.

I was initially drawn to the pose of the two subjects in the photograph, who are standing back to back and looking in opposite directions. Neither man is looking toward the photographer or viewer. It is certainly a different type of pose for two people. I also thought the lighting worked wonderfully. The image is dark with light shining in from the upper left and right corners of the image, highlighting both of the subjects' faces.

FIGURE 1.4

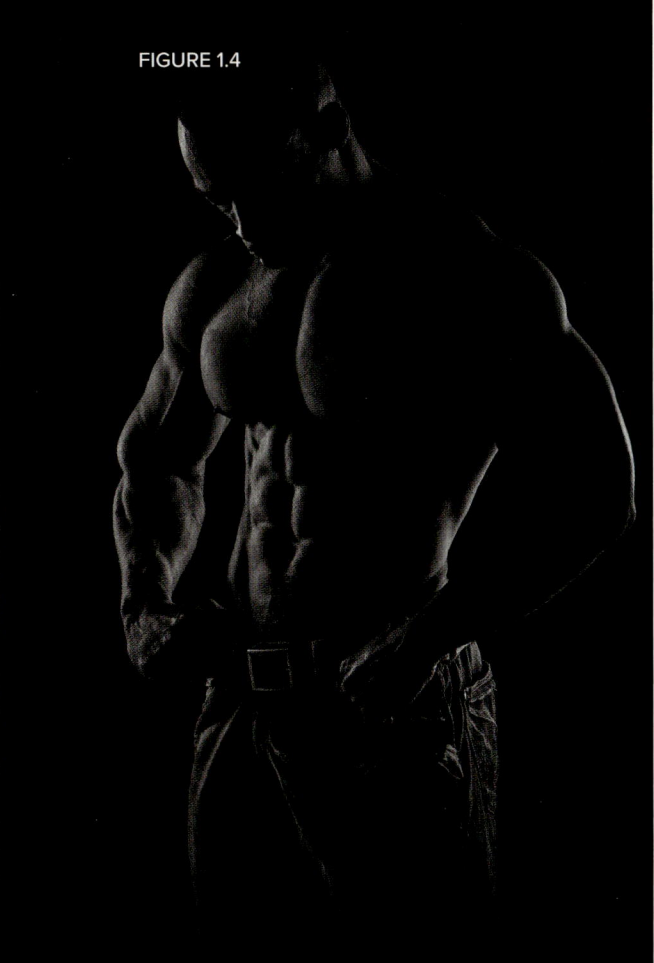

FIGURE 1.5

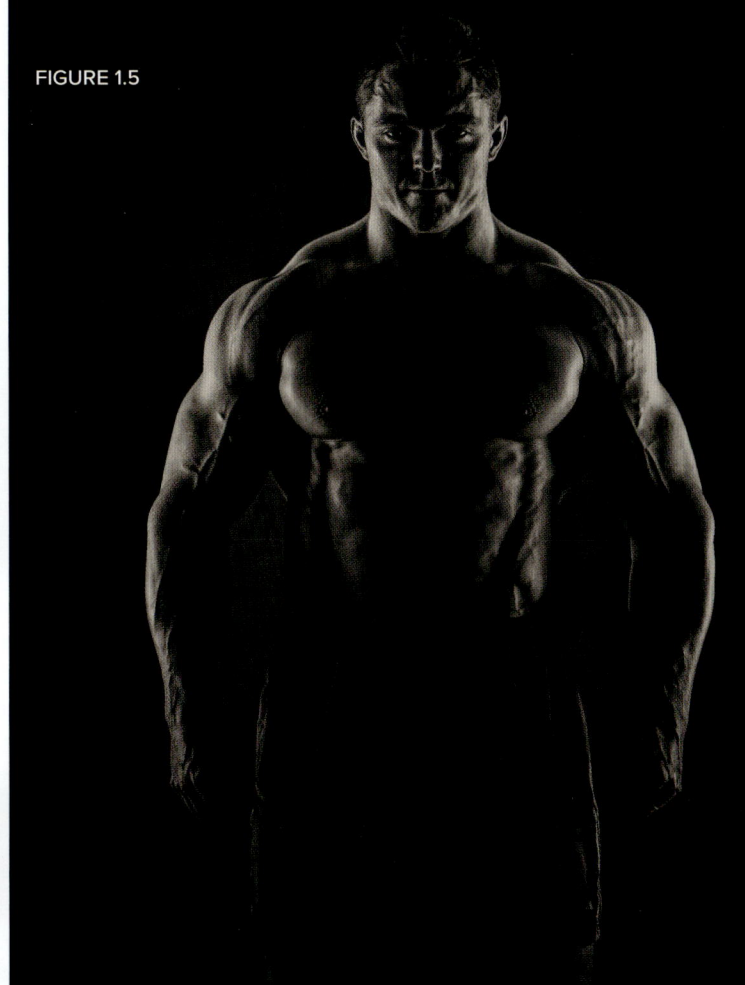

FIGURE 1.6

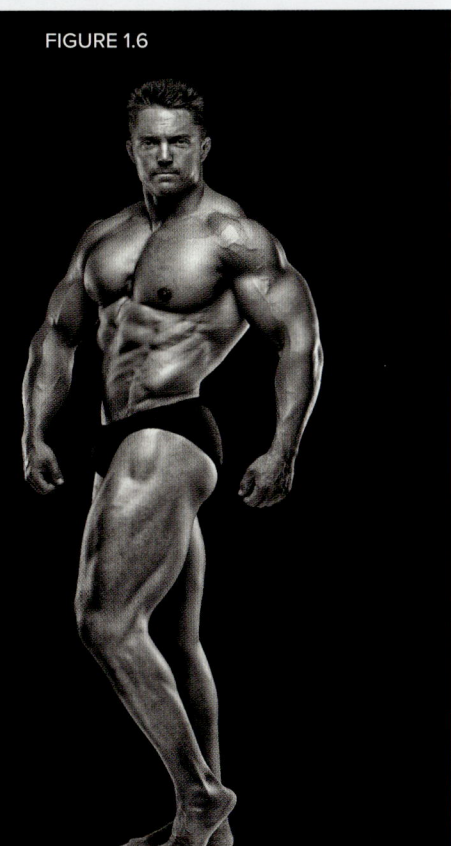

NOTE *When I talk about "copying" the work of others, I'm talking about figuring out what it is you like about the artwork and photographs you're drawn to and trying to incorporate those elements into your own work to make something new—photographing like a thief. But we don't want to become* actual *thieves; we want to respect the work and rights of our fellow photographers, and that's why I haven't included some of the images by other photographers that I discuss in this chapter and throughout the book. I'm drawn to and inspired by many different photographers, but we can only print images for which we've obtained permission to do so. In cases where we do not have permission to print a specific image, I have included a link to the image online so you can check it out.*

Straight away I thought the pose and lighting style would work great in a picture I was due to take of World Champion Kickboxer Steven "Pocket Rocket" Cook and his coach Michael Graham (**Figure 1.7**). I arranged the men so that Steven, the main character, stares confidently straight out at the viewer, while Michael looks off-camera, oozing wisdom. They stand close together because they're a team and a powerful force. We're going to be working through this picture from start to finish as one of the projects later on in this book.

TIP *One strategy that works really well for me, and I'm sure will work well for you, is to show the person you're going to be photographing what you want to do, rather than simply explaining what you want to do. This is what I did with Steven Cook in the* Killing Lincoln *example. This way the model or subject becomes excited about what you'll be working on because you've now involved them in the creative process.*

When you're organizing photo shoots, especially in the early days, go in with the intention of working on creating just one quality picture as opposed to as many pictures as possible. This will produce far better results. Also, working on perfecting one image rather than photographing as many setups as you can will demonstrate to your subject that you respect their time. They'll remember having a good experience working with you and will be much more inclined to do so again.

FIGURE 1.7

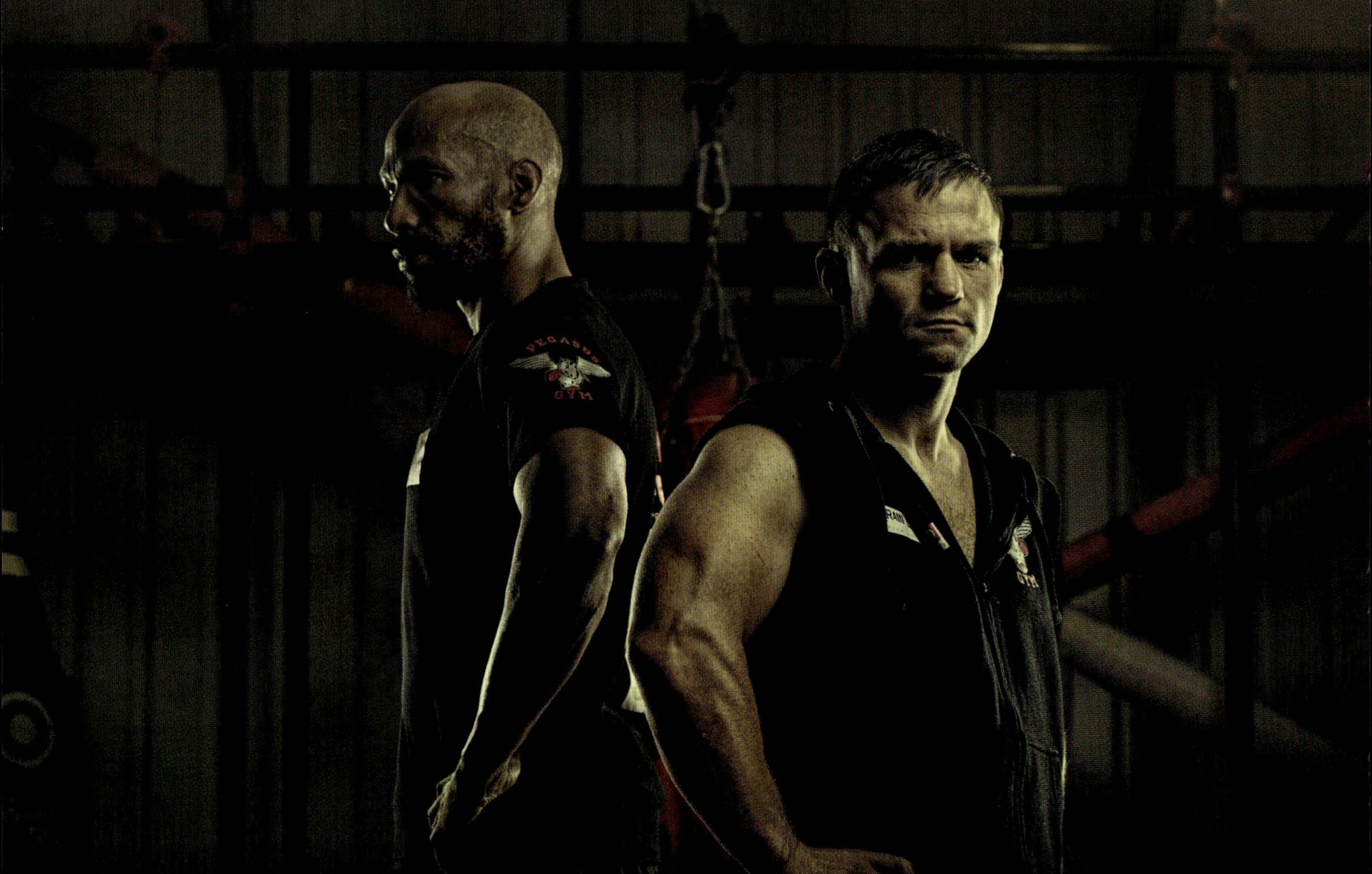

One of my all time favorite photographers is Annie Leibovitz. I just love everything about her pictures; in particular, the portraits and group photographs of celebrities she takes for publications such as *Vanity Fair*. The lighting is just so incredibly natural, as are the poses and expressions she draws out of her subjects.

Scouring the Internet one day I came across a photograph of actors Sir Patrick Stewart and Sir Ian McKellen taken by Annie. It is another somewhat dark image, with the light shining down on the subjects from above. The men sit next to one another against a textured background and make direct eye contact with the viewer. As is my usual practice, I took a screen grab of the image and stored it in my "Inspiration and Ideas" folder on my computer. This is something I do all the time and have done since day one, only back then it meant tearing pages out of magazines and sticking them in a scrapbook. Now things are so much easier with the ability to take screen grabs and snap pictures with your mobile phone.

It just so happened that a while later I was photographing a couple of guys from a group called The Bearded Villains—very stylish men with flat caps, waistcoats, and pocket watches—and the picture I'd saved earlier came to mind. I thought similar lighting, poses, and a textured background would work a treat on these guys, so that's exactly what we did; again, taking something from one image and using it in another to create something

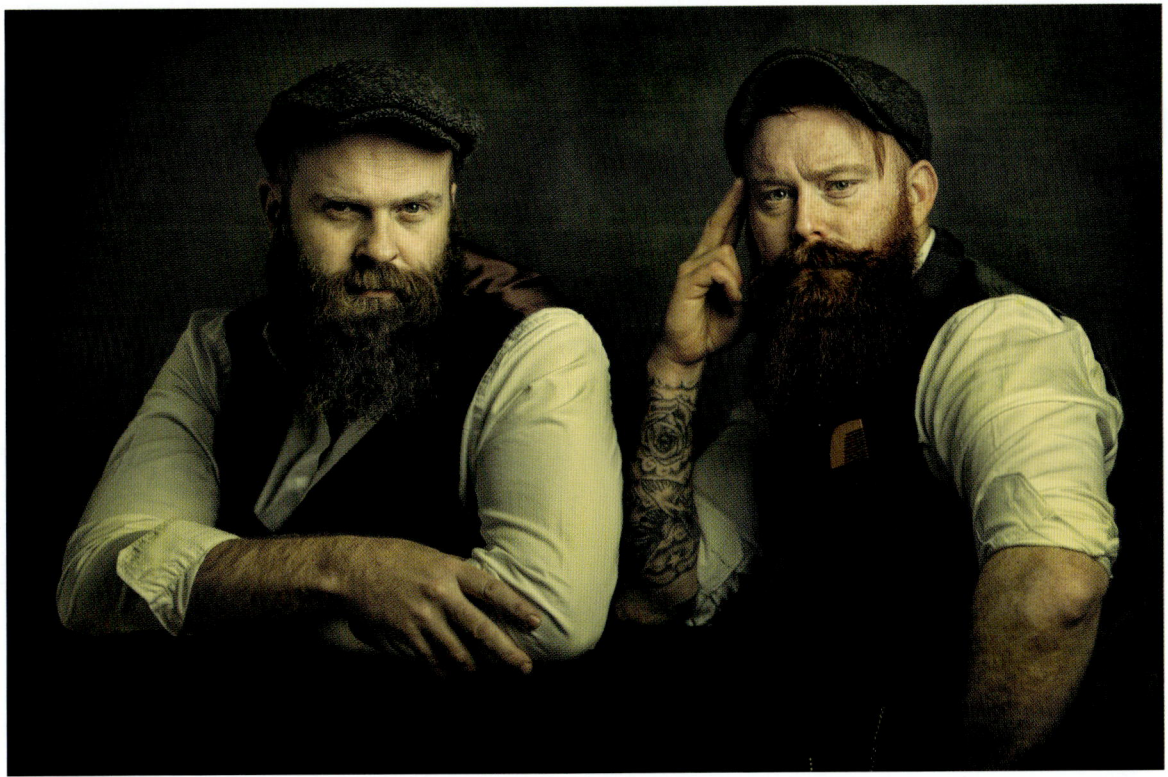

FIGURE 1.8

new and different (**Figure 1.8**). We'll go through this picture later on in the book and cover the photography and post-production from start to finish.

LEARNING FROM THE PROCESS

Sometimes I'll do something purely for the fun of it, but on the back of that it's incredible how much you can learn in the process. My buddy Dave Clayton approached me one time saying that he'd always wanted a picture taken of him made to look like the lead character Carl from Pixar's animated film *Up*. This was certainly a style of picture I'd never considered doing, but I figured the process would be a whole lot of fun, so we set the date and the planning began. Dave collected suitable clothing from thrift shops and I searched the Internet for stills from the movie to see exactly what we could work toward.

I took the pictures and then moved over to the computer and opened a still from the movie on one screen and the image of Dave on another (**Figure 1.9**). Working on this image was a great exercise in problem solving and retouching. Forcing myself to work out how to recreate the head shape and jowls, change the body composition and hair color, and match all the other tiny details was not only a great learning experience, it was also fun, and for me, that is so incredibly important (**Figure 1.10**). Plus, this project ended up being a collaboration with our dear friend Aaron Blaise—an artist and movie director who worked at Disney for over 20 years on movies such as *Aladdin*, *Beauty and the Beast*, and *Brother Bear*—who drew the background for Dave's portrait.

Due to its very nature and all the technicalities involved, photography can become very serious, so giving yourself little projects like this can not only be a great escape, but will also remind you why you got involved in photography in the first place—presumably for the fun and enjoyment of it.

Anyone who knows me knows that I'm an animal lover and that going on a safari is high on my bucket list. I'll do it one day for sure, but in the meantime one on-going project that I am constantly adding to is my "Animals" project. This is a photography and retouching project where I go to places like wildlife parks and zoos to photograph animals in captivity. I'm there for as little time as possible because I find these places quite depressing, but what I do with the photographs is use Photoshop to cut the animals out of their captive scenes and place them into new scenes I've created that have the look and feel of the animals' natural habitats. For me, doing this feels like setting the animals free and the first time I did it was actually the first time I think I ever felt emotionally moved by photography (**Figure 1.11**).

Don't worry, I'm not about to turn all heavy and deep on you, but it just affected me in that way. It was incredible to me how impactful it was to separate an animal from its environment and see how it changed the mood and overall feel of the photograph.

THOSE WHO DO NOT WANT TO IMITATE ANYTHING, PRODUCE NOTHING.

– Salvador Dali

FIGURE 1.9

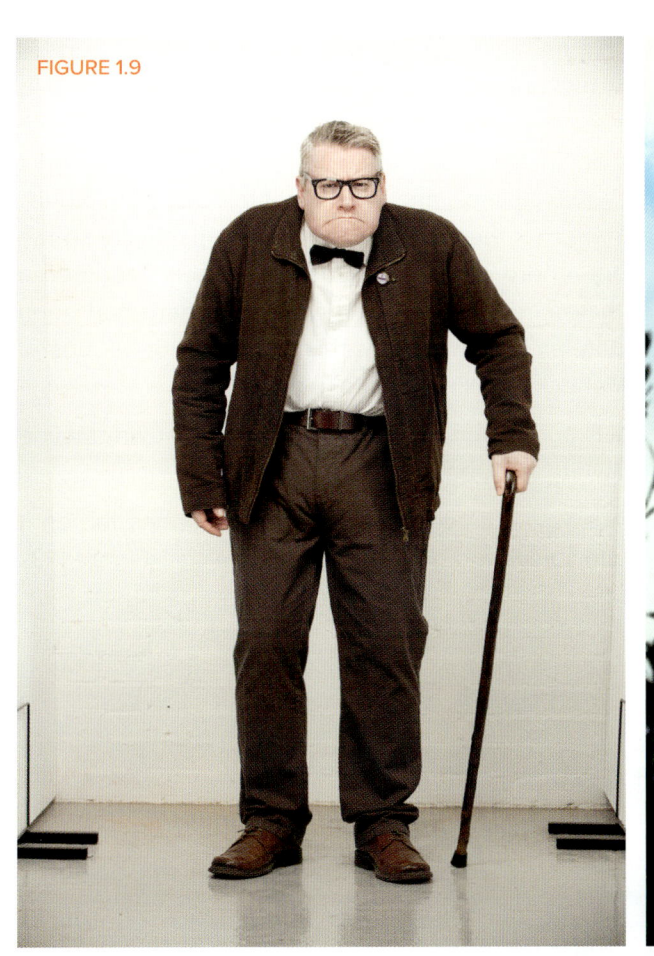

FIGURE 1.10

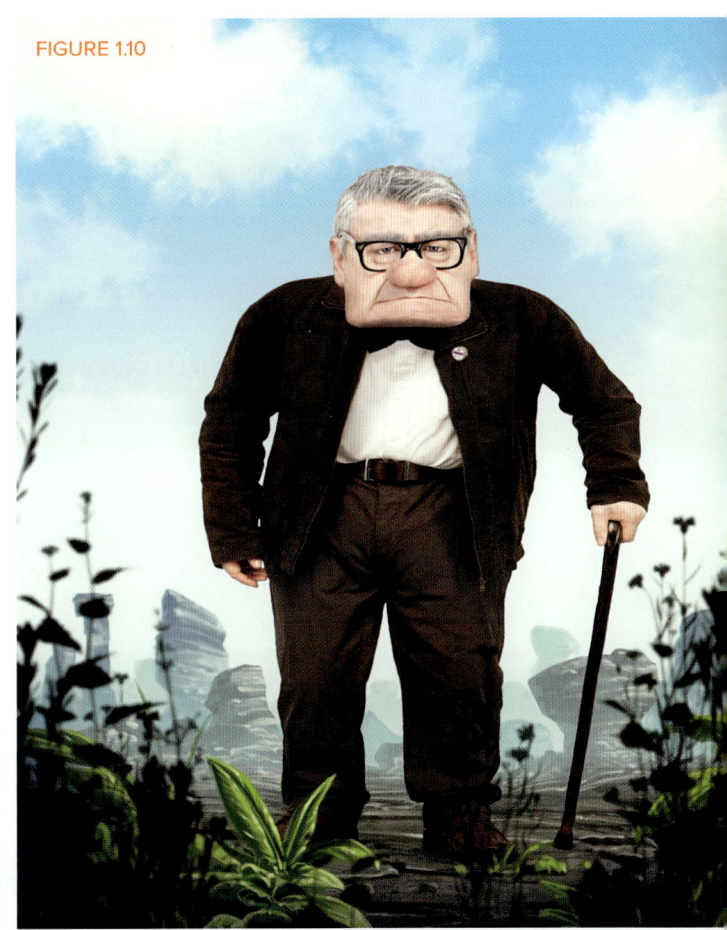

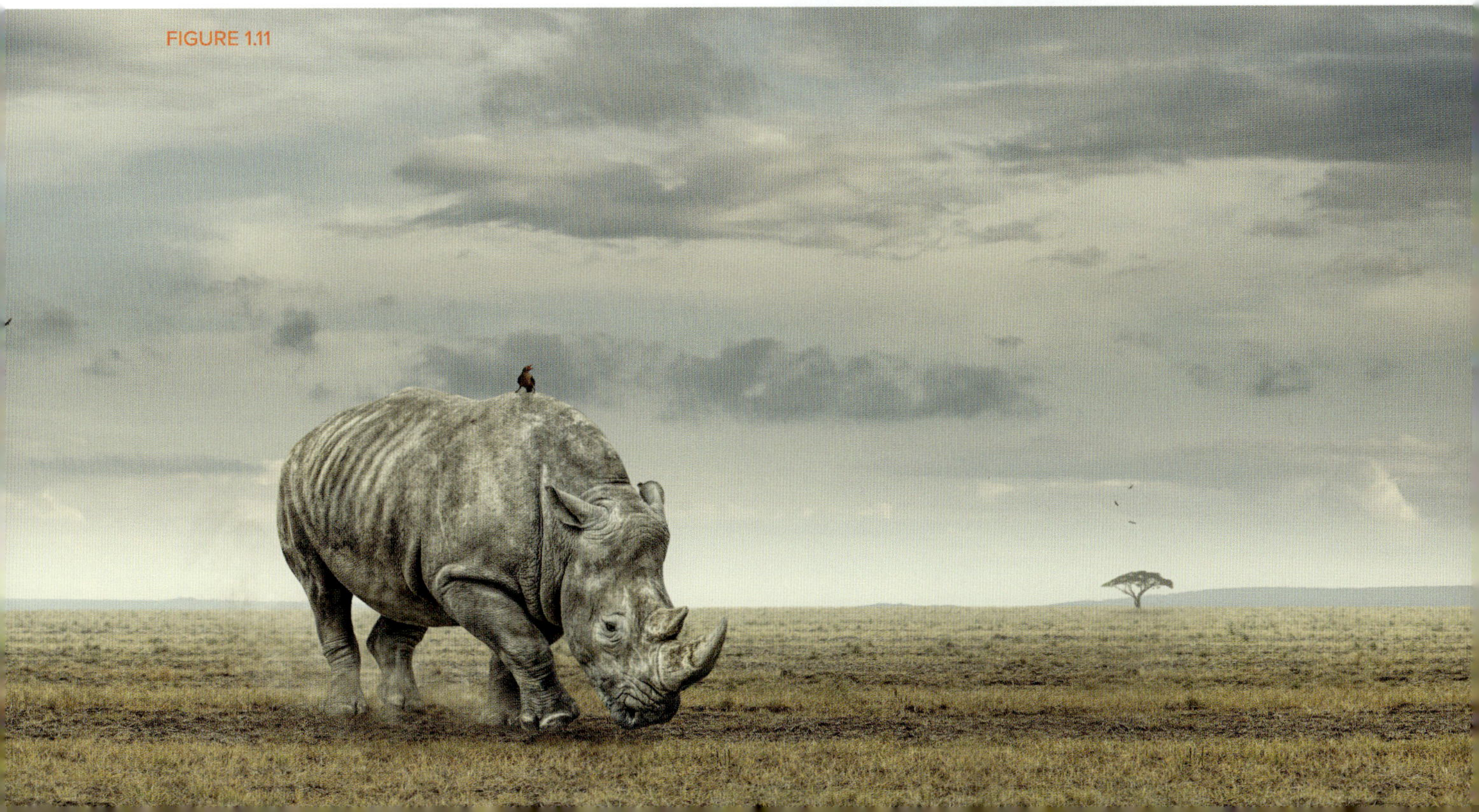

FIGURE 1.11

Shortly after starting this project I became aware of photographer Nick Brandt and his wildlife photographs from Africa (**www.nickbrandt.com**). *Never* had photography stopped me in my tracks like his work did. His use of black-and-white and relatively shallow depth of field is unique enough, but it's his ability to capture emotion that never fails to affect me. Nick tells the stories of these beautiful animals and their plight through his pictures, creating an incredibly powerful experience for the viewer. One picture in particular shows rangers holding recovered tusks from a herd of elephants that had been slaughtered by poachers. They are standing in the same composition in which the herd had been photographed some time before. I defy anyone who sees this image to not be moved emotionally. I highly recommend you check out Nick's work.

So could I "take" something from Nick Brandt's work that would enhance my own? Maybe it would just be to go with black-and-white as opposed to color?

Figure 1.12 was pretty much a throw away, but seeing Nick Brandt's images turned it around for me and inspired me to create something I'd hang on my office wall (**Figure 1.13**).

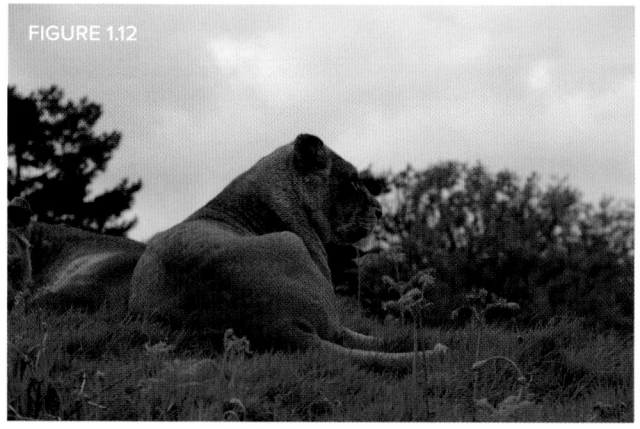

FIGURE 1.12

FIGURE 1.13

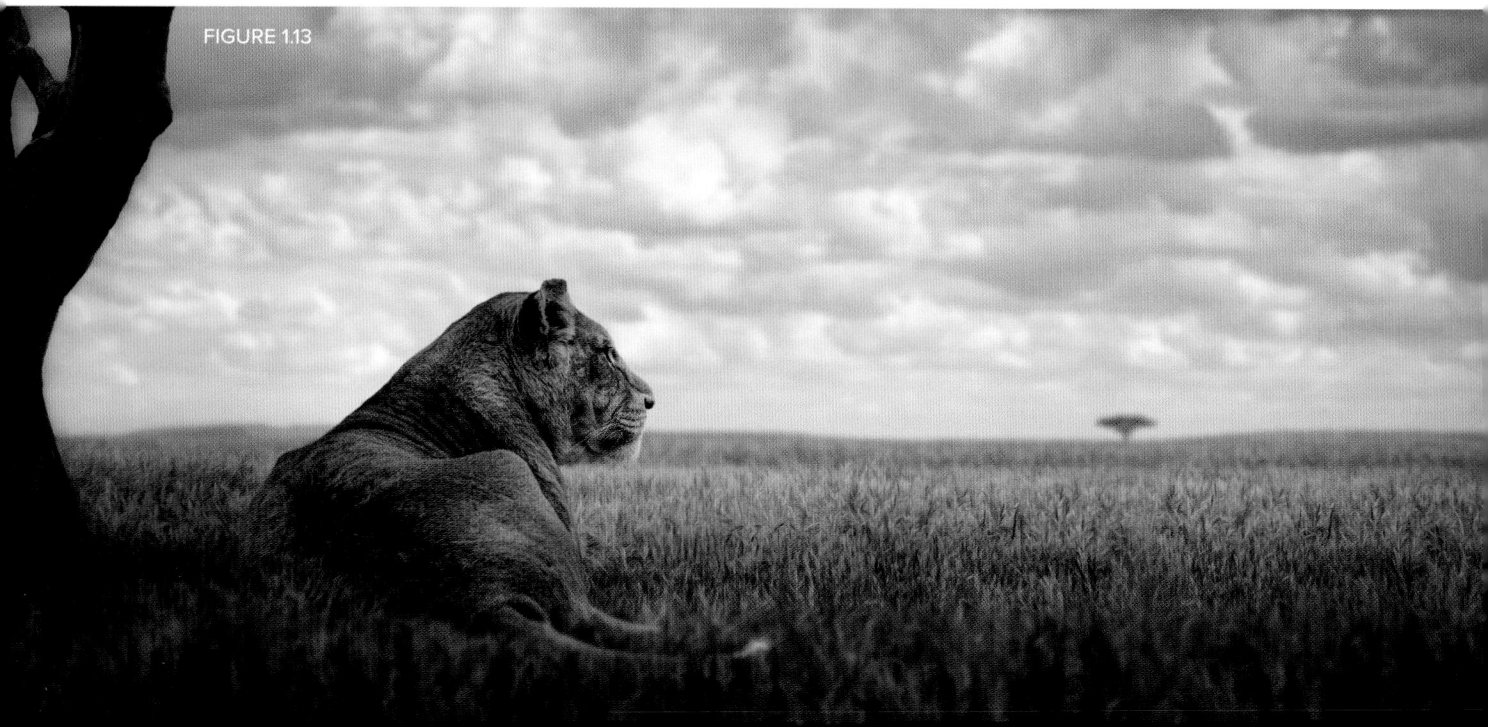

Now I'm no Nick Brandt, but trying to copy the look of one of his pictures to see how it would turn out helped me to produce my own unique piece, because no matter how hard we try to copy, we never will! The result? A piece of work that I'm actually really quite proud to have hanging on my office wall.

So copying *is* a good thing. It gives you a starting point, a beginning that you can move on from. And with time, after copying over and over again, your own style will show itself.

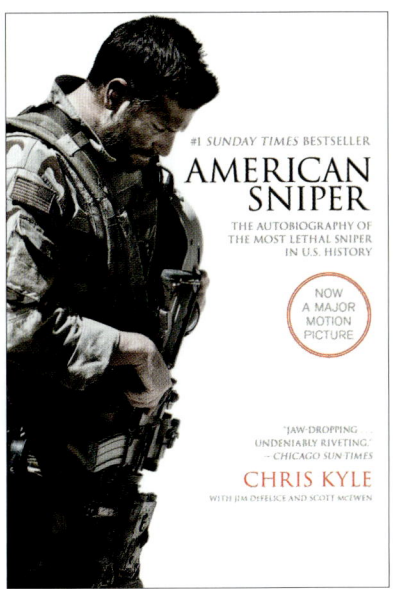

FIGURE 1.14 The original *American Sniper* book cover

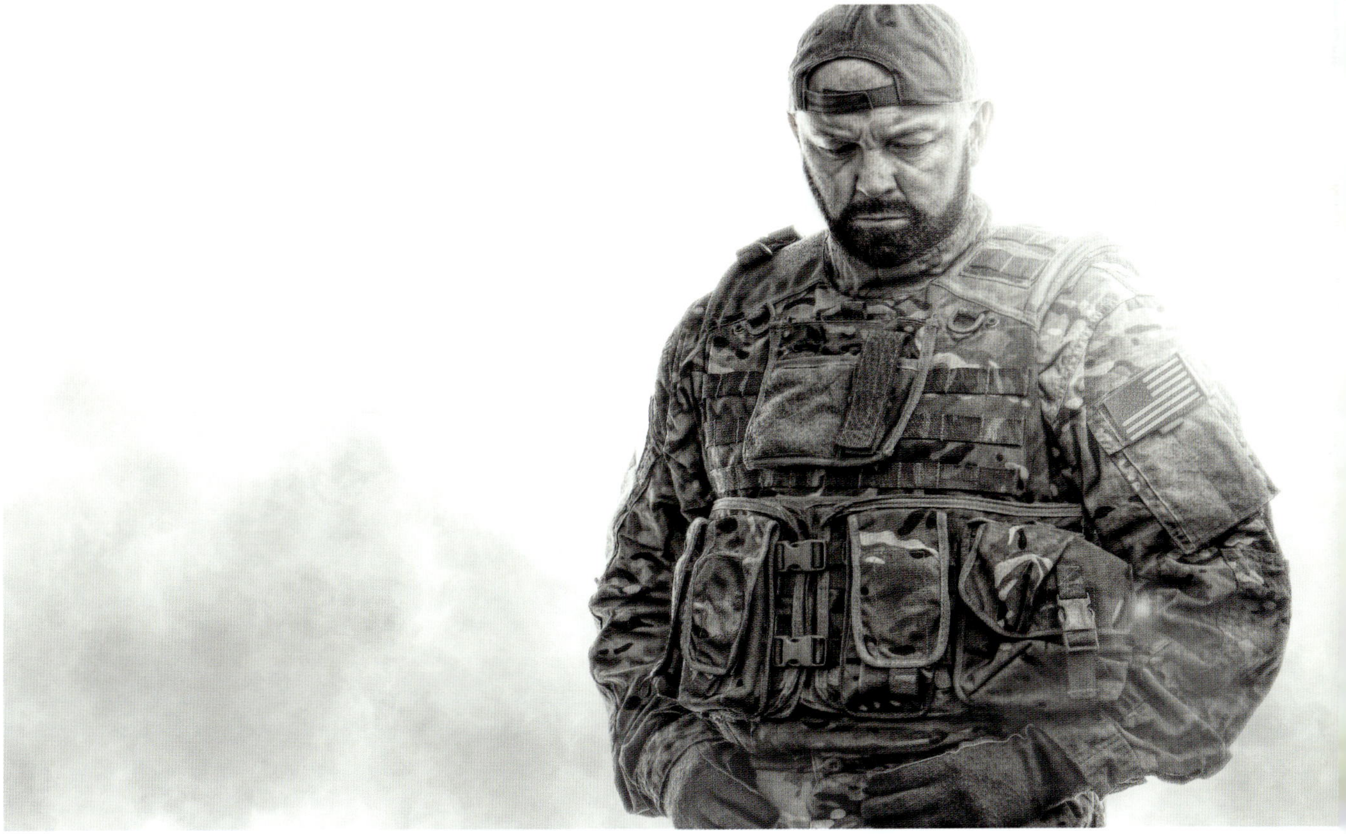

FIGURE 1.15 An image I created inspired by the *American Sniper* book cover

If you're still struggling with this whole concept of copying, or maybe you don't have a photographer in mind whose work you really like, then why not recreate a book cover, a poster, a scene from a movie, or something like that? Because one thing is for sure, copying in some form or another is vital to your growth as a photographer or digital artist!

As an artist, you'll force yourself to overcome challenges, develop your skills, and grow your portfolio. As someone in business, going through the process of planning and preparing your work will help you to hone those skills when working with clients.

My ultimate goal was to have a personal style and to be hired for the kind of work I wanted to do as opposed to taking on whatever came my way. But in the process of developing that style and those skills by copying the work of others, if someone ever posted a comment online that said, "that looks like a Joel Grimes picture or an Annie Liebovitz picture," do you think I was concerned? Heck no! That's a compliment and shows you're on your way to developing your own style. Hey, when I was bodybuilding folks would always ask the steroid question. Some of my friends who also trained used to get so wound up about this, but I took it as a compliment. Why? Well what does Joe Public think of steroids? They make you BIG, right? Well then, for them to suggest that I looked like I could have used steroids, they must have thought I was BIG. You see my point?

Photography is a whole lot of fun, and for those of us who never excelled at or were encouraged in art at school, now armed with a camera, some great software, and lots of practice, the sky really is the limit.

So from this day on you have my blessing to get out there and become a thief.

Copy lighting styles, poses, book covers, movie posters—just get out there and copy. Get inspired and watch your style and portfolio grow.

Now, let's get to work...

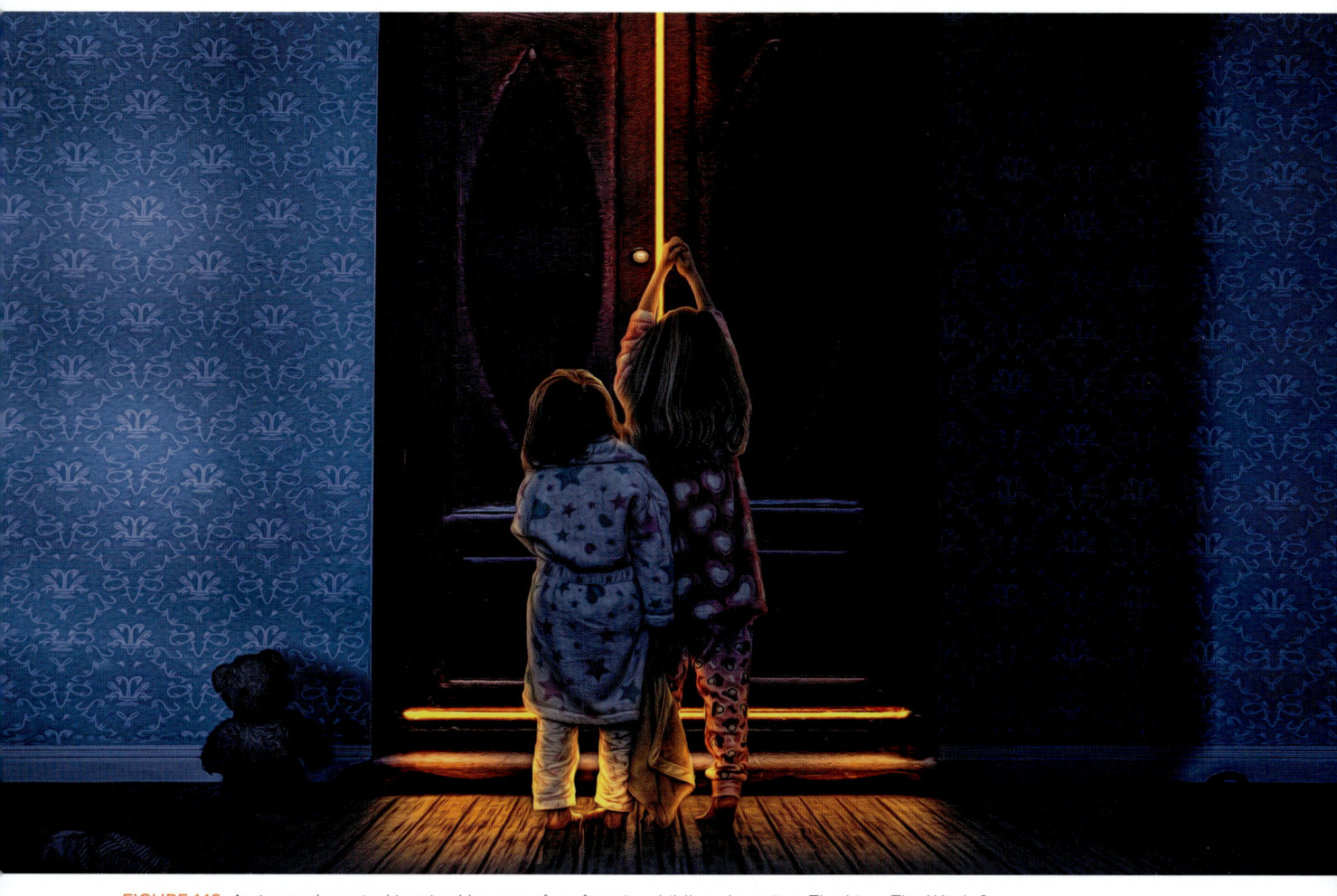

FIGURE 1.16 An image I created inspired by one of my favorite childhood movies, *The Lion, The Witch & The Wardrobe*

YOU CAN'T SHORTCUT THE SHORTCUT BECAUSE COPYING IS THE SHORTCUT.

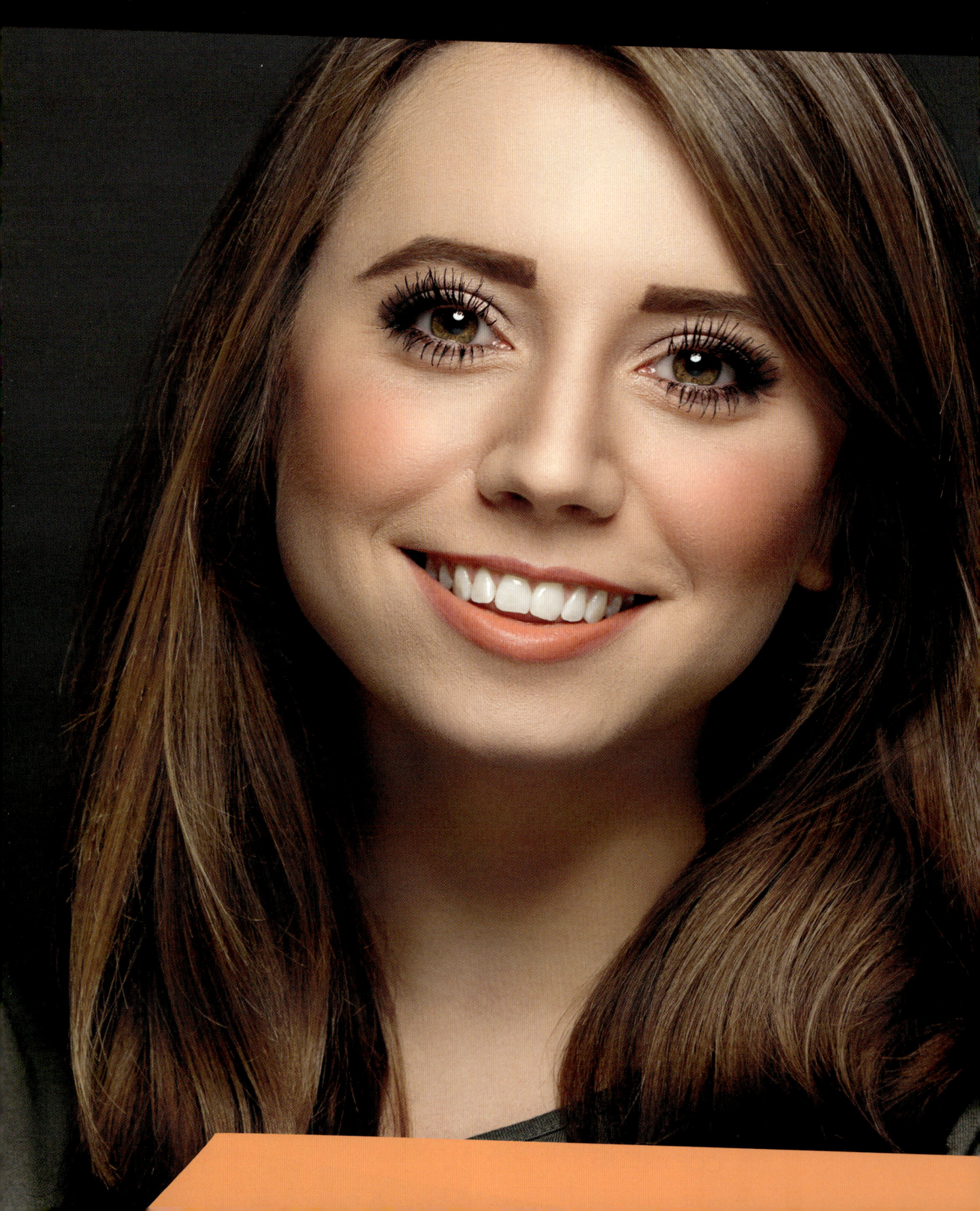

2 REVERSE ENGINEERING

Being able to look at pictures and reverse engineer, or break down, how they were lit is an incredibly useful skill. Determining how many light sources were used by examining the shadows, highlights, and catch lights and observing whether the light is soft or hard not only tests your knowledge and understanding of light, but also will help you to replicate looks and go on to create your own unique images.

In this chapter we'll look at a number of images and by studying the clues, we'll be able to pretty accurately say how each image was lit, how many lights were used, where the lights were positioned, and to some extent, what modifiers were used.

Catch lights in a subject's eyes are always a good place to start, but these days we can't trust them completely because they may have been moved or even eliminated in post-production. Fake light sources can also be added in post-production, and this can make lighting appear much more complicated that it actually is.

The goal here is to have an understanding of how a picture could have been lit. It will be easier to determine the lighting setup for some images than it is for others, and it may be that we're not one-hundred percent accurate in figuring out an exact setup, but that's not a problem because who's to say a similar type of light couldn't be achieved with a slightly different setup? The idea is to get the gray matter working by looking at the clues. This exercise, in addition to spending plenty of time behind the camera, will help you to keep building your knowledge and understanding of light and photography.

Let's start off with just a few simple setups to show how the size, position, and type of modifiers used affects the appearance of catch lights, highlights, and shadows.

SETUP 1

One of the first clues we can see in **Figure 2.1** are the catch lights in the eyes (**A**). There is one round catch light in each eye at the twelve o'clock position (top and middle). This would initially suggest the use of a single light source like a beauty dish (because it's round) on a boom.

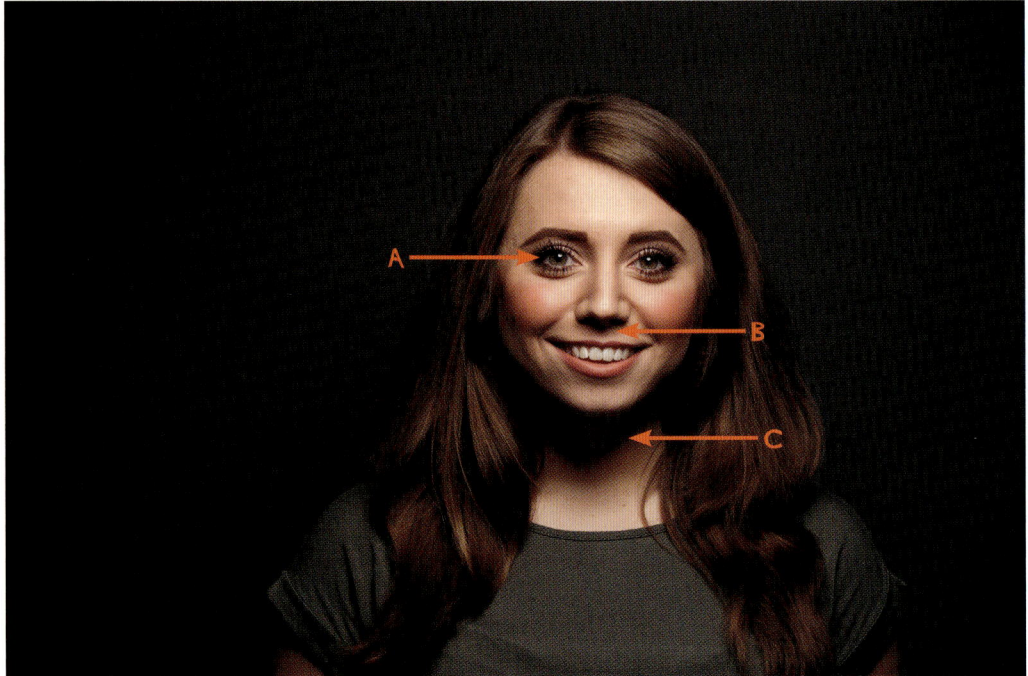

FIGURE 2.1

Looking at the shadows we can see that there is one directly beneath the model's nose (**B**) and one under her chin on her neck (**C**). The shape of the shadows—how each one comes to almost a point in the middle—would suggest that the light source was in front of the model, in line with her face on the camera axis, positioned up high and angled downward. Also note how the shadow areas on either side of the model's face are quite even, again suggesting that the light source was in line with the model's face on the camera axis.

Figure 2.2 shows a behind-the-scenes look at the lighting that created the catch lights and shadows; however, the reflector you can see at chest height was not used to create the image in Figure 2.1.

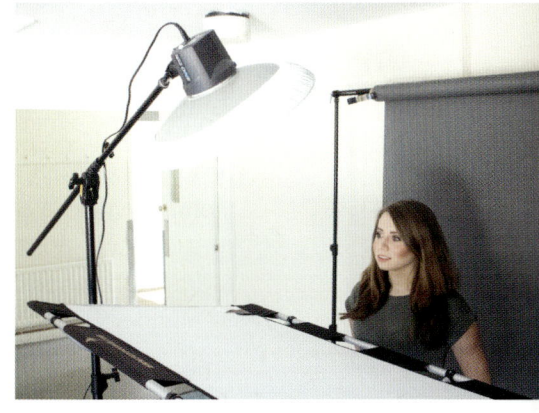

FIGURE 2.2

SETUP 2

Figure 2.3 shows what the catch lights and lighting look like with the same setup as that which was used for Figure 2.1, but this time with the reflector at chest height.

The reflector bounced light upward and the consequence of this is that the shadow areas aren't quite as dark. We can still see the shadows underneath the model's nose and chin, but they are significantly brighter than before.

In both shots, the beauty dish had material stretched over the front (**Figure 2.4**), which softened the light a touch.

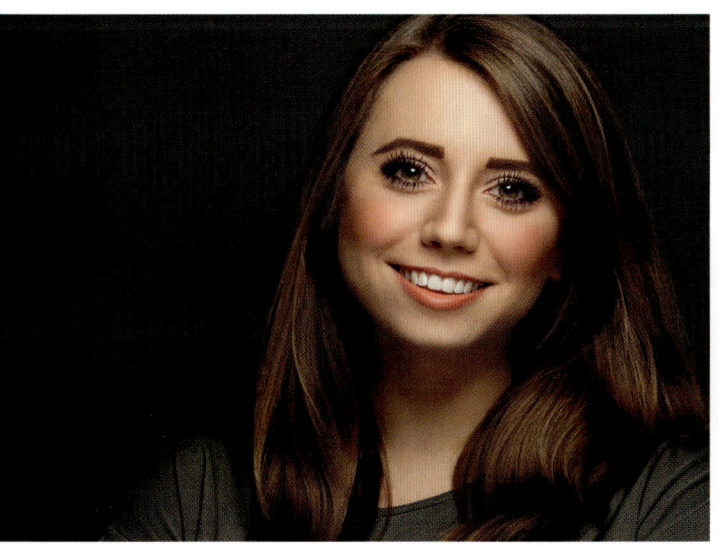

FIGURE 2.3

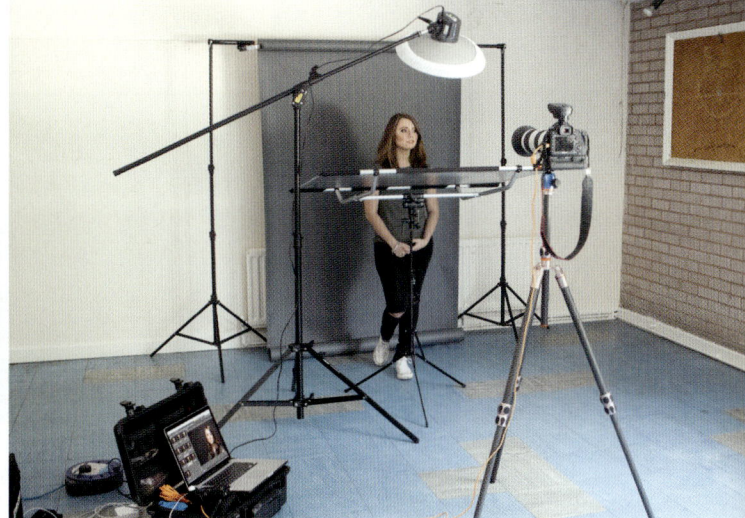

FIGURE 2.4

SETUP 3

In **Figure 2.5** just one side of the model's face is lit (**A**). This suggests that there was a light source aimed at the model directly from the side—in this case, from camera left.

We can see from the catch light (**B**) that the light source is round, which would mean it's something like a beauty dish. The catch light is in the nine o'clock position, which tells us the light was positioned at the same height as her head at camera left. The fact that the edge of the shadow runs down the middle of her face (**C**), rather than being at an angle, is another clue that the light was positioned at head height.

The area where the highlight and shadow areas meet is very pronounced and does not blend gradually, especially on the model's neck (**D**), meaning the light source was quite hard.

Figure 2.6 is a behind-the-scenes picture showing the setup. In this case, the beauty dish did not have any diffusion material other than the deflector across the front to soften the light, and it was positioned at head height and directly to the side.

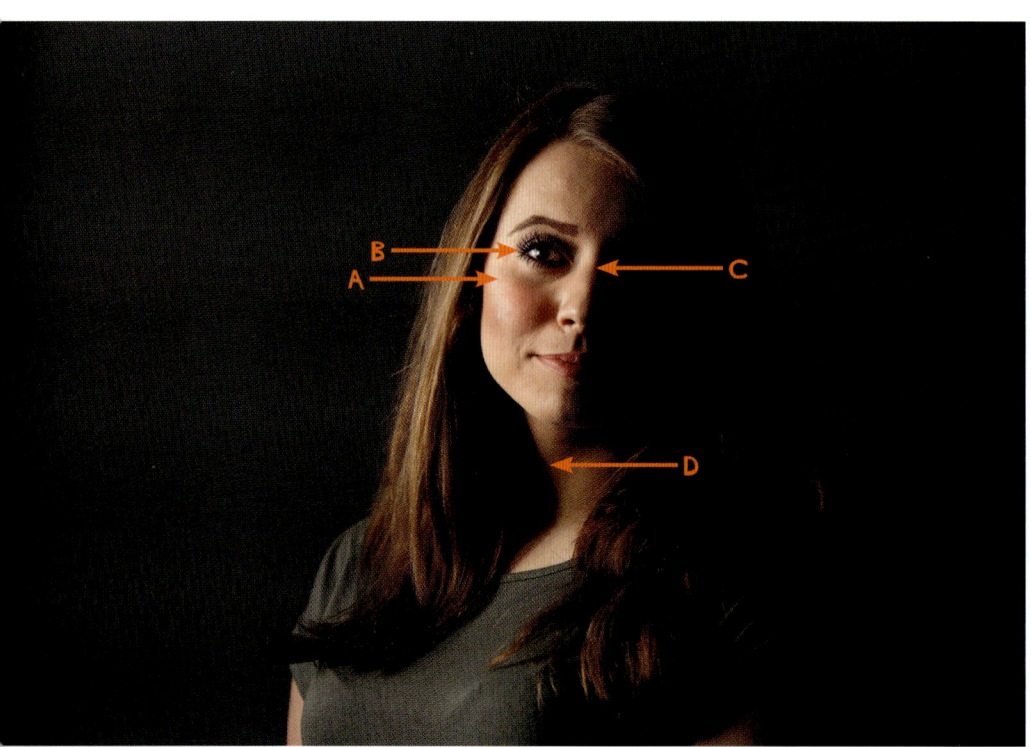

FIGURE 2.5

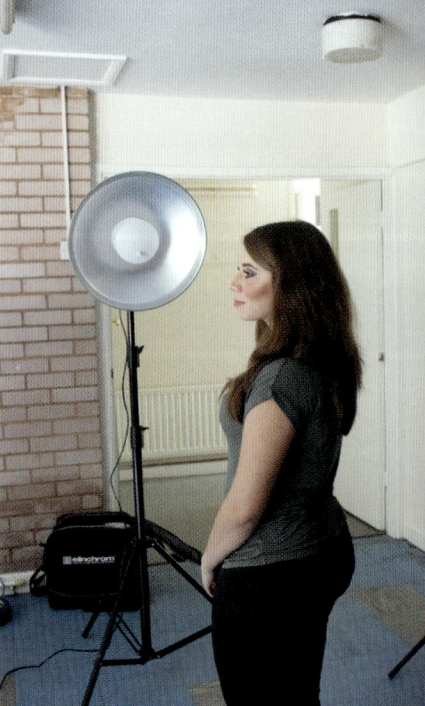

FIGURE 2.6

SETUP 4

In **Figure 2.7** we can see that, again, one side of the model's face is lit and the other side is in shadow (**A**). However, on the shadowed side of her face there is a little bit of light underneath her eye (**B**). This suggests that the light was again positioned to the side of the model at camera left. However, because some light hits the shadowed side of her face, we can tell the light was slightly in front of of the model and closer to the camera. This allows the light to reach past the model's nose and hit that part of her face.

There are two clues that tell us the light was also positioned above the model. First, the catch lights are in the ten o'clock position (**C**). Second, on the shadowed side of the model's face, more light falls on her cheek than on her eye or the part of her forehead above her eye.

The behind-the-scenes shot in **Figure 2.8** shows the lighting setup for this particular picture. The beauty dish is a relatively small light source with no diffusion material apart from the deflector over the flash bulb. It was also positioned at a greater distance from the model than it was for previous shots. This explains why the lighting is hard, by which I mean the shadow and highlight areas are pronounced and don't blend into each other gradually.

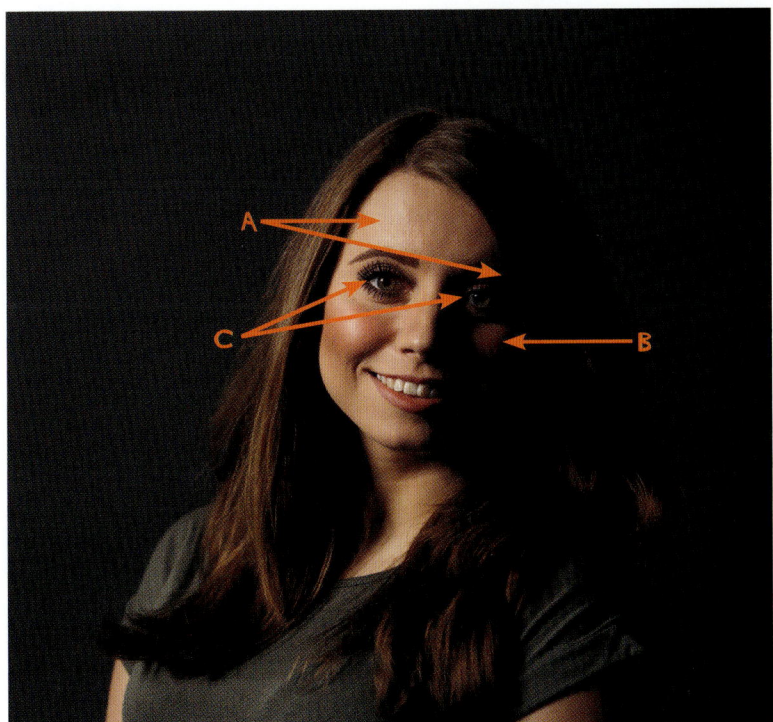

FIGURE 2.7

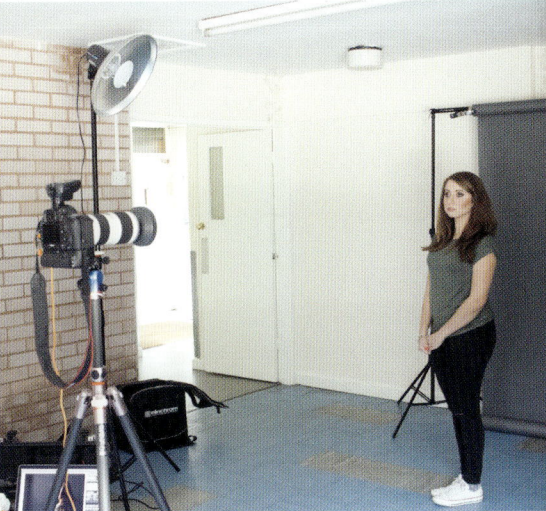

FIGURE 2.8

SETUP 5

The setup for **Figure 2.9** was very similar to the previous setup, but this time the relatively small beauty dish was replaced by a large light source—the Elinchrom Rotalux 135cm Octa.

The light source was positioned to the side and slightly in front of the model. We can tell this because one side of her face is lit and the other is in shadow (**A**), except for an area on her cheek (**B**). The light source was again positioned above the model and angled downward, which we can tell by the fact that the catch lights in her eyes (**C**) are roughly around the ten o'clock position and the light on the shadowed side of her face falls mainly on her cheek and just a little to the side of her mouth. There is not much light falling on her eye or the part of her forehead just above her eye.

Figure 2.10 is a behind-the-scenes picture showing the lighting setup that produced this particular look.

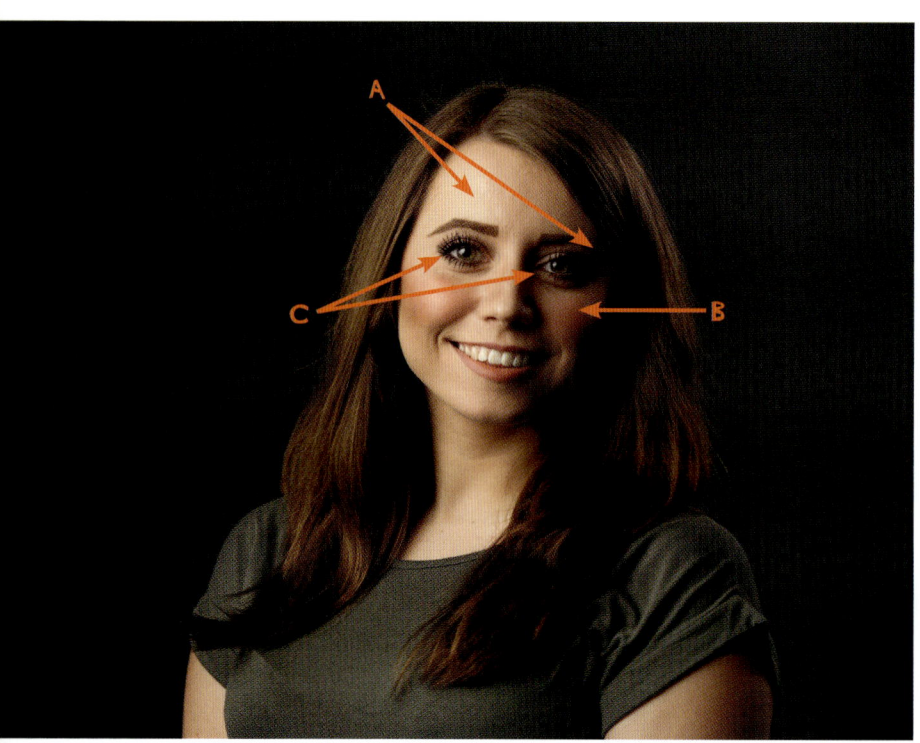

FIGURE 2.9

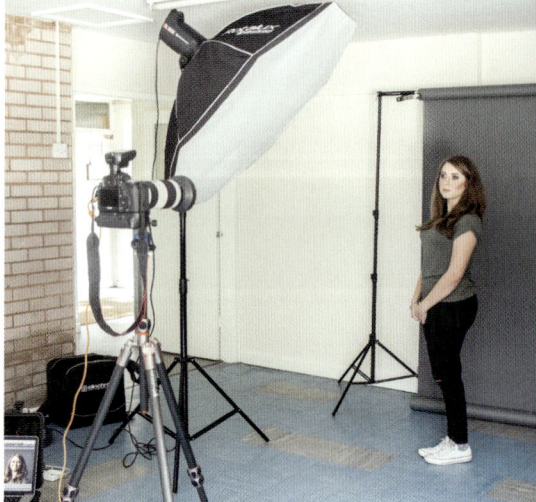

FIGURE 2.10

SETUP 6

Figure 2.11 is a silhouette created by positioning the model directly in front of the light source (**Figure 2.12**), which in this case was the Elinchrom Rotalux 135cm Octa (my favorite).

I like to use this setup when I want a clean, bright-white background behind a model. Obviously, I can't use a setup like this for full length shots, but when I use the larger 175cm version I can take three-quarter length shots from about knee height upward.

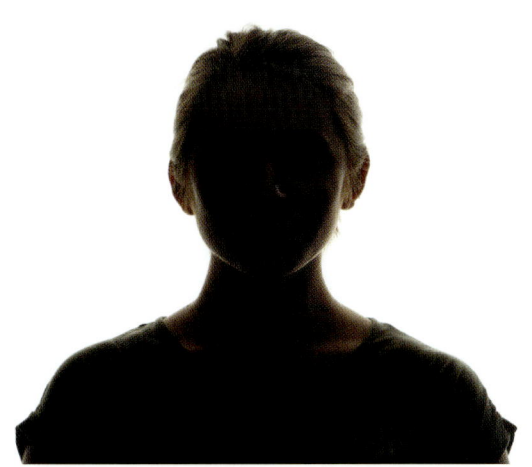

FIGURE 2.11

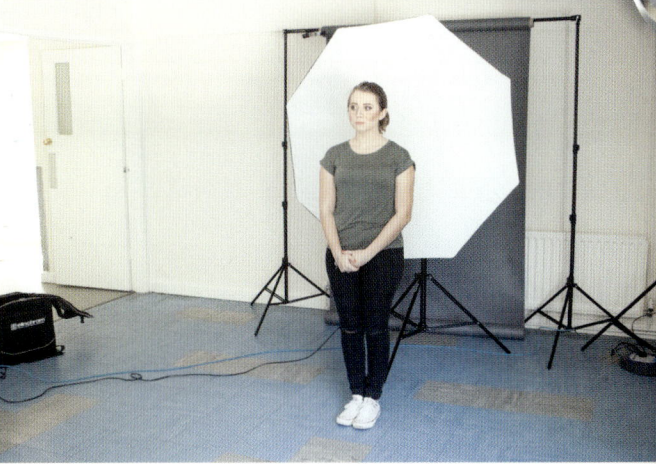

FIGURE 2.12

This is a setup I started to use after a shoot I did when a light I had positioned to the front of my subject did not go off. It turned out that I really liked the result, as did the subject in the shot, boxer Steven Cook (**Figure 2.13**).

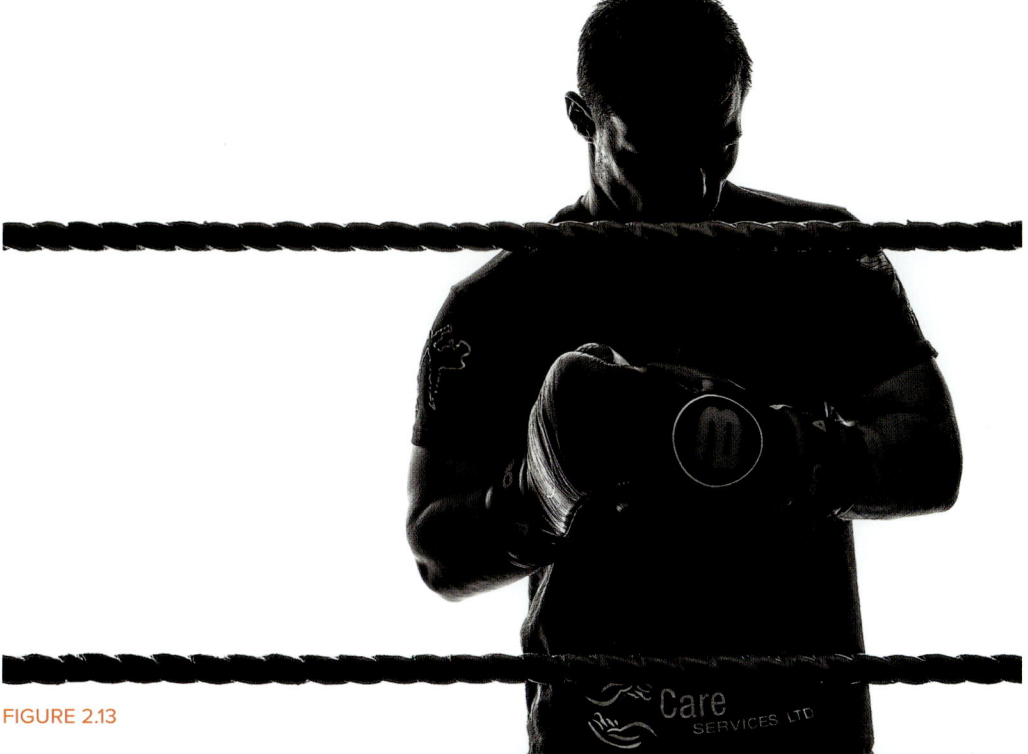

FIGURE 2.13

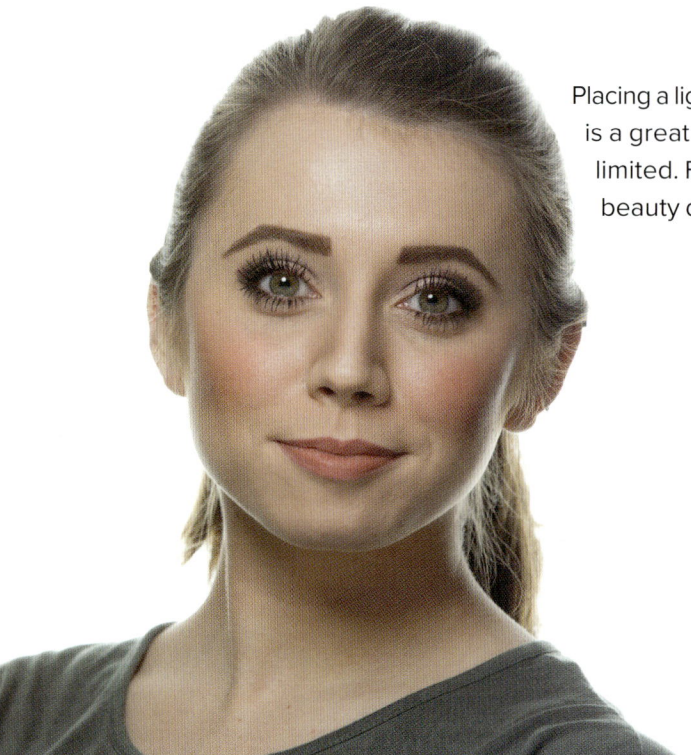

Placing a light source behind the model to create a white background is a great setup when you're shooting in an area where space is limited. For **Figure 2.14** I used this setup with the addition of the beauty dish and reflector positioned as in Setup 2 (**Figure 2.15**).

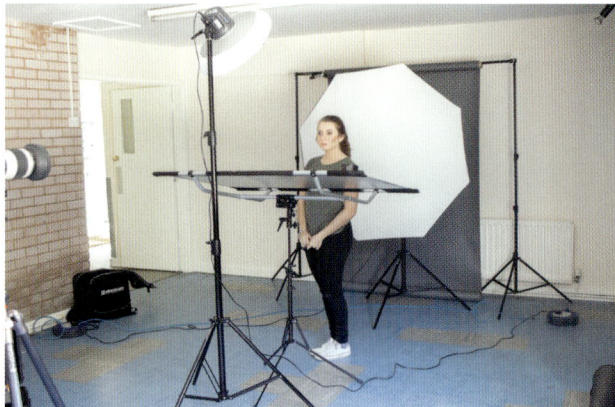

FIGURE 2.14

FIGURE 2.15

Oh, and let me share a random tip that I use when photographing someone in front of a light source like this. Invariably, doing so results in your model's ears lighting up (**Figure 2.16**), so one thing you can do to combat this is to stick a piece of gaffers tape behind their ears (**Figure 2.17**). This might sound a little crazy and you might get a few odd stares, but it'll save you a heck of a lot of time in post-production. Just don't forget to tell your model to remove it when you're done.

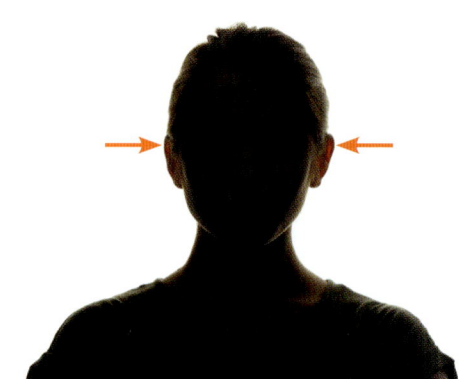

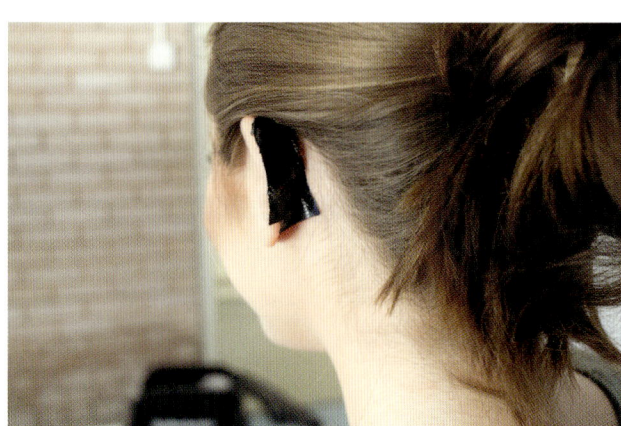

FIGURE 2.16

FIGURE 2.17

Okay, now that we've gone through some basic setups and seen a few examples of how we can look at shadows, highlights, and catch lights to get a good idea of the lighting setup used, let's take a look at some finished images from my own portfolio.

PICTURE 1

You wouldn't be wrong if you guessed that two light sources were used to create this picture (**Figure 2.18**). One light produced the bright highlight on the model's face and the highlights running down the arm and front of his coat (**A**), and another, coming from camera left, caused the shadow of the dog to fall on the model's coat (**B**).

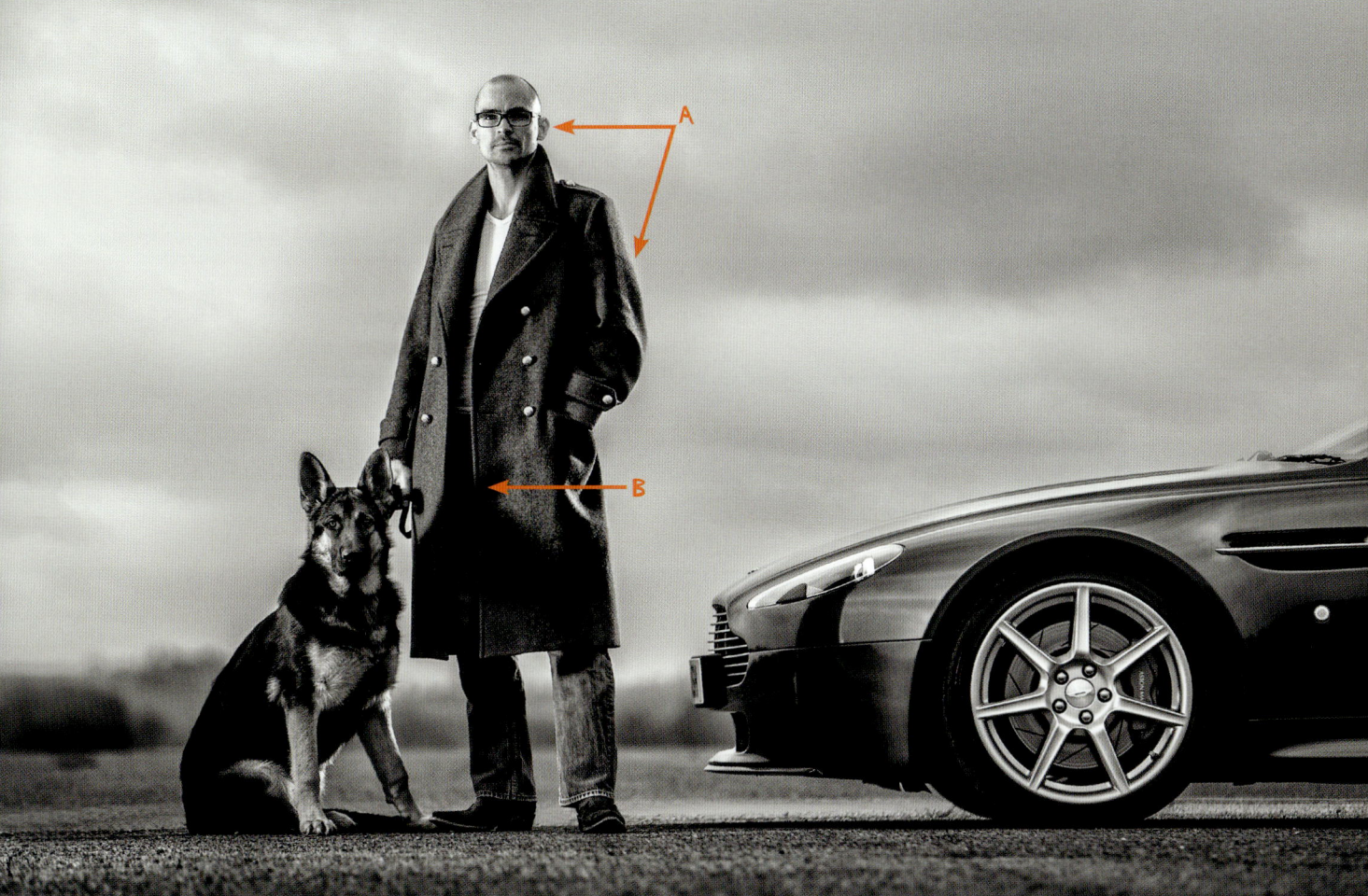

FIGURE 2.18

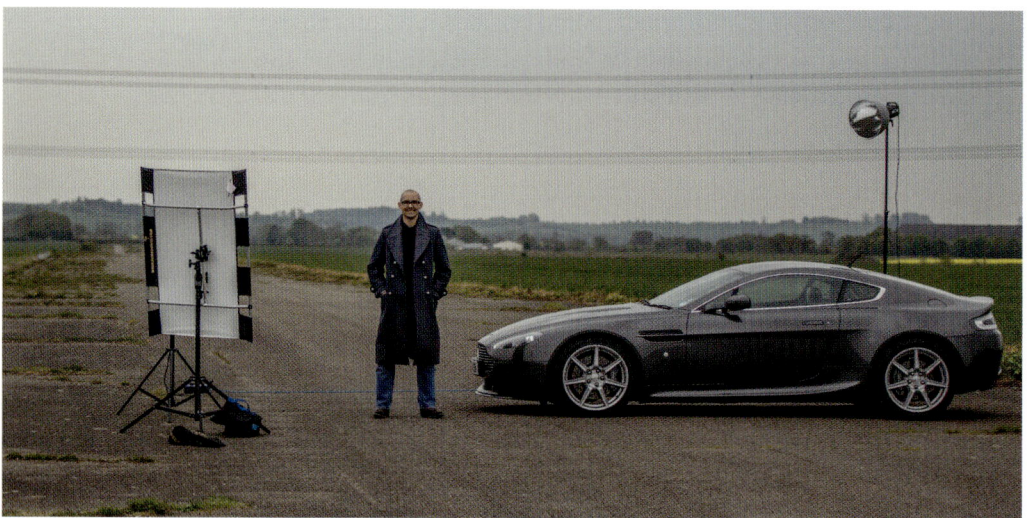

FIGURE 2.19

The actual setup is shown in **Figure 2.19**. I positioned one light at camera right, aimed at the model. I positioned a silver reflector at camera left to bounce light back onto the model. A light positioned at camera left would have worked great as well; the only reason I didn't use one was because the power cable was not long enough to reach the one power source we had on location.

This is a great example of how post-production can hide the evidence of light sources. In the native image you could clearly see the silver reflector in the front wing of the car so I used Photoshop to remove it.

PICTURE 2

For **Figure 2.20** I used just one light source positioned to the side (camera left) and slightly in front of the subjects. I placed it up high and angled down slightly, just as in Setup 5.

We can tell how the lights were positioned by looking at the highlights and shadows on most of the faces. Notice how the camera-left side of each face is lit and the camera-right side is in shadow, except for the area under each subject's eye (**A**)?

We can also see that the light was positioned at camera left by examining the shadows cast onto the floor (**B**) and the shadow on the back of my nephew Will's upper arm (**C**).

In the behind-the-scenes picture you can just about see the light source on the left-hand side (**Figure 2.21**).

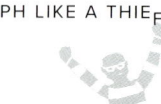

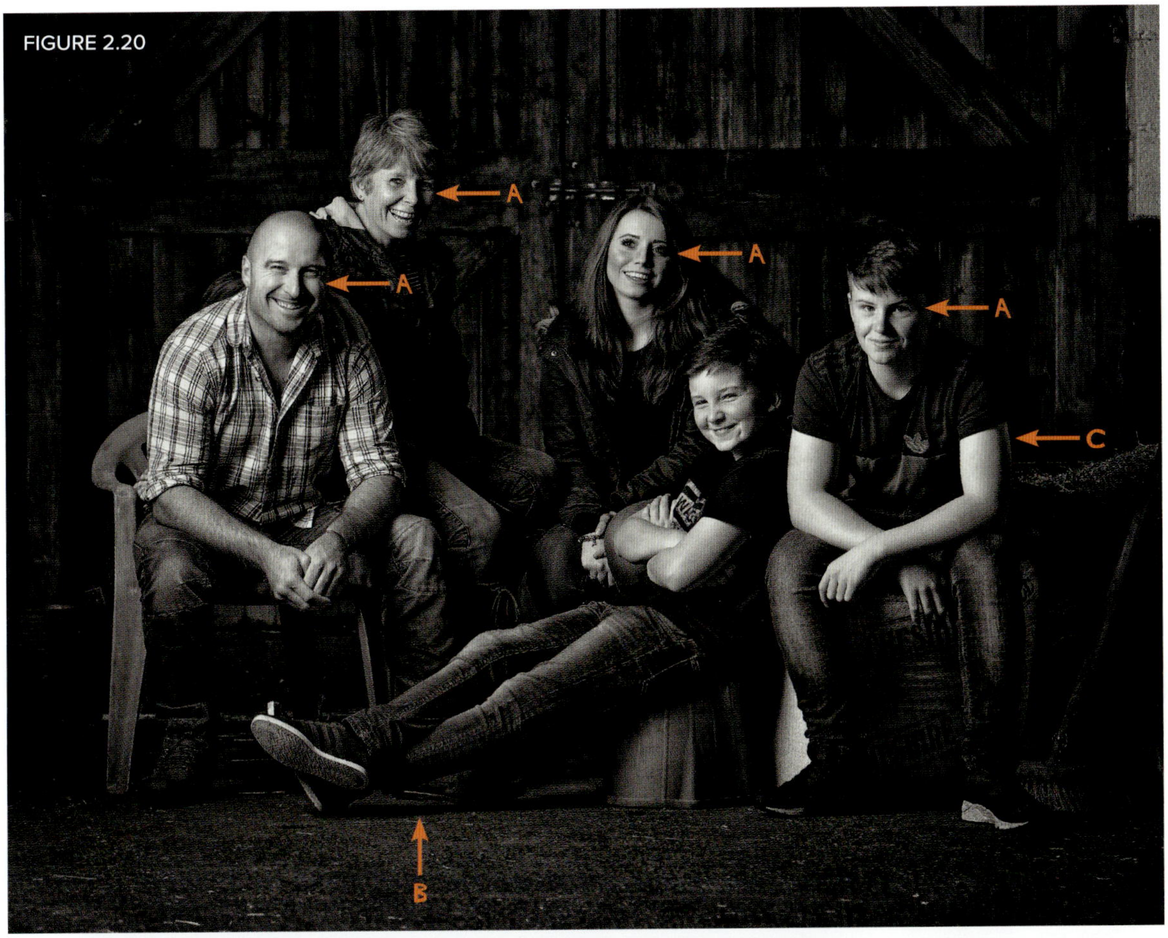

FIGURE 2.20

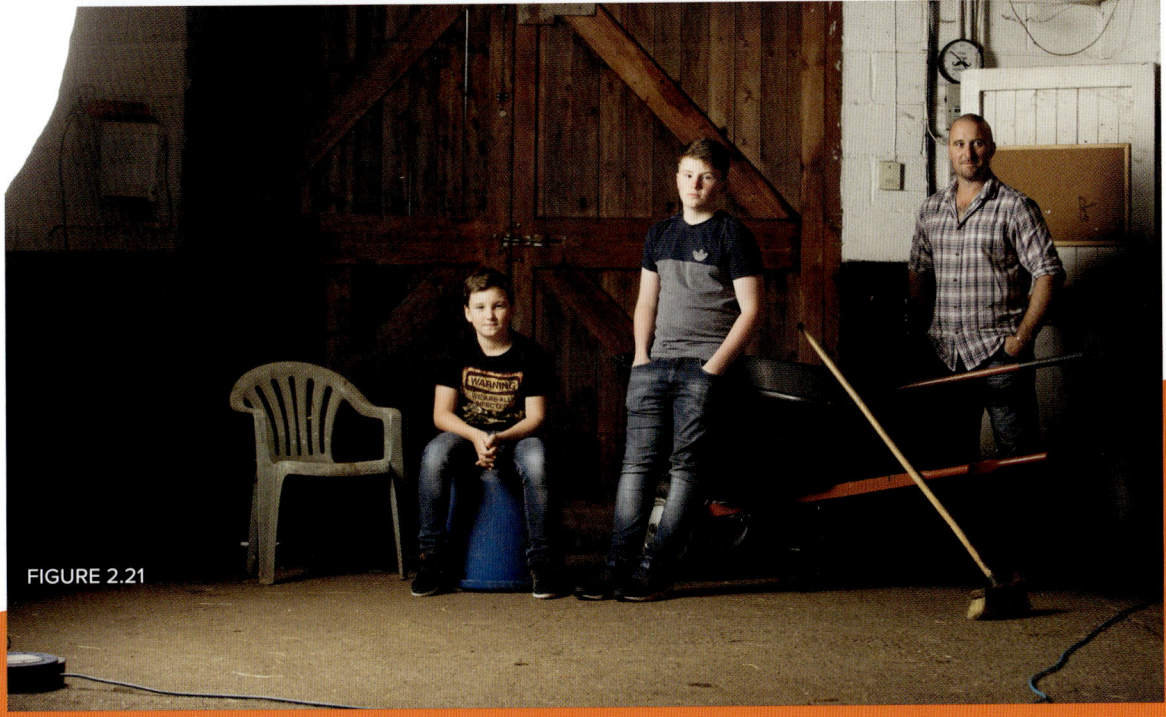

FIGURE 2.21

27

PICTURE 3

I used just one light source for **Figure 2.22**, which we can tell by looking at the shadows and highlights on the subject's face. The camera-left side of his face is lit and camera-right side is darker, except for the light around his cheek and eye (**A**).

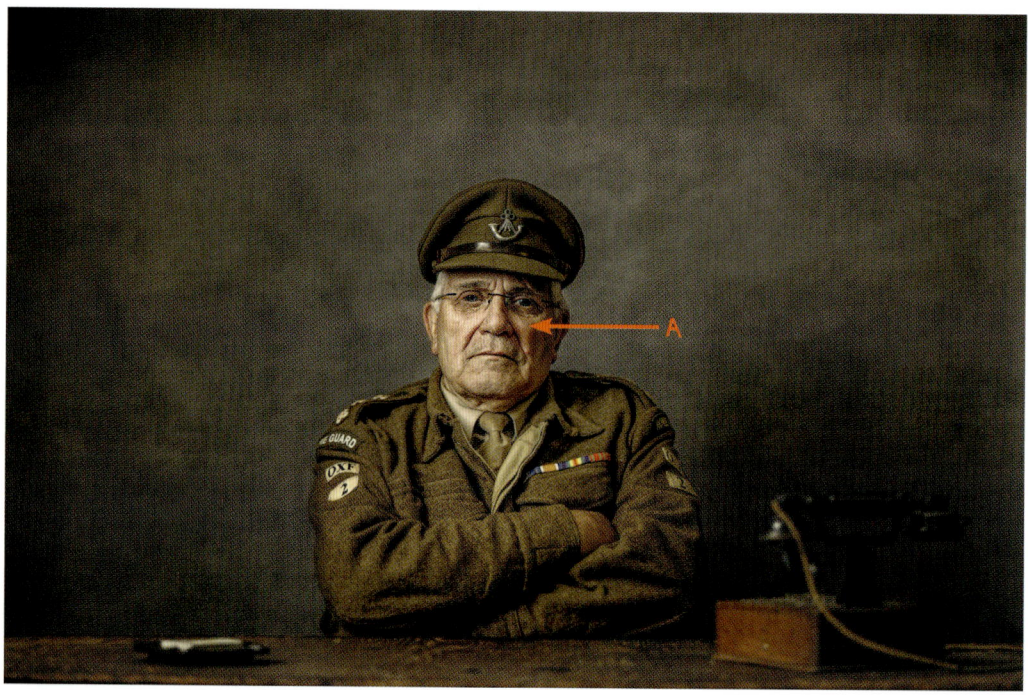

FIGURE 2.22

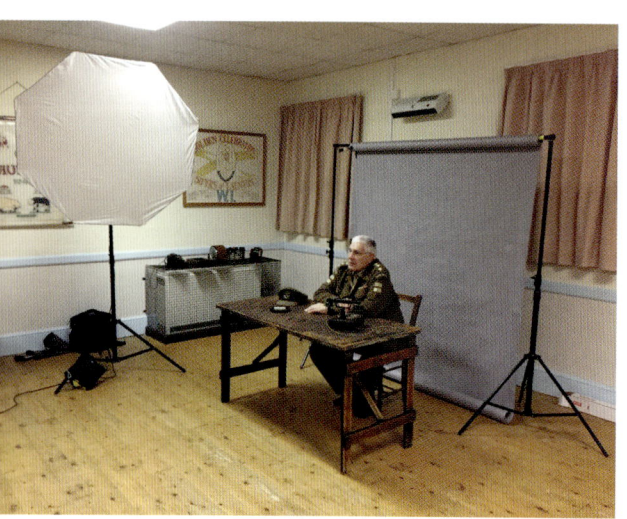

FIGURE 2.23

Going by what was covered in Setups 4 and 5, the light on the camera-right side of the subject's face would suggest the light source was positioned at camera left and in front of the subject, and here's a behind-the-scenes picture to prove it (**Figure 2.23**).

A similar setup was used for **Figure 2.24**, but on a much smaller scale. The subject, Steven Cook, was lit with a Phottix Mitros+ speedlight and the Rogue FlashBender 2 XL Pro (see chapter 3), which is a smaller light source, but because it was positioned very close to Steven it gave a softer light.

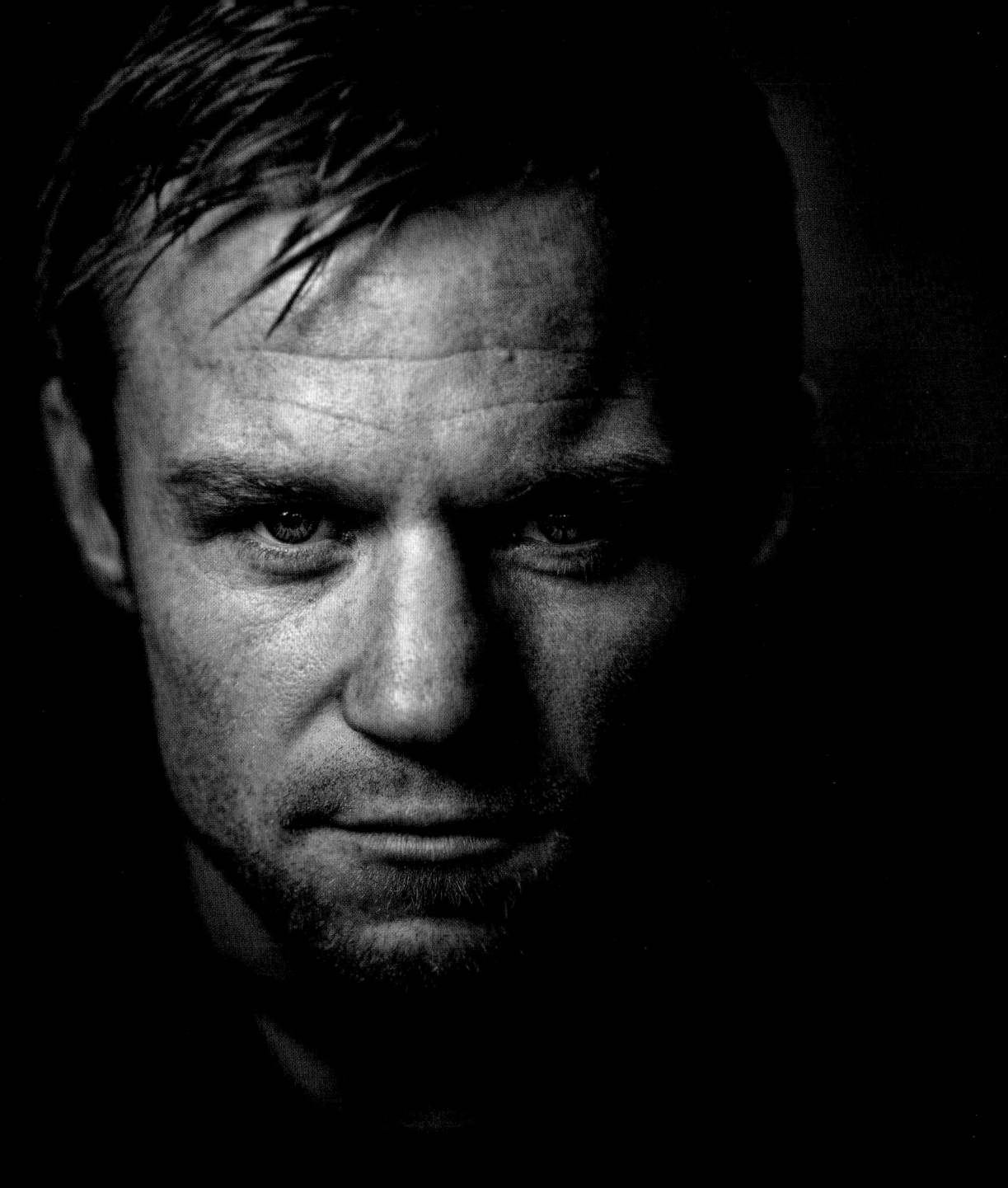

FIGURE 2.24

We can tell whether the light source was positioned higher than the model and angled down or placed directly to the side by considering the prominence of the nose shadow. When the light comes directly from the side we can see the nose shadow very clearly (**Figure 2.25**). When the light is positioned higher and angled down the nose shadow joins with the shadow around the cheek.

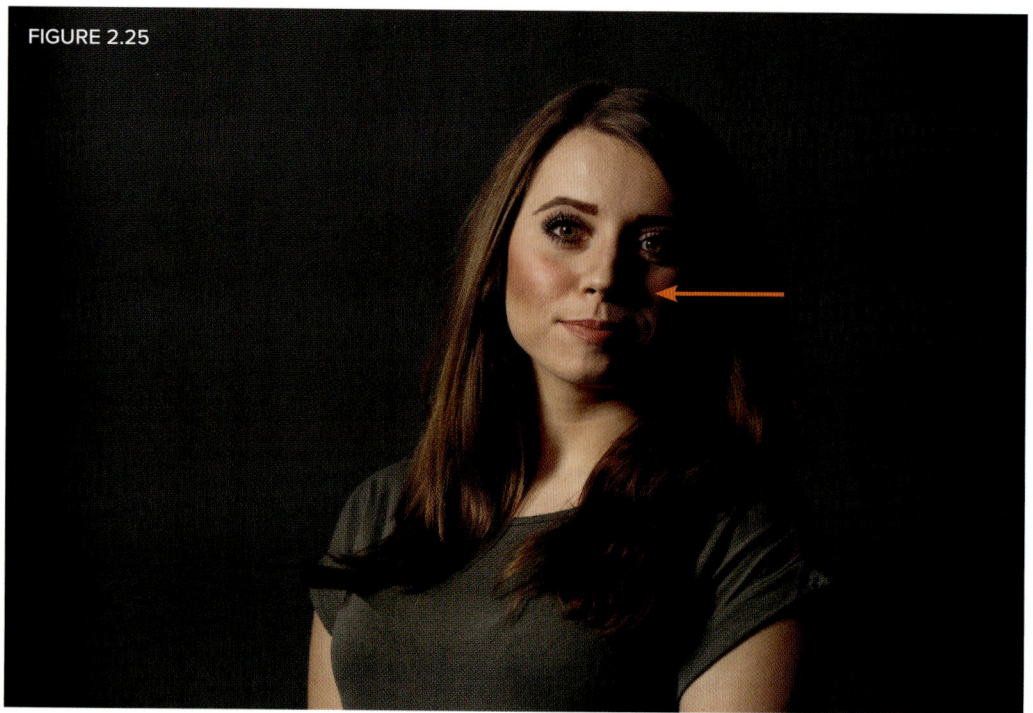
FIGURE 2.25

PICTURE 4

In **Figure 2.26** we can see that two light sources were used: one lit the side of the model's face furthest from camera (**A**) and the other lit the side of his face closest to the camera (**B**).

The setup for this started out very similar to Setup 3, with a light source—in this case, an Elinchrom Rotalux 135cm Octa—positioned directly to the side of the subject in the nine o'clock position. This would have left the side of his face nearest to the camera in shadow; however, another light was placed behind the model at camera right and aimed at that side of his face (**Figure 2.27**).

This is a great example of how moving around your subject to take photographs from different angles, rather than sticking to one camera position in front of the subject, can result in more picture options.

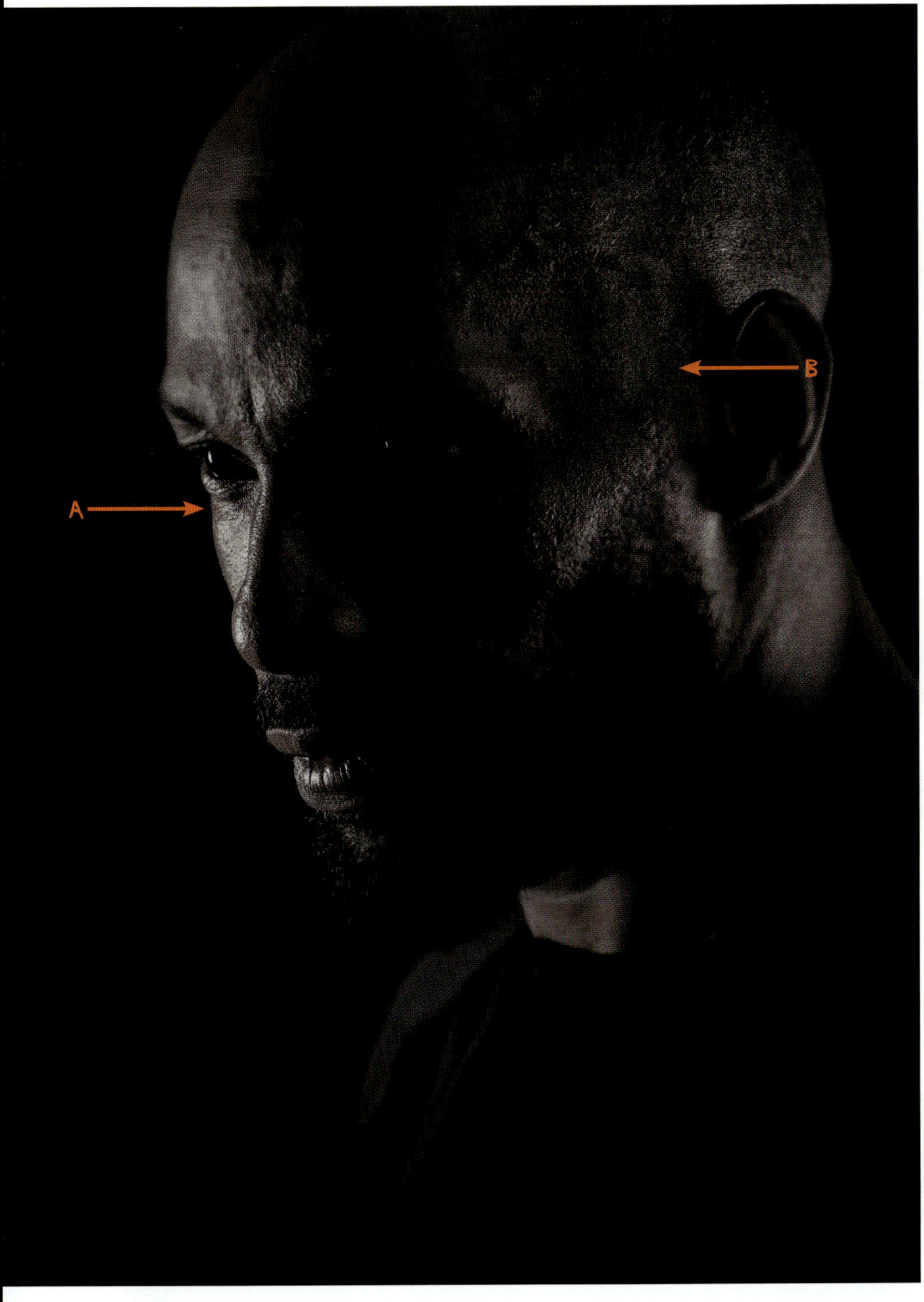

FIGURE 2.26

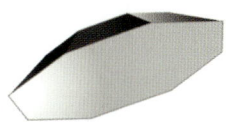

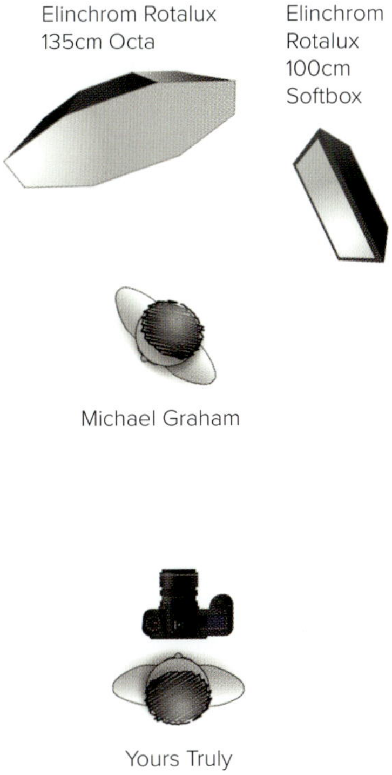

Elinchrom Rotalux 135cm Octa

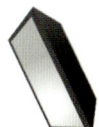

Elinchrom Rotalux 100cm Softbox

Michael Graham

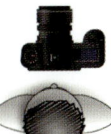

Yours Truly

FIGURE 2.27

PICTURE 5

In this portrait of World Champion Bodybuilder Nigel St Lewis (**Figure 2.28**) we can see that two light sources have been used due to the fact that both the camera-left (**A**) and camera-right (**B**) sides of Nigel are being hit with light.

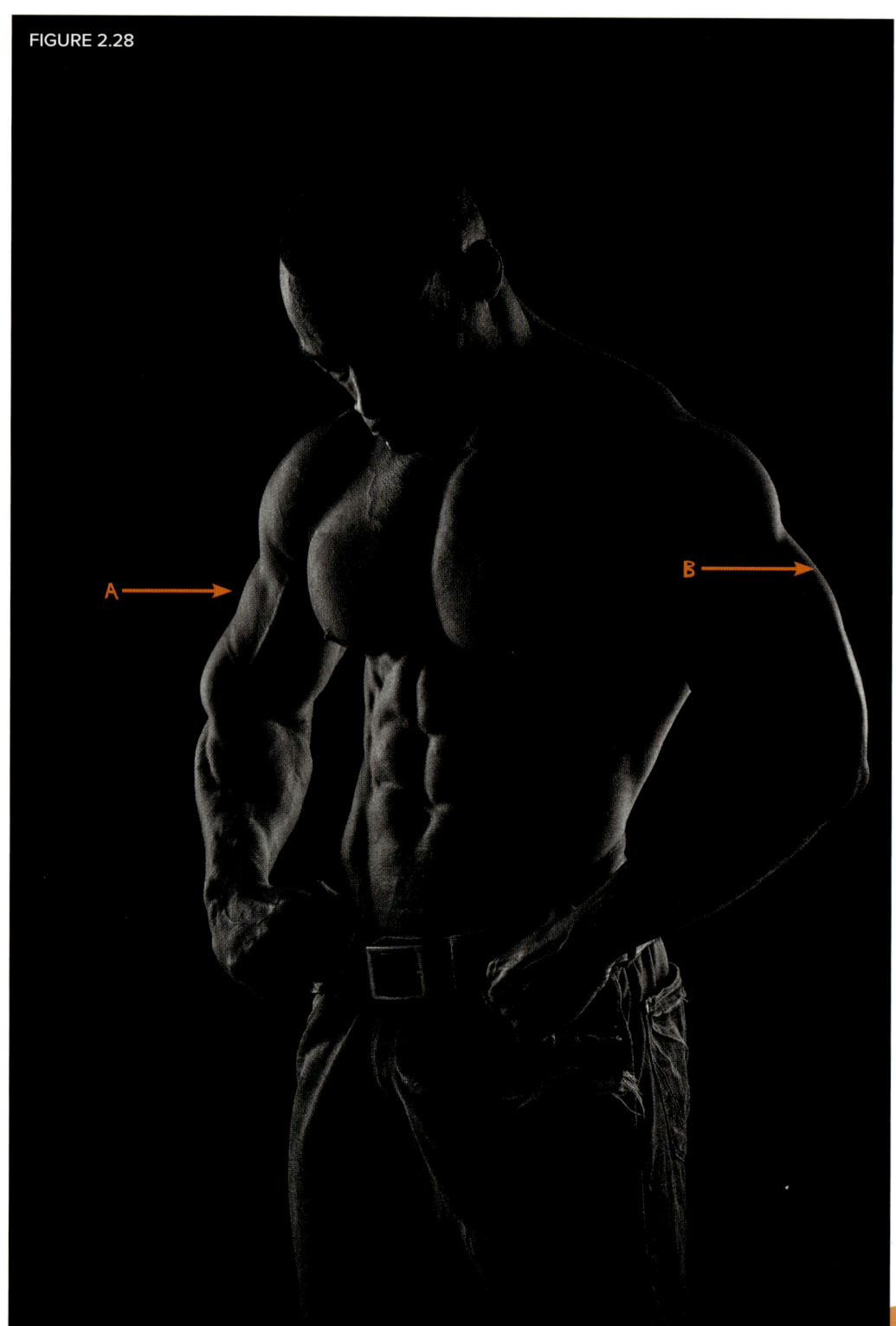

FIGURE 2.28

The light on both sides of the model is even from top to bottom. This is due to the use of strip boxes (**Figure 2.29**). The strip boxes were fitted with grids to avoid unwanted light spill, giving the light more direction and focus, which works perfectly on physique shots like this.

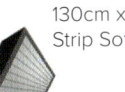
Elinchrom Rotalux 130cm x 50cm Strip Softbox

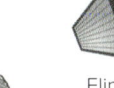
Elinchrom Rotalux 130cm x 50cm Strip Softbox

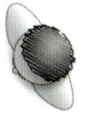
Nigel St Lewis

PICTURE 6

In this picture of boxer Nathan Graham (**Figure 2.30**) I used a single light source positioned higher than him at camera right. We can see that one main light was used because the light falls naturally in one direction. We can also see that the side of his face nearest the camera is lit and the side furthest from the camera is in shadow (**A**).

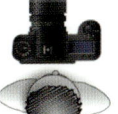
Yours Truly

FIGURE 2.29

I also used a reflector (**Figure 2.31**) to bounce a little bit of light back onto Nathan because he was wearing dark clothing and the shadows were darker than I wanted. Of course, I could have used another light source on a very low power setting, instead.

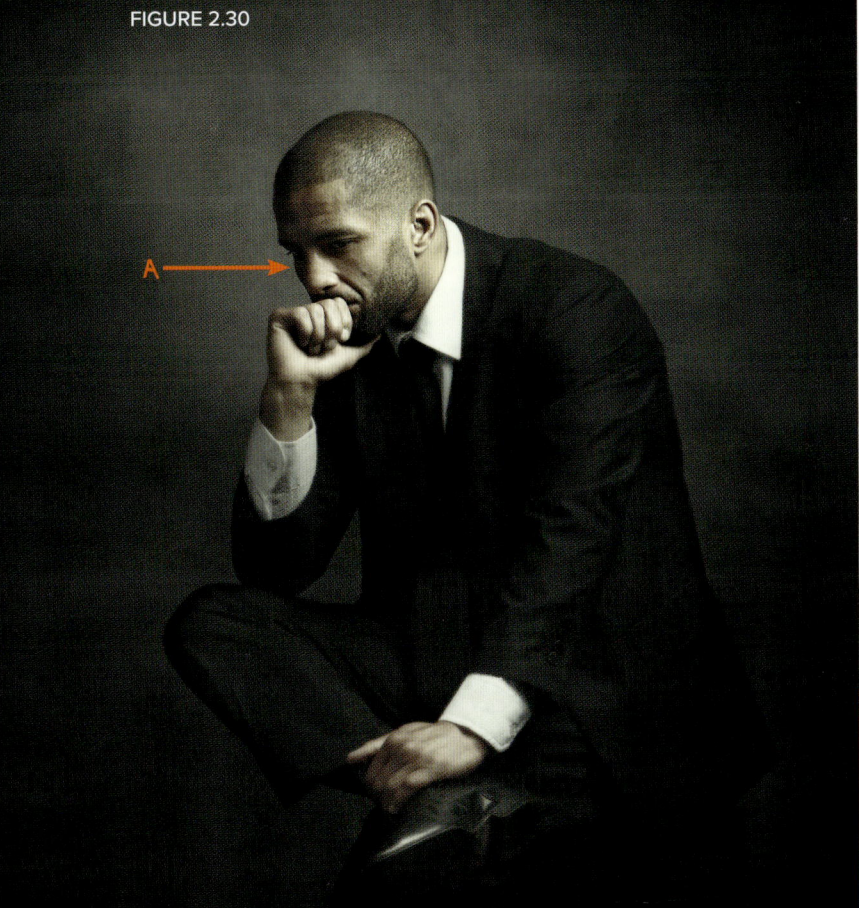
FIGURE 2.30

A →

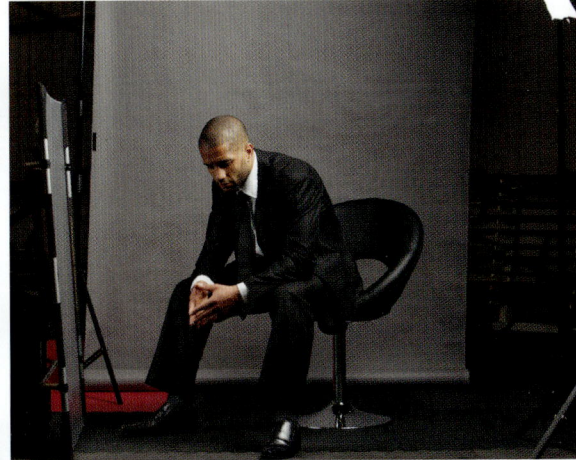
FIGURE 2.31

PICTURE 7

When you first look at **Figure 2.32** you could easily think that a large number of lights were used; however, this is another good example of how post-production can change the appearance of the lighting. In fact, just three lights were used to create this image.

Let's break it down by first looking at boxer Steven Cook on the left. We can see that there is a shadow being cast onto his shoulder and upper arm by the boxing ring rope (**A**), which would suggest that a light was positioned somewhere at camera left. This is backed up by the fact that there is light hitting the back and side of his head (**B**).

When we look at Coach Michael Zilles on the right we can see that his back is being lit (**C**), as is the back and top of his head (**D**). This would suggest that there was a light source positioned somewhere at camera right. This is backed up by the shadow we can see on the padding just above Steven's head.

FIGURE 2.32

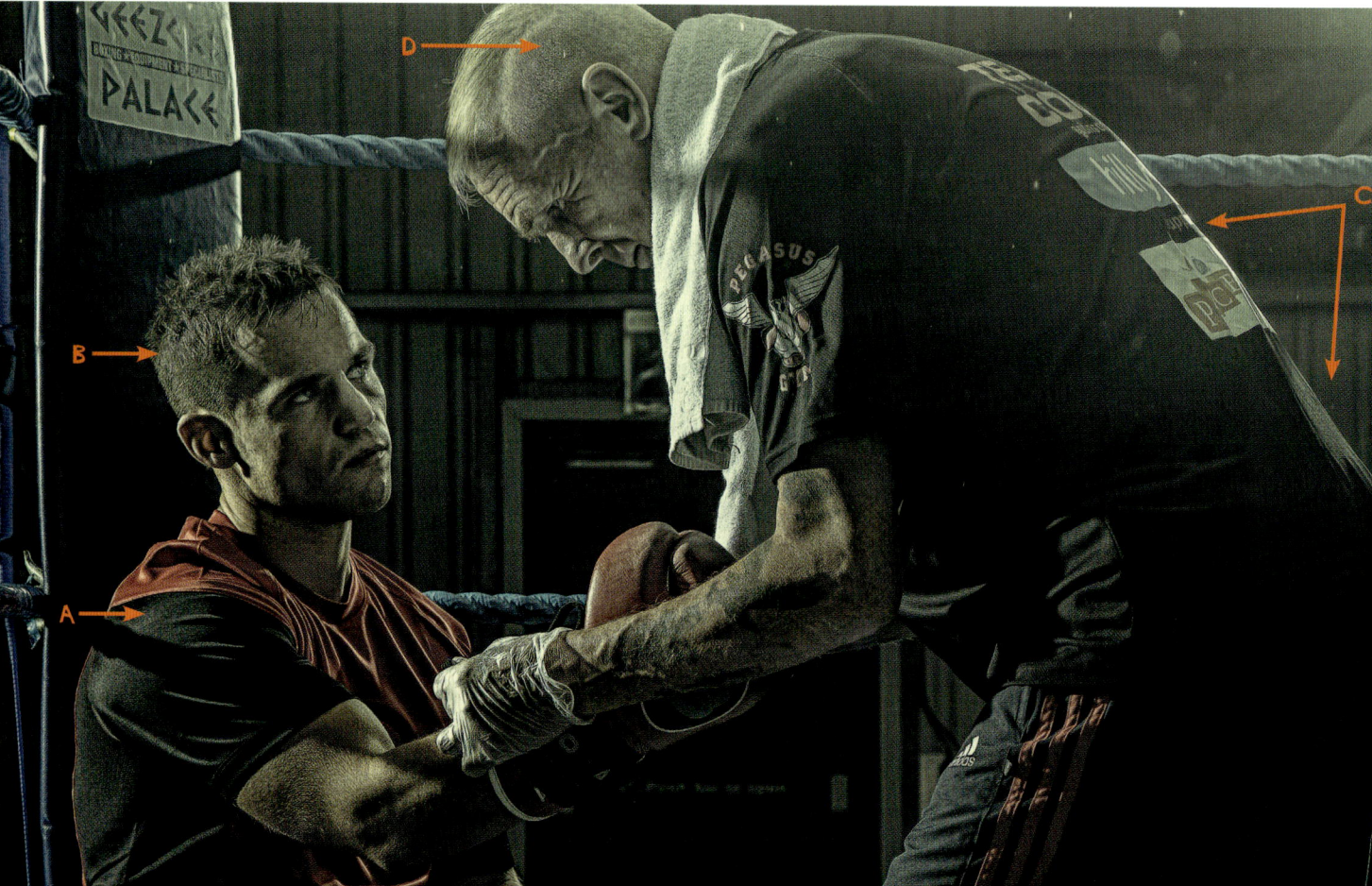

Two lights would have been sufficient, but I added a third light above the camera to fill in shadow areas on both Steven and Michael; otherwise, the picture would have been way too dark.

In the behind-the-scenes picture (**Figure 2.33**) you can see the lights at camera left and camera right. I fitted reflectors to the flash heads to mimic the kind of lighting you would get in a boxing arena.

PICTURE 8

Figure 2.34 shows the typical lighting style I use when photographing muscular physiques. Again, because of all the highlights and shadows, you could easily overthink the lighting setup, whereas, in fact, it is very simple.

First of all, when we look at the outline of physique athlete James Borne's body, we can see that the light around him (**A**) is brighter than that on the front of his body or his face. This suggests that he was being lit on either side, which is true—there was a strip box at camera left and one at camera right.

When we look the front of James we can see that the top of his head is lit and there is a shadow under his chin (**B**). There are also shadows underneath his chest muscles and armpits (**C**), which tells us there was a light source above James that was angled down.

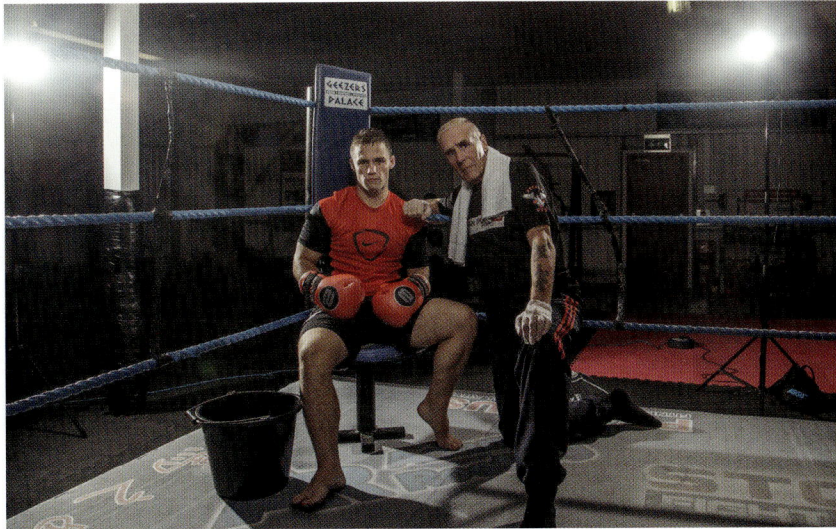

FIGURE 2.33

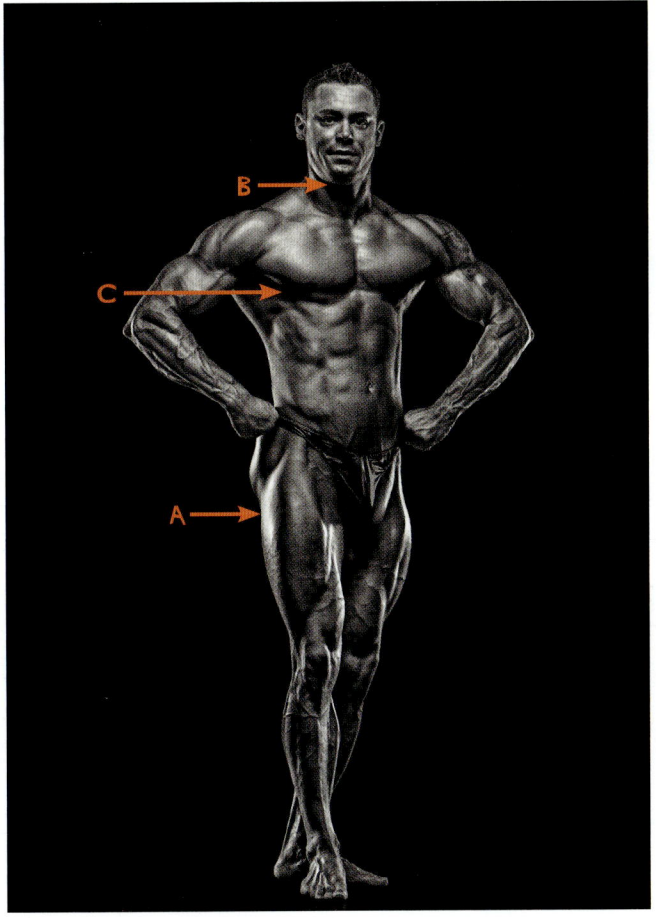

FIGURE 2.34

Figure 2.35 is a behind-the-scenes picture showing the lighting setup.

You can see that there were two strip boxes on either side of the platform, and there was an Elinchrom Rotalux 135cm Octa overhead that was pointed directly down to the ground. This light was positioned about a half meter in front of where James stood. This light illuminates areas of the body that are pronounced and deepens the shadows on areas that are recessed. The result of this is like dodging and burning in-camera so that the muscle looks much more defined.

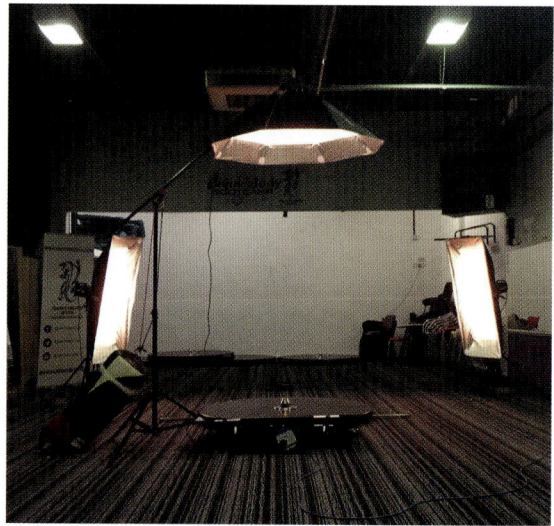

FIGURE 2.35

James was situated on a platform so that the reflector on the floor in front him was out of camera view but bounced a little bit of light back onto his lower body.

Note also that I removed the outer diffusion panels on each of the modifiers to create a light that is midway between soft and hard—a lighting style I prefer to use on muscular physiques.

PICTURE 9

This picture of physique athlete Glenn Richardson (**Figure 2.36**) is a bit misleading, to be honest, because there were actually no flash heads used. If you looked at this and thought there was a light aimed at his shoulders and back to produce the highlights on top of his shoulders, and maybe another light at the front of Glenn, you wouldn't be wrong.

In fact, this was photographed using natural, ambient light, which is something I try to do as often as possible when I'm photographing in a gym so I cause as little disruption as possible.

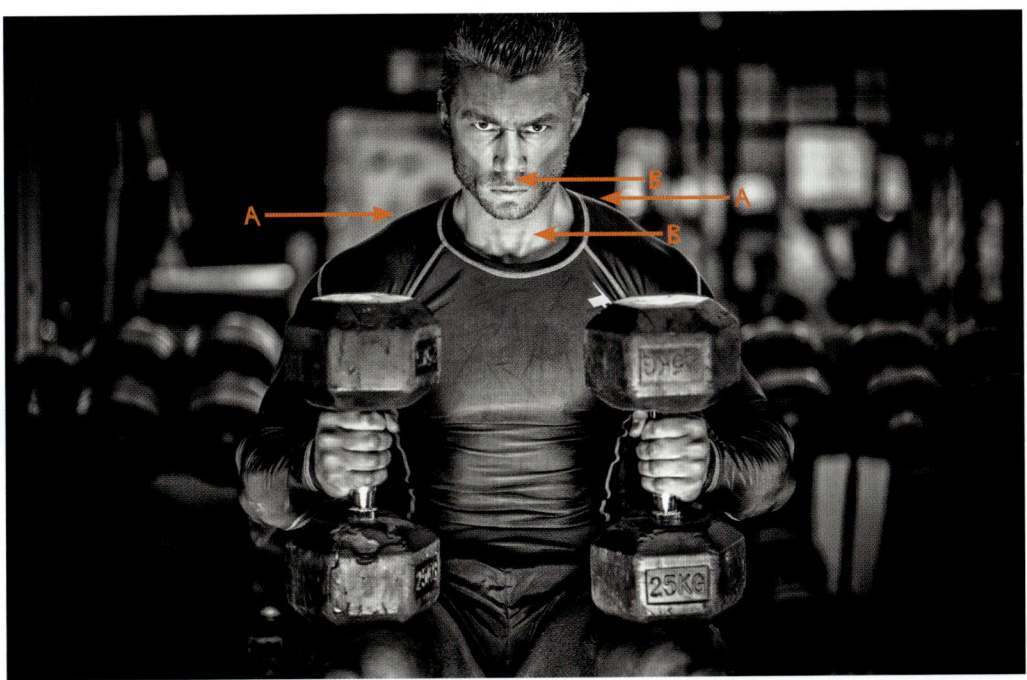

FIGURE 2.36

The light on Glenn's shoulders (**A**) comes from lights in the ceiling directly above him (**Figure 2.37**). The only other light is sunlight bounced off a silver reflector on the ground in front of Glenn, creating the uplighting effect. We can tell a light of some sort was aimed up toward Glenn because there are no shadows under his chin or nose (**B**).

So, now we've looked at just a few example pictures to get a feel for how they were lit. Reverse engineering pictures is a great exercise that can really help you gain a better understanding of light. Like I said before, the idea here isn't necessarily to be spot-on with the lighting and which modifiers were used, because similar looks can be achieved in many different ways. However, being able to see where light is being used is a great way to replicate looks, and with that knowledge, go on to create something of your own.

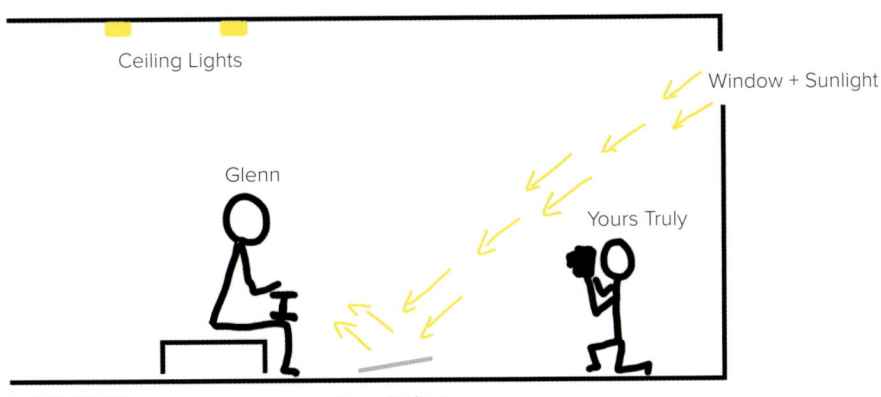

FIGURE 2.37

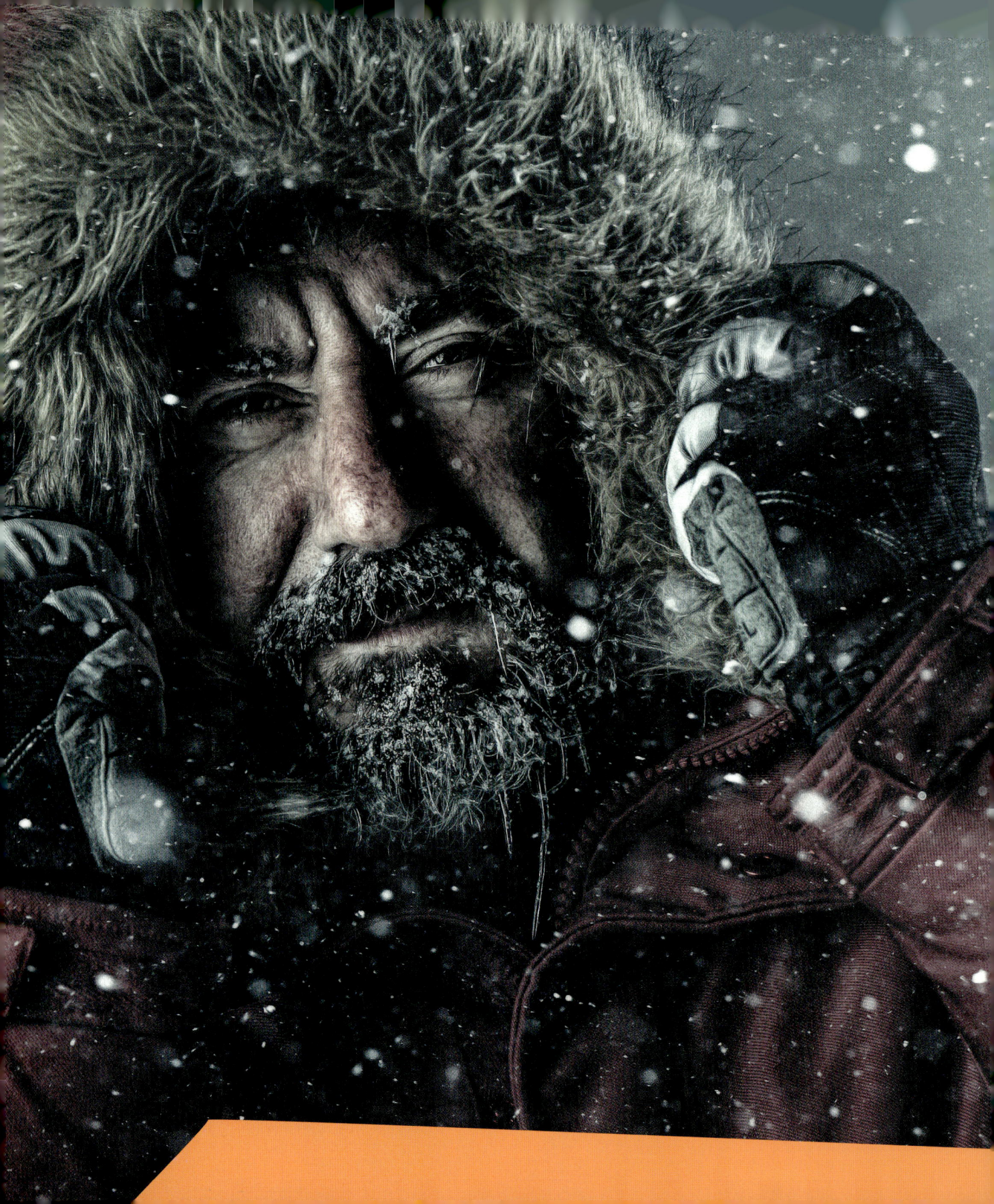

3 GEAR TALK

I'm often asked what kit I use and why. Seeing as how we're going through the whole photo shoot and post-production process in this book, I thought this would be the ideal place to share pretty much everything I use. The gear that is listed over the following pages is what I find works well for me. I've tried a lot of different equipment, and spent a lot of money, to get to the point where I'm using what best suits me, my workflow, and the kind of work I do.

I most definitely am not into the whole "my brand is better than your brand" argument because history shows that a new feature of one brand will most likely appear on another brand at some point down the line. I've jumped around trying to find what I like most more times than I can or dare say, but right now, I'm in a happy place with what I'm using.

Oh, and I think it's worth mentioning that none of the brands you see in the following pages are lining my pockets for using them. I don't get a kickback or anything for mentioning them; I use them because they fit with what I need and like, and they do it well consistently, without ever letting me down.

CAMERA

When I first started out I was shooting with a Nikon D200. I loved that camera. I started with Nikon purely because everyone I was following and learning from was using them. I had friends who were using Nikon so it was easy to share lenses and other equipment.

However, a few years down the line I changed over to Canon and that's what I'm using currently. At the time of writing this book, I'm using a Canon 5D MKIII (**Figure 3.1**). I changed over to Canon basically because it suited my workflow. I'd started shooting tethered and one thing I didn't like about using the Nikon for tethered shooting was that images were saved only to my computer,

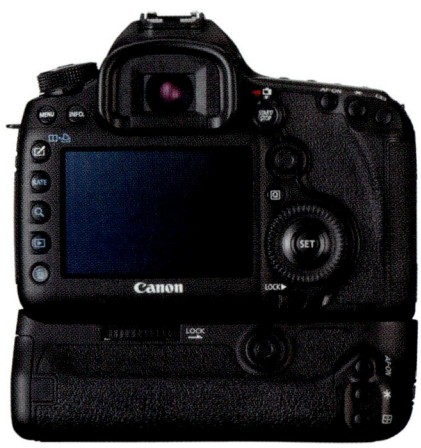

FIGURE 3.1

as opposed to both a memory card and my computer (this may not be the case now). This alone made me slightly nervous because something could happen to the computer between the shoot and getting back home, and I also found it frustrating that images would show up only on the computer as they were taken, rather than on both the back of the camera and the computer. You might be wondering why I would want to see images on the back of the camera if I'm shooting tethered. You wouldn't be wrong for questioning this; after all, the reason for shooting tethered is so that you can see the images on the big screen. But I wanted the images to appear in both places when I was teaching so that my students could look at the big screen while I looked at the camera from my position.

Long story short, I moved over to Canon because it gives me the ability to save images to both a memory card and my computer, and it also allows images to appear on both the camera and the screen it's tethered to. I also find the menu system easier to navigate, but this is purely my own taste.

As for lenses, my workhorse is the 70–200mm f/2.8L IS II USM. I also like to use the 85mm f/1.8, 100mm f/2.8 Macro, and 24–105mm f/4.0L IS, but I don't tend to use the last one quite as much.

STUDIO LIGHTING

For big-flash, studio lights and modifiers I use Elinchrom. I've tried a variety of different brands, but have found that Elinchrom fits perfectly into my workflow.

The Elinchrom ELC Pro HD 1000 flash unit (**Figure 3.2**) is a well-built, solid piece of equipment that performs well consistently. It gives me a power range of 8ws all the way up to 1000ws and has Hi-Sync technology (amongst other bells and whistles) that enables me to shoot at shutter speeds way beyond the native sync speed. And, of course, the lights can be controlled wirelessly using the Elinchrom EL-Skyport Plus HS Trigger (**Figure 3.3**).

I love Elinchrom's Rotalux modifiers, which are incredibly quick and easy to put up and take down. My most-used modifier is the Rotalux 135cm Octa Softbox (**Figure 3.4**).

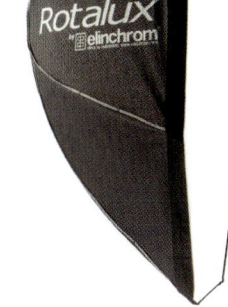

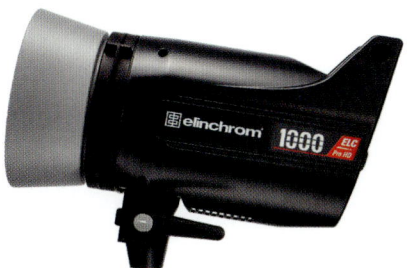

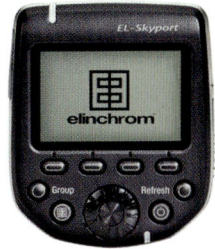

FIGURE 3.2

FIGURE 3.3

FIGURE 3.4

I also use the Elinchrom D-Lite RX One flash unit (**Figure 3.5**), which is considered an entry-level studio light, but has a built-in wireless receiver and fan and is incredibly light, making it ideal to use with a boom.

One last piece of equipment I'd like mention here is the Godox Portable Power Inverter (**Figure 3.6**), which enables me to use my indoor studio lights outdoors or in locations where power availability is an issue.

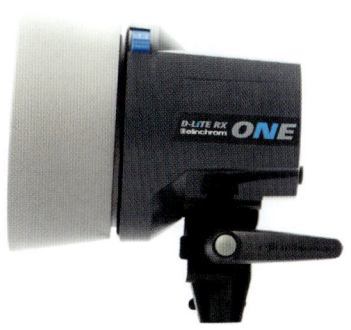

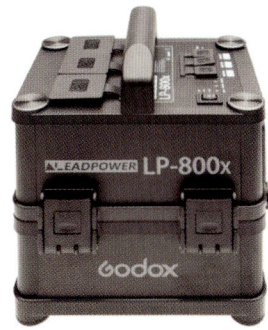

FIGURE 3.5

FIGURE 3.6

SMALL FLASH

Depending on what I'm shooting, in addition to my Elinchrom lights, I use small-battery, Speedlight-type flashes made by Phottix.

When I was shooting with Nikon cameras I had a bunch of SB800s, but I sold them all, and when I made the switch to Canon, I took some time away from Speedlights because the work I was doing didn't necessitate them.

I started using small flashes again—in this case, the Phottix Mitros+ (**Figure 3.7**)—when I put together what I call my "Anytime Anywhere Portrait Kit," which is a camera bag I tend to keep in the boot of my car whenever I go out. It contains a cheaper camera (a Canon 760D), one flash, the Phottix Odin II Trigger (**Figure 3.8**), and a Rogue FlashBender 2 XL Pro modifier.

This kit is so incredibly portable and because I always have it with me, I end up taking so many more spur of the moment portraits, many of which have ended up in my portfolio. The Phottix flashes are incredibly well made and sturdy, and the menu system makes them easy to set up and use.

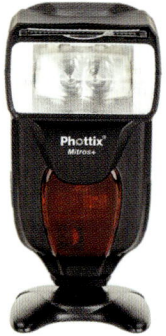 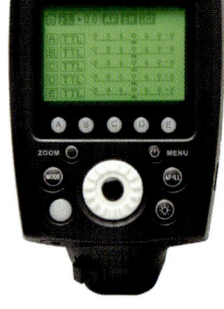

FIGURE 3.7   FIGURE 3.8

SMALL FLASH MODIFIERS

When I was putting together my "Anytime Anywhere Portrait Kit" I ended up buying quite a few different modifiers, but the one I found to be exactly what I wanted was the Rogue FlashBender 2 XL Pro (**Figure 3.9**).

This modifier is a great size (13" × 16") and it collapses down to hardly anything, plus it comes with a grid. I use this all the time when I'm taking those spur of the moment portraits because it's quick and easy to attach it to my Phottix Mitros+ flash. The person I'm photographing can hold it as well, so there is no need for a light stand.

There's a lot you can do with these modifiers by using them with or without the diffusion material and with or without the grid. Because they are so bendable, you have great control over the light.

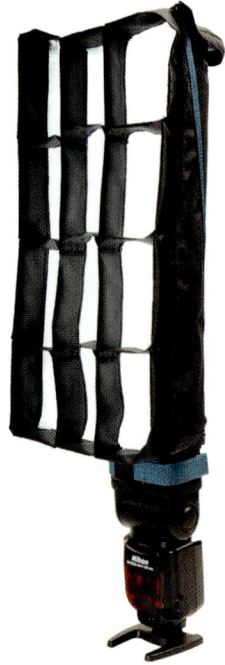

FIGURE 3.9

TRIPOD

I have tried so many different brands of tripods and I've made some costly mistakes. I've spent money on brands that were certainly cheaper than others, but after continuous use the tripods ended up breaking and I had to buy another, so this turned out to be a false economy. The saying "buy cheap, buy twice" springs to mind.

Naturally, it's advisable to invest in the best you can afford because something like a tripod should last you at least a good few years.

I use tripods made by 3 Legged Thing, specifically the Winston model (**Figure 3.10**), which ticks all the boxes for me: light, strong, sturdy, quick to put up, quick to put away, and can be used in a number of different configurations. Love it. Nothing more to be said.

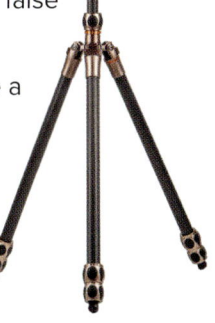

FIGURE 3.10

TETHER TOOLS

Quite simply, if you shoot tethered then the gear made by Tether Tools is a must! Tether Tools offers a wide range of tethering solutions, and one piece that I wouldn't dream of being without is what they call a JerkStopper (**Figure 3.11**). Basically, it's a small gadget that is attached to the tethering cable and your camera and prevents the cable from being pulled out of the camera, which in turn prevents damage to the socket the cable is plugged into. Damage to a socket can be a very costly repair!

The tether cables I use are bright orange, which reduces the chances of them being stepped on and pulled out of my camera or computer (**Figure 3.12**).

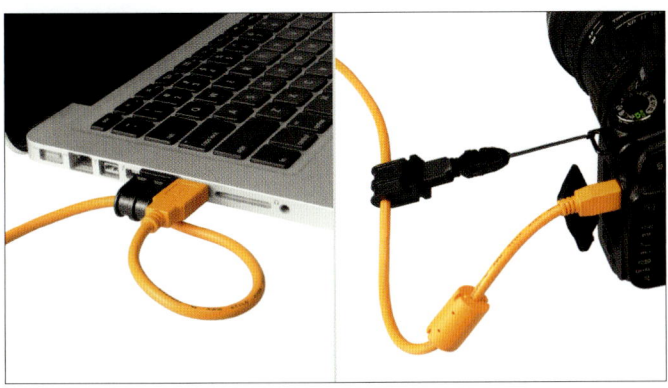

FIGURE 3.11

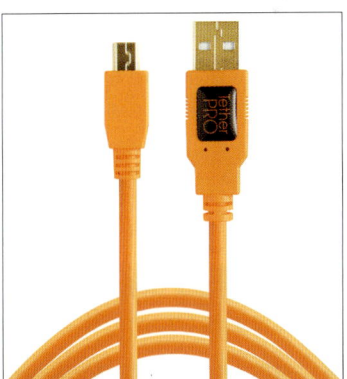

FIGURE 3.12

LIGHT METER

When I first started out a light meter was something that was completely alien to me. In fact, I was constantly told that I didn't need one nowadays with digital cameras. While that may be true to some degree, I think the reason for having and using a light meter has not changed from what it was before the age of digital photography.

I was convinced of the value of using a light meter a few years back when unbeknownst to me, there was a fault with one of my lenses. I was over in the Netherlands doing a combined workshop with my friend Frank Doorhof and I noticed that when I swapped from my Nikon 70–200mm f/2.8 lens to my Nikon 24–70mm f/2.8 the exposure was way off. A quick test with the light meter and another identical lens proved that the lens was indeed faulty.

Using a light meter helps me in a number of ways. When it comes to setting up one light or multiple lights, I can get the exposure nailed without even picking up the camera—something that seriously impresses a client, by the way.

Using a light meter also enables me to sort out the technical side of a photo shoot in a fraction of the time, and once the exposure is perfected I can make adjustments to suit what it is I'm looking for. A light meter reading gives me the best possible starting point from which I can work.

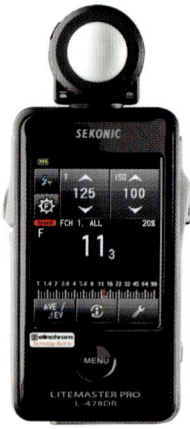

I find that using a light meter leaves me time to do what I enjoy most, which is be creative and interact with whomever it is I'm photographing.

An entry-level light meter would be perfectly adequate for most folks. However, I use the Sekonic LiteMaster Pro L-478DR EL (**Figure 3.13**), which not only gives me a digital reading, but also allows me to trigger my Elinchrom flashes and adjust their power up and down so I don't have to walk over to the flash heads or hold the Elinchrom wireless trigger.

FIGURE 3.13

FILE BACKUP SYSTEM

I'm sad to say that I was once the victim of a hard drive failure and lost lots, and I mean lots, of files. I vowed to never let that happen again; however, that being said, there is a saying that hard drives are always in one of two states: failed or about to fail.

I spent quite a while looking around for a system that would give me as much peace of mind as possible. It so happened that a friend of mine, Chris Fields of CHNO Technology, a UK specialist for the photo and video market, worked closely with a company called CRU, which manufactures backup solutions. Chris asked me a lot of questions with regard to what I would want and came up with a system that fit my needs perfectly.

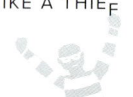

Now my files are backed up automatically in a RAID system (**Figure 3.14**) that monitors its own health and will alert me of any issues. Plus, it's set up in such a way that the backups are also backed up (**Figure 3.15**), and I use a cloud-based backup service, too. So all in all, I'm able to sleep soundly. I guess you can tell I've suffered at the hands of a hard drive failure in the past, right?

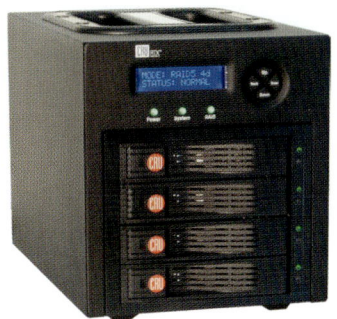

FIGURE 3.14

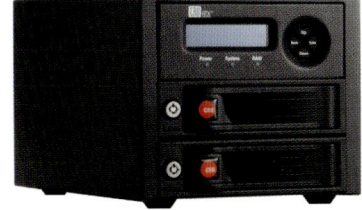

FIGURE 3.15

MONITOR

I'm often asked about my computer setup as well. At the time of writing, I use a MacBook Pro that, when purchased, was maxed out with the RAM, processor, and everything else. This sits open on a stand on my desk. Connected to this is my monitor, a BenQ SW2700PT 27-inch photography monitor that I absolutely love (**Figure 3.16**), so I have a dual monitor setup.

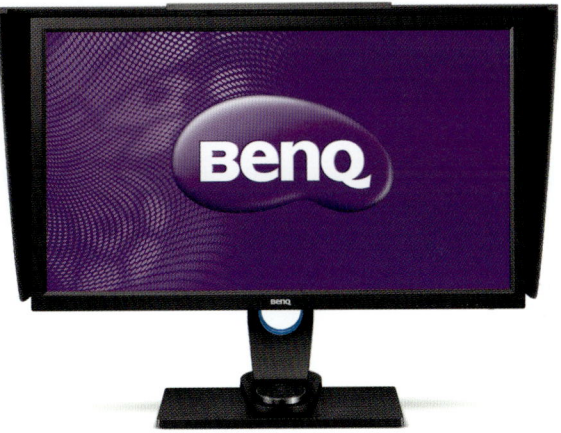

FIGURE 3.16

The colors and contrast in the screen are absolutely bang on and when it's calibrated (using my X-Rite i1 Display Pro), it gives me a superbly accurate representation of the colors, contrast, and brightness in my images. This is especially evident when I get prints back from the lab. Good quality monitors can make a world of difference for your retouching, so if you're able to, I'd highly recommend you invest in a monitor and a device for calibrating it regularly.

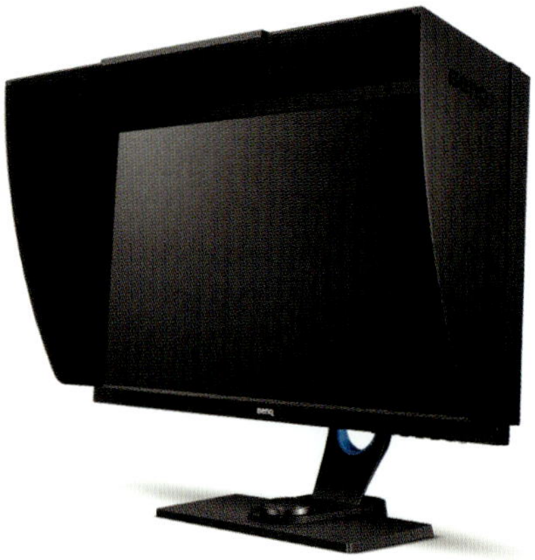

Another lifesaving feature of this particular monitor is that it comes with a screen shade (**Figure 3.17**), which prevents light from spilling onto my screen and affecting how I see the images and, in turn, how I retouch them.

PEN AND GRAPHICS TABLET

I simply couldn't and wouldn't work on my images without my Wacom pen tablet. The tablet comes in various sizes including small, medium, and large.

FIGURE 3.17

I currently use the small version of the Wacom Intuos5 Touch (**Figure 3.18**), which I find perfectly adequate because I can simply rest my wrist in one place and move my hand left and right to cover the entire screen space.

I highly recommend you consider investing in one of these. They really do change your retouching for the better.

One word of caution: When you first try using a pen tablet it may feel a little strange, but don't worry, this is completely normal since it's a different way of controlling your cursor. Stick with it for a day or two and I guarantee you'll fall completely and utterly in love with it.

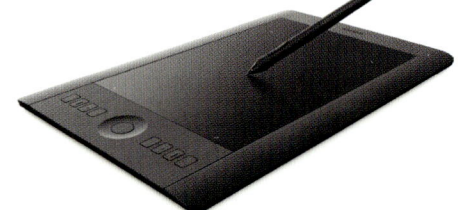

FIGURE 3.18

PLUGINS

I'm not someone who uses a multitude of third-party plugins, but there are a couple that I regularly make use of.

TOPAZ CLARITY

Topaz Labs produces a wide range of plugins for all manner of retouching and special effects needs. One I wouldn't want to be without is Topaz Clarity. Unlike Clarity in Adobe Lightroom or Camera RAW, this plugin gives you a great deal of control with the ability to finesse your images by adding in differing degrees of contrast, ranging from microcontrast to high contrast.

Throughout this book—and in chapter 4, specifically—I'll share how I use Topaz Clarity. You'll see examples of the look you can give to your images, which is quite challenging to replicate in Photoshop alone.

NIK COLOR EFEX PRO 4

Color Efex Pro, part of Google's Nik Collection, is a great plugin that has a ton of adjustments and presets you can use to give your images a completely unique look. However, you'll see throughout this book—particularly in chapter 4 where I show how I use it—that I only use a fraction of what is available.

Recently I've been using Color Efex Pro less frequently because I favor the Color Lookup image adjustment in Photoshop for colorizing my images, but I still keep it installed on my computer for the occasional times I do dive over to it.

PRINTING LAB

Despite being a self-confessed geek and loving the convenience of storing my images on electronic devices, I still believe that print is king!

Nothing beats holding a big print in your hand, and when you give a print to someone else—maybe a client—the experience for them is completely different than seeing the image on a screen. They'll walk around with the image, hold it away from their face, bring it in close, hold it in different light, turn it around to show others, and place it on display.

For every client shoot and every personal project I shoot I always give a print to whomever I photographed as a thank you. I usually get the image printed at about 18 inches on the long edge and mount it on 2mm cardstock.

I use Loxley Colour, which is based in Scotland, for all my printing, not just because of the quality of their printing and products, but also because of the service and support they provide. I couldn't want for more.

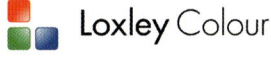

FIGURE 3.19

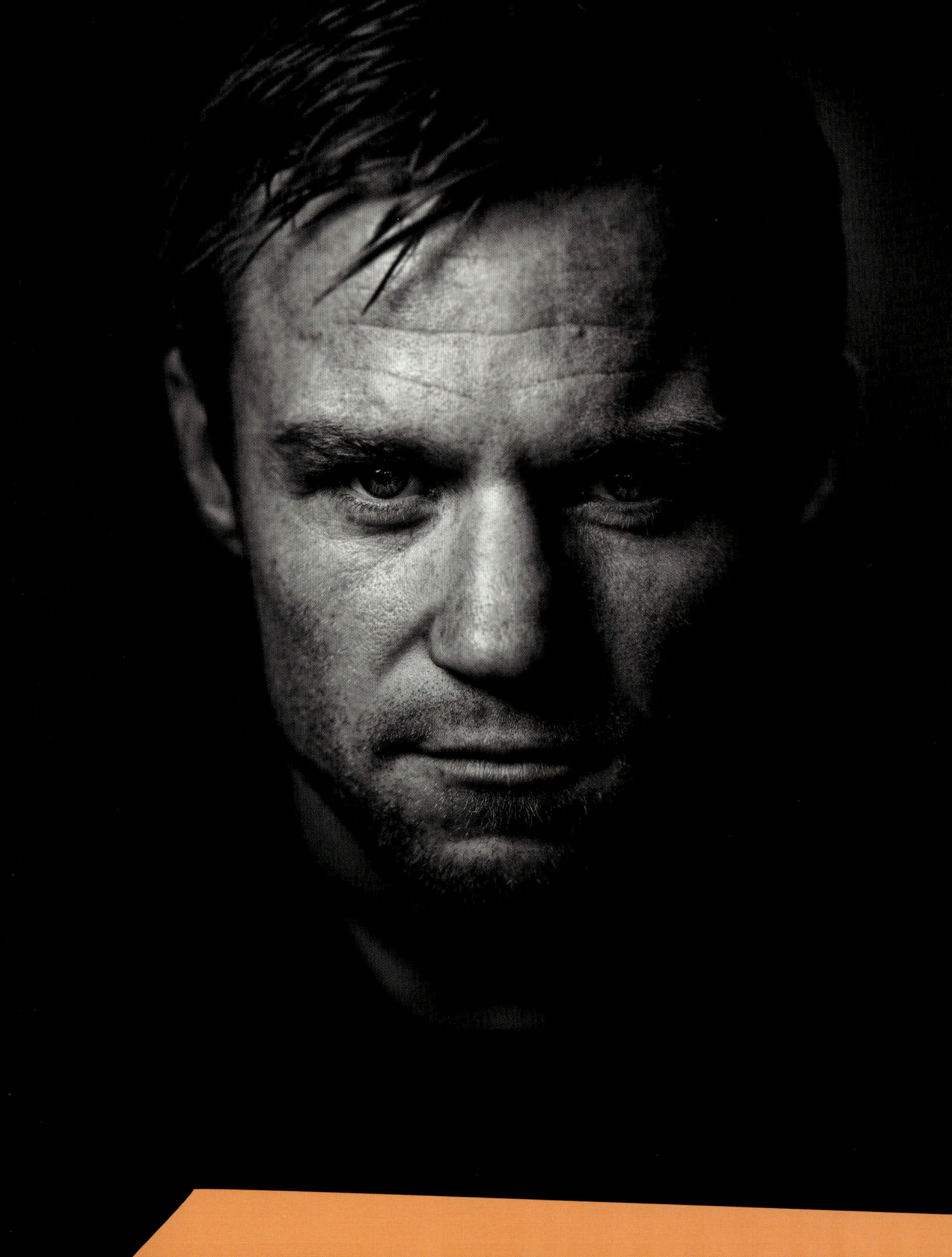

4 MY COMMONLY USED TECHNIQUES

In this chapter I thought I'd share some of the techniques I use most often. This isn't to say they're the best ones out there; there are always new techniques being discovered and Adobe is constantly adding to and enhancing the programs and tools they offer. That being said, the techniques in this chapter are the ones that give me great results, save me time, and are pretty easy to replicate again and again.

As you work through chapters 5 through 14, you'll see that I refer to this chapter on a regular basis, rather than go into depth on specific techniques repeatedly in each chapter. The idea is to save you from having to read the same words over and again, and to provide you with one place where you can find the techniques I use most often so you don't have to search through lots of pages.

To kick off, I'll take you through a shooting technique, and then we'll move onto some Photoshop techniques.

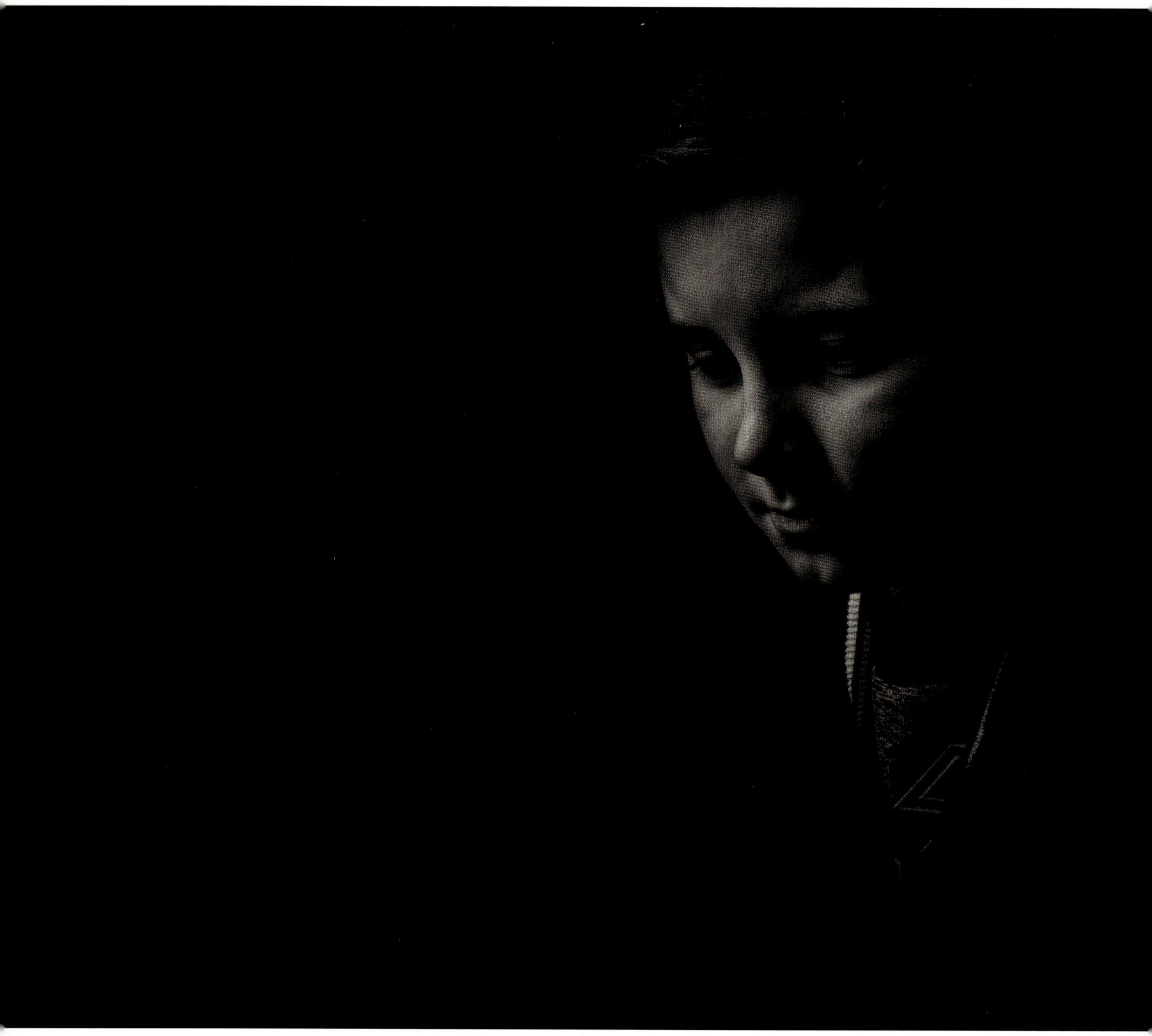

FIGURE 4.1

NOTE *Download all the image files you need to follow along step-by-step at:*
http://www.rockynook.com/photograph-like-a-thief-reference/

INVISIBLE BLACK BACKGROUND

WHAT IS THE INVISIBLE BLACK BACKGROUND?

As the saying goes, a picture is worth a thousand words, so here are before (**Figure 4.2**) and after (**Figure 4.3**) pictures to show you what I mean.

There's no question that having this technique in your photography tool bag can save you a lot of time, effort, and money. It also allows you to add a little extra creativity to your shoot and create photos that you may have thought were only possible in a studio or with a collapsible backdrop.

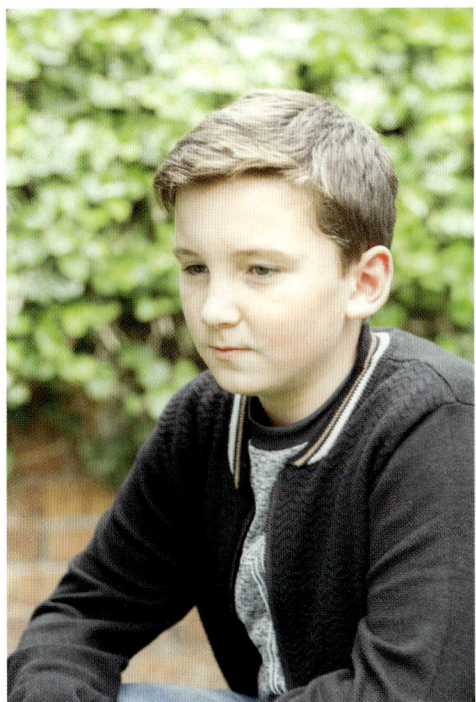

FIGURE 4.2 Before

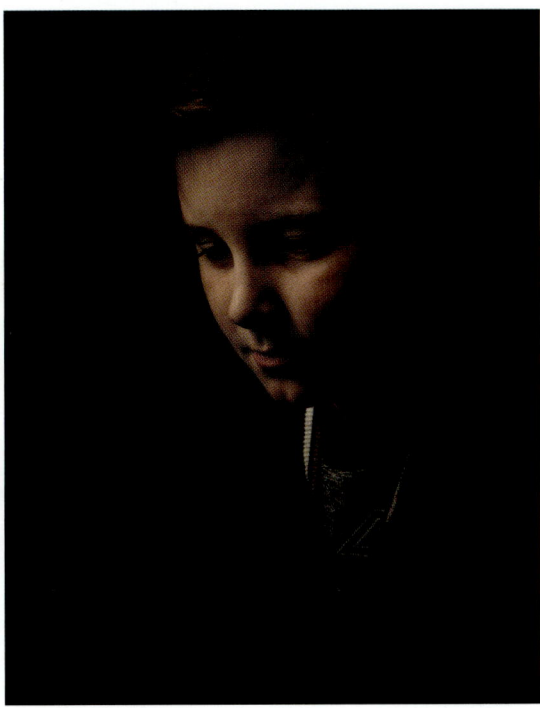

FIGURE 4.3 After

HOW DO WE ACHIEVE THE INVISIBLE BLACK BACKGROUND?

Basically, what we're looking to do is tell the camera to capture no light other than the light we introduce—in the form of a speedlight flash, for example. We don't want the camera to pick up *any* of the ambient light. By doing this we have an instant black backdrop.

This technique can be done with any camera that has a Manual mode and the ability to trigger off-camera flash—that means SLR, mirrorless, and some point-and-shoot cameras.

THERE ARE ONLY FIVE STEPS TO IT.

1. **Manual Mode** Put your camera into Manual mode. Yes, now you are in control of the shutter speed, aperture, and ISO. From this point on you're telling the camera what to do rather than allowing the camera to make the decisions and give you the picture it thinks you want.

2. **ISO** Set your camera to its lowest possible ISO. The ISO dictates how sensitive your camera's sensor is to light. A low number like 200 means it's less sensitive to light, whereas a higher number like 1600 means it's more sensitive to light. The higher the ISO number, the more noise there will be in your photograph, particularly in the shadow areas. Seeing as how we're looking to make a black backdrop, we're not concerned with how sensitive the camera is to light, so keep the ISO as low as possible. My Nikon D3 can go down to ISO 100, which means the camera won't be very sensitive to light at all and the final picture will be nice and clean with minimal noise.

3. **Shutter Speed** Set your camera to its maximum flash sync speed. This is the maximum shutter speed at which your camera and flash can work together; any faster than this and your camera's shutter will open and close too quickly to allow all the light from your flash to fill the camera's sensor. Common maximum sync speeds are around 1/200s to 1/250s. Although we could quite easily make the scene completely black by using an incredibly high shutter speed like 1/8000s, the problem with this is that the shutter will open and close so quickly that none of the light from the flash will hit the sensor. So we must stick to the maximum sync speed that allows our cameras and flashes to work together.

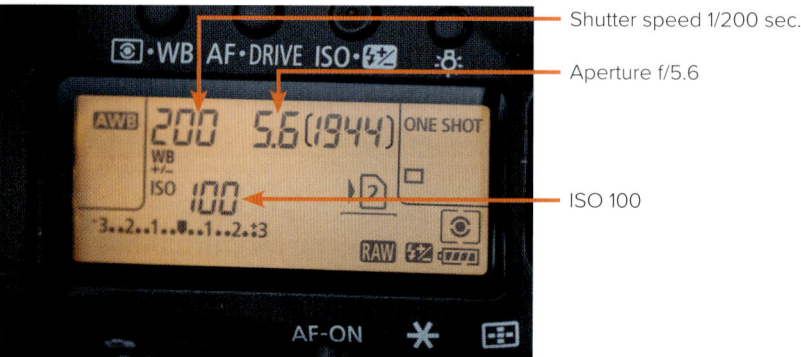

FIGURE 4.4

4. **Aperture** The final setting on your camera is the aperture, or the f-number. Knowing roughly what f-number to use will become second nature after you've done this a few times. The best thing to do is choose f/5.6 and go from there. Once you're at this stage, take a photo of your subject and see what results you get. The objective here is to see absolutely nothing on your camera display; you should see a completely black screen. If you see a bit of the environment then clearly some ambient light is creeping into the

scene. All you have to do to fix this is close down your aperture a little. For example, if you're capturing some ambient light at f/8.0 (**Figure 4.5**), then try stopping down to f/11 or even f/16 (**Figure 4.6**) and see what that gives you.

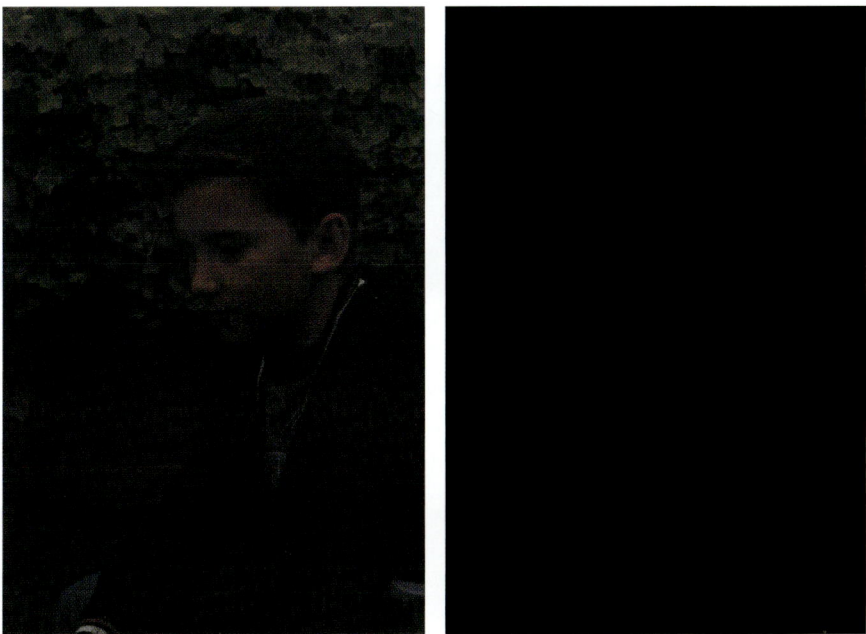

FIGURE 4.5 The scene is not quite completely black.

FIGURE 4.6

5. **Flash** Now you've set the scene with your camera and you have a completely black screen. The final step is to bring in the flash. Where you prefer to position your flash and what modifier you use is entirely up to you, depending on the look you want to achieve. I find I get great results with a 60-inch reflective umbrella (**Figure 4.7**). This is a great piece of equipment that creates beautiful light, and I can use a peg to close it down and control how much light I want and where I want it to fall (**Figures 4.8** and **4.9**).

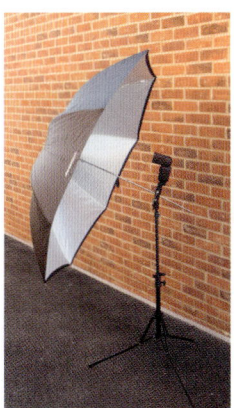 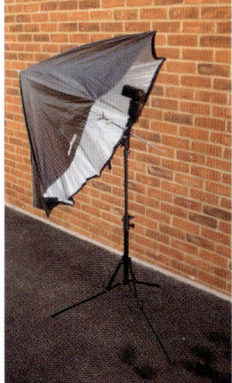 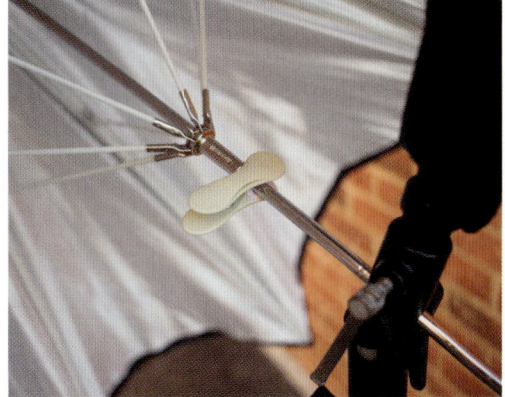

FIGURE 4.7   FIGURE 4.8   FIGURE 4.9

Again, after doing this a few times, experience will dictate what power level you use for the flash. Until that time, just pick a power level (1/4 power, for example) then take a shot and see what you get. If you want more light, increase the power of the flash in increments until you get what you want. If the light from the flash is too bright, simply lower the power level in increments.

As a rule, the shutter speed controls the amount of ambient light that gets through to the sensor and the aperture controls the flash power. But with this technique, once you've set the shutter speed and aperture to give you a black background, you really need to leave them alone and control the power of the flash manually.

Because this technique requires the use of off-camera flash, you need to have a way to trigger your flash. I use PocketWizards, which are the industry-standard radio triggers. They're reliable and work at ridiculous distances, but they do have a price tag to match. There are lots of alternative ways to trigger your flash, including using a simple sync cable to connect your camera to your flash (with obvious limitations) or using an infrared trigger. Nikon users can use their camera's built-in flash to trigger another flash using the Nikon Creative Lighting System. You can even get budget radio triggers off eBay that seem to work just fine.

In summary, there are five steps for creating an invisible black background:

1. Set your camera to Manual mode.

2. Select the lowest ISO (200 or lower, if possible).

3. Set the shutter speed to the maximum flash sync speed (around 1/250s or 1/200s).

4. Select an aperture (use f/5.6 as a starting point).

5. Bring in the flash.

That, quite simply, is all there is to it. I've deliberately not gone into too much technical detail to explain this because I want this to be a simple "how to" tutorial, but if you want to know all the technical ins and outs of this technique, I'll gladly pass on recommendations for books that will cover it.

A COUPLE OF THINGS TO NOTE

1. If you're using this technique indoors, be aware that the light from the flash may bounce off of light-colored walls, which will light up the room and destroy your black backdrop. My advice when using this technique indoors would be to restrict where the light falls by using a modifier such as a Honl Photo Speed Grid or Lastolite Ezybox, or to close down your reflective umbrella.

2. If you're using speedlights outside on a bright afternoon, you will have to close down your aperture so much (to f/22, for example) that your speedlights won't be powerful enough to reach the sensor. The answer here is to find a covered or shady area in which to photograph, or better yet, to wait for the sun to ease off a little. This technique can be done in the middle of the afternoon on a bright sunny day, but that would call for much more powerful lighting, which would cost a lot more money.

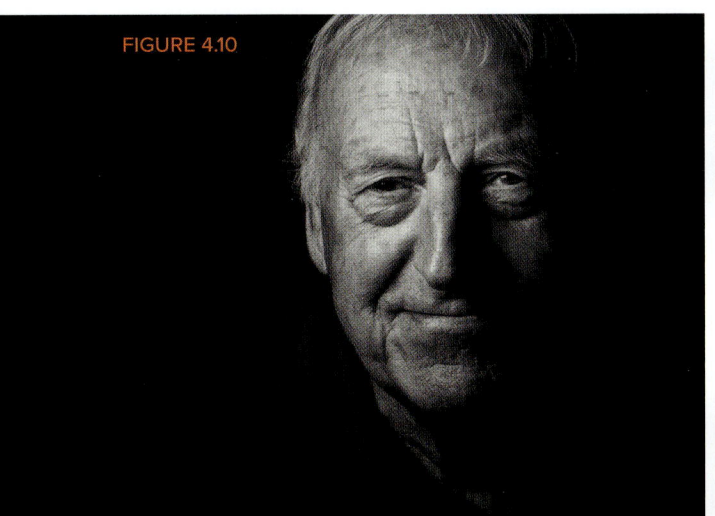

FIGURE 4.10

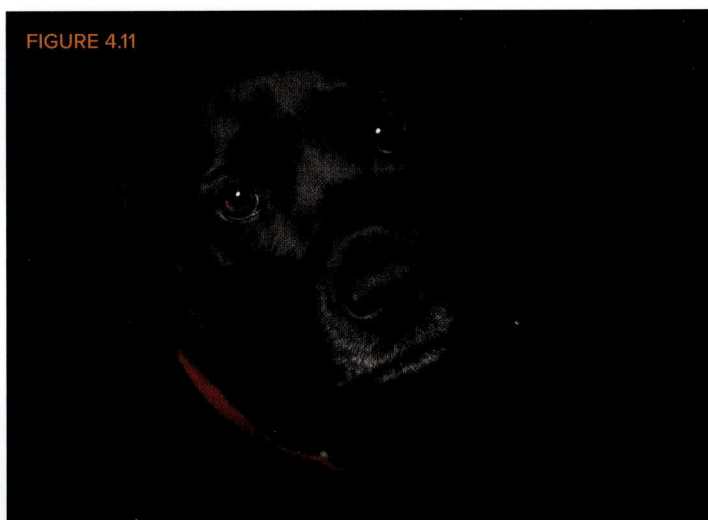

FIGURE 4.11

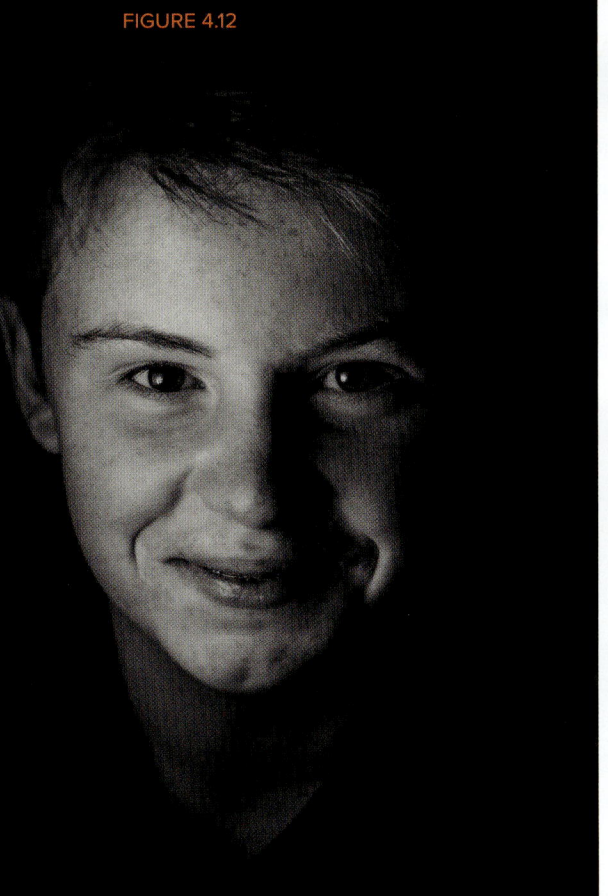

FIGURE 4.12

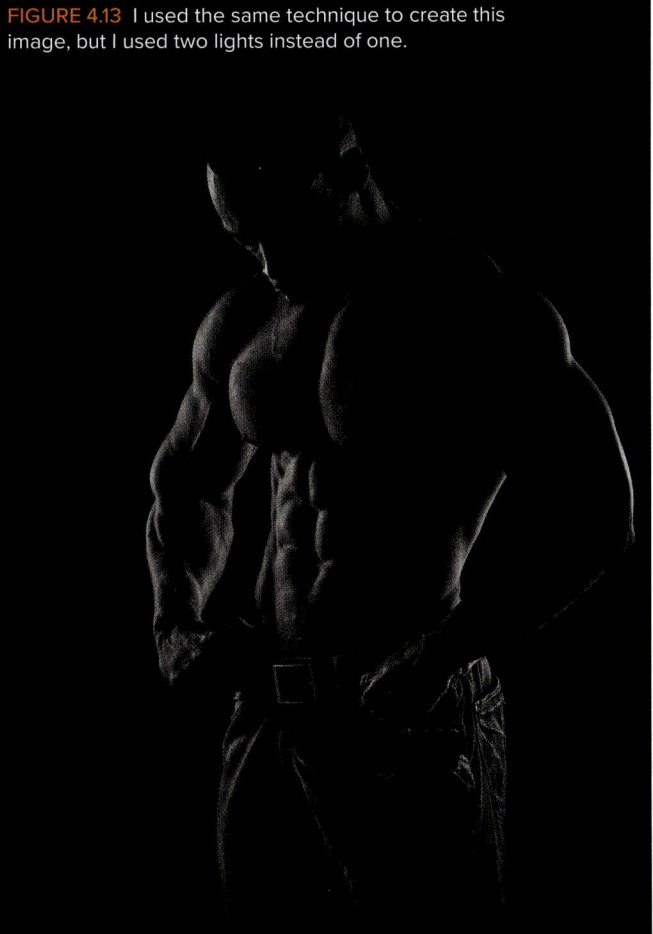

FIGURE 4.13 I used the same technique to create this image, but I used two lights instead of one.

COLORIZING

With Photoshop there are countless techniques and tools for colorizing pictures: Levels, Curves, Hue/Saturation, Selective Color adjustment layers, and the list goes on. The techniques you use, as is always the case with Photoshop, depend a lot on your personal preference, so there's no right or wrong way as long as you can get the results you're after.

That said, I have two preferred ways to colorize my pictures and create a specific mood and atmosphere. I use a plugin, which at the time of writing happens to be Color Efex Pro 4 from Google's Nik Collection, or I use Color Lookup Tables (LUTs) in Photoshop. In this section I'll show you how I typically use both of these tools. Let's kick off with LUTs, which is my go-to method for colorizing my images.

During the time I've used Photoshop I've tried many different methods for colorizing my images to achieve the mood and atmosphere I'm after. I still make use of Curves, Selective Color adjustment layers, and the Color Efex Pro 4 plugin, but with the introduction of Color Lookup Tables in Photoshop, I'm finding I choose to use them more than any other method. I love how I can create my own custom looks by combining a number of Color Lookup Table Adjustment layers, adjusting their Opacity, and experimenting with different Blend Modes.

PHOTOSHOP COLOR LOOKUP TABLES (LUTS)

Color Lookup Tables are located in the Adjustments panel in Photoshop. You may be tempted to simply click on each preset to see what its effects look like; however, if you combine presets, vary their Opacity, and maybe even change their Blend Modes, the possibilities are endless.

We'll go through the entire retouching process for this series of Home Guard pictures in chapter 8, but for now I'll explain how I used Color Lookup Tables to create the look I was after.

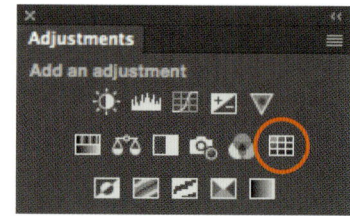

FIGURE 4.14

1. Click the Color Lookup icon in the Photoshop Adjustments panel to add a Color Lookup adjustment layer (**Figure 4.14**).

2. In the Color Lookup properties, select TensionGreen.3DL from the top menu labeled 3DLUT File (**Figure 4.15**). In the Layers panel, lower the opacity of this adjustment layer to 30%.

3. Add a second Color Lookup adjustment layer and select EdgyAmber.3DL from the 3DLUT File dropdown menu (**Figure 4.16**). In the Layers panel, lower the opacity of this adjustment layer to 20%.

4. Add a third Color Lookup adjustment layer and select FoggyNight.3DL from the 3DLUT File dropdown menu (**Figure 4.17**). In the Layers panel, lower the opacity of this adjustment layer to 20%.

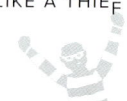

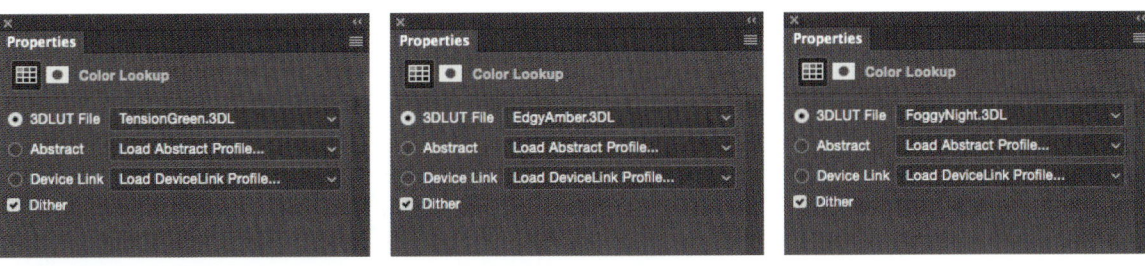

FIGURE 4.15

FIGURE 4.16

FIGURE 4.17

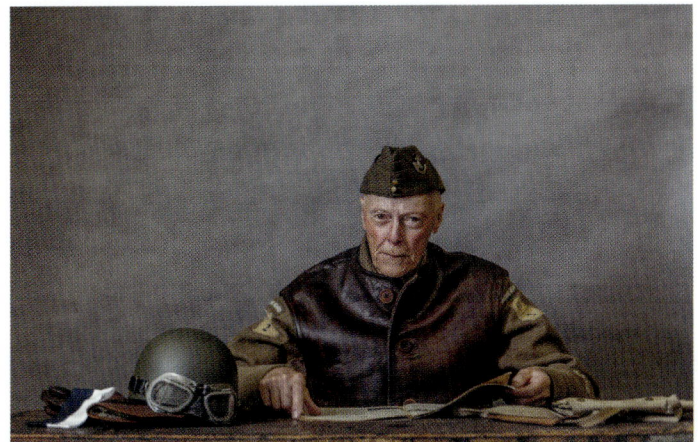

FIGURE 4.18 Before

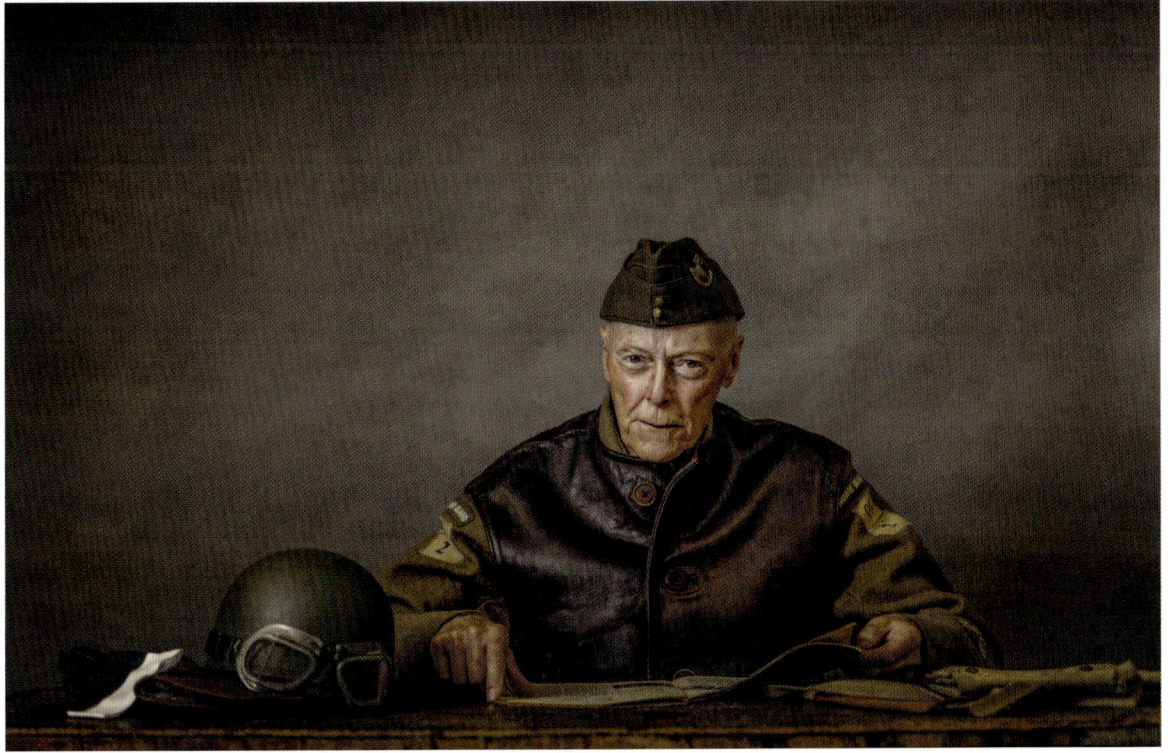

FIGURE 4.19 After

COLOR EFEX PRO 4

There are so many different filter sets to choose from in Color Efex Pro 4, but to be honest, I only ever make use of three of them: Cross Processing, Cross Balance, and Colorize. These tend to give me the look I'm after. Let's walk through an example of how to use them.

1. In Photoshop, open the Color Efex Pro 4 plugin by going *Filter > Nik Collection > Color Efex Pro 4*. Choose the Cross Processing preset (**Figure 4.20**), and then select Y06 from the Method drop-down menu and set the Strength to 55% (**Figure 4.21**). Then click on Add Filter.

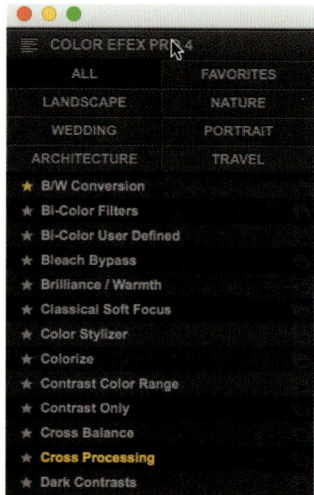

FIGURE 4.20

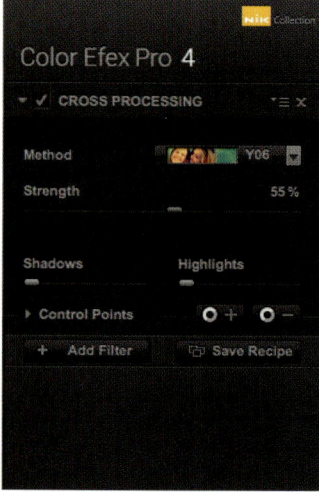

FIGURE 4.21

2. Click on the Cross Balance preset (**Figure 4.22**), and then select Tungsten to Daylight (1) from the drop-down menu and set the Strength to 70% (**Figure 4.23**). Then click on Add Filter.

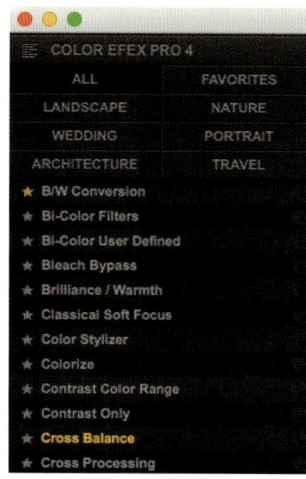

FIGURE 4.22

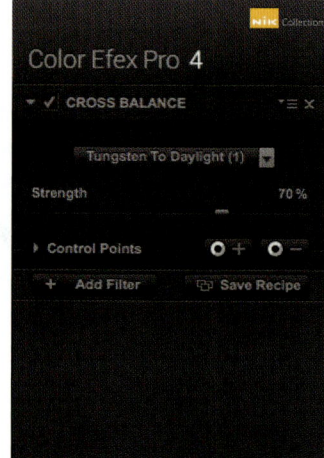

FIGURE 4.23

3. Click on the Colorize preset (**Figure 4.24**), and then choose 2 from the Method drop-down menu and set the Strength to 15% (**Figure 4.25**). Then click on Add Filter.

Like I said, when I do use the Color Efex Pro 4 plugin, I tend to use these three presets and experiment with the options within them.

When you've created a look you like by combining filters, you can click on Save Recipe so that in the future you can apply the same combination of filters with just one click.

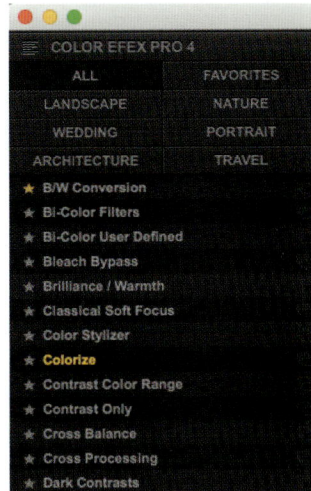

FIGURE 4.24

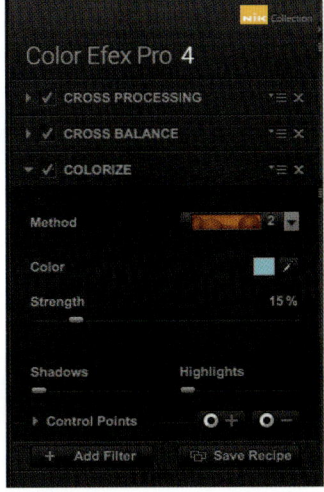

FIGURE 4.25

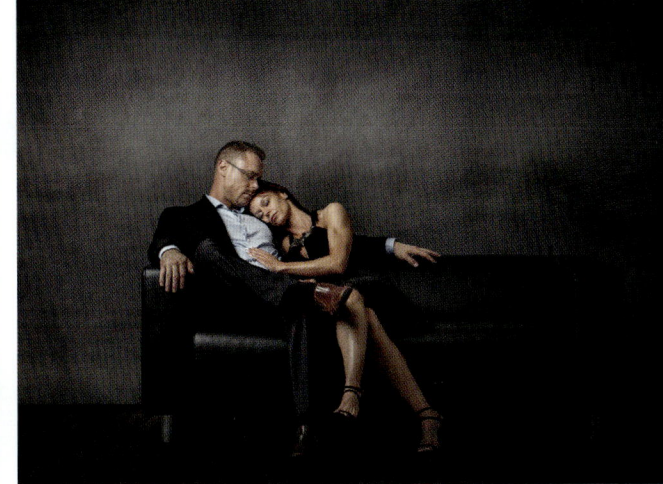

FIGURE 4.26 Before

FIGURE 4.27 After

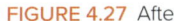

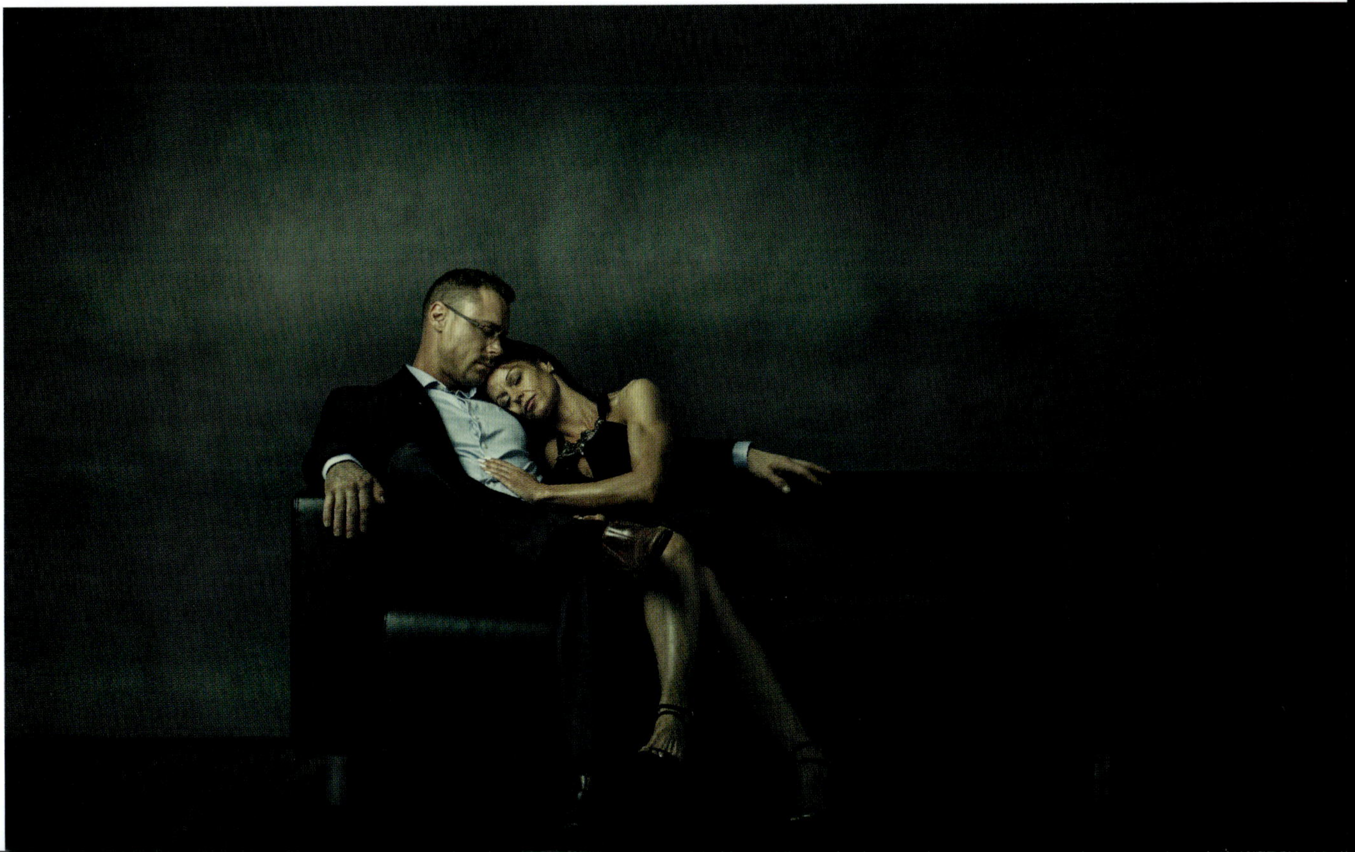

CONTRAST

Although there are lots of ways to add contrast to your pictures in Photoshop and Lightroom, I have two preferred methods for doing so. When I use them all depends on the look they give me.

TOPAZ CLARITY

Let's start with my go-to, which is a plugin from Topaz Labs called Topaz Clarity.

There's not much to show you here because although this plugin has lots of presets and adjustments available, I have found that I get the exact results I'm looking for with just two sliders: Micro Contrast and Low Contrast. These sliders can be found on the right-hand side of the plugin window (**Figure 4.28**).

My normal rule of thumb is to increase Micro Contrast the most and increase Low Contrast a little less, as shown in **Figure 4.28** where Micro Contrast is set to 0.25 and Low Contrast is set to 0.09.

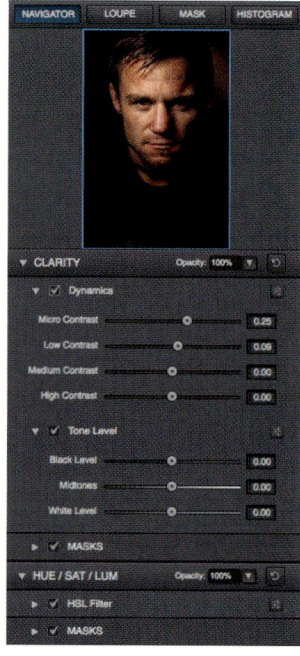

FIGURE 4.28

Figures **4.29** and **4.30** show the before and after versions of the image. The results of Topaz Clarity may not be quite as visible in this book as they are on your computer screen or in a photographic print (that's when you can really see the difference). However, you can see that it increased the texture in the skin (**Figure 4.30, A**) and darkened the shadowed side of Steven's face (**B**).

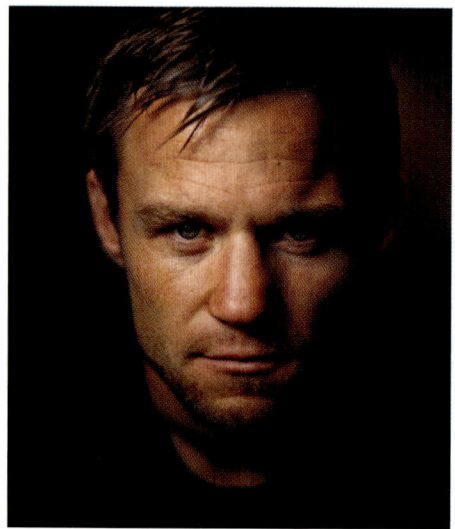

FIGURE 4.29 Before

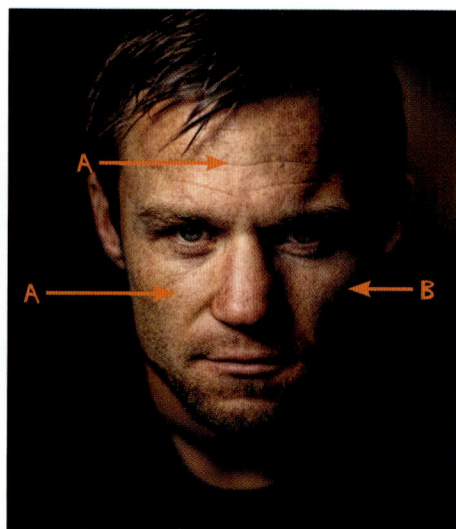

FIGURE 4.30 After

I also applied a black-and-white conversion (**Figure 4.31**), which works really well with the grungy, textured look created by the Topaz Clarity plugin. When I had this image printed on metal by Loxley Colour the result was outstanding! The portrait took on an almost three-dimensional look as it appeared to come forward off the print toward the viewer.

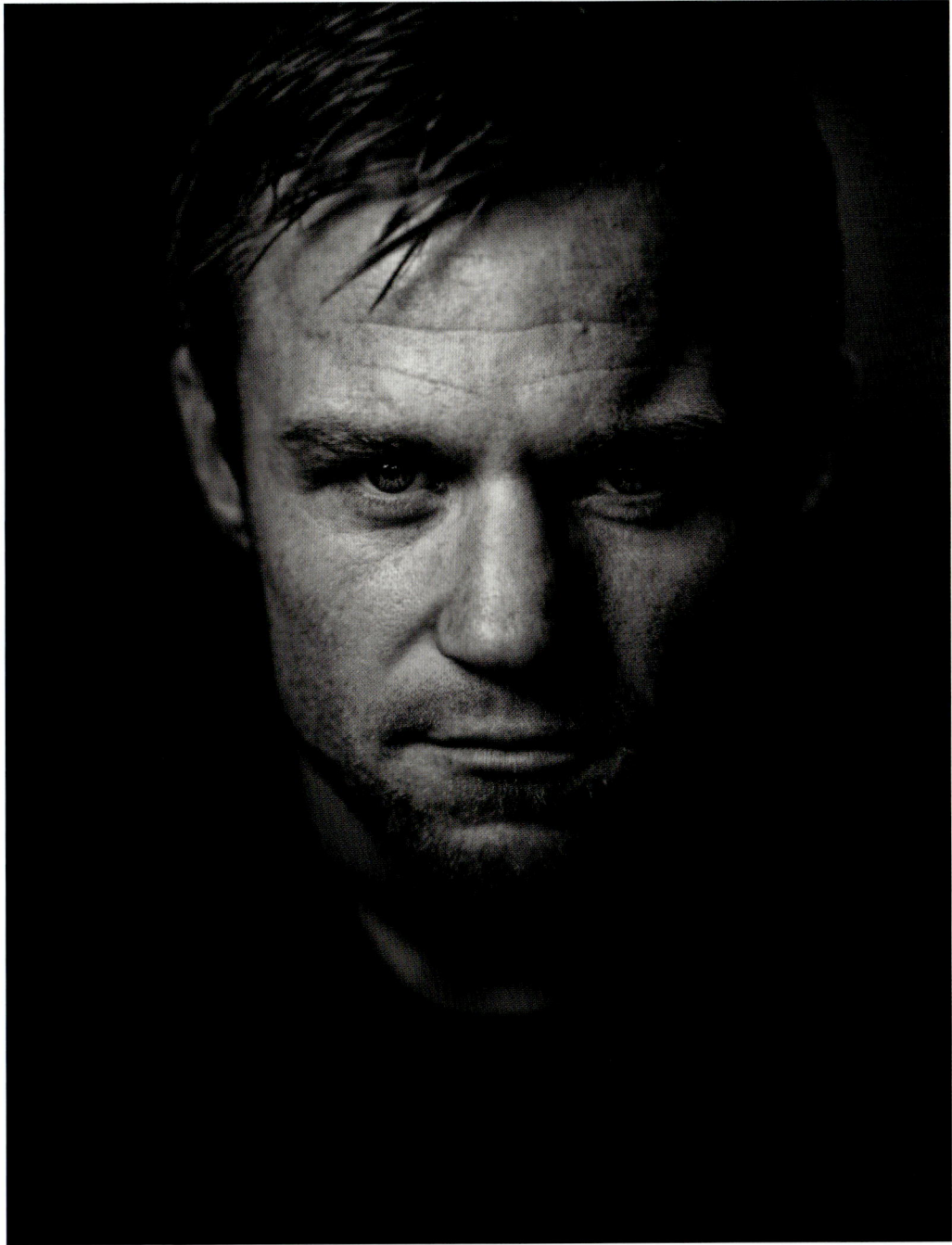

FIGURE 4.31 Black-and-white conversion

UNSHARP MASK

I tend to use Photoshop's Unsharp Mask filter in the final stages of a retouch. I don't have any reason for doing it this way other than habit, but it's a great technique for adding contrast without bringing in the grunge look. It also allows you to add substantial contrast to your pictures without causing any halos or color shift, which can sometimes happen when you use other methods for adding contrast.

Unsharp Mask is found in the *Filter > Sharpen* menu (**Figure 4.32**). When using this technique, you will achieve the best results by keeping the Amount and Radius values the same (i.e., if you increase the Amount, then increase the Radius to the same value). Keep the Threshold at 0 (**Figure 4.33**).

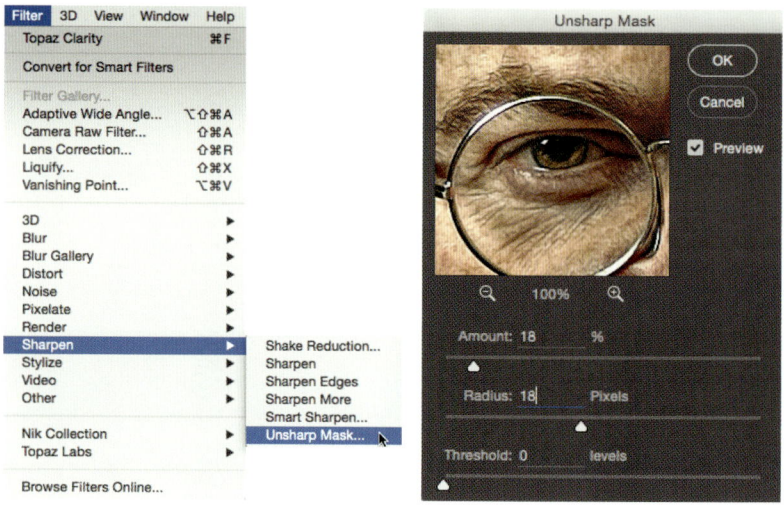

FIGURE 4.32   FIGURE 4.33

I generally increase the Amount and Radius to no more than 20–25. If you go much higher than that the image can begin to look overly processed. You'll see this when we go through some of the projects in later chapters if you try adjusting the settings a little higher than I suggest.

In **Figure 4.35** you can see that I increased the contrast, but in a very subtle way, without increasing detail in the skin or giving it a grungy feel. Plus, there are no halos. The overall result is much more natural, especially around the cheeks (**A**) and eyes (**B**).

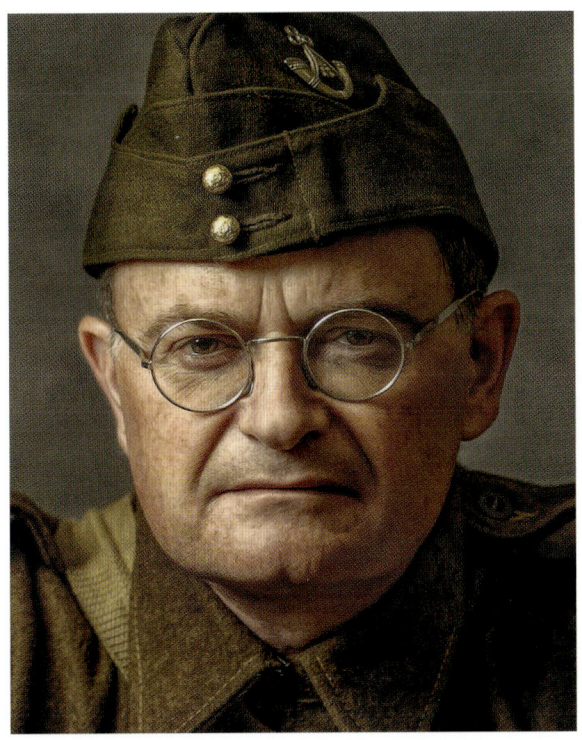

FIGURE 4.34 Before

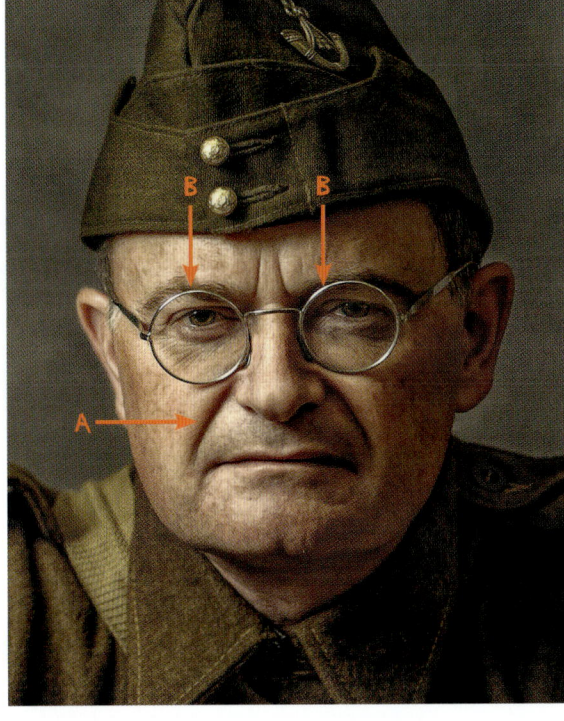

FIGURE 4.35 After

DETAILS TECHNIQUE

I first saw this technique demonstrated by photographer and digital artist Calvin Hollywood. He renamed it Freaky Amazing Details. It's a great technique for adding microcontrast and enhancing details in your pictures. It can also give your pictures a grungy kind of look, so you have to choose the pictures you use it on wisely.

1. In the Layers panel make sure you have a merged layer at the top of the layer stack. Hold down the Command key (Mac) or Ctrl key (PC) and press the letter J twice to create two copies (**Figure 4.36**).

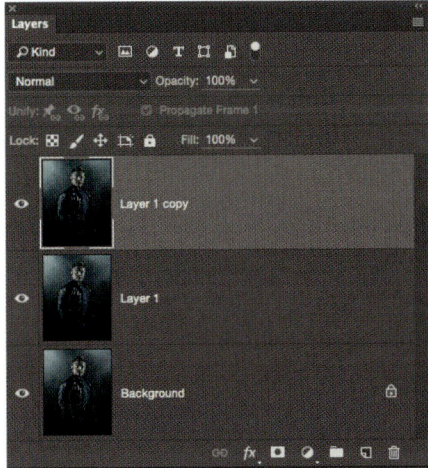

FIGURE 4.36

2. Hold down the Shift key and click on the layer beneath the top layer so that both are selected (**Figure 4.37**). Go to *Layer > New > Group from Layers* (**Figure 4.38**), name the group "details," and click OK. With the details group selected in the Layers panel, change the Blend Mode to Overlay (**Figure 4.39**).

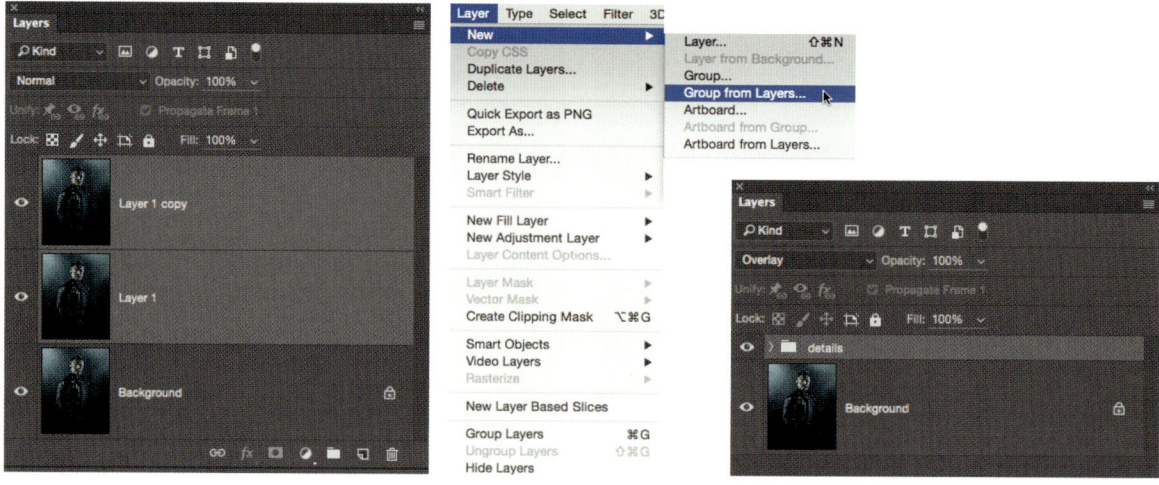

3. Expand the details group in the Layers panel so that you can see each layer. Change the Blend Mode of the topmost layer in the group to Vivid Light (**Figure 4.40**), and then go to *Image > Adjustments > Invert* (**Figure 4.41**).

4. Next we're going to use a filter to enhance details in the image. To give us the flexibility of making changes to this filter at a later stage, let's convert the layer into a Smart Object by selecting *Filter > Convert for Smart Filters* (**Figure 4.42**).

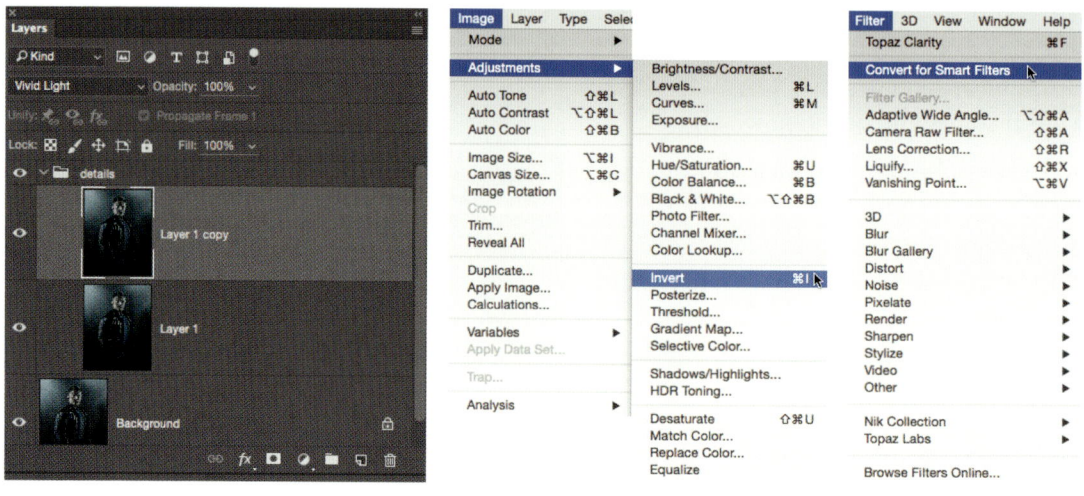

5. To enhance details in the image, go to *Filter > Blur > Surface Blur* (**Figure 4.43**). Dial in an amount of around 20 for the Radius and 15 for the Threshold (**Figure 4.44**). Feel free to experiment with these amounts to achieve the level of detail and the look you are after.

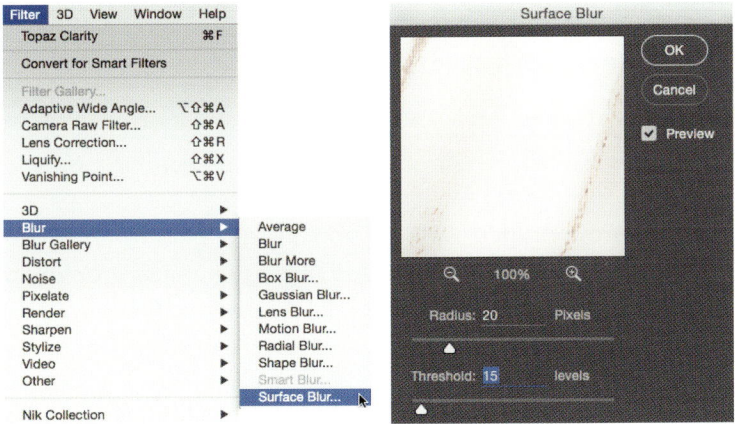

FIGURE 4.43

FIGURE 4.44

Figures 4.45 and **4.46** show before and after versions of the image. You can see more texture and detail in certain areas, such as in the T-shirt and jacket (**Figure 4.46, A**). However, you have to be careful not to overdo it when you use this technique because halos may start to appear (**B**). To avoid this, you can apply this effect to only certain parts of a picture. On pictures that contain a lot of detail, such as cars, motorbikes, or people carrying kit like a soldier, the Details technique can work an absolute treat.

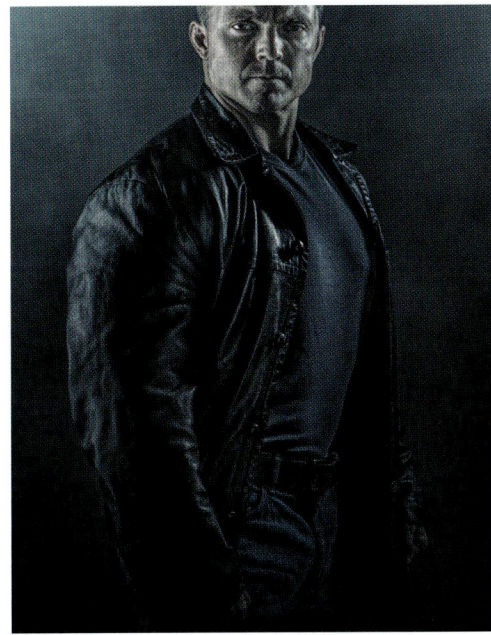

FIGURE 4.45 Before

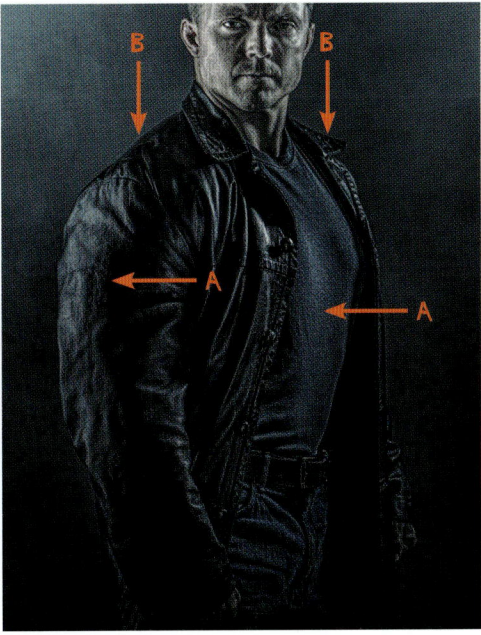

FIGURE 4.46 After

6. The details have been enhanced across the entire picture, but if you want to apply this filter only to certain areas of the image (the model's clothing, in this example), simply add a black Layer Mask to the details group by holding down the Option key (Mac) or Alt key (PC) and clicking on the Layer Mask icon at the bottom of the Layers panel. This will hide the effect. Then use a white, round, soft-edged brush to paint over the areas where you want the effect to be visible.

DODGE & BURN

Dodging and burning has been around since, well, the beginning of photography. I never ventured into the world of film, so I never experienced mixing chemicals, developing pictures, and dodging and burning in a darkroom. Although we're now well into the age of digital photography, the art and process of dodging and burning is still as important as ever, but nowadays with Photoshop, Lightroom, and so on, there are many ways to do so.

In this tutorial I'll take you through a technique that makes use of Photoshop's Dodge and Burn Tools. This technique is nondestructive, so it gives you a lot of flexibility.

1. Add a new layer to the top of the layer stack by holding down the Option key (Mac) or Alt key (PC) and clicking on the New Layer icon at the bottom of the Layers panel. In the New Layer dialog box, name the layer "dodge and burn" (**Figure 4.47**). Select Soft Light from the Mode drop-down menu, place a checkmark in the Fill with Soft-Light-neutral color (50% gray) checkbox, and click OK.

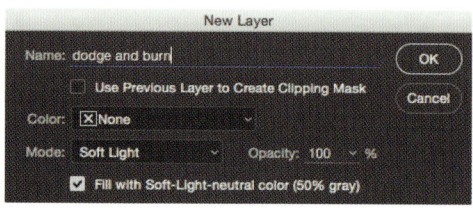

FIGURE 4.47

2. Select the Dodge Tool from the toolbar (**Figure 4.48**). In the options bar at the top of the screen, leave the Range set to Midtones (this makes no difference because we're going to be working on a 50% gray layer), lower the Exposure (strength) to around 5%, and keep a checkmark in the Protect Tones checkbox (**Figure 4.49**).

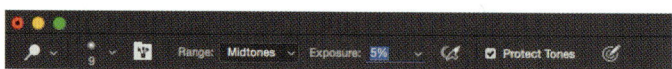

FIGURE 4.48   FIGURE 4.49

TIP *It's best to keep the Exposure setting fairly low so that you build up the effect gently. When dodging and burning, it's easy to do too much without realizing it.*

3. Now you're all set to start dodging and burning. There's so much that can be said about how to do it, but let's keep it simple and say that the main objective here is to brighten the bright parts and darken the dark parts. You can toggle quickly between the Dodge Tool and the Burn Tool by simply holding down the Option key (Mac) or Alt key (PC). The advantage of doing this as opposed to manually changing to the Burn Tool is that the settings remain the same. For example, if you're using the Dodge Tool at 5% Exposure, the Burn Tool will also stay at 5% Exposure. **Figure 4.50** shows the areas I generally work on.

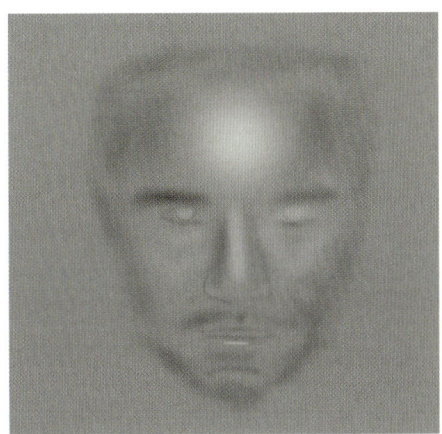

FIGURE 4.50

TIP *To see only the gray layer you're working on, hold down the Option key (Mac) or Alt key (PC) and click on the eye icon next to the gray (dodge and burn) layer in the Layers panel. This will turn every other layer off. To go back to normal view, hold down the Option key (Mac) or Alt key (PC) again and click where the eye icon for the gray (dodge and burn) layer would be.*

4. Some people choose to dodge and burn on the gray layer using a combination of black and white brushes, and this works just fine. However, the reason I choose not to is so that I can set my foreground color to 50% gray by clicking on the foreground color and setting the HSB to 0, 0, 50 (**Figure 4.51**). Then when I'm dodging and burning, if I need to remove or reduce an area I can quickly select a brush and paint over the area with this 50% gray color at whatever opacity I choose (**Figure 4.52**).

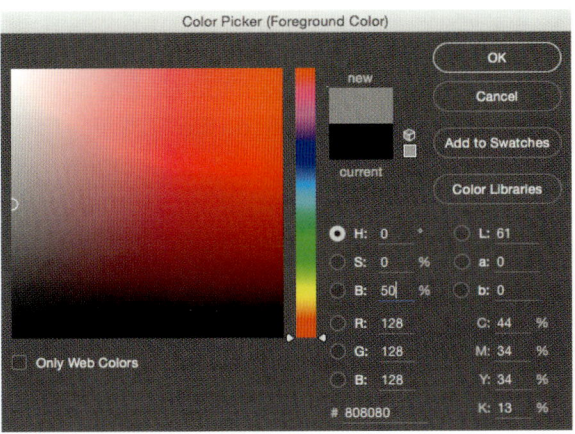

FIGURE 4.51

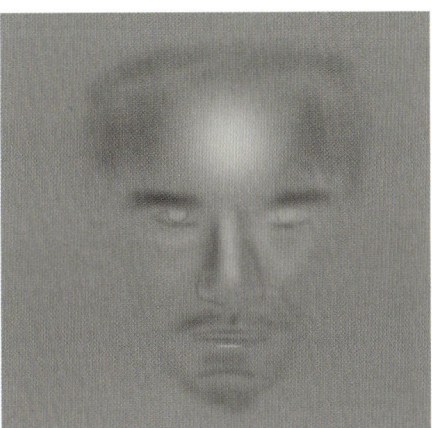

FIGURE 4.52

5. Another great reason to dodge and burn on a 50% gray layer is that it makes it easier to blend areas together. The real skill with dodging and burning is making the highlight and shadow areas you've enhanced blend into each other naturally. On this gray layer, we can do that after the fact by selecting an area (**Figure 4.53**) and using Gaussian Blur to create a smooth transition between highlights and shadows (**Figure 4.54**).

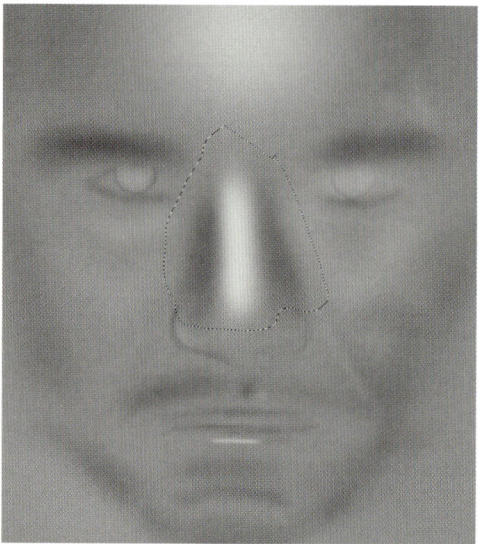

FIGURE 4.53

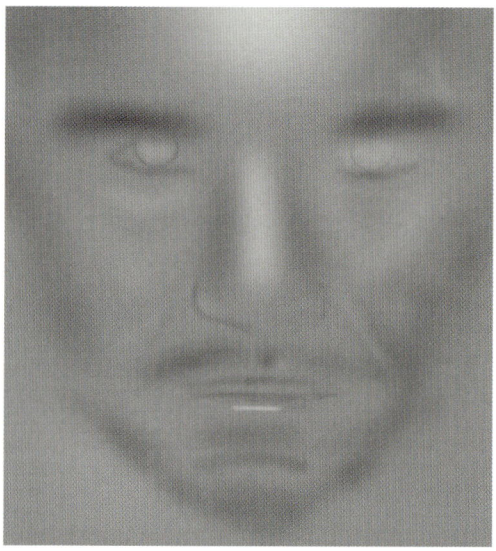

FIGURE 4.54

Dodging and burning can make such a difference in your pictures. It allows you to highlight specific areas to which you want to guide the viewer and adds much more depth and dimension.

The one final tip I'd offer is to take your time. Do a little and then step away from your picture and return a few minutes later. When you do this you'll see your picture with fresh eyes and will instantly know if you need to do more, or if you went too far and need to reduce the effect. It's easy to reduce the effect when you're working on the 50% gray layer.

SKIN SMOOTHING

I think it's fair to say that when it comes to retouching techniques there is a seemingly endless number of ways to smooth skin. From blurring techniques to third-party plugins, all of them will produce different results. However, when it comes to portrait retouching the goal should be to show smooth skin that retains a level of texture and ultimately looks realistic.

In this tutorial I want to take you through a technique that I turn to again and again because it helps me achieve exactly that. It maintains texture and looks realistic, and I have total control over how much of the effect I wish to apply depending on the subject.

1. Open your image in Photoshop and create a duplicate layer by going to *Layer > New > Layer via Copy*, or by using the keyboard shortcut Command + J (Mac) or Ctrl + J (PC). Rename the duplicate layer "smooth skin" (**Figure 4.55**). We do this so our original is safe, but also, as you'll see later, so we can use it to control exactly how smooth we want the skin to be.

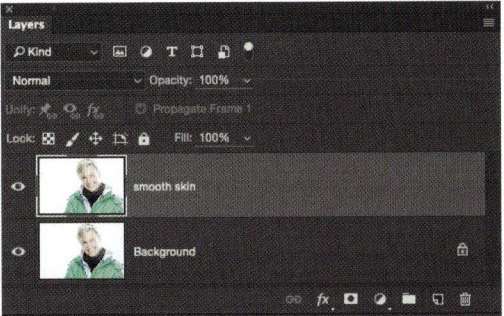

FIGURE 4.55

2. With the smooth skin layer selected in the Layers panel, change the Blend Mode to Vivid Light (**Figure 4.56**). This will create what looks like a very high-contrast version of our picture. Next, go to *Image > Adjustments > Invert* (**Figure 4.57**), or simply use the keyboard shortcut Command + I (Mac) or Ctrl + I (PC).

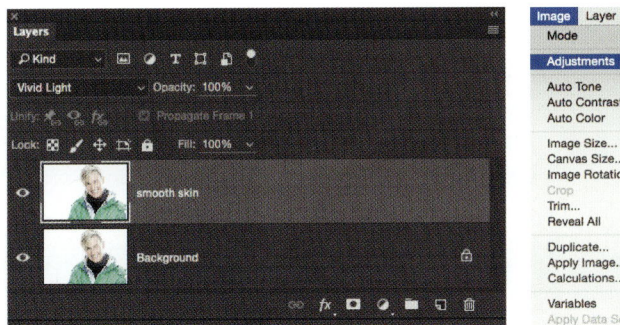

FIGURE 4.56

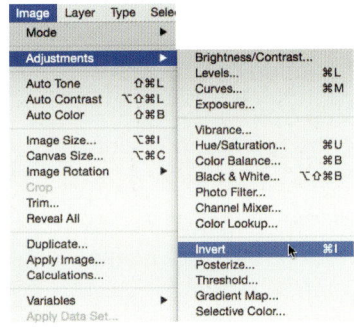

FIGURE 4.57

3. Go to *Filter > Other > High Pass*. For a high-resolution picture, a Radius of around 20 Pixels will be perfect (**Figure 4.58**). For a lower-resolution image, you'll need to input a lower amount. Now we need to add a small amount of blur, so go to *Filter > Blur > Gaussian Blur*, and for a high-resolution image, a Radius of around 3 Pixels is all we need (**Figure 4.59**).

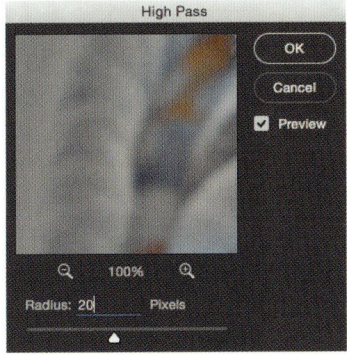

FIGURE 4.58

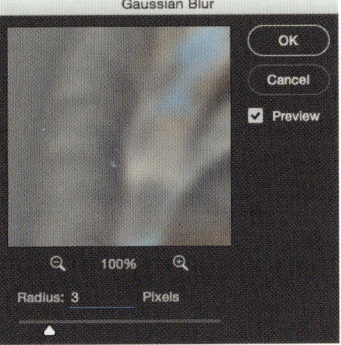

FIGURE 4.59

4. The actual smoothing has now been applied; however, at this stage our picture doesn't look quite right and we've lost the highlights and blacks in the important areas (**Figure 4.60**). So the next step is to click on the fx icon at the bottom of the Layers panel and choose Blending Options from the popup menu (**Figure 4.61**).

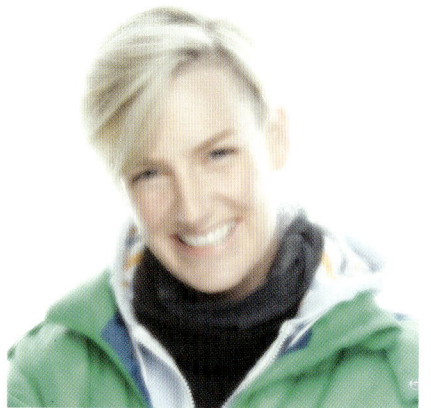

FIGURE 4.60

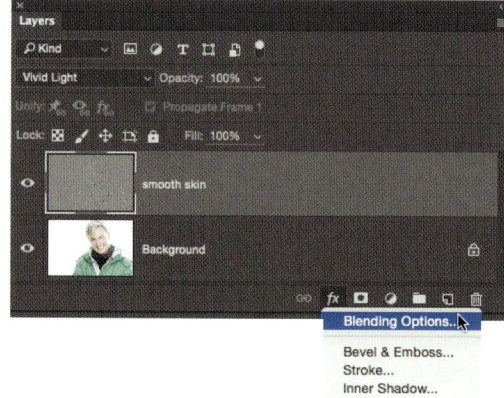

FIGURE 4.61

Within the Blending Options are the Blend If sliders, which we can use to make the image look more normal while retaining the smoothness we have applied. First we'll use the top Blend If slider labeled "This Layer." Hold down the Option key (Mac) or Alt key (PC) and click on the black marker at the far left to split the marker in half. Drag one half of the marker to the right until you get a reading of approximately 0/200 (**Figure 4.62**).

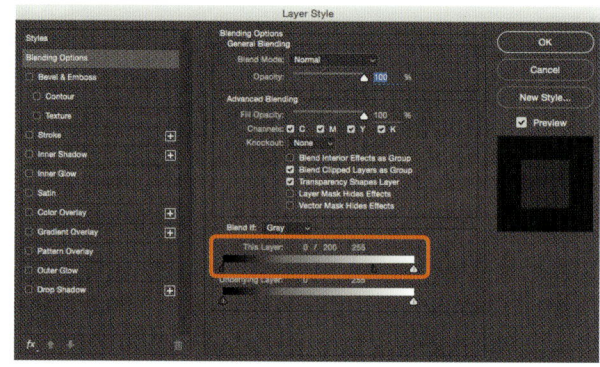

FIGURE 4.62

5. The previous step brought back some of the lighter parts of the image, so now we need to bring back the darker areas, particularly the areas around the eyes, nose, and mouth. Hold down the Option key (Mac) or Alt key (PC) and click on the white marker at the far right to split it in half. Drag it to the left until you get a reading of approximately 60/255 (**Figure 4.63**).

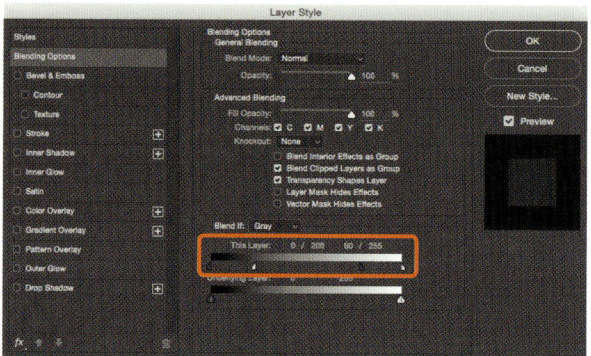

FIGURE 4.63

6. At this stage we've applied smoothing to our entire picture, including our subject's hair and teeth and the background. The softening is actually a little too much, so we need to restrict where the effect is applied and reduce it to the desired amount. To do this, simply hold down the Option key (Mac) or Alt key (PC) and click on the Layer Mask icon at the bottom of the Layers panel. This hides the smoothing. With a soft white brush at 100% Opacity, paint the effect back in over the skin, then lower the Opacity of the layer to around 40% (**Figure 4.64**).

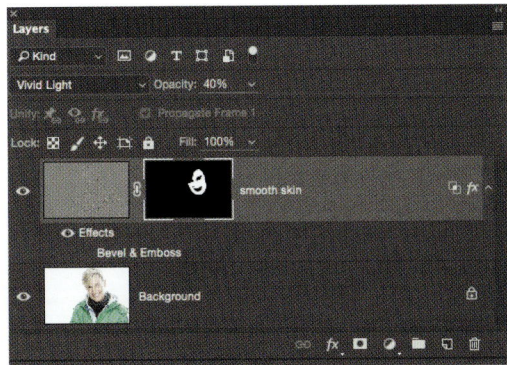

FIGURE 4.64

7. We've now given our subject smooth skin and maintained a realistic amount of detail and texture. We could stop at this point and carry on retouching other areas; however, I find that adding in a touch more contrast at this stage finishes the smoothing effect quite nicely. I do this by creating a merged layer at the top of the layer stack. Go to *Select > All*, then *Edit > Copy Merged*, then *Edit > Paste*, and finally *Filter > Sharpen > Unsharp Mask*. An Amount of 10%, Radius of 10, and Threshold of 0 works just fine (**Figure 4.65**).

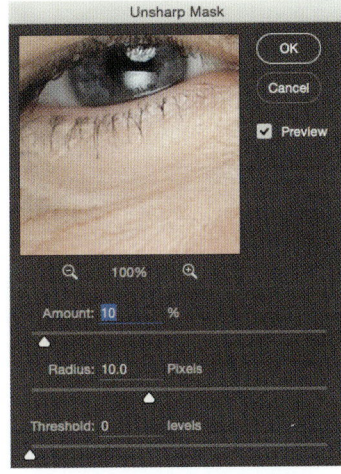

FIGURE 4.65

In **Figure 4.67** the skin under the eyes is smoother (**A**), but you can still see the natural lines; they're just more subtle. The overall look and feel of the skin is softer, but it still has texture (**B**), so the image looks natural and believable.

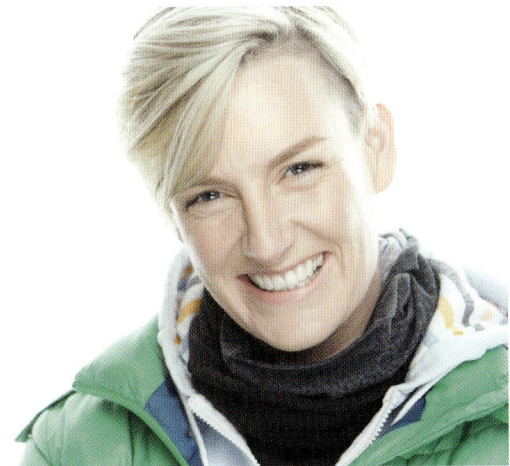

FIGURE 4.66 Before

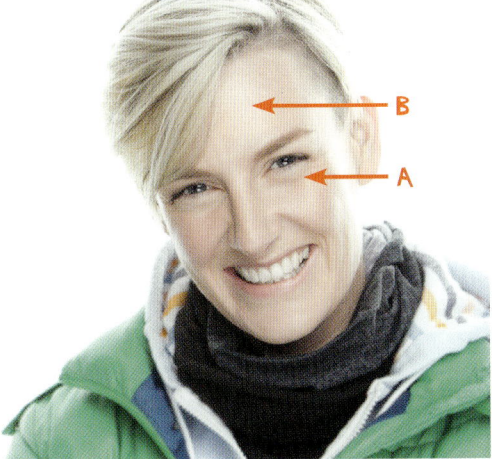

FIGURE 4.67 After

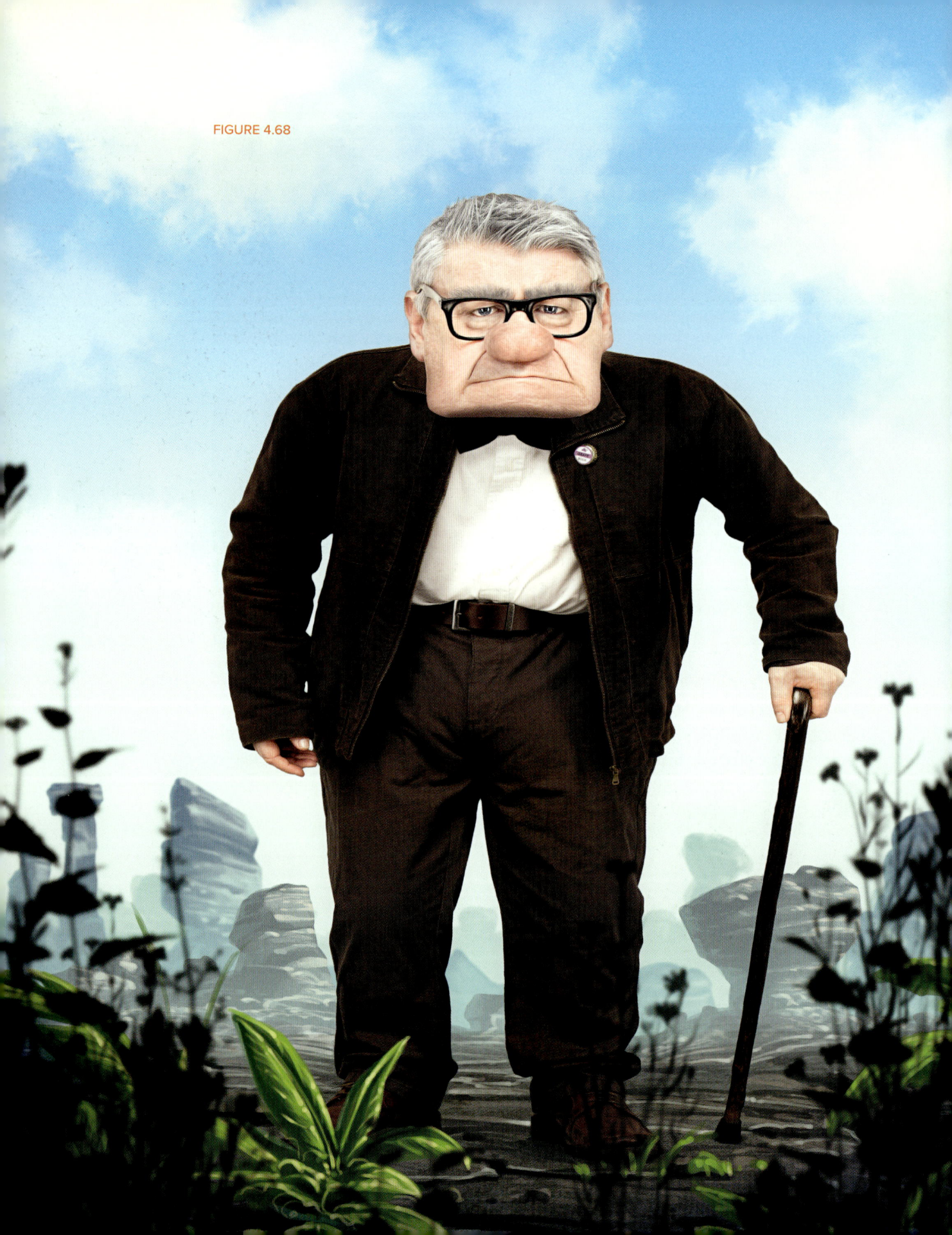

FIGURE 4.68

SELECTIONS & CUTOUTS TUTORIAL 1

As Photoshop continues to advance, it is becoming easier and less frustrating to make accurate selections and cutouts. The introduction of the Quick Selection Tool was quite literally a game changer for many.

However, despite the advancement in Photoshop's Selection Tools, there's still no "one-click fix" or tool that will work on every image. Each image is different and offers up it's own challenges, so as a Photoshop user it's a good idea to build up an understanding of as many ways to make selections as possible. This way, no matter what challenge you encounter, you'll be able to call upon a tool or technique that will work for you, and you'll be able to combine techniques to achieve the result you're after.

In this tutorial I'll take you through one of the ways I use the Quick Selection Tool. Most of the time the Quick Selection Tool will do a great job; however, I have found that sometimes you need to use it to make two separate selections and then add them together. This is often the case when selecting a person. While the Quick Selection Tool works great on the body area, it's not as accurate when it comes to picking up all those fine hairs on a person's head.

Let's go through the steps so you can see what I mean.

1. Choose the Quick Selection Tool (keyboard shortcut: W) and click and drag the selection cursor over the body area of our character, including the walking stick. We can see the area we're selecting because it is surrounded by what is commonly called the "marching ants" (**Figure 4.69**). We can exclude areas like the one between his arm and his body from the selection by holding down the Option key (Mac) or Alt key (PC) and dragging the cursor within them. Don't select the head, just go straight across the tops of the shoulders (**Figure 4.70**).

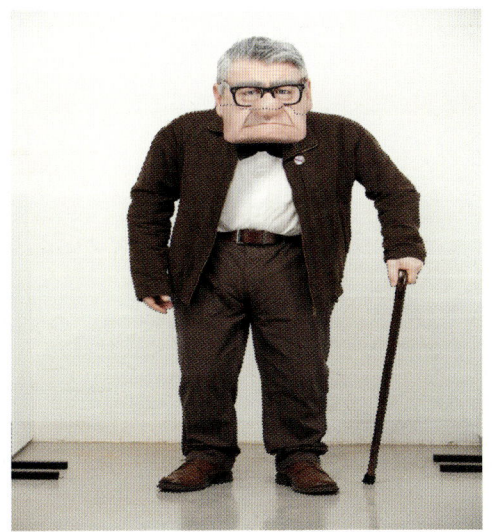

FIGURE 4.69

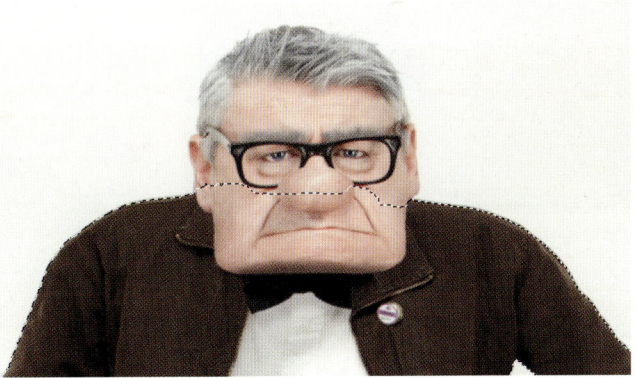

FIGURE 4.70

2. Once you have finished using the Quick Selection Tool, press Q on the keyboard to enter Quick Mask mode. I have Photoshop set up so that the red overlay covers the areas that have been included in the selection. However, Photoshop's default setting is to cover the unselected areas with the red overlay, which I actually find a little confusing. To set up Photoshop the way I use it, which I think is much easier when using Quick Mask, double-click

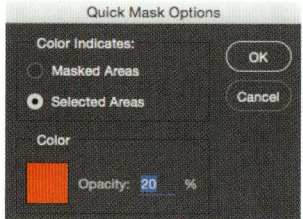

FIGURE 4.71

on the Quick Mask icon at the bottom of the toolbar, turn on Selected Areas, and press OK (**Figure 4.71**). Now press Q on the keyboard to show the selected areas covered in the red overlay.

3. Now that we're in Quick Mask mode we can hold down the space bar and click and drag to move around the image and see if there are any areas that need to be added to or excluded from the selection. To add an area, choose a brush (B) and paint over the area with black (**Figure 4.72**). To exclude an area, paint with white. Once you're finished, press Q to exit Quick Mask mode.

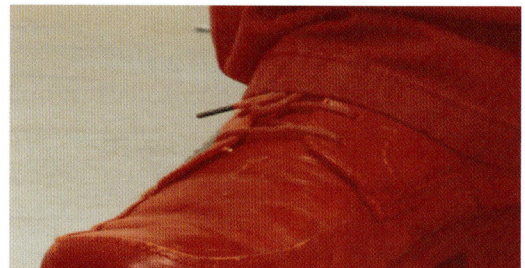

FIGURE 4.72

4. Now we need to save the selection. With the marching ants still visible, go to *Select > Save Selection*. In the dialog box type in something like "BODY" for the Name and click OK (**Figure 4.73**). Then go *Select > Deselect*.

5. Our next step is to make a selection of the head and hair. To do this, use the Quick Selection Tool (W), as we did in step 1 (**Figure 4.74**).

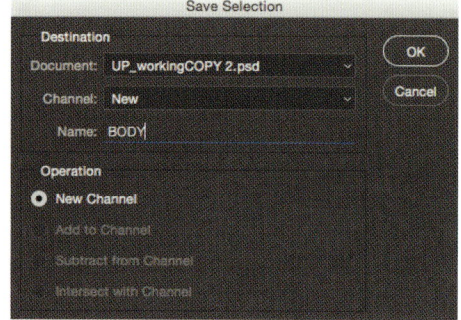

FIGURE 4.73

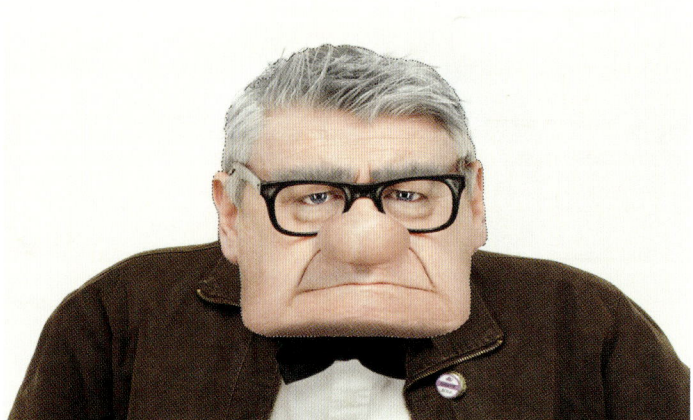

FIGURE 4.74

6. With a selection around the head active, click on Select and Mask in the options bar at the top of the screen (**Figure 4.75**). With the View Mode set to On White (this

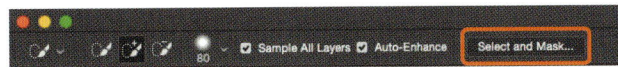

FIGURE 4.75

depends on personal preference) put a checkmark next to Smart Radius and increase the Radius slider to help Photoshop pick up any fine hairs it missed when we used the Quick Selection Tool (**Figure 4.76**). Don't increase this too much or it will ruin the selection. I found a radius of 6 pixels to be enough here. Next, use the Refine Radius Tool to brush around the outer edge of the character's head to pick up any extra fine hairs. Before exiting the Select and Mask dialog, choose Selection from the "Output To" drop-down menu at the bottom of the dialog box, and then click OK.

7. Now we are back in the Photoshop work area and the head and hair is surrounded by marching ants. To save this selection go to *Select > Save Selection*, name it "HEAD," and click OK. Then go *Select > Deselect*.

8. Now we need to combine the two selections. Go to the Channels tab and drag the BODY channel over the New Channel icon to create a copy. Double-click on the name of this channel copy and rename it CUTOUT (**Figure 4.77**). Hold down the Command key (Mac) or Ctrl key (PC) and click on the HEAD channel thumbnail to activate the marching ants (**Figure 4.78**). Go to *Edit > Fill*, choose White from the Contents menu, and click OK (**Figure 4.79**). Then go to *Select > Deselect*. We have now combined the two selections.

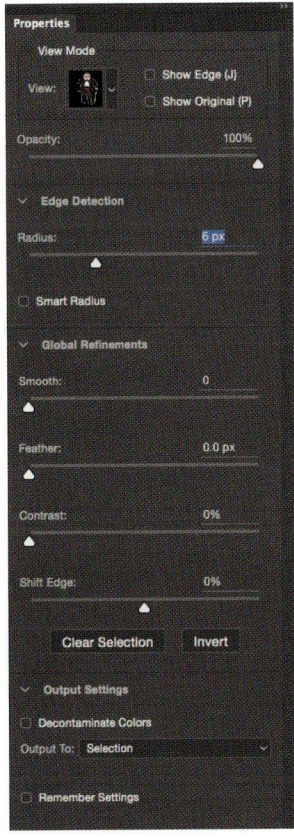

FIGURE 4.76

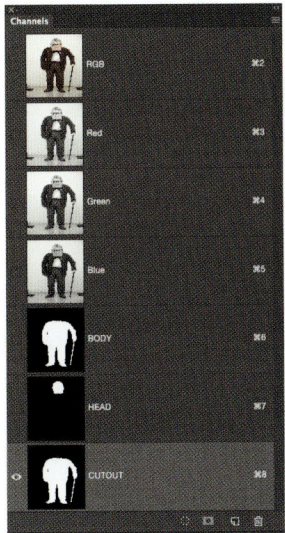

FIGURE 4.77

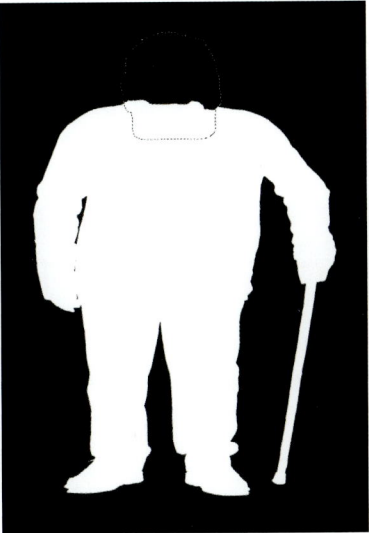

FIGURE 4.78

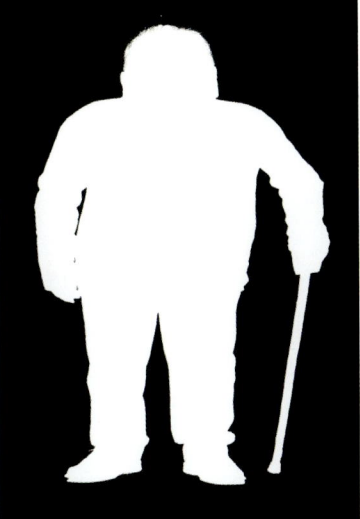

FIGURE 4.79

9. Click once on the RGB channel thumbnail to return to the normal image view, then click on the Layers tab. Go to *Select > Load Selection* and choose CUTOUT from the Channel drop-down menu. This is the channel we created by combining the two selections. Now click OK, and the marching ants will appear around the body and head of our character, showing that the two selections were combined and we now have one complete selection. With the selection active (marching ants), click the Layer Mask icon to cut out the character from the background (**Figure 4.80** and **4.81**). Then use the Move Tool (V) to click and drag the character into your background scene (**Figure 4.82**).

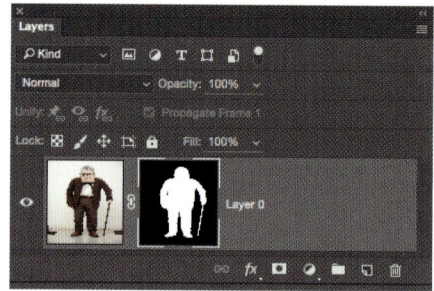

FIGURE 4.80

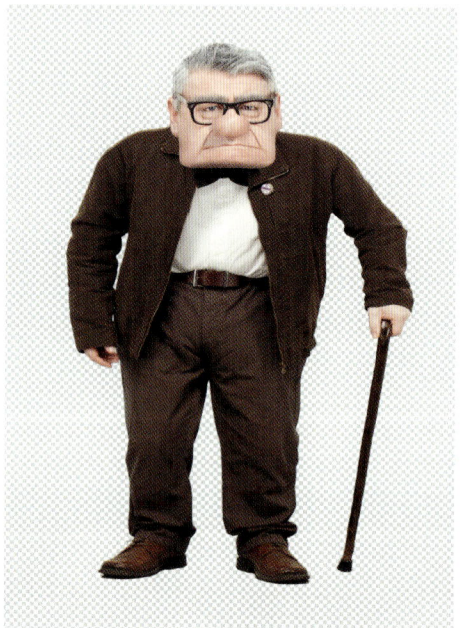

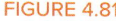

FIGURE 4.81

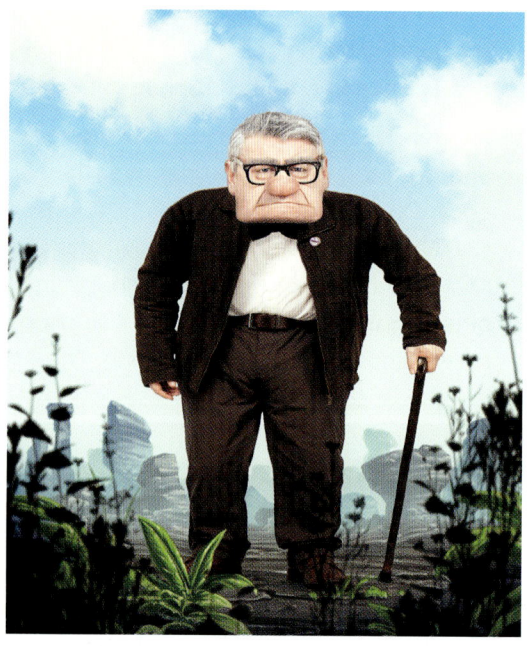

FIGURE 4.82

SELECTIONS & CUTOUTS TUTORIAL 2

In this tutorial I'll take you through another selection and cutout, but this time we'll make it one that could potentially be quite challenging. I'll show you how we can use a brush in Photoshop and make a few changes to it's behavior so that we can "fake" the cutout and speed up the process considerably. First we'll look at why we would want to do this.

1. Let's start by using the Quick Selection Tool to make as accurate of a selection of the mouse as we can, but don't worry too much about making it perfect. You'll likely notice that the selection process starts off well, but when we work around areas such as the tail, the selection goes off track somewhat. To bring the selection back close to the mouse and remove unwanted areas from the selection, hold down the Option key (Mac) or Alt key (PC) while dragging (**Figure 4.83**).

2. Now that we have a fairly accurate selection of our mouse, click on Select and Mask in the options bar. Because the mouse is so close in tone and contrast to the background, using Select and Mask doesn't produce as good of a result as we'd like (despite it being the all-new singing-and-dancing selection method). Using Smart Radius and the Refine Edge Brush to pick up some of the fine hairs produces a cloudy, smudged effect around the mouse (**Figure 4.84**). It's times like this when we can turn to other Photoshop tools to speed up the process and fake the cutout.

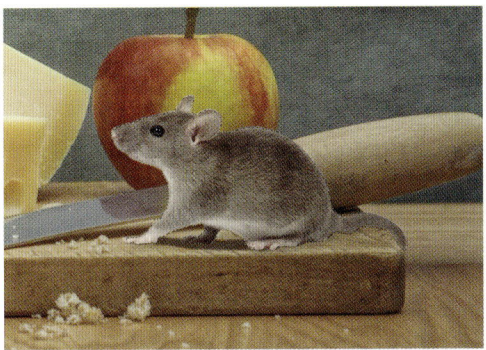

FIGURE 4.83

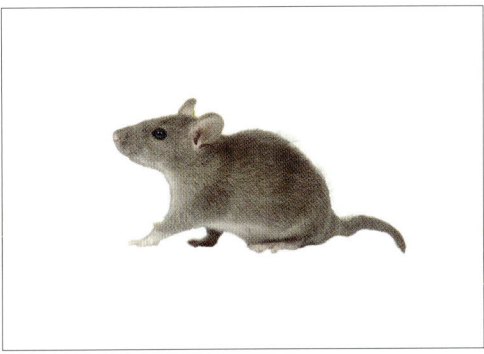

FIGURE 4.84

3. Click Cancel to exit the Refine Edge dialog box and return to the original picture of the mouse with the selection we made with the Quick Selection Tool still active. Click on the Layer Mask icon. So that we can clearly see what we are doing as we cut out the mouse, let's add a blank layer below the mouse by holding down the Command key (Mac) or Ctrl key (PC) and clicking on the New Layer icon at the bottom of the Layers panel. Then go to *Edit > Fill*, choose White from the Contents dropdown menu, and click OK (**Figure 4.85**).

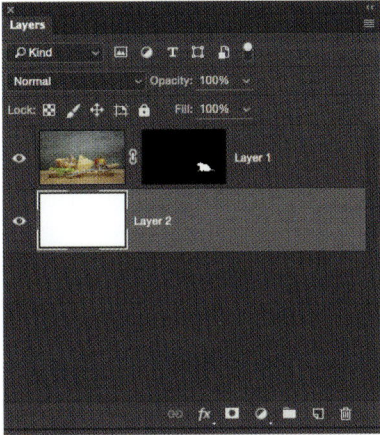

FIGURE 4.85

4. Click on the layer mask attached to the mouse layer, and then choose a round, hard-edged brush from the toolbar (**Figure 4.86**). Click on the brush options to ensure there are no settings applied to affect how the brush behaves. With this hard-edged brush and a black foreground color, paint around the perimeter of the mouse to paint away part of the mouse's body and fur (**Figure 4.87**). Decrease the size of the brush as you go along areas such as the tail.

5. At this point, the cutout of the mouse doesn't look realistic; however, we can now use a brush that is preinstalled in Photoshop to create the look of fur. Go to the Brush Preset Picker and scroll down until you see brush number 112, which looks like a single blade of grass (**Figure 4.88**). Click on this brush preset and then open the Brush panel (**Figure 4.89**). At the bottom of the Brush panel there is a preview of what the brush will look like if it's used with the presets currently applied. We can make changes to these settings so that the brush behaves differently.

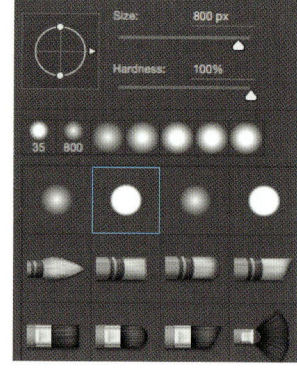

FIGURE 4.86

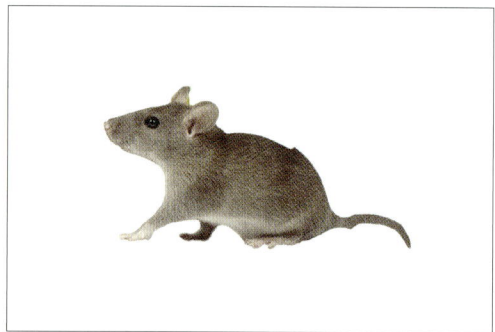

FIGURE 4.87

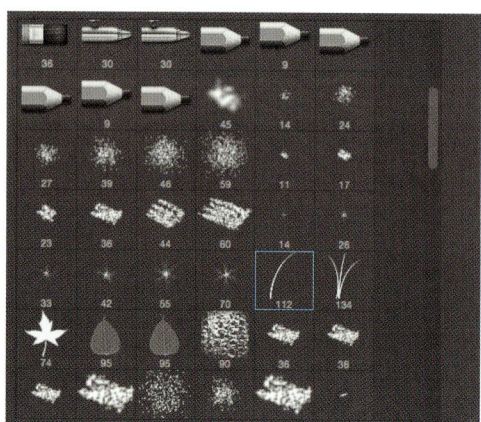

FIGURE 4.88

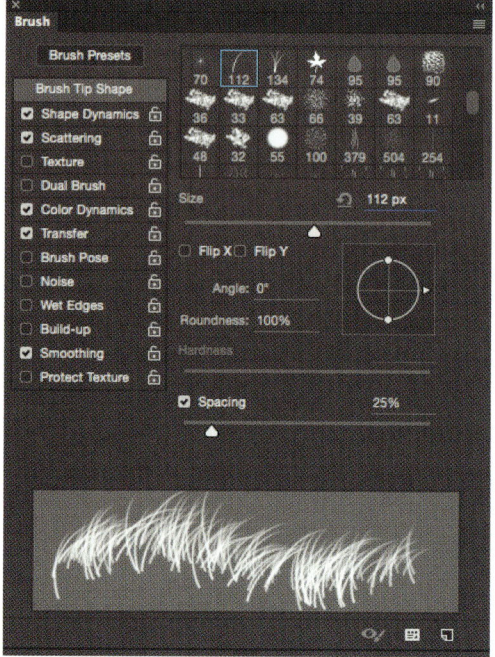

FIGURE 4.89

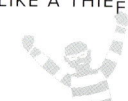

6. The Brush Tip Shape tab contains an option that allows us to change the angle at which the brush is applied. This is very useful for painting along the contour of the mouse. We can also adjust Spacing so that the brush strokes gather tighter together, which is great for creating fake fur (**Figure 4.90**). Click on Shape Dynamics and set the Size Jitter to around 10% (**Figure 4.91**). This will slightly vary the size of each brush stroke that is applied. Leave Scattering at its default settings and uncheck Color Dynamics, Transfer, and Smoothing (**Figure 4.92**).

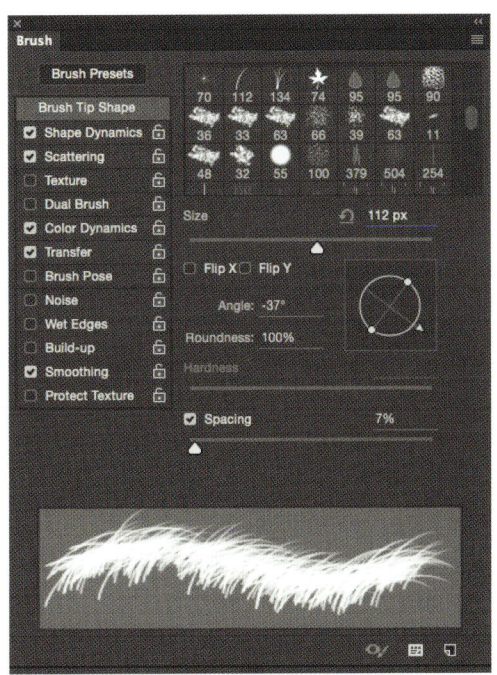

FIGURE 4.90

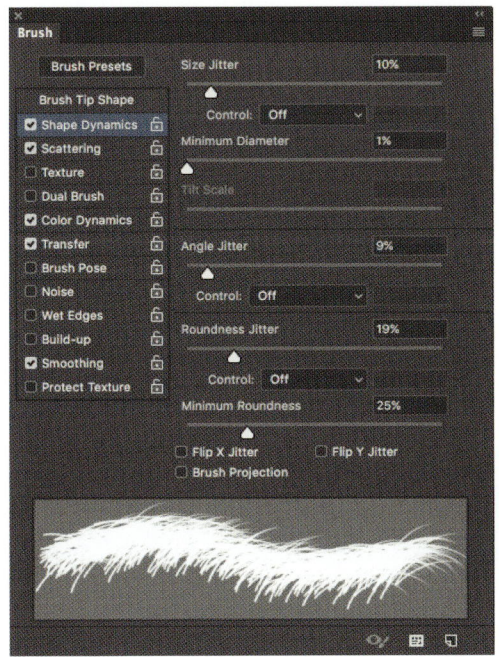

FIGURE 4.91

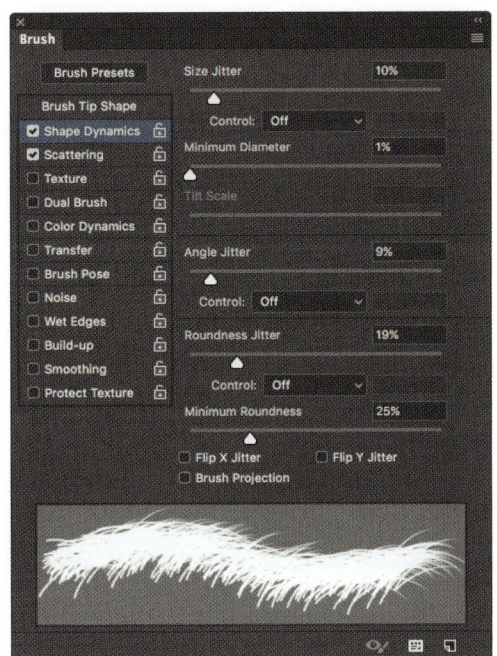

FIGURE 4.92

7. With the brush settings in place, change the foreground color to white. Then use the fur brush we just created to paint along the perimeter of the mouse to reveal what was previously hidden. Now that we are using this new brush, the parts of the mouse we painted away are revealed as fur (**Figure 4.93**). As we paint around the mouse, we can dive back into the Brush panel to alter the Size and Angle of the brush to suit the area we are brushing over. After we've painted around the mouse to reveal the fur,

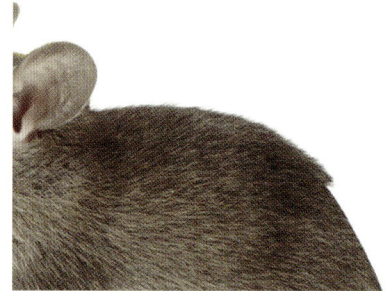

FIGURE 4.93

we can then use the Move Tool to drag the mouse off the original picture, but we'll bring the layer mask with it in case we need to make any adjustments later.

8. Having taken the time to create this fake fur brush, you'll most definitely want to save it as a preset so that you can use it in the future without having to go through the previous steps each time. Open the Brush panel and click on the Create New Brush icon in the bottom-right corner. In the dialog box that appears, give the new brush an appropriate name and then click OK (**Figure 4.94**). From now on, you'll be able to choose this brush from the Brush Presets (**Figure 4.95**).

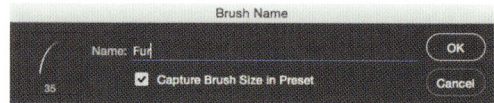

FIGURE 4.94

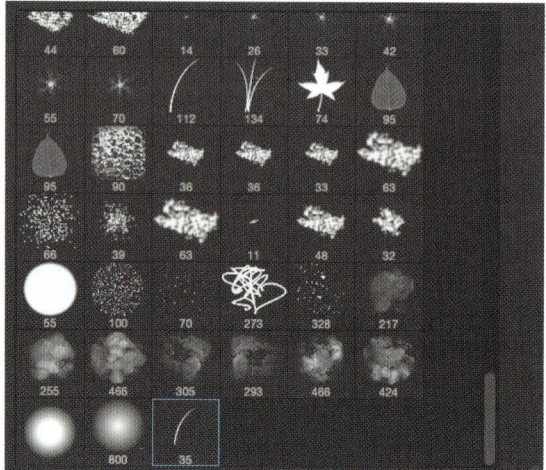

FIGURE 4.95

TIP *Brushes are undoubtedly one of the most powerful tools we have at our disposal in Photoshop, especially when it comes to creating composites. For **Figure 4.96** I modified a pre-installed brush (134) with my own settings to create the look of grass. I created this composite of a lioness from a selection and cutout using the exact same method I described in the previous tutorial. I used my modified version of brush 134 to paint over parts of the lioness with the shape of grass so that she appears to be sitting in the grass.*

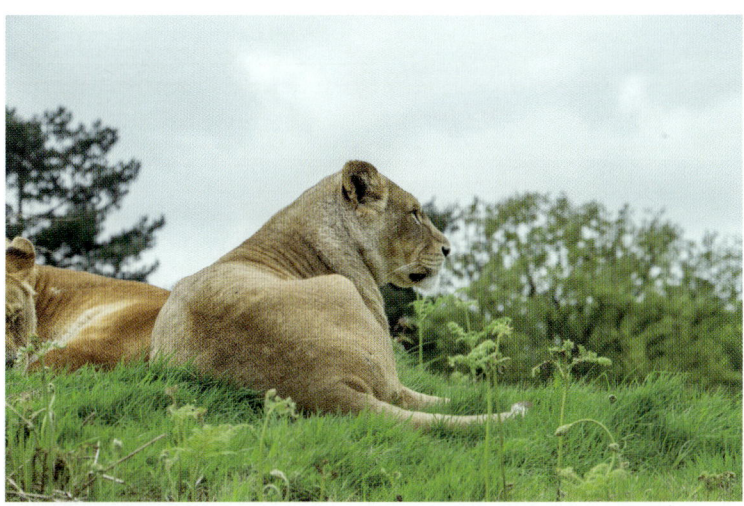

FIGURE 4.96 Before

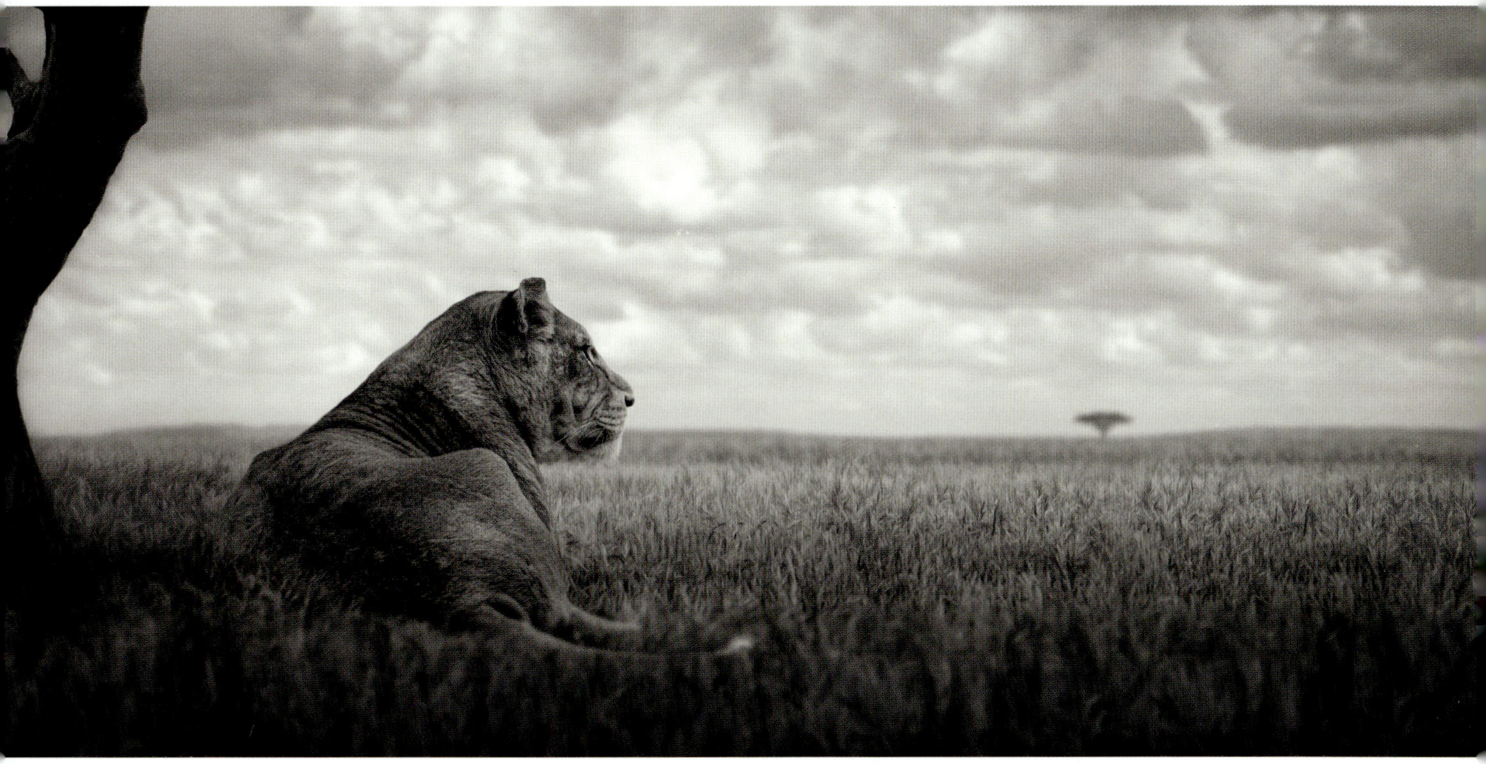

FIGURE 4.97 After

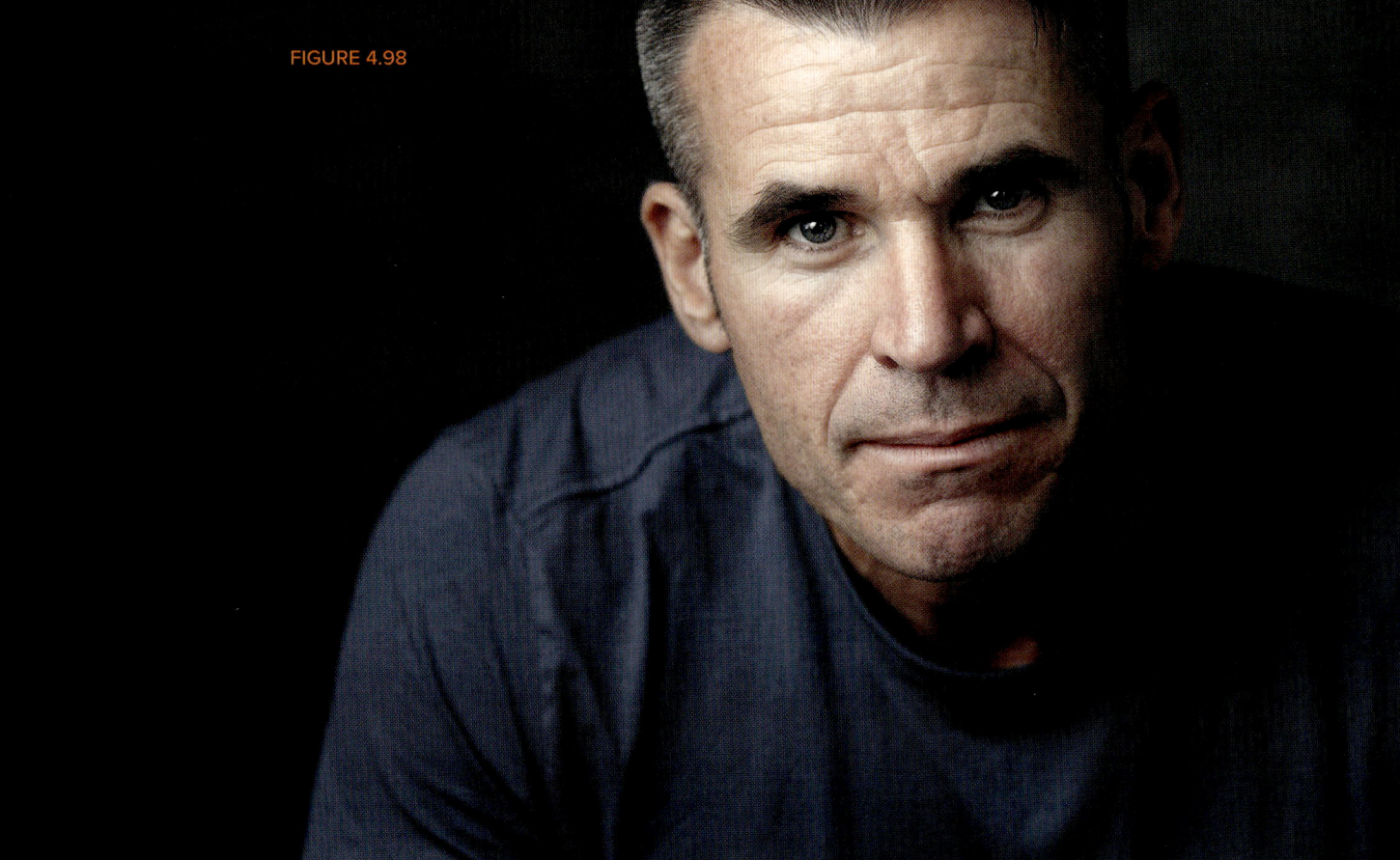

FIGURE 4.98

AMAZING EYES

This tutorial is all about my favorite way to enhance eyes, make them sharp, and add color. Of course, there are many more techniques we could use, especially with the likes of the Adjustment Brush in Camera RAW and Lightroom, but I just find that the following technique gives the eyes that extra punch, which gives the portrait much more impact.

This is a quick and easy technique that gives you a lot of control and is completely non-destructive, so you can always dive back in and make adjustments at a later stage if you want to.

1. We're going to use a Quick Mask to select the eyes first, so we'll need to modify its default settings. Double-click on the Quick Mask icon in the toolbar (**Figure 4.99**). In the Quick Mask Options dialog tick the Selected Areas checkbox and click OK (**Figure 4.100**).

2. Press Q to enter Quick Mask mode. Choose a soft-edged round brush (about 25% hardness; **Figure 4.101**) and a black foreground color, and then paint around the inside of the eye (**Figure 4.102**). If you paint over too much, change the foreground color to white and paint it away.

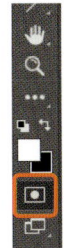
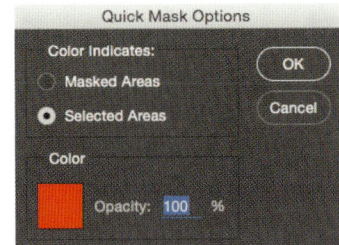
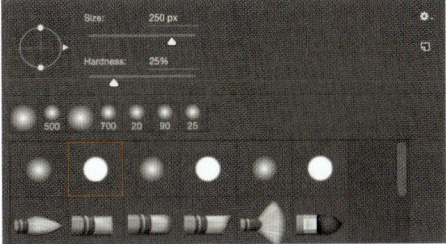

FIGURE 4.99   FIGURE 4.100   FIGURE 4.101

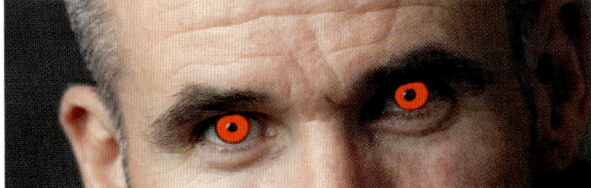

FIGURE 4.102

3. Press Q to exit Quick Mask mode. Now you'll see the marching ants indicating the areas you manually selected using the Quick Mask (**Figure 4.103**). With the selection visible, add a Selective Color adjustment layer by clicking on the corresponding icon in the Adustments panel (**Figure 4.104**).

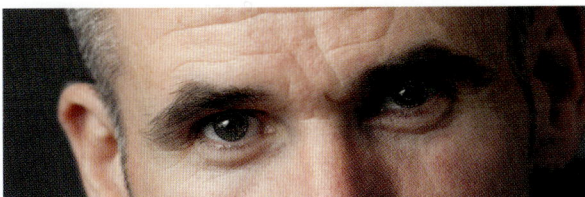
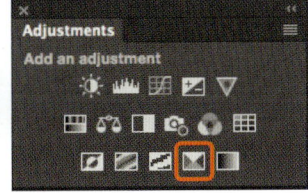

FIGURE 4.103   FIGURE 4.104

4. Change the Blend Mode of the Selective Color adjustment layer to Linear Dodge (Add) (**Figure 4.105**), and you'll see that the eyes brighten considerably (**Figure 4.106**). This is a great way to see what color the eyes are so we know what colors to enhance.

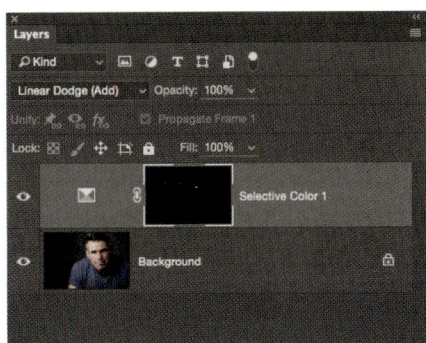
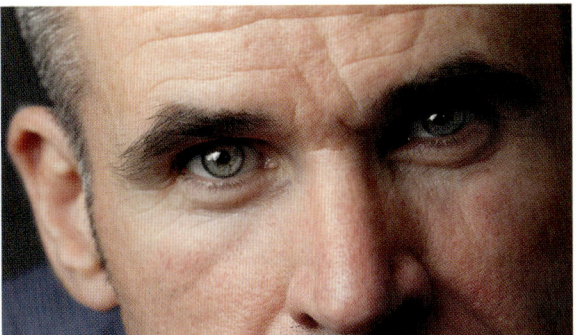

FIGURE 4.105   FIGURE 4.106

5. In the Selective Color Properties, choose Neutrals from the Colors menu, and then use the sliders to enhance or change the color of the eyes (**Figure 4.107**).

6. Choose Blacks from the Colors menu and use the Black slider to increase or decrease contrast in the eye (**Figure 4.108**). Moving to the right increases contrast and moving to the left decreases contrast.

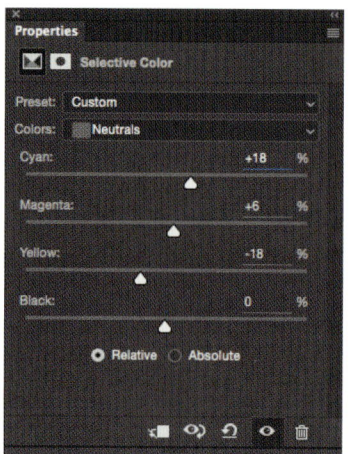

FIGURE 4.107

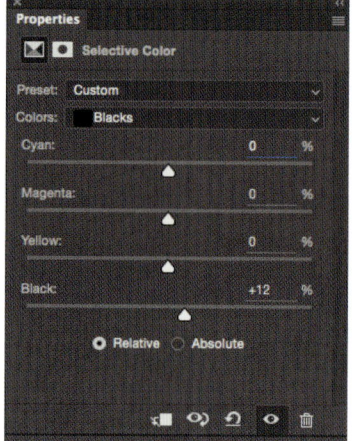

FIGURE 4.108

7. In the Layers panel, lower the Opacity of the Selective Color adjustment layer to around 40%. Then add a new blank layer to the top of the layer stack and name it "sharpness" (**Figure 4.109**).

8. Choose the Sharpen Tool from the toolbar (**Figure 4.110**). In the options at the top of the screen choose a Strength of 30% and ensure that the Sample All Layers and Protect Detail checkboxes are ticked (**Figure 4.111**).

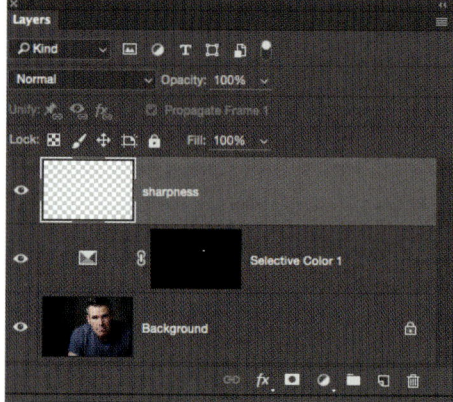

FIGURE 4.109

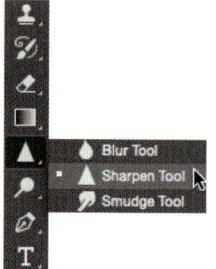
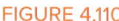

FIGURE 4.110

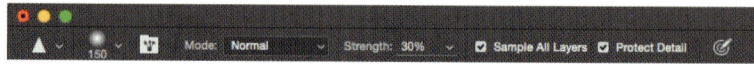

FIGURE 4.111

Now simply paint over the eyes to sharpen them. One thing to note here is that the Sharpen Tool works like a spray can, so the more times you cover an area without lifting off, the more the effect builds up.

Notice how the eyes have much more impact in **Figure 4.113**. The color and highlights have been increased (**A**) and you can see much more of the texture and detail in the eyes (**B**).

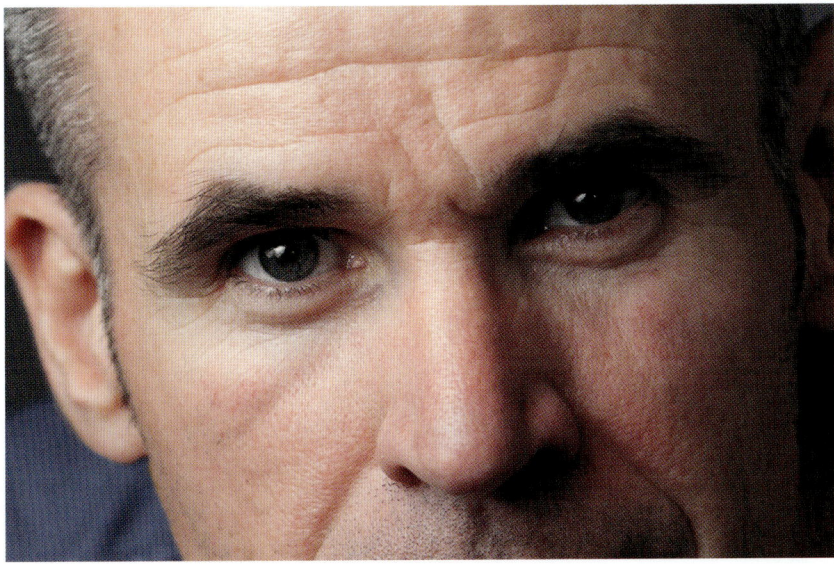

FIGURE 4.112 Before

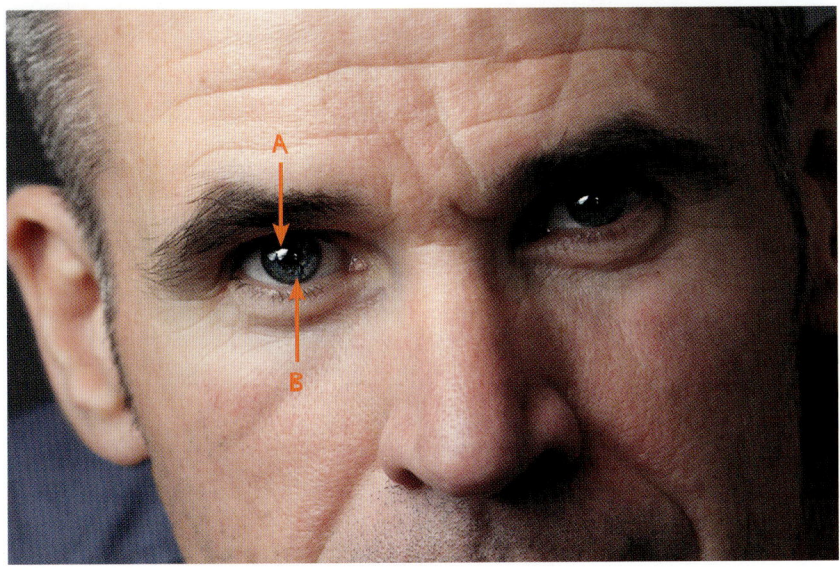

FIGURE 4.113 After

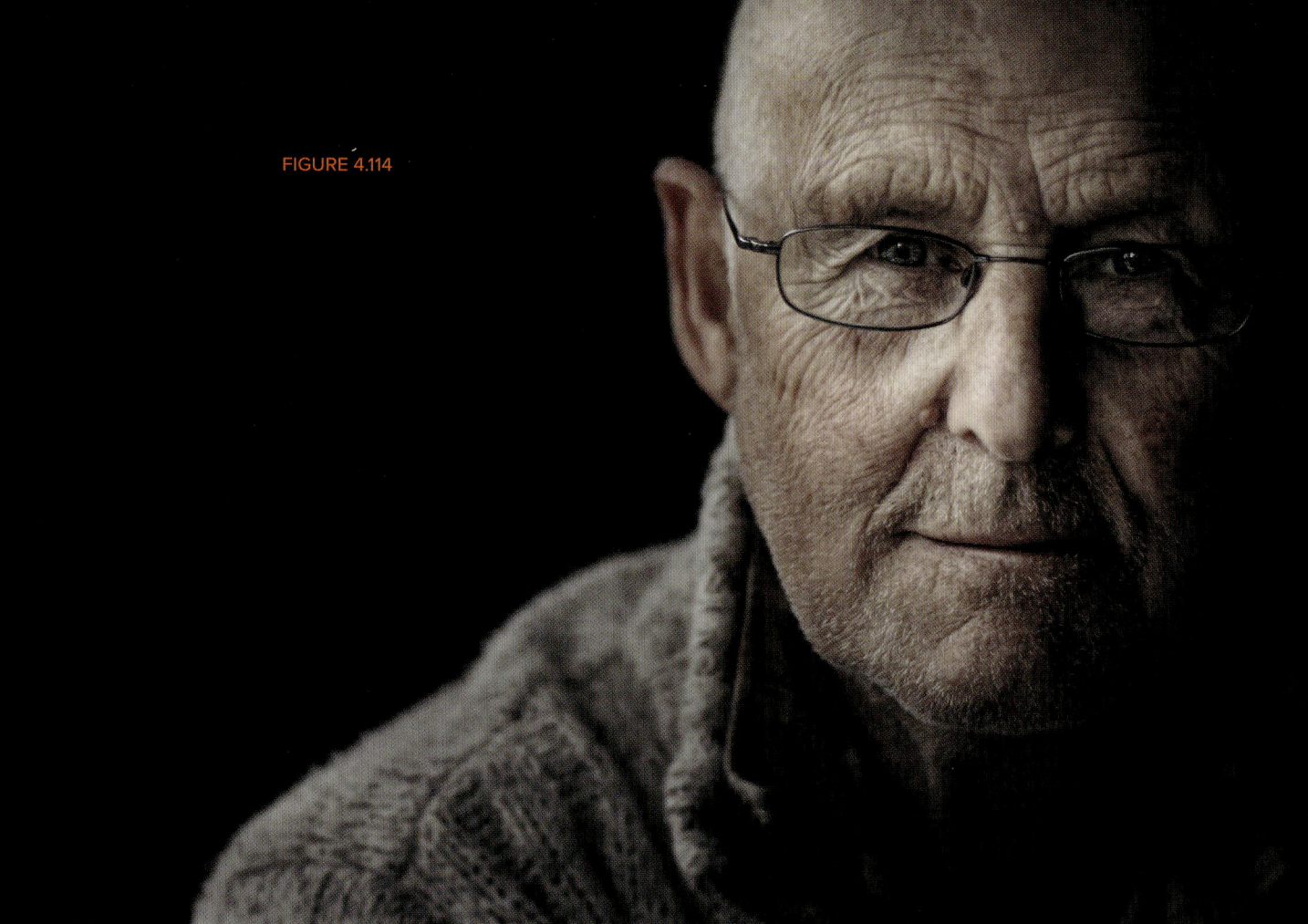

FIGURE 4.114

BUILDING DEPTH

When we look at a picture we're naturally drawn to the brightest and sharpest areas of the picture, and it's these areas combined with the areas that have more contrast that give a picture its depth and dimension. The areas that are sharper and more contrasty appear to be closer to the viewer, and vice versa.

Armed with this knowledge, I started applying it to my portraits, but in layers, so that it appears as though the subjects are actually coming forward off the screen or page. Let's walk through how I do it.

1. Starting off in Adobe Camera RAW (or Lightroom), add Sharpening first. For male portraits I usually add an Amount of 40 (**Figure 4.115**). Then hold down the Option key (Mac) or Alt key (PC) and click and drag the Masking slider to restrict the sharpening to the subject's face. This is indicated by the areas that show up as white (**Figure 4.116**).

2. Select the Adjustment Brush, increase Sharpening to around 40, and paint over any facial hair and the eyes to add extra sharpening (**Figure 4.117**).

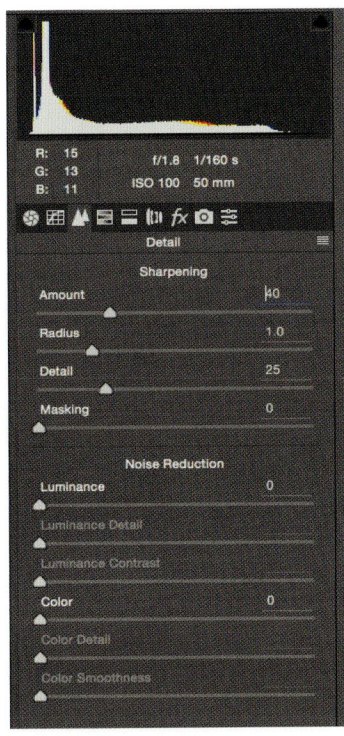

FIGURE 4.115

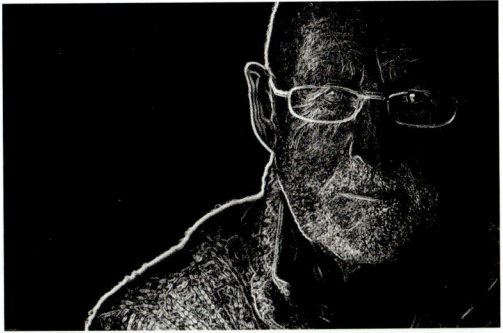

FIGURE 4.116

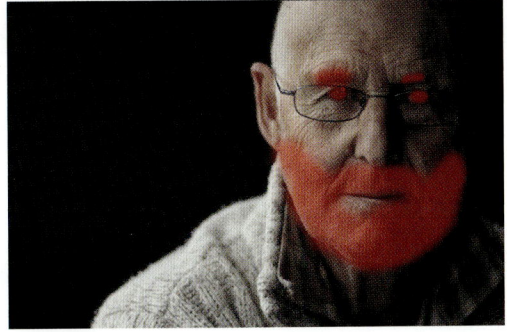

FIGURE 4.117

3. Click OK to apply the adjustments and send the image back into Photoshop. If you're using Lightroom, go to *Photo > Edit > Edit in Adobe Photoshop*.

This is the stage at which I'll usually do some dodging and burning on the face and enhance the eyes using the techniques discussed earlier in this chapter.

4. Go to *Filter > Sharpen > Unsharp Mask* (**Figure 4.118**) and input an Amount and Radius of 10 pixels each (**Figure 4.119**). This adds contrast to the entire picture.

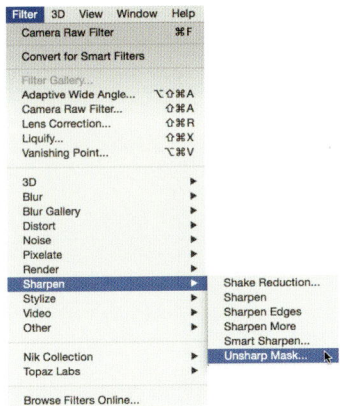

FIGURE 4.118

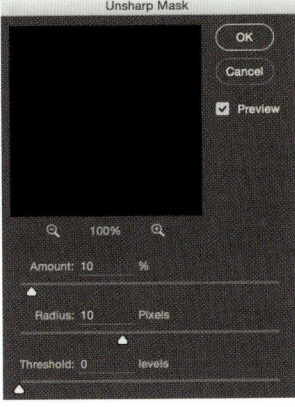

FIGURE 4.119

5. Double-click on the Quick Mask icon in the toolbar (**Figure 4.120**). In the Quick Mask Options dialog, tick the Selected Areas checkbox and click OK (**Figure 4.121**).

Press Q to enter Quick Mask mode. Use a round, soft-edged brush and a black foreground color to paint inside the face, leaving a small gap around the outer edge (**Figure 4.122**). Press Q again to exit Quick Mask mode, and the marching ant selection will be visible (**Figure 4.123**).

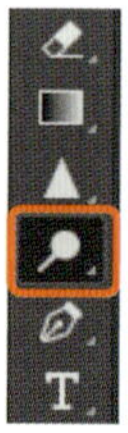

FIGURE 4.120

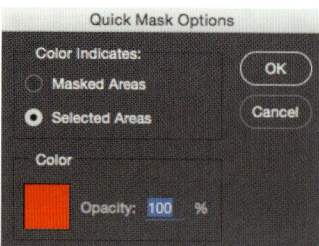

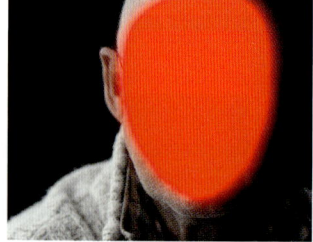

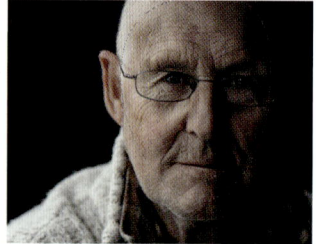

FIGURE 4.121

FIGURE 4.122

FIGURE 4.123

6. Now press Command + F (Mac) or Ctrl + F (PC) to apply the last-used filter, which in this case is Unsharp Mask. This adds additional contrast in the face. Press Command + D (Mac) or Ctrl + D (PC) to remove the marching ant selection.

7. Repeat steps 5 and 6, but this time use Quick Mask mode to select a smaller area of the face (**Figure 4.124**), and reapply the Unsharp Mask filter.

8. Repeat steps 5 and 6, but this time use Quick Mask mode to select just the eyes, nose, and mouth (**Figure 4.125**), and reapply the Unsharp Mask filter.

Of course, you could use higher values for Amount and Radius in the Unsharp Mask filter, but even with the settings used here you can see how it adds focus to the main areas of the face (eyes, nose, and mouth) and creates greater depth and dimension.

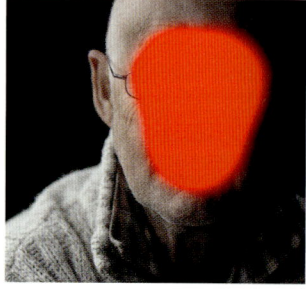

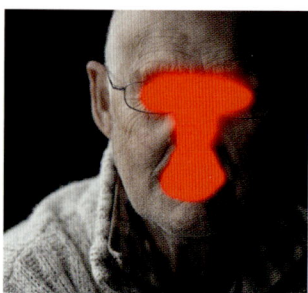

FIGURE 4.124

FIGURE 4.125

Figure 4.127 has more impact than the original image. The results aren't necessarily earth-shattering, but there is definitely a difference, and when it comes to retouching, it's the small differences that make the biggest impact. Figure 4.126 looks flat and smooth, whereas in Figure 4.127 the face has much more definition, especially around the eyes, nose, and mouth. The shadows around the eyes are deeper (A) and the highlights are slightly brighter, particularly in the eyes and around the rim of the glasses. The detail and contrast around the mouth and chin and in the facial hair has increased (B). The clarity in these areas combined with the slight blurriness of the outer areas of the face makes the eyes, nose, mouth stand out more.

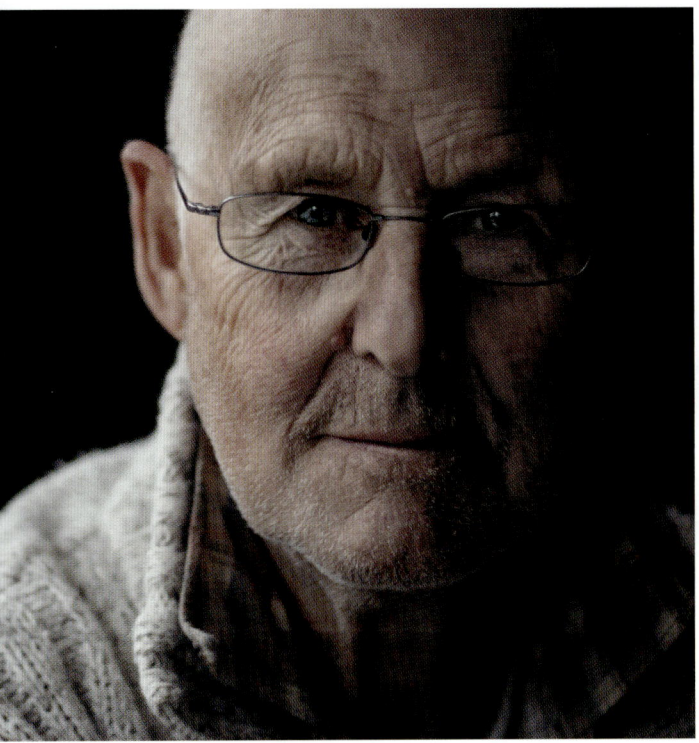

FIGURE 4.126 Before

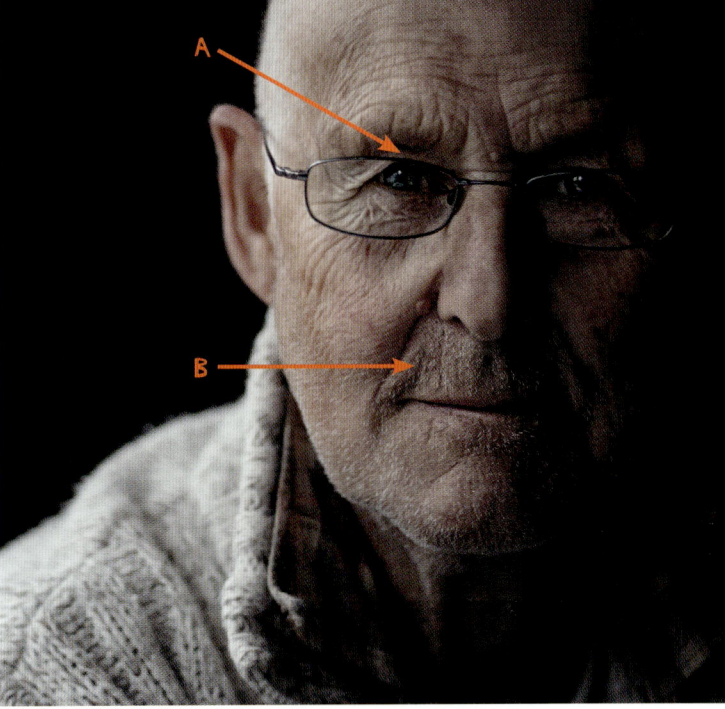

FIGURE 4.127 After

FREQUENCY SEPARATION

In this tutorial I want to take you through a simplified version of what I believe is possibly the very best retouching technique you'll ever learn and use: frequency separation.

As you'd expect with Photoshop and post-production, there are many ways to achieve similar results, and that's no different when it comes to frequency separation. But what is frequency separation? Well, in the simplest terms, this technique allows us to separate the color in an image from the content. By doing so we can then work on either without affecting the other.

Frequency separation is used a lot in beauty retouching, but it can be useful for working on almost any image. In this tutorial, I'll show you how you can use it to remove a shadow from a face quickly, easily, and realistically.

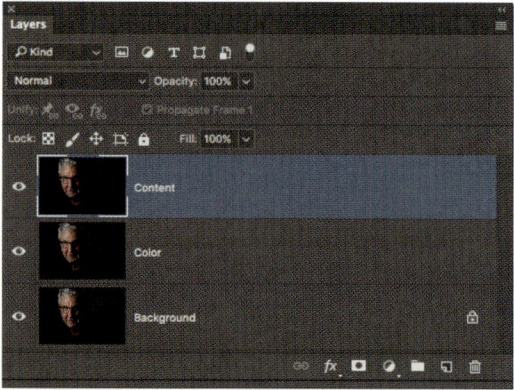

FIGURE 4.129

1. To start off we need to create two new layers, one for the color and one for the content. To do this, hold down the Command key (Mac) or Ctrl key (PC) and press the letter J twice. Rename the first copy "color" and the second copy, which will be the uppermost layer in the layer stack, "content" (**Figure 4.129**).

2. Turn off the content layer by clicking on the eye icon to the left of the layer, and then click on the color layer (**Figure 4.130**). Go to *Filter > Blur > Gaussian Blur* and add in an amount that doesn't completely blur out your picture to the point that it becomes unidentifiable, but rather so that it loses all sharpness and detail. For this image, a Gaussian Blur Radius of 30 Pixels is just about right. We are left with what is, in effect, color in the shape of a face (**Figure 4.131**). Click OK.

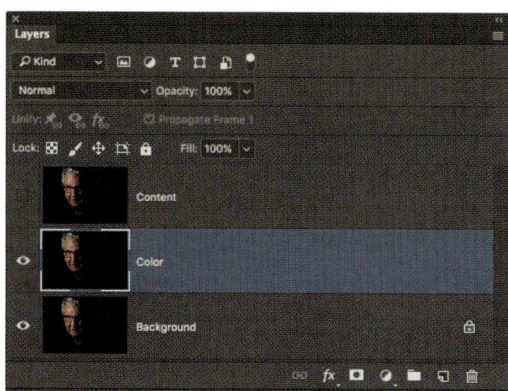

FIGURE 4.130

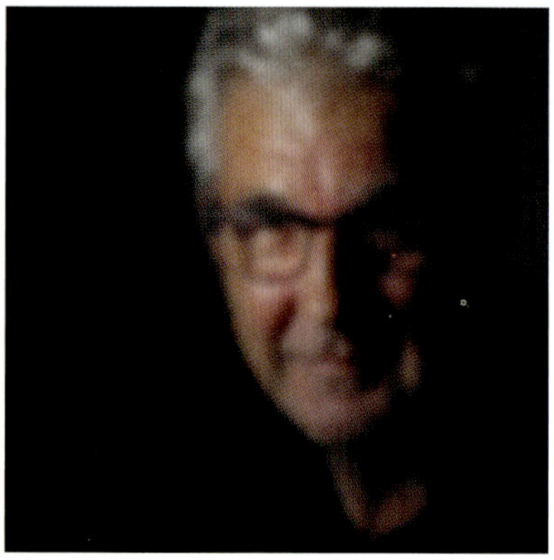

FIGURE 4.131

3. Click on the eye icon for the content layer so that the layer becomes active (**Figure 4.132**). Then go to *Image > Adjustments > Brightness/Contrast*, and in the small dialog that appears, click on the Use Legacy checkbox to turn it on. Adjust the Contrast to -50 and click OK (**Figure 4.133**). **Note:** For this technique to work it's vital that Use Legacy is checked before the Contrast amount is added.

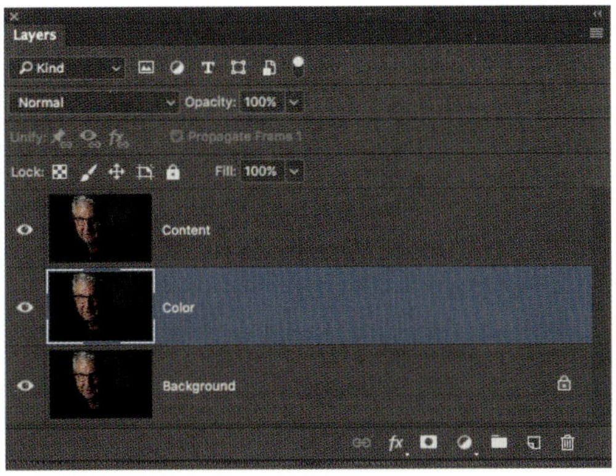

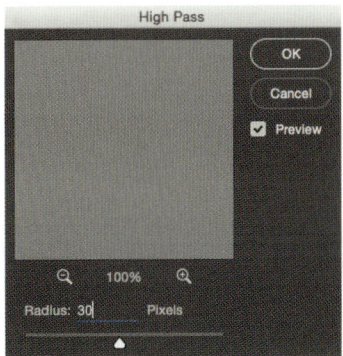

FIGURE 4.132

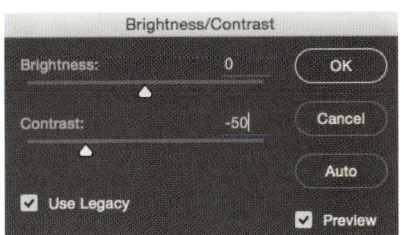

FIGURE 4.133

4. Now go to *Filter > Other > High Pass*, and for the Radius, add in the same amount as you did for the Gaussian Blur (in this example, 30 Pixels; **Figure 4.134**). Click OK. In the Layers panel, change the Blend Mode of the content layer to Linear Light (**Figure 4.135**).

5. Click on the color layer in the Layers panel, and then add a new blank layer so that it is placed underneath the content layer. Rename this layer "remove shadow" (**Figure 4.136**). Choose the Clone Stamp Tool from the toolbar. In the options at the top of the screen, set the Exposure to 10% and select Current and Below from the Sample drop-down menu.

FIGURE 4.134

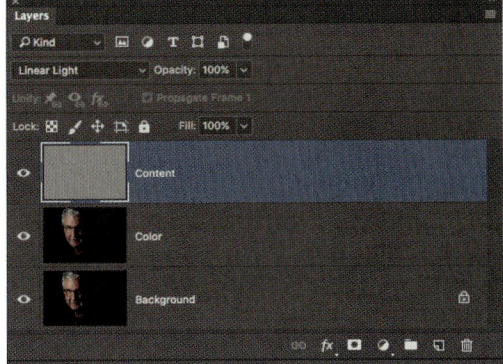

FIGURE 4.135

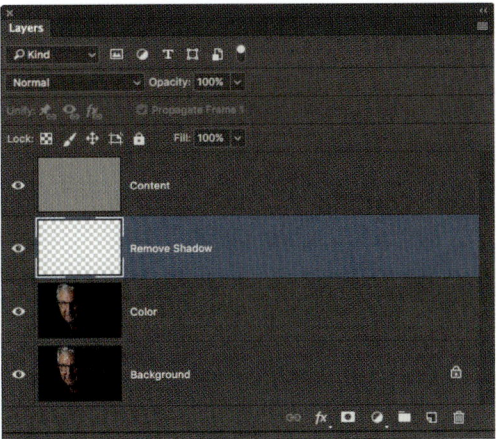

FIGURE 4.136

6. Zoom in to the area of the face where the shadow is. With the Clone Stamp Tool selected, hold down the Option key (Mac) or Alt key (PC) and click on either side of the shadow to sample skin color (**Figure 4.137**). Then paint over the shadow with a few strokes in each area to build up the color so that the shadow is lightened and takes on the color of the skin. The trick here is to continually sample the skin color on either side of the shadow as you work, and to do so with a low opacity setting on the Clone Stamp Tool, so that the blend is much more realistic.

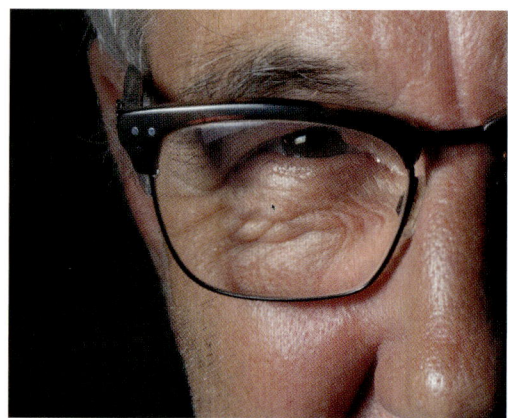

FIGURE 4.137

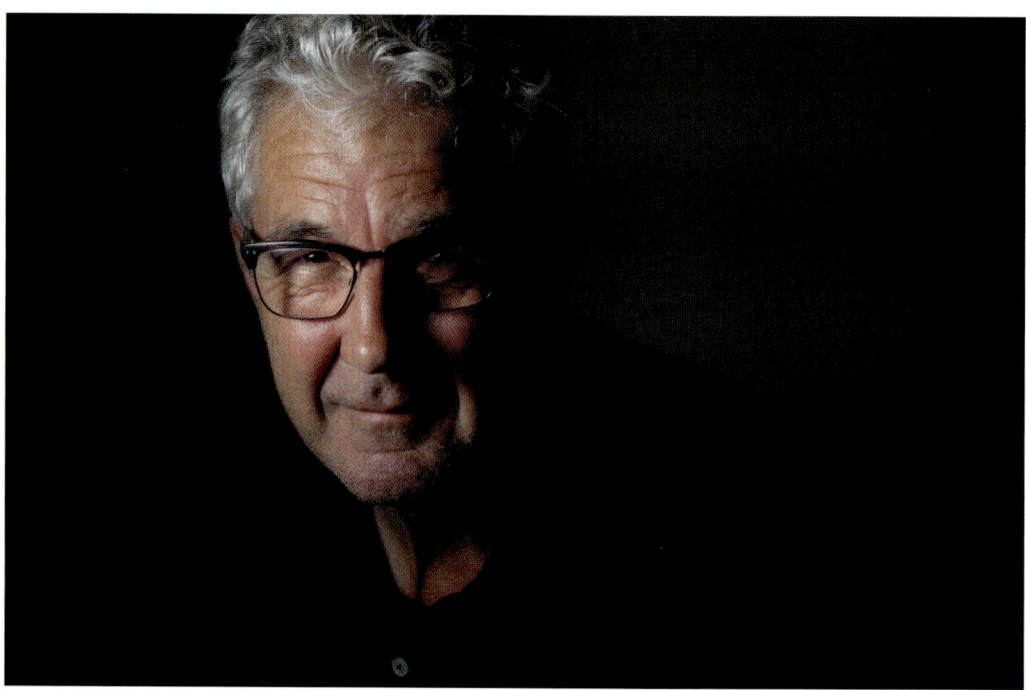

FIGURE 4.138 Before

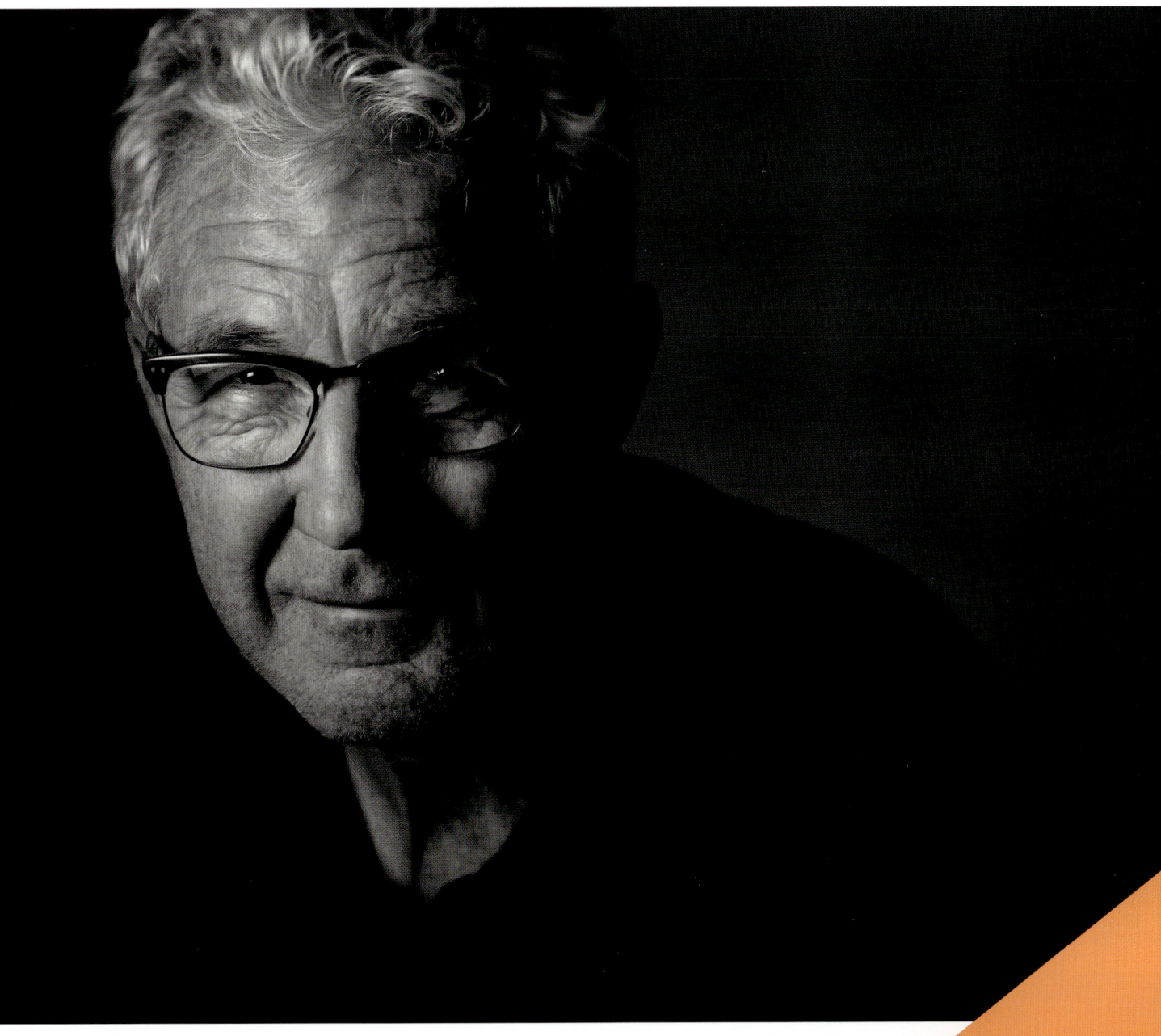

FIGURE 4.139 After

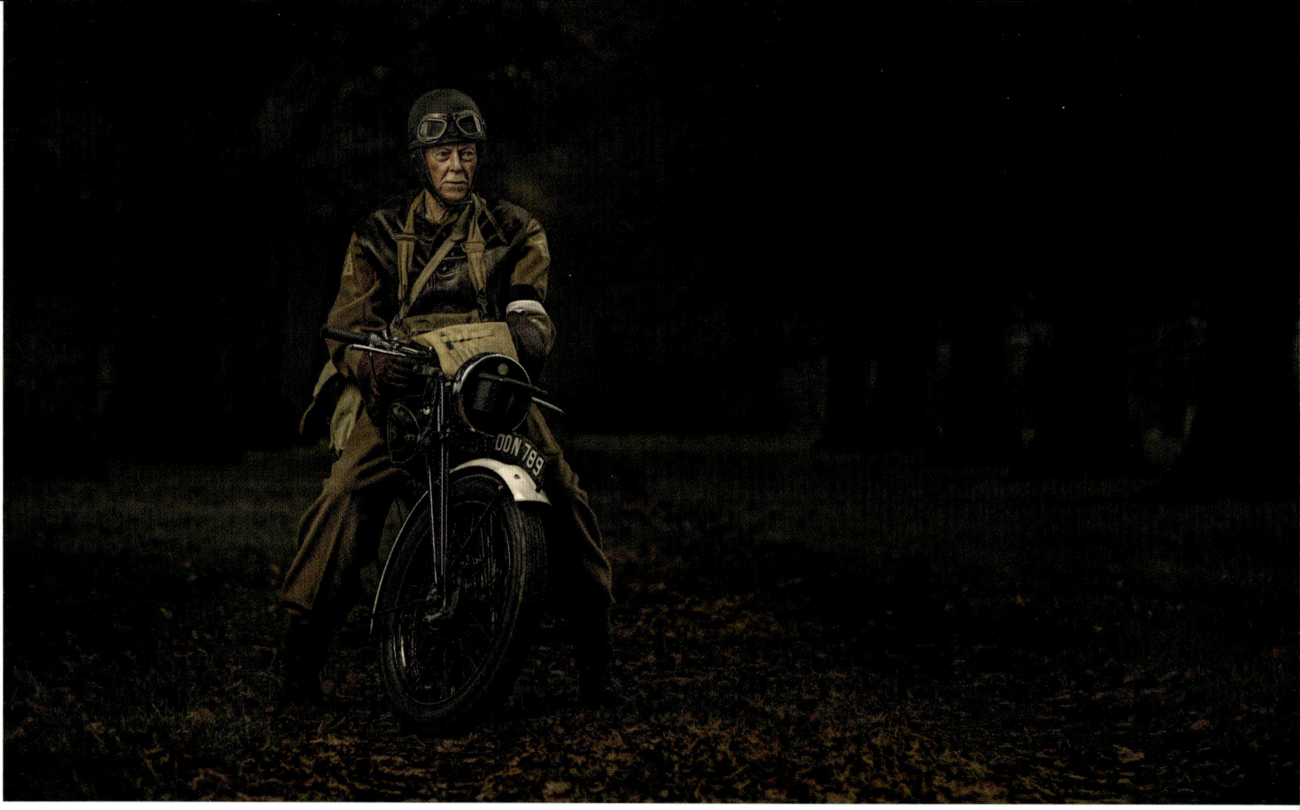

CARTOON OR PAINTERLY EFFECT

I've never really known what to call this effect, so I tend to say it gives your images a cartoon or painterly look. Some folks have told me that it almost makes my pictures look like paintings (**Figure 4.140**), and I'm frequently asked if I use a third-party plugin to create the effect.

I actually create this effect by using Photoshop's Reduce Noise filter in a slightly different way than it's normally used.

TIP *When you use Photoshop, it's always worth experimenting with sliders. See what happens when you take them to their maximum and minimum settings, when you use them in conjunction with a Blend Mode, and so on. Experimenting like this will help you to discover new effects and techniques.*

I tend to apply this painterly effect toward the end of the retouching steps, and I apply it to most, if not all, of my images to some degree. It works great on skin, giving it an almost waxy texture, as well as on images with a lot of detail.

1. Create a copy of the layer containing your image by pressing Command + J (Mac) or Ctrl + J (PC). If you have more than one layer in the layer stack, start by adding a merged layer to the top of the stack by going to *Select > All*, then to *Edit > Copy Merged*, and then to *Edit > Paste* [or by pressing Shift + Option + Command + E (Mac) or Shift + Alt + Ctrl + E (PC)]. Rename this layer "look." Create a duplicate of the layer by pressing Command + J (Mac) or Ctrl + J (PC) and rename this new layer "sharpness." Finally,

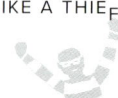

turn off the visibility of the sharpness layer by clicking on the eye icon, and then click on the look layer so it is active (**Figure 4.141**).

2. Go to *Filter > Noise > Reduce Noise* (**Figure 4.142**). In the Reduce Noise dialog, increase Strength to 7 (or up to 10 depending on the look you're after), leave every other slider at 0, and click OK (**Figure 4.143**).

This has added the waxy look I mentioned, but in doing so, it has made the picture lose sharpness in areas such as the eyes, parts of the motorbike, and so on. To fix this, click on the sharpness layer and turn on its visibility (**Figure 4.144**), go to *Filter > Other > High Pass*, dial in a Radius of 1 Pixel (**Figure 4.145**), and click OK. Change the Blend Mode of the sharpness layer to Hard Light (**Figure 4.146**).

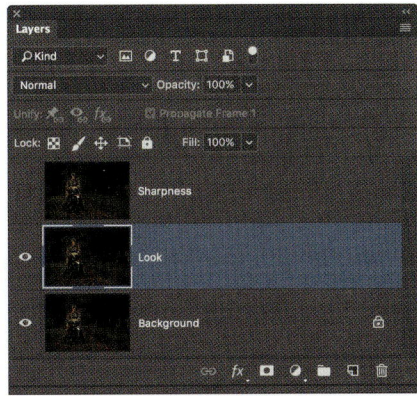

FIGURE 4.141

Now if you toggle the visibility of the sharpness layer on and off, you'll see how some of the sharpness has returned due to our use of the High Pass Filter.

I tend to finish off by adding in some contrast using the Unsharp Mask technique I explained on page 62.

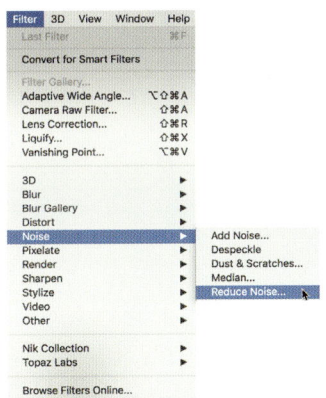

FIGURE 4.142

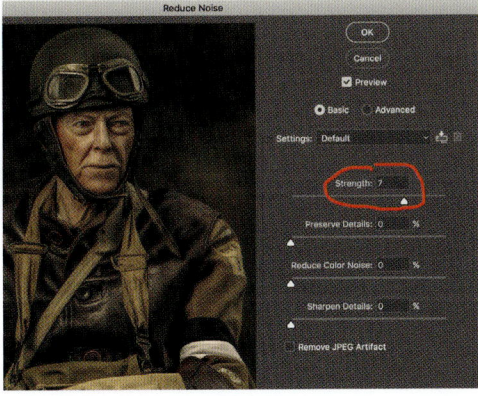

FIGURE 4.143

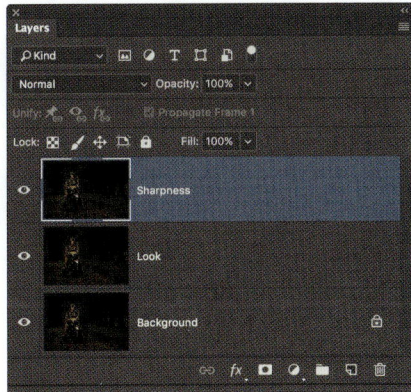

FIGURE 4.144

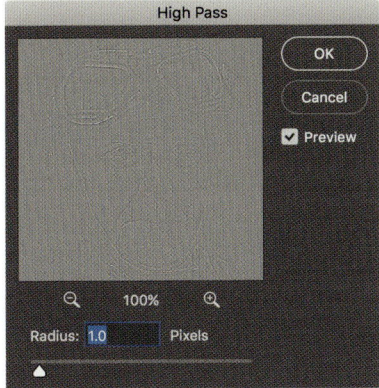

FIGURE 4.145

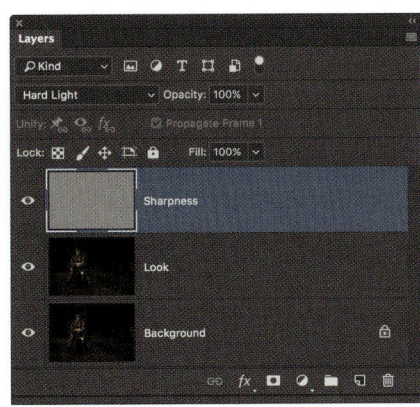

FIGURE 4.146

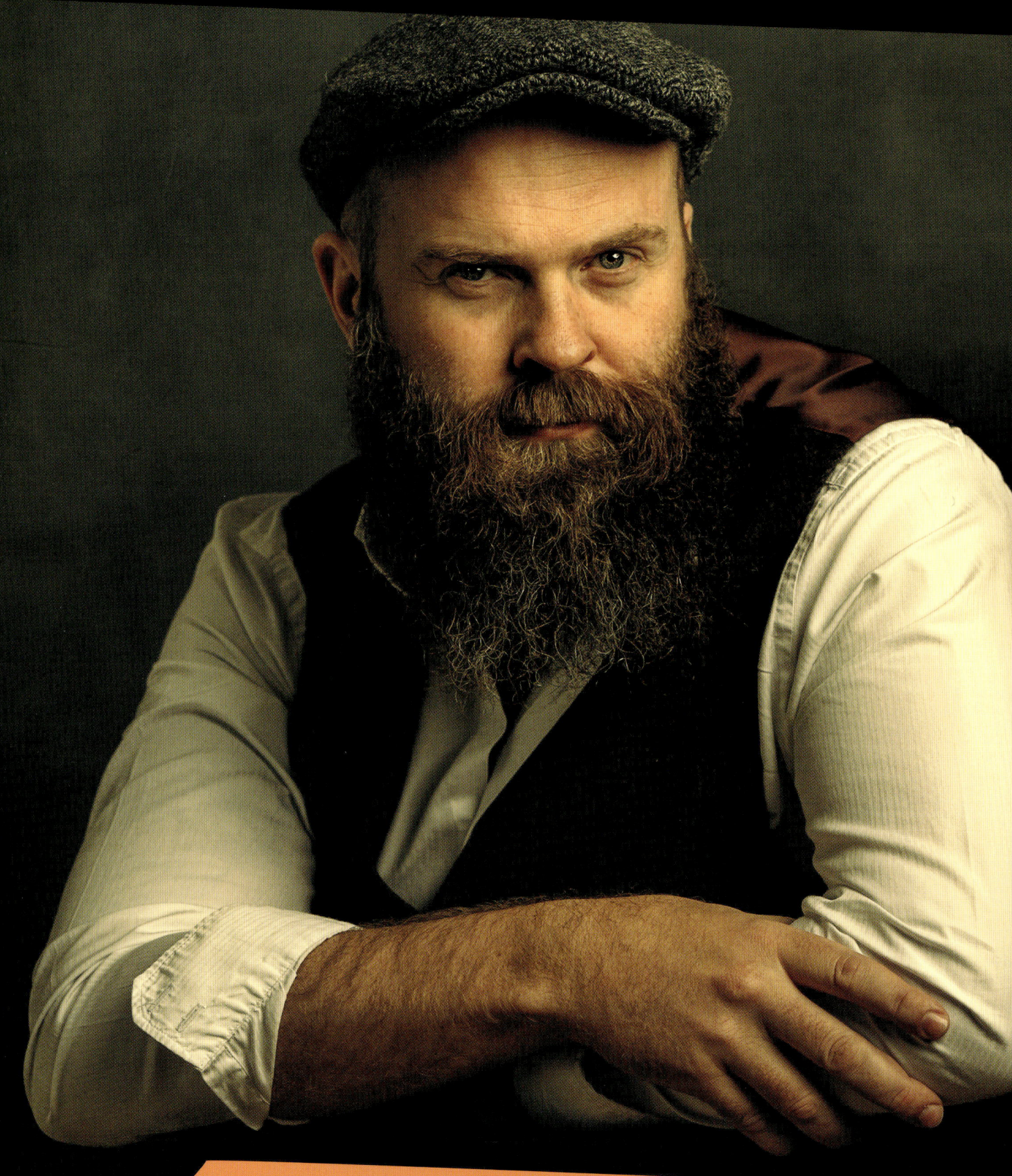

5 ANNIE LEIBOVITZ INSPIRED

I guess it's fair to say that if you're into photography, you have heard of and seen the work of Annie Leibovitz. She is well known for her celebrity portraits and Vanity Fair covers, and who can forget her iconic portrait of then-pregnant Hollywood actress Demi Moore? And, of course, there's also her series of portraits of HRH Queen Elizabeth II.

Some of her work includes elaborate, purpose-designed and -built sets with multiple lighting rigs, but it's her simplistic one-light portraits that I'm particularly drawn to, for both the way in which the images are post-processed and the wonderful expressions Annie draws from the subjects in front of her camera.

In early 2016, I had the opportunity to photograph some members of a worldwide organization called the Bearded Villains, which isn't what you might first think; it is actually an organization for lovers of beards. We're not talking overnight stubble here, but rather quite substantial facial hair.

It doesn't stop there. The clothing worn by these guys is very much like the styles worn on a popular TV drama series in the United Kingdom called *Peaky Blinders*: waistcoats, flat caps, fob watches, you get the idea, right? I was definitely excited about the picture, possibilities, but was undecided about which way to go in terms of lighting, setup, and post-production.

That is, until I saw a picture by Annie Leibovitz of actors Sir Patrick Stewart and Sir Ian McKellen (you can see this image at: http://bit.ly/PLAT_annie). As soon as I saw the picture, I knew the look would be perfect for my Bearded Villains portrait. The pose is unconventional. Both men are looking toward the photographer, but they are seated in such a way that their bodies are facing different directions. Sir Patrick Stewart is leaning sideways a bit, toward Sir McKellen. Sir McKellen is seated with his upper body facing Sir Stewart, but his face is turned toward the photographer.

The color grading in the image really adds to the mood, as does Annie's use of a textured canvas background. And as for the expressions on the actors' faces, well, they're quite perfect!

As is common practice for me, I forwarded a copy of the Annie Leibovitz picture to both of the models I would be photographing so they could get a feel for what we'd be looking to do. Needless to say, they loved it and the date for the shoot was set.

REVERSE ENGINEERING

In the photograph taken by Annie Leibovitz there is a gradual blending of shadows and highlights on the men's faces, which indicates that soft lighting has been used. There are no harsh, defined areas where the shadows and highlights meet, so for our picture we'll be using softboxes with both the inner and outer diffusion panels fitted.

Looking at the eyes of the subjects in a photo is always a good way to see how many lights and what types of lights were used. In this picture we can't get in close enough to see what types of lights were used, but we can see that there's just one catch light, which tells us that there was one light source. (Of course, there's always a chance that other catch lights were removed during post-production, but we'll go with the likelihood that the catch lights have not been touched and will stick with one light source for our image.)

So we know that just one light source was used and it was a soft light, but what about the placement and direction of the light? When we look at the picture we can clearly see which direction the light is coming from by looking at the shadows on both faces. The camera-left side of each man's face is shaded and the camera-right side is brighter, meaning the light was positioned at camera-right.

To summarize, we can confidently replicate the look of the original Annie Leibovitz picture using just one, soft light source. In this case, we'll use the Elinchrom Rotalux 135cm Octa Softbox. We'll place it at camera right, slightly in front of our subjects so that some of the light from the softbox also lights up the opposite sides of the faces a little. We can experiment with this to find the look we're after in our picture.

THE SETUP

I took what I learned by reverse engineering Annie Leibovitz's picture and used just one light for my setup (**Figure 5.1**). Instead of the Oliphant painted canvas background Annie regularly uses, I made use of a gray, seamless roll of paper. In the post-production steps, I'll show you how to easily fake it and make it look similar to the canvas she uses.

In **Figure 5.2** you can see that I shot the portrait with my camera tethered to my MacBook Pro. I kept the original Annie Leibovitz picture on my computer screen so that I could check back on the posing and lighting.

The gray, seamless paper I used for a backdrop was hung so that it just touched the floor. There was no need to roll it out onto the floor because we were shooting from about waist height upward. In **Figure 5.3** you can see a white panel positioned opposite the light. I placed it there to see if we needed to bounce some light onto the subjects, but as it turned out, we didn't need it for the final picture so we left it out.

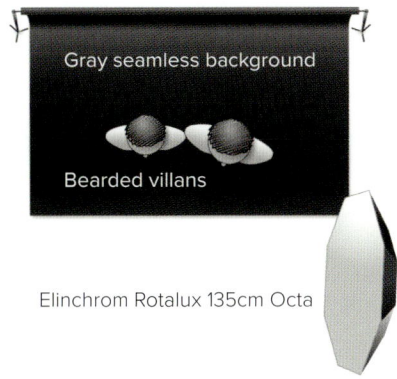

Elinchrom Rotalux 135cm Octa

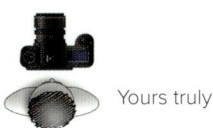

Yours truly

FIGURE 5.1

Notice how the softbox is positioned slightly in front of the subjects and angled down just a touch. This positioning enabled us to predominantly light one side of the faces and add mainly shadow to the other.

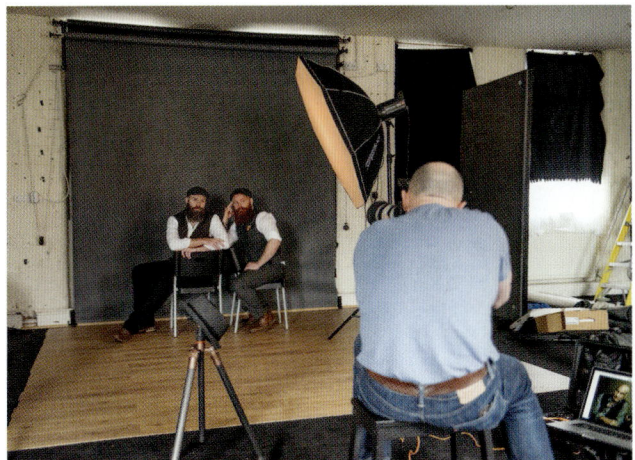

FIGURE 5.2 Shooting tethered to my MacBook Pro with Tether Tools cabling

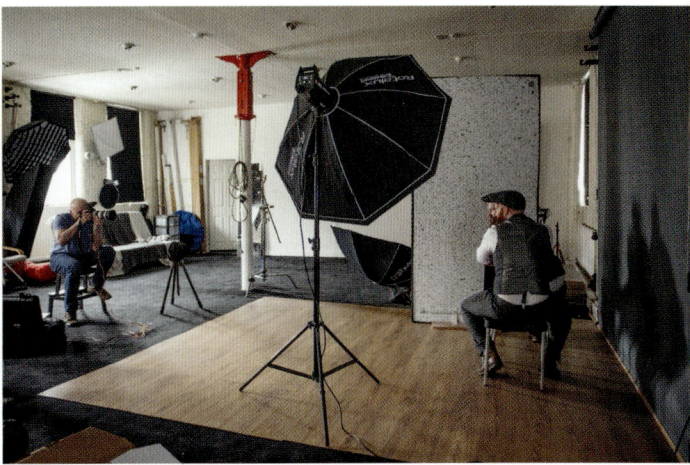

FIGURE 5.3

CAMERA SETTINGS

For this shoot I used my Canon EOS 5D Mark III with the Canon EF 70–200mm f/2.8 IS II lens.

Because the subjects were sitting side by side and roughly in the same focal plane, I opted for an aperture of f/4.5. An aperture of f/4.0 would have been enough but my index finger must have knocked it by accident. Therefore, the light from the Octa was metered at f/4.0. The ISO could have happily been down as low as ISO 100, but ISO 400 still gives us a clean, noise-free file.

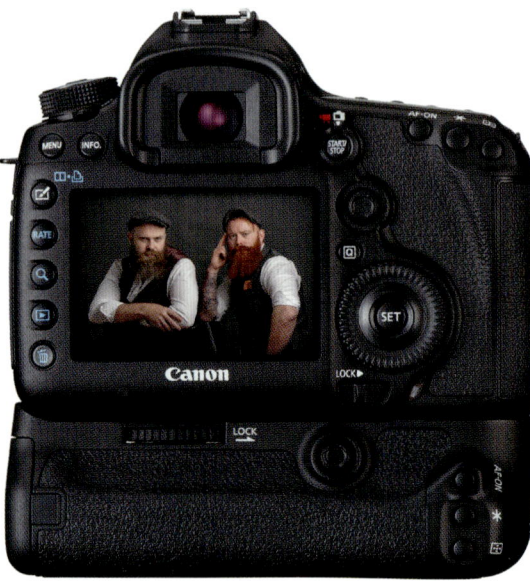

FIGURE 5.4

MODE Manual

ISO 400

APERTURE f/4.5

SHUTTER SPEED 1/200 sec.

LENS Canon 70–200mm f/2.8 IS II USM

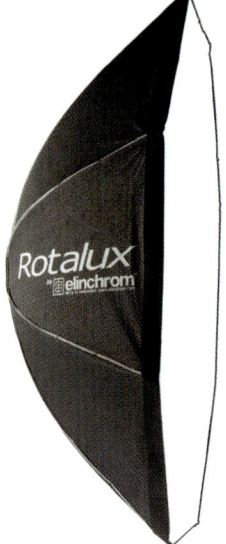

GEAR GUIDE

For this particular setup I used an Elinchrom Rotalux 135cm Octa Softbox (**Figure 5.5**) and an Elinchrom ELC Pro HD 1000 flash head (**Figure 5.6**). I use Elinchrom lights and modifiers most of the time because they're durable and easy to use.

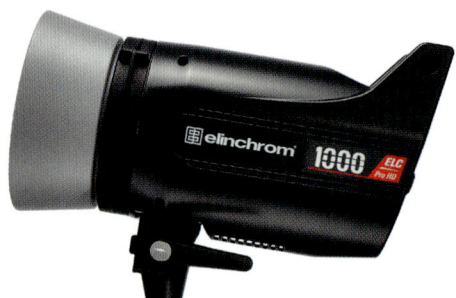

FIGURE 5.5   FIGURE 5.6

SMALL FLASH GEAR GUIDE

The setup for this picture could certainly be achieved with small flashes or speedlights because nowadays there are so many modifiers and accessories we can use. The only obvious disadvantage of a small-flash setup is the lack of a modeling light to get the position of the light exactly right, but a few test shots should get it sorted out quickly enough.

Based on what is available on the market at the time of writing, you could achieve a similar lighting setup with a small flash or speedlight and a Lastolite Ezybox II Octa Large 1.2m (**Figure 5.7**).

POST-PROCESSING

The post-processing for this picture is actually quite simple and realistically could be done from start to

FIGURE 5.7

finish in about 10–15 minutes, so it's a great image to start with. The use of the gray, seamless paper background is what adds so much to the picture, as you'll see when we add texture to it to give it a look that's fairly similar to that of the Oliphant canvas backgrounds Annie likes to use.

We'll also be color grading the picture, which is what will give the portrait its overall mood and will work so well with the models, what they're wearing, and their expressions. A really important part of the retouching process is getting everything to work together so that we end up with a great final image.

We'll kick off by sorting out an issue with sharpness and you'll see how a filter in Photoshop can really save an image. This isn't a technique you want to make a habit of using, but it's incredibly handy when you need it.

 **NOTE** *Download all the files you need to follow along step-by-step at: http://www.rockynook.com/photograph-like-a-thief-reference/*

1. **Figure 5.8** is the original, as-shot, RAW image in Lightroom. Even though we'll be altering the overall color later on, it's always a good idea to give ourselves the best starting point. To help with this, I used a gray card during the photo shoot (a ColorChecker Passport from X-Rite; **Figure 5.9**). With this image open in the Develop Module in Lightroom, simply select the White Balance Tool (**W**) and click on the card.

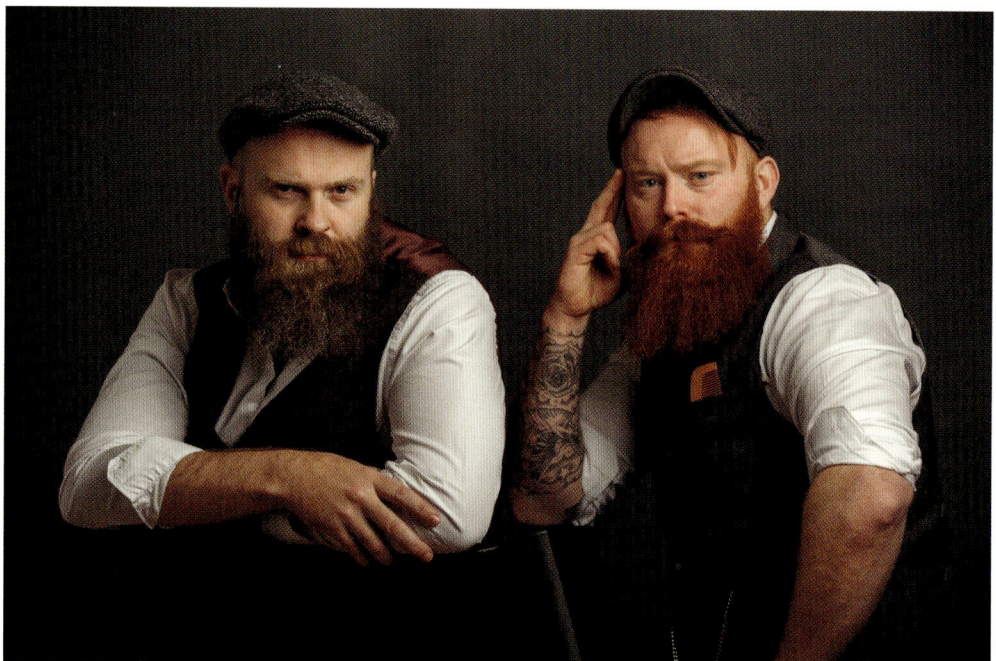

FIGURE 5.8 Original RAW image

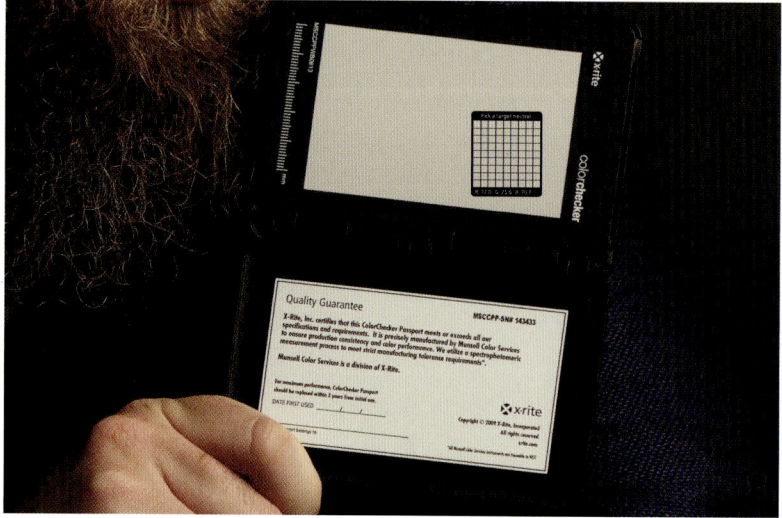

FIGURE 5.9 X-Rite ColorChecker Passport

2. Return to the Grid View (**G**) and with the photograph that contains the gray card selected, hold down the Shift key and click on the original RAW image (the one we want to retouch). With both images now selected,

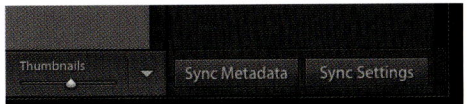

FIGURE 5.10

click on Sync Settings in the bottom-right corner of the screen (**Figure 5.10**) to bring up the Synchronize Settings properties. We only want to sync the white balance, so click Check None to deselect all of the adjustments, and then click on the White Balance and Process Version checkboxes and click OK (**Figure 5.11**).

Figures 5.12 and **5.13** show the image before and after setting the correct white balance.

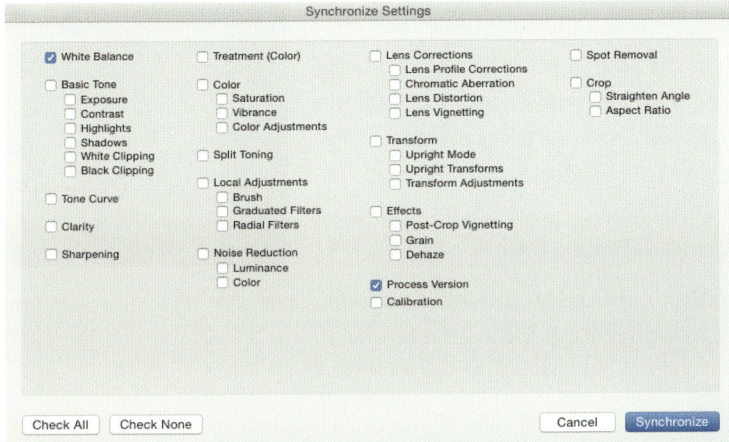

FIGURE 5.11

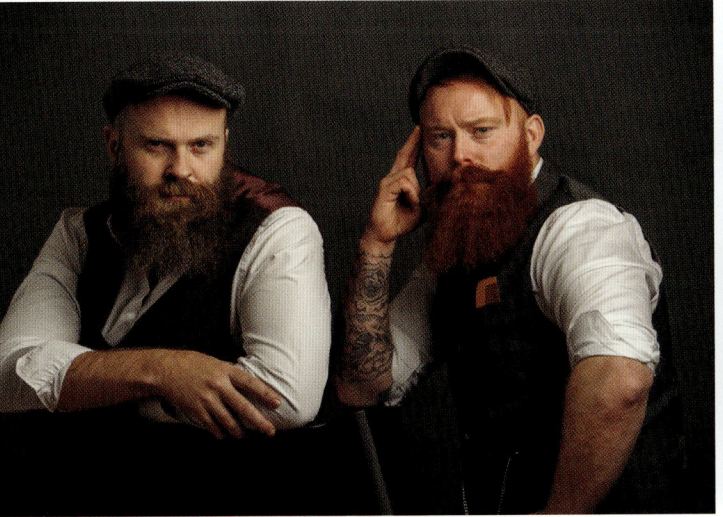

FIGURE 5.12 Before (uncorrected white balance)

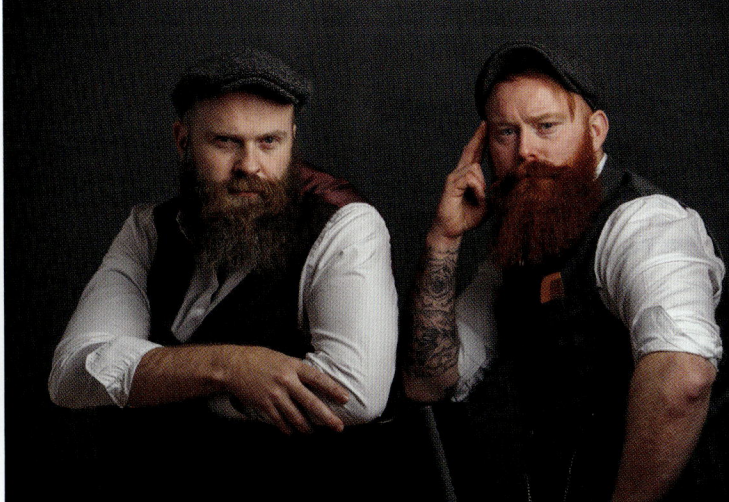

FIGURE 5.13 After (corrected white balance based on gray card)

3. The next thing we want to do is bring out just a little more detail, especially in the shadow areas. To do this, press **D** to go to the Develop Module, and then in the Basic tab, increase the Shadows slider to around +30 and drag the Highlights slider down to around -60 (**Figure 5.14**).

4. When I originally worked on this photograph, it was at this stage that I noticed one of the guys was sharper than the other (left-hand side is sharp, right-hand side is ever-so-slightly soft). We will fix this in Photoshop in the next step, but for now let's just add some overall sharpening to the image. Click on the Detail tab and in the Sharpening section, increase the Amount to around 40 (**Figure 5.15**). Leave the Radius and Detail sliders at their default settings of 1.0 and 25. Hold down the Option key (Mac) or Alt key (PC) while increasing the Masking slider to around 80 to restrict where the sharpening is applied—we mainly want it on the guys' faces and hair and not on the background (**Figure 5.16**).

Now we'll dive over to Photoshop, sort out that softness issue, and carry on working through the retouching.

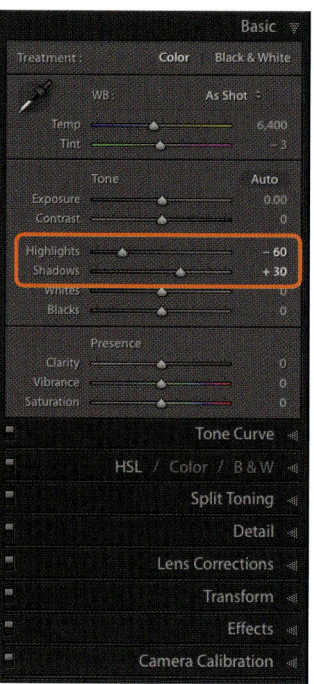

FIGURE 5.14

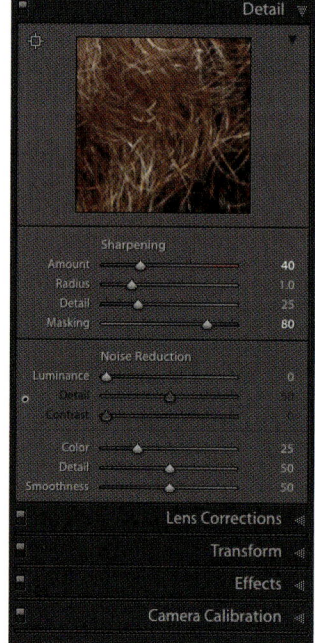

FIGURE 5.15

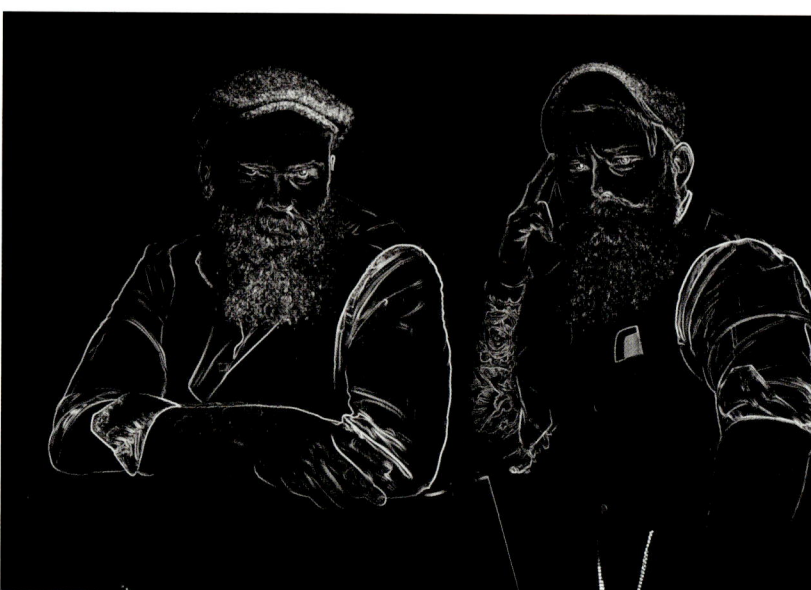

FIGURE 5.16 The white areas indicate where the sharpening is being applied

5. Because we only covered a few steps in Lightroom, we aren't going to send the file over to Photoshop as a Smart Object. If we had made lots of corrections, I would suggest converting the file to a Smart Object because that would give us the flexibility to alter the corrections later if we wanted or needed to. But in this case, we're good to go, so go to *Photo > Edit In > Adobe Photoshop CC*, or simply press Command + E (Mac) or Ctrl + E (PC).

In step 6 we're going to use the Shake Reduction filter, which is only available in the Creative Cloud Subscription version of Photoshop, so it may not be available to you if you are using an older version of the software. Hopefully you won't make the same mistake I did during your photo shoots, and you won't ever need to use this filter.

6. With the image open in Photoshop, create a duplicate copy by pressing Command + J (Mac) or Ctrl + J (PC). Then go to *Filter > Sharpen > Shake Reduction* (**Figure 5.17**). In the Shake Reduction interface, reposition the frame over the face of the man on the right side of the picture. This specifies an area for the Shake Reduction filter to analyze. Leave the settings at their defaults and click OK (**Figure 5.18**).

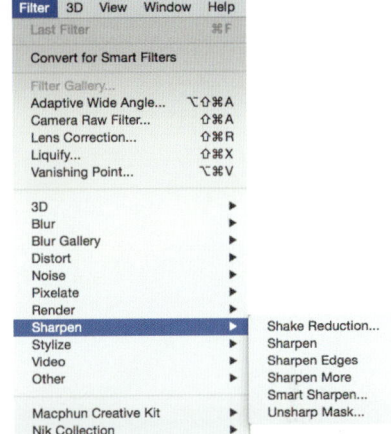

FIGURE 5.17

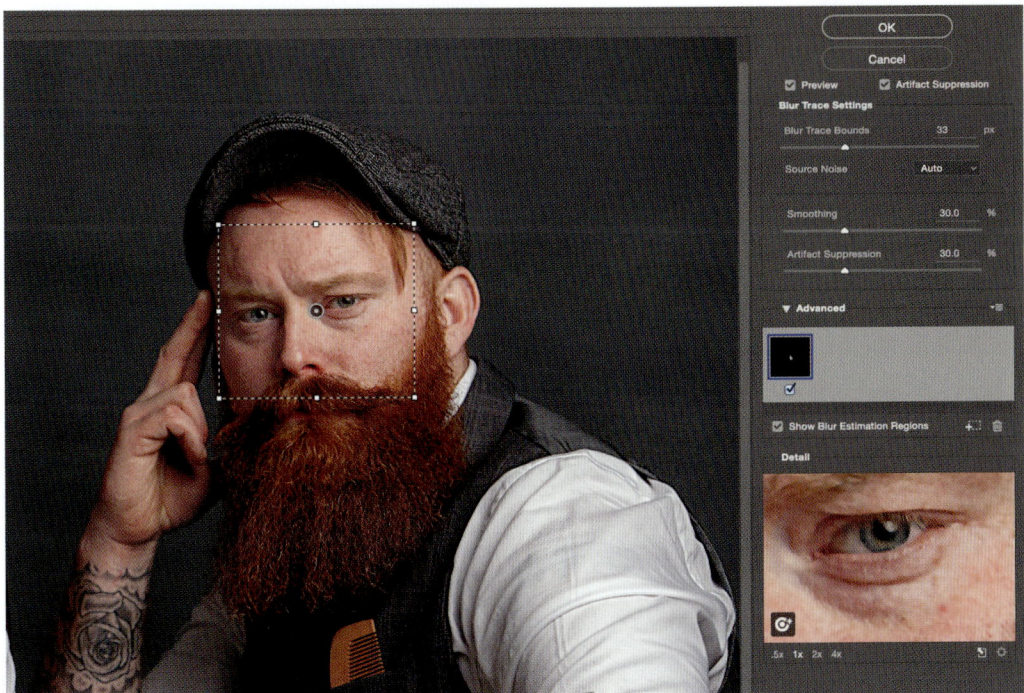

FIGURE 5.18

Depending on the file, the results from the Shake Reduction filter can be quite impressive, and it can certainly help to save a picture.

If you look at **Figures 5.19** and **5.20** you can clearly see the difference this filter makes, especially in the eyes.

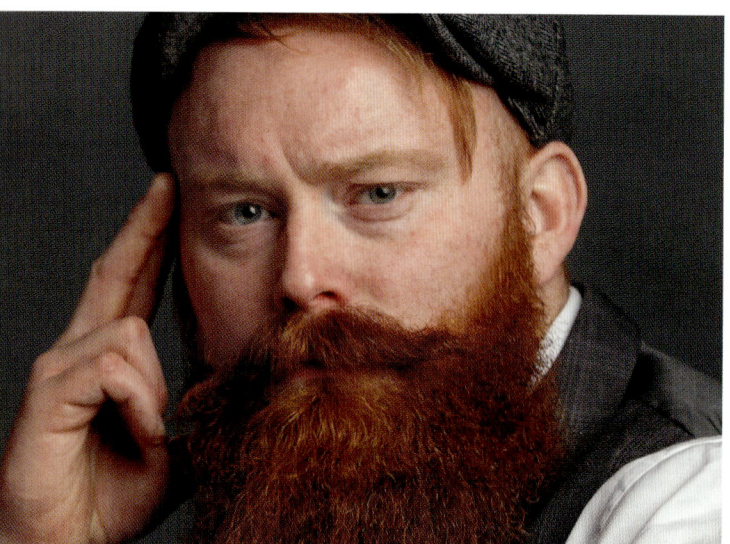

FIGURE 5.19 Before Shake Reduction

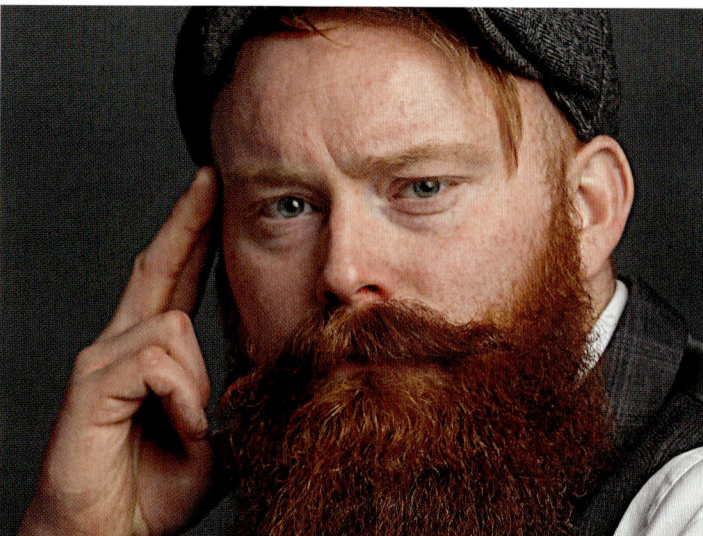

FIGURE 5.20 After Shake Reduction

7. Rename the layer "shake reduction" (**Figure 5.21**). We only want the sharpness over the guy's face, so first add a black layer mask by holding down the Option key (Mac) or Alt key (PC) and clicking on the Layer Mask icon at the bottom of the Layers panel. This will hide the results of the Shake Reduction filter. Then choose a white foreground color and a soft-edged brush and paint over the face to reveal the results of the filter in the desired areas.

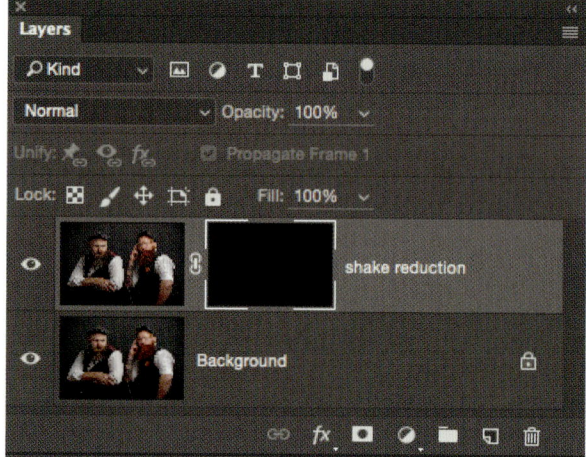

FIGURE 5.21

8. Now that we're back in focus and on track, let's get on with the creative side of retouching. We'll start off with the eyes. We're going to be using a Quick Mask at some point because it's a great way to see what we're selecting, but first we need to set it up.

   Double-click on the Quick Mask icon in the toolbar (**Figure 5.22**). In the Quick Mask Options dialog box, make sure that Selected Areas is checked and click OK (**Figure 5.23**).

   Use the Elliptical Marquee Tool to select both eyes of the man on the right side of the picture (**Figure 5.24**).

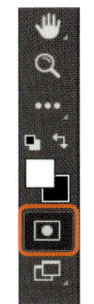

FIGURE 5.22

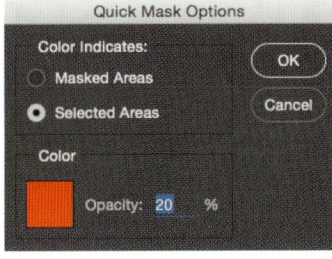

FIGURE 5.23

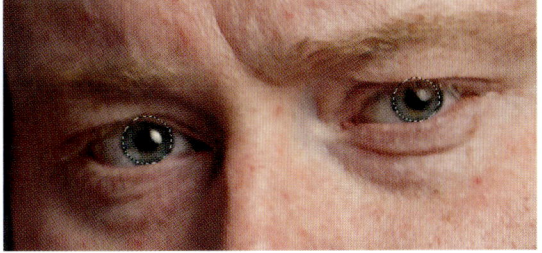

FIGURE 5.24 Both eyes are selected

TIP *Hold down the Shift key while dragging out an ellipse to make it perfectly round. Once you have made one selection, hold down the Shift key while selecting the other eye to keep both selections active.*

9. Now we need to tidy up the selections so that they include only the centers of the eyes and not the eyelids or other surrounding areas. Press **Q** to enter Quick Mask mode. The outline of the red overlay (our selected area) is very defined (**Figure 5.25**), so we need to soften this. Go to *Filter > Blur > Gaussian Blur* and add in around 2px Radius of Blur, then click OK (**Figure 5.26**).

   With a white foreground color and a round, soft-edged brush set to about 30% Hardness, paint over the areas of red overlay that you want to remove (eye lids and pupils; **Figure 5.27**).

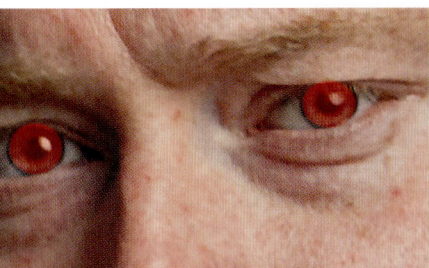

FIGURE 5.25 Defined selection outline

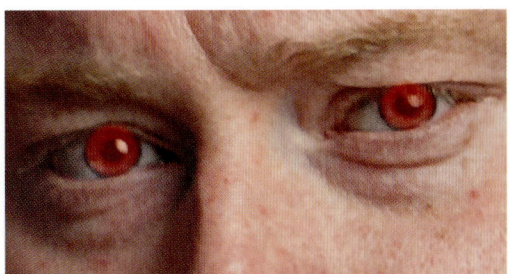

FIGURE 5.26 Selection outline softened with Gaussian Blur

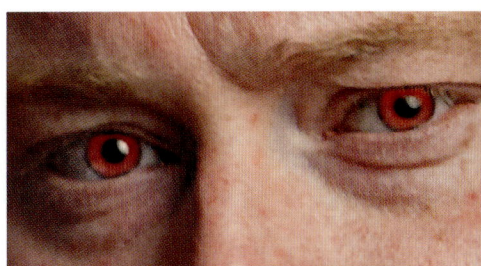

FIGURE 5.27 Painting with white in Quick Mask mode removes the red overlay from unwanted areas

10. Press **Q** to exit Quick Mask mode and click on the Selective Color adjustment layer icon (**Figure 5.28**). In the Selective Color properties, change the Colors menu to Neutrals (**Figure 5.29**). Then in the Layers Panel, change the Blend Mode of the Selective Color adjustment layer to Linear Dodge (Add) (**Figure 5.30**).

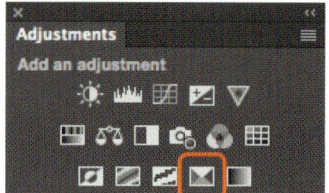

FIGURE 5.28

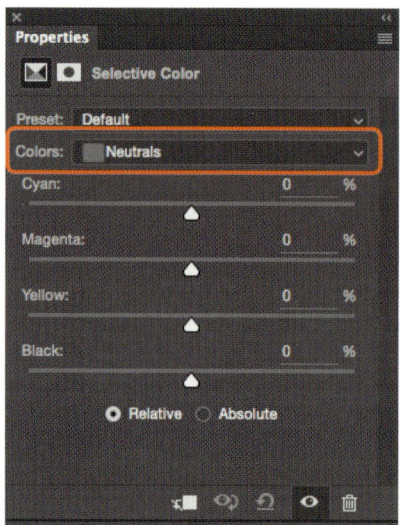

FIGURE 5.29

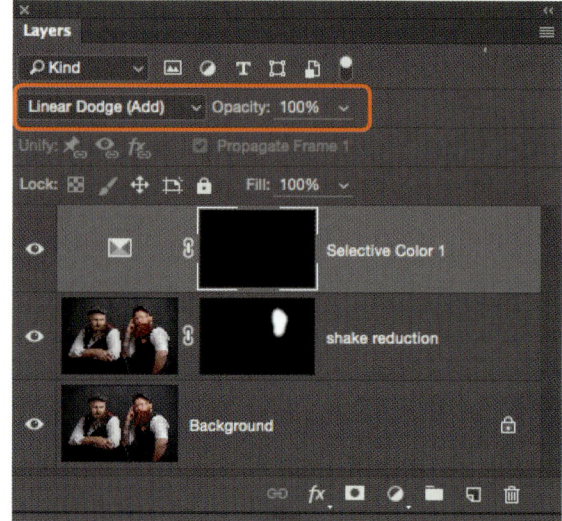

FIGURE 5.30

11. Reduce the Opacity of the Selective Color adjustment layer to around 20% (**Figure 5.31**). In the Selective Color properties, adjust the sliders to make the eyes bluer. In my example, I set Cyan +22, Magenta +24, and Yellow -14 (**Figure 5.32**). If you want to add more contrast in the eyes, change the Colors menu from Neutrals to Blacks and drag the Black slider to the right. In this example, I increased the Blacks to +45% (**Figure 5.33**).

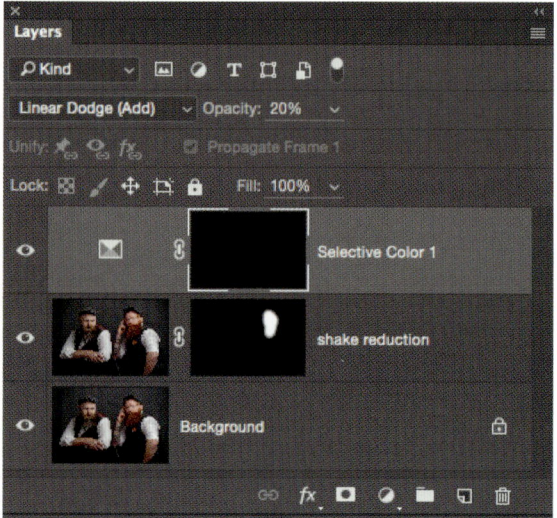

FIGURE 5.31 Opacity of Selective Color adjustment layer lowered to 20%

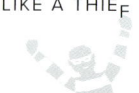

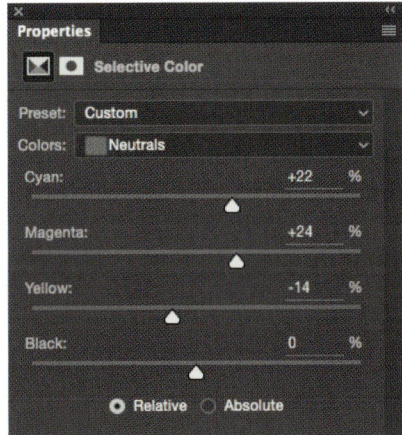

FIGURE 5.32

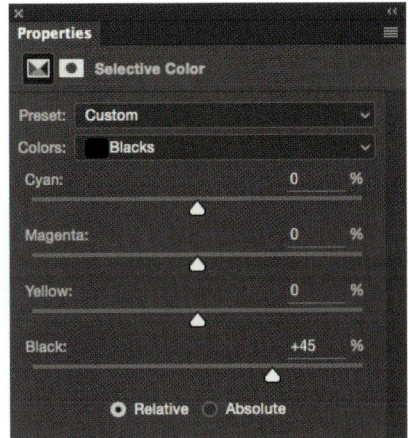

FIGURE 5.33 Increase contrast by choosing Blacks from the Colors menu and dragging the Blacks slider to the right

Repeat steps 8–11 to enhance the other man's eyes, but choose settings and colors that suit your taste.

12. Next we'll sharpen the eyes a little more to give them some pop. Add a new blank layer to the top of the layer stack and rename it "Sharpen Eyes" (**Figure 5.34**). Select the Sharpen Tool from the toolbar (**Figure 5.35**) and in the options bar at the top of the screen, set Strength to 50% and put checkmarks in the Sample All Layers and Protect Detail checkboxes (**Figure 5.36**). Paint over the middle of the eyes on both gentlemen a few times to add some sharpening.

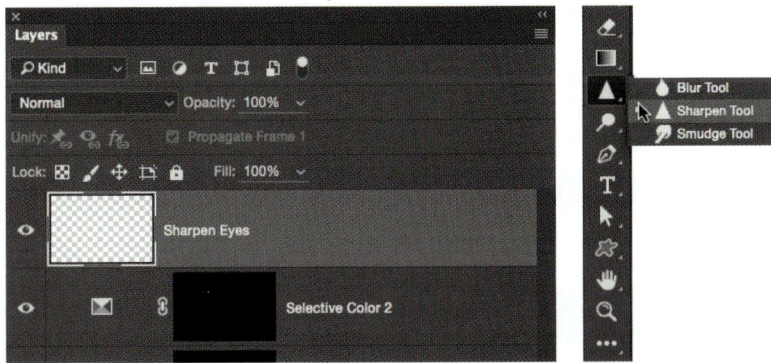

FIGURE 5.34   FIGURE 5.35

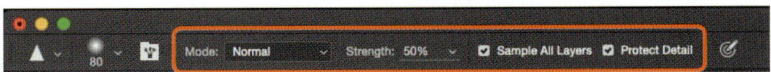

FIGURE 5.36

We can see the effects of the three simple layers by looking at the before and after images (**Figures 5.37** and **5.38**).

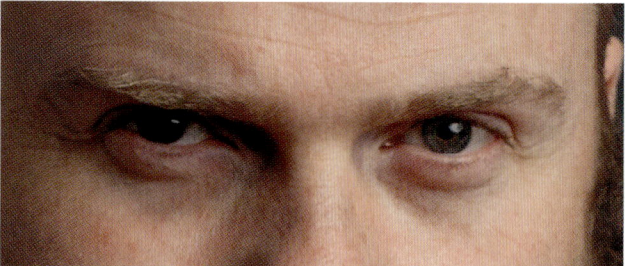

FIGURE 5.37 Before

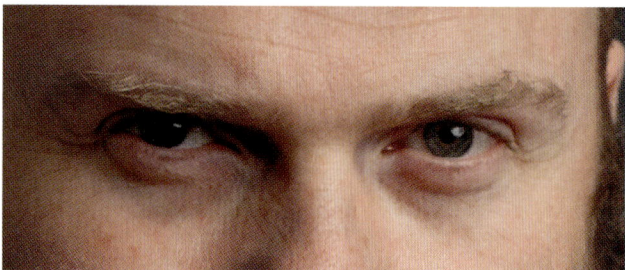

FIGURE 5.38 After

13. It's good to keep things organized, so let's put all of the eye adjustment layers into a group. With the uppermost layer (Sharpen Eyes) active, hold down the Shift key and click on the Selective Color 1 layer (**Figure 5.39**). Now both Selective Color adjustment layers and the Sharpen Eyes layer are highlighted. Then go to *Layer > New > Group From Layers* (**Figure 5.40**) and name this group "Eyes."

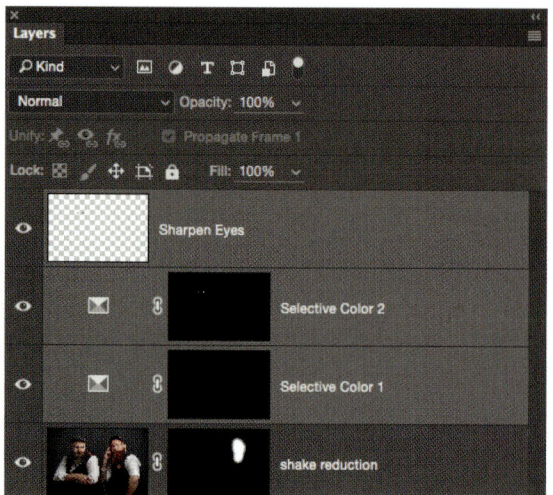

FIGURE 5.39

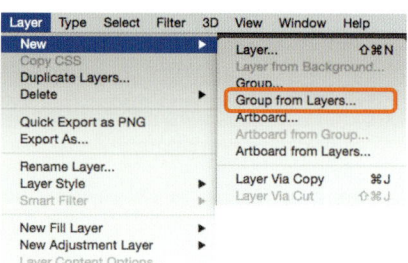

FIGURE 5.40

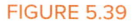

14. Next let's tidy up both men's shirts by fixing the double iron lines on the sleeves (**Figure 5.41**). Add a new blank layer to the top of the layer stack and name it "Shirts." Then choose the Clone Stamp Tool from the toolbar (**Figure 5.42**) and in the options bar at the top of the screen, put a checkmark in the Aligned checkbox and select All Layers from the Sample menu (**Figure 5.43**).

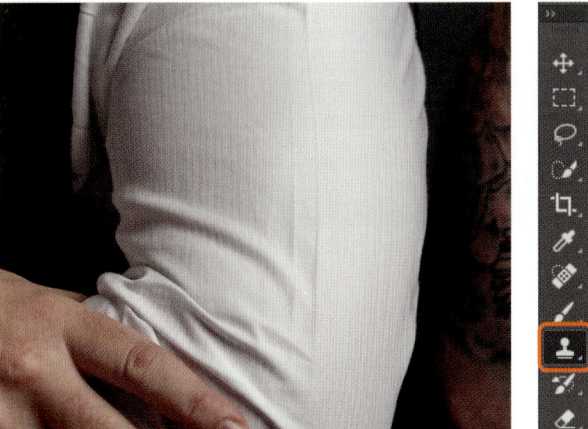

FIGURE 5.41   FIGURE 5.42

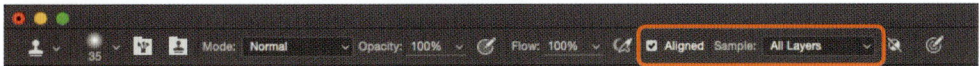

FIGURE 5.43

Hold down the Option key (Mac) or Alt key (PC) and click to sample a smooth part of the shirt from either side of the iron crease. Place the cursor over the crease and drag upward or downward to cover it with the sampled area of the shirt.

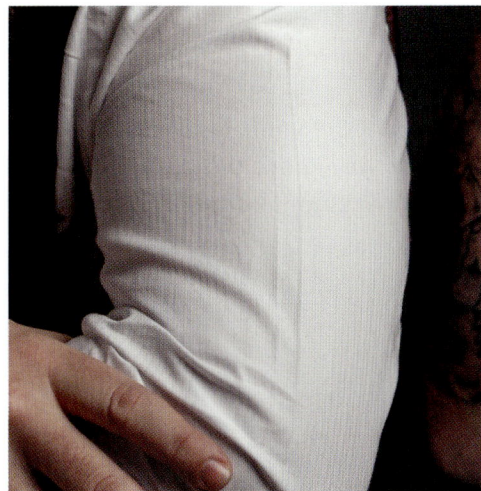

FIGURE 5.44 Before

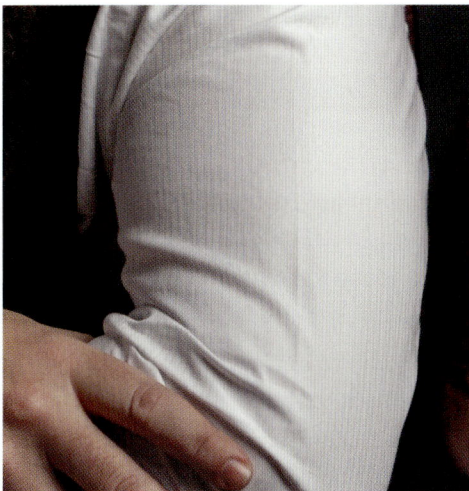

FIGURE 5.45 After

15. Next we'll be doing some dodging and burning to give our subjects added depth and dimension. To do this, we'll use the technique I use most often, which is the 50% gray layer method I went over in chapter 4 (page 66).

    Add a new blank layer to the top of the layer stack by going to *Layer > New > Layer*. In the New Layer dialog, rename the layer "Dodge & Burn," change the Mode to Soft Light, place a checkmark next to Fill with Soft-Light-neutral color (50% gray), and click OK (**Figure 5.46**).

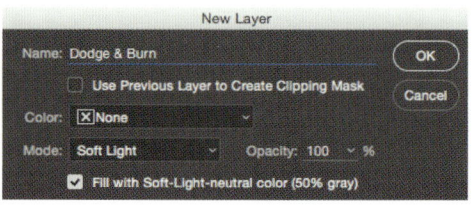

FIGURE 5.46

16. Press the **D** key to set the foreground and background colors in the toolbar to their defaults of black and white. Click on the foreground color and in the Color Picker, set H: 0, S: 0, B: 50; then click OK (**Figure 5.47**). Next, choose the Dodge Tool (**O**) and in the options bar at the top of the screen, leave Range set to Midtones, set Exposure to 5–10%, and put in a check in the Protect Tones checkbox (**Figure 5.48**).

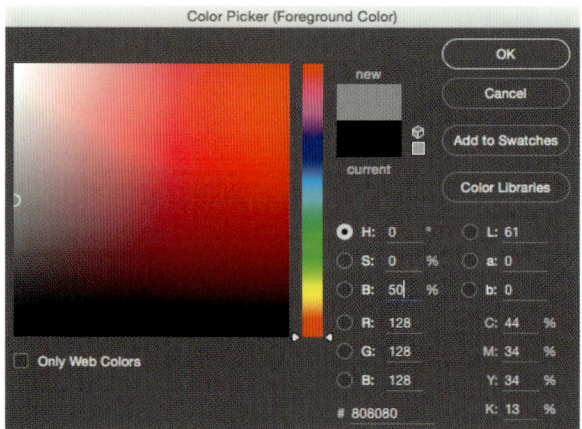

FIGURE 5.47

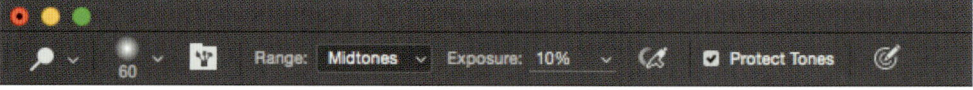

FIGURE 5.48

17. Start working over both faces by increasing highlight (brighter) areas with the Dodge Tool. Hold down the Option key (Mac) or Alt key (PC) to turn the Dodge Tool into the Burn Tool. Toggling between the two tools this way keeps the options bar settings the same for both. Use the Burn Tool to add some midtone or shadow areas on either side of where the Dodge Tool has been used. Release the Option key (Mac) or Alt key (PC) to go back to the Dodge Tool.

    As you're dodging and burning, if you want to see only the gray layer, hold down the Option key (Mac) or Alt key (PC) and click on the eye icon of the Dodge & Burn Layer in the Layers panel. In **Figure 5.49** you can see where I applied dodging and burning in my retouching of this image.

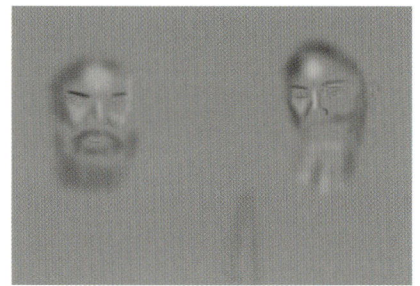

FIGURE 5.49

The result is subtle, as it should be when dodging and burning because you want to maintain a natural look. However, you should be able to see that the shadow and midtone areas are now slightly darker and the highlight areas are slightly brighter. For example, notice how the eyebrows and the shadow side of each face are a touch darker. Although this is just a slight change, it does help to add shape and dimension to the men's faces.

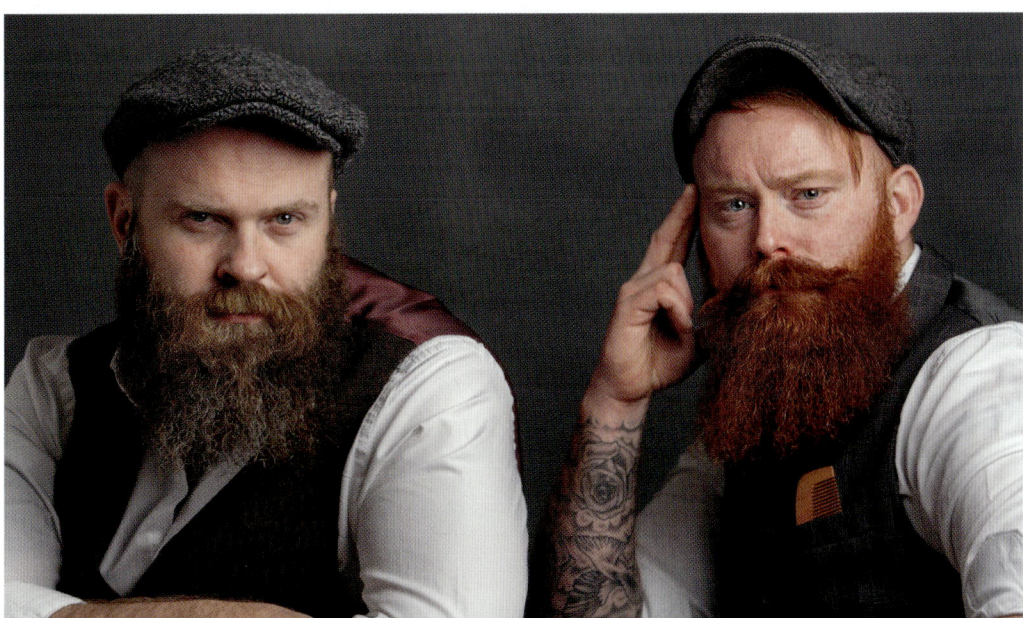

FIGURE 5.50 Before dodging and burning

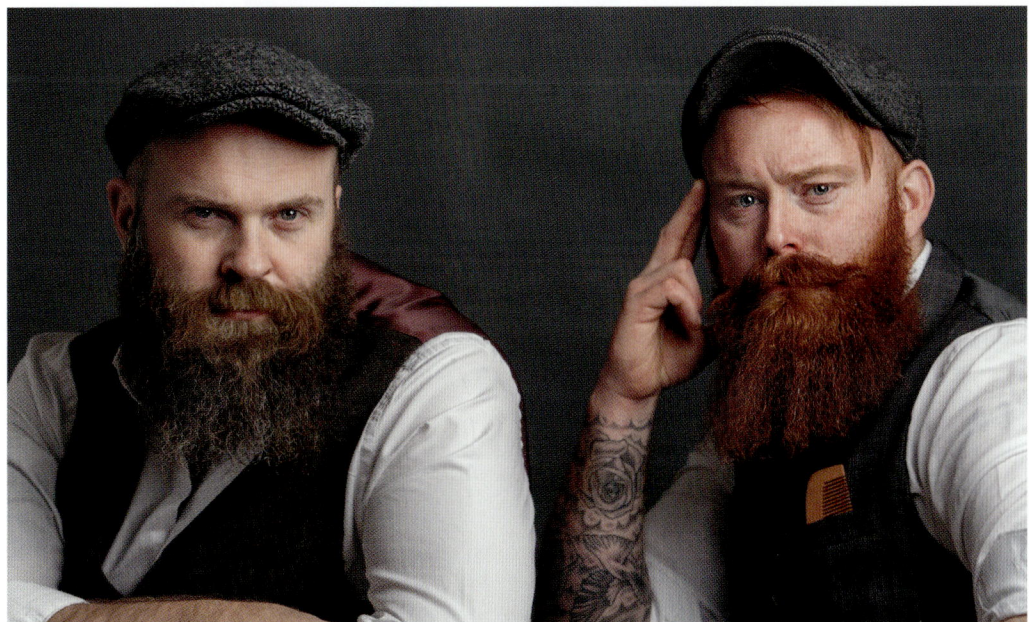

FIGURE 5.51 After dodging and burning

18. There's a couple of areas we need to tidy up. Add a new blank layer to the top of the layer stack and rename it "Tidy Up." Select the Clone Stamp Tool, and in the options bar at the top of the screen, ensure that All Layers is selected in the Sample menu. Then hold down the Option key (Mac) or Alt key (PC) and click to sample an area of the background on the far left of the picture, then use this sample to clone away the dark area in the bottom-left corner (**Figure 5.52**).

Use the Clone Stamp Tool to cover the hole in the back of the left-hand chair and the plastic joint-line going down the side of the right-hand chair (**Figure 5.53**). In the options bar, change the brush Opacity to 50%, and then clone over the slightly shiny area going down the side of the right-hand chair (**Figure 5.54**).

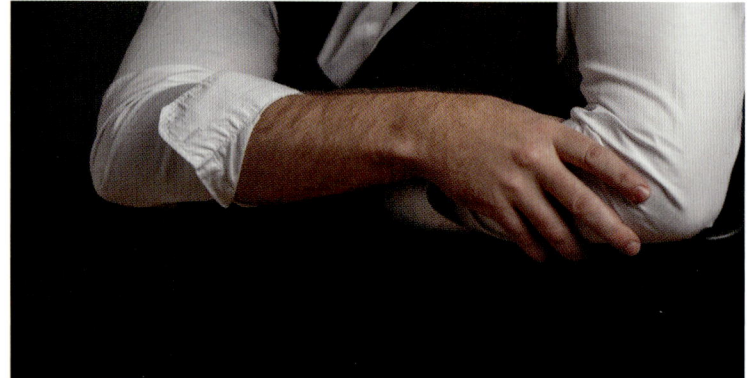

FIGURE 5.52

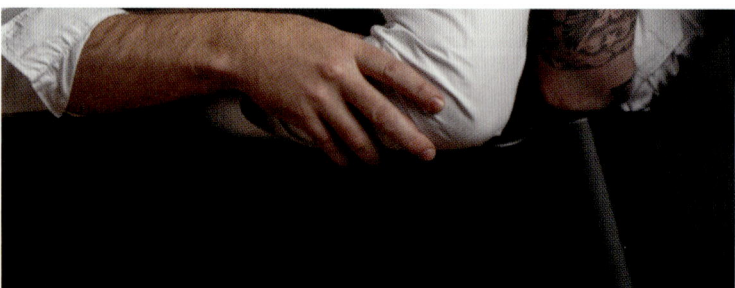

FIGURE 5.53

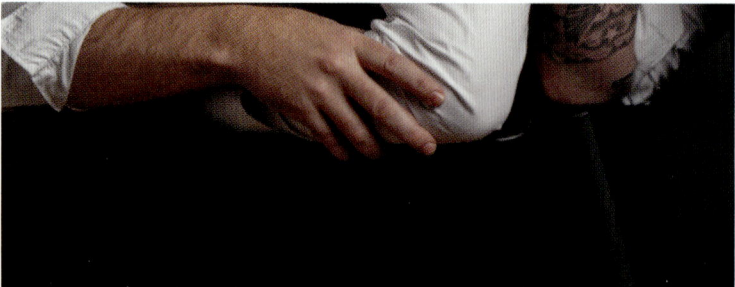

FIGURE 5.54

19. Next we'll add some texture to the background to give it the look of the Oliphant painted, textured canvas. This is where the gray, seamless-paper backdrop comes in.

Textures can come from literally everywhere: floors, walls, pavement, and so on. For this step, we'll use a texture that you can get for free from Adobe Add-ons (https://creative.adobe.com/addons) in an Add-on called Adobe Paper Textures Pro. There are many textures available, but we'll use one called Burnished Clay. I've added the Texture file to the book's webpage: rockynook.com/photograph-like-a-thief-reference/.

Once you've downloaded the Texture file, go to *File > Place Embedded* (or *File > Place*, depending on the version of Photoshop you are using), navigate to the file on your hard drive, and click OK. The Texture will be added to the top of the layer stack (**Figure 5.55**).

We need to remove all color from the Texture layer; otherwise, when we blend it onto the gray background it just won't look good. The layer is currently a Smart Object, so first we need to convert it into a regular layer by going to *Layer > Rasterize > Smart Object* (**Figure 5.56**). Now go to *Image > Adjustments > Desaturate* to remove the color from the layer.

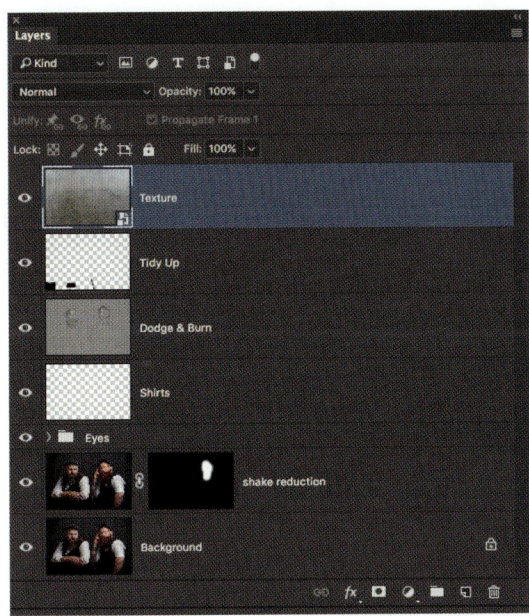

FIGURE 5.55

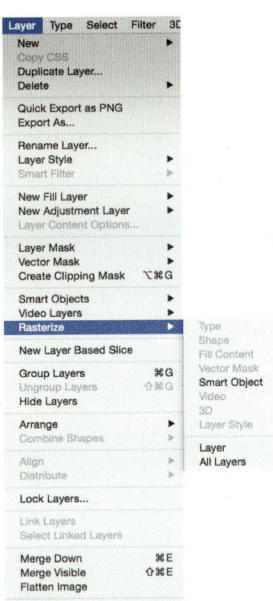

FIGURE 5.56 Rasterize will convert the Smart Object into a regular layer

20. To add the texture to the gray background, change the Blend Mode of the Texture layer from Normal to Overlay. Now we see the two gentlemen again, but the texture is overlaid on them and their clothing in addition to the background. To remove the texture from the men so that it covers only the background, click on the Layer Mask icon at the bottom of the Layers panel (**Figure 5.57**).

With the foreground color set to black in the toolbar, choose a normal round brush with a Hardness of about 30% (**Figure 5.58**), and then paint over both gentlemen and the chairs so that the texture is only visible on the background.

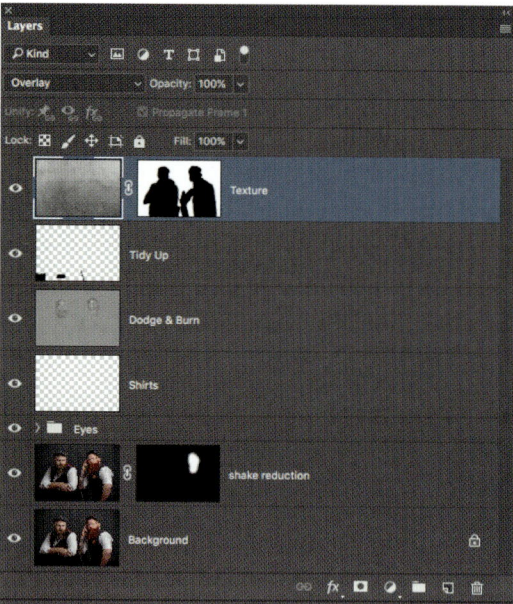

FIGURE 5.57

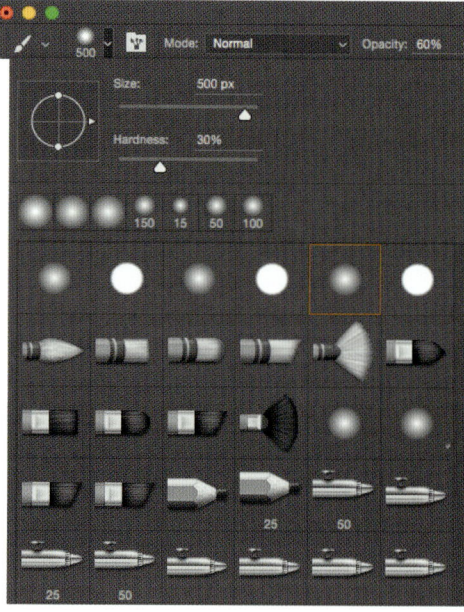

FIGURE 5.58

NOTE *You could use the Soft Light Blend Mode instead of the Overlay Blend Mode to add the texture to the gray seamless background. The difference between the two is that Overlay adds more contrast.*

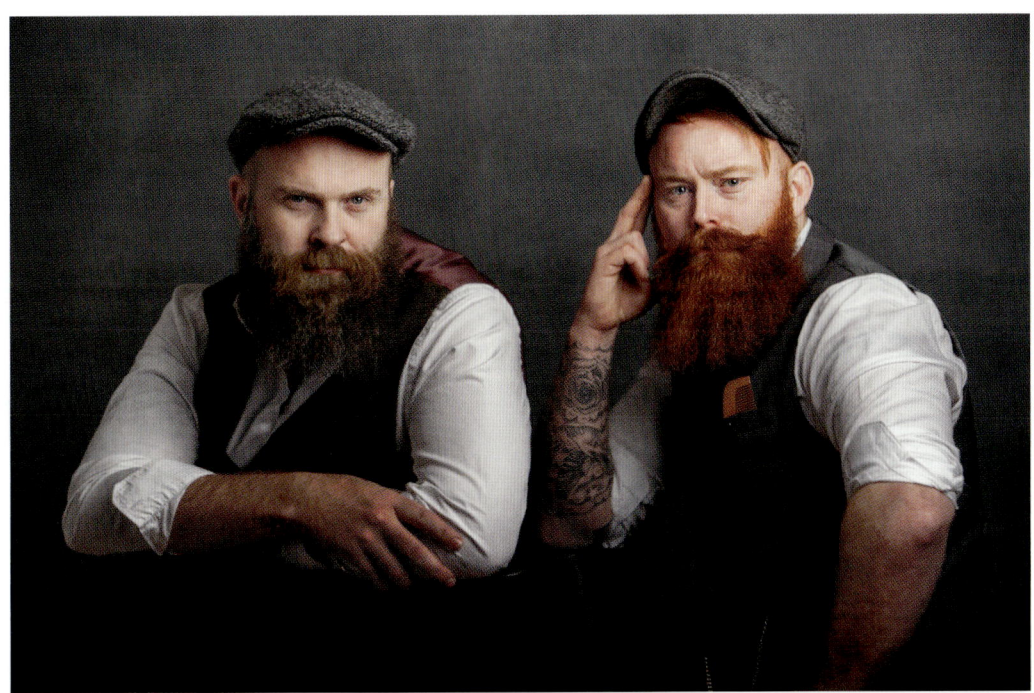

FIGURE 5.59 Texture has been added, but it's visible over the entire picture

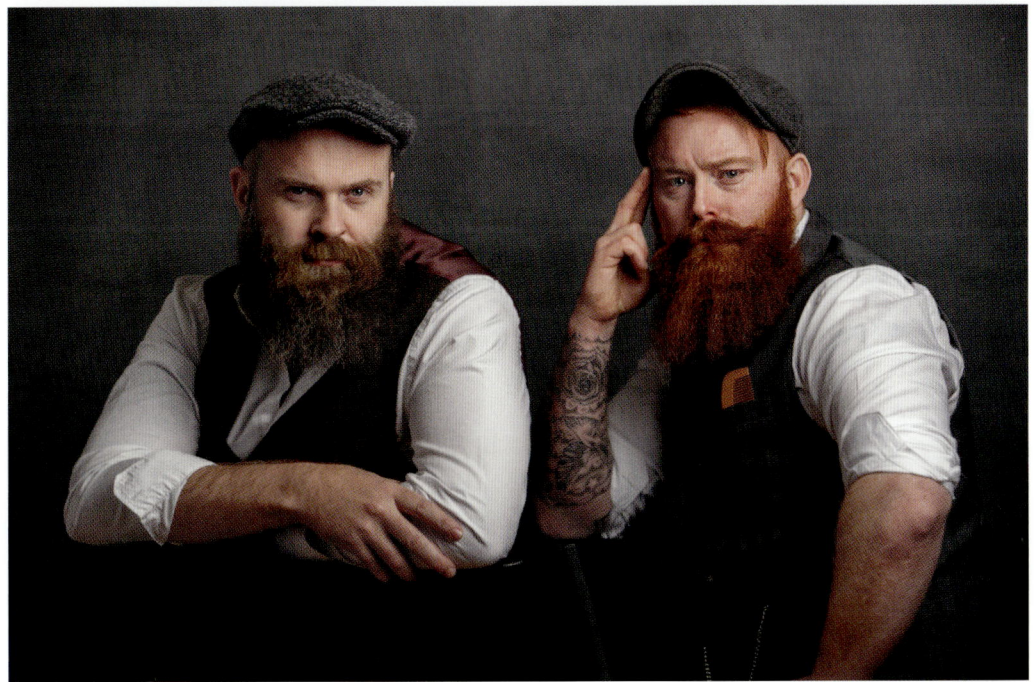

FIGURE 5.60 A Layer Mask has been applied so that the texture is only visible on the gray background

21. If we take another look at the picture by Annie Leibovitz, we can see that there's definitely some color grading that has added a slight green tint. We'll do something similar to our picture in the following steps.

As I explained in chapter 4 (page 56), there are a few methods I use to color grade my pictures. For this picture we're going to use some Adjustment layers that also include LUTs (Lookup Tables).

Click on the Color Lookup adjustment layer icon (**Figure 5.61**) and in the Color Lookup properties, select TensionGreen.3DL from the 3DLUT File menu (**Figure 5.62**). As with any Adjustment layer in Photoshop, because it's on its own layer, we can control the strength of the adjustment by changing the Opacity. Lower the Opacity of this first adjustment to around 40% (**Figure 5.63**).

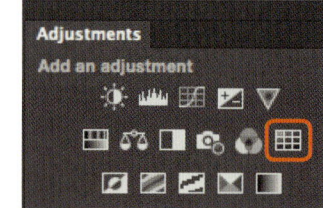

FIGURE 5.61 The Color Lookup adjustment layer icon

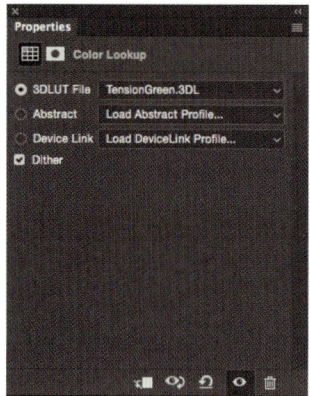

FIGURE 5.62

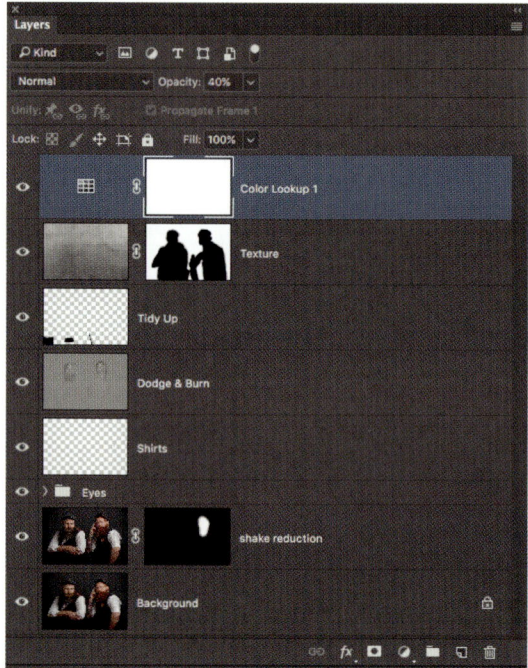

FIGURE 5.63 Lower the Opacity of the Color Lookup adjustment layer to 40%

22. Add another Color Lookup adjustment layer and choose EdgyAmber.3DL from the 3DLUT File menu (**Figure 5.64**). Lower the Opacity of the layer to 15%. Add one more Color Lookup adjustment layer and choose Crisp_Warm.look from the 3DLUT File menu (**Figure 5.65**). Lower the opacity of the layer to 40%. You can see the Layers panel with the three Color Lookup adjustment layers in **Figure 5.66**.

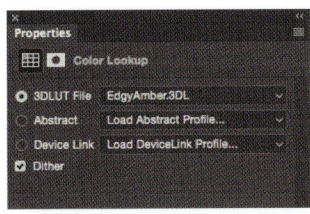

FIGURE 5.64

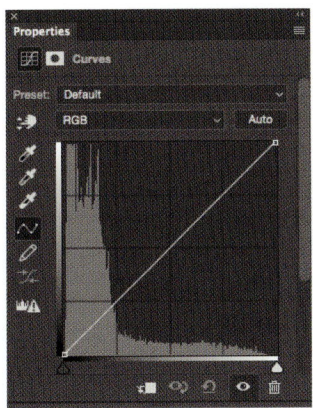

FIGURE 5.65

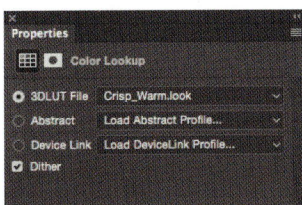

FIGURE 5.66 Three Color Lookup adjustment layers

23. Now let's add a Curves adjustment layer to add a bit of warmth (yellow) to the mix and bring back some detail in the shadow areas.

Click on the Curves adjustment layer icon. By default, the grid within the Curves adjustment properties is 4 × 4 (**Figure 5.67**), but for this step we need more squares to make an accurate adjustment. To break the grid into more squares (10 × 10; **Figure 5.68**) hold down the Option key (Mac) or Alt key (PC) and click once on the grid.

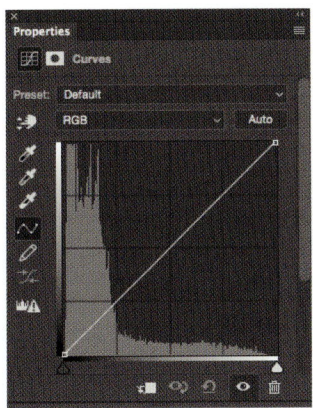

FIGURE 5.67 4 × 4 grid

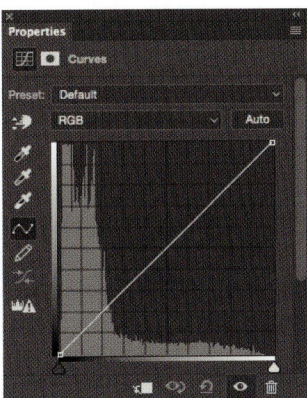

FIGURE 5.68 10 × 10 grid

Now click on the RGB menu in the Curves adjustment properties and select Blue (**Figure 5.69**). Click on the blue point in the top-right corner of the grid and drag it downward one complete square to add yellow to the picture (**Figure 5.70**).

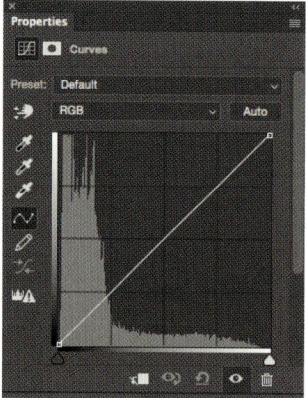

FIGURE 5.69 Choose Blue to adjust the blue channel

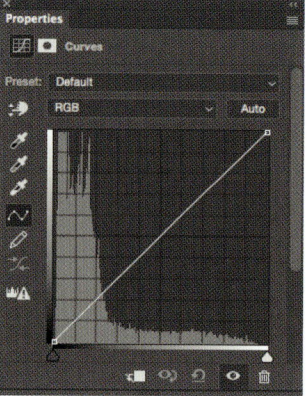

FIGURE 5.70 Add Yellow (warmth) to the picture by dragging the top of the blue line downward

24. Change from Blue back to RGB, then click on the point in the bottom-left corner of the grid and drag it upward about half a square to lighten up the darker areas of the image (**Figure 5.71**).

25. At this stage, it's just a matter of finessing the picture and experimenting to get the final look. Add a merged layer to the top of the layer stack by pressing and holding Shift + Option + Command + E (Mac) or Shift + Alt + Ctrl + E (PC). Rename the layer "FT" (Finishing Touches; **Figure 5.72**).

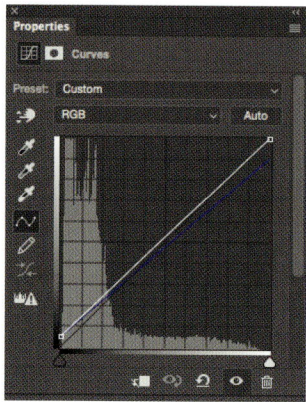

FIGURE 5.71 Lighten the shadow areas by dragging the bottom of the RGB line upward

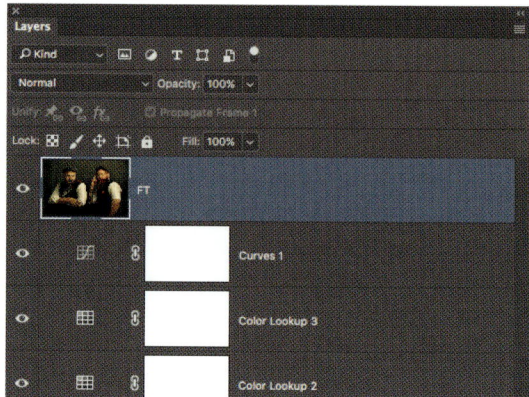

FIGURE 5.72

Let's add some contrast to give the picture a bit more punch, depth, and dimension. We'll use one of my favorite plugins, Topaz Clarity. If you don't have Topaz Clarity, there is an alternative technique you can use that I explain in chapter 4 (page 62); however, the result isn't quite the same.

Go to *Filter > Topaz Labs > Topaz Clarity* and in the Topaz Clarity dialog, adjust Micro Contrast to 0.17 and Low Contrast to 0.11 and click OK (**Figure 5.73**). There's no magic to these settings; I just think they work well for this picture. I tend to adjust only these two sliders when I use Topaz Clarity.

26. Now we're out of the Topaz Clarity plugin and back in Photoshop. There's just one little thing I want to do to this picture before it's pretty much finished, and that's reduce the annoying (well, I think it is) highlight on the chair on the left (**Figure 5.74**). Select the Clone Stamp Tool (S) and set the Opacity to 50% in the options bar. Hold down the Option key (Mac) or Alt key (PC) and sample an area under the highlight. Then brush just once across the highlight area to reduce it just enough (**Figure 5.75**).

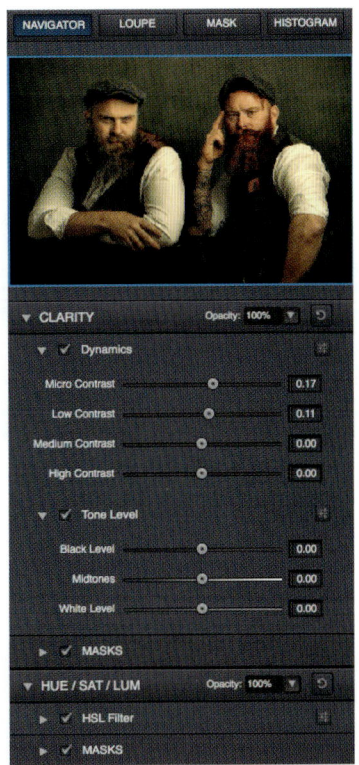

FIGURE 5.73

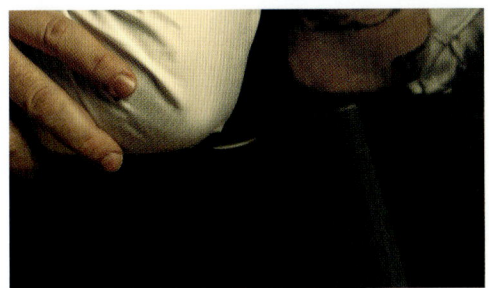

FIGURE 5.74 Highlight on the left-hand chair

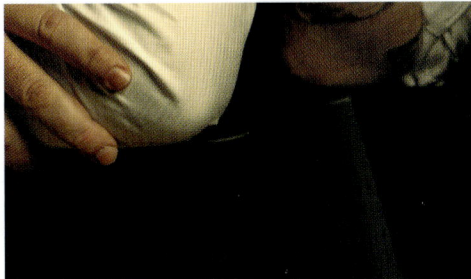

FIGURE 5.75 The highlight has been reduced by using the Clone Stamp Tool at 50% Opacity

Okay, I think we're pretty much finished now. However, just to be sure, at this stage I ALWAYS save the file, step away, and come back to it a few hours later, or maybe even the next morning. When I come back to the picture I see it with fresh eyes and I can determine whether I need to do more. For this chapter, we're all done.

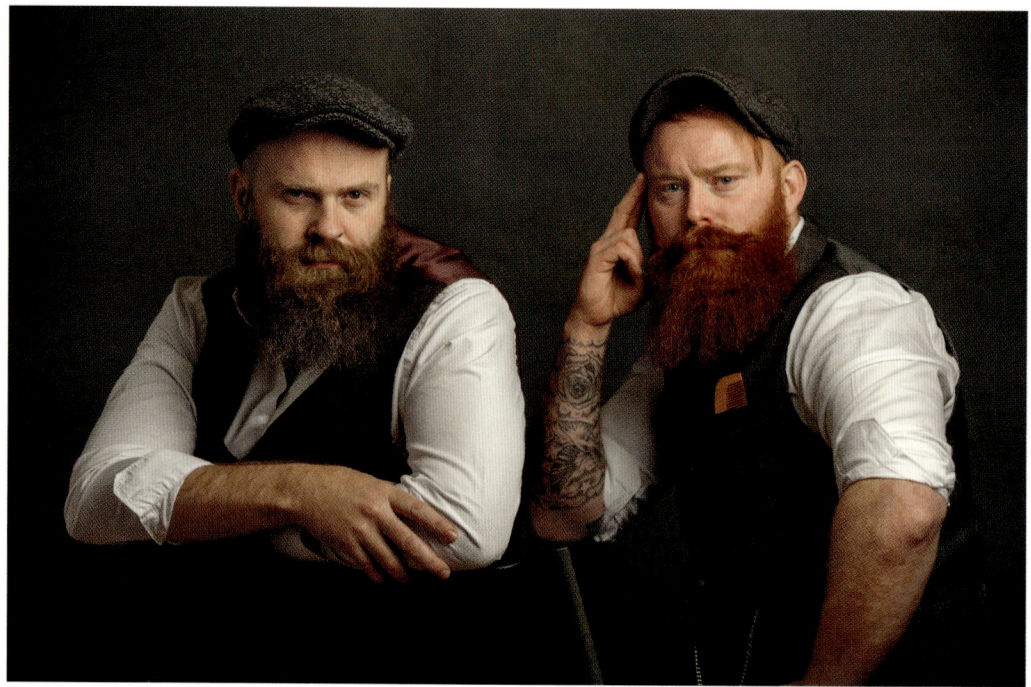

FIGURE 5.76 Original RAW image

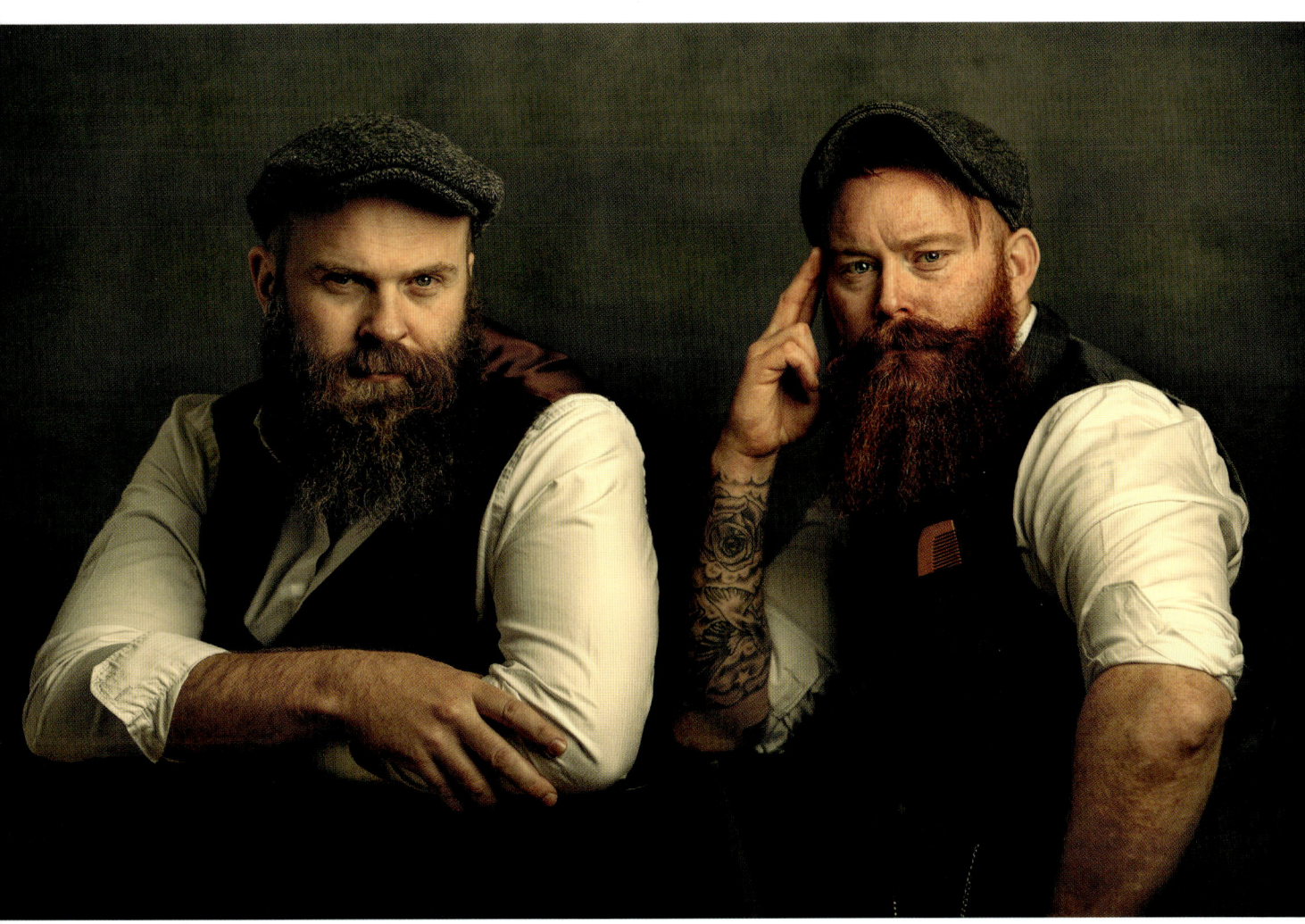

FIGURE 5.77 Final retouched image

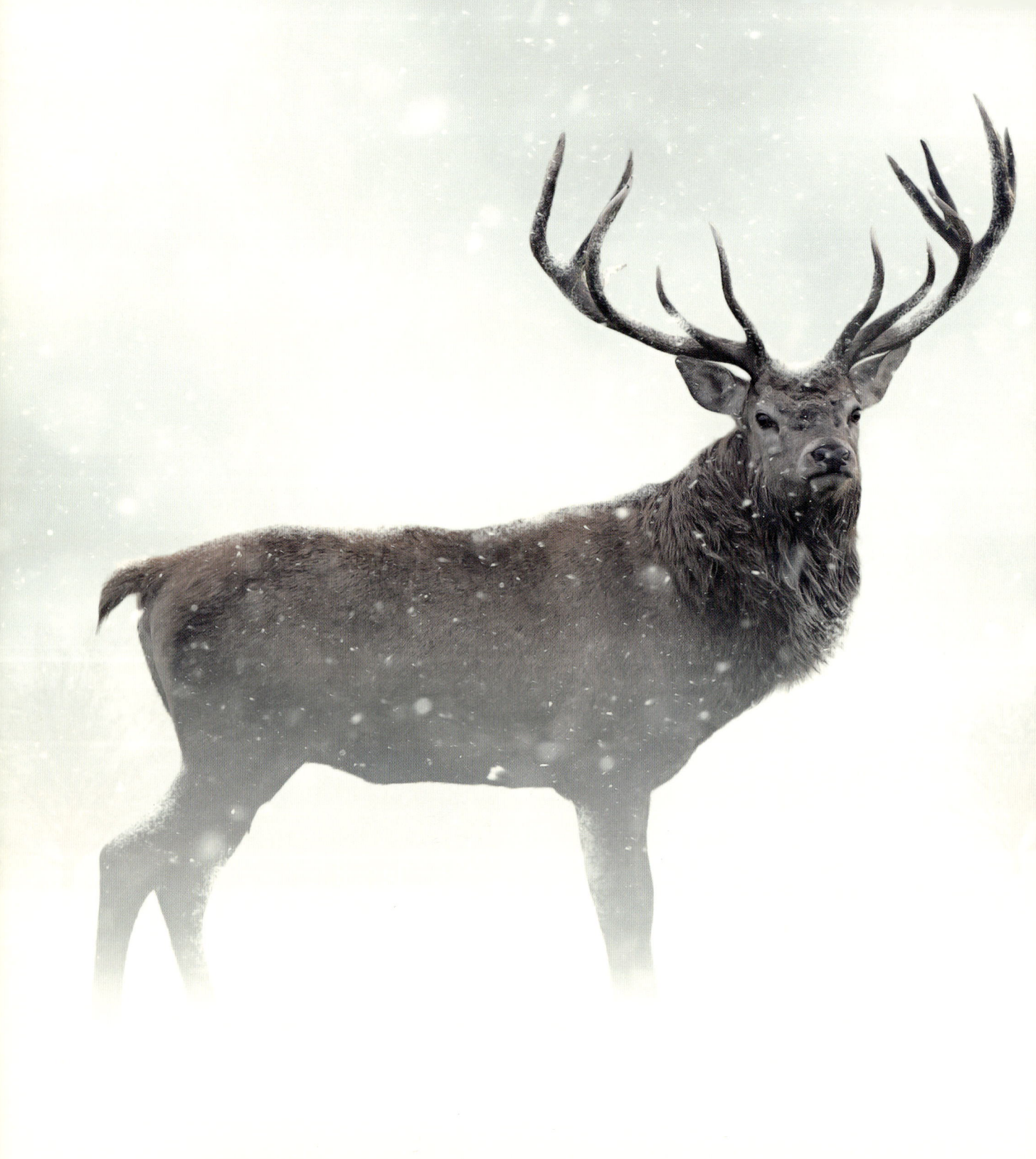

6 INTERNET INSPIRED

I've always been an animal lover. When I was young my parents had what's called a smallholding here in the UK, which is a small, self-sufficient farm with just a few livestock such as cows, sheep, goats, and, of course, the obligatory chickens roaming free.

Photographing wildlife is something I haven't done often enough. I keep telling myself that I should just take off for a few days with a tent and supplies and go into the countryside to photograph nature and take some time out—yeah, that's my idea of bliss for sure.

I've never been on a safari, although it is high up on my wish list, but I started a personal project some time ago where I photograph animals in captivity, such as in wildlife parks and zoos. Then I use Photoshop to cut them out of their surroundings, create scenes that look like their natural habitats, and place them in those scenes. In my mind, this sets them free, if that makes sense. In chapter 10 I'll take you through one of these pictures, which was inspired by the work of wildlife photographer Nick Brandt.

One picture I wanted to create, although not part of my Animals project, was of a stag out in the Highlands of Scotland, amongst the heather with mountains in the distance. With this image in mind, I headed out with a friend to a nearby farm during the mating season to photograph a stag. I planned to later go to Scotland to photograph the scenery so I could put the images together, but this never happened. For some reason, I lost the motivation to work on the image, despite having taken the stag photographs, and I ended up putting it on the back burner for another day.

One day I happened to be browsing wildlife photographs on the 500px website and on the website of my friend Moose Peterson, who is a photographer and Nikon Ambassador. I often browse 500px and the websites of other photographers whose work I love, not just to see great images, but also to look for inspiration.

One particular wildlife photograph that Moose had taken stuck with me. It is a photograph of a bison in the middle of what looks like a pretty fearsome blizzard (**Figure 6.1**). It is truly a beautiful image and it immediately made me think of my photographs of the stag, inspiring me to create a picture of the stag in the snow instead of the expected Scottish Highlands scene.

FIGURE 6.1 Photograph © Moose Peterson

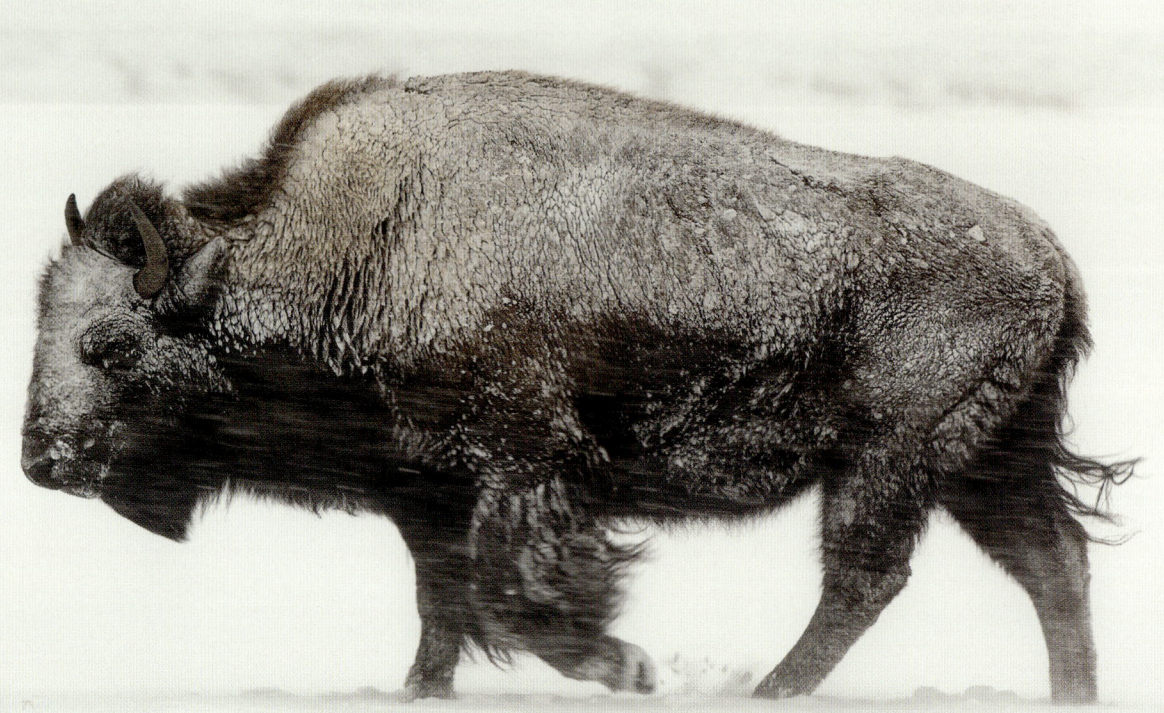

REVERSE ENGINEERING

There's actually nothing to reverse engineer for this chapter because there's no particular picture from which we're looking to copy elements like lighting. However, this is a good opportunity to talk about observing.

Without a doubt, one of the best things you can do as a photographer and digital artist, especially when creating composite images like we are in this chapter, is to get outside and observe your surroundings. Examine how shadows behave, look at their characteristics, look at reflections, look at what happens to the color of distant objects, and on and on.

Taking the time to regularly observe what "real life" is like, as opposed to guessing what something should look like, can save you a ton of time in post-production and will take your images to the next level (to use a well-known phrase).

For example, I shot **Figure 6.2** purely to make use of the sky in a future picture, but let's look at it for a moment. Look at the distant trees and hills and notice how in addition to being out of focus, they also have a blue color cast, whereas the foreground is much warmer. This kind of information is vital when it comes to putting your images together and making them believable.

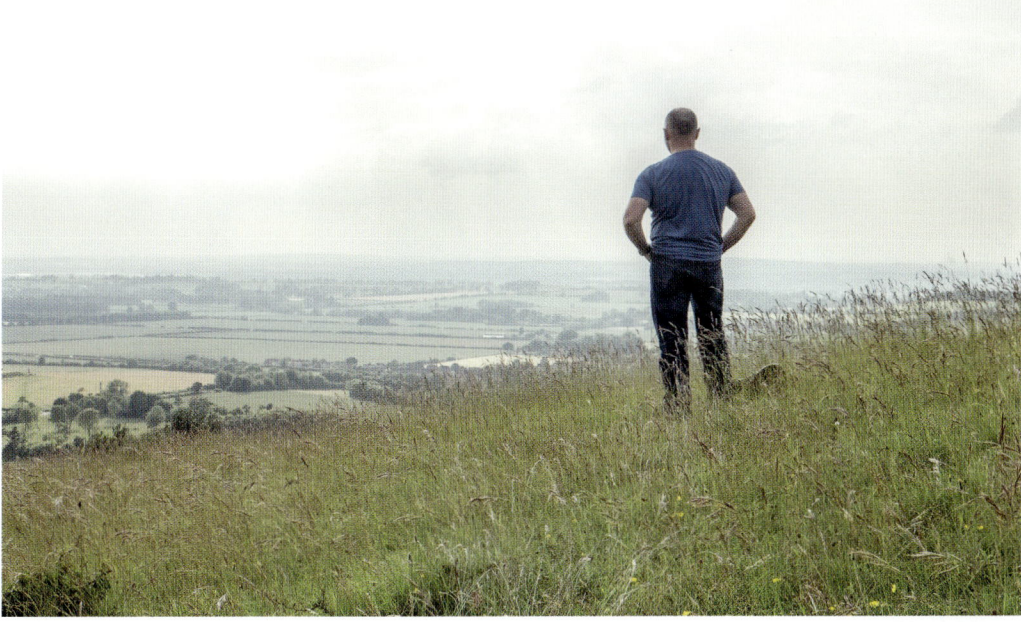

FIGURE 6.2

In this chapter, we're going to create a snow scene. Notice how in the bison picture the lighting is even and soft. Light is reflected from the white snow, filling in shadow areas and making the scene brighter. It may be a little difficult to see here, but the moving snowflakes nearest the camera are much larger and blurrier than those further into the picture, which is to be expected. And, of course, there's a subtle cool tint to the image that makes us feel cold just looking at it.

We can use all of this information to create our own believable snow scene, as you'll see in the following pages.

CAMERA SETTINGS

I knew I was going to cut the deer out of its original background in post-production, and the light wasn't particularly bright when I shot the photograph, so I chose an aperture of f/2.8.

I set the camera to Aperture Priority mode so it would only change the shutter speed. An ISO of 640 gave me a shutter speed in the 1/1000s range, which would pretty much guarantee a tack-sharp frozen deer even if it decided to move. As for focusing, I set the camera to Servo mode so that it would constantly react as I tracked the deer.

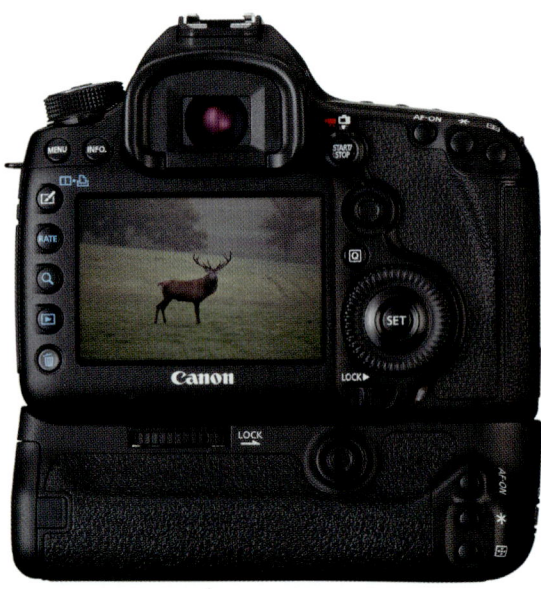

FIGURE 6.3

MODE Aperture Priority

ISO 640

APERTURE f/2.8

SHUTTER SPEED 1/1000 sec.

LENS Canon 70–200mm f/2.8 IS II USM

GEAR GUIDE

There isn't much to cover in terms of gear because it was just me and my camera (**Figures 6.4** and **6.5**).

Had I thought about it, I most certainly would have used a monopod or even a tripod when photographing the stag, but I was with a large group and didn't know how much space we'd have and…yeah, I know, it sounds like I'm making excuses.

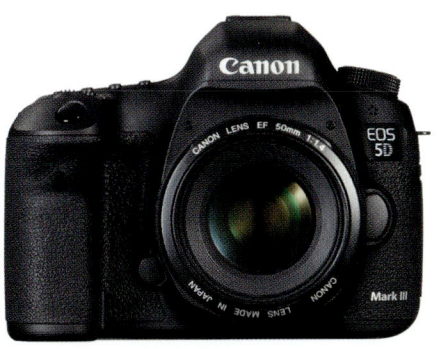

FIGURE 6.4 Canon EOS 5D Mark III

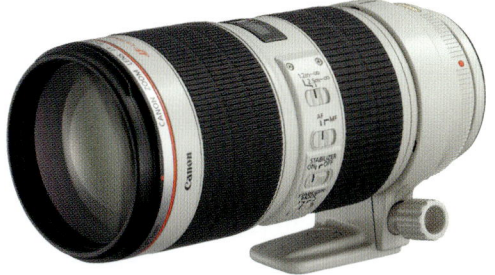

FIGURE 6.5 Canon 70–200mm f/2.8L IS II USM

POST-PROCESSING

There's quite a few steps involved in taking this picture from the original selection and cutout to the final snow scene. We'll start off in Adobe Photoshop Lightroom, but if you don't use Lightroom you can follow the exact same steps in Adobe Camera RAW. Once we've completed the RAW conversion, we'll head over to Photoshop to build the image up step-by-step and create effects that simulate real life so our final image is believable. We'll use Smart Filters and Adjustment layers so we can dive in and make changes later if we need to, without having to redo lots of steps.

Once you've gone through the steps in this chapter, why not create a snow scene using your own pictures? Instead of the deer you could insert your family members or the family dog.

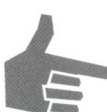

NOTE *Download the image file you need to follow along step-by-step at: http://www.rockynook.com/photograph-like-a-thief-reference/*

1. We'll start with the original, out-of-camera picture. Although we're going to be doing a cutout a little later on, there's just a few things we need to tidy up to give us the best starting point.

   Grab the Crop Tool (**R**) and bring in the sides, top, and bottom so that there is a smaller frame around the deer (**Figure 6.6**). Then bring your cursor outside of the crop handles and drag up to rotate and straighten the image (**Figure 6.7**).

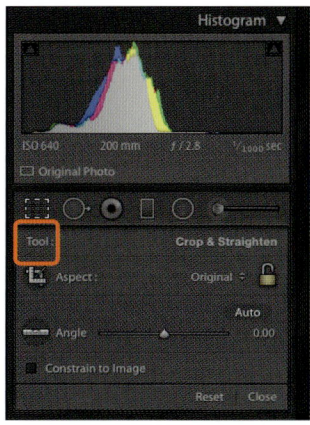

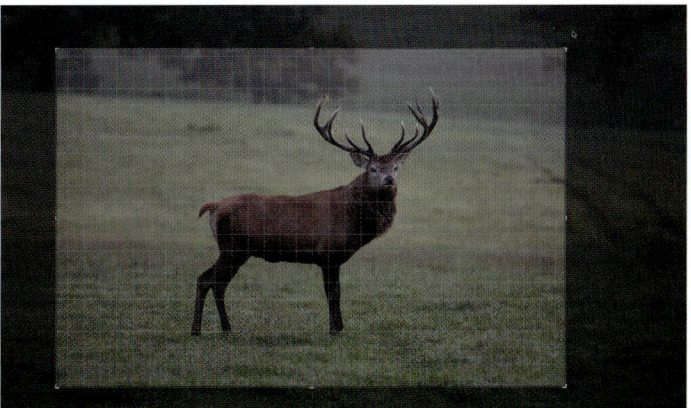

FIGURE 6.6

FIGURE 6.7

2. Now we need to bring out a little more detail in the deer. Even though the deer will be partially obscured by snow in the final image, the image will improve if the shadow areas reveal a bit more and the overall brightness of the deer is increased.

   In the Basic tab, start by increasing the Exposure slider to around +0.55 and the Shadows slider to +65 (**Figure 6.8**). The adjustment caused by the Shadows slider is subtle, but it does tend to flatten the image out, so we'll move the Clarity slider to around +20 to bring back a little midtone contrast.

3. Next we'll sharpen the image. Click on the Detail tab, and in the Sharpening section, increase the Amount to around 35 (**Figure 6.9**). Then hold down the Option key (Mac) or Alt key (PC) and click and drag the Masking slider to the right. When we do this our image turns black and white, with black indicating areas that are not being sharpened and white indicating those that are (**Figure 6.10**). The further right we drag the Masking slider, the more we restrict where the sharpening is applied. Since we want the sharpening mainly confined to the deer, dragging the slider to around 77 will be just fine.

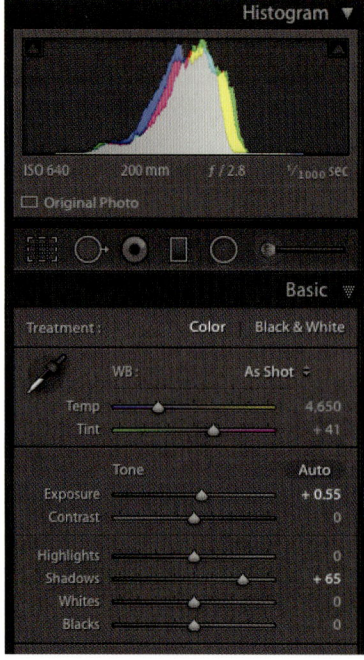

FIGURE 6.8

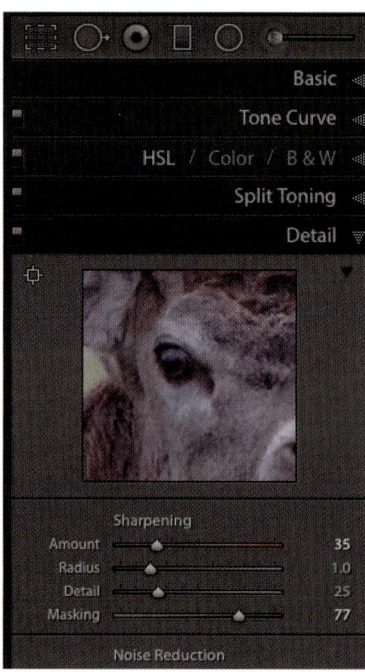

FIGURE 6.9

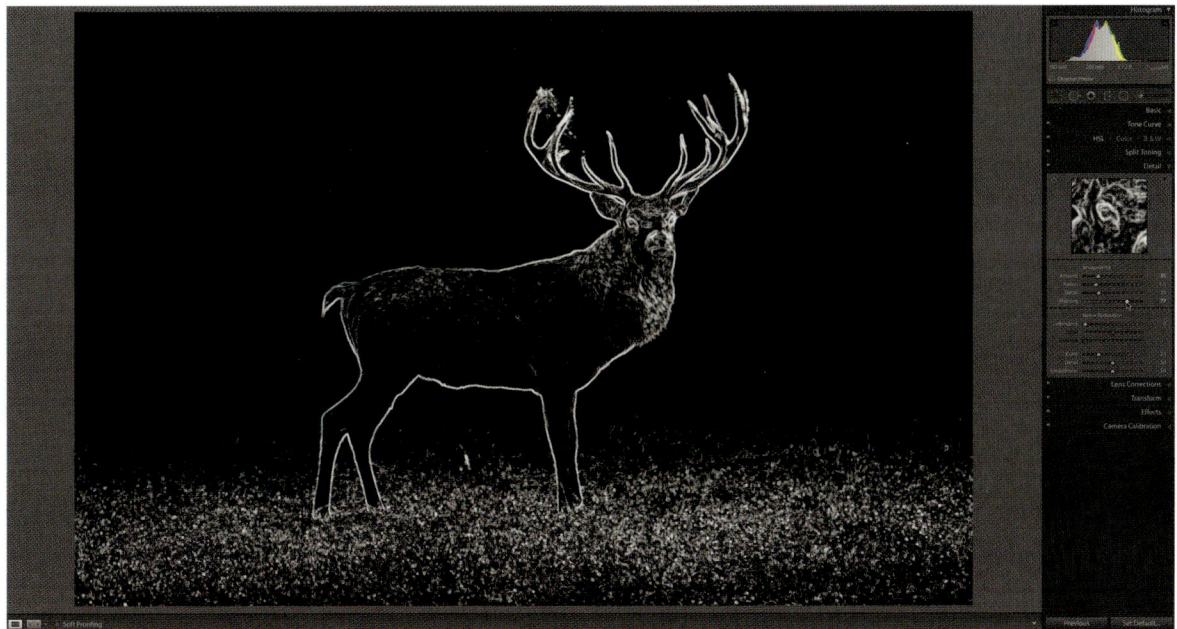

FIGURE 6.10 In the Masking view, white indicates areas where sharpening is applied

4. Because we increased the Exposure and Shadow sliders and added some sharpening, there's some noise in the picture. Before heading over to Photoshop, zoom in with a ratio of 2:1 (**Figure 6.11**) to enlarge the deer on the screen and the noise will become more noticeable. In the Detail tab, under Noise Reduction, increase the Luminance value to around 25, the Radius to 60, and the Contrast to 20 (**Figure 6.12**).

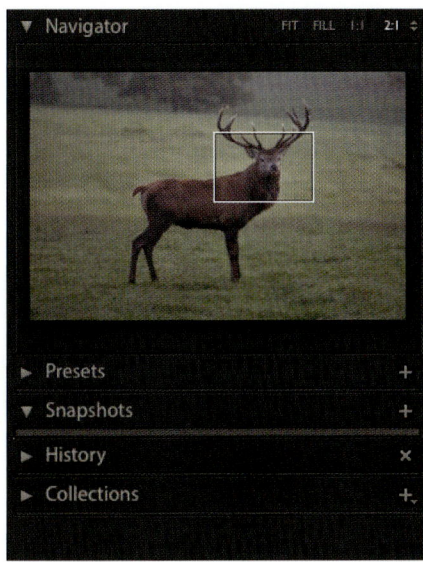

FIGURE 6.11

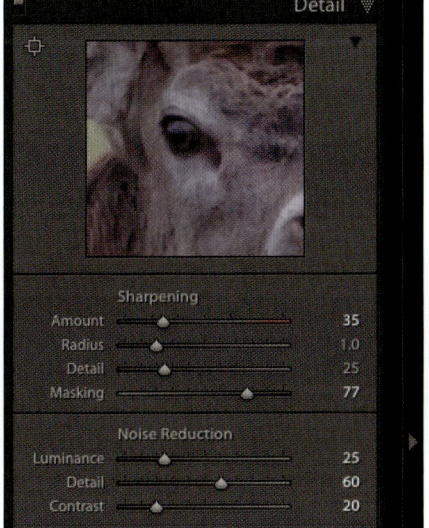

FIGURE 6.12

Figures **6.13** and **Figure 6.14** show the before and after versions of the deer image.

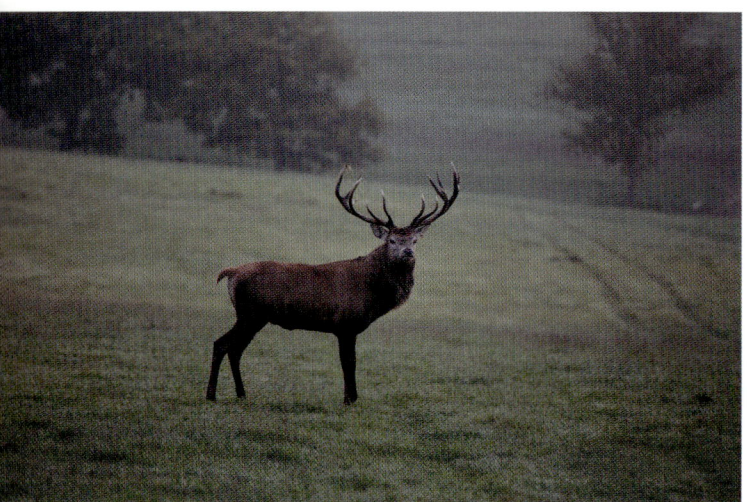

FIGURE 6.13 Before RAW Processing

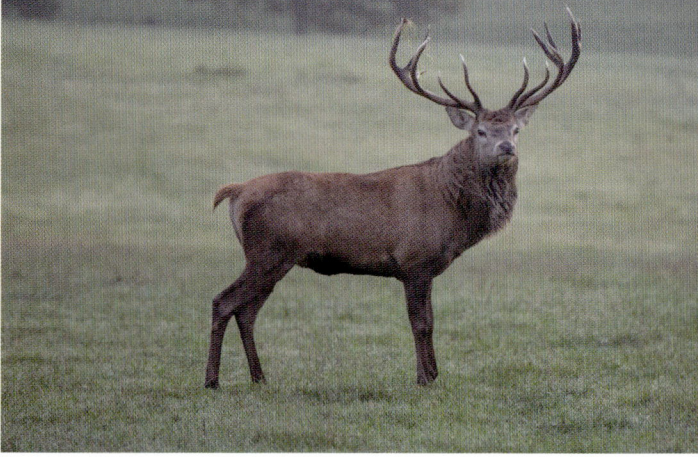

FIGURE 6.14 After RAW processing and ready for Photoshop

5. Go to *Photo > Edit In > Edit In Adobe Photoshop* (**Figure 6.15**).

Now we're going to make a selection and cut the deer out of its original background. With the Quick Selection Tool, start making a selection of the deer by clicking and dragging over it (**Figure 6.16**).

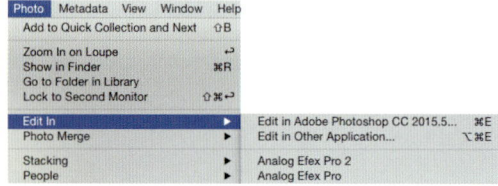

FIGURE 6.15

If the Quick Selection Tool has included any areas that you don't want to select (**Figure 6.17**), hold down the Option key (Mac) or Alt key (PC) and drag the cursor over those areas to remove them from the selection (**Figure 6.18**).

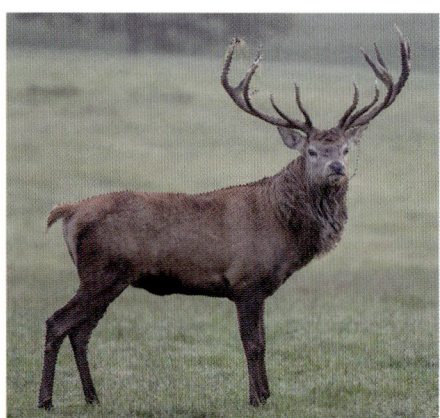

FIGURE 6.16

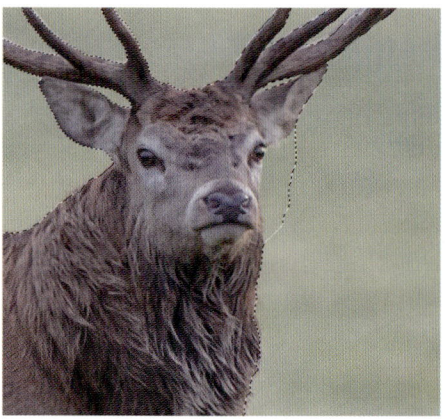

FIGURE 6.17 The Quick Selection Tool has included part of the background in the selection

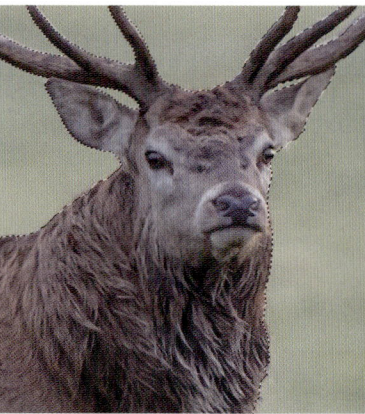

FIGURE 6.18 The background has been removed from the selection

NOTE *Don't expect to get a perfect selection with the Quick Selection Tool. Bright parts of the deer's antlers and its fur are quite challenging, so we'll be using other techniques to pick up those areas next.*

6. Now that we've made as good of a selection as we can with the Quick Selection Tool (without spending too much time laboring over it), let's finesse the selection. First, because getting to this stage has taken a little time, we'll save the current selection by going *Select > Save Selection* (**Figure 6.19**). Name the selection "Deer 1" and click OK (**Figure 6.20**).

7. Double-click on the Quick Mask icon in the toolbar (**Figure 6.21**), make sure that Selected Areas is checked in the Quick Mask options (**Figure 6.22**), and click OK. Now you'll see that the deer is covered with a red overlay, which makes it much easier to see and work with the selection.

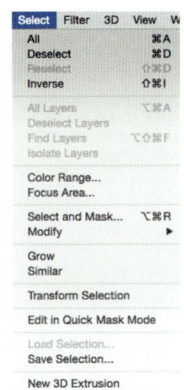

FIGURE 6.19

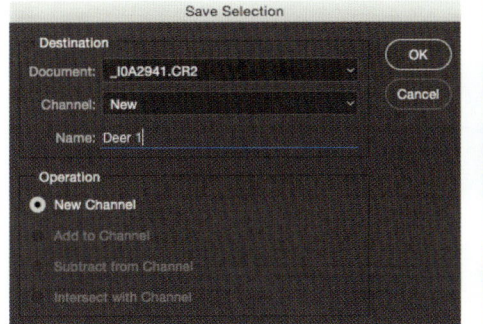

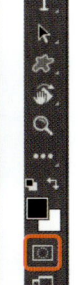

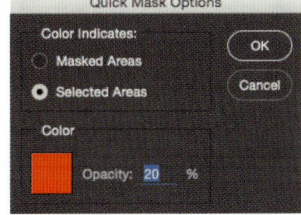

FIGURE 6.20   FIGURE 6.21   FIGURE 6.22

NOTE *By default, Quick Mask is set to Masked Areas, which means the area that is NOT included in the selection is covered with the red overlay. I prefer it when the selected area is covered in the red overlay, but this is just a personal preference.*

Choose a normal round brush (**B**) with a Hardness of about 90% (**Figure 6.23**), zoom in to the antlers, and start painting over them to add or remove areas from the selection. Don't include the bit of grass hanging off of them.

Now that we've finished working on the antlers, press **Q** on the keyboard to exit Quick Mask mode and you'll see the marching ants selection around the deer (**Figure 6.26**). Again, to be safe, save the selection by going *Select > Save Selection*. Name the selection "Deer 2" and click OK (**Figure 6.27**).

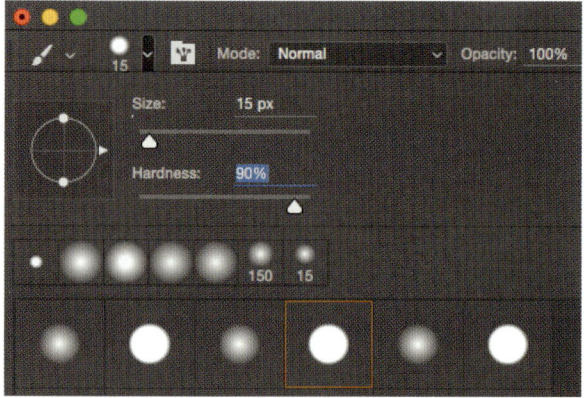

FIGURE 6.23

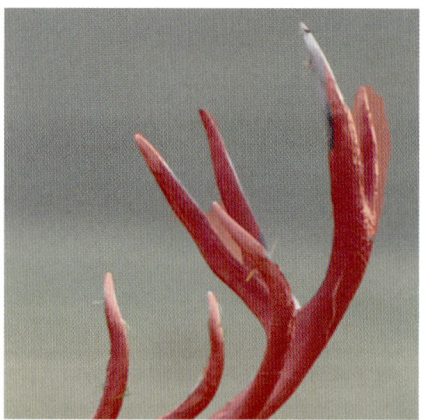

FIGURE 6.24 Painting an area black will add it to the selection (red overlay)

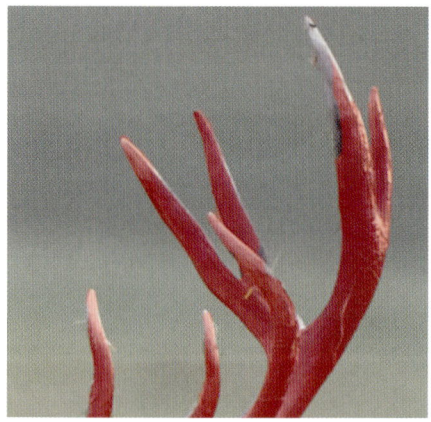

FIGURE 6.25 Painting an area white will remove it from the selection

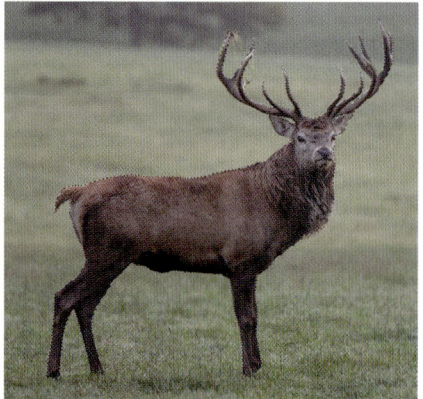

FIGURE 6.26

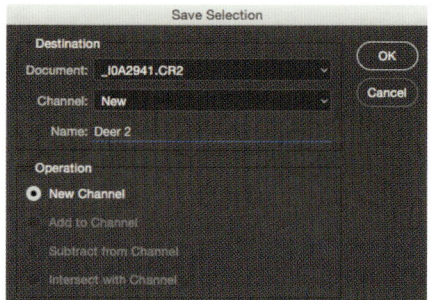

FIGURE 6.27

8. Press **W** on the keyboard to choose the Quick Selection Tool, and then click on Select and Mask in the options bar (**Figure 6.28**). (Note: If you are not using the subscription version of Photoshop, then click on Refine Edge.)

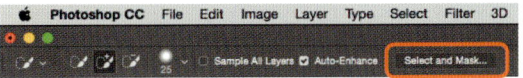

FIGURE 6.28

We're not going to do much in here because I found that trying to pick up too many of the fine hairs affects the selection we've already been working on (especially if you turn on Smart Radius). With the Refine Edge Brush Tool, paint down the front of the deer (his neck) to pick up the fine hair in this area (**Figure 6.29**). Then paint around the deer's tail, across the top of his back, and along his underside (**Figure 6.30**). Click OK to exit Select and Mask or Refine Edge.

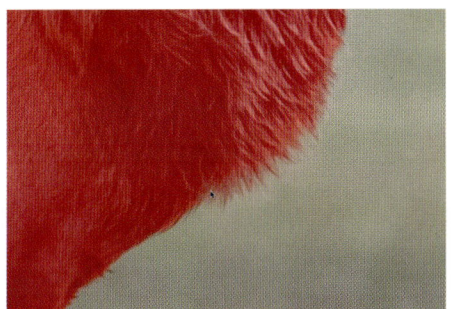

FIGURE 6.29

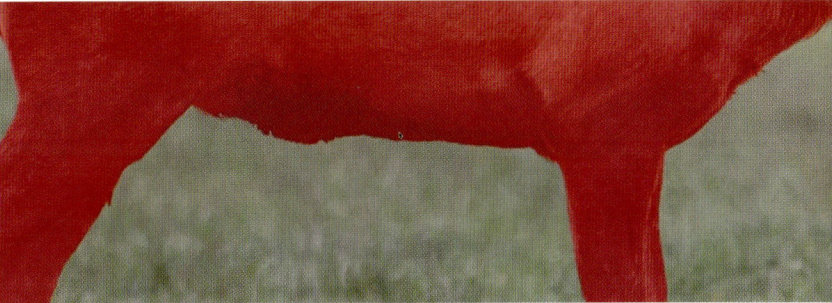

FIGURE 6.30

9. Once again, let's save the selection by going to *Select > Save Selection*. This time, name the selection "Deer Final" and click OK (**Figure 6.31**).

With the marching ants selection still active around the deer, click on the Layer Mask icon at the bottom of the Layers panel (**Figure 6.32**). This hides the background and gives us a cutout of the deer that we will add into the snow scene (**Figure 6.33**).

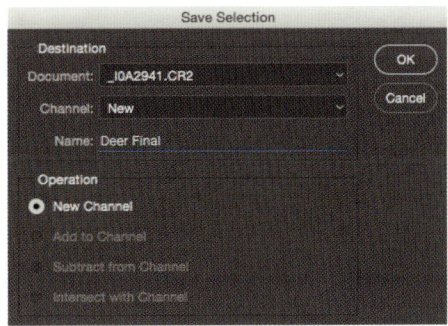

FIGURE 6.31

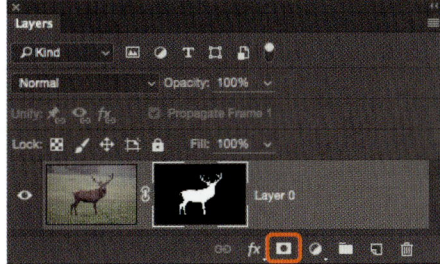

FIGURE 6.32 When a selection is active, clicking the Layer Mask icon hides everything outside of the selection

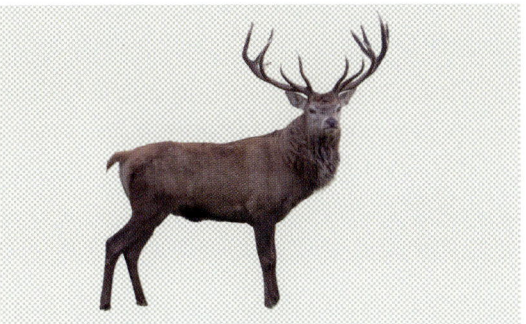

FIGURE 6.33 The deer cutout

10. Before we start building the new snow scene we'll remove the remaining grass from the antlers. Click on the thumbnail of the deer in the Layers panel so that it is surrounded by the white frame. Grab the Clone Stamp Tool (**S**) (**Figure 6.34**) and uncheck the Aligned checkbox in the options bar at the top of the screen (**Figure 6.35**).

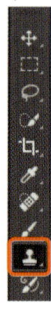

Hold down the Option key (Mac) or Alt key (PC) and click on areas of the antlers that have grass nearby to sample a clean area (**Figure 6.36**), and then clone over the grass (**Figure 6.37**). Keep Option-clicking (Mac) or Alt-clicking (PC) different areas to sample and clone so that the cloning doesn't look repetitive and obvious.

FIGURE 6.34

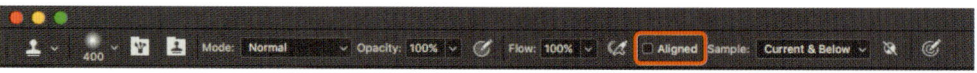

FIGURE 6.35

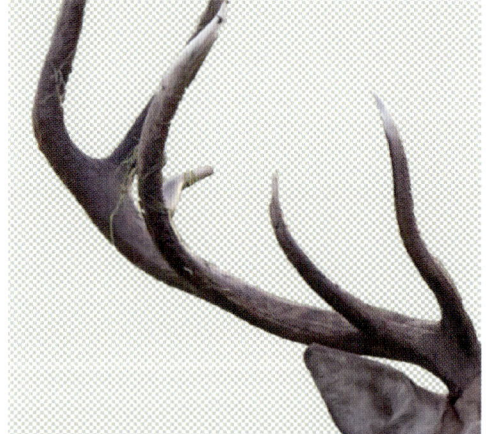

FIGURE 6.36 Grass on the antlers from the original picture

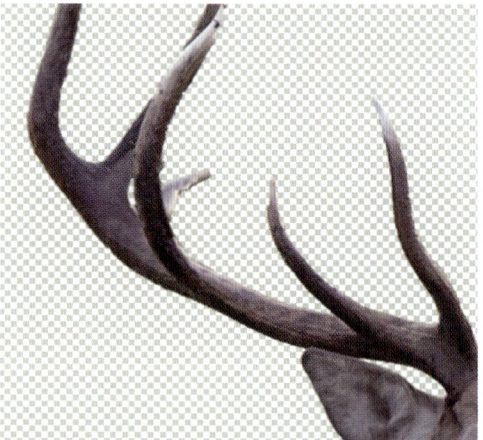

FIGURE 6.37 The grass has been cloned away with the Clone Stamp Tool

NOTE *We don't have to be careful about cloning outside of the deer because the Layer Mask will hide it.*

11. Rename this layer "Deer." Go to *Layer > New Fill Layer > Solid Color* (**Figure 6.38**), name the layer "Sky," and click OK.

Open the Color Picker and set the RGB values to R: 194, G: 206, and B: 210 (**Figure 6.39**), then click OK. Drag this Layer to position it beneath the Deer layer in the Layers panel (**Figure 6.40**).

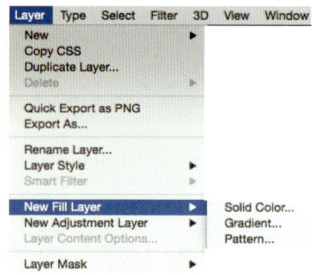

FIGURE 6.38

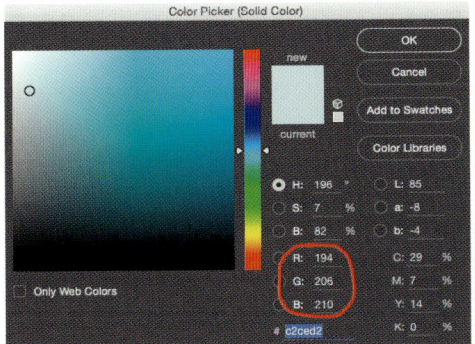

FIGURE 6.39

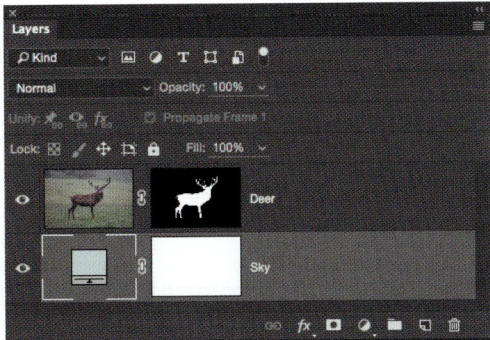

FIGURE 6.40

12. Hold down the Command key (Mac) or Ctrl key (PC) and click on the New Layer icon in the Layers panel to add a blank layer to the very bottom of the layer stack. Rename this layer "Background" (**Figure 6.41**). Choose the Crop Tool (**C**) and drag the crop handles outward to increase the canvas area. The grid intersections should be positioned approximately as they are in **Figure 6.42**. Press Return (Mac) or Enter (PC) to set the crop in place.

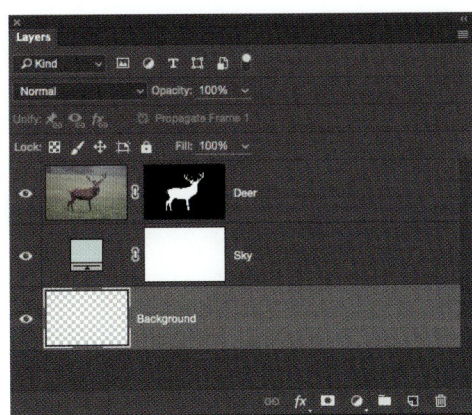

FIGURE 6.41

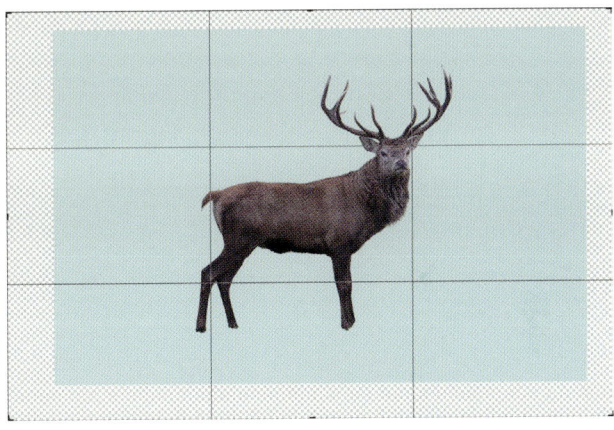

FIGURE 6.42 The Crop Tool can be used to increase the canvas size

13. Now we'll add in the ground. Grab the Marquee Tool (**M**) from the toolbar and drag out a selection of the lower part of the picture. You can see in **Figure 6.43** that I selected an area that extends from the bottom edge of the picture up to just above the deer's knee joints. With the selection in place, go to *Edit > Fill* and select White from the Contents menu (**Figure 6.44**). Click OK, and then go to *Select > Deselect*.

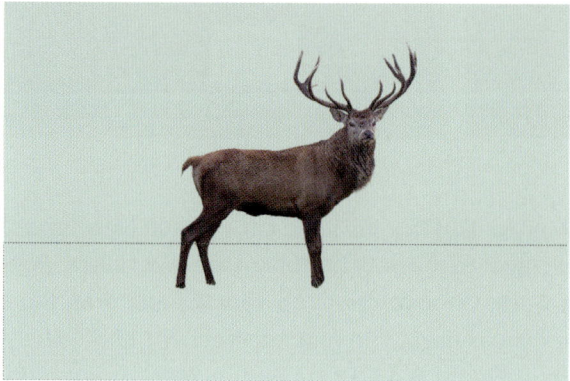

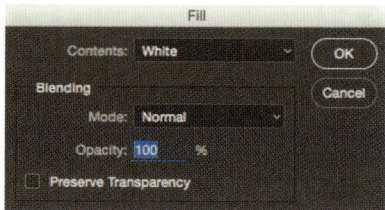

FIGURE 6.43   FIGURE 6.44

It's very unlikely for a horizon line to be perfectly straight, so we'll warp it a little bit in our picture to make it look more realistic. Go to *Edit > Transform > Warp* (**Figure 6.45**), and then click and drag inside the Warp grid to make the horizon line a little more wavy (not too much, though; **Figure 6.46**). Press Return (Mac) or Enter (PC) to set the line.

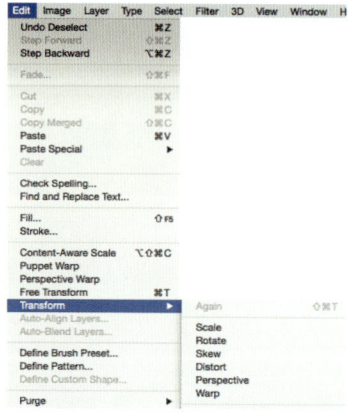

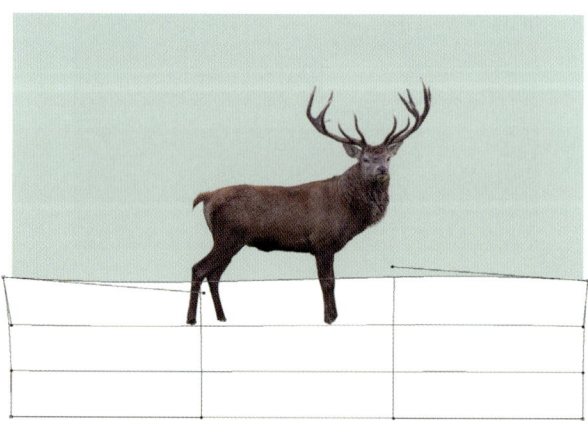

FIGURE 6.45   FIGURE 6.46

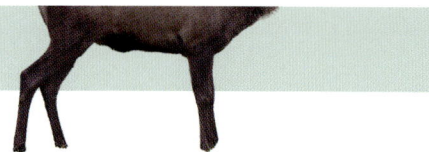

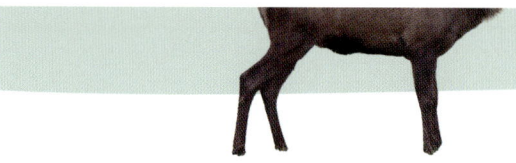

FIGURE 6.47 Before Warp – the horizon line looks too straight

FIGURE 6.48 After Warp – the horizon line looks more natural with a slight curve

14. Next we'll blend the feet into the ground we've just created by making use of the Layer Mask on the Deer layer and a brush.

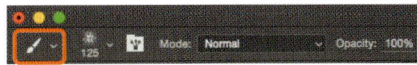

FIGURE 6.49

Press **B** to go to the Brush Tool, and in the options bar at the top of the screen, click to open the Brush Preset Picker (**Figure 6.49**). From there, choose Brush 59, which looks a spray-can effect (**Figure 6.50**).

We need to make some changes to the brush so that it behaves how we want it to, so open up the Brush panel (**Figure 6.51**). At the bottom of this panel we can see a real-time representation of what the brush will look like as we use it. Set Size to 125 px and Spacing to 7%.

Click on Shape Dynamics on the left side of the panel and increase Size Jitter to 14% (**Figure 6.52**). This controls the amount of variation between each brushstroke.

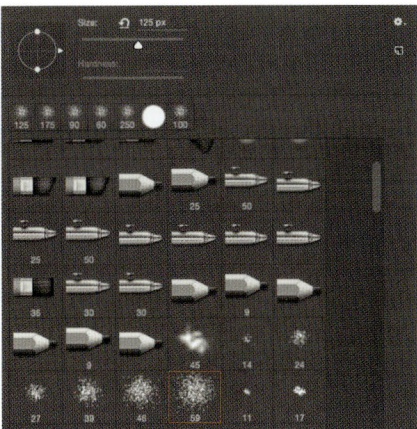

FIGURE 6.50

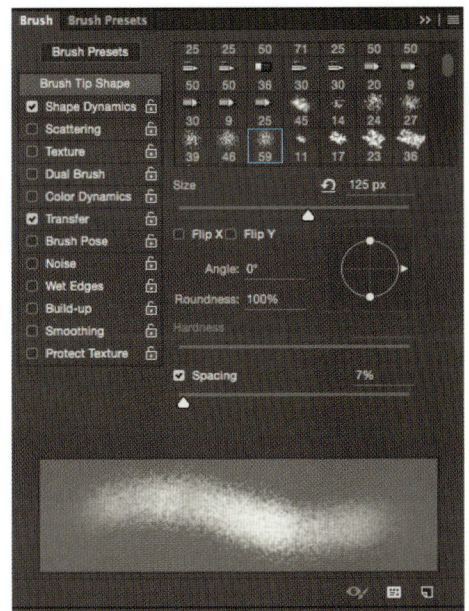

FIGURE 6.51

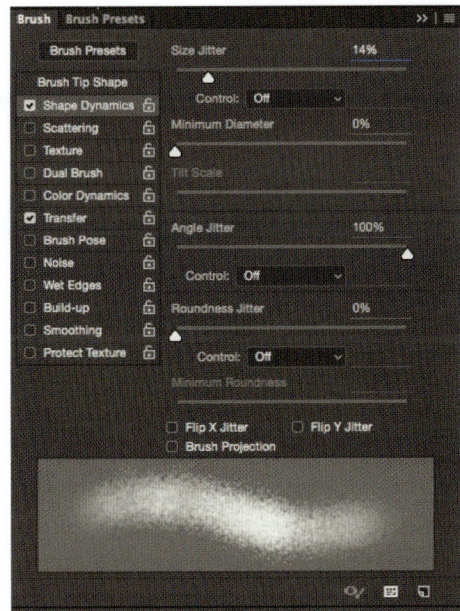

FIGURE 6.52

Finally, click on Transfer and increase Opacity Jitter to 100%. If you're using a pressure-sensitive tablet and pen like those made by Wacom, turn on Pen Pressure (**Figure 6.53**).

Then simply zoom in on the lower portion of the picture, and with a black foreground color, use the brush we've created to apply a few strokes over the bottom of each leg to make it look like the deer is standing in snow (**Figure 6.54** and **Figure 6.55**).

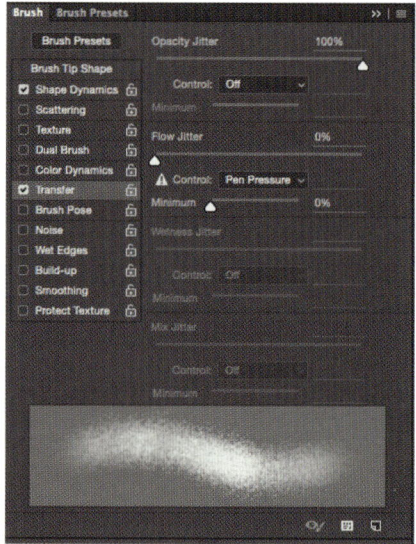

FIGURE 6.53

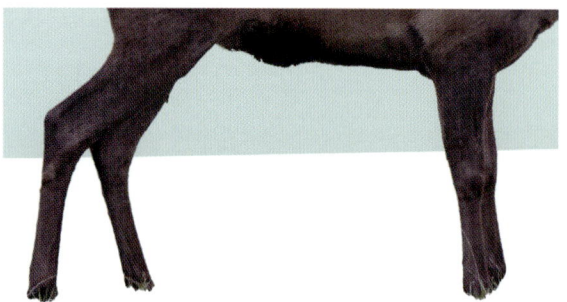

FIGURE 6.54 Before

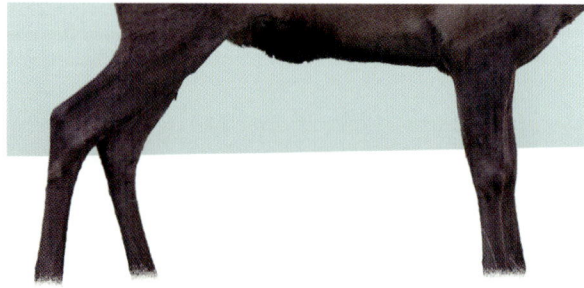

FIGURE 6.55 After

15. Hold down the Option key (Mac) or Alt key (PC) and click once on the Deer Layer Mask in the Layers panel to show it in the main part of the workspace. Choose the Blur Tool (**Figure 6.56**), and in the options bar, set Strength to 20% (**Figure 6.57**). Apply a few strokes over each of the deer's hooves to blend the previous brushstrokes so they don't look so hard and sharp (**Figure 6.58**). This will again add to the realistic look of the image.

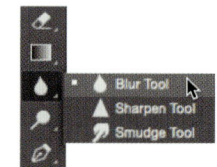

FIGURE 6.56

Hold down the Option key (Mac) or Alt key (PC) and click once on the Layer Mask in the Layers panel to return to normal, full-color view.

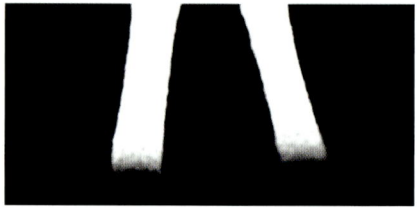

FIGURE 6.58 Blur the brushstrokes to help them blend in with the scene

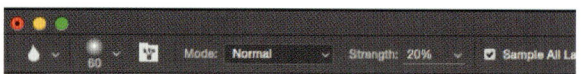

FIGURE 6.57

16. Now we're going to start adding in some trees in the distance. Click on the Sky layer in the Layers panel, and then add a new blank layer above it by clicking on the New Layer icon at the bottom of the Layers panel. Rename this layer "Tree – Left" (**Figure 6.59**).

I use the subscription-based version of Photoshop CC, which has tools that enable me to render all kinds of trees. I can control the branches, the amount of leaves, the color, and so much more. However, if you are using a standalone version of Photoshop, you'll need to use a

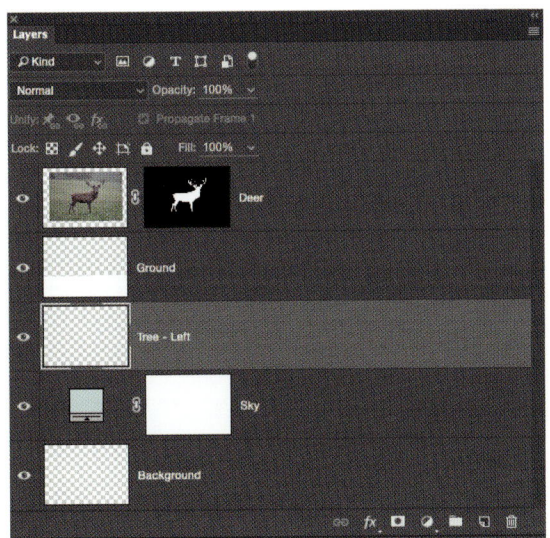

FIGURE 6.59

different method to add trees. You can use stock images or your own photographs, for example.

NOTE *If you're adding in stock images or your own photographs of trees, I have a great video on my YouTube channel that shows how to cut them out from their background. Just visit www.youtube.com/glyndewis, and check out Episode 76 in my Weekly Show Playlist.*

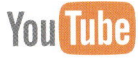

If you're using Photoshop CC, go to *Filter > Render > Tree* (**Figure 6.60**), and in the Base Tree Type menu choose 12: Ash Tree (**Figure 6.61**). Now we can make the tree look exactly how we want it to by adjusting the sliders as follows: Light Direction: 5; Leaves Amount: 2; Leaves Size: 101; Branches Height: 83; Branches Thickness: 107. Leave Default Leaves and Randomize Shapes checked, and then click OK.

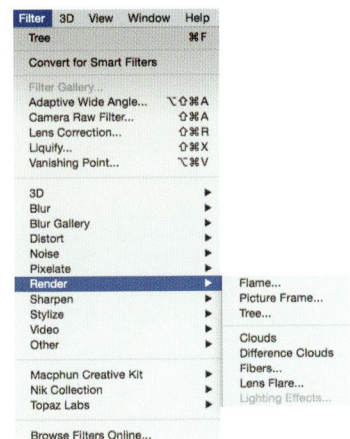

FIGURE 6.60

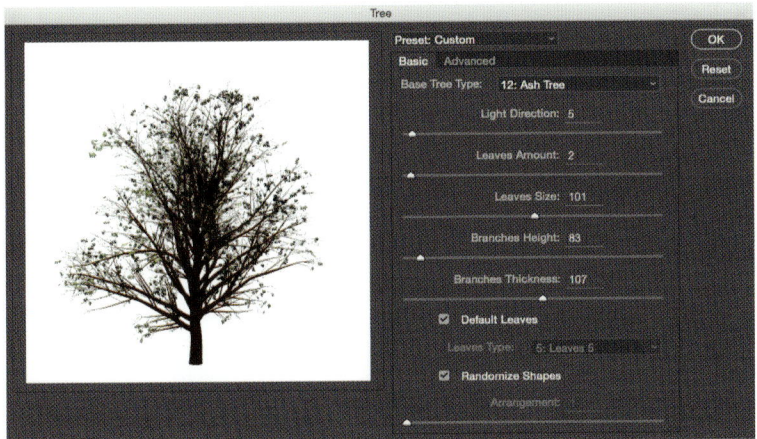

FIGURE 6.61 Adjusting the sliders changes the look of each type of tree

17. Resize the tree by going to *Edit > Free Transform* [or pressing Command + T (Mac) or Ctrl + T (PC)]. Hold down Shift + Option (Mac) or Shift + Alt (PC) and click on a corner handle and it drag inward. Reposition the tree to the left of the deer (**Figure 6.62**) and press Return (Mac) or Enter (PC).

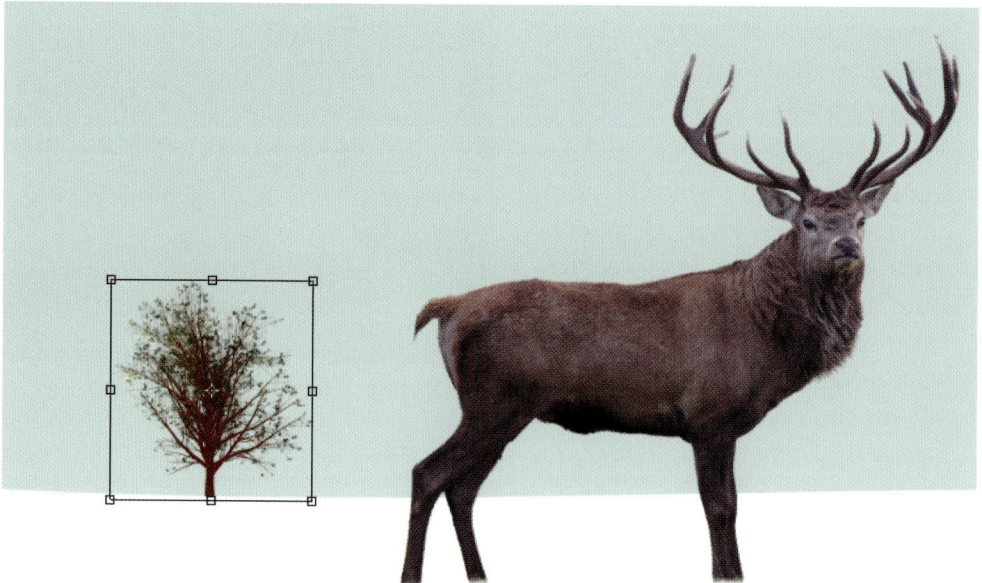

FIGURE 6.62

18. We need to make the tree darker since it is supposed to be way in the distance and we shouldn't be able to see quite so much color. Hold down the Option key (Mac) or Alt key (PC) and click on the Levels icon in the Adjustments panel to add a Levels adjustment layer. In the dialog box that appears, name the adjustment "Darken Tree – Left" and put a check next to Use Previous Layer to Create Clipping Mask (**Figure 6.63**). Click OK.

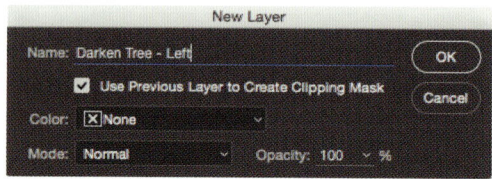

FIGURE 6.63

Darken the tree by dragging the midtone slider in the Levels properties to the right so it reads 0.70 (**Figure 6.64**). Click on the Tree – Left layer in the Layers panel and lower its Opacity to 50% (**Figure 6.65**), which will make the tree look like it's off in the distance.

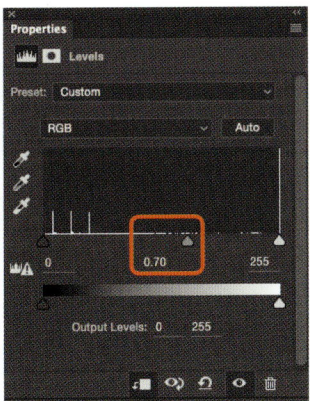

FIGURE 6.64

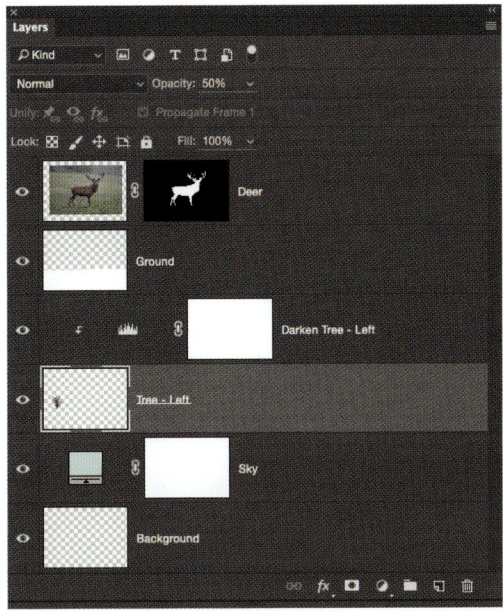

FIGURE 6.65 Lowering the opacity of the tree lowers the contrast, which is characteristic of distant objects

19. The last thing we'll do to the tree is blur it slightly, because objects obviously lose their sharpness when they're further away. With the Tree – Left layer selected, go to *Filter > Convert for Smart Filters* (**Figure 6.66**), and then to *Filter > Blur > Gaussian Blur*. Set Radius to 1.5 Pixels and click OK (**Figure 6.67**).

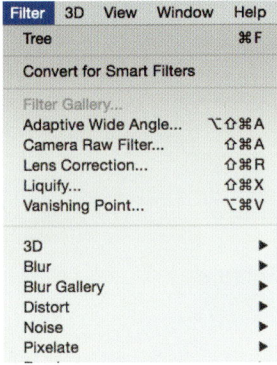

FIGURE 6.66

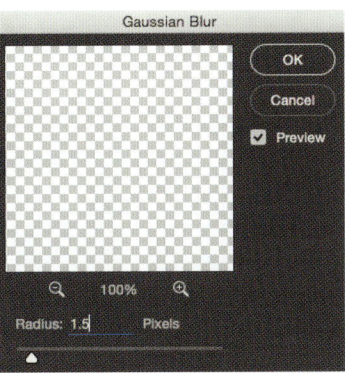

FIGURE 6.67 Adding a small amount of blur helps make the tree appear as though it's far away

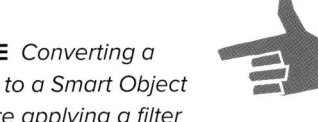

NOTE *Converting a layer to a Smart Object before applying a filter gives us much more flexibility because it enables us to go in at a later stage and adjust the filter without having to redo lots of steps.*

20. Repeat steps 16–19 to add a tree in front of the deer and another tree further over to the right (**Figure 6.68**).

Vary the tree settings in step 16 each time so the trees aren't identical. Set the Opacity of the layer with the middle tree to 60% (**Figure 6.69**), and add Gaussian Blur with a Radius of 2 Pixels. Set the Opacity of the layer with the tree on the far right to 50% (**Figure 6.70**), and add Guassian Blur with a Radius of 1 Pixel.

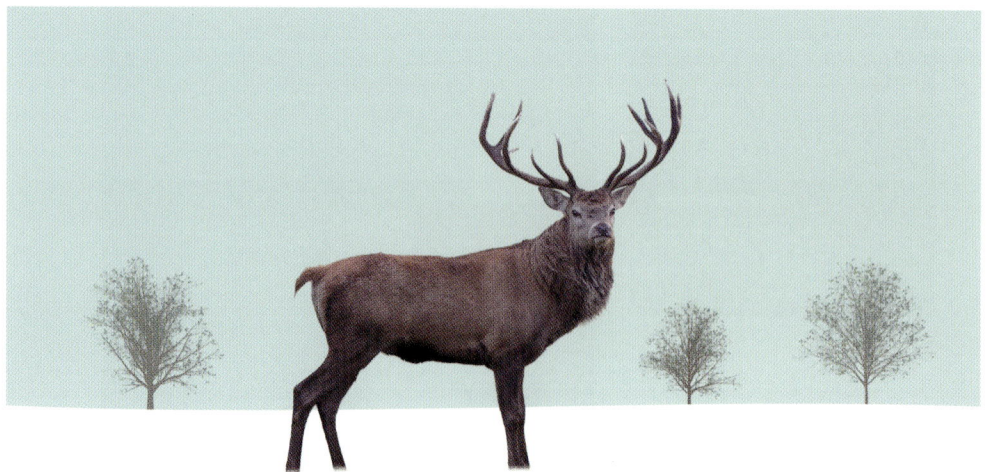

FIGURE 6.68

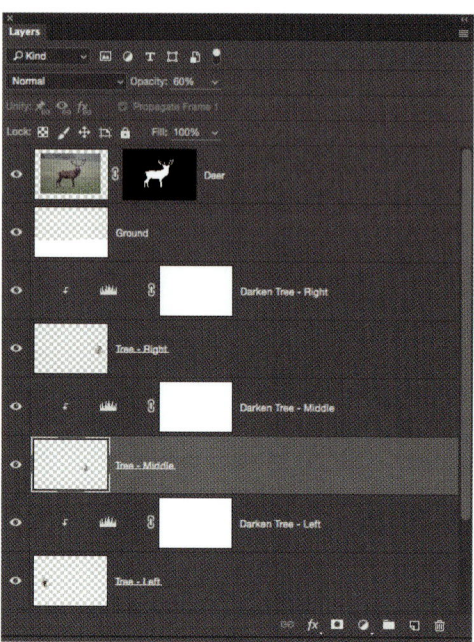

FIGURE 6.69

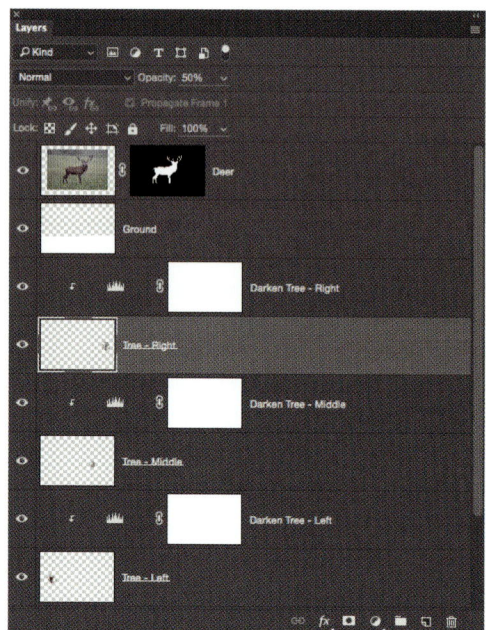

FIGURE 6.70 Varying the opacity, size, and level of blur for each tree will add to the realistic look of the final picture by making the trees appear closer or further away.

TIP *Getting out and about and simply observing your surroundings can go a long way toward helping you with your retouching. Notice how distant objects have lower contrast and appear to have a blue cast over them.*

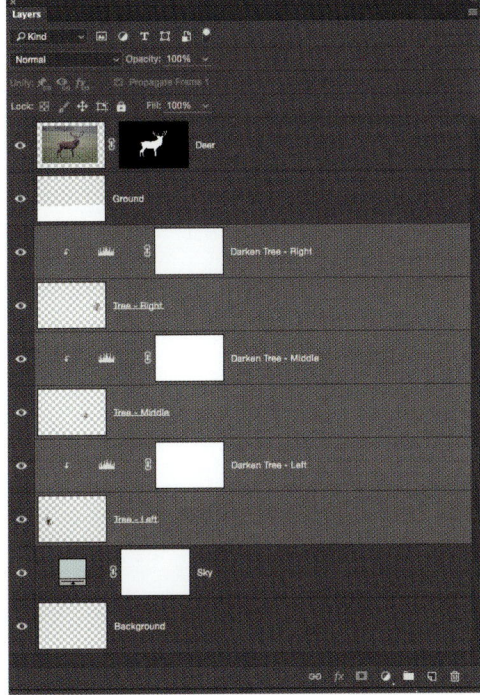

FIGURE 6.71

21. By now the Layers panel is starting to build up, so let's just tidy things up a bit by putting all the tree layers into a group. Click on the Levels adjustment named Darken Tree – Right, hold down the Shift key, and click on the layer named Tree – Left (**Figure 6.71**). Then go to *Layer > New > Group from Layers* (**Figure 6.72**), name the group "Trees," and click OK.

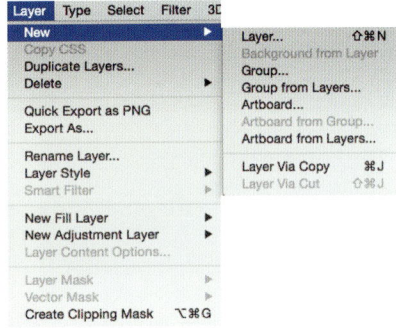

FIGURE 6.72

22. The next thing we'll do is add in some mist, which will add to the atmosphere of the picture and help to create a feeling of depth.

Add a new blank layer above the Tree group by clicking on the New Layer icon at the bottom of the Layers panel. Press **D** to set the foreground and background colors in the toolbar to their defaults of black and white, and then go to *Filter > Render > Clouds* (**Figure 6.73**).

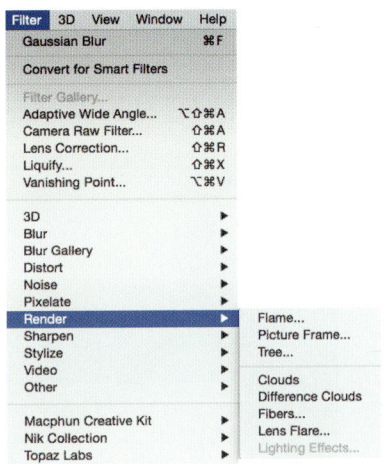

FIGURE 6.73

Click on the eye icon of the Deer layer to turn off this layer's visibility while we work on the mist (**Figure 6.74**).

Select the Marquee Tool (**M**) and drag out a small rectangle in the middle of the layer that contains the clouds. Then go to *Layer > New > Layer via Copy* to put this rectangular selection onto its own layer (**Figure 6.75**). Rename this layer "Mist," and then delete the original clouds layer.

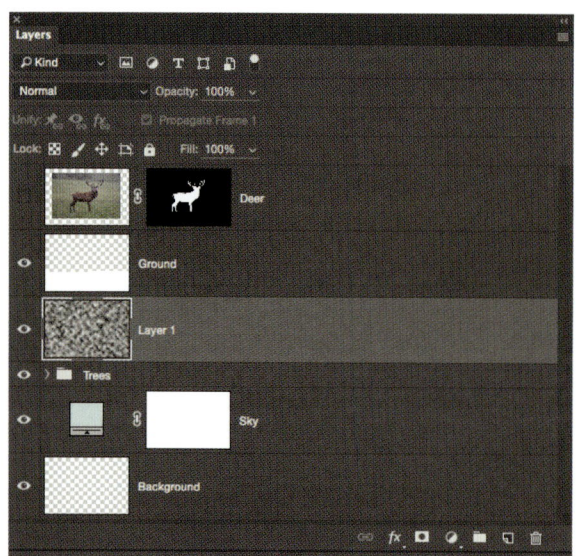

FIGURE 6.74

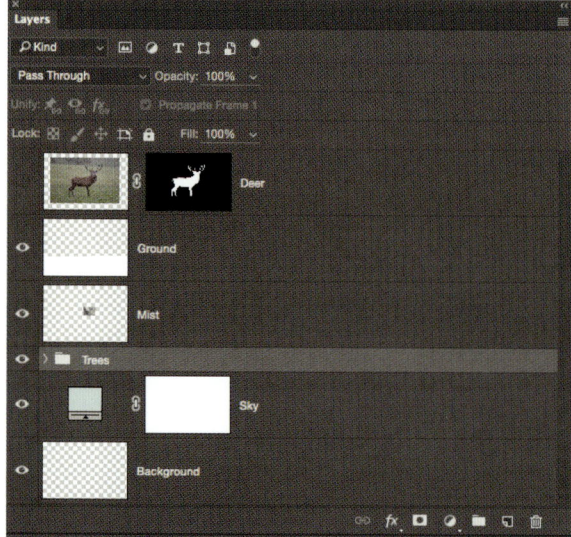

FIGURE 6.75

23. With the Mist layer selected in the Layers panel, go to *Edit > Free Transform*, and while holding down Shift + Option (Mac) or Shift + Alt (PC), click on a corner handle and drag outward until the frame is outside of the canvas area (**Figure 6.76**). Press Return (Mac) or Enter (PC).

FIGURE 6.76

Hold down the Option key (Mac) or Alt key (PC) and click on the Levels icon in the Adjustments panel to add a Levels adjustment layer. Name this adjustment "Lighten Mist" and click OK. In the Levels adjustment properties, drag the black Output Levels marker to the right until you reach 100 (**Figure 6.77**).

In the Layers panel, lower the Opacity of the Mist layer to around 70%. Then click to reveal the eye icon on the Deer layer and turn on its visibility.

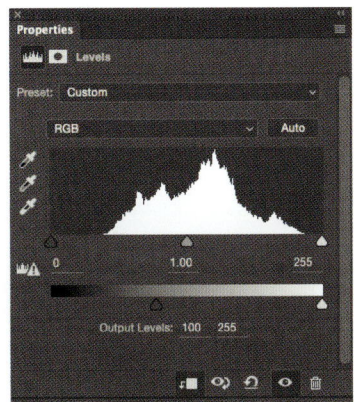

FIGURE 6.77

24. Soon we'll be adding in some snowfall, but before we do that, let's make it look like the deer has some snow on him. We'll do this with a brush that is similar to the one we used earlier when we blended the deer's legs into the ground.

Click on the Deer layer in the Layers panel and add a new blank layer above it by going to *Layer > New > Layer*. In the properties, name the new layer "Deer Snow" and check the Use Previous Layer to Create Clipping Mask checkbox (**Figure 6.78**).

Note: We use a clipping mask so that when we paint to add snow onto the deer, the snow will only appear on the deer and not on other parts of the image. The clipping mask restricts the snow so it is only visible per the layer mask below.

Press **B** to select the Brush Tool. Click on the Brush Preset Picker in the options bar at the top of the screen and choose Spatter Brush number 27 (**Figure 6.79**).

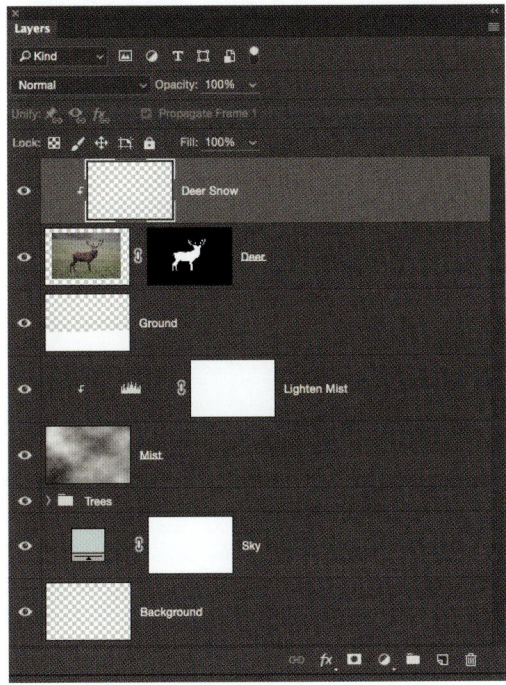

FIGURE 6.78

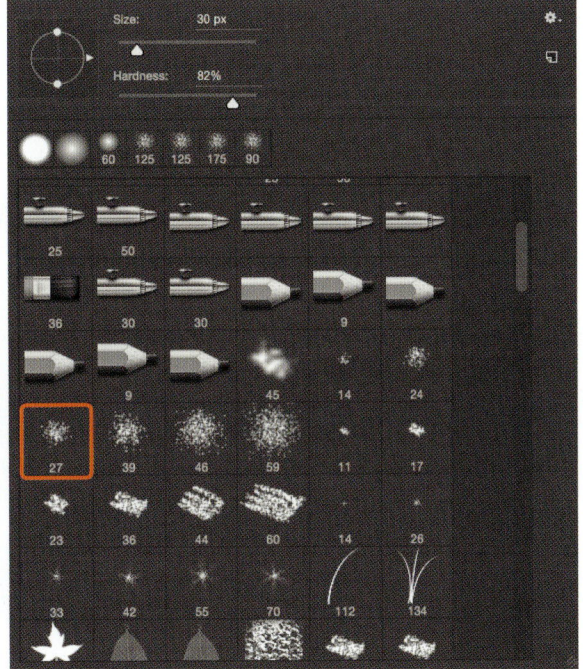

FIGURE 6.79

Open the Brush panel, and in the Brush Tip Shape section, set Size to 80 px and Spacing to 40% (**Figure 6.80**).

Click on Shape Dynamics and set Size Jitter to 25% and Angle Jitter to 100% (**Figure 6.81**).

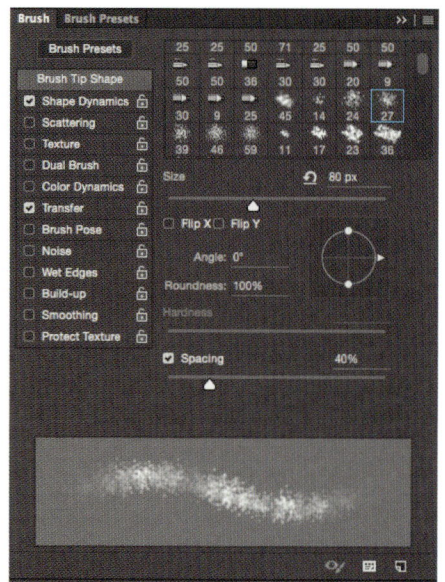

FIGURE 6.80

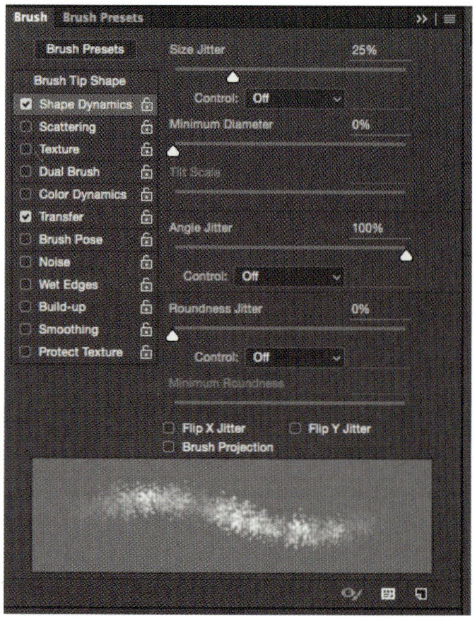

FIGURE 6.81

Click on Transfer and set Opacity Jitter to 100% (**Figure 6.82**). If you're using a pressure-sensitive tablet and pen, choose Pen Pressure from the Control menu.

With a white foreground color, paint over the areas of the deer where you want to add snow (**Figure 6.83**).

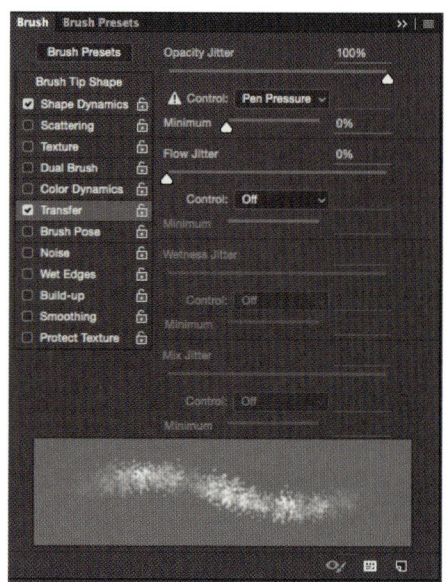

FIGURE 6.82

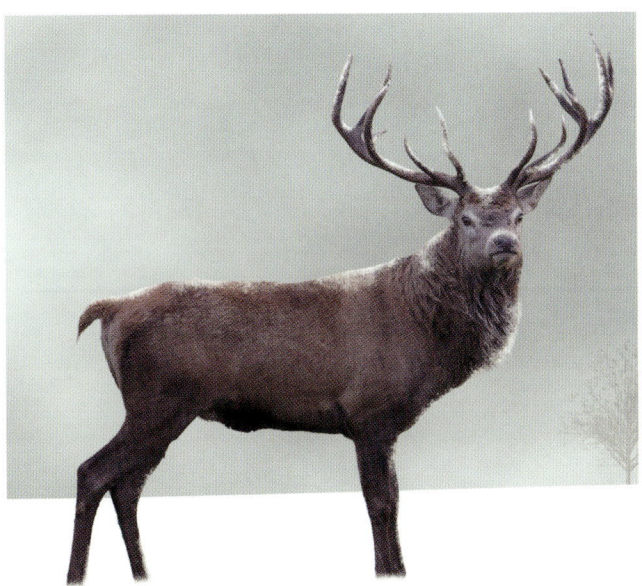

FIGURE 6.83

25. Let's add a little bit of blur to this snow to make it look lighter and fluffier. Go to *Filter > Convert for Smart Filters*, and then go to *Filter > Blur > Gaussian Blur*. Set Radius to 1 Pixel and click OK.

26. Looking at the image now, I think we need to brighten the background and the deer a little. Start by clicking on the Lighten Mist Levels adjustment layer (**Figure 6.84**). In the properties, move the midtone slider to the left until you hit 3.00 (**Figure 6.85**).

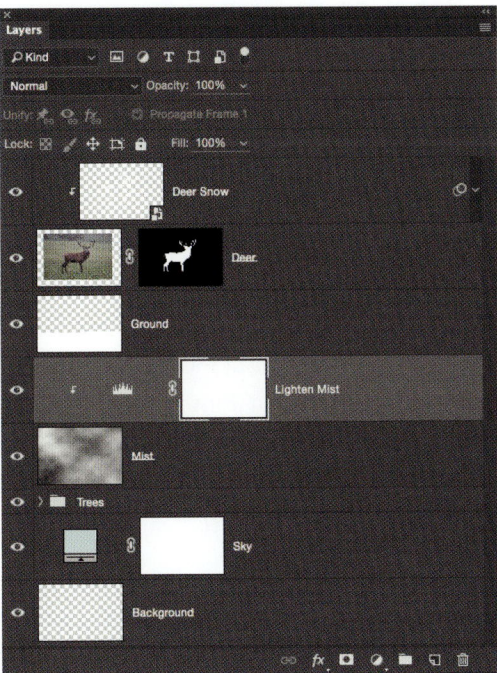

FIGURE 6.84

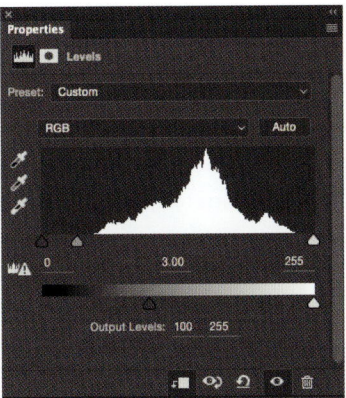

FIGURE 6.85

27. Click on the Deer Snow layer in the Layers panel, and then click on the Levels icon in the Adjustments panel to add a Levels adjustment layer. Rename this layer "Brighten," and in the properties, drag the midtones slider to the left until you reach 1.26 (**Figure 6.86**). With a round, soft-edged brush and a black foreground color, randomly paint on the layer mask (**Figure 6.87**). Make sure to paint over the deer's face to bring back some of the contrast that this adjustment layer reduced. Leaving contrast on the face draws attention to it, which is what we want.

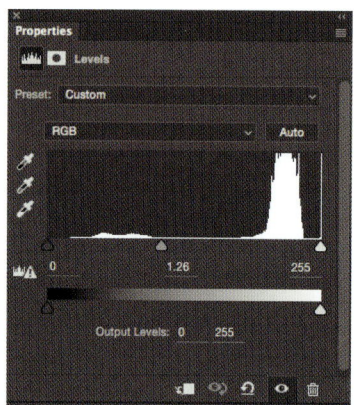

FIGURE 6.86

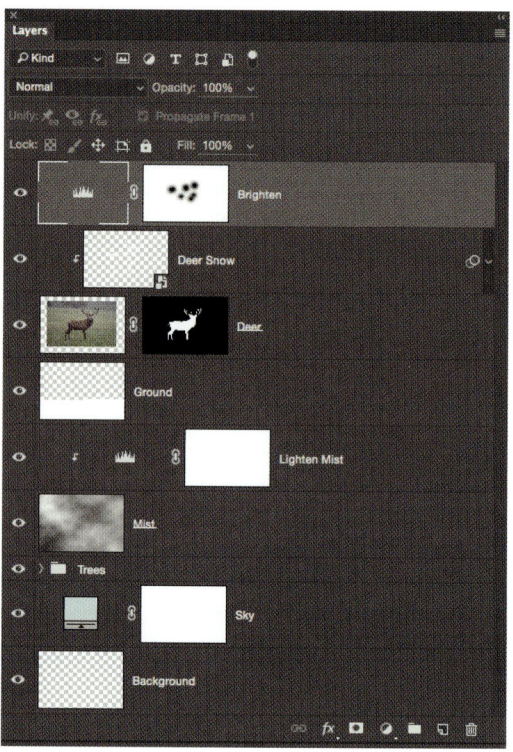

FIGURE 6.87

28. Next we'll add some mist in the foreground. But before we do, I want to soften the horizon line because to me it looks a little too sharp, especially since it's supposed to be in the distance. Click on the Ground layer, and then go to *Filter > Convert for Smart Filters*, followed by *Filter > Blur > Gaussian Blur*. Set Radius to 1 Pixel and click OK.

Add a new layer to the top of the layer stack and rename it "Mist 2." Set the foreground color in the toolbar to white, and then press **G** to select the Gradient Tool. In the options bar at the top of the screen, open the Gradient Picker and choose the second gradient, which is called Foreground to Transparent (**Figure 6.88**). Hold down the Shift key and click and hold at the bottom of the deer's front leg. Without letting go, drag upward to the top of the deer's shoulder and then release (**Figure 6.89**). This adds a mist effect to the lower part of our picture (**Figure 6.90**).

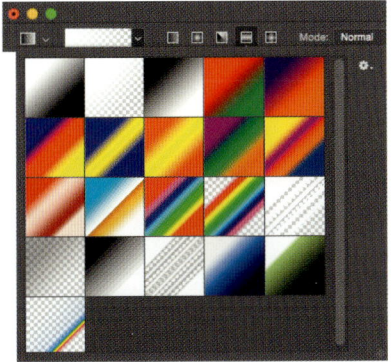

FIGURE 6.88

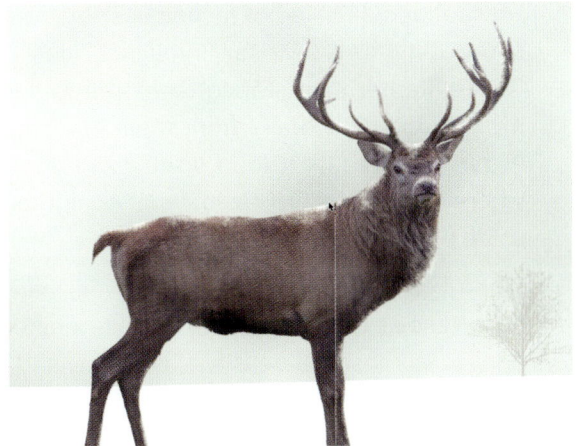

FIGURE 6.89

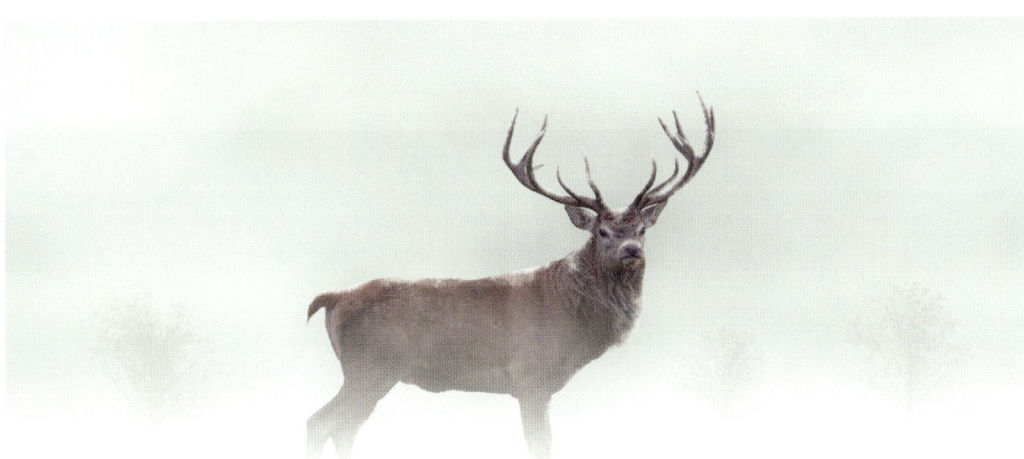

FIGURE 6.90 The mist effect is added by using a simple Foreground to Transparent gradient

29. There are only a few more steps, and the next step is to add in snowfall. There are many techniques for creating snow, and I've recorded videos over on my YouTube channel (www.youtubecom/glyndewis) showing exactly that; however, the very best snow I've found for use in Photoshop is from my friend Renee Robyn (www.reneerobynphotography.com; **Figure 6.91**). In the Stock section of her website she has a whole host of textures and effects that you can purchase. The snow packs are individual files that you can drag into your image as layers.

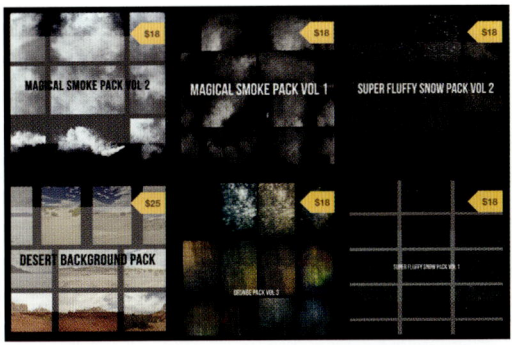

FIGURE 6.91

Having tried all kinds of techniques for creating snow, I still turn to these individual files from Renee. Rather than storing them in a folder on my computer, I actually store them in a catalog within my Creative Cloud so that I have them wherever I go, regardless of what computer I'm using (**Figure 6.92**).

30. When it comes to adding the snow layers that I got from Renee's website, I like to add a few different ones to increase the density of the snow and create depth. For this image, I added a layer of snow that shows snowflakes on a black background to the top of the layer stack (**Figure 6.93**). To remove the black, all we have to do is change the Blend Mode of the layer to Screen (**Figure 6.94**).

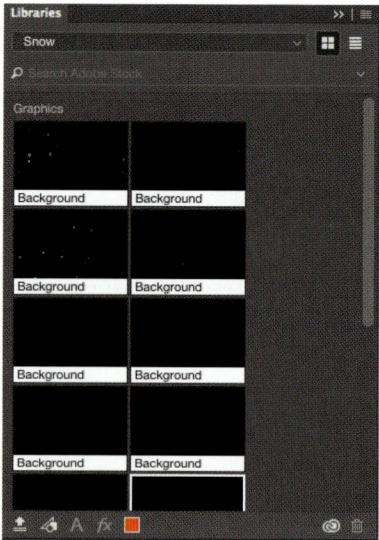

FIGURE 6.92 The Creative Cloud Library where I store files that I use often

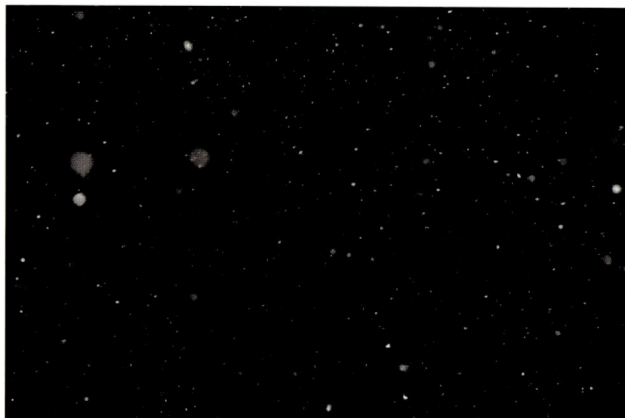

FIGURE 6.93

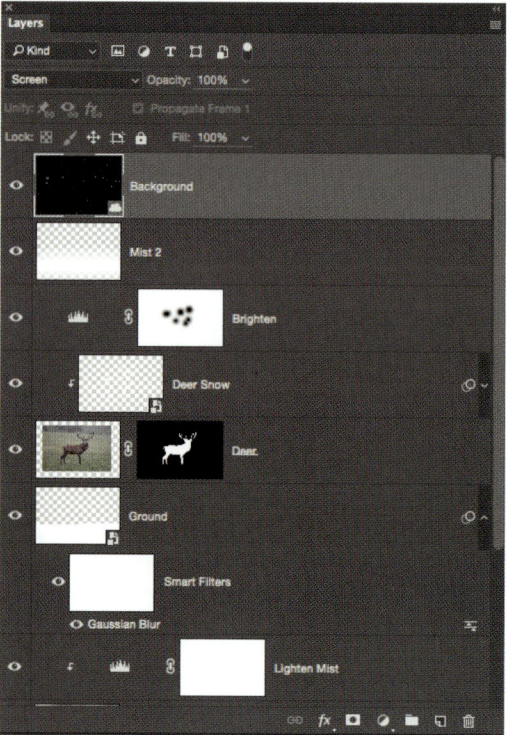

FIGURE 6.94

I may add up to six different snow layers. When the snow looks dense enough, I'll put all the snow layers into a group by clicking on the uppermost snow layer, holding down my Shift key, clicking on the first snow layer, and then going to *Layer > New > Group from Layers* (**Figure 6.95**).

31. Finally, to finish the picture off we'll make it look a bit cooler by changing the color slightly with a Hue/Saturation adjustment layer.

    Start by adding a new layer to the top of the layer stack and renaming it "Noise." Go to *Edit > Fill*, choose 50% Gray from the Contents menu, and click OK. Then go to *Filter > Noise > Add Noise*, set Amount to 3%, select Gaussian, and put a check in the Monochromatic checkbox (**Figure 6.96**). Click OK. Change the Blend Mode of the Noise layer to Soft Light (**Figure 6.97**) to hide the gray and reveal our picture, which now has added noise and texture.

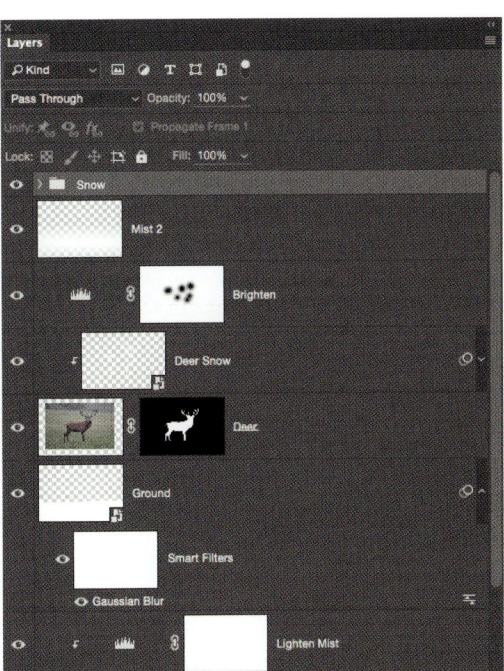

FIGURE 6.95 Adding multiple snow layers increases the depth and variation of the snow

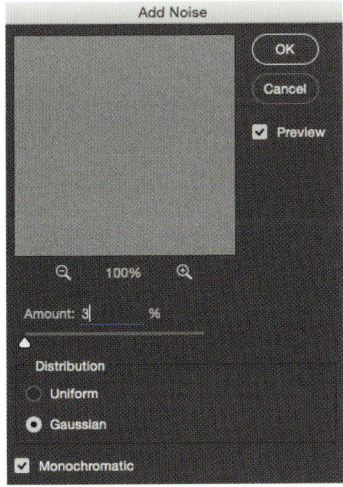

FIGURE 6.96

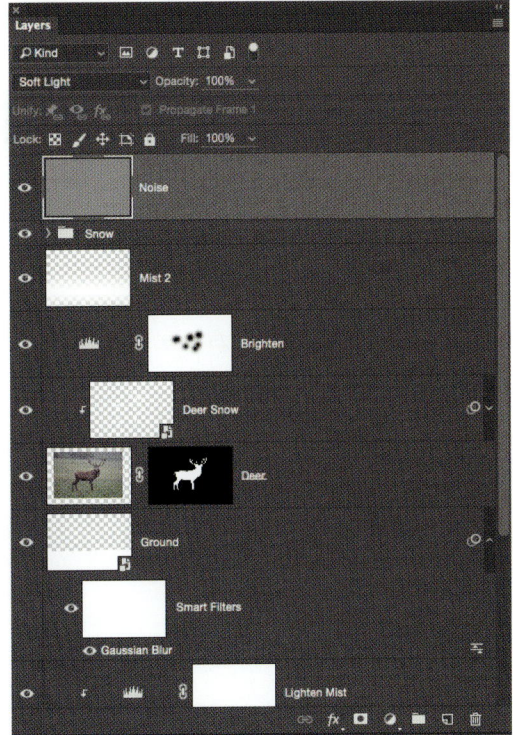

FIGURE 6.97

Hold down the Option key (Mac) or Alt key (PC) and click on the Hue/Saturation icon in the Adjustments panel to add a Hue/Saturation adjustment layer. Name this adjustment "Cool" and click OK. In the Hue/Saturation properties, click the Colorize checkbox and dial in Hue: 215 and Saturation: 25 (**Figure 6.98**). Lower the Opacity of the layer to 30%.

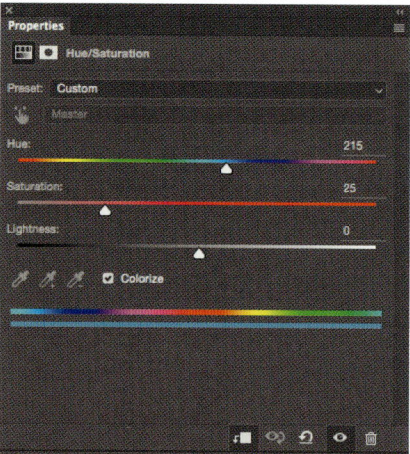

FIGURE 6.98

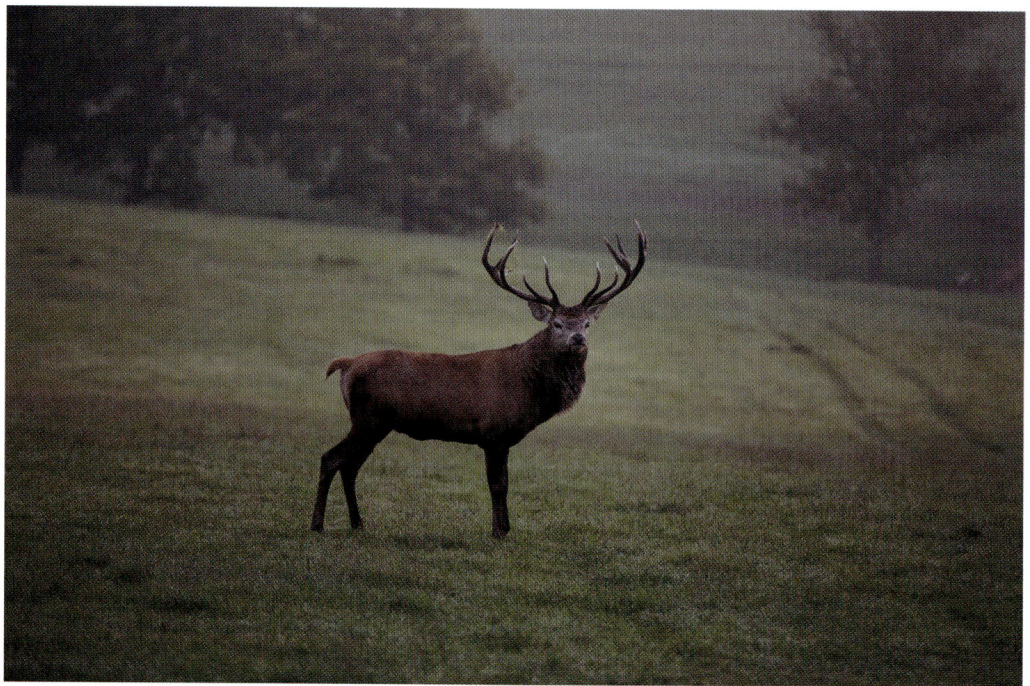

FIGURE 6.99 Original photograph

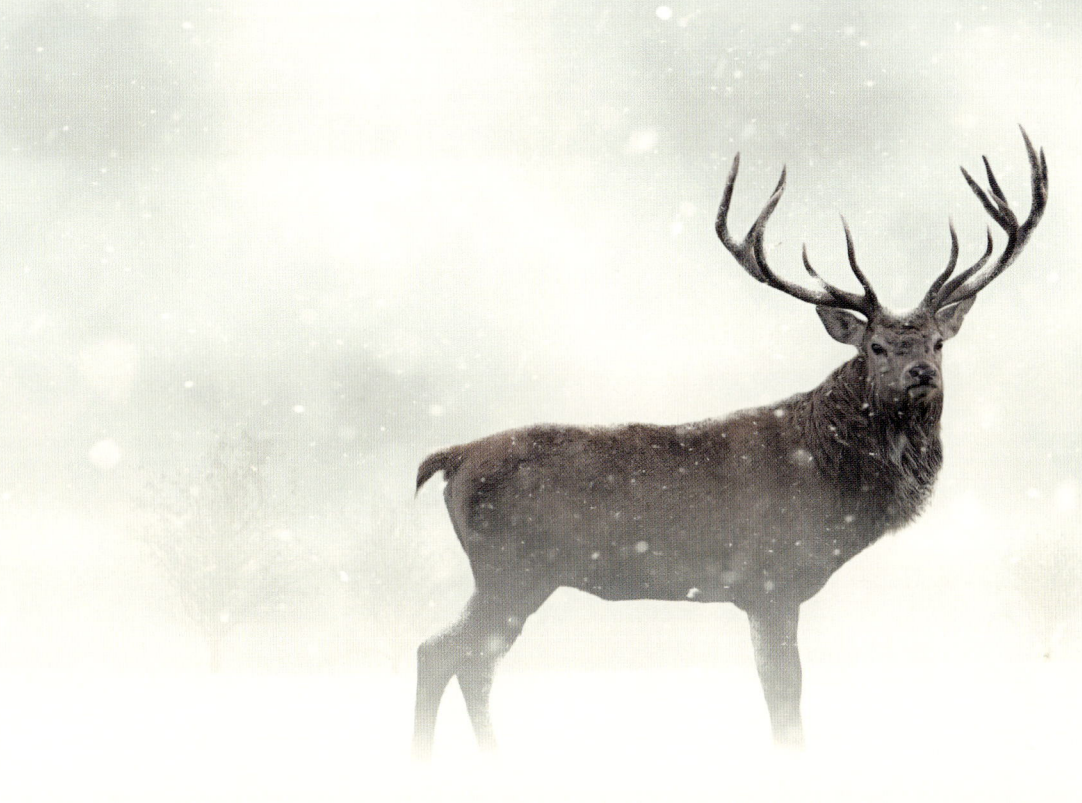

FIGURE 6.100 Final deer in snow composite

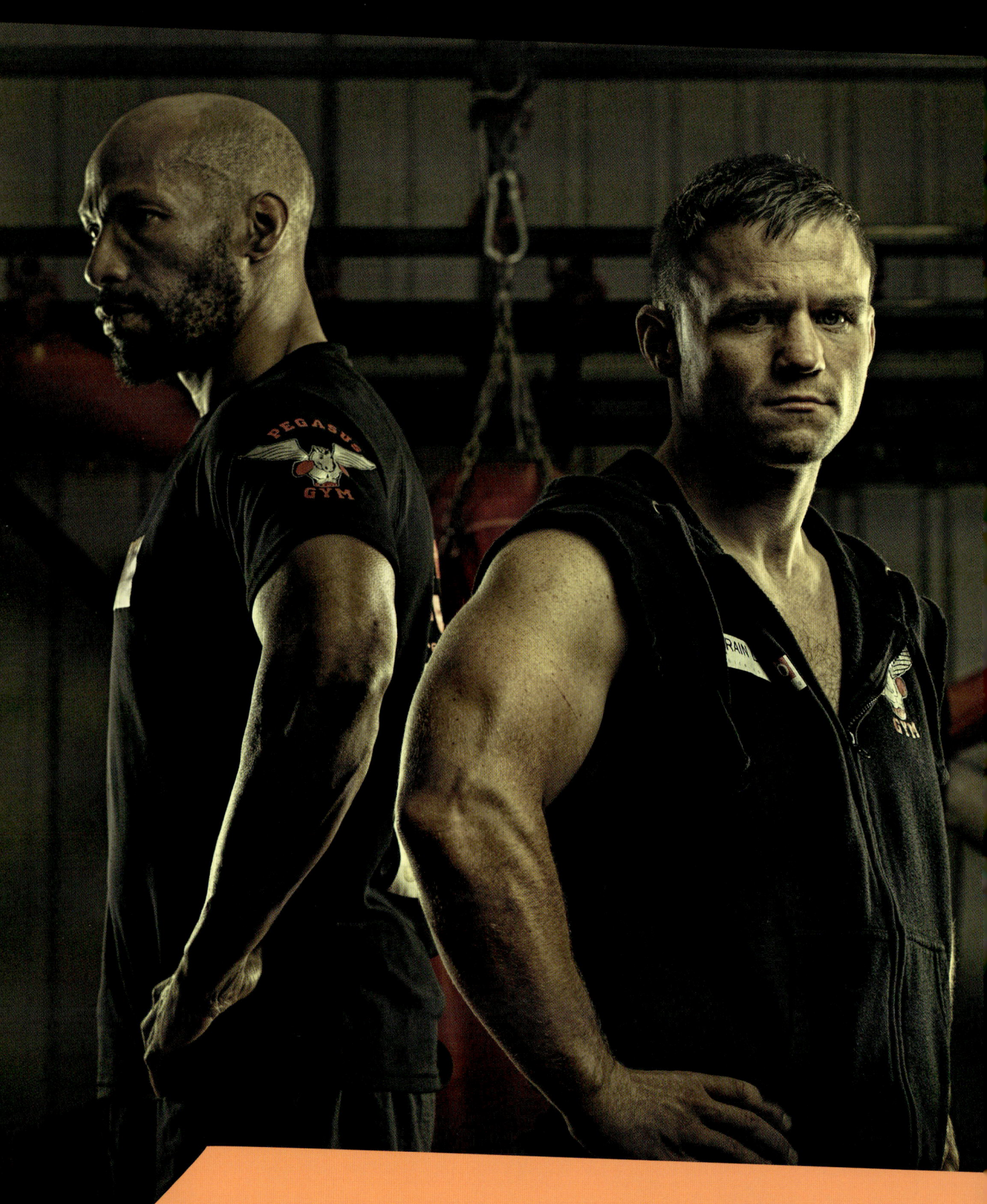

7 JOEY LAWRENCE INSPIRED

The very first time I became aware of Joey Lawrence was back when the first *Twilight* movie was released. Now don't get me wrong here, I'm not saying I'm a fan of the *Twilight* series (truth be told, I've never seen one of them), but I do remember being in London and seeing the good ol' London buses adorned with promotional pictures for the new movie—images that Joey had photographed at the crazy-young age of 18.

There's no mistaking a Joey Lawrence picture. His use of light, which the majority of the time seems to be just one light source, and the ever-so-slightly desaturated and cool look he gives his images during post-processing really appeals to me. As does the wide variety of subject matter he photographs, from musicians and movie stars to people in places such as Ethiopia and beyond.

One evening I was browsing around the Internet looking for inspiration and ideas for a new picture when I came across a picture that Joey had made for a docudrama on the National Geographic Channel called *Killing Lincoln*. You can see the image at: http://bit.ly/PLAT_joeyl.

Posing people together is always a challenge, so what initially drew me to this picture is how the key characters are pretty much standing back-to-back. This certainly isn't the way you would ordinarily position people, but here it works so well. I knew straight away where I could make use of this.

At the time, I was working on an ongoing photography project with World Champion Kickboxer Steven Cook and we'd been thinking about making a portrait of him and his coach, Michael Graham. Rather than try to explain what I wanted to do, I texted Steven the *Killing Lincoln* picture and told him I'd like to create something similar in terms of the pose and lighting. The next day it was game on, and we were off to the gym to shoot the picture.

REVERSE ENGINEERING

In the picture by Joey Lawrence we can see that the lighting is quite soft because there is no hard, defined line where the highlights and the shadows meet, but rather they gently blend into each other. That would suggest soft lighting, so we're going to say that soft boxes with both their inner and outer diffusion panels have certainly been used.

We can also say that the John Wilkes Booth character has been lit with cross lighting. The side of his face that's furthest away from the camera is well lit, and there is a triangular pattern of light underneath his eye and on his cheek on the side that's nearest the camera. This would certainly suggest that a light source is coming from the right-hand side of the frame and is slightly in front of John Wilkes Booth.

The profile of the Abraham Lincoln character is lit by a very defined white light going down his face onto his chest and hands. This light is even and defined, which suggests the possible use of a strip box positioned at the left-hand side of the frame.

Speaking of profiles, when we look back at John Wilkes Booth, although it's not quite as obvious, we can see that his profile has also been lit, and this light is brighter than that coming from the cross lighting. This tells us that a third light has been used, which could be something like a strip box placed at the right-hand side of the frame.

In summary, I think we can be pretty confident that three lights were used: two strip lights coming in from the left and right to illuminate the profiles of our characters, and the light source coming in from the right to provide cross lighting. The cross lighting also adds a little bit of fill light to the front of both characters to prevent the shadows from becoming too dark, which is important because both characters are wearing dark clothing. Having watched plenty of Joey Lawrence behind-the-scenes videos, I'm fairly confident that he used something like the Elinchrom Rotalux 135cm Octa Softbox.

THE SETUP

The diagram in **Figure 7.1** shows the approximate positioning of the lights I used for the photograph of Steven Cook and Michael Graham.

Rather than photograph in a studio, we decided to set up on location in Pegasus Gym so we could include an array of training equipment in the picture (**Figures 7.2** and **7.3**). This adds to the atmosphere and sets the scene.

FIGURE 7.1

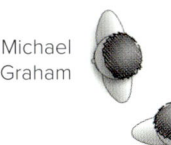
Elinchrom Rotalux
130cm x 50cm Soft Box

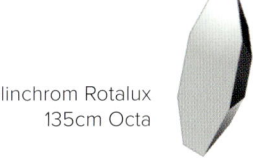
Elinchrom Rotalux
130cm x 50cm Soft Box

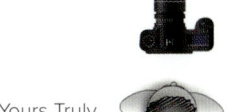
Michael
Graham

Steven Cook

Elinchrom Rotalux
135cm Octa

Yours Truly

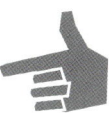

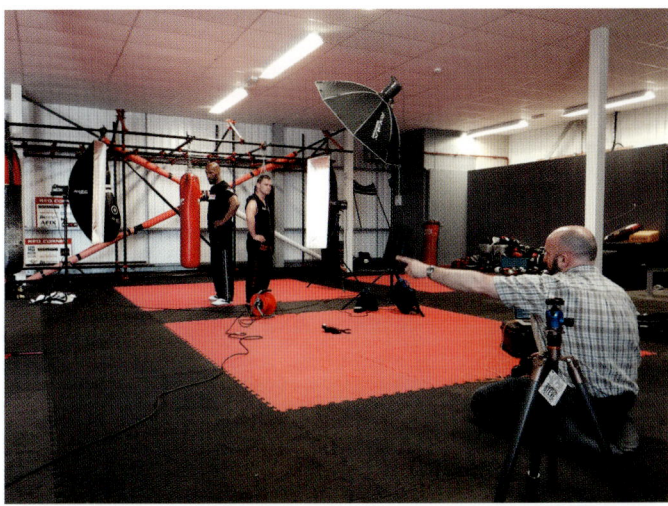

FIGURE 7.2

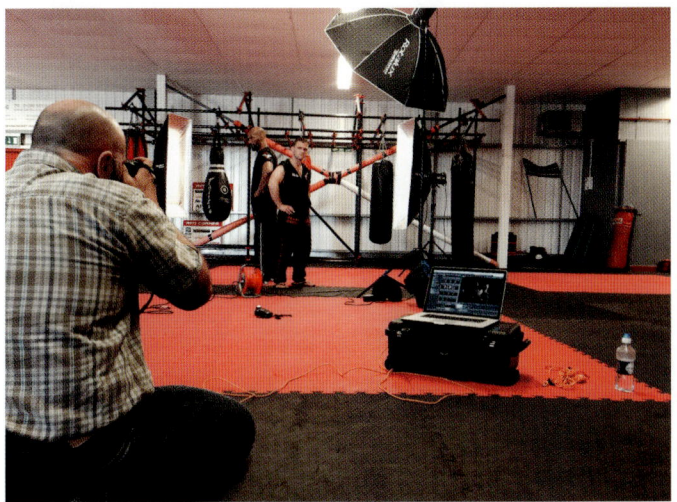

FIGURE 7.3 Tethered shooting with the images uploading directly into Adobe Photoshop Lightroom

NOTE *Notice how the outer diffusion panel on each softbox has been removed, leaving just the inner diffusion panel. I did this to create a light that is slightly harder than that in Joey Lawrence's* Killing Lincoln *photograph and is more fitting for Steven and Mike.*

CAMERA SETTINGS

I chose to use an aperture of f/5.6 to keep the subjects sharp and the background slightly out of focus. Therefore, the main light (the Octa) was metered to give a reading of f/5.6, and the two strip lights profiling Steven and Mike were metered approximately 1 stop brighter.

I kept the ISO low to give me the cleanest possible file with no noise. I used a shutter speed of 1/125s because it's a good sync speed and it allowed enough of the ambient light from the studio into the picture.

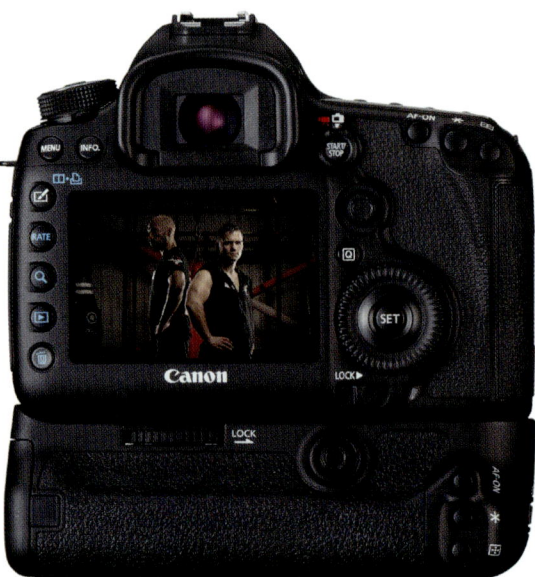

FIGURE 7.4

MODE Manual

ISO 100

APERTURE f/5.6

SHUTTER SPEED 1/125 sec.

LENS 85mm f/1.8

GEAR GUIDE

For this setup I used two Elincrhom Rotalux 50 × 130cm Strip Softboxes (**Figure 7.5**), an Elinchrom Rotalux 135cm Octa Softbox (**Figure 7.6**), an Elinchrom ELC Pro HD 1000 flash head (**Figure 7.7**), and an Elinchrom D-Lite RX One flash head (**Figure 7.8**).

As you can see, I like to use Elinchrom lights and modifiers, but this is just my personal preference, of course.

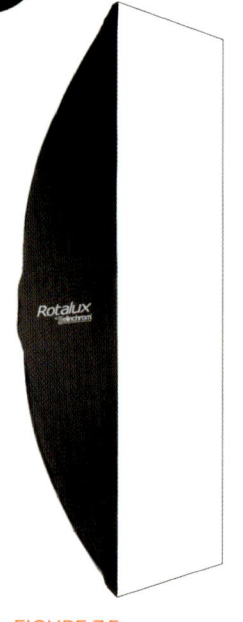

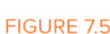

FIGURE 7.5   FIGURE 7.6

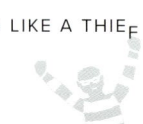

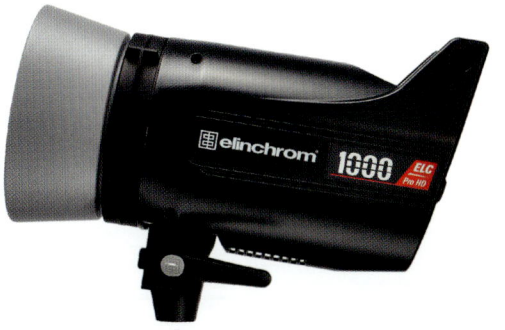

FIGURE 7.7

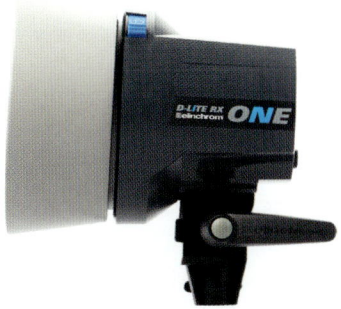

FIGURE 7.8 I use D-Lite RX One on a boom or whenever I need to position a light up high because it's incredibly light.

SMALL FLASH GEAR GUIDE

For those of you who tend to favor using speedlights as opposed to big, powerful, studio-style lights, nowadays there are so many modifiers available to us that are produced by a range of companies.

To achieve a look that is very similar to that provided by my three-light setup, you could use your speedlights with modifiers such as the Lastolite Hotrod Strip Softbox 30cm (**Figure 7.9**) and Lastolite Ezybox II Octa (**Figure 7.10**).

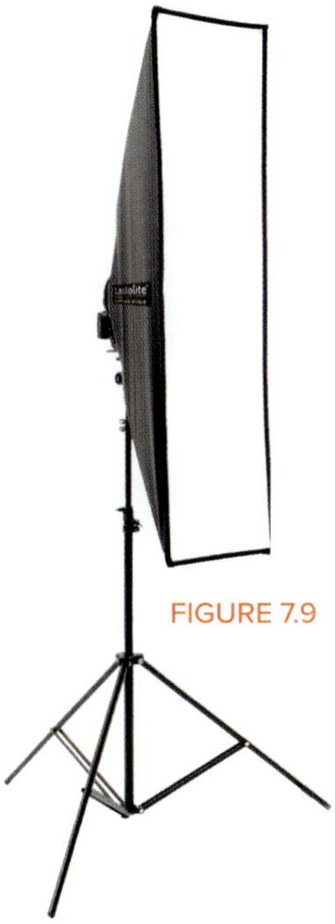

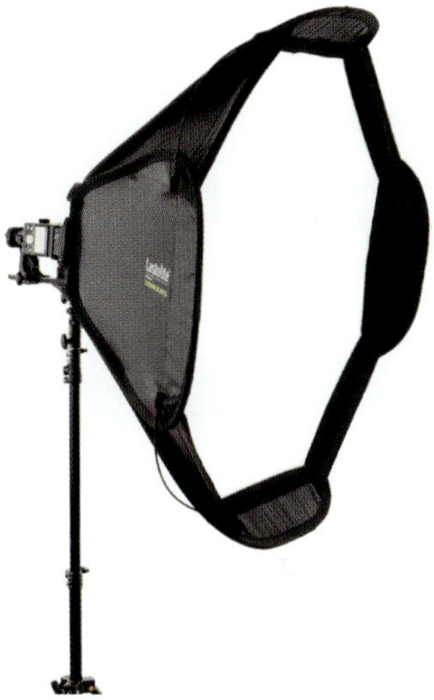

POST-PROCESSING

Some of the adjustments we're going to make to this picture are obvious, like adding in texture and an overall color grading, but there's also some that are not so obvious. In the original RAW image, Steven is sharp and in focus, whereas parts of Michael are slightly out of focus. The difference isn't huge, but even so, we can definitely improve the image very quickly using a filter in Photoshop. I'll also show you one sneaky little technique that I use on almost all male portraits to make them appear much more powerful. Overall though, there isn't a huge amount of work that needs to be done to get this picture to where we want it to be. But of course, if you're going to "steal" this setup and look, you can go on to add your own touches, too.

FIGURE 7.9

FIGURE 7.10

NOTE *Download the image file you need to follow along step-by-step at: http://www.rockynook.com/photograph-like-a-thief-reference/*

1. Here's the original, as-shot, RAW image open in Lightroom. Even though we'll be altering the overall color later on, it's always a good idea to give yourself the best starting point, so let's fix the white balance. As luck would have it, the back wall in the gym was a neutral grey, so all we have to do is select the White Balance Tool (**W**) and click on an area just above Steven's head (**Figure 7.11**).

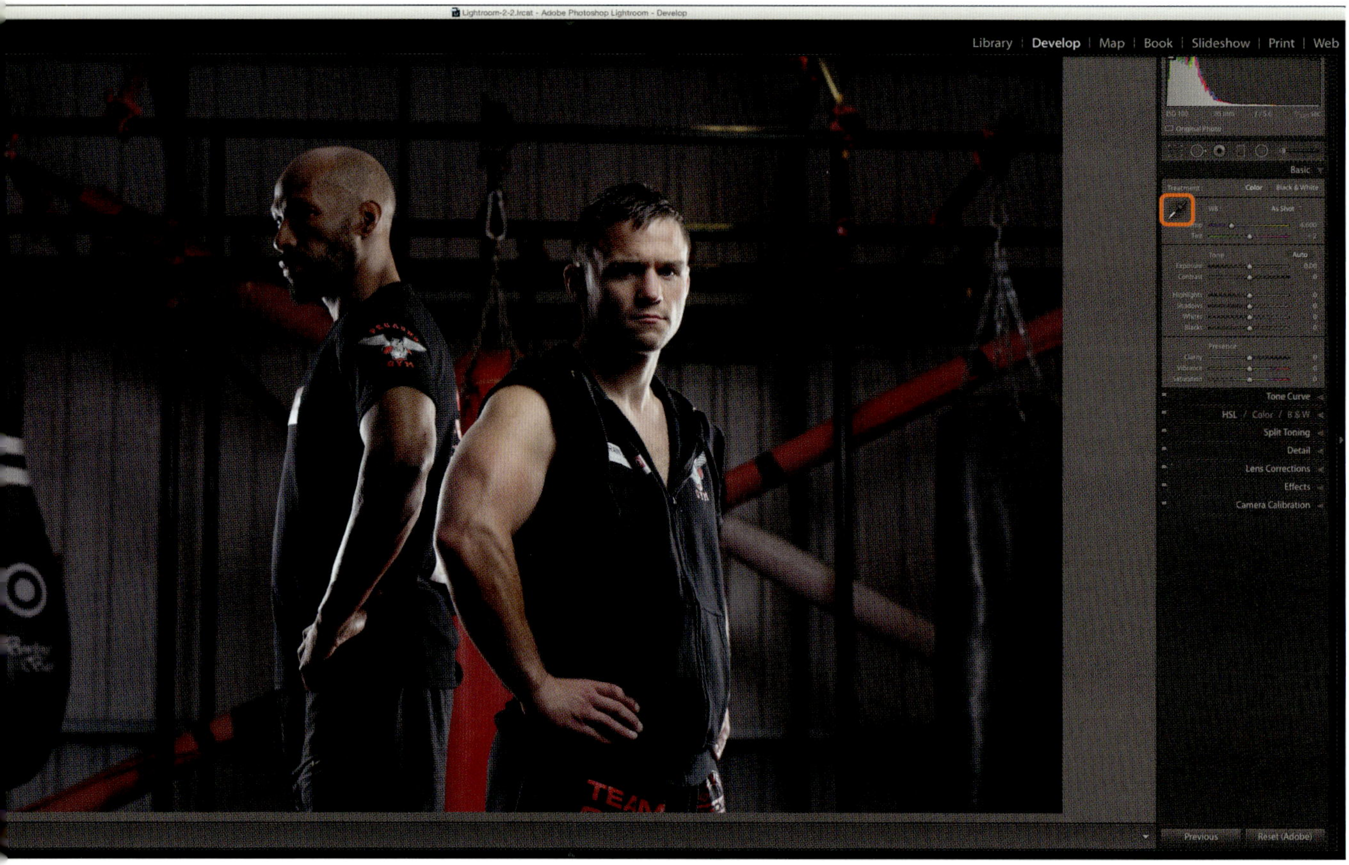

FIGURE 7.11

2. Next we need to straighten the image. To do this, click on the Crop Tool (**R**) and then the Angle Tool (**Figure 7.12**). Bring the cursor over into the image area, click on an area along the top of the back wall, and without releasing, drag out a line to the right following the line of the back wall (**Figure 7.13**). Then release. This has straightened our picture, so now we'll alter the composition slightly by dragging the crop handles in from the bottom and top. Press Return (Mac) or Enter (PC).

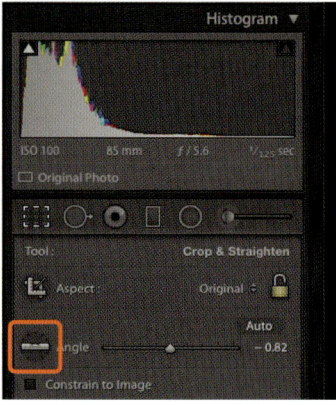

FIGURE 7.12

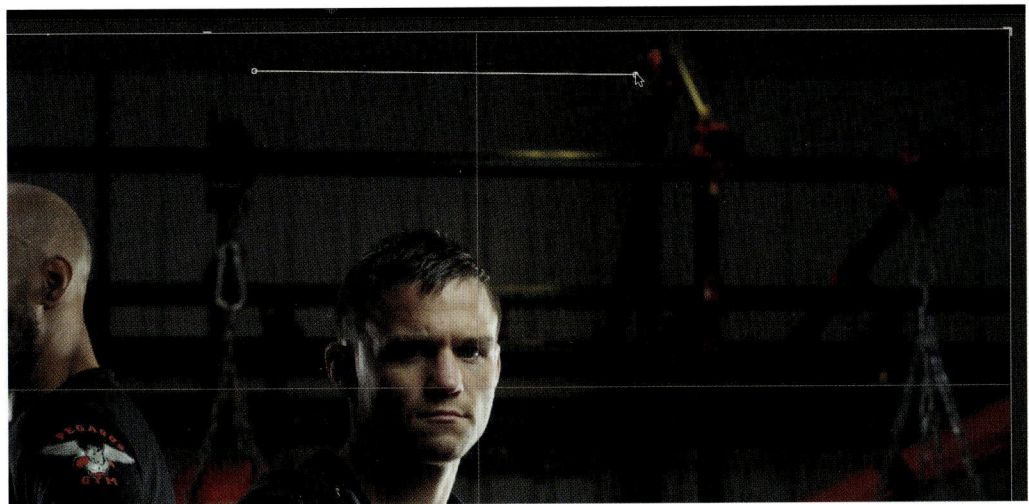

FIGURE 7.13

3. Because both Steven and Michael are wearing dark clothing, the shadow areas could use a little more detail. We can sort this out a by dragging the Shadows slider in the Basic Panel all the way to the right to reach +100 (**Figure 7.14**). Looking at Steven's face, we can see that we also need to reduce the highlights a little by dragging the slider to the left to around -14.

4. Let's brighten the shadow areas on both Steven and Michael's faces so that their eyes show up a little more. Select the Adjustment Brush (**K**), and then double-click on the word Effect to reset all the sliders to zero. Increase the Shadows slider to 50 (**Figure 7.15**) and turn on Show Selected Mask Overlay (**Figure 7.16**).

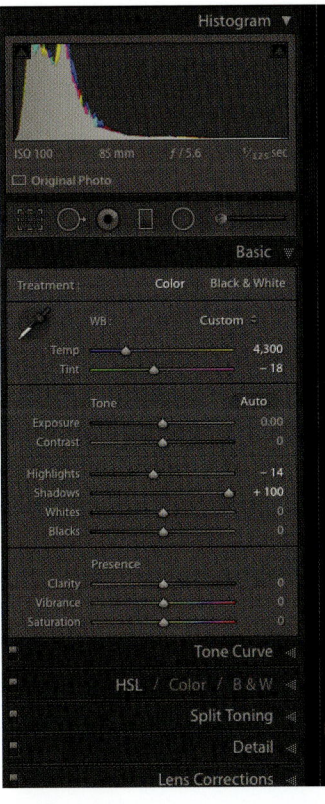

FIGURE 7.14

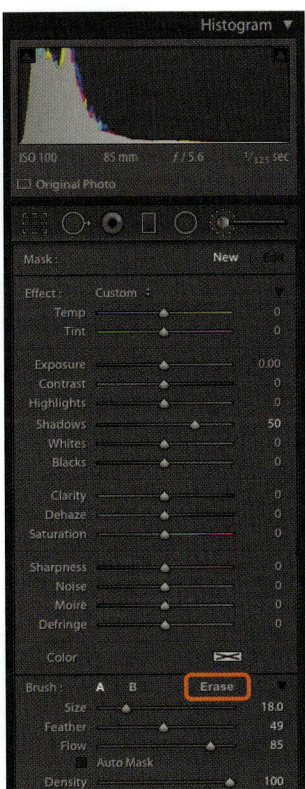

FIGURE 7.15

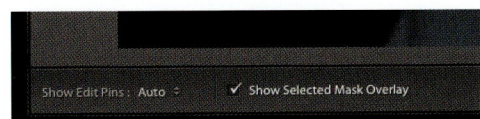

FIGURE 7.16

Brush over Steven and Michael's faces so that you see the red overlay covering only the shadow areas you want to enhance (**Figure 7.17**). If you paint over unwanted areas, click on Erase at the bottom of the Adjustment Brush Panel and paint over the areas to remove the red overlay. Turn off Show Selected Mask Overlay (**O**), and then increase or decrease the Shadows slider to taste. (Note: I increased the Shadows slider to 100.)

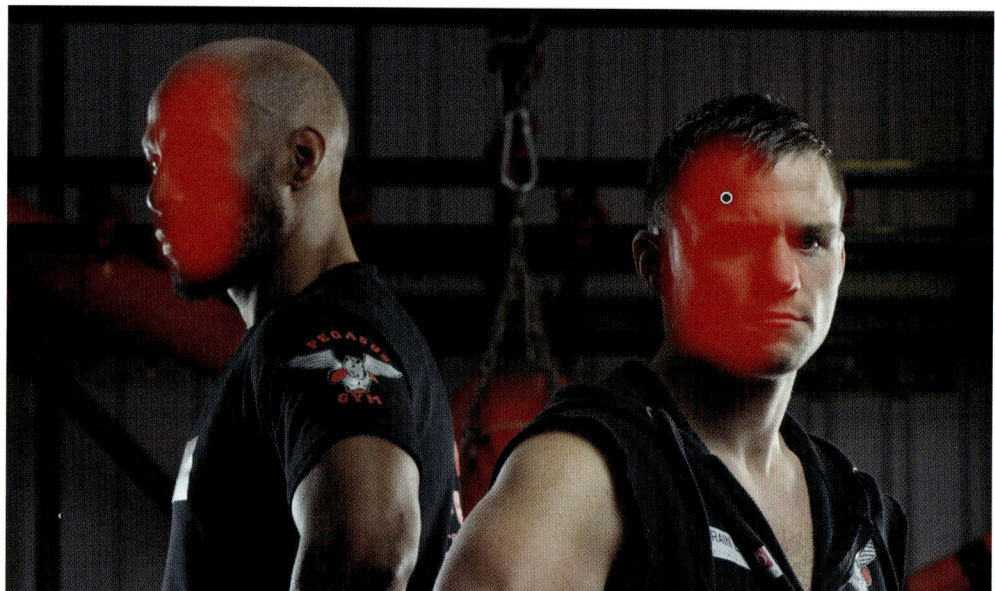

FIGURE 7.17

5. I always like to add sharpening at this stage in Lightroom because I feel it does such a great job and also because we can use the masking slider to quickly and easily control which areas are sharpened. Open the Detail tab, and in the Sharpening section, increase Amount to around 50 (**Figure 7.18**). I tend to use this amount quite often on male portraits. Leave the Radius and Detail sliders at their defaults of 1.0 and 25. While holding down the Option key (Mac) or Alt key (PC), click and drag the Masking slider to the right to around 80. The black-and-white mask on the image indicates what is (white) and isn't (black) being sharpened (**Figure 7.19**).

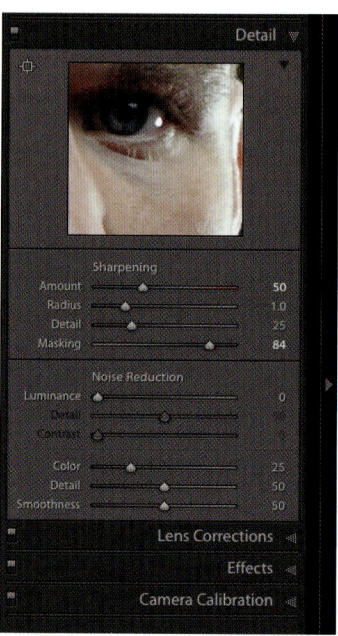

FIGURE 7.18

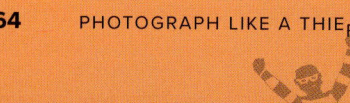

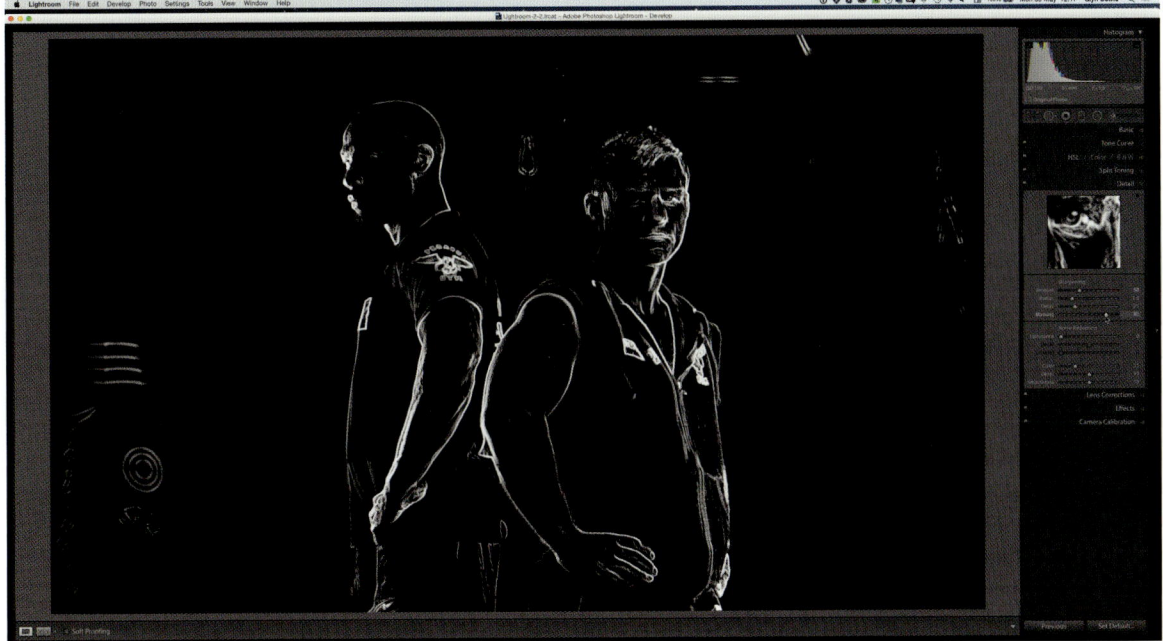

FIGURE 7.19 White areas on the mask indicate the areas that are being sharpened

6. Before heading into Photoshop, we'll shape the light to draw more attention to Steven and Michael by adding in a vignette. Open the Effects tab and drag the Amount slider to -40. Leave all other sliders at their defaults (**Figure 7.20**).

7. Now we're now ready to send this file over into Photoshop. Ordinarily, I would send the file as a Smart Object so I could continue working nondestructively. However, we haven't done any major steps so far, so we can send it to Photoshop as a regular layer by going to *Photo > Edit In > Edit In Adobe Photoshop CC* (**Figure 7.21**), or simply press Command + E (Mac) or Ctrl + E (PC: Ctrl).

8. Now that we're in Photoshop, let's sort out that sharpness issue on Michael. We'll do this with the Shake Reduction filter, which is not a filter I tend to use all that much, thankfully, but when I have used it it's does a great job. Of course, it has its limitations, but for the right picture it can really save the day.

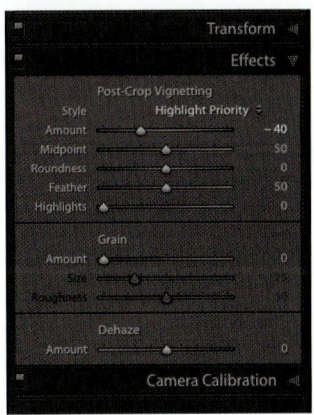

FIGURE 7.20

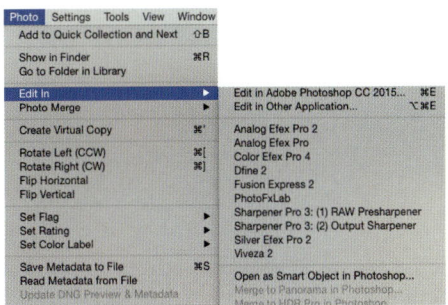

FIGURE 7.21

Press Command + J (Mac) or Ctrl + J (PC) to create a copy of the background layer, and then go to *Filter > Sharpen > Shake Reduction*. In the Shake Reduction dialog, drag the square boundary over Michael's face and resize it by dragging on the outer handles (**Figure 7.22**). I tend to use the default settings and very rarely adjust them, so once the filter has finished processing, just click OK.

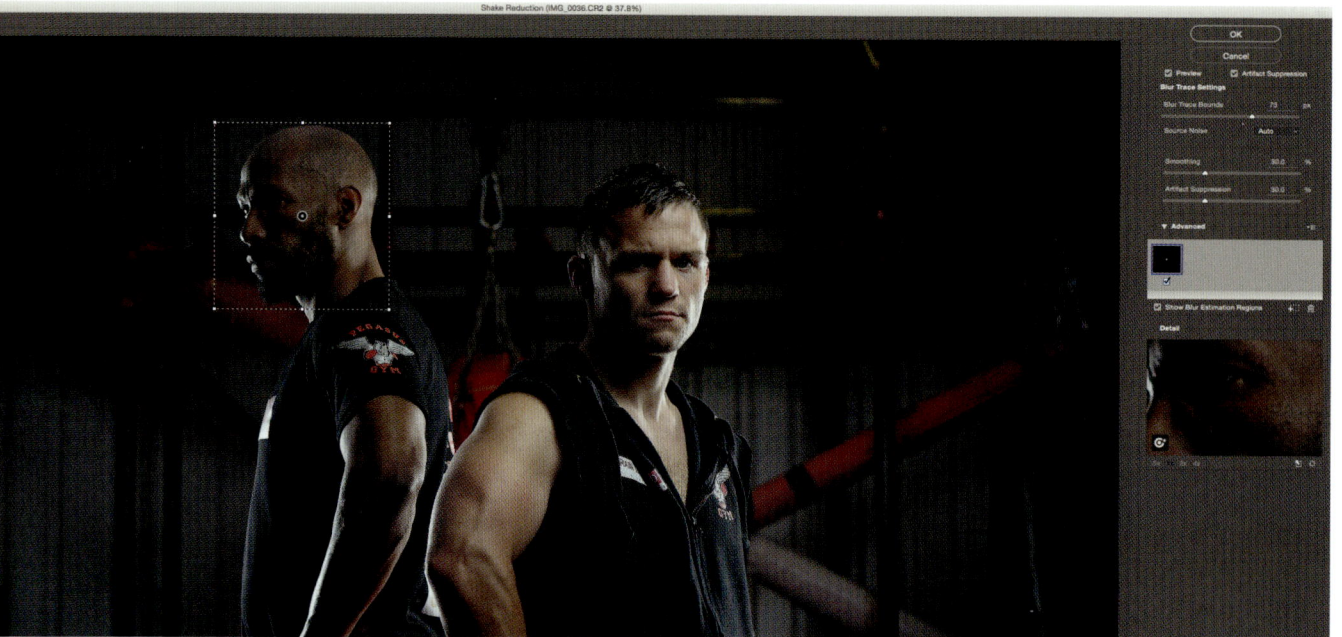

FIGURE 7.22

9. We want to apply the Shake Reduction filter mainly on Michael's face, so we'll mask out the other areas. Hold down the Option key (Mac) or Alt key (PC) and click on the Add Layer Mask icon at the bottom of the Layers panel (**Figure 7.23**). This adds a black layer mask that hides the results of the Shake Reduction filter. Press D on the keyboard, and then with a normal, round, soft-edged brush (**B**), paint over Michael's face to reveal the results of the Shake Reduction filter. Rename this layer "Reduce Shake."

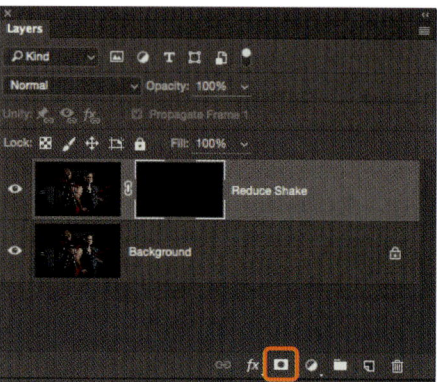

FIGURE 7.23

You can see the results of the Shake Reduction figure by looking at **Figure 7.24** (before) and **7.25** (after). Naturally, this filter has limitations, but on an image such as this, the results can be very impressive.

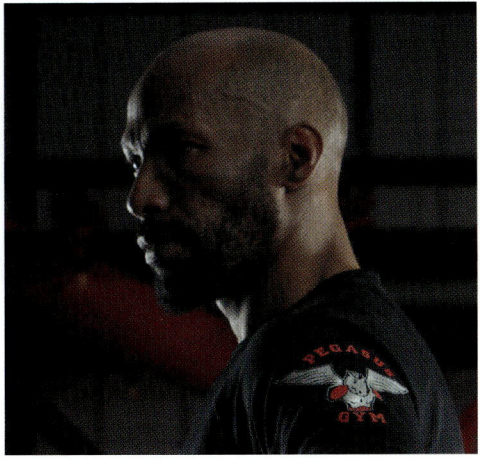

FIGURE 7.24 Before Shake Reduction

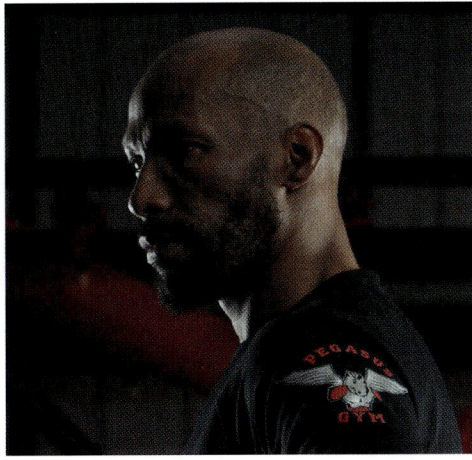

FIGURE 7.25 After Shake Reduction

10. Now here's that sneaky tip you can use to give male portraits a little more power: Add a merged layer to the top of the layer stack by pressing Command + Option + Shift + E (Mac) or Ctrl + Alt + Shift + E (PC), or by going to *Select > All*, then *Edit > Copy Merged*, then *Edit Paste*. Rename this layer "Widen." Then go to *Edit > Free Transform*, and in the options bar at the top of the screen, change the width (W) to 105% (**Figure 7.26**) and press Return (Mac) or Enter (PC). At first it's hard to see any difference, but try turning the layer on and off by clicking the eye icon to the left of the layer, and you'll see the change.

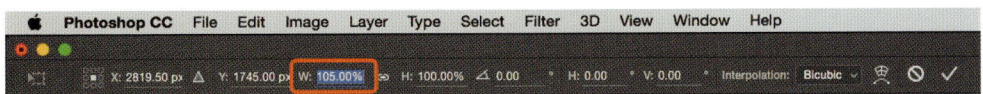

FIGURE 7.26

TIP *When using this Free Transform trick to give male portraits more power, increase the width to anywhere between 100% and 105%, but avoid going any further than that; otherwise; you'll stretch the image too much and it will be obvious that you've done something to alter it. This trick could also be used on female portraits, but you may want to go to 95% instead of 105%.*

11. We could do with a little body reshaping, mainly because of the way the clothing is hanging on both Steven and Michael. We'll do this with the Liquify Filter. Thanks to an update, we can now use the Liquify Filter as a Smart Object. This means we can alter any changes we make later, as opposed to having to completely redo them from scratch.

Add another merged layer to the top of the layer stack by pressing Command + Option + Shift + E (Mac) or Ctrl + Alt + Shift + E (PC). Rename this layer "Liquify" (**Figure 7.27**). Go to *Filter > Convert for Smart Filters*, then *Filter > Liquify*.

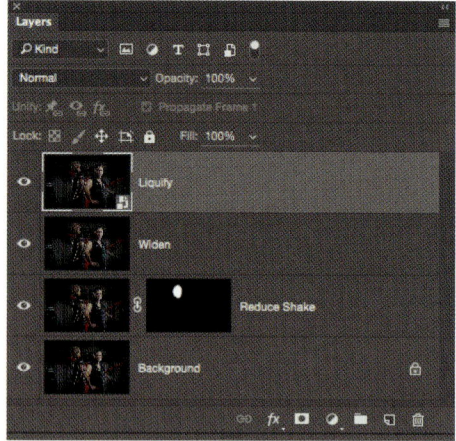

FIGURE 7.27

First we're going to work on Michael's T-shirt. In the Liquify filter dialog, choose the Freeze Mask Tool (**F**) (**Figure 7.28**) and paint over some of the area in front of Michael, his arm, and his hand to protect them from being affected. The areas you paint will be covered with a red overlay (**Figure 7.29**). Now choose the Forward Warp Tool (**W**) and increase the Size to around 1000. (Tip: You can increase or decrease the size by using the right and left bracket keys.) Then press down and drag the circle to the right over Michael's T-shirt to bring it in at the waist (**Figure 7.30**).

Repeat this process on Steven to bring in the lower area of his top.

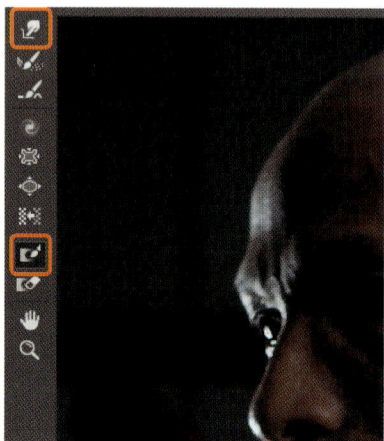

FIGURE 7.28 Freeze Mask Tool (bottom square) and Forward Warp Tool (top square)

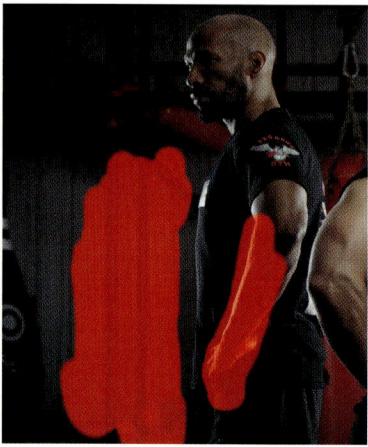

FIGURE 7.29 The Freeze Mask protects areas from being affected when you use tools in the Liquify filter dialog

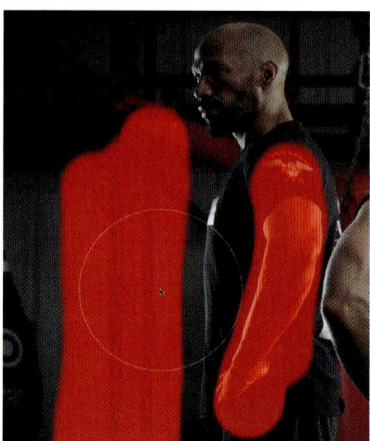

FIGURE 7.30

12. Now we'll give this picture a bit more punch (no pun intended) by using the third-party plugin Topaz Clarity from Topaz Labs. I love the way this plugin allows you to control different levels of contrast, from Micro to High, and although I only use a fraction its features, I really do like the results I get with it. I use only the Micro Contrast and Low Contrast sliders since these tend to add much more texture and dimension to skin, which is what we're after. Generally, I'll increase Micro Contrast to around 0.25 and Low Contrast to 0.10 (**Figure 7.31**). After you've adjusted the sliders, click OK.

13. In Joey Lawrence's *Killing Lincoln* photograph, there's definitely some smoke or fog that adds to the atmosphere, and I think adding this to the picture of Steven and Michael would work really well. Add a new blank layer to the top of the layer stack, and then press D on the keyboard to set the foreground and background colors to their defaults of black and white. Next go to *Filter > Render > Clouds*, and Photoshop will add the most unrealistic-looking clouds ever! Grab the Rectangular Marquee Tool and drag out a selection in the middle of these Photoshop Clouds (**Figure 7.32**). Press Command + J (Mac) or Ctrl + J (PC) to create a new layer containing this selected area of clouds. Rename this layer "smoke" (**Figure 7.33**).

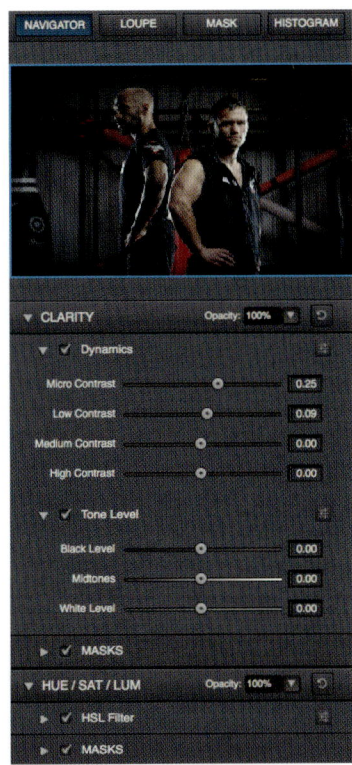

FIGURE 7.31 Using the Micro Contrast and Low Contrast sliders is a great way to enhance texture in skin and clothing

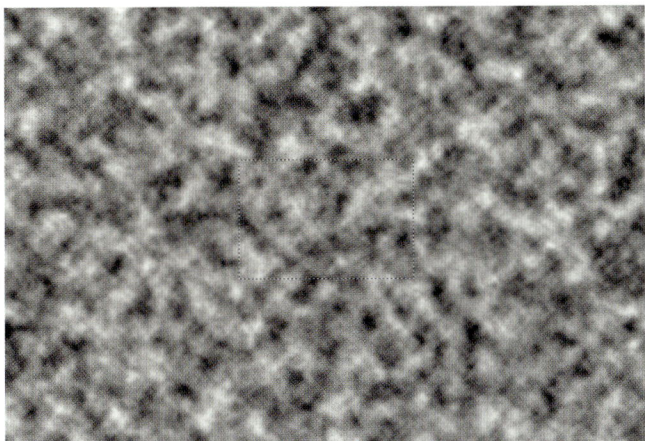

FIGURE 7.32 Use the Marquee Tool to select a small area of the Photoshop Clouds

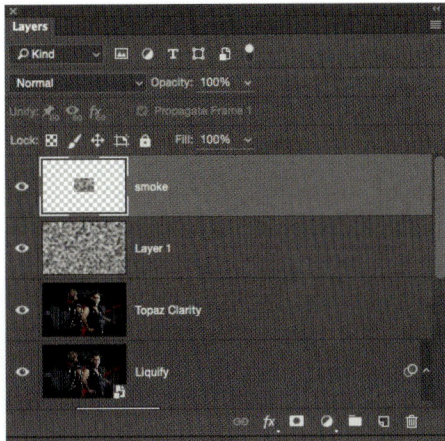

FIGURE 7.33

14. We don't need the original layer containing the Photoshop Clouds filter so we can just delete it. Now click on the smoke layer and zoom out a bit so that there is some space around the image in the main workspace. Then go to *Edit > Free Transform*. Hold down Shift + Option (Mac) or Shift + Alt (PC) and click on a corner transform handle and drag it outward to make the smoke layer much, much bigger (**Figure 7.34**). Press Return (Mac) or Enter (PC), and then lower the Opacity of the smoke layer to around 25% (**Figure 7.35**).

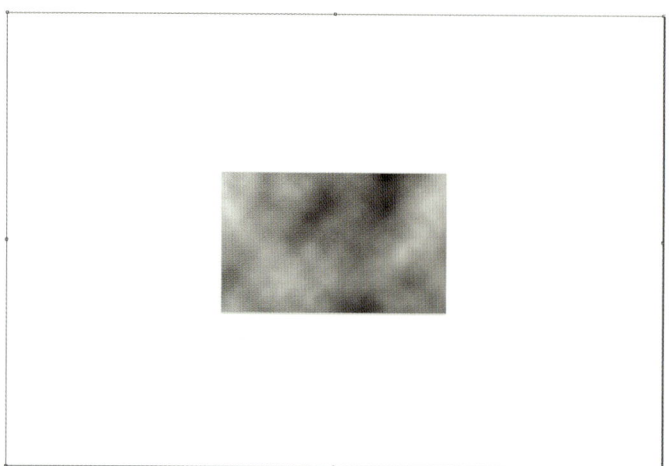

FIGURE 7.34

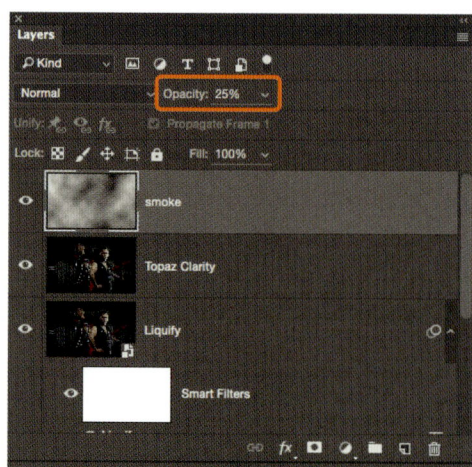

FIGURE 7.35

15. It looks like there are some lights in the upper-left and upper-right corners of the *Killing Lincoln* photograph, so we'll add a couple of fake lights in the corners of our picture as well. We'll use what I call The World's Simplest Lighting Effect, because it really is exactly that.

Add a new blank layer to the top of the layer stack and rename it "Light Left." With a white foreground color and a normal, round soft-edged brush, click once in the center of the picture (**Figure 7.36**).

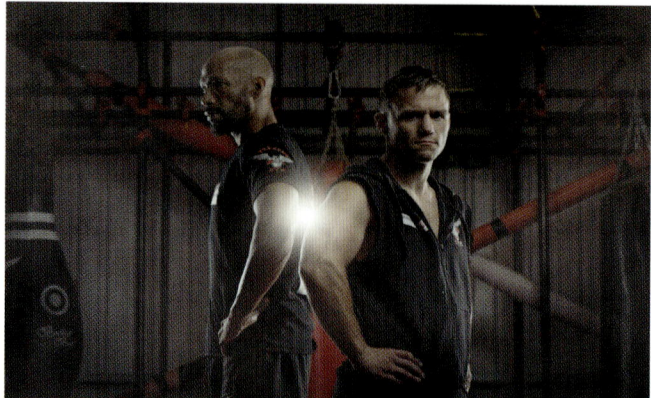

FIGURE 7.36

Zoom out and then go to *Edit > Free Transform*. Hold down Shift + Option (Mac) or Shift + Alt (PC) and drag outward to increase the size (**Figure 7.37**), and then press Return (Mac) or Enter (PC). Select the Move Tool and click and drag the "light" into the top-left corner of the picture so that only the soft area is visible and the center is outside of the picture area. Lower the Opacity to around 80%. Copy the Light Left layer by holding down Command + J (Mac) or Ctrl +J (PC) + J, rename it "Light Right," and use the Move Tool to drag the "light" across to the upper-right corner (**Figures 7.38** and **7.39**).

The next steps are where we add the finishing touches and these are subject to personal taste. I'll take you through the steps I did to get to my final image, but it's worth noting that I generally perform these steps after taking a break and then returning to the picture. Giving yourself some time away from the screen will help you to look at your picture with fresh eyes and instantly see what you need or want to do.

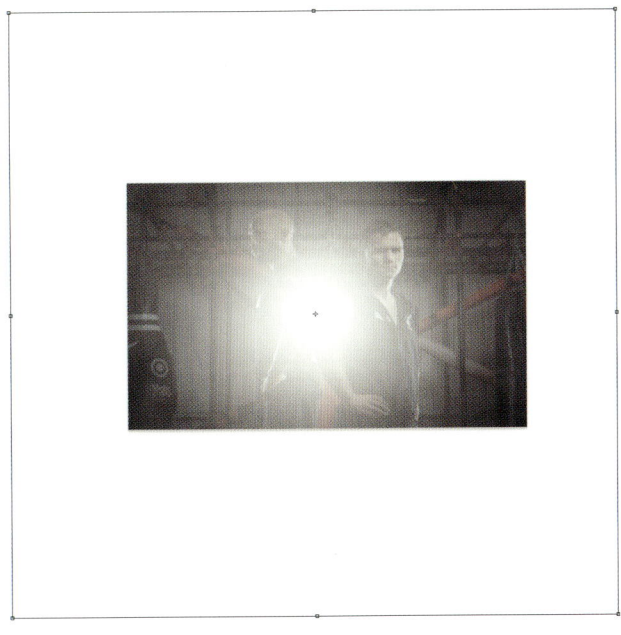

FIGURE 7.37

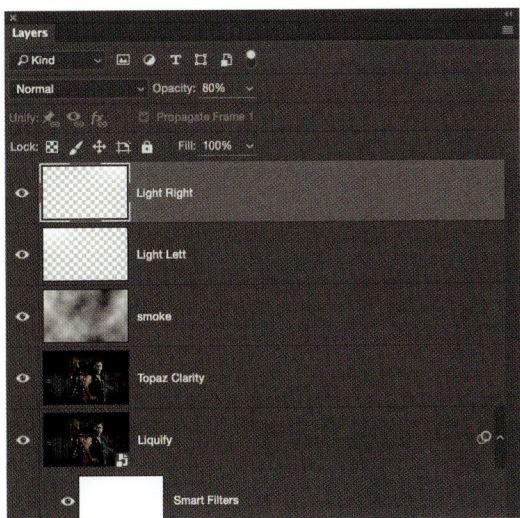

FIGURE 7.38

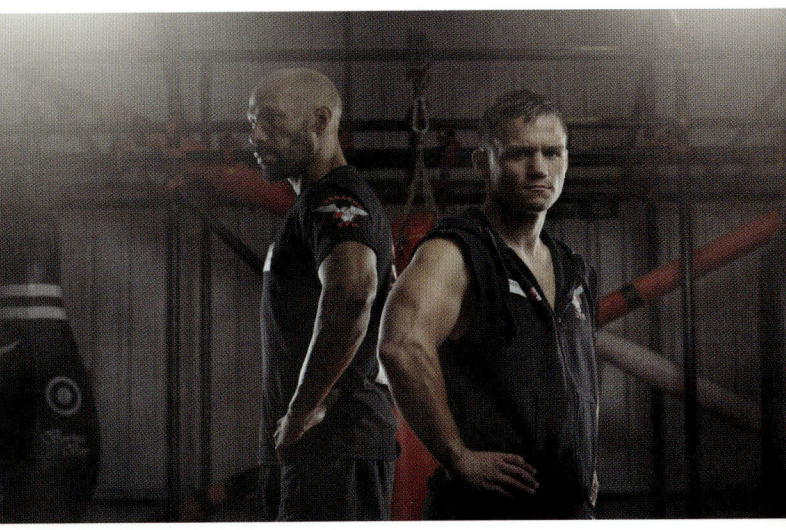

FIGURE 7.39

16. Add a merged layer to the top of the layer stack by pressing Command + Option + Shift + E (Mac) or Ctrl + Alt + Shift + E (PC). Now we're going to use the Nik Collection Color Efex Pro 4 plugin to color grade the picture. As I mentioned in chapter 4 (page 56) there are alternative plugins and techniques you can use here, but at the time of writing this book, I favor this Nik Collection plugin from Google.

Open the plugin by going to *Filter > Nik Collection > Color Efex Pro 4*. Choose Cross Processing and select Y06 from the Method menu (**Figure 7.40**). Increase the Strength slider to 60 and click OK (**Figure 7.41**).

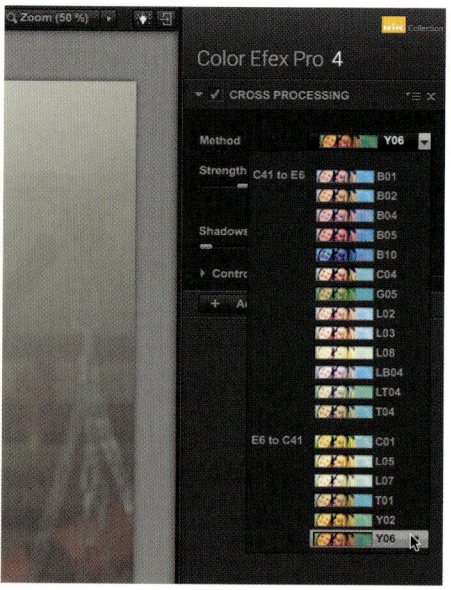

FIGURE 7.40

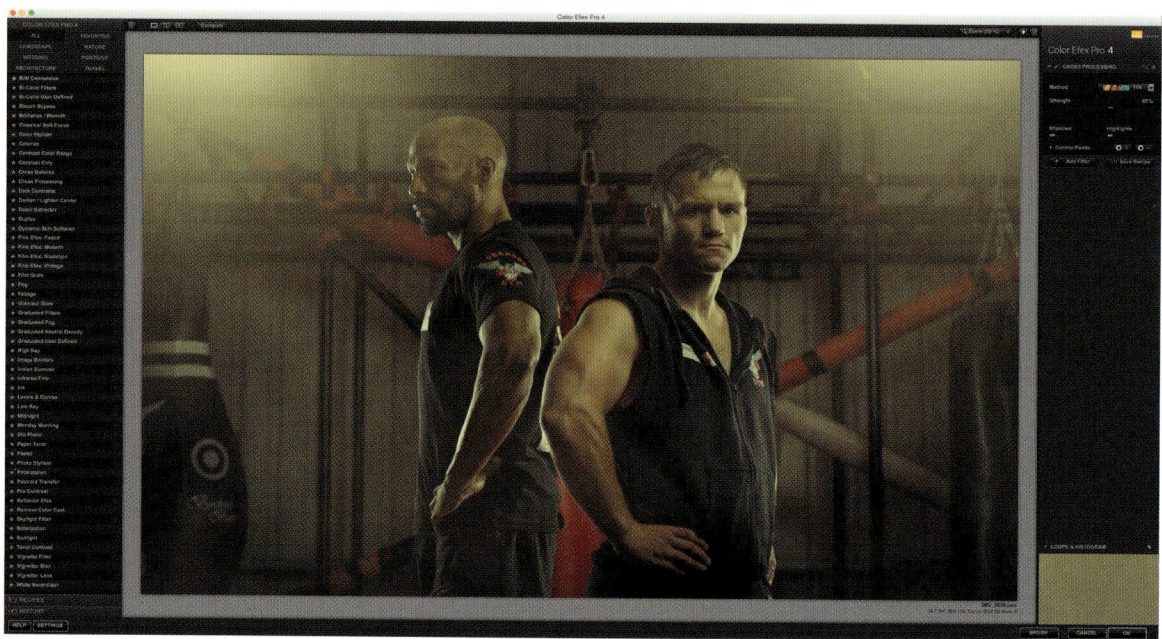

FIGURE 7.41

17. We'll use the Nik Collection Silver Efex Pro 2 plugin to desaturate the image. Go to *Filter > Nik Collection > Silver Efex Pro 2*. Use the default Neutral black-and-white filter that is applied when you first enter the plugin, increase the Structure to 40% (**Figure 7.42**), and click OK. Once you're back in Photoshop, lower the Opacity of this layer to around 25% (**Figure 7.43**).

18. To finish off I think we need to add a little more contrast and texture to the picture to increase the drama and mood. To do this, we'll make one more visit to Topaz Clarity. Press Command + Option + Shift + E (Mac) or Ctrl + Alt + Shift + E (PC) to add a merged layer to the top of the layer stack, rename it Topaz Clarity, and go *Filter > Topaz Labs > Topaz Clarity*. Click OK to use the previous settings.

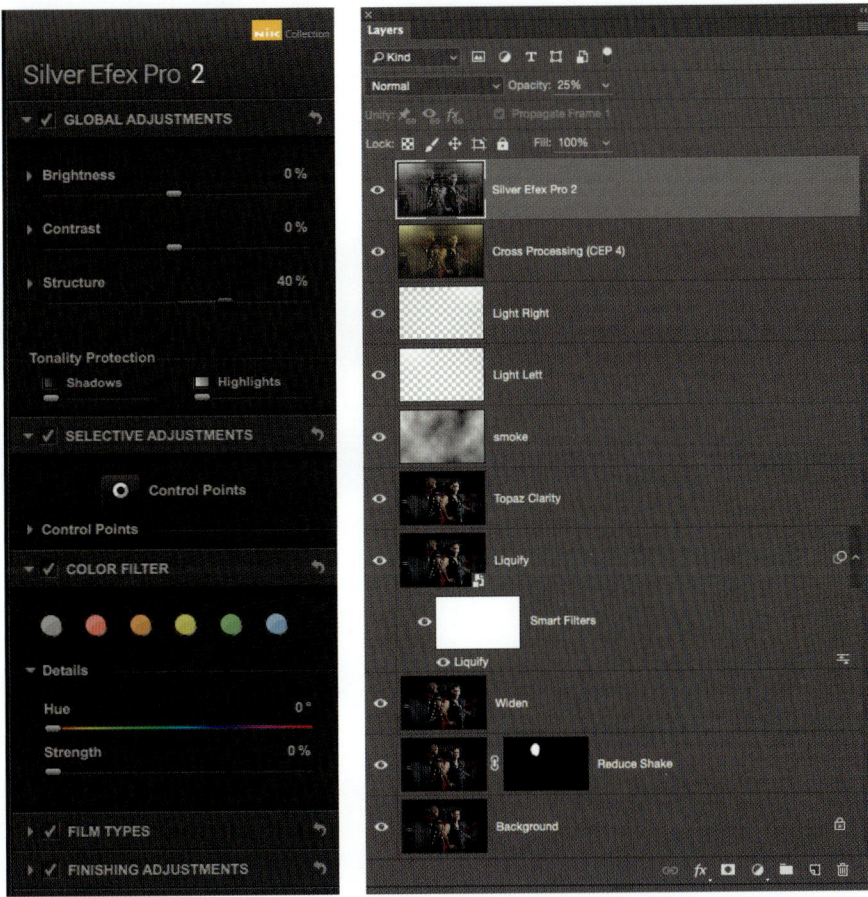

FIGURE 7.42　　　FIGURE 7.43

As I said, adding these final finishing touches is very much a matter of personal taste. I'll often dive in and out of plugins and try out different Photoshop techniques until I get the look I'm after (**Figure 7.44**).

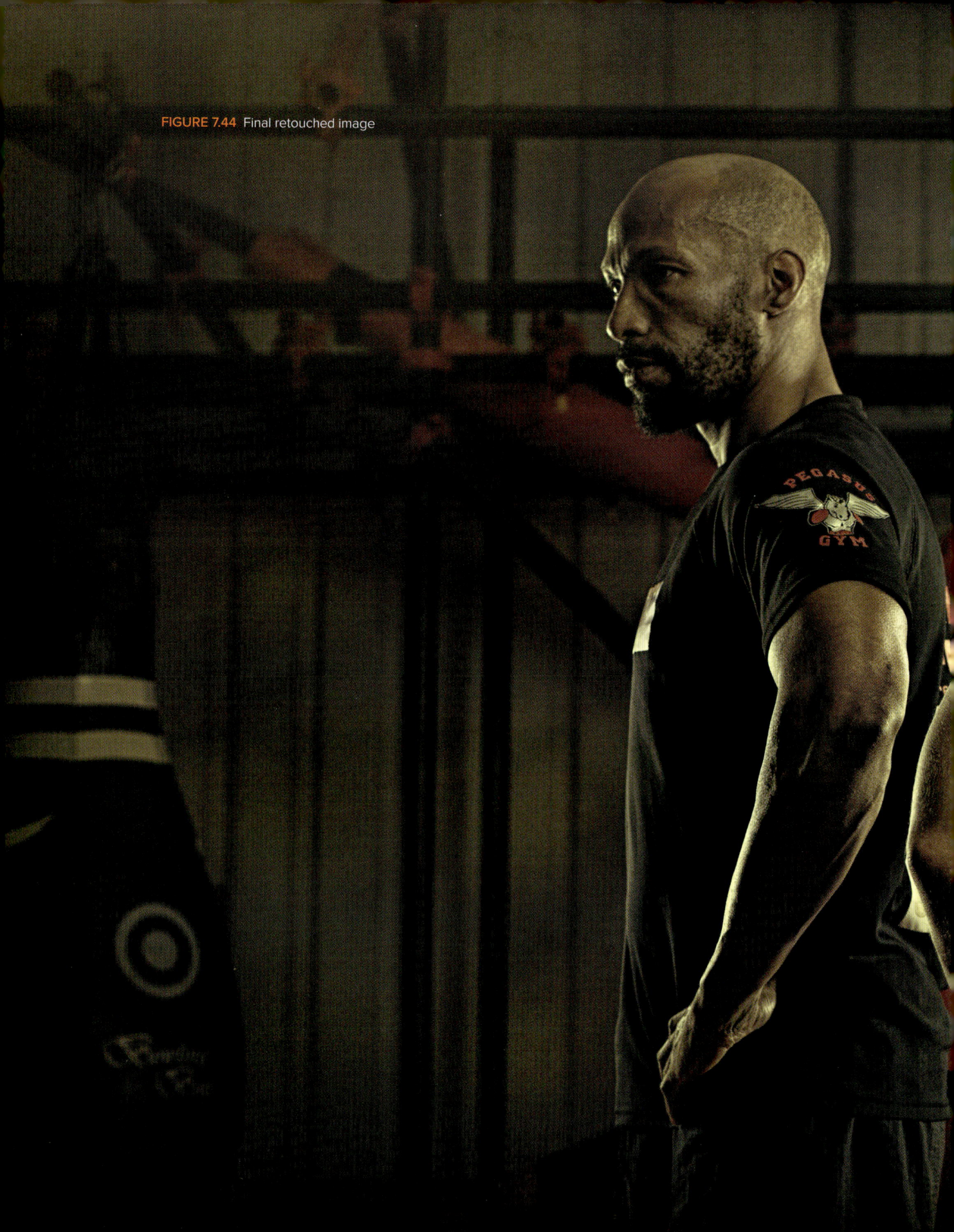

FIGURE 7.44 Final retouched image

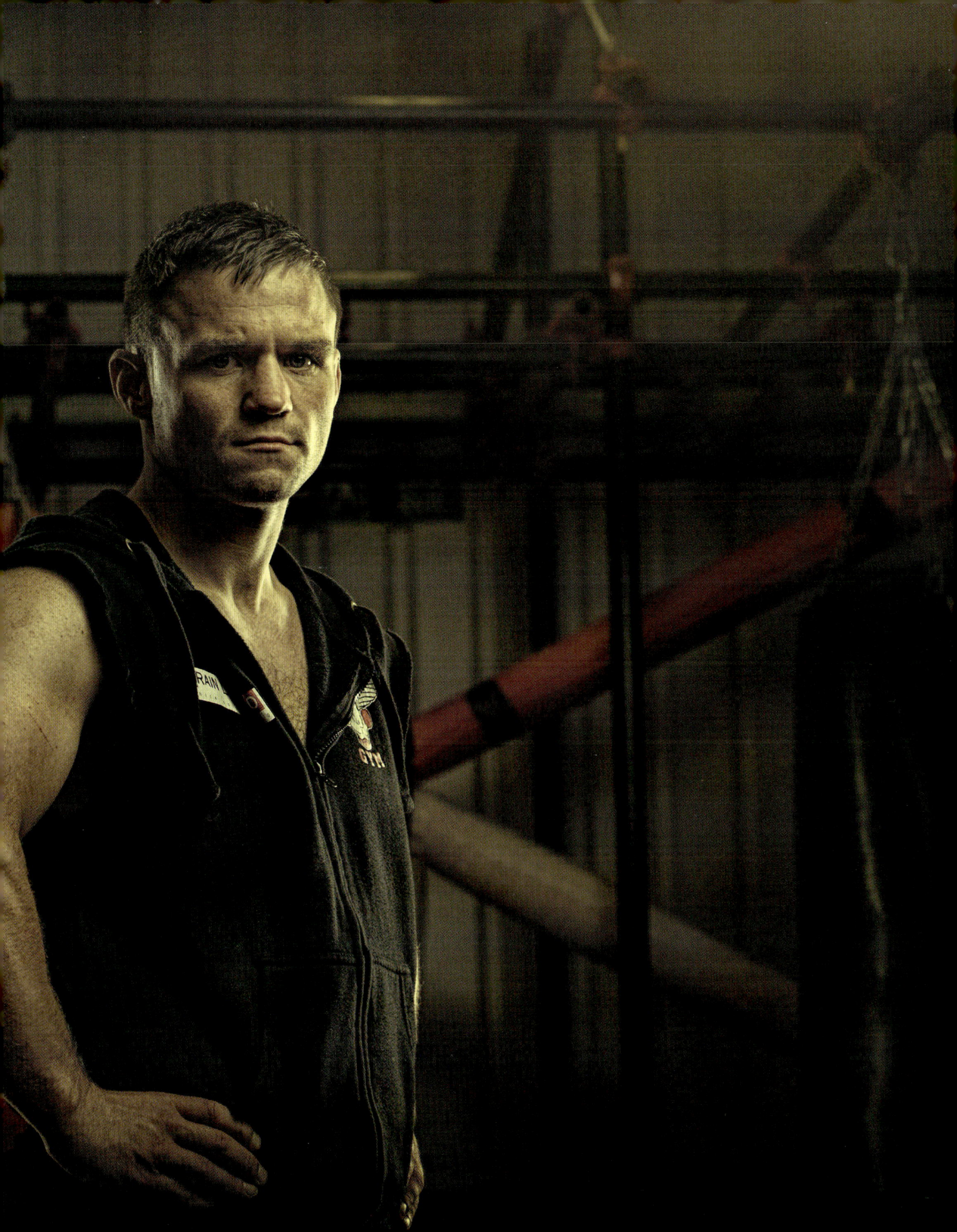

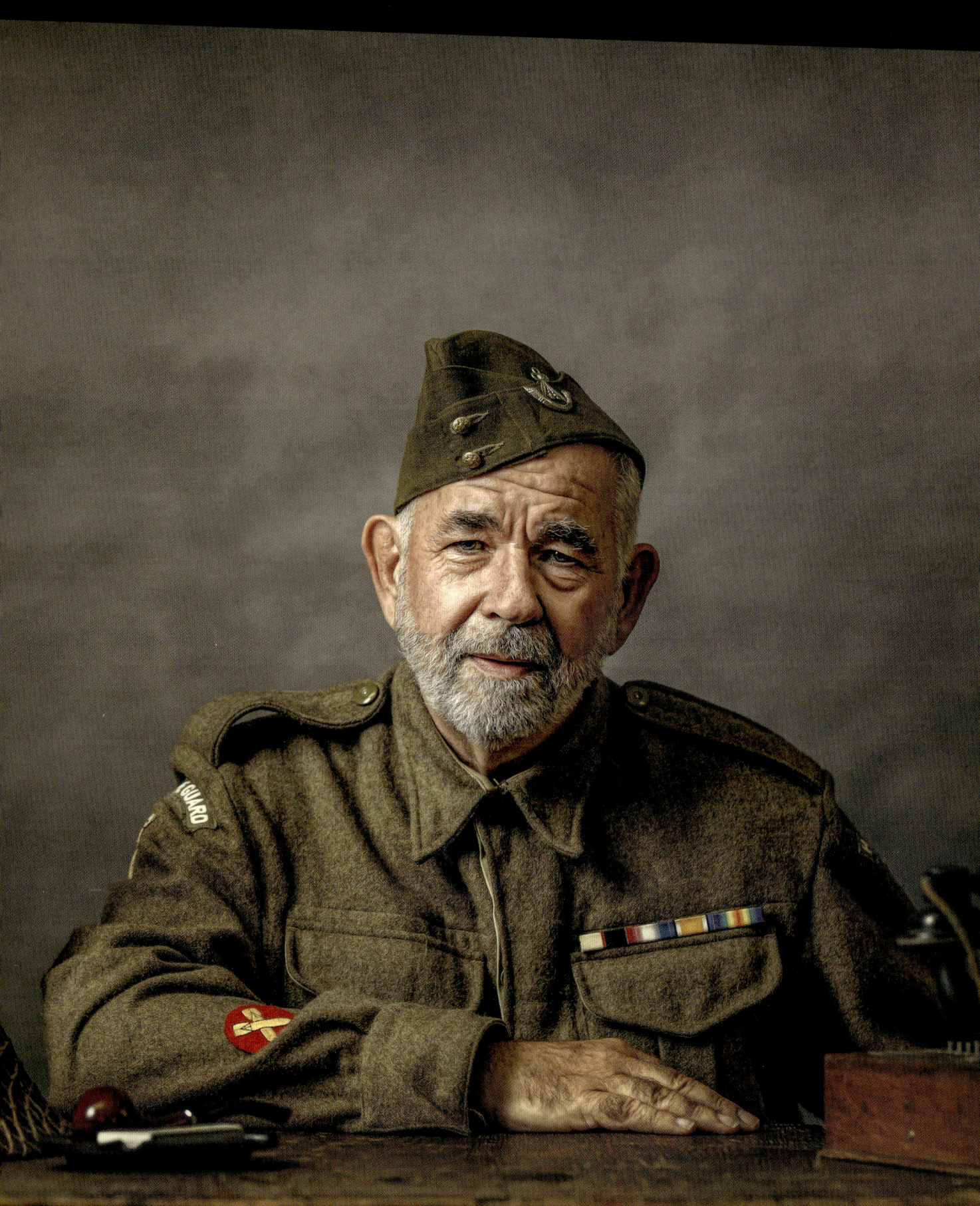

8 WORLD WAR II INSPIRED

I've always been fascinated by anything to do with the 1940s, especially the history around World War II.

My uncle is an author and while conducting research for his books, he met and became friends with a wonderful gentleman by the name of Richard "Dick" Rutter, who had been awarded the Military Medal (MM) for bravery during the conflict in Normandy. Dick served alongside my granddad, who had passed a number of years before we met Dick, so it was wonderful to develop a friendship with him and hear fascinating stories from his years of service. I visited Normandy with my wife, Anne, and I contacted my Uncle Jeff to see if he could shed any light on areas where my granddad would have been all those years before. He responded, "I can do better than that, I'm over there tomorrow," and the following day we were given a tour of the area with commentary. My uncle was able to point out locations where my granddad would have walked, where he was injured, and so much more. It was a truly wonderful and emotional experience.

To be honest, I never intended to include any pictures like this one of the Oxfordshire Home Guard in this book, but while I was working on earlier chapters, my wife and I watched the modern version of *Dad's Army* one evening and I absolutely loved it. That got me thinking about how great it would be to start a project photographing folks from that era or folks who reenact military history and belong to Living History Associations.

I mentioned this to my dear friend Barry, who happened to know of such a group, and the rest, as they say, is history.

What's the moral of the story? If you've got an idea, share it. There's always someone who knows someone who may be exactly what you're looking for.

THE SETUP

The idea here was to keep the lighting and setup simple and classic, so I ended up using a very similar setup to that of the Bearded Villains picture in chapter 5, except for a slight change in the light positioning (**Figure 8.1**).

The photo shoot was held in a local village hall where the Home Guard hold their biweekly meetings. Those of you who are familiar with the original *Dad's Army* TV series or who have seen the more recent movie will appreciate the authenticity of this.

These images were from the very first photo shoot I did with the group, so my intention was to cause as little disruption as possible, keep everything simple, and leave them with a good impression and great results—just what you need if you're hoping to work with the same people again.

I positioned the octa to the side and slightly in front of the subject to create a cross-lighting effect. In **Figure 8.2** you can see how I angled it down to prevent it from causing strange shadows that would have resulted from the light hitting the nose directly from the side.

In **Figure 8.3** and **8.4** you see the distance between the octa and the subject, and also how it was turned slightly away from the subject so that the feathered edge of the light was used.

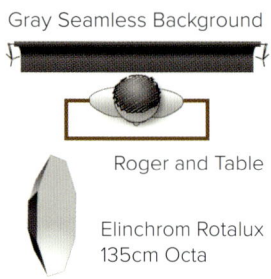

Gray Seamless Background

Roger and Table

Elinchrom Rotalux 135cm Octa

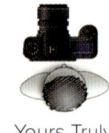

Yours Truly

FIGURE 8.1

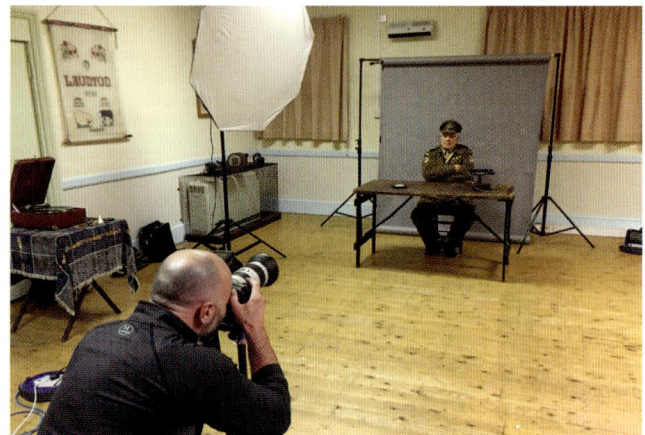

FIGURE 8.2

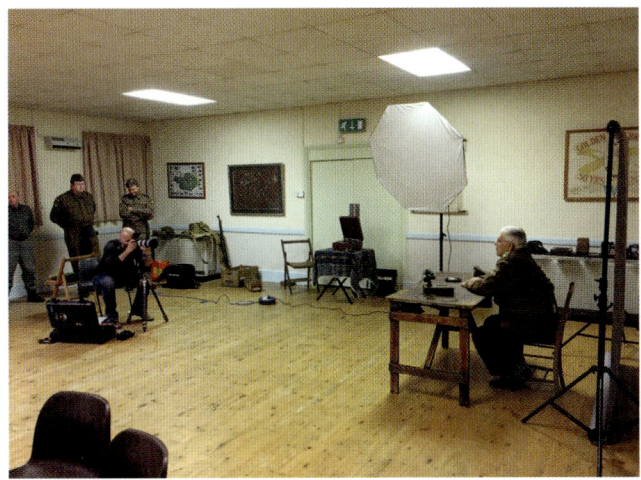

FIGURE 8.3

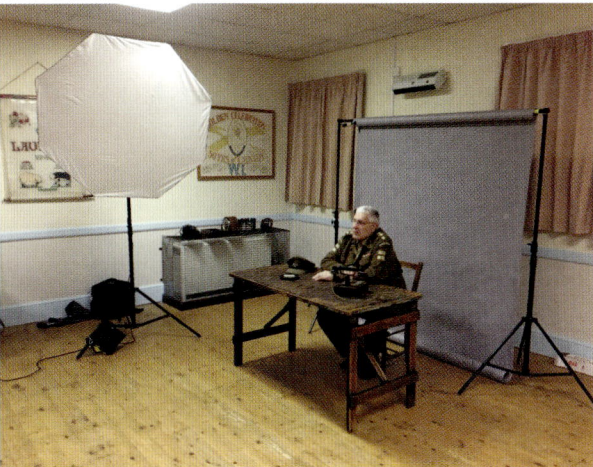

FIGURE 8.4

Shooting tethered (**Figure 8.5**) is a MUST and is something I will ALWAYS do unless I'm shooting outside and the weather isn't suitable. Viewing your images on a big screen as you shoot allows you to see so much more detail, and you'll catch stuff you'd likely miss if you were only looking at the pictures on the back of your camera (regardless of how good your camera screen is). I prefer to have my laptop resting on top of my Peli Case (**Figure 8.6**), keeping it as low to the ground as possible, as opposed to putting it on a stand. It's been knocked over too many times by either me or someone else, and reactions akin to those of Peter Parker have thankfully saved it from crashing to the floor.

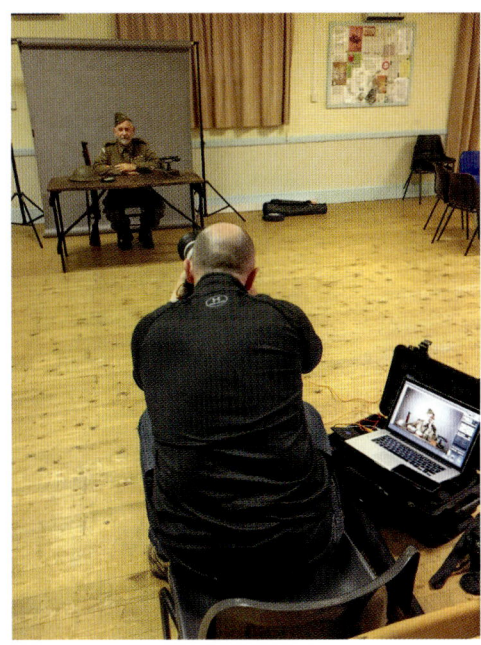

FIGURE 8.5

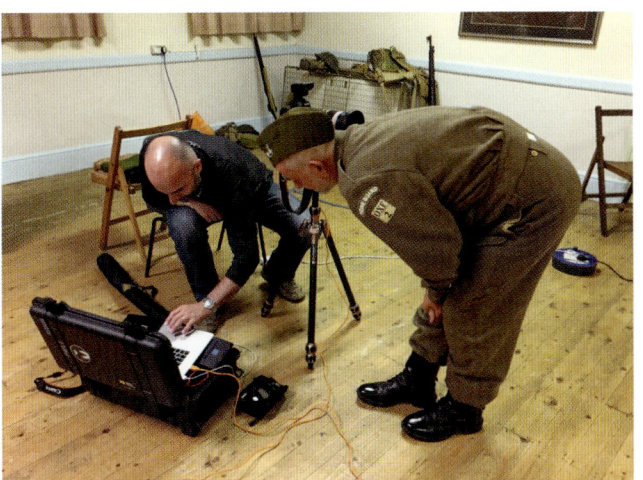

FIGURE 8.6

In **Figure 8.7** you can see that I also used a tripod. This ensured that everything was tack-sharp and that each image in the series was taken from the same height. It also allowed me to take some of the photographs without tucking myself in behind the camera—an action that can make your subjects immediately tense up. Instead, I could just gently rest my finger on the camera and shoot pictures while looking at and talking to the subject. I've found that sometimes this can produce much better results.

CAMERA SETTINGS

My intention with this series was to create images that draw the viewer's attention primarily to the subject's face, so I opted to shoot with an aperture of f/2.8. The main light

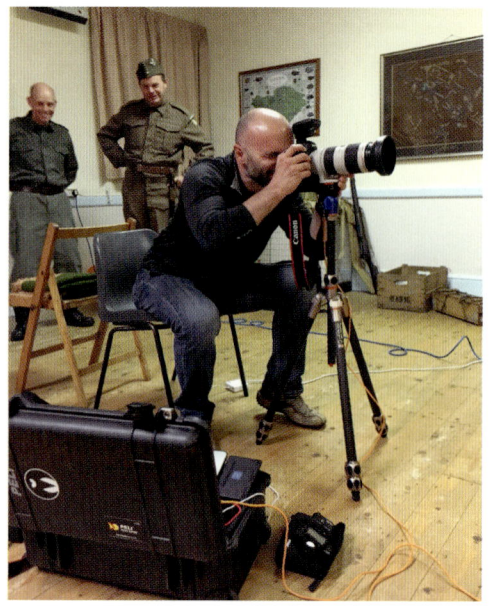

FIGURE 8.7

(the octa) was metered to give a reading of f/2.8, but I used an ISO of 400 and a shutter speed of 1/60sec to also allow enough ambient light into the scene.

For modern cameras, an ISO of 400 results in a perfectly clean, low-noise to noise-free image, and a shutter speed of 1/60sec was perfectly fine since the subjects were still and the camera was mounted on a tripod. Incidentally, the lens I used has Image Stabilization built-in, but when my I have my camera on a tripod I turn this off to prevent any movement caused by the workings inside.

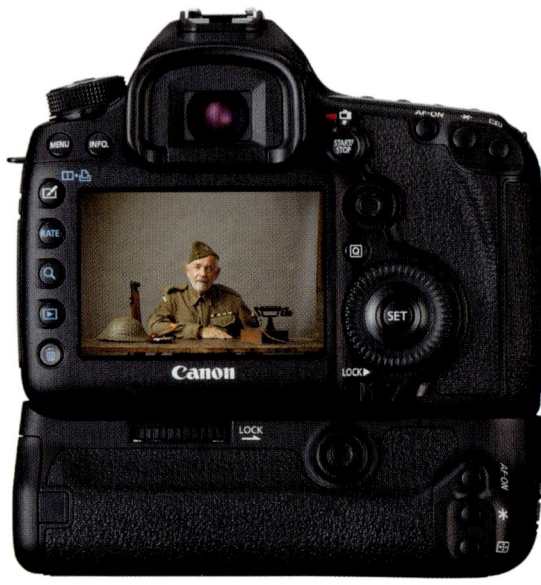

FIGURE 8.8

MODE Manual

ISO 400

APERTURE f/2.8

SHUTTER SPEED 1/160 sec.

LENS Canon 70–200mm f/2.8L IS II USM

GEAR GUIDE

For this shoot, I used an Elinchrom Rotalux 135cm Octa Softbox (**Figure 8.9**) and an Elinchrom ELX Pro HD 1000 flash head (**Figure 8.10**).

I prefer to use Elinchrom lights and modifiers because they are durable and easy to use.

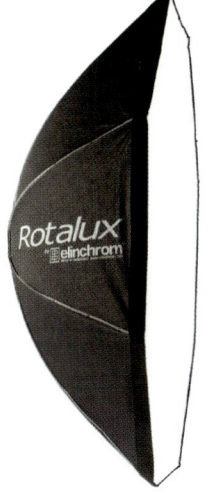

FIGURE 8.9

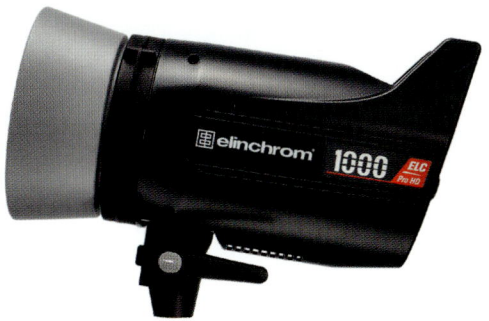

FIGURE 8.10

SMALL FLASH GEAR GUIDE

The setup for this picture could certainly be achieved with small flashes or speedlights because nowadays there are so many modifiers and accessories we can use. The only obvious disadvantage of a small-flash setup is the lack of a modelling light to get the position of the light just right, but a few test shots should get it sorted quickly enough.

Based on what is available on the market at the time of writing, you could achieve a similar lighting setup with a small flash or speedlight and a Lastolite Ezybox II Octa Large 1.2m (**Figure 8.11**).

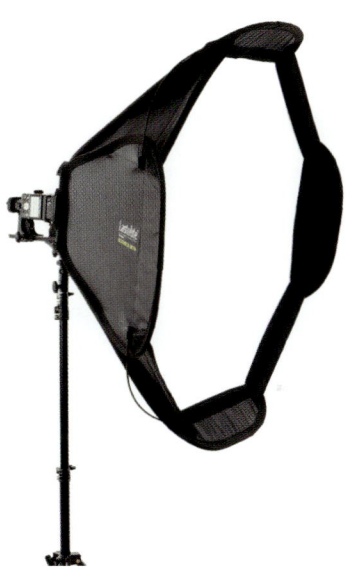

FIGURE 8.11

POST-PROCESSING

The post-processing for this image, and all the others in my ongoing Home Guard project, was so important to get right. Although it's relatively simple and subtle, I think it's a great example of how knowledge of post-production techniques is vital for the modern day photographer. Maybe that's just my opinion, but for this image and the others to work, they needed more than lighting props, expression, and pose. I wanted the images to look like they are from the 1940s, and the finishing touches in Lightroom and Photoshop are what helped to bring it all together and create the feel I was after.

In the steps that follow you'll also learn how I add extra depth and dimension to a portrait to make it feel like it's almost coming forward from the screen or print, which really adds to the overall impact.

NOTE *Download all the files you need to follow along step-by-step at: http://www.rockynook.com/ photograph-like-a-thief-reference/*

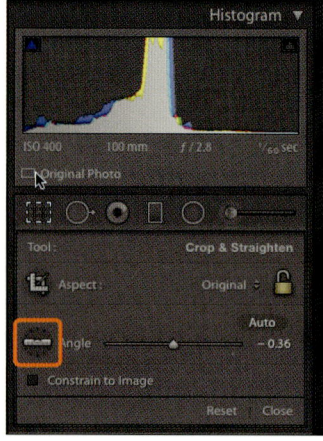

1. Here we have the original, RAW image open in Lightroom (but you could just as well have it open in Camera RAW). We'll start by leveling out and cropping the image. Grab the Crop Tool (**R**) and click on Angle to activate the Straighten Tool (**Figure 8.12**).

   Click on the top edge of the desk on the far left side of the picture, and then drag the Straighten Tool over to the far right side of the desk and click on the top edge (**Figure 8.13**). This straightens the image.

FIGURE 8.12

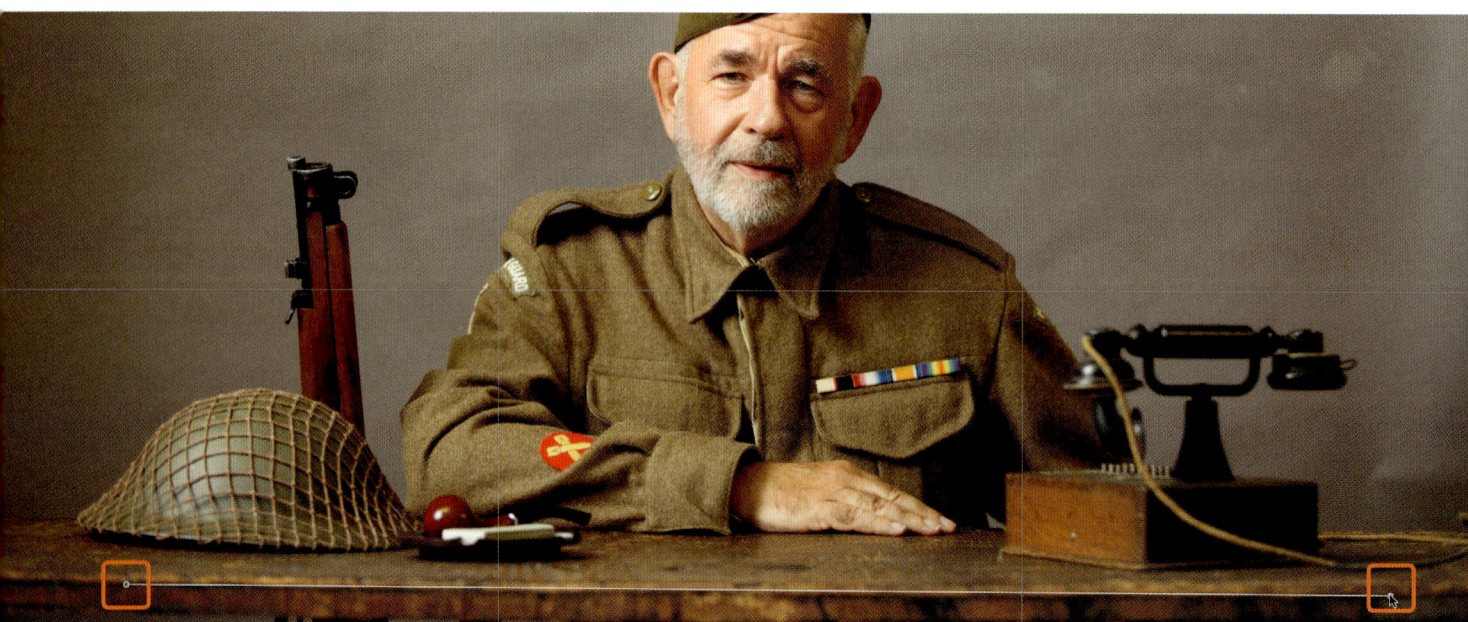

FIGURE 8.13

2. With the Crop Tool still active, hold down the Shift key to crop in proportion, click on the bottom right crop handle, and drag upward until the area on the right that is not covered by the gray background is excluded (**Figure 8.14**). Press Return (Mac) or Enter (PC).

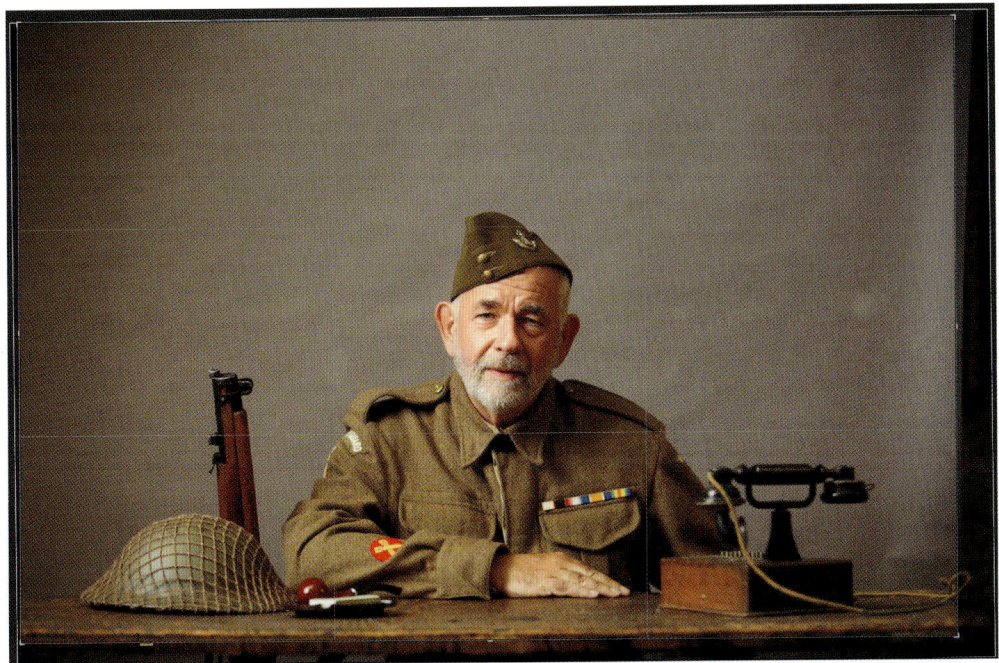

FIGURE 8.14

3. In the Develop tab, click on the White Balance Selector (**Figure 8.15**), then click on the gray background next to the subject's head (**Figure 8.16**).

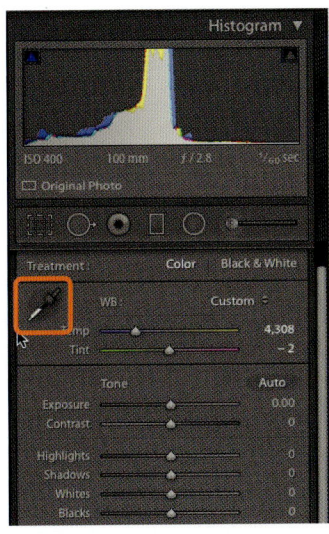
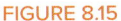

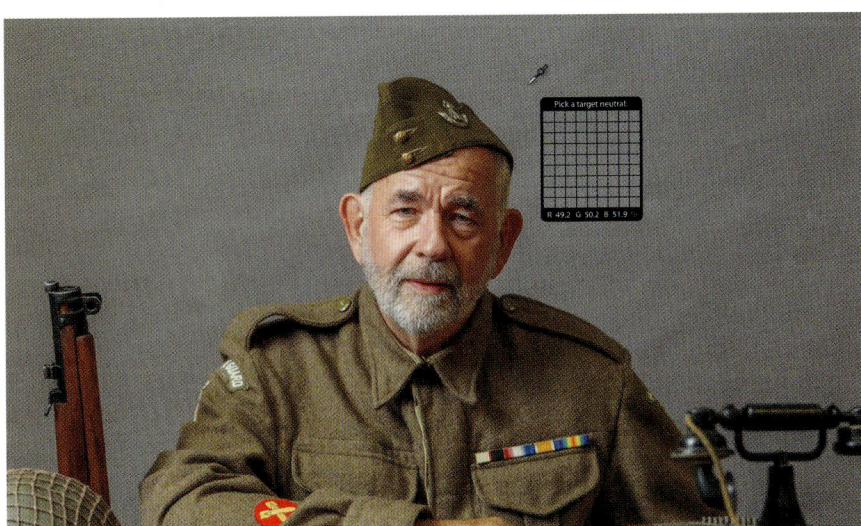

FIGURE 8.15

FIGURE 8.16

4. Now that we've corrected the basics, let's get on with creating the look. Start by increasing the Shadows slider to +100 and decreasing the Highlights slider to -100 (**Figure 8.17**).

5. Open the Detail tab and increase the Sharpening Amount to 40 (**Figure 8.18**). Leave the Radius and Detail sliders at their default amounts of 1.0 and 25, respectively. This is generally the amount I sharpen portraits when I want to get the look we're after for this image, which will end up with lots of detail. However, we've just sharpened the entire picture, including the background, and we want to restrict the sharpening mainly to the point of interest, which is our subject.

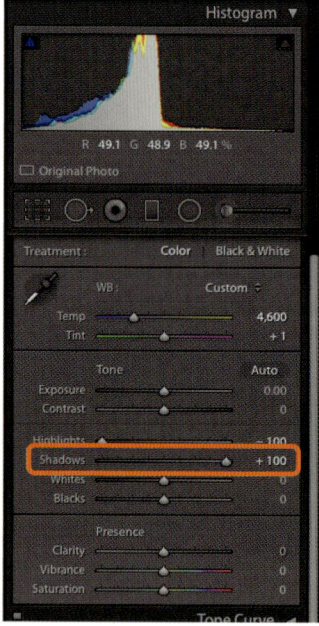

FIGURE 8.17

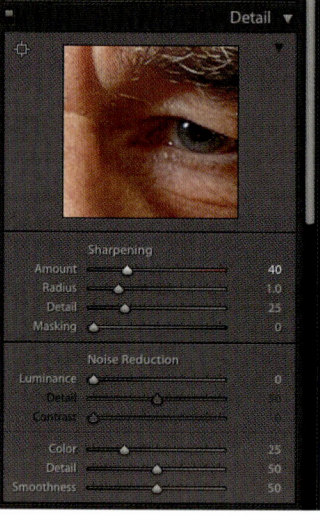

FIGURE 8.18

To do this, hold down the Option key (Mac) or Alt key (PC), click on the Masking slider, and drag to the right. As we do this, our work area turns white, indicating the areas where the sharpening is applied (i.e., all over). As we drag to the right, black is introduced, and this is where sharpening is not being applied (**Figure 8.19**).

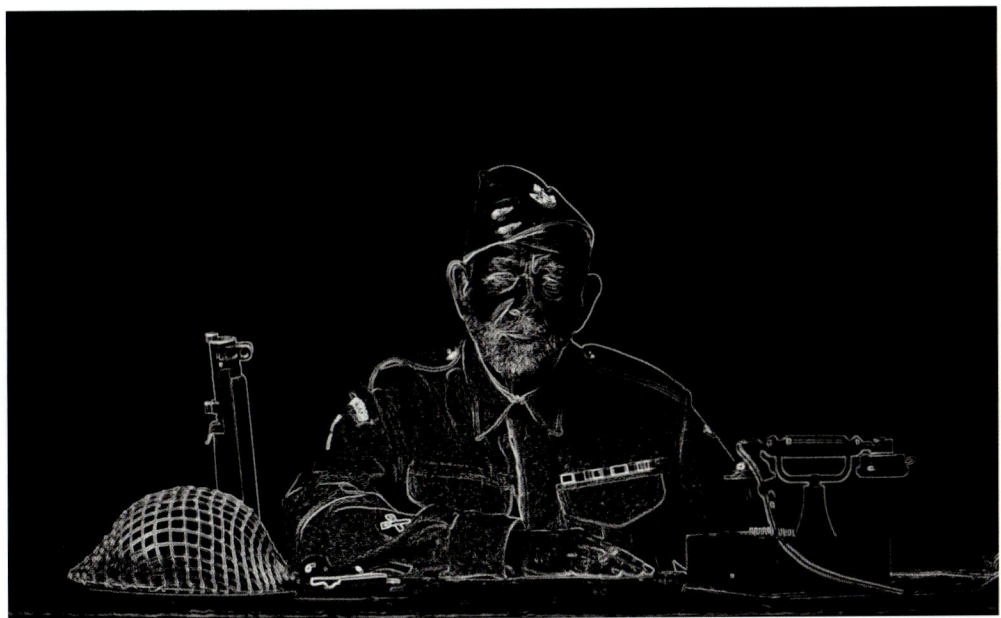

FIGURE 8.19

We just want to sharpen the subject and, to some degree, the items on the table, so dragging the Masking slider to around 85 is enough (**Figure 8.20**).

6. The last thing we'll do in Lightroom (or Camera RAW) before heading over to Photoshop is in the Lens Correction tab. Simply click on Enable Profile Corrections, and Lightroom will load in the specific profile corrections relevant to the lens you used during the shoot. In this case, we can see that my Canon 70–200mm f/2.8 has been loaded in (**Figure 8.21**).

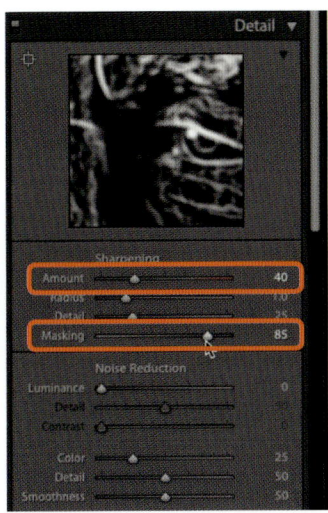

FIGURE 8.20

FIGURE 8.21

This is something I do religiously to ensure I am working with the best possible image file. You can see the difference it makes to the image in the before and after examples shown in **Figure 8.22** and **8.23.** The most significant change is in the vignetting.

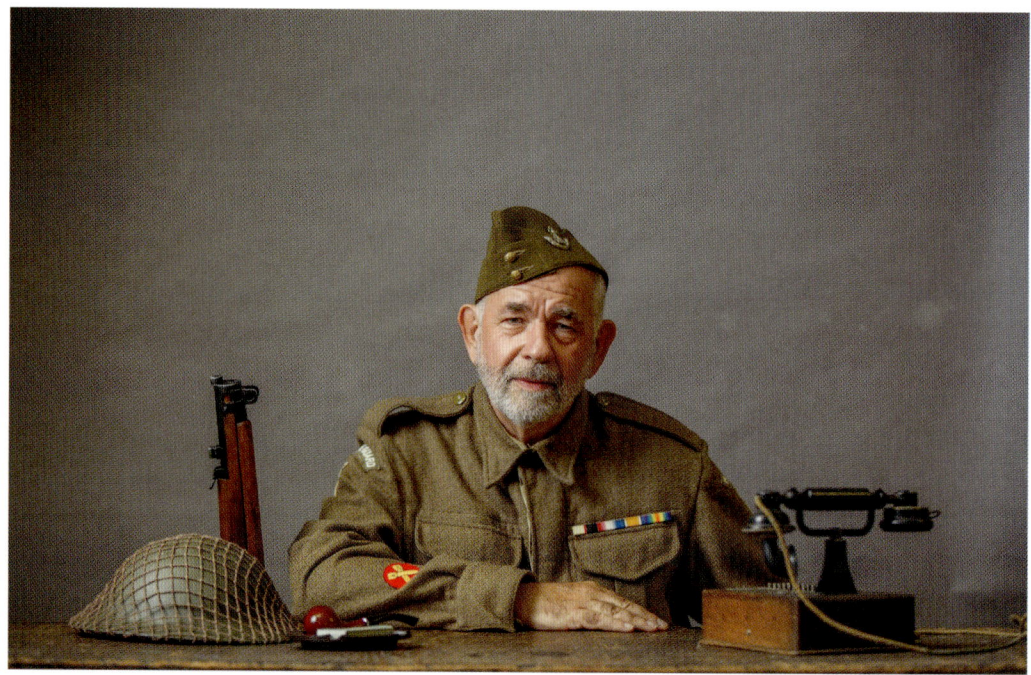

FIGURE 8.22 Before Profile Corrections

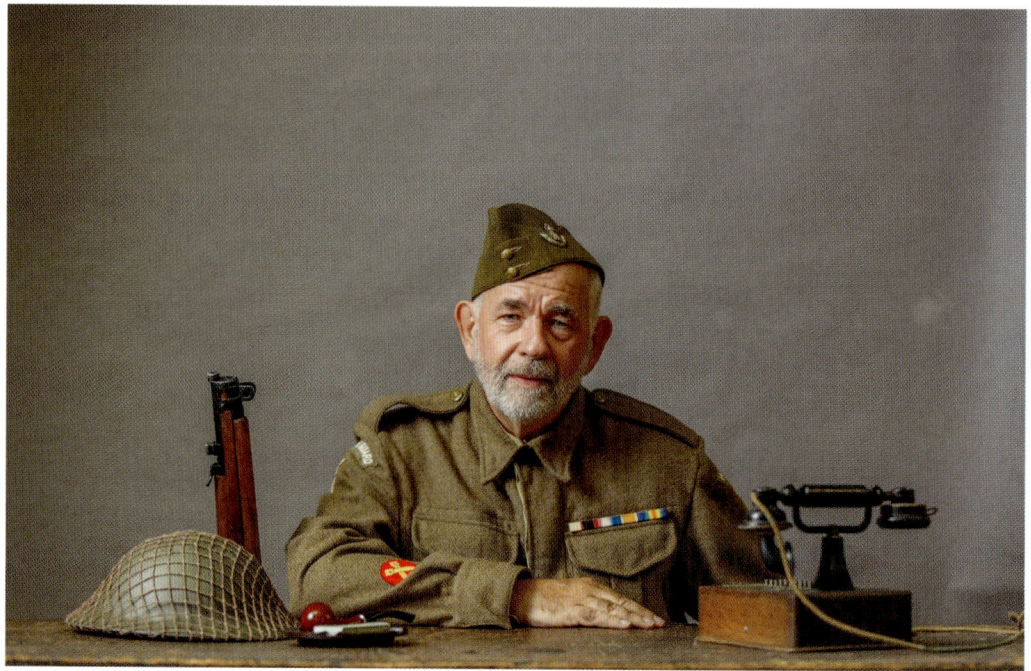

FIGURE 8.23 After Profile Corrections

7. We're now finished in Lightroom (or Camera RAW) so let's get to work in Photoshop. We'll send the image into Photoshop as a regular layer as opposed to a Smart Object because we haven't done much to it at this point. If we had already made a lot of adjustments, I would likely send the file to Photoshop as a Smart Object so that we could make changes later, if necessary, without having to redo lots of work. Go to *Photo > Edit In > Edit In Adobe Photoshop* (**Figure 8.24**).

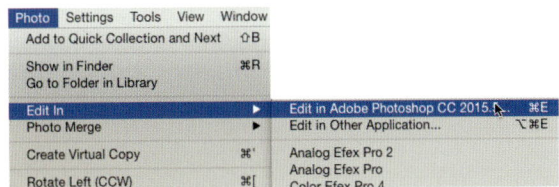

8. Now that we're in Photoshop we'll quickly clean up the background. Grab the Patch Tool (**J**; **Figure 8.25**) and make selections around the areas on the right side of the image where there are marks on the gray background (**Figure 8.26**). Drag the selections to clean areas of the background, and Photoshop will replace the areas you originally selected by blending in information from the clean areas.

   The crease in the bottom-right corner of the image (**Figure 8.27**) can also be fixed with the Patch Tool. Simply make a selection around it and drag the selection to a clean area, and you're done.

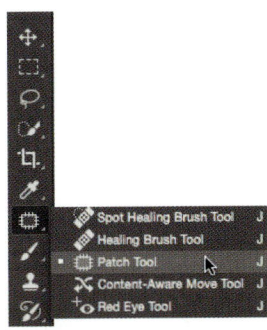

FIGURE 8.25

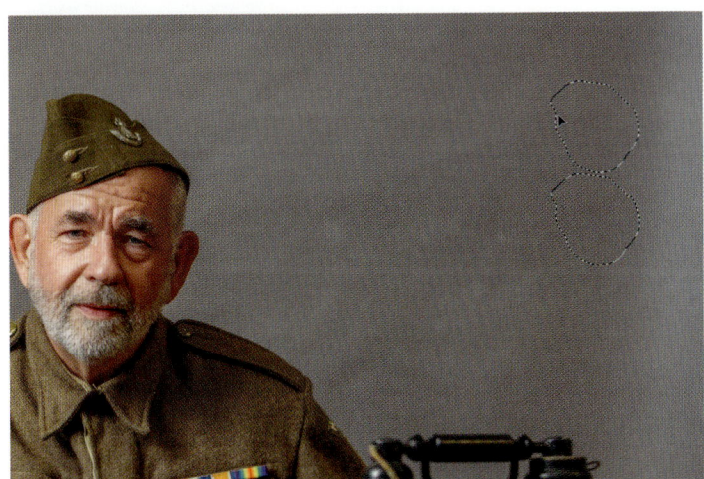

FIGURE 8.26

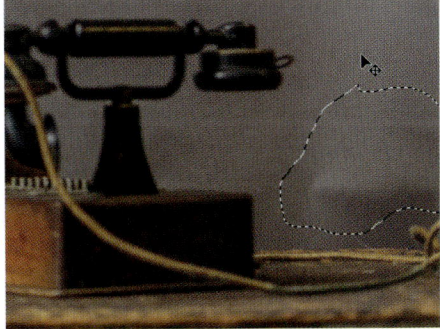

FIGURE 8.27

9. Now we're going to enhance the subject's eyes. Be sure to read the section that covers this in chapter 4 (page 82) because it contains detailed instructions that will help you to do this correctly.

Zoom in on the subject's eyes, select a black foreground color, and grab a round brush about 10px in size with a Hardness of 25% (**Figure 8.28**).

Press Q to enter Quick Mask mode. Paint over the center of both eyes so that the red overlay covers the iris (**Figure 8.29**).

Press Q to exit Quick Mask mode. The area we painted over is now a selection (marching ants; **Figure 8.30**). With the selection active, add a Selective Color adjustment layer (**Figure 8.31**), and then change the Blend Mode of the layer to Linear Dodge (**Figure 8.32**). This brightens the eyes considerably (**Figure 8.33**).

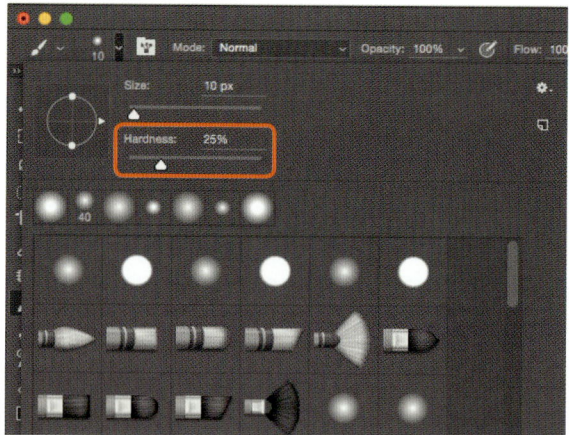

FIGURE 8.28

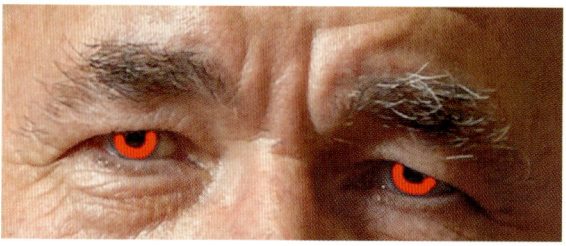

FIGURE 8.29

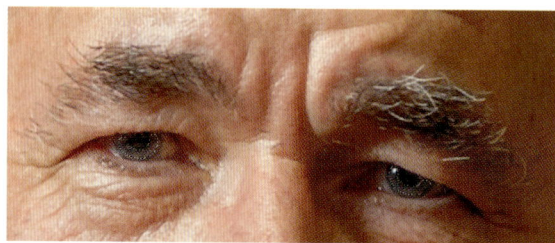

FIGURE 8.30

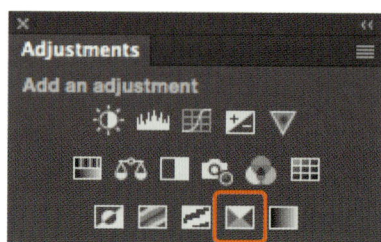

FIGURE 8.31

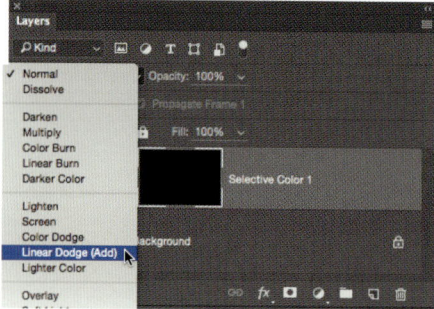

FIGURE 8.32

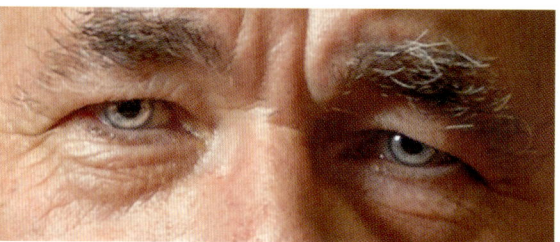

FIGURE 8.33

10. In the Selective Color properties, select Neutrals from the Colors menu, and then use the sliders to enhance the color of the Roger's eyes. Let's do this by changing Cyan to +12, Magenta to +7, and Yellow to -19 (**Figure 8.34**).

We can also add more contrast to the eyes by changing the Colors menu to Blacks and increasing the Black slider to around +20 (**Figure 8.35**).

Lower the Opacity of this Selective Color adjustment layer to 50% (**Figure 8.36**).

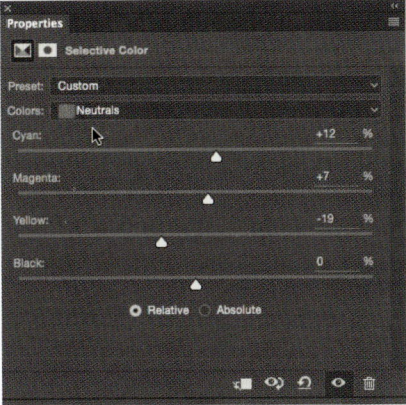

FIGURE 8.34

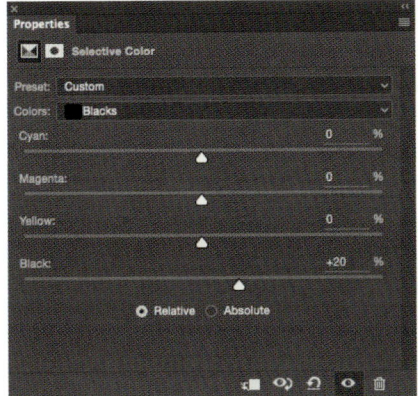

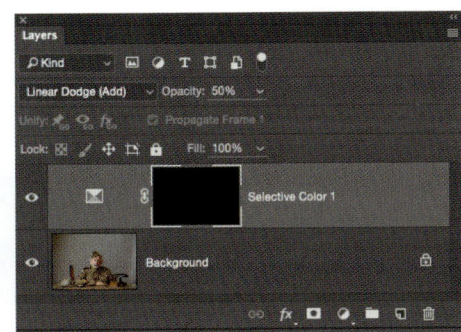

FIGURE 8.35

FIGURE 8.36

11. Add a new blank layer to the top of the layer stack and rename it "sharpen eyes" (**Figure 8.37**). Grab the Sharpen Tool from the toolbar (**Figure 8.38**), and in the options bar at the top of the screen, set the Strength to 30% and make sure that the Sample All Layers and Protect Detail checkboxes are checked (**Figure 8.39**).

Now paint around the middle of the eye to add some sharpening.

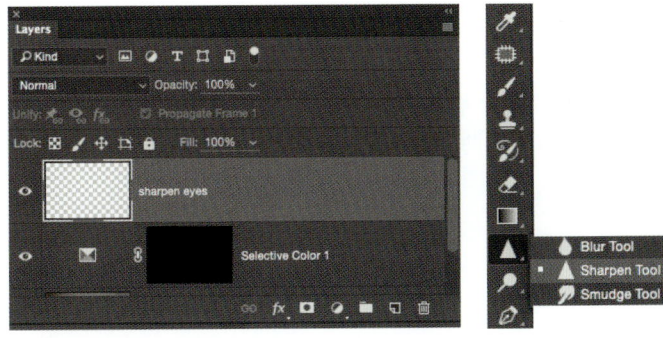

FIGURE 8.37

FIGURE 8.38

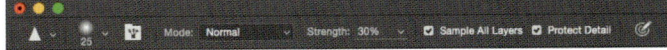

FIGURE 8.39

NOTE *The Sharpen Tool works like a spray can in that the more times you go over the same area without lifting off, the more the effect builds up.*

12. There are a few hot areas on Roger's face on the end of his nose and above and below his right eye (**Figure 8.40**), so we'll quickly fix those. Add a new blank layer to the top of the layer stack and rename it "skin shine."

Grab the Healing Brush from the toolbar (**Figure 8.41**), and in the options bar at the top of the screen, ensure that Mode is set to Darken, Source is set to Sampled, and Sample is set to Current & Below (**Figure 8.42**).

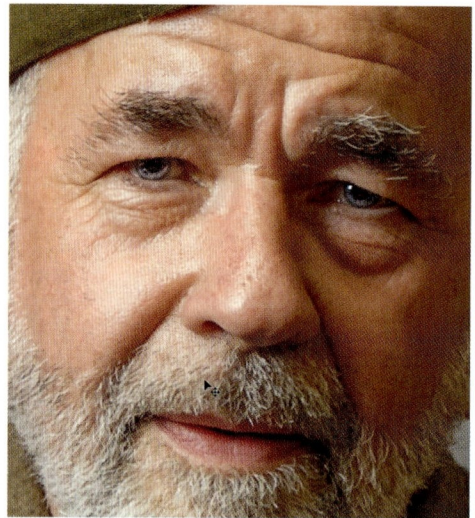

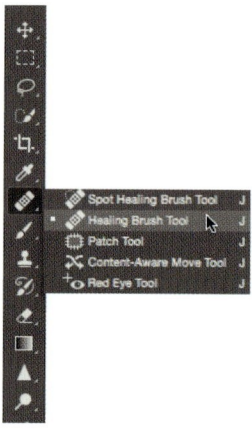

FIGURE 8.40

FIGURE 8.41

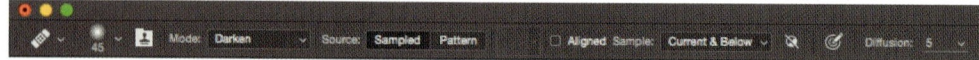

FIGURE 8.42

Hold down the Option key (Mac) or Alt key (PC) and click to sample a nearby area of skin that has no shine. Then brush over the areas with shine. Try to sample areas of skin near the areas you want to fix so that you get similar color and tone. Once you're finished, lower the Opacity of the skin shine layer to around 50% so that a little of the skin shine still shows through. This will make the fix look much more realistic.

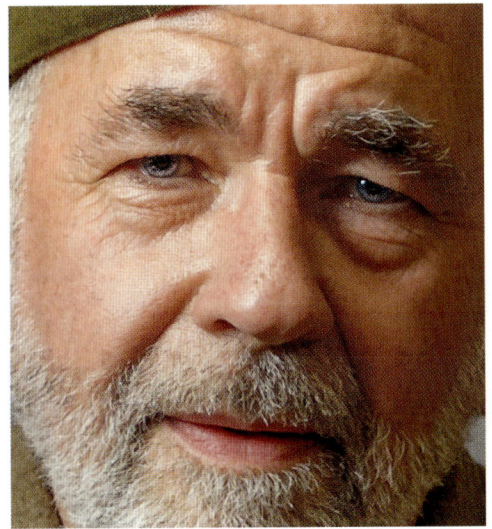

FIGURE 8.43 Before

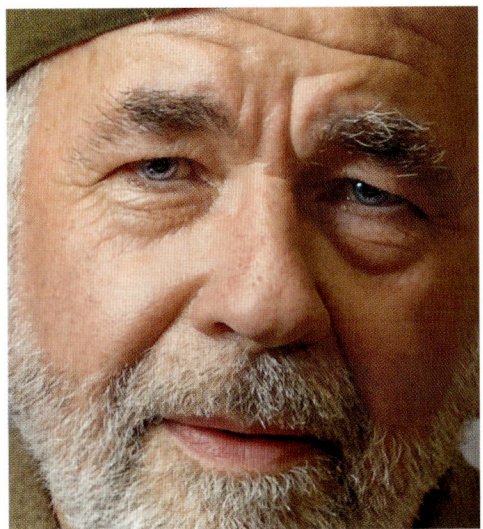

FIGURE 8.44 After

13. Next we'll do some dodging and burning using the technique I covered in chapter 4 (page 66). Go to *Layer > New > Layer*, and in the New Layer dialog box, rename this layer "dodge and burn," change the Mode to Soft Light, and check the Fill with Soft-Light-neutral color (50% gray) checkbox (**Figure 8.45**). Click OK.

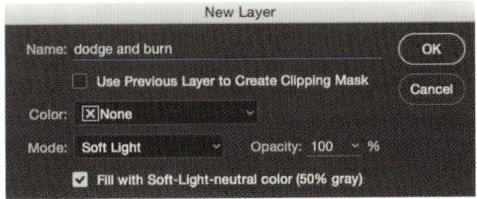

FIGURE 8.45

Grab the Dodge Tool from the toolbar (**O**), and in the options bar at the top of the screen, set Exposure to around 5% and make sure Protect Tones is checked (**Figure 8.46**). Leave Range set to Midtones; to be honest, this makes no difference because we're going to be working on a 50% gray layer anyway.

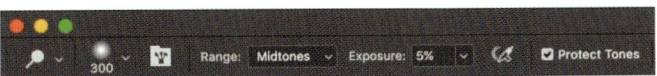

FIGURE 8.46

We don't need to be excessive here; we just want to enhance some areas of highlight and shadow. In the 50% gray layer, you can see where I have worked the most, brightening and darkening areas (**Figure 8.47**).

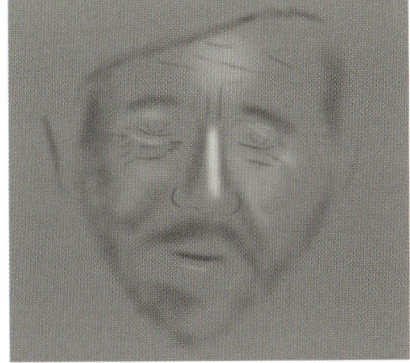

FIGURE 8.47

You can see the overall effect of the dodging and burning when you compare **Figures 8.48** and **8.49**. I didn't do too much and the differences are actually quite subtle. Notice that I only worked on Roger's face. This is because I want the face to have a lot of depth and dimension in the final picture.

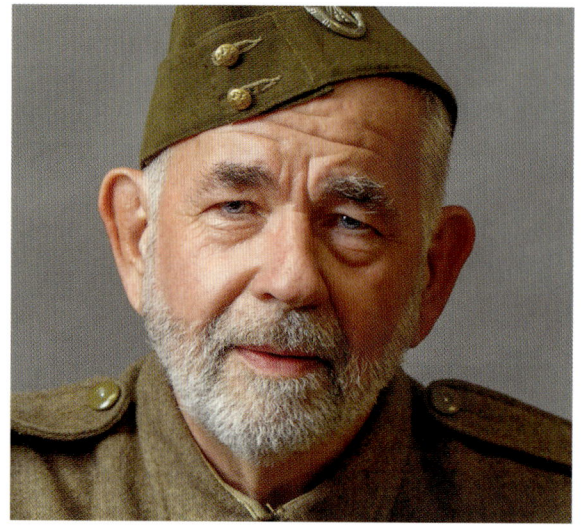

FIGURE 8.48 Before

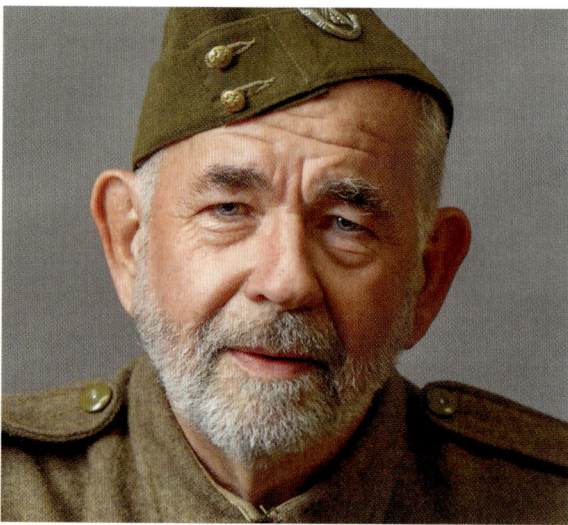

FIGURE 8.49 After

14. Now we'll add some texture to the background, which is so incredibly easy and effective when you shoot with some gray paper behind your subject. This technique is great for folks who don't want to shell out lots of cash for a painted canvas background like the ones used by Annie Leibovitz (chapter 5).

I've added a texture file to the book's webpage: rockynook.com/photograph-like-a-thief-reference/. Once you've downloaded the texture file, go to *File > Place Embedded* (or *File > Place*, depending on the version of Photoshop you are using), navigate to the file on your hard drive, and click OK. This will place our texture at the top of the layer stack (**Figure 8.50**). Press Return (Mac) or Enter (PC) to set the texture in place. The texture will cover the entire image at this point.

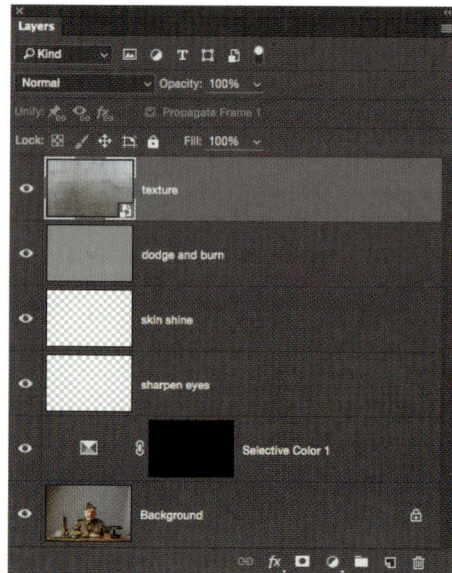

FIGURE 8.50

We don't need this texture layer to be a Smart Object, which is what it becomes when you use the Place Embedded command, so go to *Layer > Rasterize > Layer* to change it to a regular layer (**Figure 8.51**).

We'll use a Blend Mode to attach this texture to the original gray paper, but before we do that, we need to remove any color from it; otherwise, it just won't look right. Go to *Image > Adjustments > Desaturate* (**Figure 8.52**) and change the Blend Mode of the texture layer to Overlay (**Figure 8.53**).

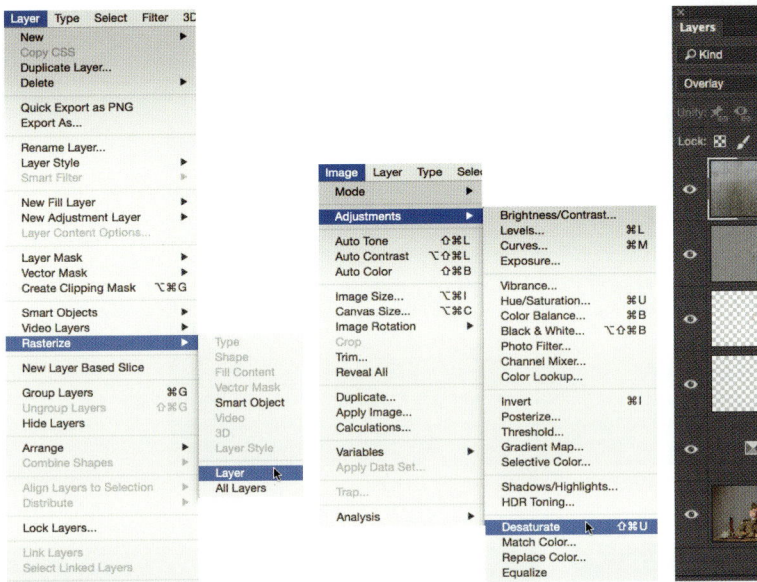

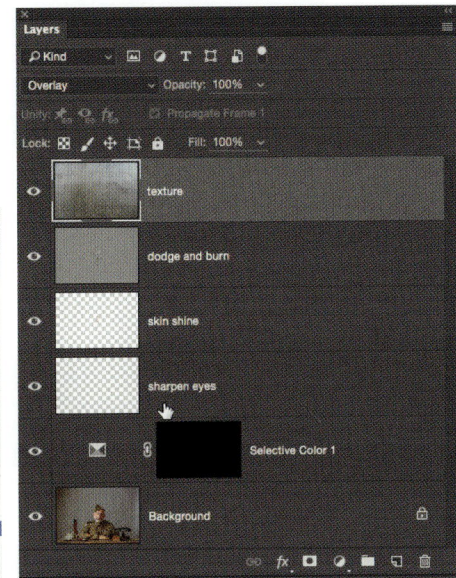

FIGURE 8.51   FIGURE 8.52   FIGURE 8.53

15. Changing the Blend Mode has added the texture onto the background; however, it also covers everything else, including Roger, the table, and everything on it. To remove the texture from these parts of the image so it covers only the background, add a Layer Mask to the texture layer, and with a round brush at about 30% Hardness and a black foreground color at 100% Opacity, paint over the areas where you don't want the texture to appear.

NOTE *Using a brush at around 30% Hardness makes it easier to paint along areas that are next to the gray background. If we used a soft brush, it would be very difficult to keep within areas without spilling over onto the background.*

Click on the thumbnail of the texture in the Layers panel (**Figure 8.54**), and then go to *Filer > Blur > Gaussian Blur* and set Radius to 4 Pixels (**Figure 8.55**). Click OK to blur the background a touch.

Lower the Opacity of the texture layer to 60%.

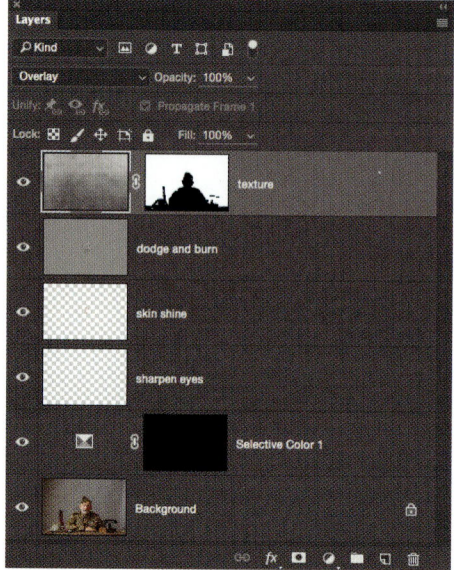

FIGURE 8.54

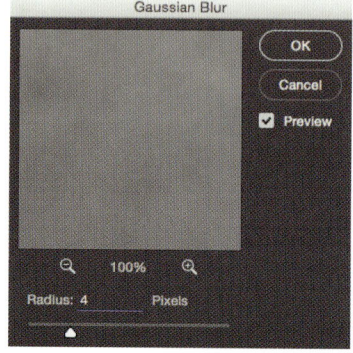

FIGURE 8.55

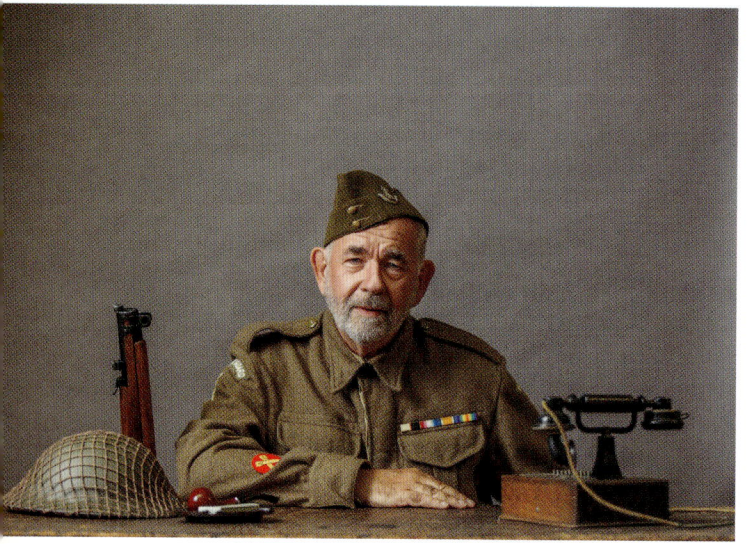

FIGURE 8.56 Without texture

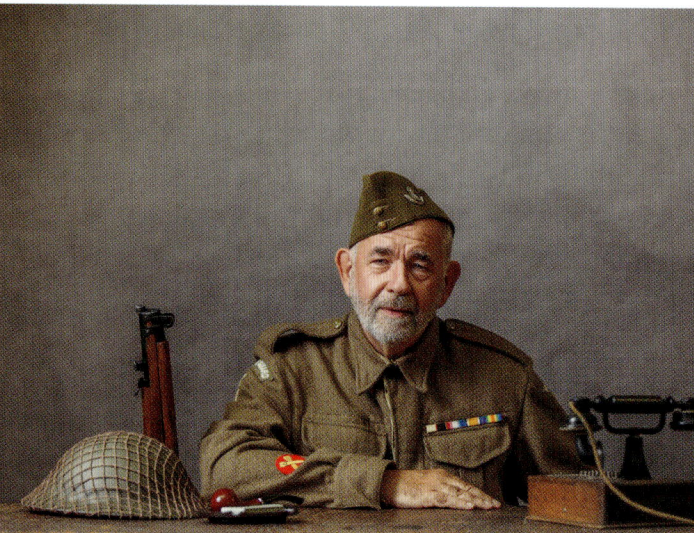

FIGURE 8.57 With texture

16. Add a merged layer to the top of the layer stack by going to *Select > All*, then to *Edit > Copy Merged*, and then to *Edit > Paste*. Alternatively, you can use the keyboard shortcut Shift + Option + Command + E (Mac) or Shift + Alt + Ctrl + E (PC). Rename this layer "contrast."

Now we'll use the Topaz Clarity plugin to start creating some depth and dimension in the picture. You can also use any of the other contrast methods I mentioned in chapter 4 (page 60).

However, I must admit that I do find the Topaz Clarity plugin gives my images something I can't quite replicate with any other tools or techniques, and it's one of the very few plugins I choose to invest in.

Go to *Filter > Topaz Labs > Topaz Clarity* (**Figure 8.58**). In the controls on the right side of the screen, increase Micro Contrast to 0.25, Low Contrast to 0.13, and Medium Contrast to 0.05, and click OK (**Figure 8.59**).

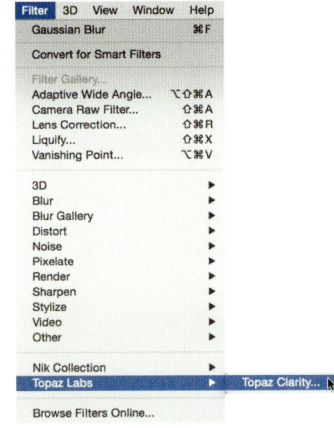

FIGURE 8.58

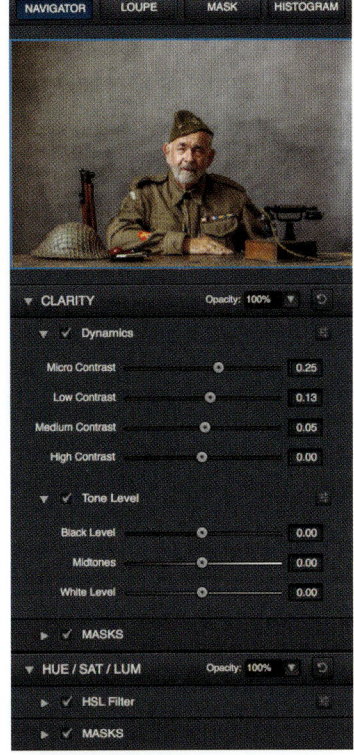

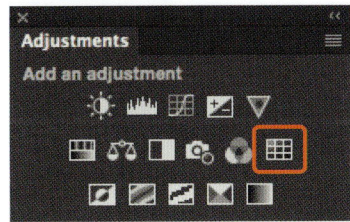

FIGURE 8.59

17. The next step is to color grade the picture to give it the right mood. We'll do this using Color Lookup adjustment layers, which are without doubt my favorite way to color grade pictures.

Click on the Color Lookup icon in the Adjustments panel to add a Color Lookup adjustment layer (**Figure 8.60**).

In the Color Lookup properties, select TensionGreen.3DL from the top menu labeled 3DLUT File (**Figure 8.61**). In the Layers panel, lower the Opacity of this Adjustment layer to 30%.

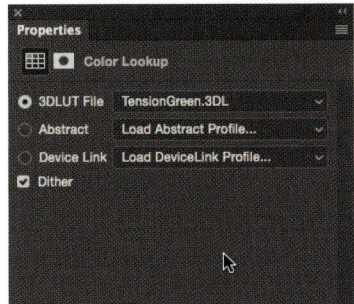

FIGURE 8.60

FIGURE 8.61

18. Add a second Color Lookup adjustment layer and select EdgyAmber.3DL from the 3DLUT File menu (**Figure 8.62**). In the Layers panel, lower the Opacity of this Adjustment layer to 20%.

19. Add a third Color Lookup adjustment layer and choose FoggyNight.3DL from the 3DLUT File menu (**Figure 8.63**). In the Layers panel, lower the Opacity of this Adjustment layer to 20%.

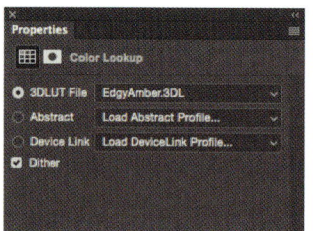

FIGURE 8.62

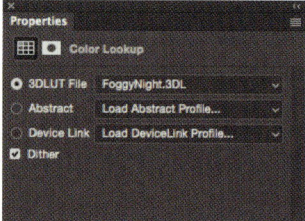

FIGURE 8.63

20. Add a merged layer to the top of the layer stack and rename it "shadow detail" (**Figure 8.64**). Then go to *Filter > Camera RAW Filter*, increase the Shadows slider to +50, and click OK (**Figure 8.65**).

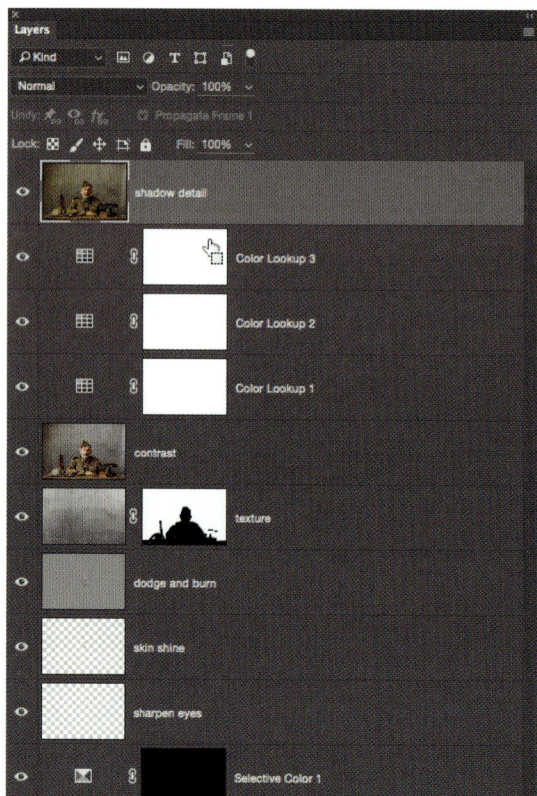

FIGURE 8.64

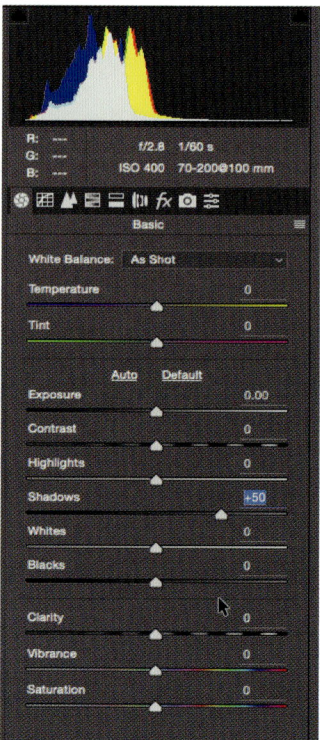

FIGURE 8.65

21. Create a copy of this shadow detail layer by pressing Command + J (Mac) or Ctrl + J (PC) and rename the layer "contrast 2" (**Figure 8.66**).

Now add contrast using the same method you used in step 16—in my case, the Topaz Clarity plugin. Go to *Filter > Topaz Labs > Topaz Clarity*, input the same settings as before (Micro Contrast: 0.25, Low Contrast: 0.13, and Medium Contrast: 0.05), and click OK (**Figure 8.67**).

22. Hold down the Option key (Mac) or Alt key (PC) and click on the Layer Mask icon at the bottom of the Layers panel to add a black Layer Mask (**Figure 8.68**). This will hide the effects of the contrast we have just added.

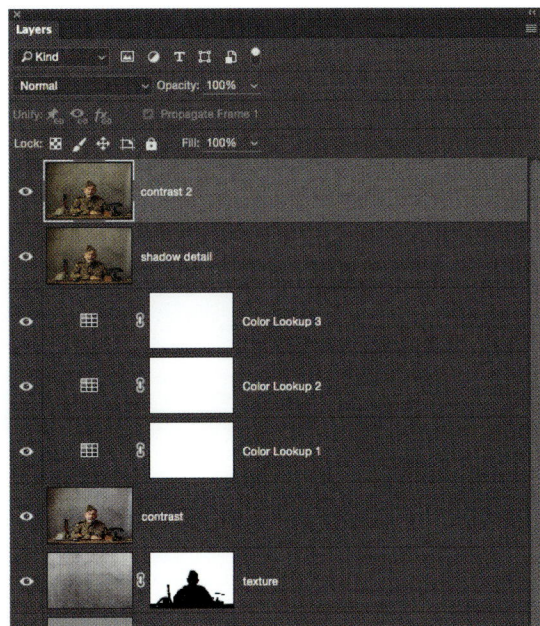

FIGURE 8.66

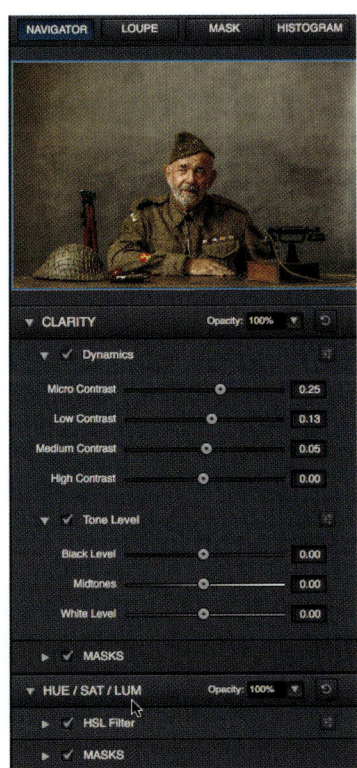

FIGURE 8.67

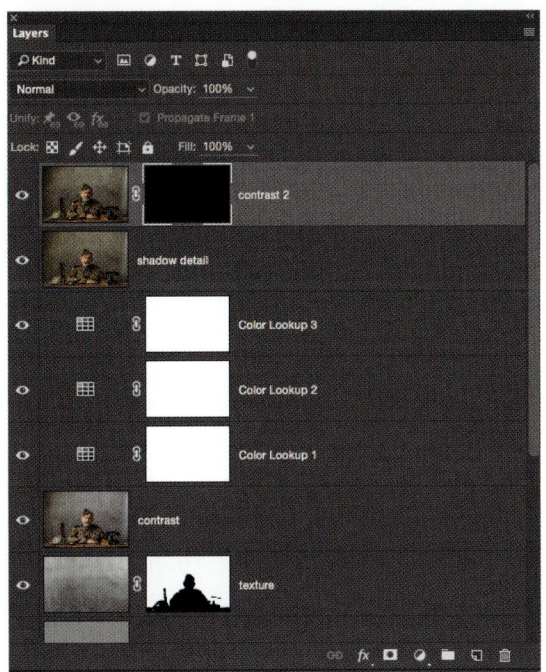

FIGURE 8.68

Choose a round, soft-edged brush with a white foreground color and an Opacity of 80%, and paint over Roger's clothing and hat to bring back the contrast effect.

Lower the Opacity of the brush to 60% and paint to bring the effect back on Roger's face.

Figures **8.69** and **8.70** show the image before and after adding contrast.

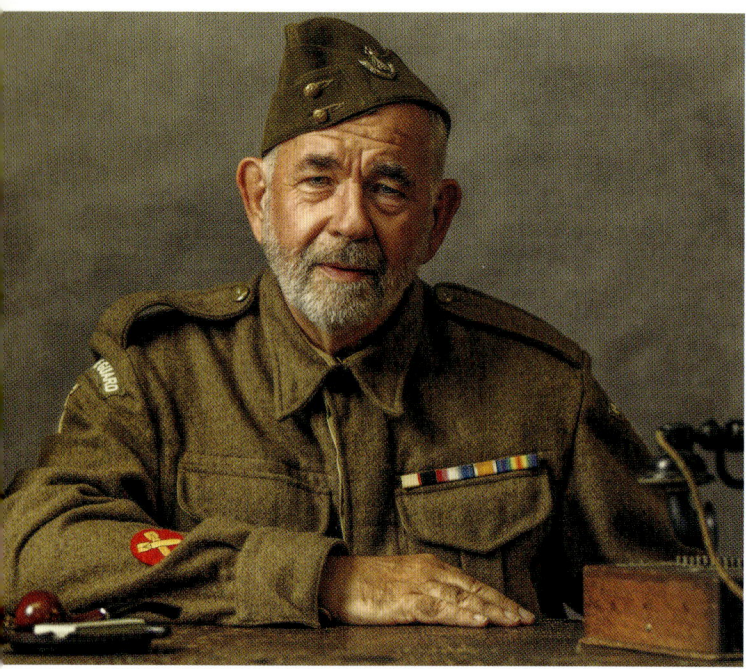

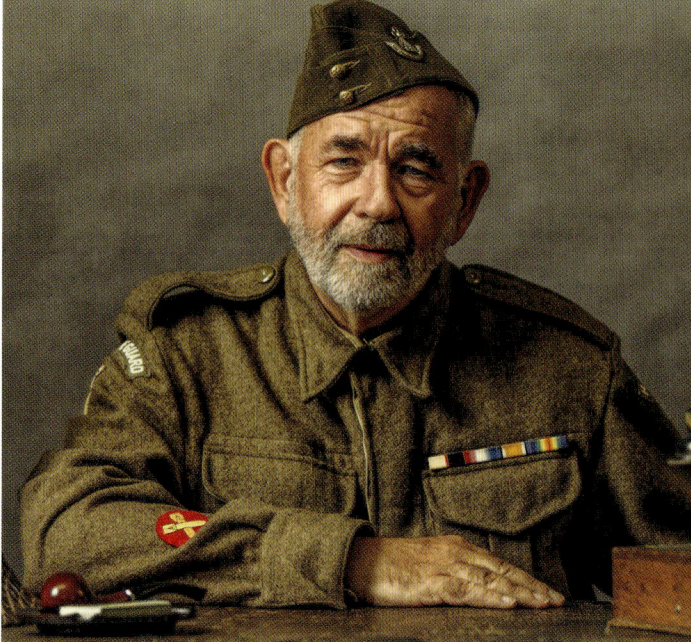

FIGURE 8.69 Before

FIGURE 8.70 After adding contrast to Roger's clothing and face

23. Frequently, I like to add what I call a painterly look to my pictures, which improves the look of skin and areas with lots of detail. I guess it's more of a waxy kind of look than a painterly look, but you'll see what I mean.

Start by adding a merged layer to the top of the layer stack by going to *Select > All*, then to *Edit > Copy Merged*, and then to *Edit > Paste* [or by pressing Shift + Option + Command + E (Mac) or Shift + Alt + Ctrl + E (PC)]. Rename this layer "look." Create a duplicate of the layer by pressing Command + J (Mac) or Ctrl + J (PC) and rename this new layer "sharpness." Finally, turn off the visibility of the sharpness layer by clicking on the eye icon, and then click on the look layer so it is active (**Figure 8.71**).

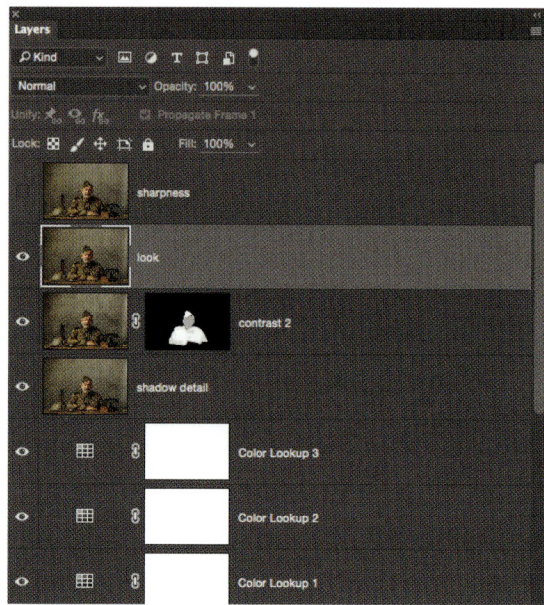

FIGURE 8.71

24. Go to *Filter > Noise > Reduce Noise* (**Figure 8.72**). In the Reduce Noise dialog, increase Strength to 7, leave every other slider at 0, and click OK (**Figure 8.73**).

This has added the waxy look I mentioned, but in doing so, it has made the picture lose sharpness in areas such as the eyes, hair, and so on. To fix this, click on the sharpness layer and turn on its visibility (**Figure 8.74**), go to *Filter > Other > High Pass*, dial in a Radius of 1 Pixel (**Figure 8.75**), and click OK. Change the Blend Mode of the sharpness layer to Hard Light (**Figure 8.76**).

Now if you toggle the visibility of the sharpness layer on and off, you'll see how some of the sharpness has returned due to our use of the High Pass Filter.

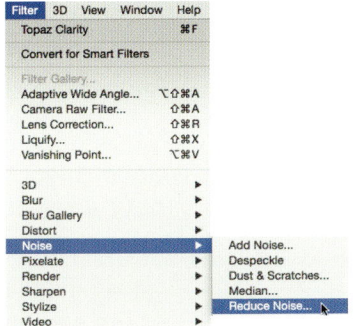

FIGURE 8.72

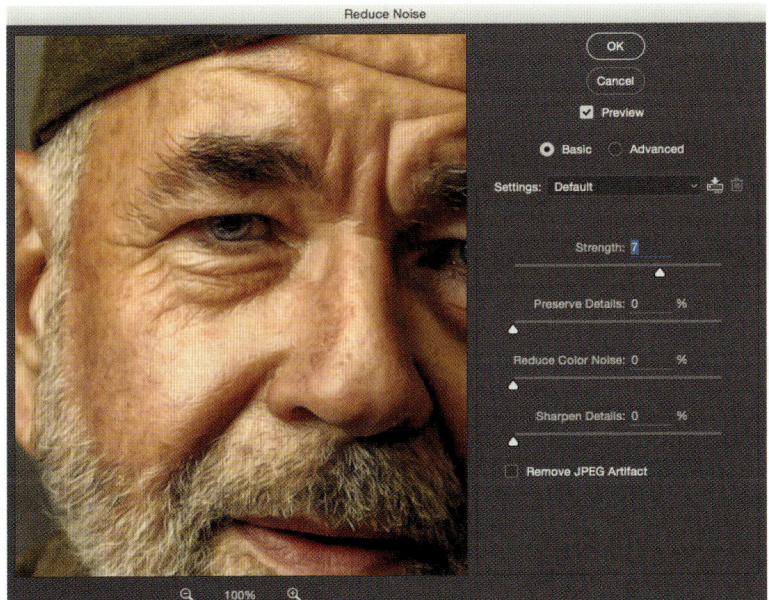

FIGURE 8.73

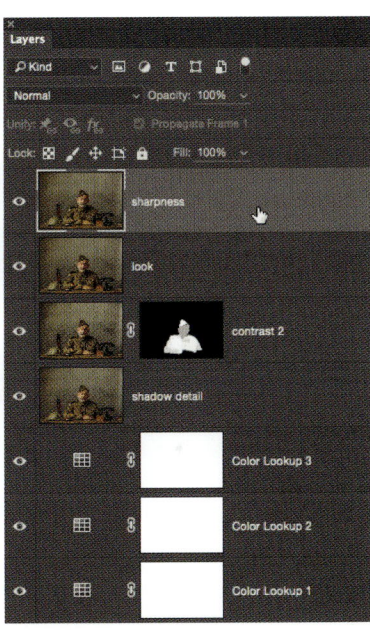

FIGURE 8.74

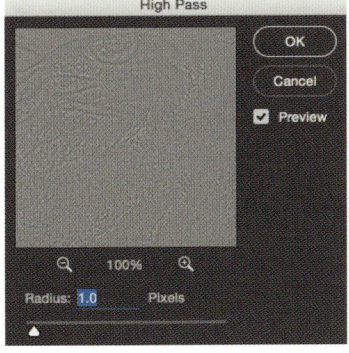

FIGURE 8.75

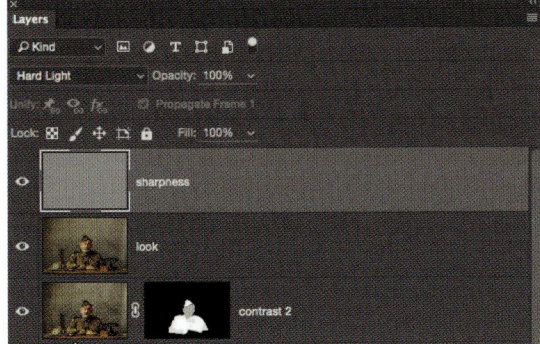

FIGURE 8.76

25. All we have left to do is add some finishing touches, which will include shaping the light in Camera RAW to create more atmosphere and adding a little more contrast to Roger's face so that it stands out even more. So, create one final merged layer to the top of the layer stack and rename it "FT" (Finishing Touches).

Go to *Filter > Camera RAW Filter*, and in the Camera RAW window, choose the Radial Filter (**J**) (**Figure 8.77**). Click on Roger's face and drag outward to create an ellipse (**Figure 8.78**). In the settings on the right side of the screen, lower the Exposure to around -1.35 (**Figure 8.79**).

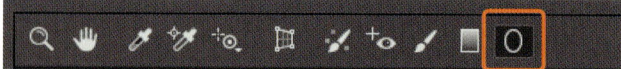

FIGURE 8.77

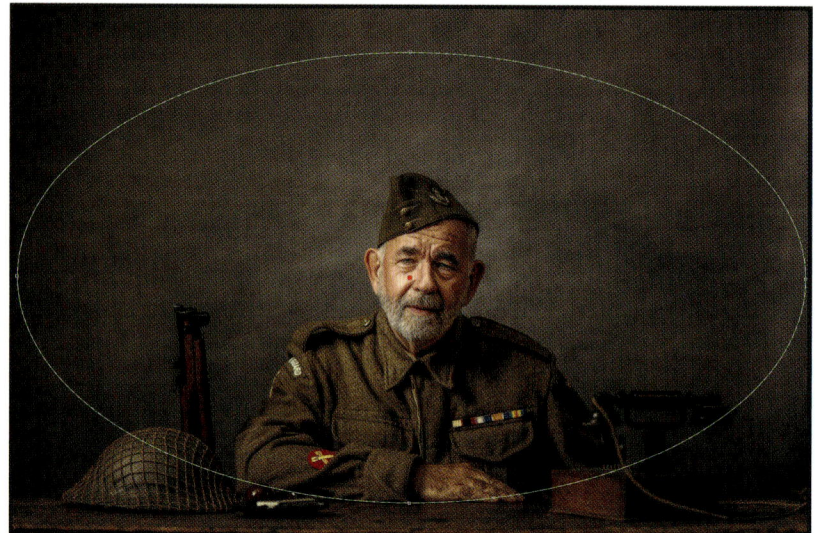

FIGURE 8.78

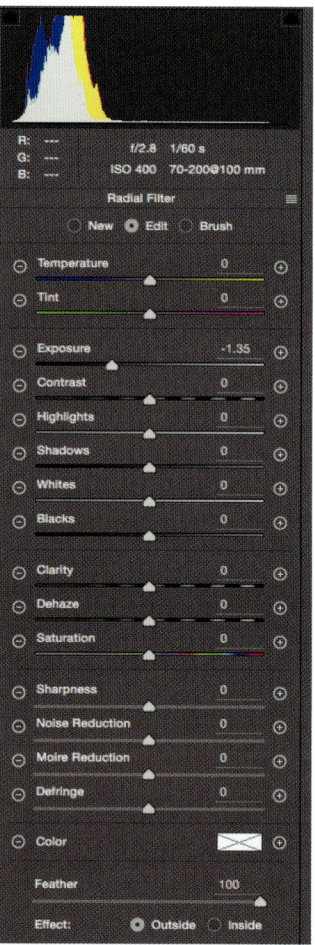

FIGURE 8.79

26. Click on the Graduated Filter icon (**Figure 8.80**) and drag a gradient from the top of the image to about a quarter of the way down the image (**Figure 8.81**). In the settings on the right, dial in an Exposure of -0.95 (**Figure 8.82**).

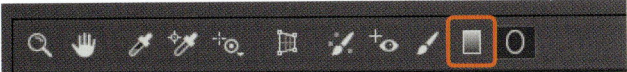

FIGURE 8.80

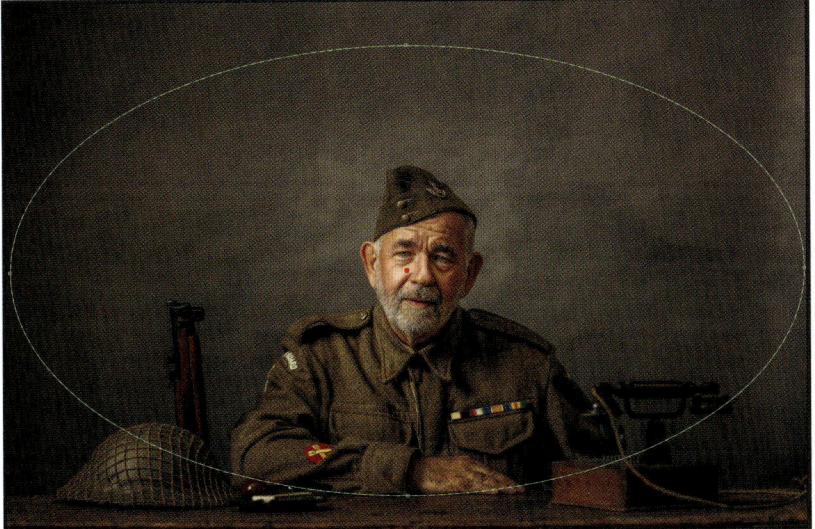

FIGURE 8.81

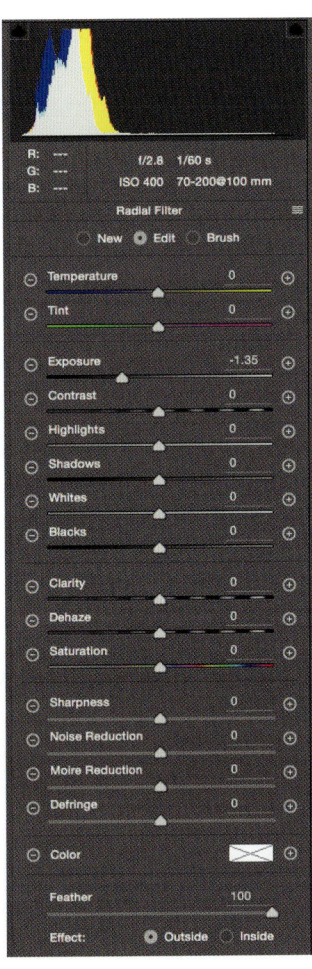

FIGURE 8.82

27. In the settings under Graduated Filter, select New (**Figure 8.83**), and then drag in from the right side of the image (**Figure 8.84**) to darken it using the same settings as before (Exposure: -0.95).

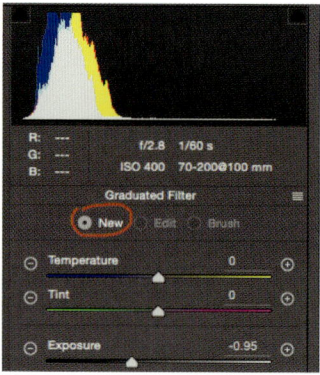

FIGURE 8.83

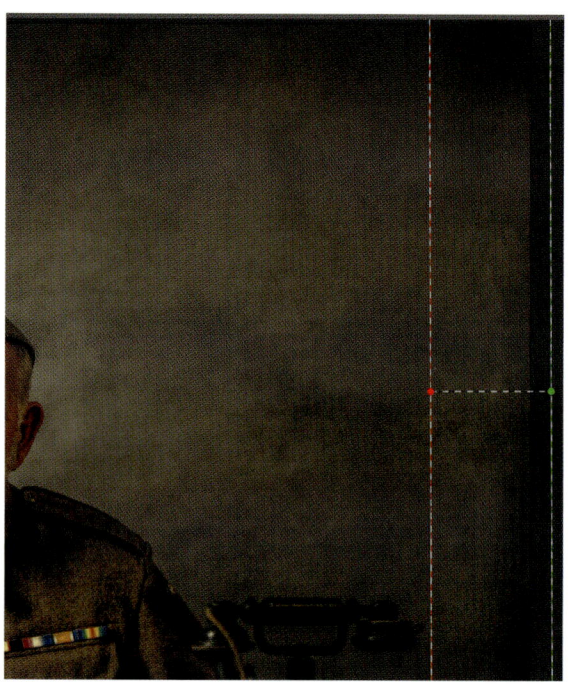

FIGURE 8.84

28. Create a copy of the FT layer by pressing Command +J (Mac) or Ctrl + J (PC). Then go to *Filter > Sharpen > Unsharp Mask* (**Figure 8.85**) and dial in an Amount of 18%, a Radius of 18 Pixels, and a Threshold of 0 levels, and click OK (**Figure 8.86**)

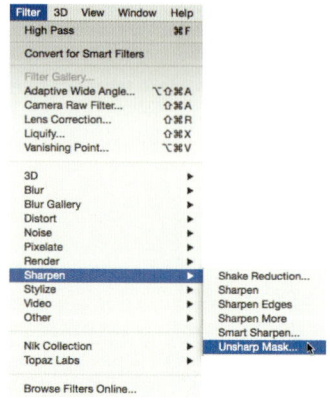

FIGURE 8.85

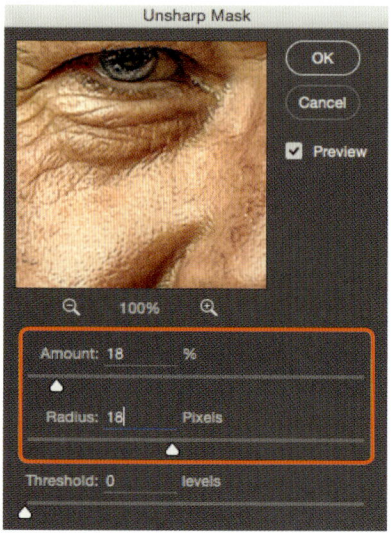

FIGURE 8.86

Hold down the Option key (Mac) or Alt key (PC) and click on the Layer Mask icon at the bottom of the Layers panel to add a black Layer Mask. This will hide the results of the Unsharp Mask Filter (**Figure 8.87**). With a round, soft-edged brush and a white foreground color at 100% Opacity, paint over Roger's face to reveal the effects of the Unsharp Mask Filter (**Figure 8.88**). Rename this layer "contrast 3."

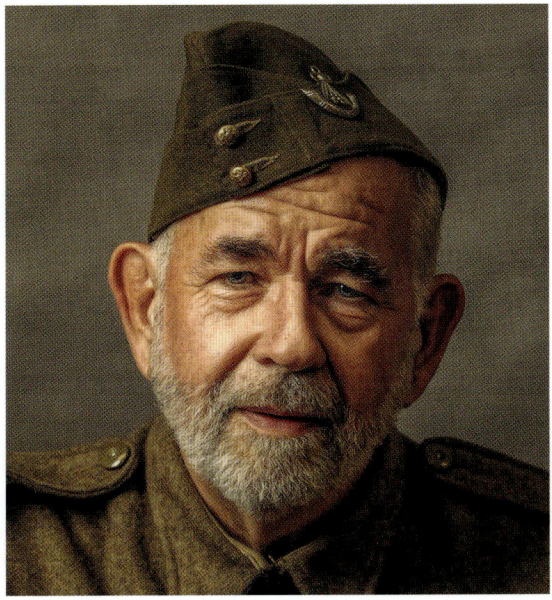

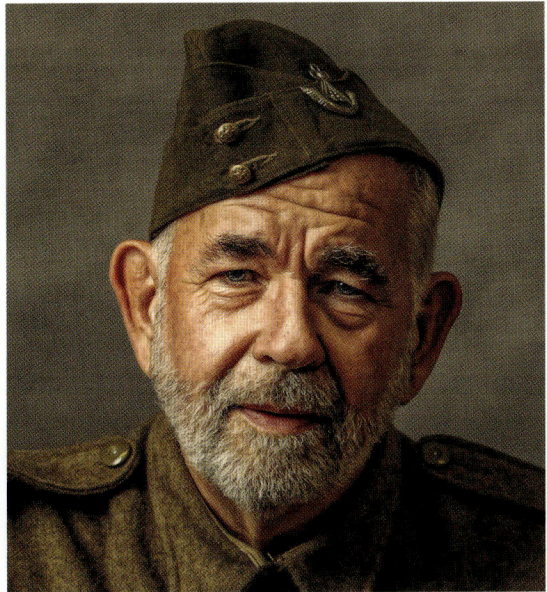

FIGURE 8.87 Before application of the Unsharp Mask Filter

FIGURE 8.88 After application of the Unsharp Mask Filter. A Layer Mask has been added so that the effects are visible only on Roger's face.

29. Finally, we'll desaturate the image a touch. Press the D key to set the foreground and background colors to their defaults of black and white, and then click on the Gradient Map icon in the Adjustments panel to add a Gradient Map adjustment layer (**Figure 8.89**). Lower the Opacity of this layer to 15% (**Figure 8.90**).

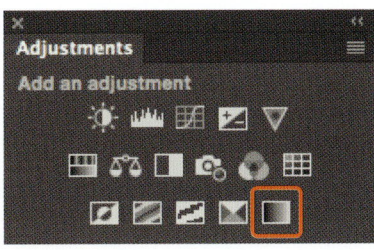

FIGURE 8.89

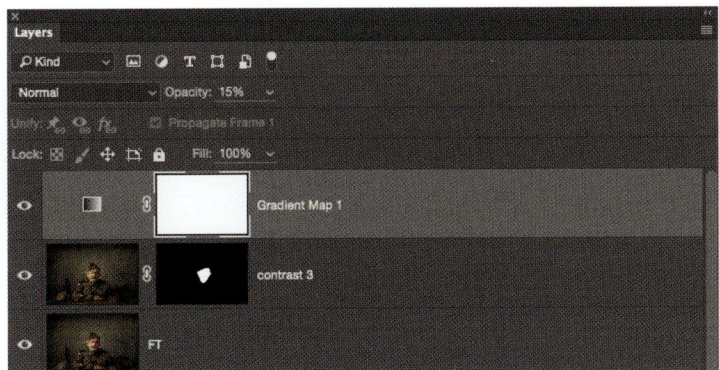

FIGURE 8.90

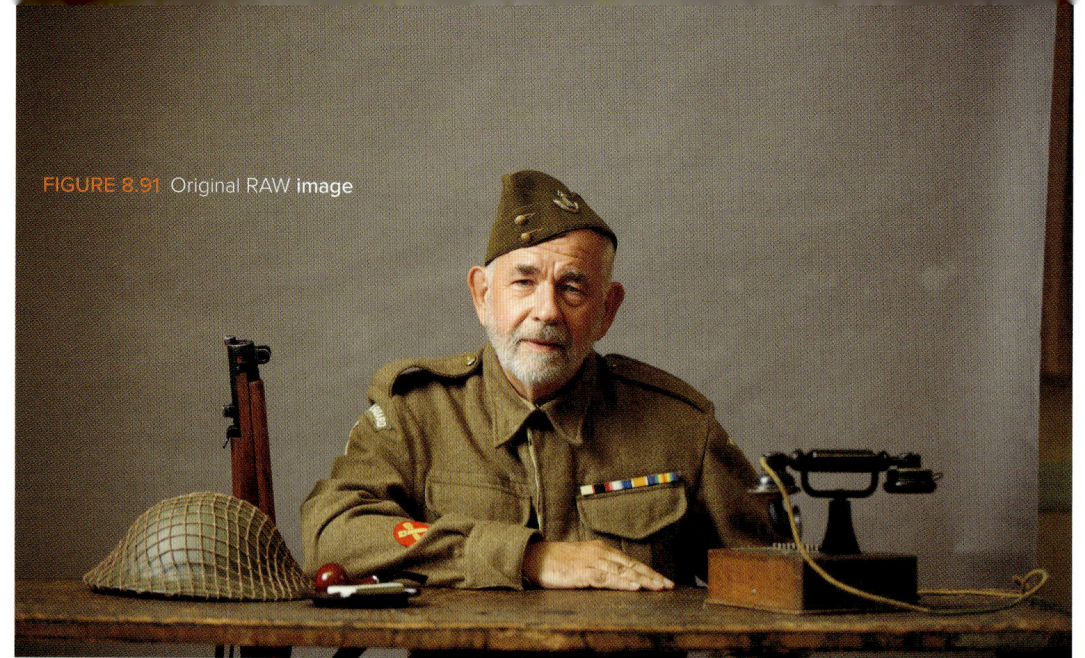

FIGURE 8.91 Original RAW image

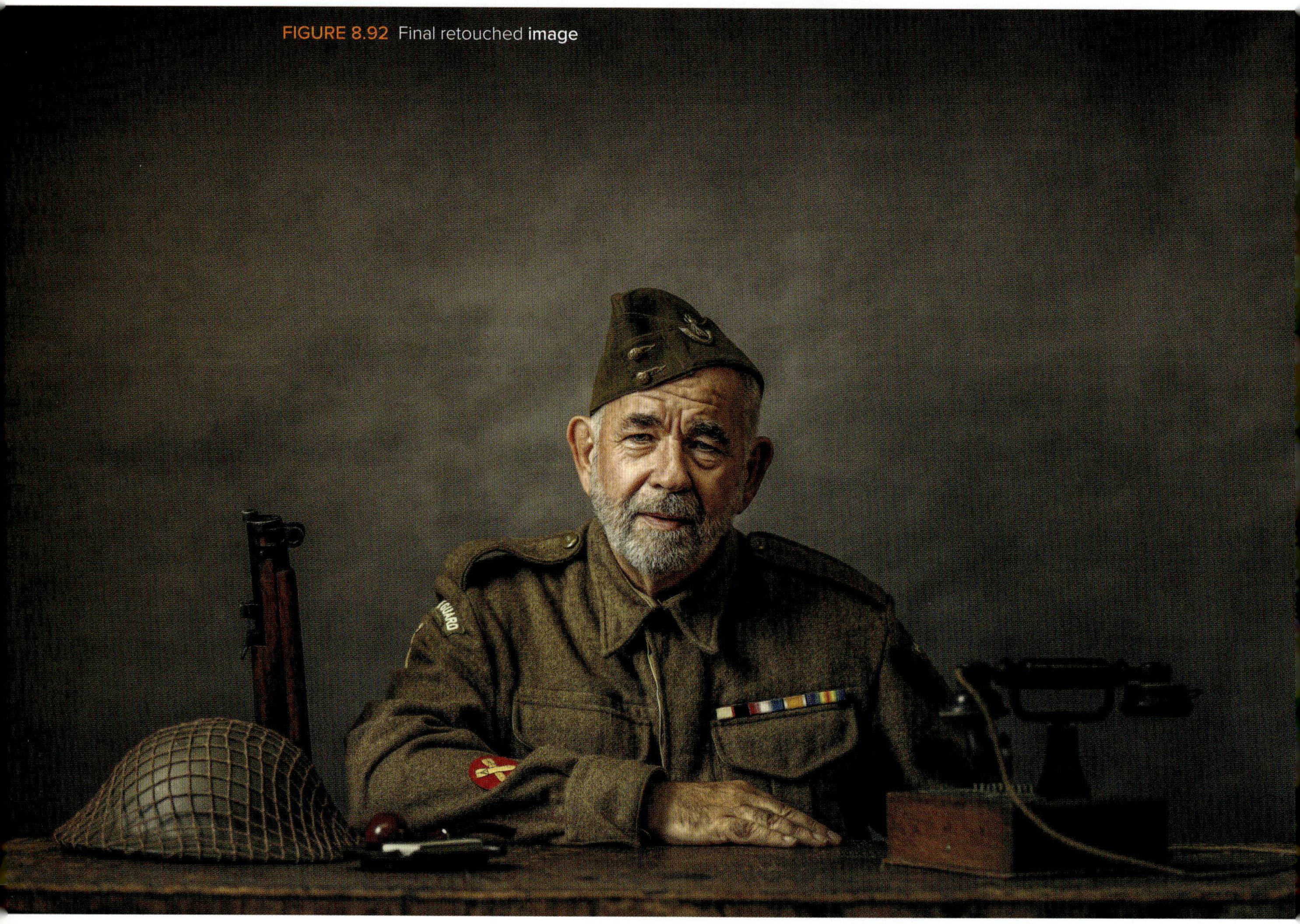

FIGURE 8.92 Final retouched image

Wherever and whenever possible, I'd always advise you to save your files with all the layers intact. This is great not only because it allows you to redo steps later if you need to, but also because you can replicate a look from one image to another by looking at each layer for reference. This proved to be extremely useful when I was retouching other images from this particular photo shoot with the Oxfordshire Home Guard (**Figures 8.93–8.97**).

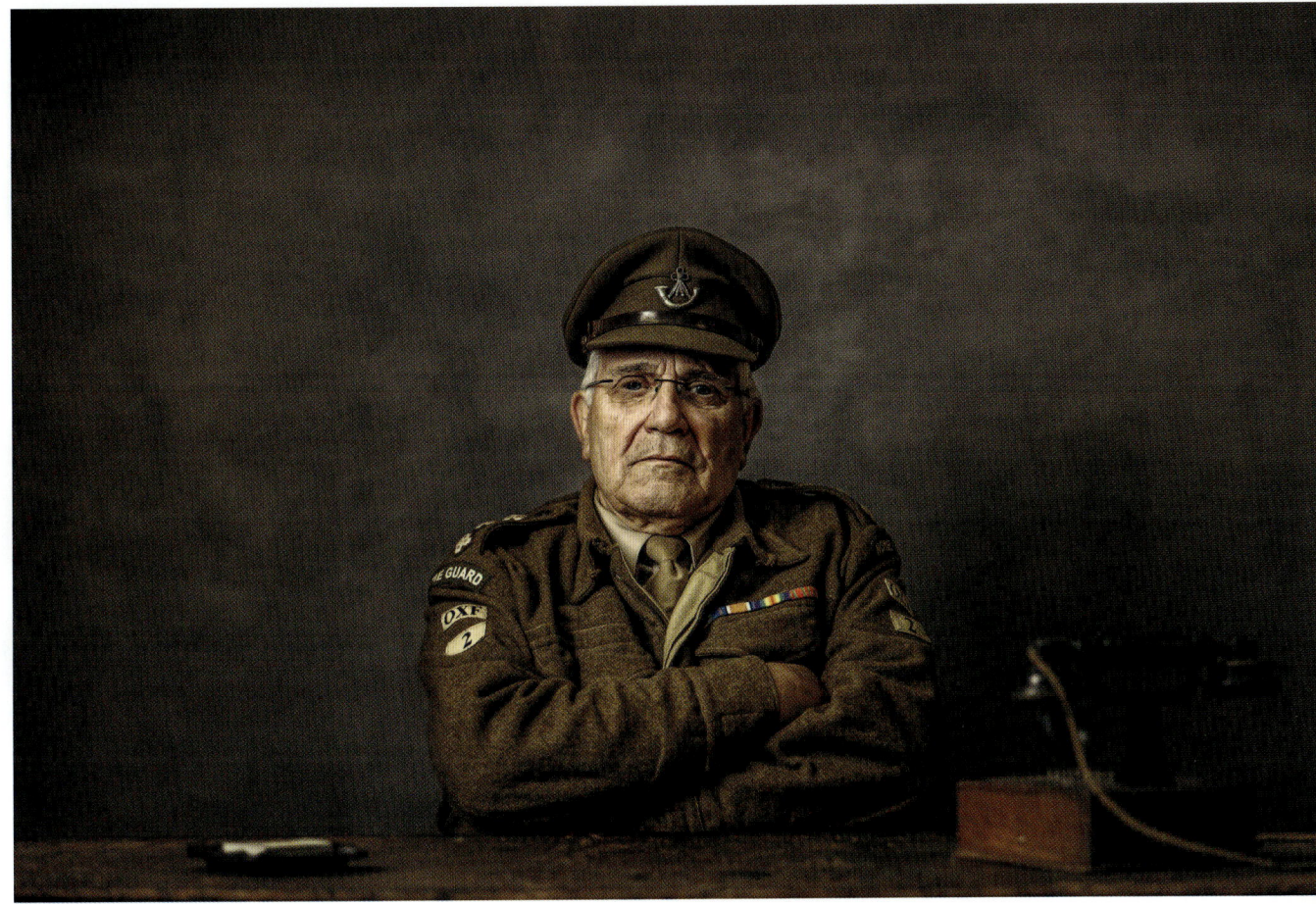

FIGURE 8.93

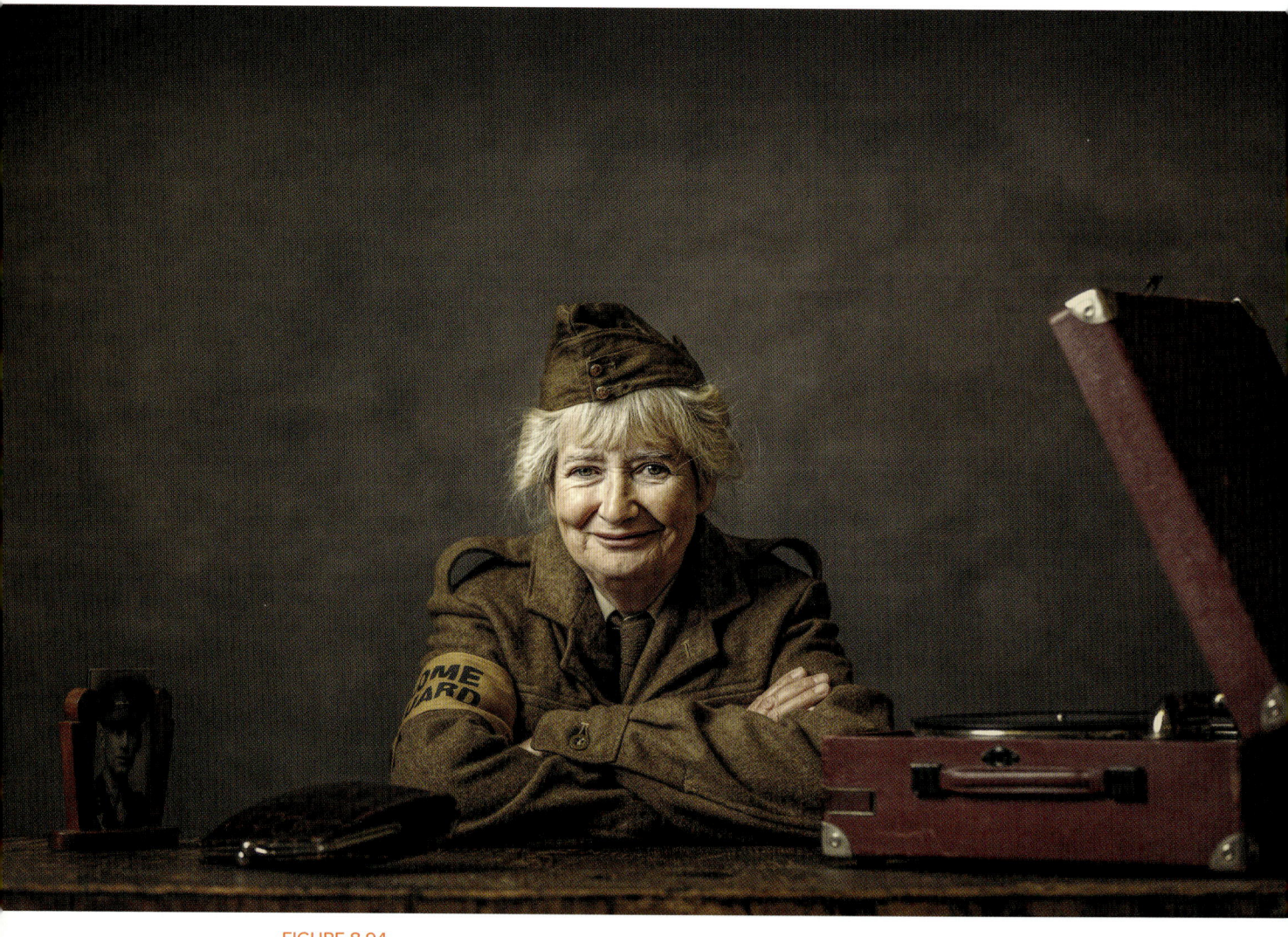

FIGURE 8.94

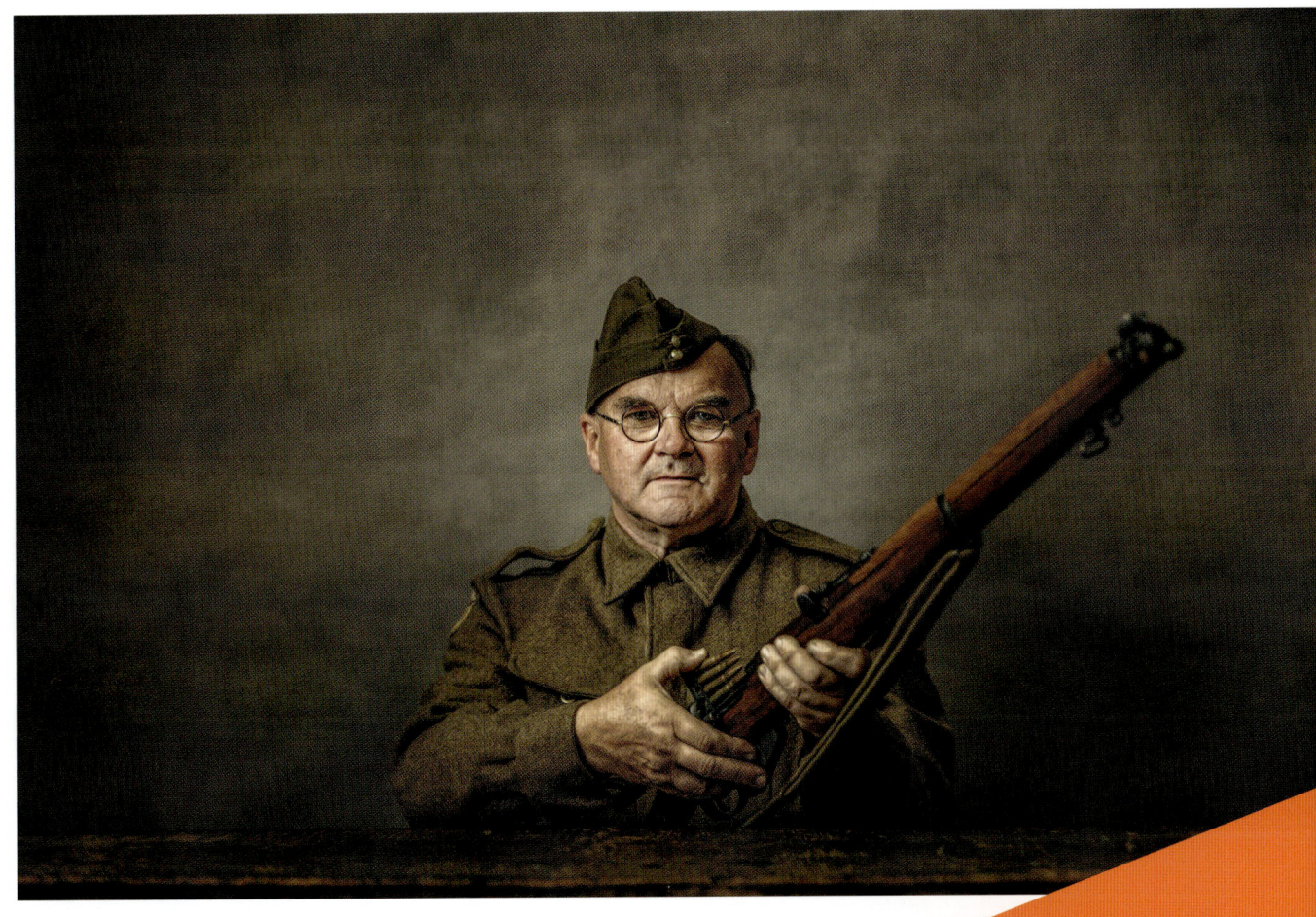

FIGURE 8.95

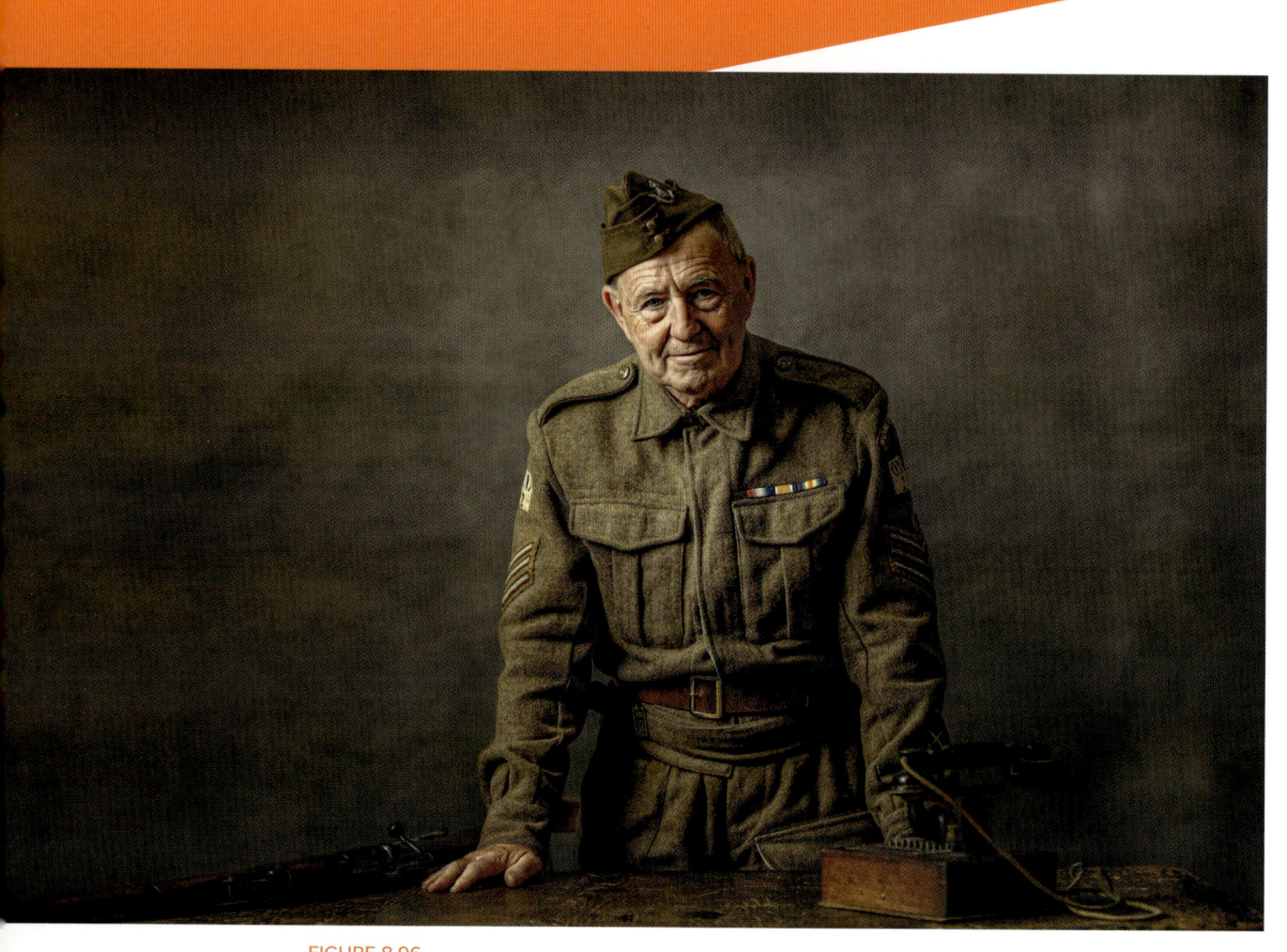

FIGURE 8.96

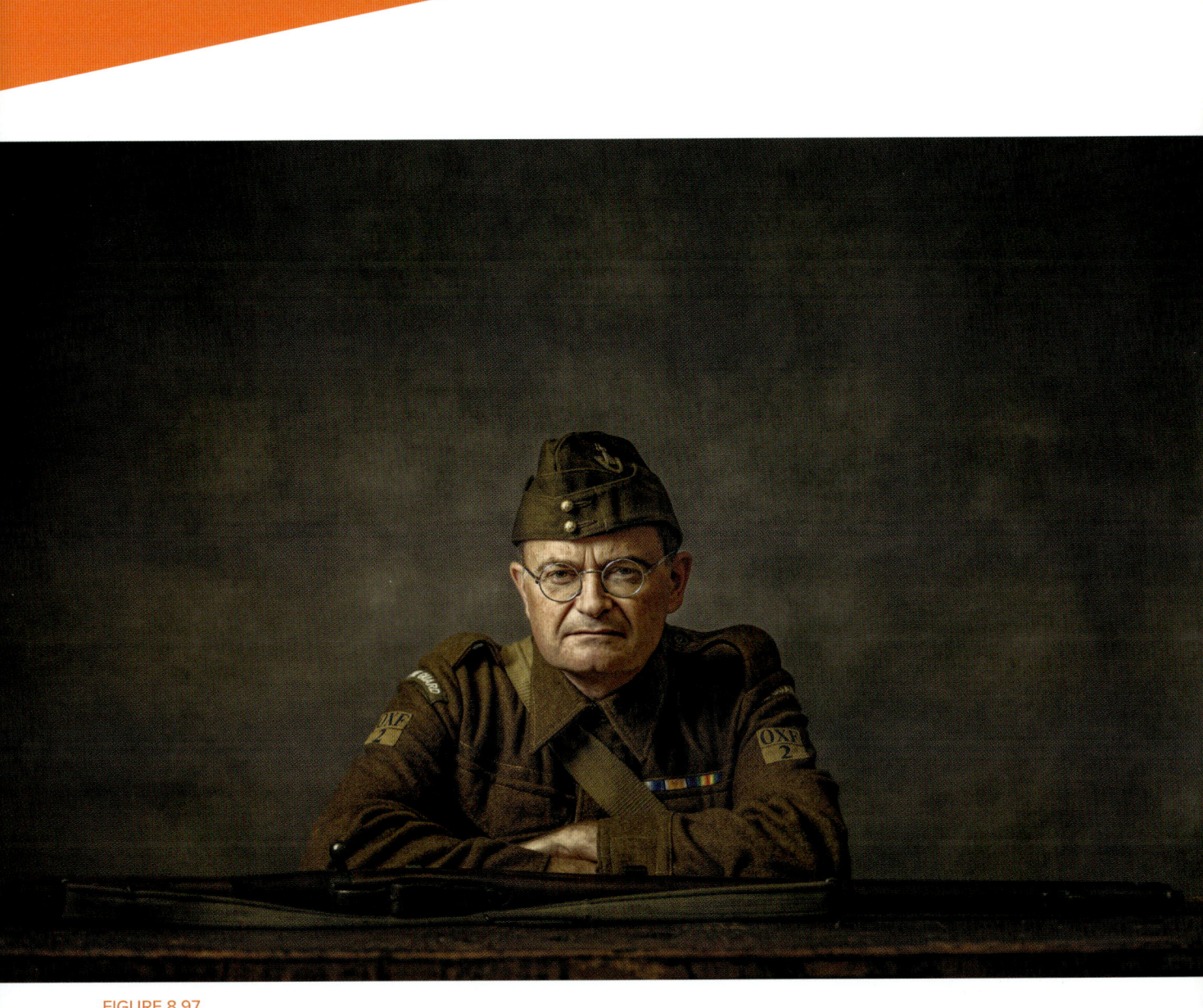

FIGURE 8.97

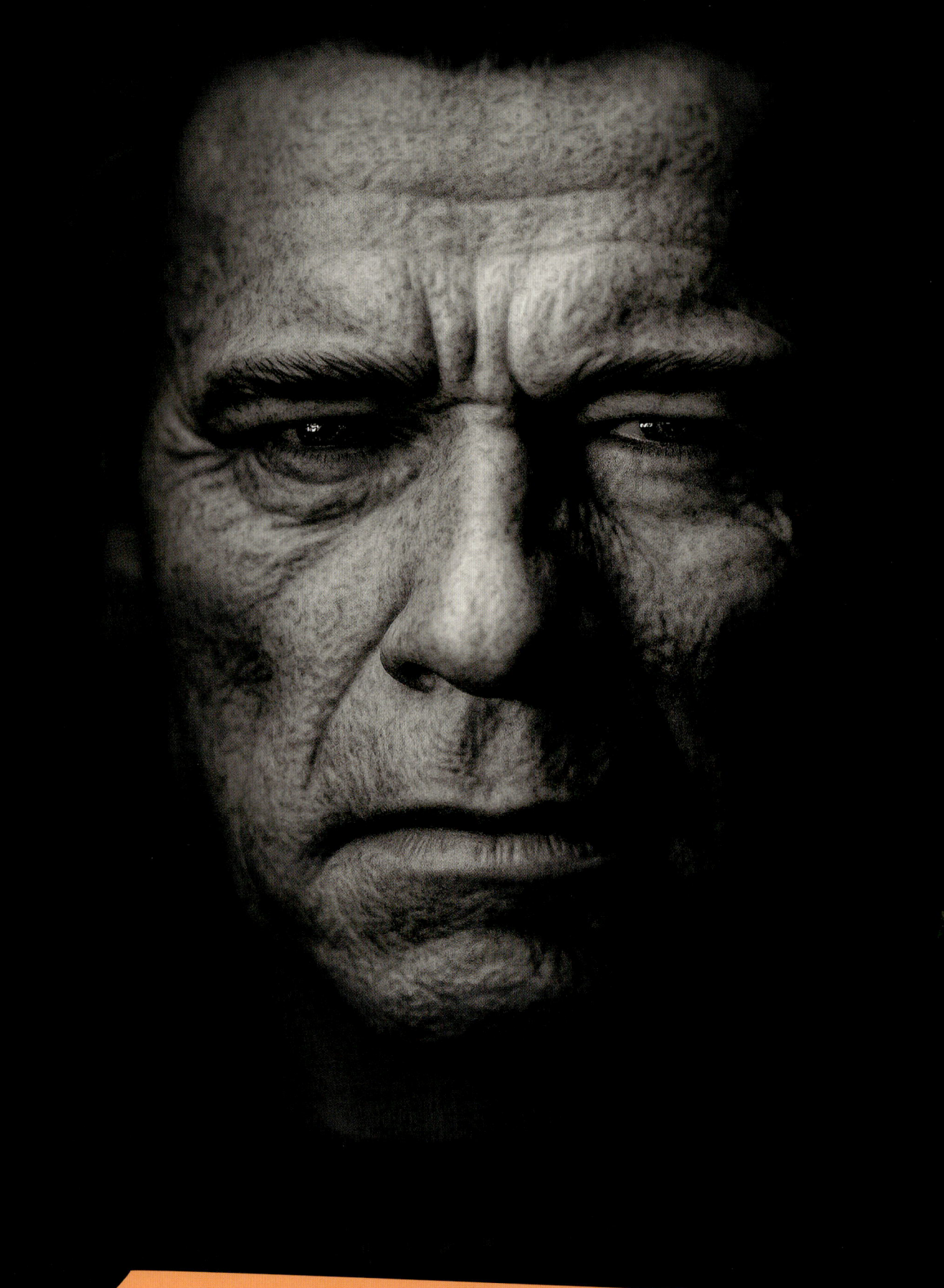

9 ACTION MOVIE INSPIRED

If you ask anyone who knows me who I would most like to photograph, they'll tell you it's Arnold Schwarzenegger. Unfortunately, that hasn't happened just yet, but I'm still holding out. In the meantime, the Hot Toys action figure we'll be working on in this chapter is a darn convincing alternative.

Originally, having just seen the new *Terminator Genisys* movie, I purchased the Hot Toys action figure with the intention of creating a Terminator-themed picture similar to one of the original posters. However, as time went on, I thought that was a little cliché and expected, and because of the incredible detail in the action figure, I decided I'd go for a portrait instead of compositing a new background, lighting effects, debris, and other effects.

This tends to happen to me from time to time. I initially approach a shoot 100% convinced of the way I want to go, but after the shoot I'm not so convinced. In the past, when I was just starting out, I would have doggedly carried on regardless of how I felt about it, but I've discovered over time to trust my instinct. Slowing down and being open to alternative ideas is what allows you to produce your very best work.

There's quite a bit to cover here, so we better get started, but before we do I have a word of warning...The force in these action figures is strong. Buy one, and the urge to buy another is almost overpowering. So far, I'm managing to resist, but Lord only knows for how long!

REVERSE ENGINEERING

Because I decided to see if I could make a convincing and life-like portrait of the Arnold action figure, instead of creating a *Terminator* movie—inspired image, there's no specific photograph I used for inspiration. However, I opted to do a portrait with a lighting style similar to that of Annie Leibovitz's work, with a single light source coming from the side and slightly in front of the subject. In fact, it's pretty much the same lighting I used in chapters 5 and 8, but obviously on a much smaller scale.

I also chose to make this a low-key portrait with a technique that I call The Invisible Black Background, which I covered in chapter 4. This technique allows me to create a portrait with a completely black background, regardless of whether I'm photographing indoors or outdoors, and without having an actual black background set up. This look is perfect for this portrait of Arnold—well, for his action figure, at least.

THE SETUP

For this picture, I used the Invisible Black Background technique I discussed in chapter 4 (page 51). I could have just put up a piece of black cardboard behind the Arnold figure, but I was shooting tethered to my main computer on my desk and my large Benq screen was great for seeing the images as they came in, so checking the focus, sharpness, and lighting was that much easier with this setup (**Figure 9.1**).

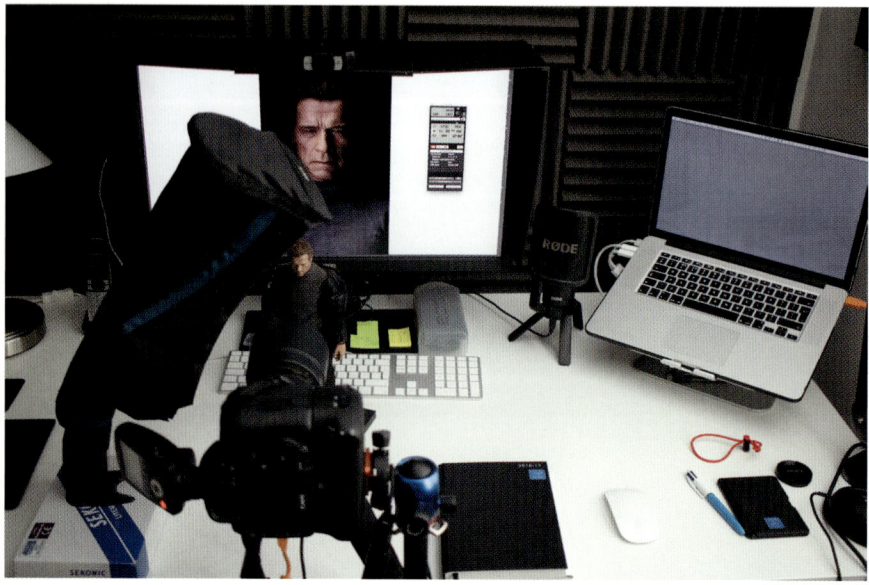

FIGURE 9.1

Also, despite working in such a small area, using the light modifiers with the grids attached meant that there was minimal light spill, so getting a completely black background was super easy.

I went for a cross-lighting setup with just one light positioned to the left of the camera and slightly in front of the Arnold figure. This meant that the side of the figure's face nearest the flash was lit and only a small area on the opposite side was lit (**Figure 9.2**).

I placed the flash on top of a box and covered the lower part of the modifier with my diary so that the light was restricted to the top half of the model (**Figure 9.3**).

I angled the camera and lens upward so I was photographing up toward the model, which gives the portrait more impact and power.

TIP *In addition to shooting tethered, I used a cable release to prevent any movement of the camera while I photographed the Arnold action figure with the macro lens.*

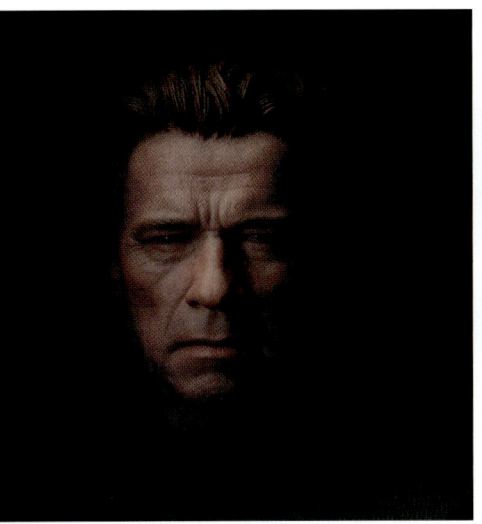

FIGURE 9.2

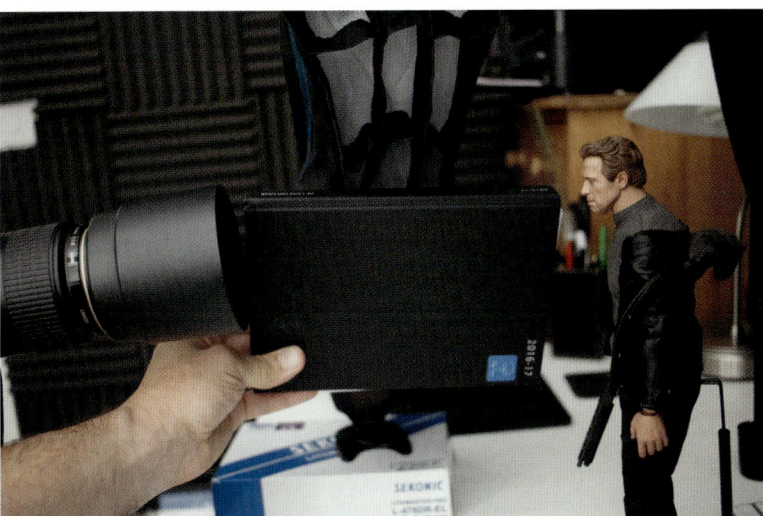

FIGURE 9.3

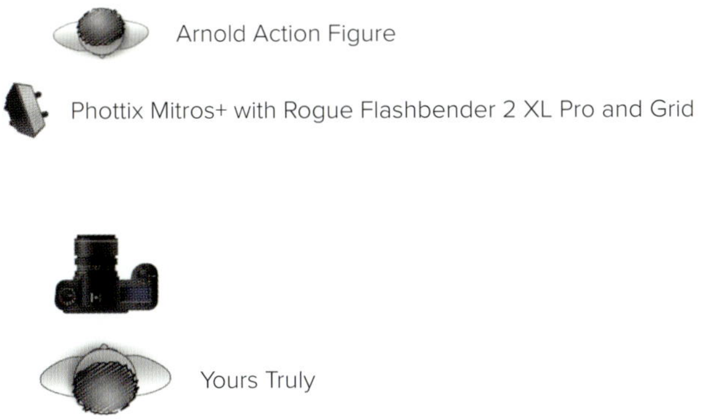

 Arnold Action Figure

 Phottix Mitros+ with Rogue Flashbender 2 XL Pro and Grid

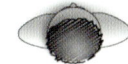

Yours Truly

FIGURE 9.4

CAMERA SETTINGS

Despite shooting in a tight area and having a computer screen behind the Arnold action figure, I was able to get a completely black background with an aperture of f/8.0.

Of course, using the grid on the Rogue light modifier was key here because it allowed me to get directional light that didn't affect anything other than the action figure. This is something to always be mindful of when using the Invisible Black Background technique. This is rarely an issue in a large indoor space or outdoors, but when you're close to walls and in a tight space it's important to use a modifier that controls the light and gives it direction.

I kept the ISO at 100 to make the sensor as least sensitive to light as possible and to get the cleanest possible file.

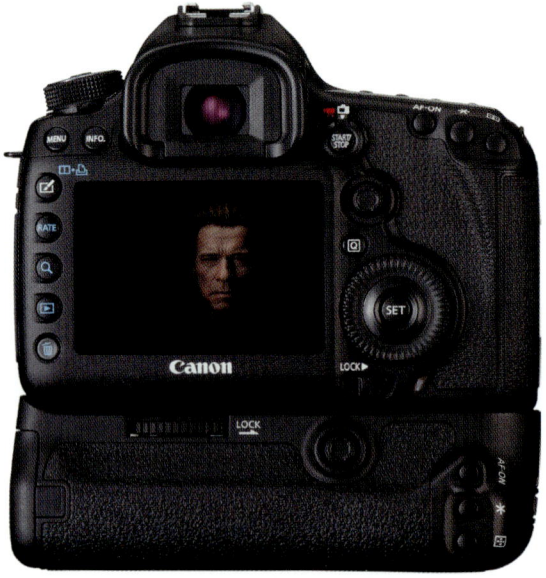

FIGURE 9.5

MODE Manual

ISO 100

APERTURE f/8.0

SHUTTER SPEED 1/125 sec.

LENS Canon EF 100mm f/2.8 Macro USM

GEAR GUIDE

For this shoot I used a small flash, namely my Phottix Mitros+ TTL Transceiver (**Figure 9.6**), and a Rogue light modifier (**Figure 9.7**) that is easy to attach and that also came with a grid to control light spill.

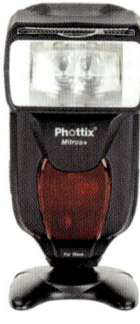

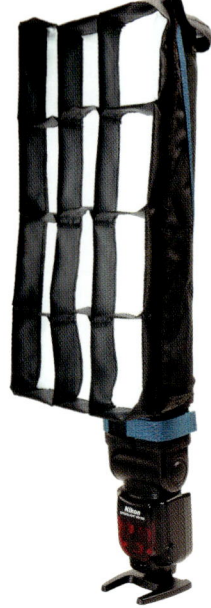

FIGURE 9.6   FIGURE 9.7

This was actually the first time I'd shot with or ever needed to use a macro lens. I opted for the Canon EF 100mm f/2.8 Macro USM (**Figure 9.8**), which is not the top-end macro lens from Canon, but it certainly did a great job for this shoot. I didn't want to invest in the more expensive model because I have no idea how many times I'll use it.

I mounted my camera on a 3 Legged Thing Winston tripod to keep it nice and steady (**Figure 9.9**).

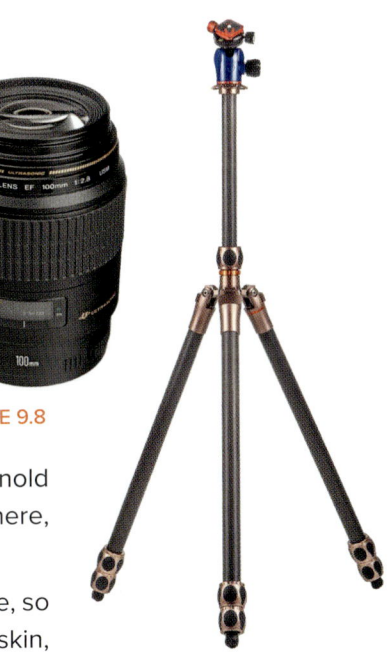

FIGURE 9.8

POST-PROCESSING

So now the photo shoot has been done and it's time to bring the Arnold action figure to life. We're going to go through quite a few steps here, despite the fact that the portrait has a simple black background.

Our main goal is to make the portrait look as believable as possible, so we'll be enhancing the eyes, adding more detail and texture to the skin, and dodging and burning to enhance the highlight and shadow areas. I'll also show you a bit of what I call depth building, which involves adding

FIGURE 9.9

increasing layers of contrast, light, and sharpness to make it appear as though the portrait is coming forward from the screen. This works especially well when you print the images.

Right, let's get to work.

NOTE *Download the file you need to follow along step-by-step at: http://www.rockynook.com/ photograph-like-a-thief-reference/*

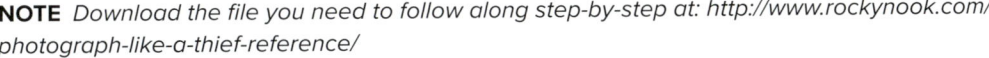

1. As always, we'll start in Lightroom, but if you're not a Lightroom user you can also use Camera RAW, seeing as how the programs are exactly the same in the Develop Module. But to be honest, we're going to do very little in here anyhow.

   Let's begin by sorting out the composition of our picture using the Crop Tool (**R**). For this portrait, I prefer to have Arnold positioned on the right side of the frame, so we'll crop from the top just above his hairline and bring in the right side to position him in the Rule of Thirds grid. I don't often follow such rules, but for this portrait it definitely works (**Figure 9.10**).

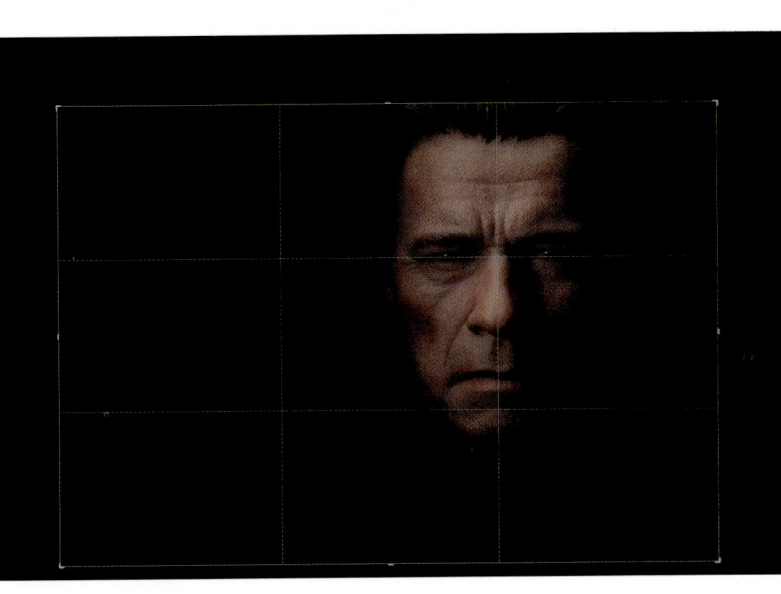

FIGURE 9.10

2. Now that we have the composition sorted, let's tidy up some of the dust and scratches on the figure before moving over into Photoshop. Select the Spot Removal Tool (**Q**) and set it to Heal (**Figure 9.11**), and then clean up some of the obvious dust spots and scratches, such as on Arnold's hair and forehead (**Figure 9.12**). To make this easier, zoom in on these areas by going to a 1:1 view in the Navigator (**Figure 9.13**).

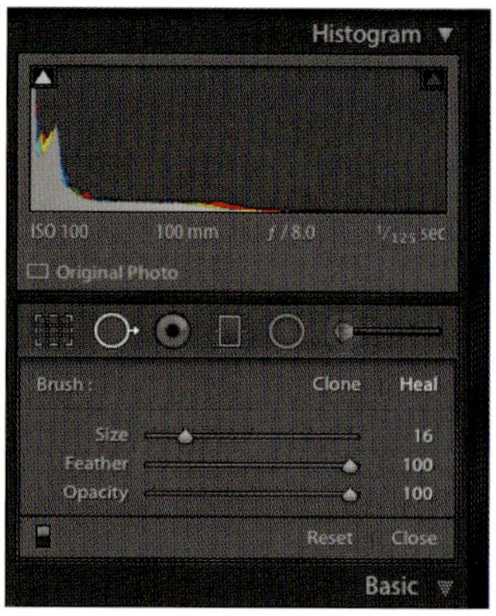

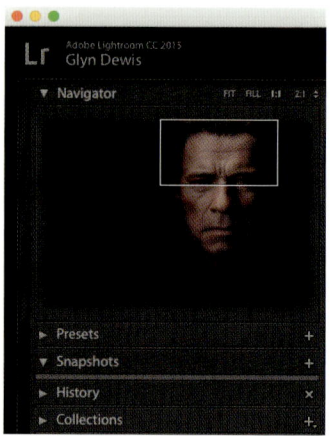

FIGURE 9.11

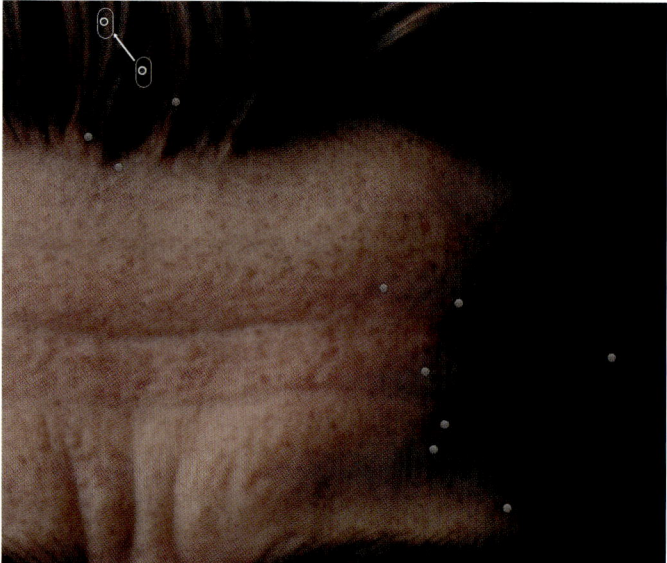

FIGURE 9.12

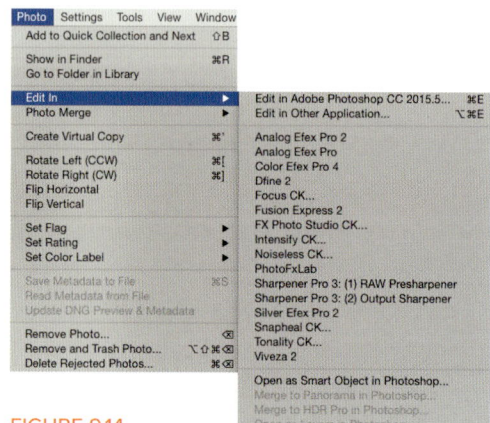

FIGURE 9.13

3. Press Q or click on the Spot Removal Tool icon to exit, and now we'll send our picture over into Photoshop by going to *Photo > Edit In > Open as Smart Object in Photoshop* (**Figure 9.14**).

4. Now we're going to enhance Arnold's eyes. Go to *Filter > Camera RAW*. Zoom in on the eyes so they're nice and big on the screen, and then choose the Adjustment Brush (**Figure 9.15**).

FIGURE 9.14

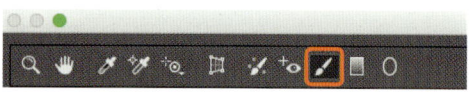

FIGURE 9.15

Set the Exposure to around +0.50 and paint over both eyes. Turn on the Mask so that the red overlay clearly shows the area being affected by the Adjustment Brush (**Figure 9.16**).

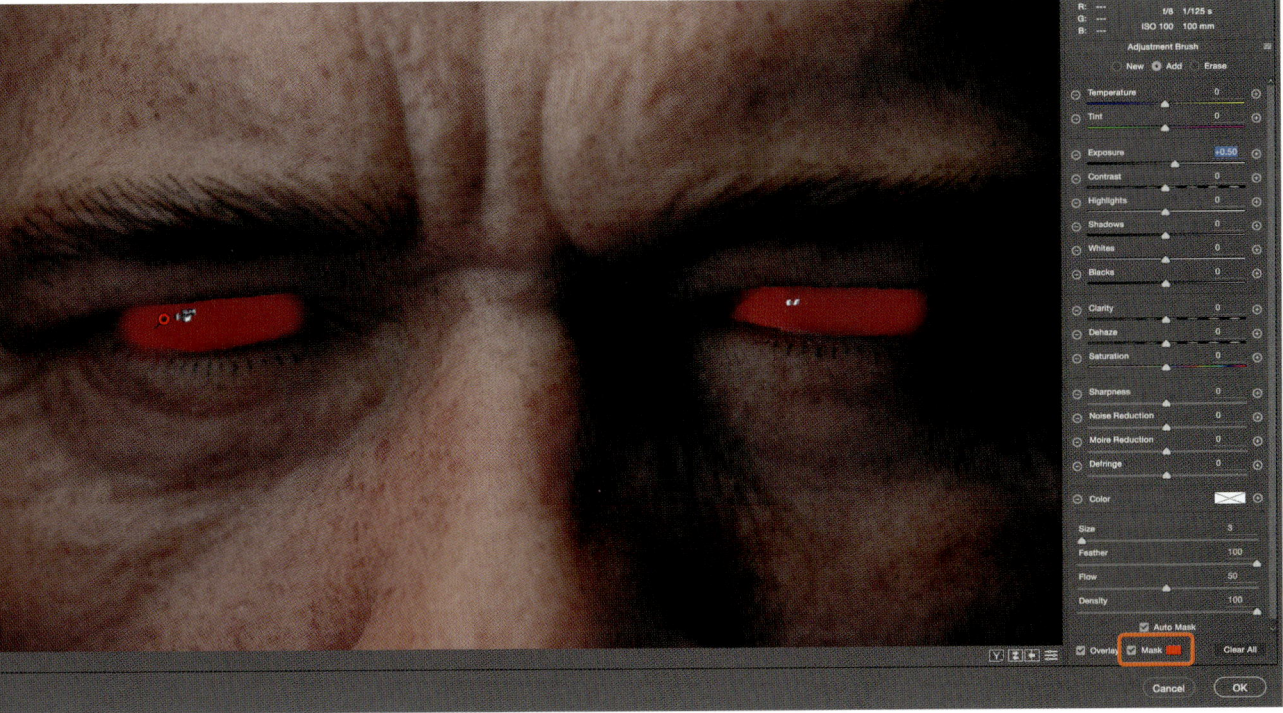

FIGURE 9.16

To remove the adjustment from specific areas, click on Erase (**Figure 9.17**) and brush over the unwanted areas.

5. To me it looks like the white of the figure's right eye is not quite as bright as that of the left, despite the fact that the light is coming from camera left (the figure's right). So to even out the eyes, make sure the Adjustment Brush is still selected and click New (**Figure 9.18**), and then paint over the eye on the left side of the picture (the figure's right eye) with the Exposure again set to +0.50. Click OK to exit Camera RAW and return to Photoshop.

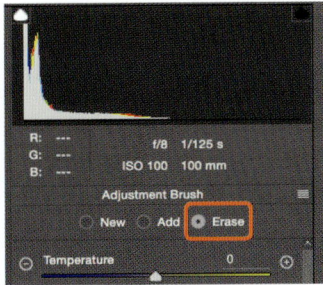

FIGURE 9.17

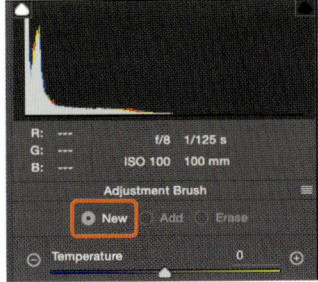

FIGURE 9.18

6. Now we'll use a Quick Mask to select the middle (cornea) of both eyes, but before we do, double-click on the Quick Mask icon in the toolbar (**Figure 9.19**), and in the Quick Mask Options, ensure that Selected Areas is checked and click OK (**Figure 9.20**).

Now choose a round, soft-edged brush with a black foreground color from the toolbar, press Q or click on the Quick Mask icon in the toolbar, and paint over the cornea of both eyes. If you paint over some unwanted areas, simply change the foreground color to white and paint over them again to remove them.

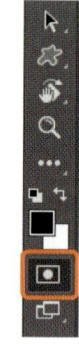

FIGURE 9.19

When you have covered the middle of the eyes with the Quick Mask overlay, press Q or click on the Quick Mask icon to exit Quick Mask mode, and the marching ants will indicate the areas you have selected (**Figure 9.21**).

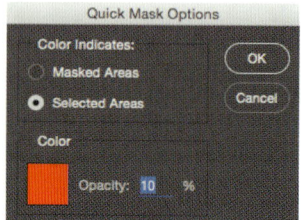

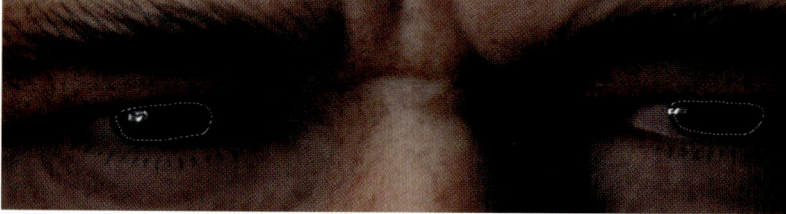

FIGURE 9.20

FIGURE 9.21

7. With the marching ants selection visible, click on the Selective Color icon in the Adjustments panel to add a Selective Color adjustment layer. In the Layers panel, change the Blend Mode from Normal to Linear Dodge (Add) (**Figure 9.22**). When you do this you'll see that Arnold's eyes get a lot brighter (**Figure 9.23**). We can adjust the Opacity of the layer to control how much brighter the eyes are, but don't do that just yet because it's easier to see the color change we're going to make when the eyes are nice and bright.

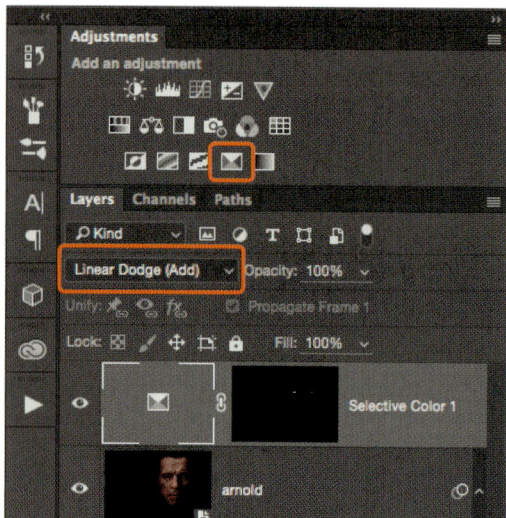

FIGURE 9.22

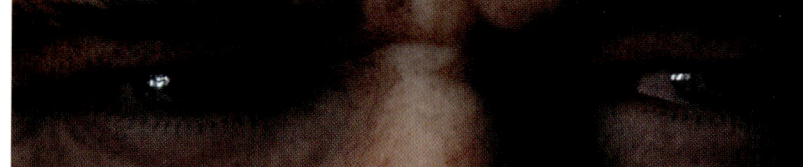

FIGURE 9.23

8. In the Selective Color Properties, select Neutral from the Colors menu. We can now use the Cyan, Magenta, and Yellow sliders to dial in a color for the eyes. In this example, lets go for Cyan: +1, Magenta: +8, and Yellow: -20.

We can also add in some contrast by changing the Colors menu to Blacks and dragging the Black slider to +3 (**Figure 9.24**).

NOTE *Although we're going to be turning this portrait into a black-and-white image, changing the eye color can have a big impact on how the eyes convert. Plus, I thought this was a pretty neat technique to share with you.*

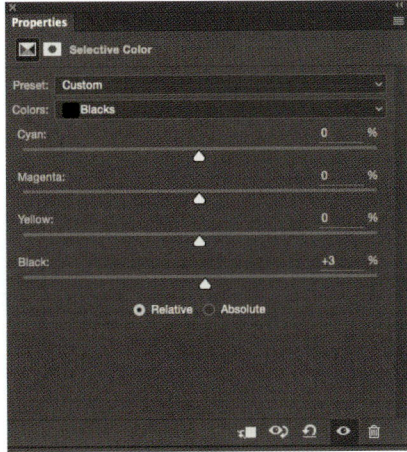

FIGURE 9.24

9. Now we can add some sharpening to the eyes to make them stand out even more. What's really cool here is that we can do this on a blank layer, so it doesn't add to the file size and it's nondestructive.

Add a new blank layer to the top of the layer stack and rename it "Eye Sharpen" (**Figure 9.25**). Grab the Sharpen Tool from the toolbar (**Figure 9.26**), and in the options bar at the top of the screen, set Strength to 30% and put a checkmark next to Sample All Layers (**Figure 9.27**).

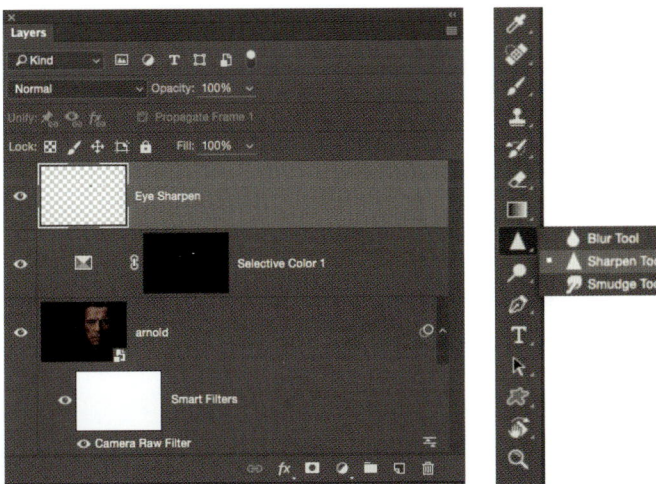

FIGURE 9.25

FIGURE 9.26

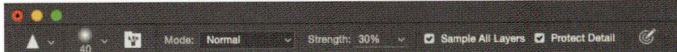

FIGURE 9.27

Now paint over both eyes to sharpen them. You can see the difference this makes in **Figures 9.28** and **9.29**.

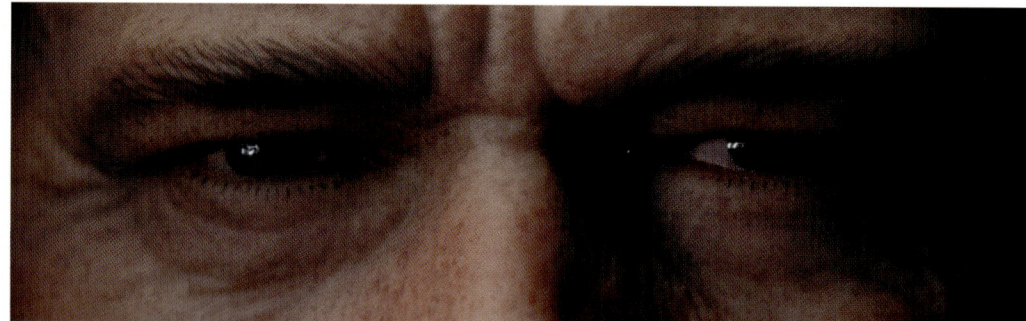

FIGURE 9.28 Before sharpening

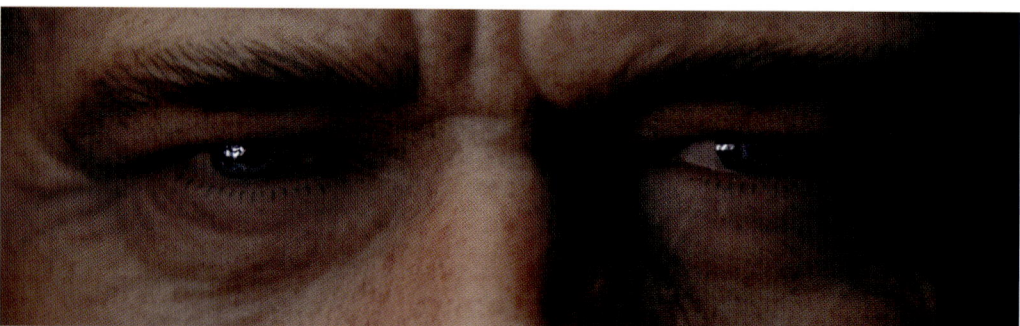

FIGURE 9.29 After sharpening

10. Let's keep things nice and organized by putting the layers affecting the eyes only into a group. With the Eyes Sharpen layer selected, hold down the Shift key and click on the Selective Color 1 adjustment layer below so both layers are selected (**Figure 9.30**). Then go to *Layer > New > Group from Layers*, rename the group "Eyes," and click OK. Lower the Opacity of this group to 80%.

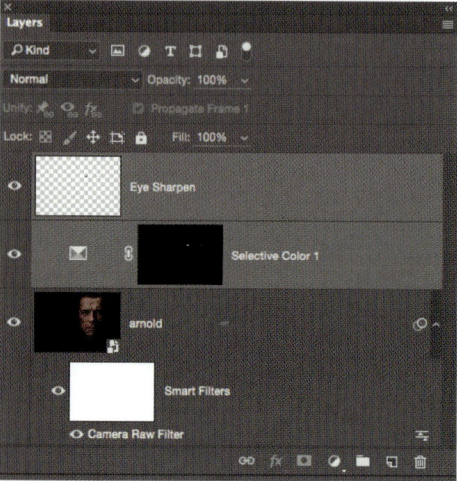

FIGURE 9.30

11. Now we'll add some depth to the portrait and make it look a little more alive with dodging and burning. We'll use the 50% Gray Layer technique that I covered in chapter 4 (page 66). Add a new blank layer by going to *Layer > New > Layer*. In the New Layer properties, rename the layer "Dodge & Burn," change the Mode to Soft Light, put a checkmark next to Fill with Soft-Light-neutral color (50% gray), and click OK (**Figure 9.31**).

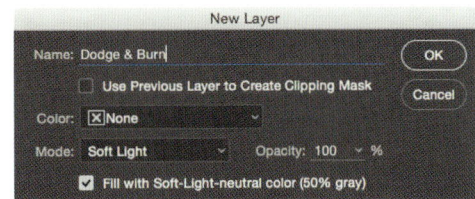

FIGURE 9.31

12. Choose the Dodge Tool (**O**) from the toolbar, and in the options at the top of the screen, leave Range set to Midtones, set Exposure to 10%, and tick the Protect Tones checkbox (**Figure 9.32**).

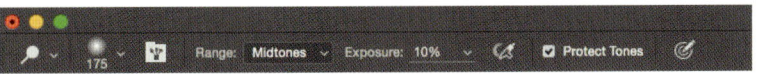

FIGURE 9.32

Use the Dodge Tool to paint over the brighter areas of Arnold's face to enhance them. Hold down the Option key (Mac) or Alt key (PC) to activate the Burn Tool with the same settings and darken the areas on either side of the highlights and the other darker areas of the image.

This is all very dependent on personal taste and how you want the image to look, but you can see the areas I enhanced in **Figure 9.33**.

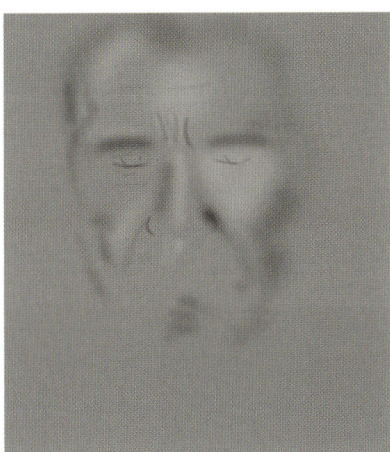

FIGURE 9.33 The 50% gray Dodge & Burn layer showing the areas I brightened and darkened to add more depth and dimension to Arnold's portrait

NOTE *To see just the gray layer, hold down the Option key (Mac) or Alt key (PC) and click on the eye icon of the Dodge & Burn layer. To return to normal view, simply do the same thing again.*

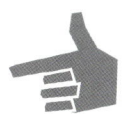

You can see the effects of the dodging and burning by comparing the before (**Figure 9.34**) and after (**Figure 9.35**) images.

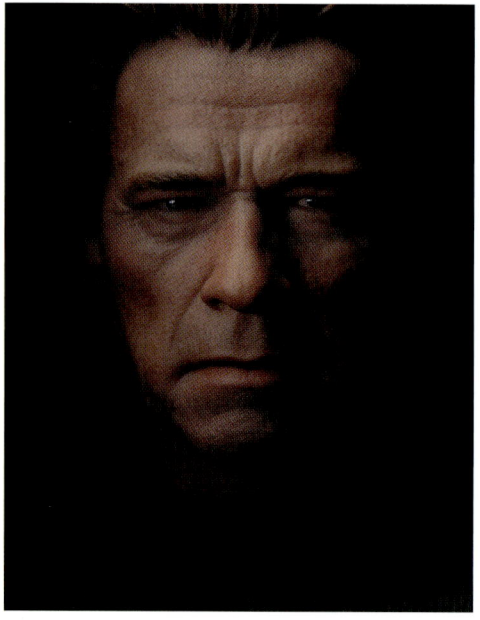

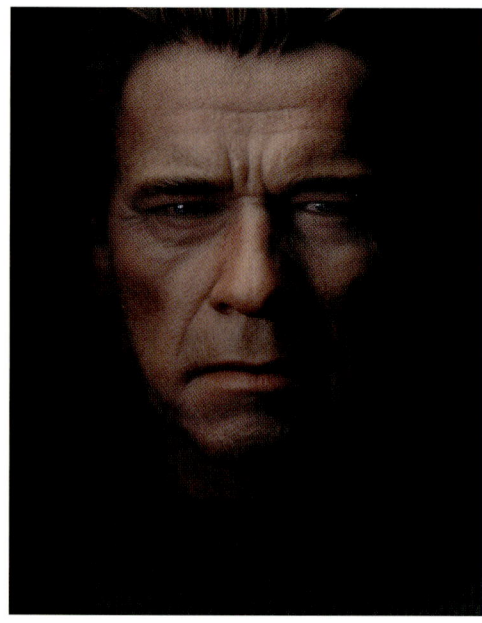

FIGURE 9.34 Before dodging and burning

FIGURE 9.35 After dodging and burning

TIP *If you want to increase the effect of the dodging and burning, you can duplicate the Dodge & Burn layer by pressing Control + J (Mac) or Control + J (PC).*

13. Although we're working with an action figure, I want to make it look as real and lifelike as possible. I'm sure you'll agree that the Hot Toys action figure is incredibly detailed, but there are some areas that need to be cleared up if we're going to "Sell the Fake," to quote Joel Grimes.

    The hairline is a giveaway that the figure is made of molded plastic, but I'll share a quick fix for that in just a bit. First we need to fix some of the color that's missing (**Figure 9.36**).

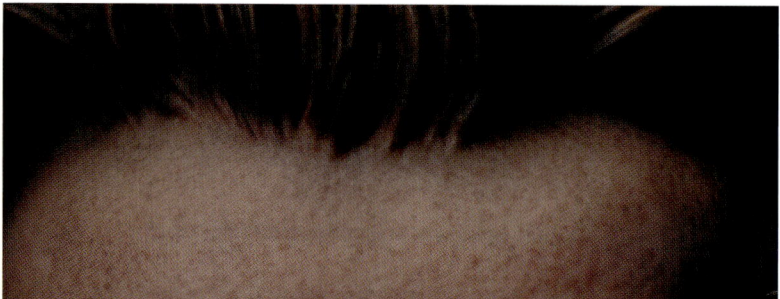

FIGURE 9.36

Add a new blank layer and rename it "Hair." Grab the Clone Stamp Tool (**S**), and in the options at the top of the screen, set the Opacity to 30%, tick the Aligned checkbox, and select All Layers from the Sample menu (**Figure 9.37**). Hold down the Option key (Mac) or Alt key (PC) and click to sample an area of brown hair near an area where the color is missing. Then brush over the areas missing color with the Clone Stamp Tool to gradually cover them with the brown hair. Doing this with a reduced opacity, rather than cloning over the areas at 100%, helps to build the effect gradually.

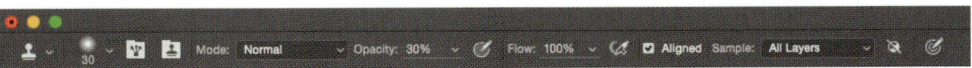

FIGURE 9.37

14. Before we move on to my favorite part, where we'll take this portrait go to a whole new level by enhancing the skin texture and contours, let's fix the eyes because they're bugging me a little. The eye on the right side of the picture looks a little too bright for my taste, so we'll bring it down. This is where working nondestructively like we have been comes in extra handy.

    Double-click on the bottom Smart Object layer named "arnold" (**Figure 9.38**). This takes us into Camera RAW where we can adjust some of the retouching steps we performed earlier. Choose the Adjustment Brush and make sure that both the Overlay and Mask checkboxes are turned on (**Figure 9.39**).

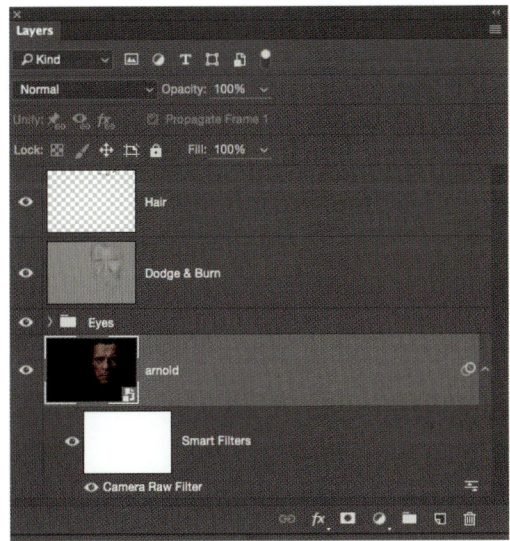

FIGURE 9.38

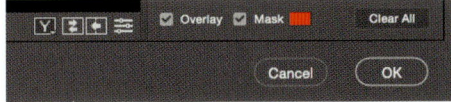

FIGURE 9.39

Hover over both pins with your cursor to identify which one turns on the red overlay for both eyes (**Figure 9.40**). When you identify the correct pin, click on it to make it active. Now choose Erase (**Figure 9.41**) and paint away the red overlay covering the eye on the right side of the frame to remove the brightening (**Figure 9.42**). Click OK to return to Photoshop.

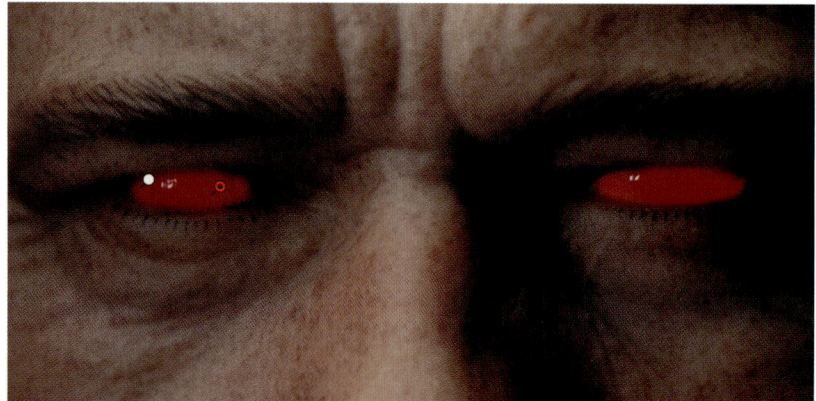

FIGURE 9.40

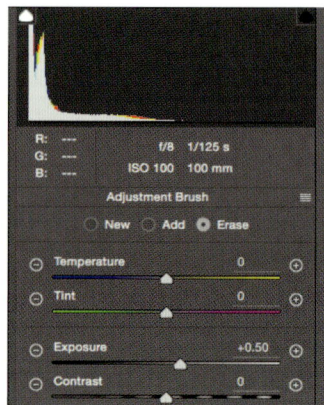

FIGURE 9.41

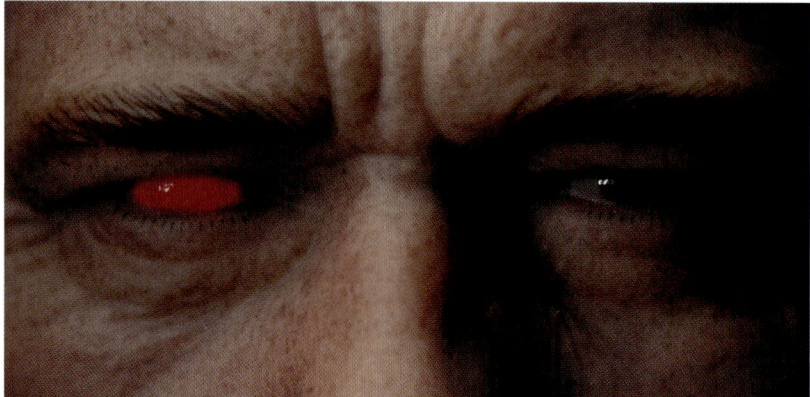

FIGURE 9.42 Camera RAW adjustment removed from eye on right side of frame

15. Click on the Hair layer in the Layers panel, and then go to *Select > All*, then *Edit > Copy Merged*, then *Edit > Paste* to create a merged layer at the top of the layer stack. Rename this layer "Clarity."

Now we're going to use one of my favorite plugins, Topaz Clarity, to enhance the skin texture and contours. The results of this are quite fantastic and make a huge difference in the portrait.

As I mentioned in chapter 4, at this stage you could also use Clarity within the Camera RAW Filter or the Details technique (page 63) as an alternative to Topaz Clarity. However, in all honesty, neither of these produces results that are as good as Topaz.

Go to *Filter > Topaz Labs > Topaz Clarity*, and on the right side of the Topaz window, increase Micro Contrast to around 0.28 and Low Contrast to around 0.14 (**Figure 9.43**). Click OK.

Notice how the plugin has enhanced the skin texture, and with the settings we've applied, it makes the model look older, which works perfect for this picture.

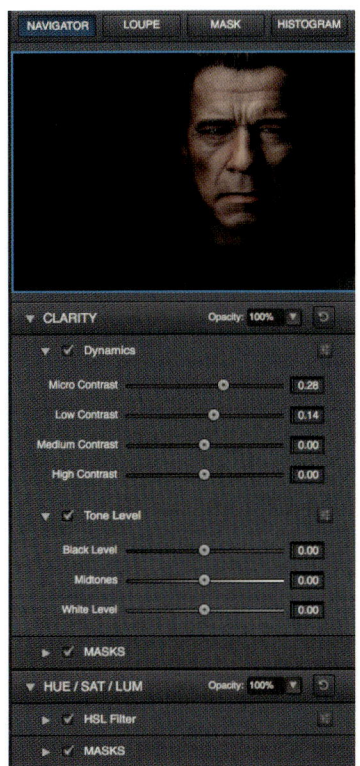

FIGURE 9.43

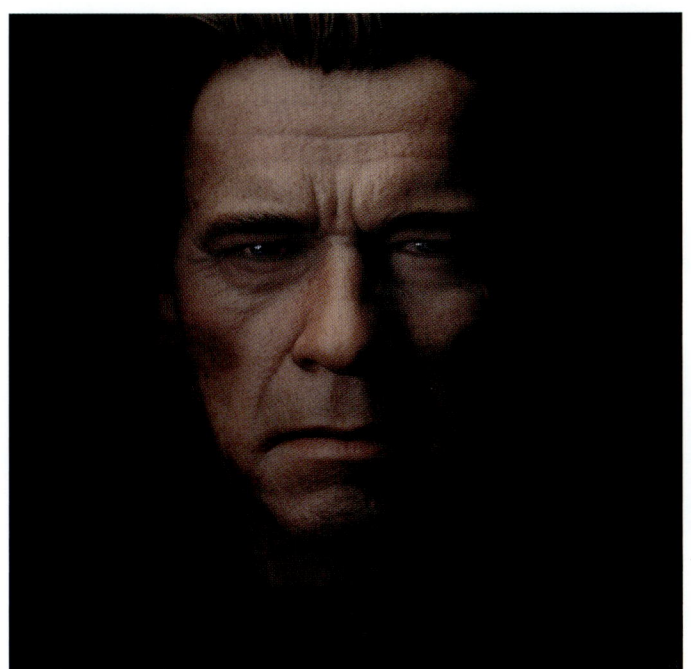

FIGURE 9.44 Before Topaz Clarity

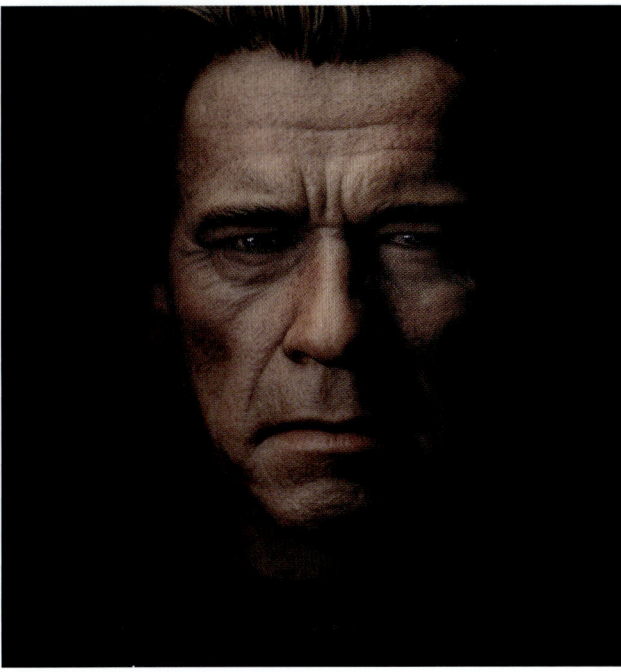

FIGURE 9.45 After Topaz Clarity

16. One way I like to add even more depth and dimension to portraits is by adding layers of contrast. We'll do that here by choosing a black foreground color in the toolbar and selecting a round, soft-edged brush. Press Q or click on the Quick Mask icon in the toolbar to enter Quick Mask mode, and then paint over an inner area of the face to include the eyes, nose, and mouth (**Figure 9.46**).

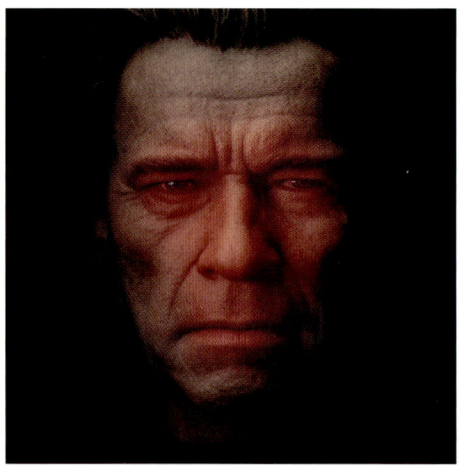

FIGURE 9.46

Press Q to exit Quick Mask mode, and the marching ants will show the selected area of the face. Go back to Topaz Clarity and reapply the settings we used in Step 15 (Micro Contrast: 0.28, Low Contrast: 0.14) and click OK.

Now go to *Edit > Fade*, and in the Fade properties, reduce Opacity to 80% and click OK (**Figure 9.47**). This reduces this second Topaz Clarity effect a little bit. Go to *Select > Deselect* to remove the marching ants selection.

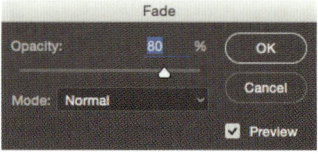

FIGURE 9.47

17. Okay, now let's sort out that hair and add just a little extra blur to help hide the fact that's it's molded.

Click on the Clarity layer and create a duplicate layer by pressing Command + J (Mac) or Ctrl + J (PC). Rename this layer "Blur Hair." Then go to *Filter > Blur Gallery > Iris Blur* (**Figure 9.48**). Click in the center of the disc that appears and drag it on top of Arnold's nose, then click on the outer points to resize and reposition the blur ellipse (**Figure 9.49**).

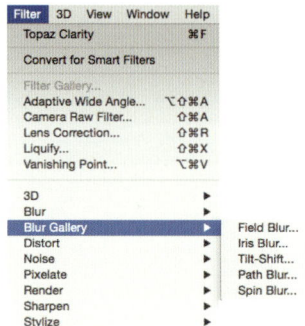

FIGURE 9.48

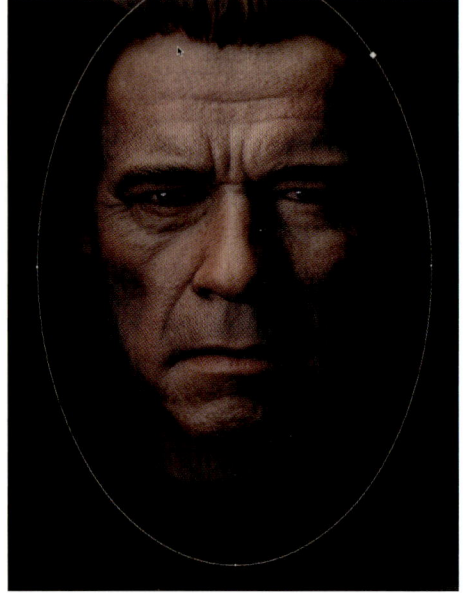

FIGURE 9.49

A Blur Amount of 15 px is enough to achieve the effect we're after (**Figure 9.50**). Click OK.

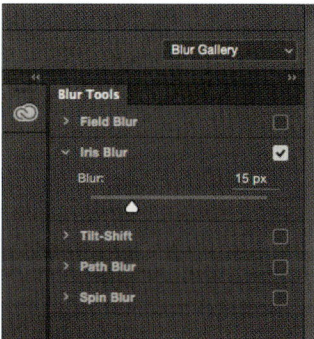

 TIP *The adjustable inner pins control how the blur fades in toward the center. If you click on one of the adjustment pins and drag it in or out, the other pins move proportionally. To adjust a pin on it's own, hold down the Option key (Mac) or Alt key (PC) and drag the pin in or out.*

18. Now let's turn this portrait into a black-and-white image. There are a lot of ways this can be done with Photoshop, Camera RAW, or plugins. The method I choose all depends on the picture because I've certainly found that there isn't one technique that works on every image.

FIGURE 9.50

Here we'll use a good old Gradient Map. With the foreground and background colors set to their defaults of black and white, click on the Gradient Map icon in the Adjustments panel to add a Gradient Map adjustment layer (**Figure 9.51**).

This immediately gives us a pretty decent conversion, but we can tweak it now to get exactly what we're after. Click on the gradient bar in the Gradient Map properties (**Figure 9.52**) to opens the Gradient Editor (**Figure 9.53**).

Click on the White Point and drag it to the left until the Location amount reaches 75% (**Figure 9.54**), then click OK.

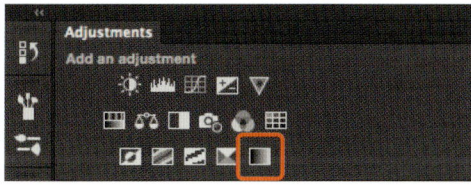

FIGURE 9.51

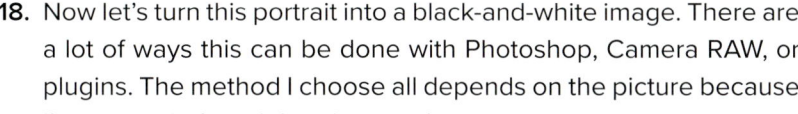

FIGURE 9.52

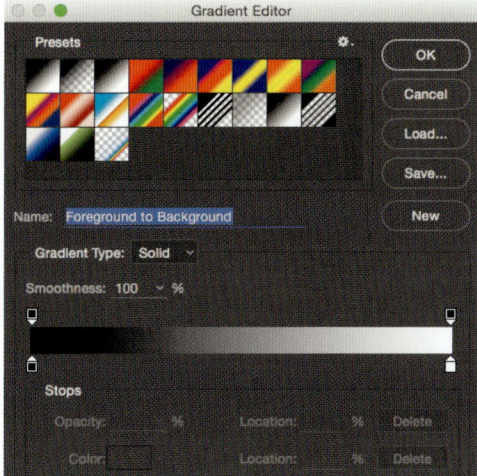

FIGURE 9.53

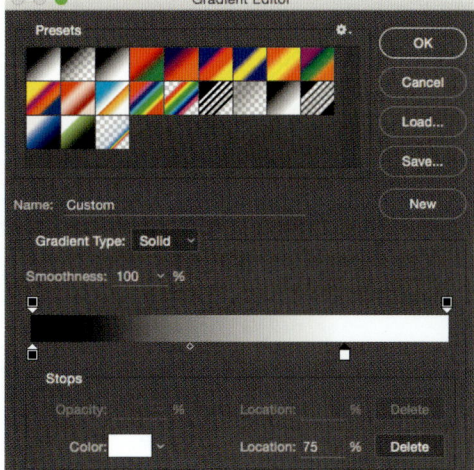

FIGURE 9.54

19. We have just a couple more things to do before the picture is finished, or at least before it's a good time to step away for a while. Let's add some finishing touches by first bringing back a bit of detail in the shadow areas. Add a Levels adjustment layer and drag the bottom-left point directly upward to just under halfway up the first small square (**Figure 9.55**).

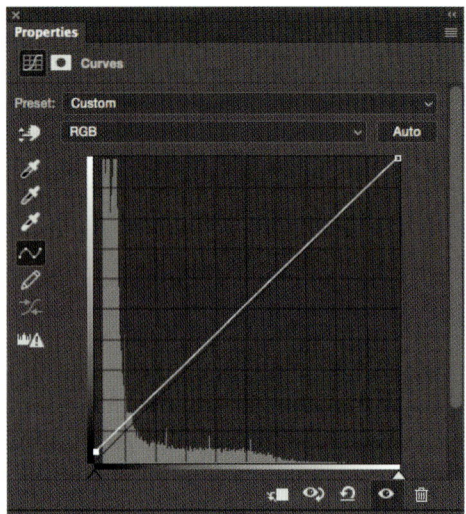

FIGURE 9.55

Create a merged layer at the top of the layer stack by going to *Select > All*, then to *Edit > Copy Merged*, and then to *Edit > Paste*. Rename this layer "FT" for Finishing Touches.

Go to *Filter > Camera RAW*, and in the Camera RAW window, choose a Radial Gradient (**Figure 9.56**).

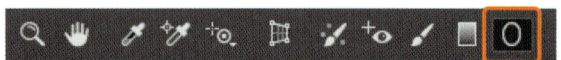

FIGURE 9.56

Click and drag out a gradient that covers Arnold's face (**Figure 9.57**). Dial in an Exposure of +0.15 and choose Inside under Effect at the bottom of the panel (**Figure 9.58**).

Click New in the Radial Filter panel to add another gradient, and this time click and drag out a gradient from the center to further outside Arnold's face (**Figure 9.59**).

Dial in an Exposure of -0.55 and choose Outside under Effect at the bottom of the panel (**Figure 9.60**). Click OK.

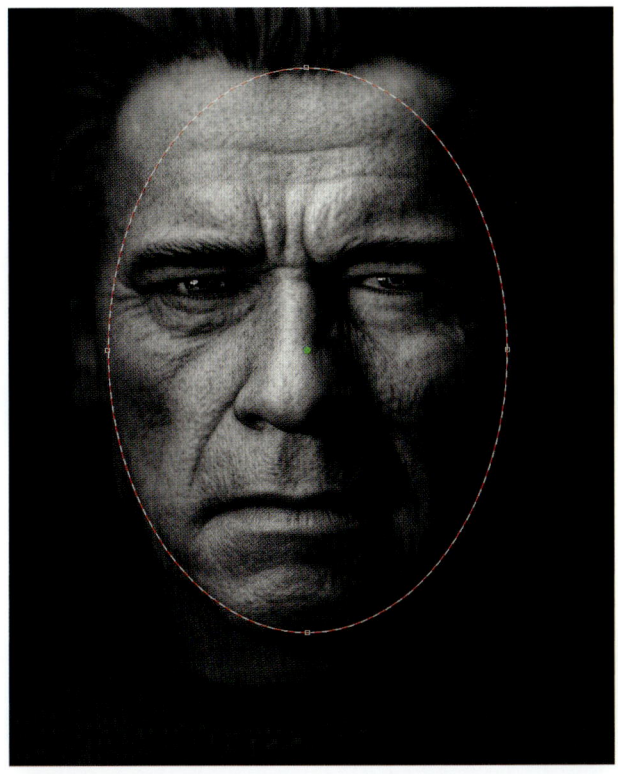

FIGURE 9.57

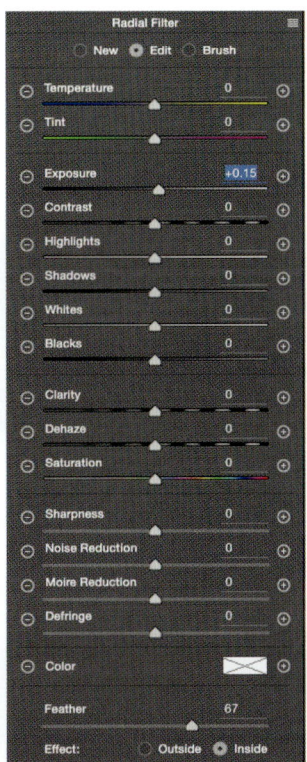

FIGURE 9.58

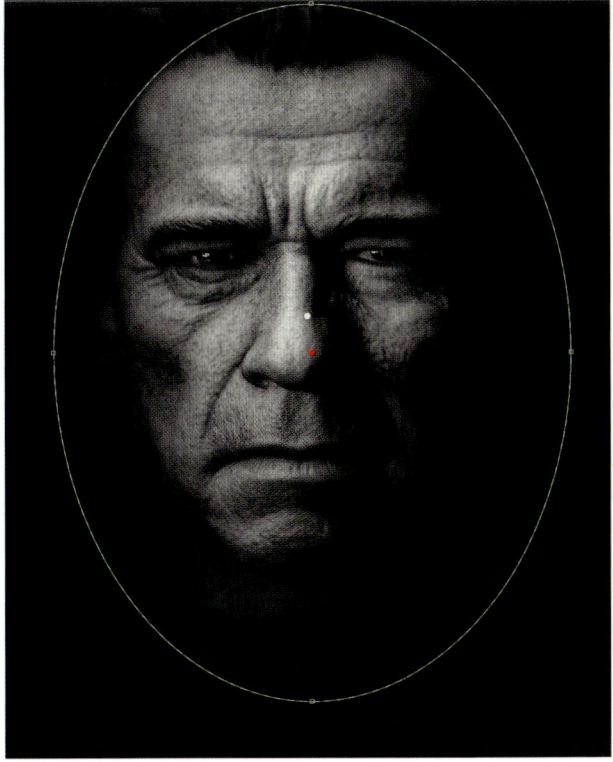

FIGURE 9.59

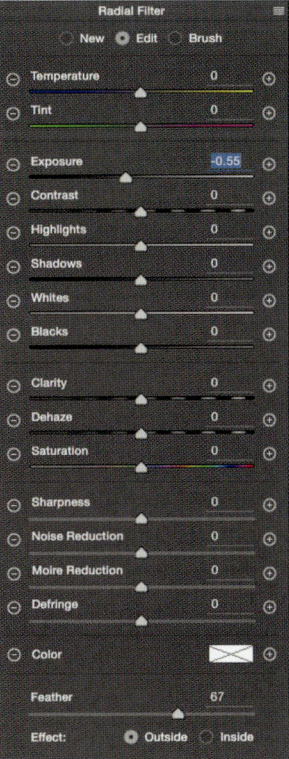

FIGURE 9.60

Now would be a good time to step away from the computer and come back later with fresh eyes. This way you'll see what you have done much clearer and will be able to tell straight away what you need to do, if anything, to finish the picture completely.

As an extra finishing touch, I added the painterly skin texture effect that I covered in chapter 4 (page 94), but this is a decision I made based purely on personal taste.

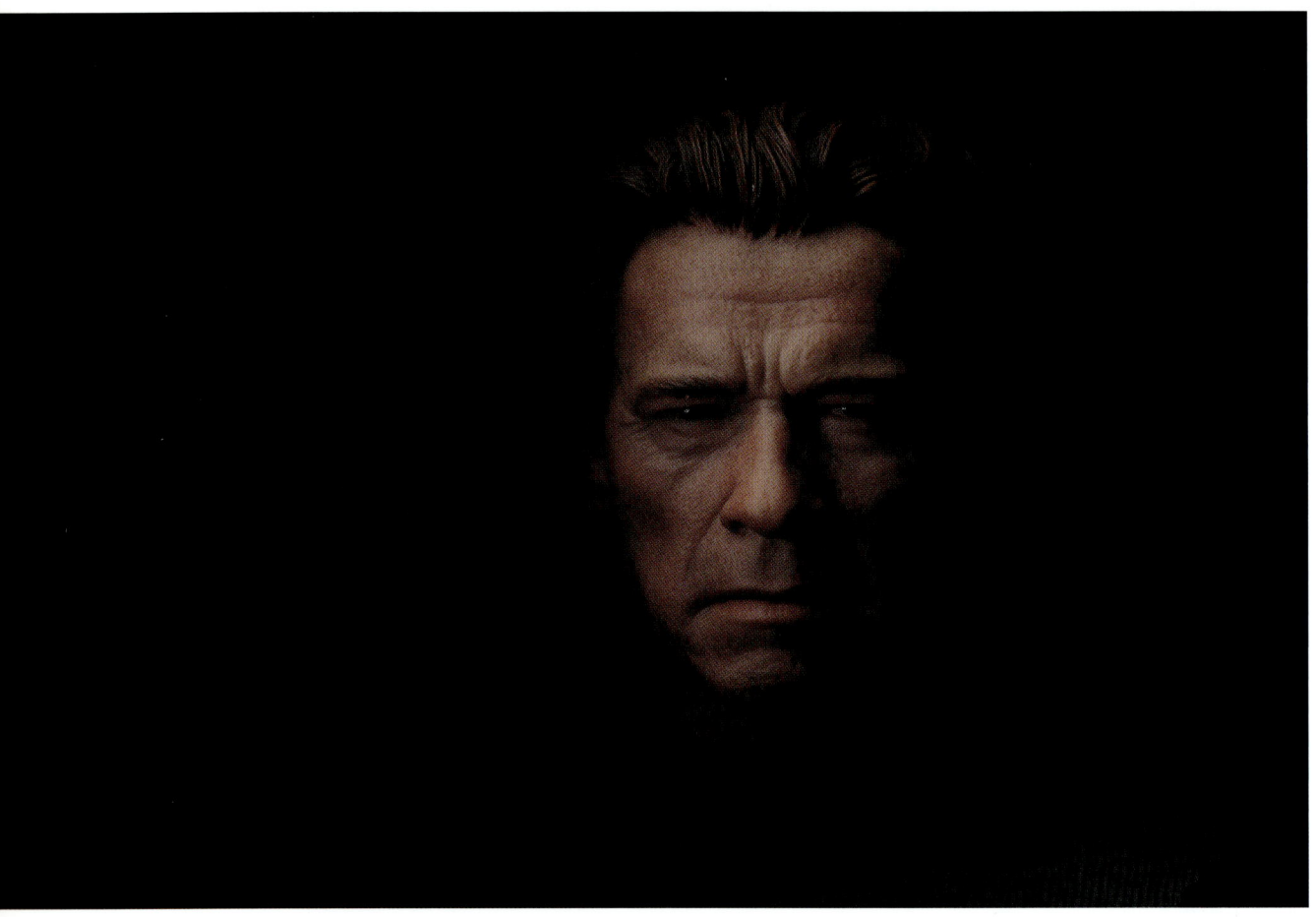

FIGURE 9.61 Original RAW image

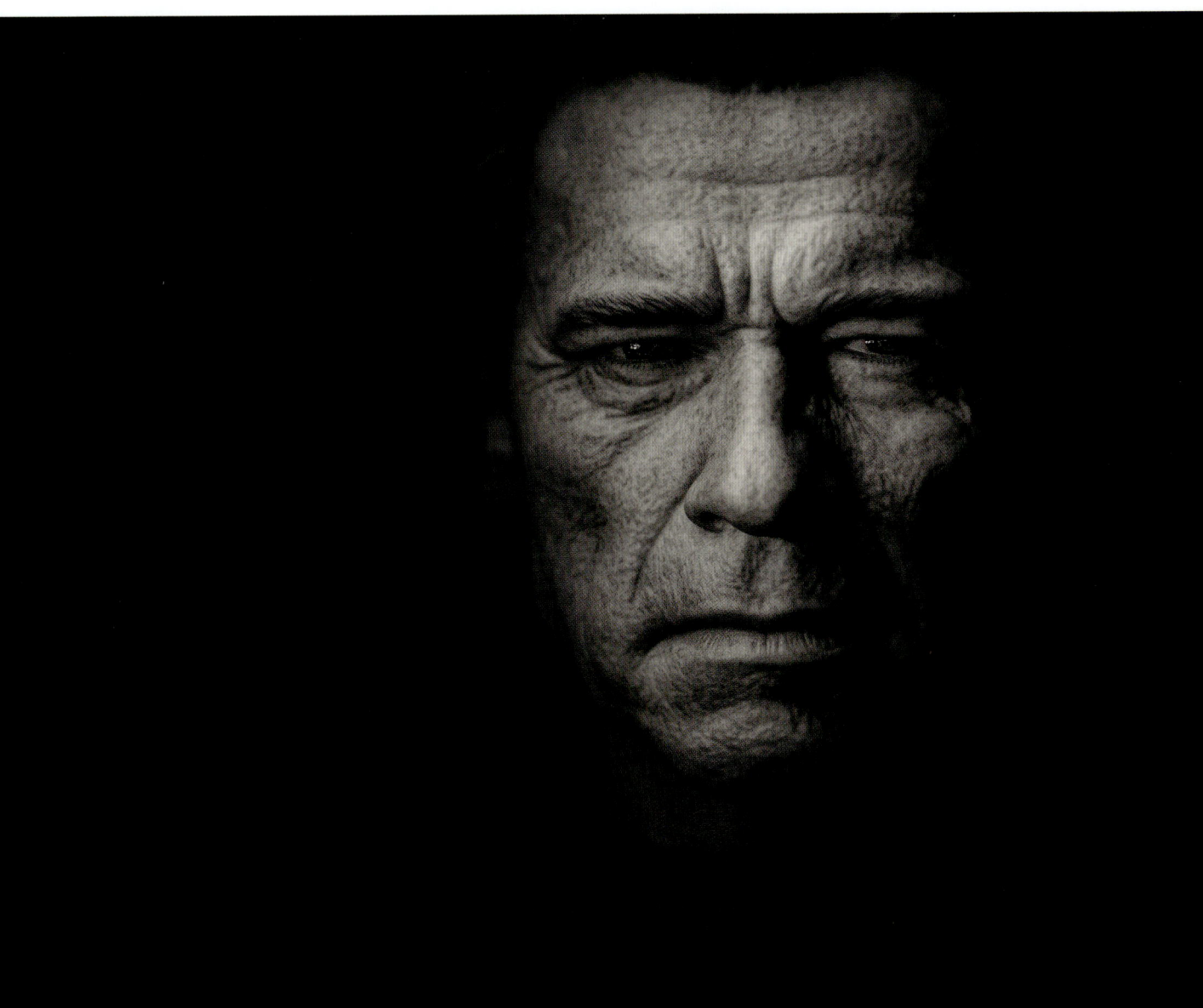

FIGURE 9.62 Final retouched image

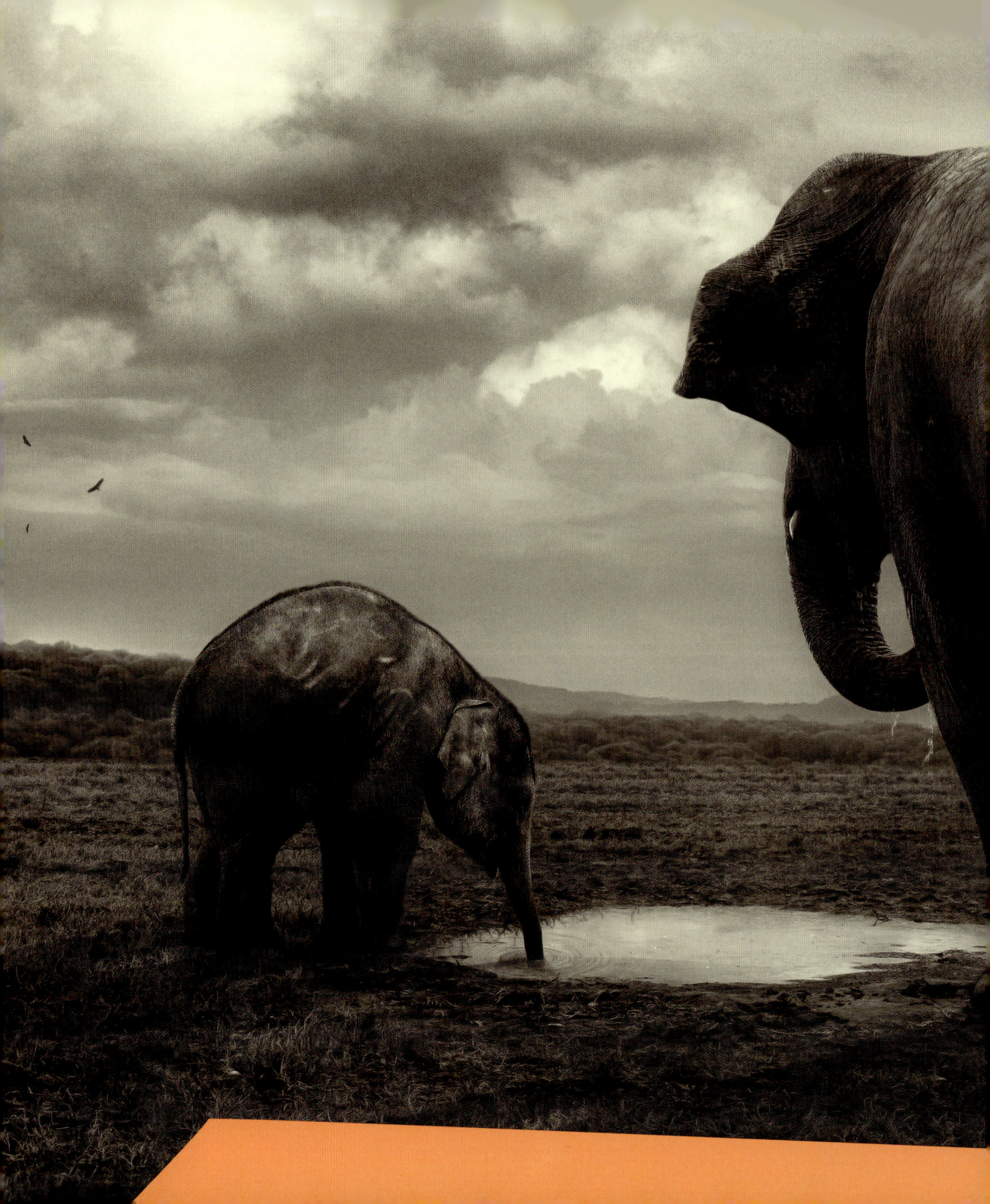

10 NICK BRANDT INSPIRED

Ever since I was a little kid I've loved animals. High up on my bucket list is to one day go on a safari and see wild animals out in their natural habitat, behaving as they should.

Until that day arrives, I have an ongoing project that I simply call my Animals project, which I've mentioned in previous chapters. I visit wildlife parks and photograph animals such as lions, giraffes, zebras, and so on. Then I use Photoshop to cut them out of the scene in which I photographed them, create a new scene that resembles their natural habitat, and place them in it. It almost feels like I'm setting them free and I find some comfort in it.

Visiting the wildlife parks is bittersweet, and many times I've found myself becoming quite upset seeing these beautiful animals in enclosures, but I know the places I visit are there for reasons such as protecting the species, breeding programs, and animal rescue. This project gives me the best of both worlds, bringing together photography and wildlife.

Shortly after starting this project I came across the work of photographer Nick Brandt, and for the first time ever, I was completely stopped in my tracks. Never before had photography generated such an emotion in me!

Nick Brandt is an English photographer who photographs exclusively in Africa and creates simply breathtaking pictures that you can't help but be moved by. Nick's images are predominantly black and white, and it is this combined with the emotion he portrays in his pictures that has made him one of my photography heroes, for want of a better phrase. I highly recommend you take a look at Nick's work on his website: www.nickbrandt.com.

Clearly, Nick's work has had an impact on me, and ever since I was introduced to his photographs and books, his style has very much influenced my Animals project. I now focus more on the emotion and story within the picture and I convert many of my images to black and white, rather than simply creating a scene and placing animals into it.

In this chapter, I'm going to take you through one of my Animal images step-by-step. I originally photographed some Indian elephants in a wildlife park in the UK, and then I created a new scene of the mother and baby at a watering hole.

CAMERA SETTINGS

I knew I was going to cut the elephants from their original background in post-production, so I shot the image with an aperture of f/8.0, which meant the elephants were sharp and in focus from front to back.

I set my camera to Aperture Priority mode, so the camera only changed the shutter speed. The ISO was set to 200 to get a shutter speed in the 1/100sec range, which is actually quite slow for nature photography. Thankfully, the Elephants were quite still. As for focusing, I put the camera in Servo Mode so that it would constantly adjust to compensate for movement.

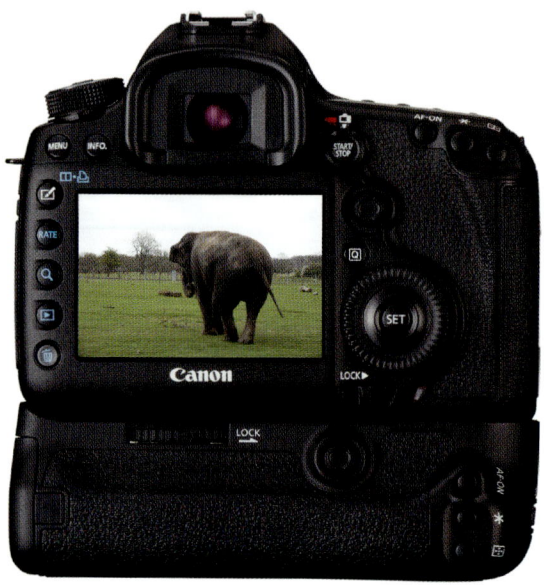

FIGURE 10.1

MODE Aperture Priority

ISO 200

APERTURE f/8.0

SHUTTER SPEED 1/100 sec.

LENS Canon 24-105mm f/4.0L IS USM

GEAR GUIDE

There isn't much to cover in terms of gear because it was just me and my camera (**Figures 10.2** and **10.3**). Ideally, I would have used a monopod or even a tripod for added stability.

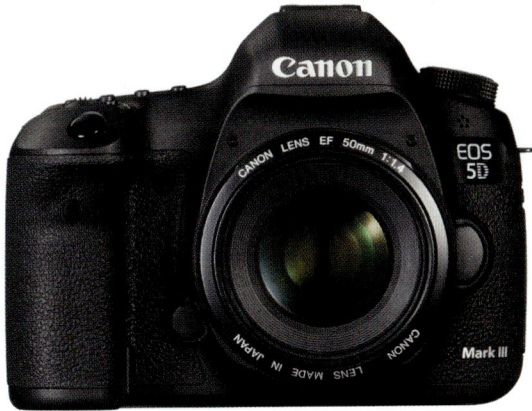

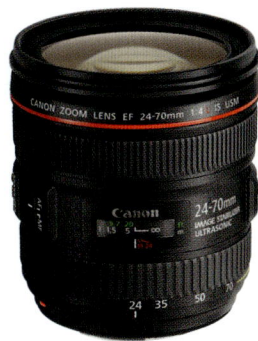

FIGURE 10.2 Canon EOS 5D Mark III

FIGURE 10.3 Canon EF 24–70mm f/4L IS USM

POST-PROCESSING

We'll start off by building the scene into which we're going to add our two elephants. The background scene is made up of different elements that I photographed over a period of time, partly because I had the idea of this specific picture in my head, but also because this picture is part of an ongoing project and I've found that having ongoing projects means you think about them all the time without even realizing it.

That might sound kind of strange, but the image of the water hole is a perfect example of this. I was driving to see a friend near where I live and I saw a herd of cows standing next to it in the middle of a field. Truth be told, one of the cows actually made the water hole, but we won't go into the finer details. Anyway, I had a camera in the car, as I always do, so I pulled over, took the picture, and was on my way.

NOTE *Download all the files you need to follow along step-by-step at: http://www.rockynook.com/ photograph-like-a-thief-reference/*

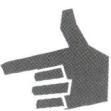

1. We'll start off by opening the grass.dng file in Camera RAW or Lightroom (it makes no difference which one you use) and simply straightening the horizon line. With the Straighten Tool (**A**; **Figure 10.4**) click on the top of the grass line on the left side of the picture and then drag a line along the grass line to the right and click again (**Figure 10.5**). Press Return (Mac) or Enter (PC) and then click on Open Image in the bottom-right corner of the screen to send the image into Photoshop.

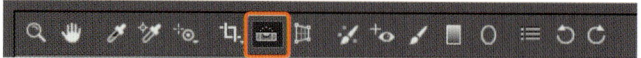

FIGURE 10.4

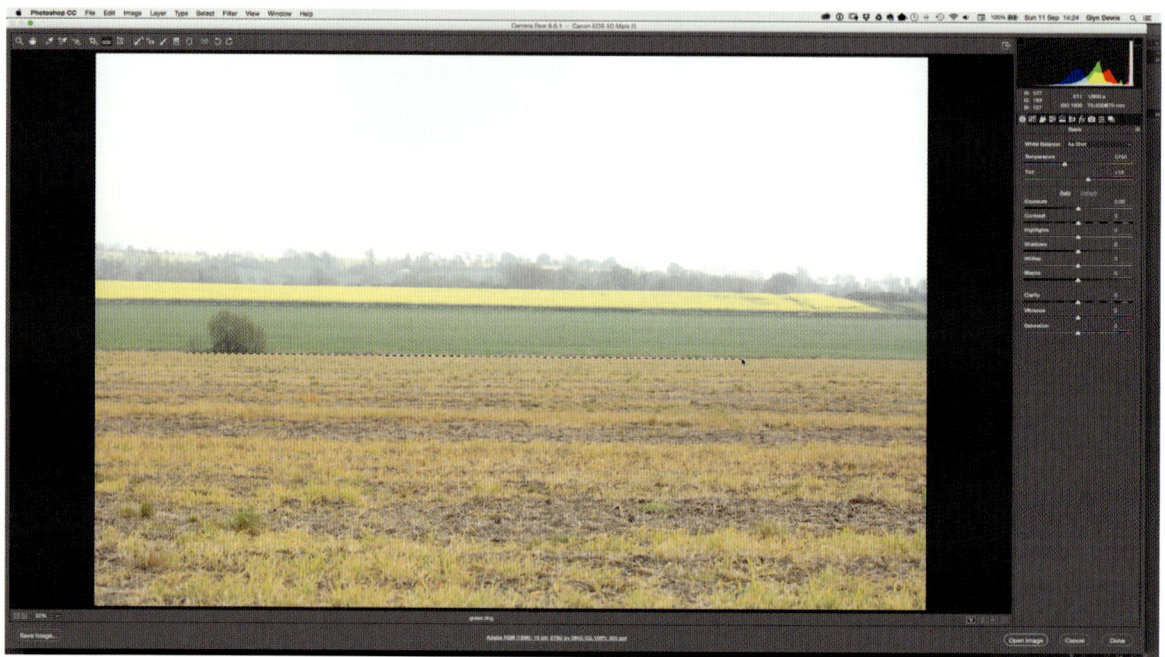

FIGURE 10.5

2. Now we're going to add the trees. Go to *File > Place Embedded* (**Figure 10.6**; *File > Place* in earlier versions of Photoshop), navigate to the trees.dng file, and click PLACE. We're not going to do anything to the trees at this stage, so when they open in Camera RAW, just click OK to place the trees file at the top of the layer stack (**Figure 10.7**).

Press Return (Mac) or Enter (PC) to set the image in place and remove the transform box from around it (**Figure 10.8**).

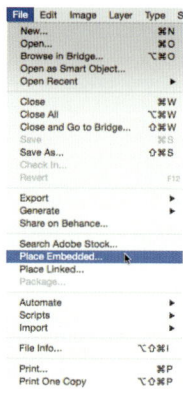

FIGURE 10.6

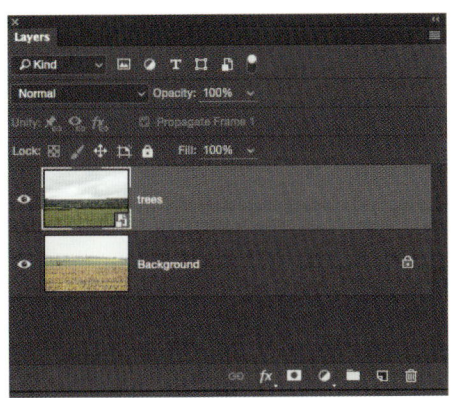

FIGURE 10.7

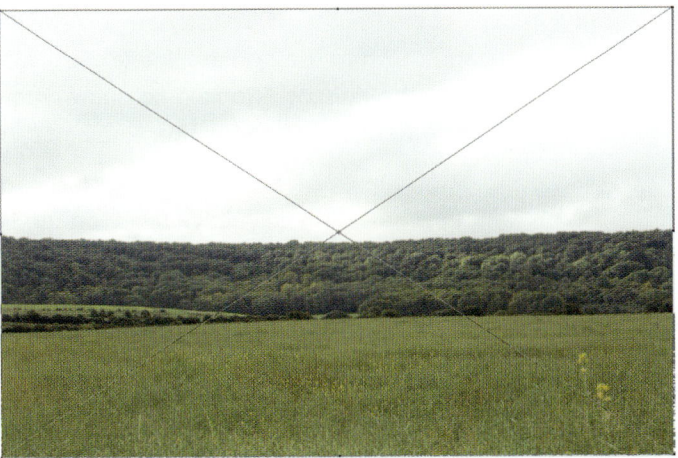

FIGURE 10.8

3. Lower the Opacity of the trees layer to around 40%. Select the Move Tool (**V**) and press the down arrow on your keyboard a few times to move the tree line lower on the horizon line (**Figure 10.9**). This makes the trees look like they're farther away.

4. Change the Opacity of the trees layer back to 100%, then click on its eye icon to turn off its visibility (**Figure 10.10**).

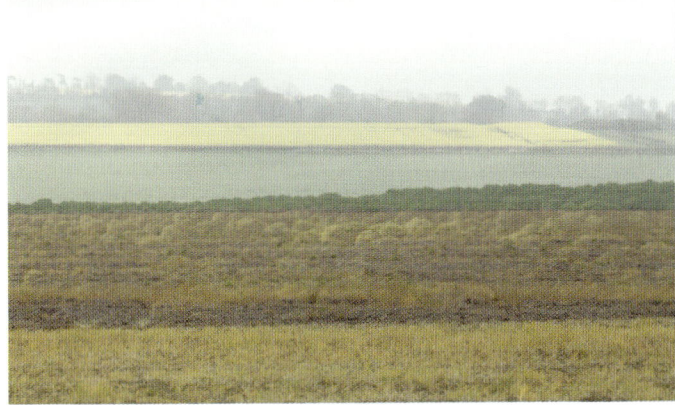

FIGURE 10.9

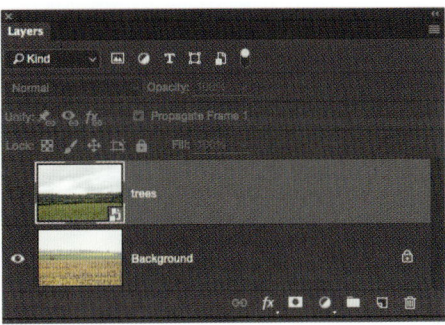

FIGURE 10.10

Select the Rectangular Marquee Tool (**M**) and drag out a selection from the top of the image down to the horizon line (**Figure 10.11**). Now we need to feather this selection so that the horizon line isn't so sharp and defined. Go to *Select > Modify > Feather* (**Figure 10.12**), add in a Feather Radius of just 1 pixel, and click OK (**Figure 10.13**).

Click on the eye icon for the trees layer to turn on its visibility, and with the marching ants selection still active, click on the Layer Mask icon to add a new Layer Mask (**Figure 10.14**).

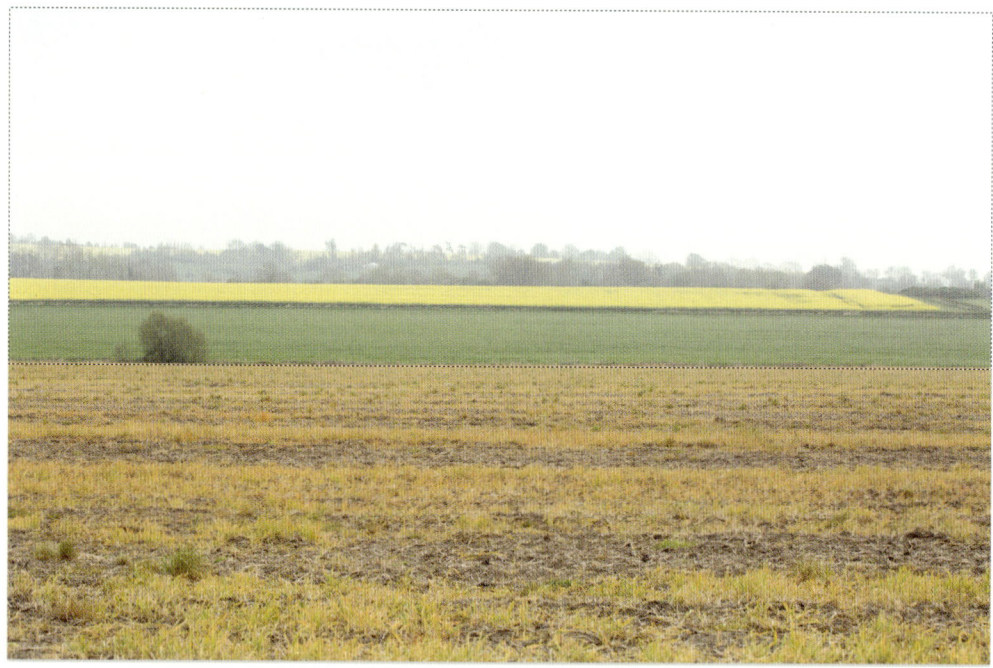

FIGURE 10.11

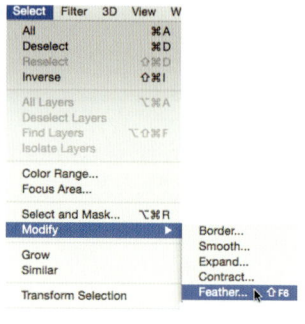

FIGURE 10.12

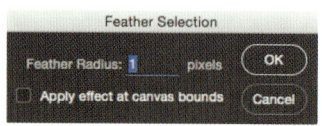

FIGURE 10.13

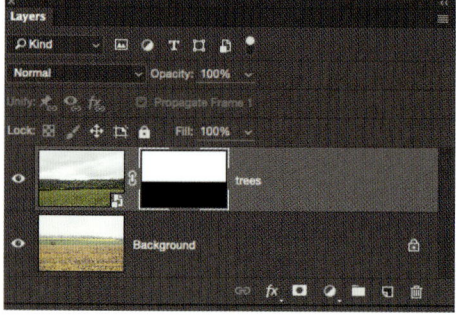

FIGURE 10.14

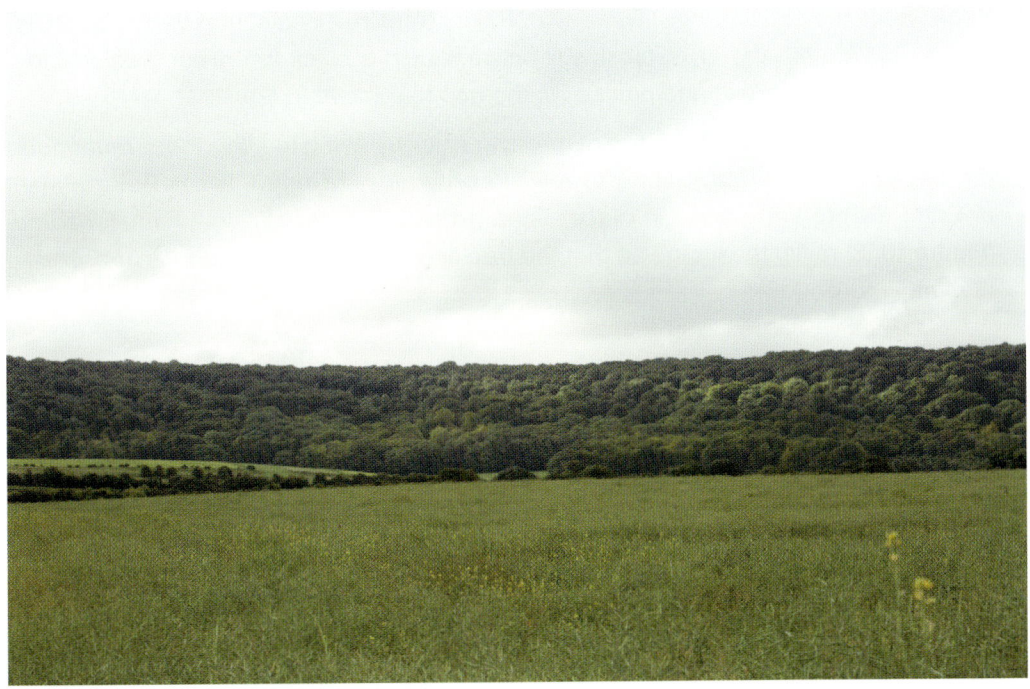

FIGURE 10.15 Before adding a Layer Mask to the selection

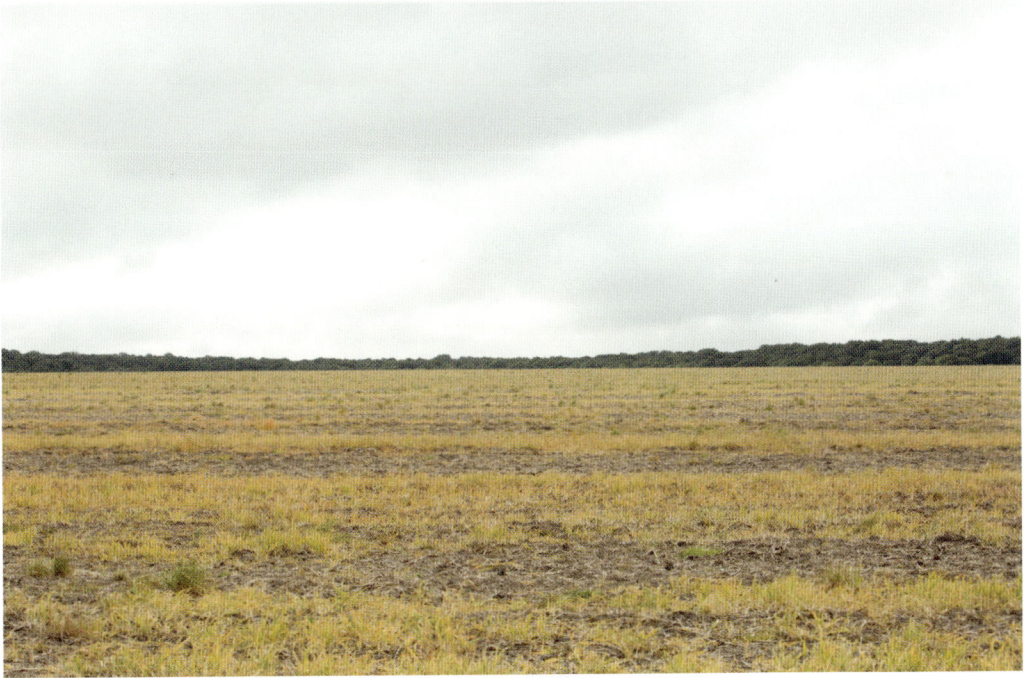

FIGURE 10.16 After adding a Layer Mask to the selection. Note how the selected area is visible and everything else in the trees layer is now concealed.

5. Because we moved the trees layer down, you may notice a gap at the top of the picture (**Figure 10.17**). With the layer mask still active, select a black foreground color and a round, soft-edged brush and paint over the gap to remove it.

6. Add the trees_2.dng file to the top of the layer stack by going to *File > Place Embedded* (or *File > Place*) and navigating to the file on your hard drive. Press Return (Mac) or Enter (PC) to set the file in place. Then go to *Edit > Transform > Flip Horizontal* (**Figure 10.18**) to flip the image so that the tree line rises up on the right as opposed to the left (**Figure 10.19**).

FIGURE 10.17

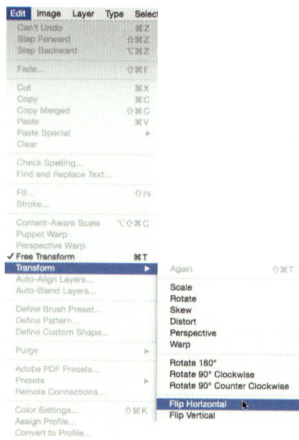

FIGURE 10.18

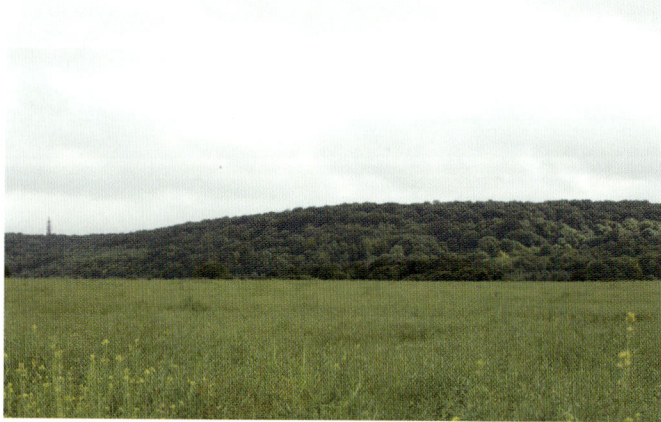

FIGURE 10.19

7. Lower the Opacity of the trees_2 layer to around 40%, and then use the Move Tool (**V**) and the arrow keys to position the layer so that the spot at which the tree line rises up is on the far right side of the image (**Figure 10.20**).

Change the Opacity of the trees_2 layer back to 100%. Hold down the Option key (Mac) or Alt key (PC), click on the layer mask attached to the trees layer in the Layers panel, drag it up to the trees_2 layer, and release (**Figure 10.21**). This creates a copy of the Layer Mask so that now the lower part of the trees_2 layer is concealed as well.

8. With a black foreground color and a round, soft-edged brush, paint on the Layer Mask to cover the other areas of the trees_2 layer that we don't want to include (**Figures 10.22** and **10.23**).

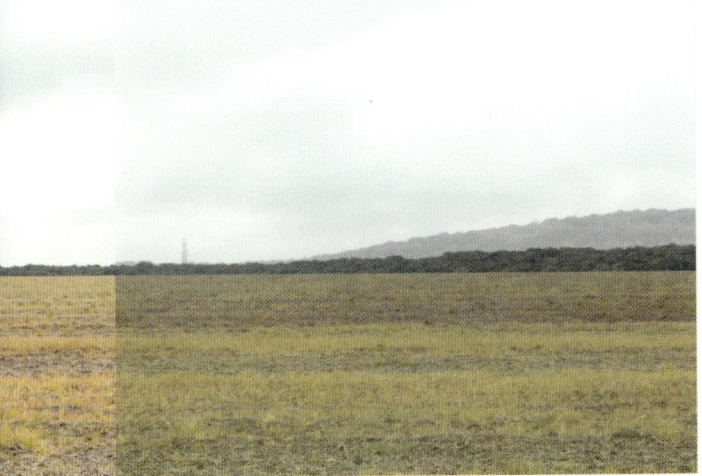

FIGURE 10.20

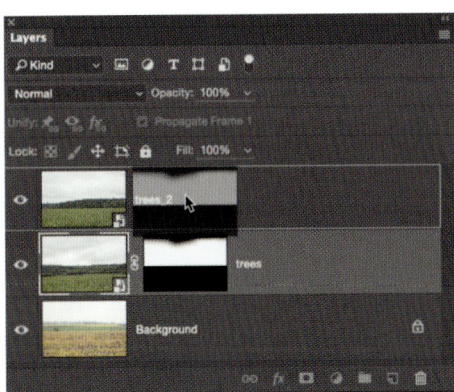

FIGURE 10.21

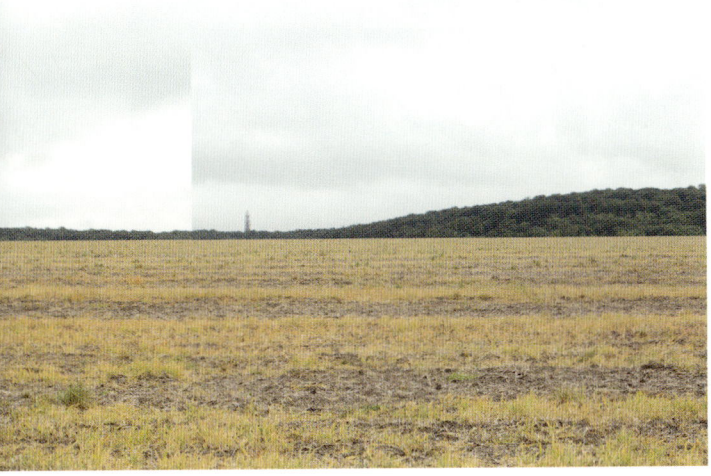

FIGURE 10.22 Before

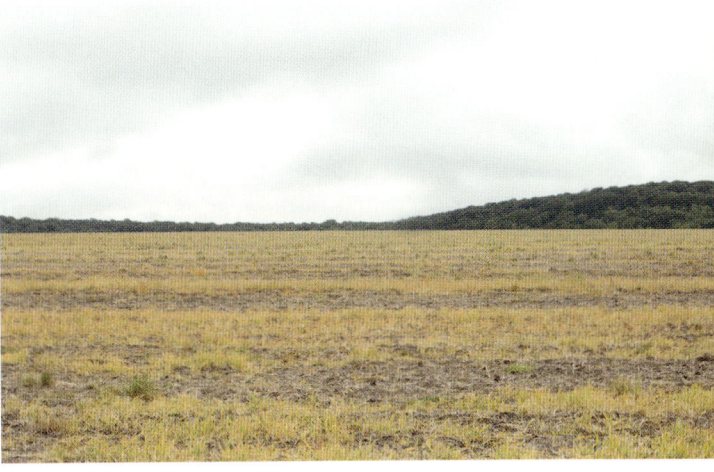

FIGURE 10.23 After

9. If you've worked through chapter 6, you may remember me talking about how getting out and about and looking around to see how things look in real life can help you with your retouching work. If not, here's a reminder (**Figure 10.24**).

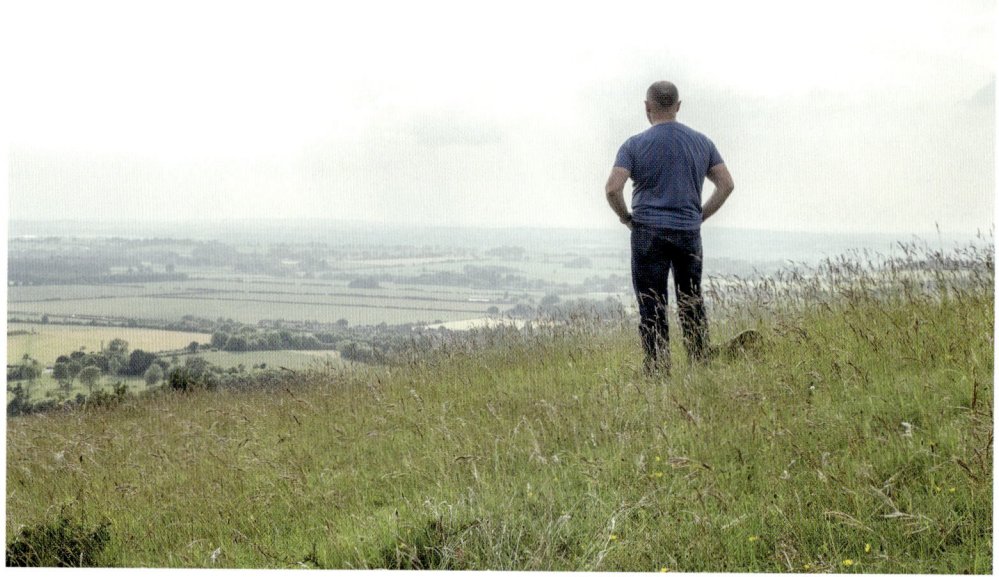

FIGURE 10.24

Notice how there is much less contrast, a slight haze, and a blue color cast near the horizon line. We can use this knowledge to make our new tree line appear farther away. This will eventually be a black-and-white image, so there's no need for us to add the blue color cast, but we can certainly reduce the contrast and add a little bit of haze.

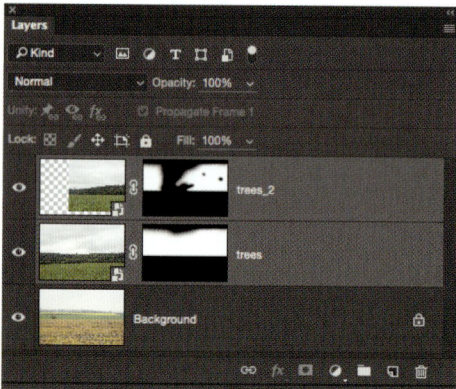

FIGURE 10.25

To do this, click on the uppermost layer, and then hold down the Shift key and click on the trees layer beneath it so that both layers are active (**Figure 10.25**). Then go to *Layer > New > Group from Layers,* name the group "trees," and click OK.

Click on the Brightness/Contrast icon in the Adjustments panel (**Figure 10.26**) to add a Brightness/Contrast adjustment layer. In the Properties, activate the Clipping Mask so that the adjustments we make affect only what is directly beneath the Adjustment layer (in this case, the trees), and drag the Contrast slider to the right to -50 (**Figure 10.27**).

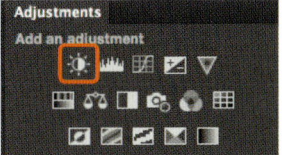

FIGURE 10.26

Add another Brightness/Contrast adjustment layer with the exact same settings we just used to reduce the contrast even further (**Figure 10.28**). (Note: Make sure to activate the Clipping Mask.)

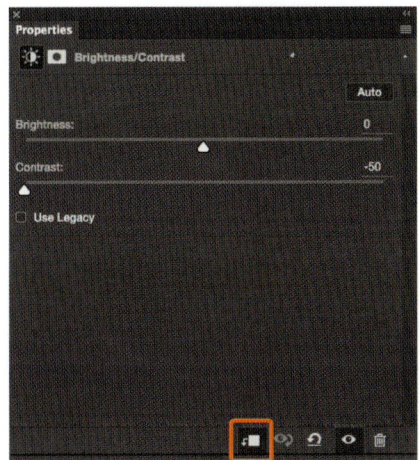

FIGURE 10.27 Clipping Mask activated and Contrast at -50

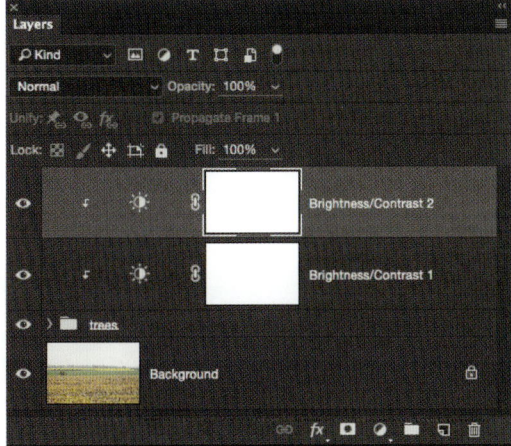

FIGURE 10.28

10. To add some haze, add a new blank layer to the top of the layer stack and rename it "haze." Then go *Edit > Fill,* and in the Fill properties, choose White from the Contents menu and click OK (**Figure 10.29**). Lower the Opacity of the haze layer to around 15% (**Figure 10.30**).

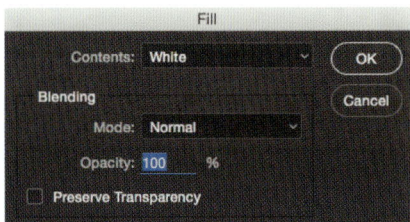

FIGURE 10.29

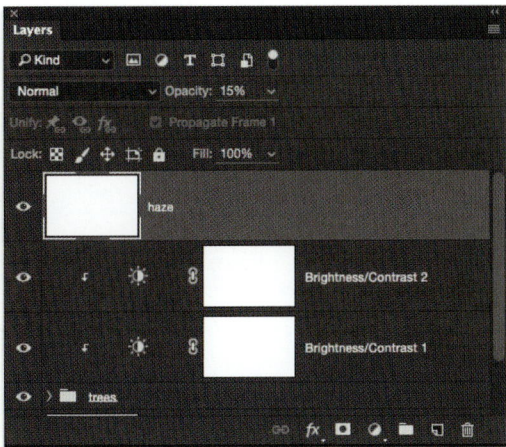

FIGURE 10.30

11. This haze layer is currently affecting the entire picture, but we only want it to cover the trees, so let's select the Rectangular Marquee Tool (**M**) and drag out a selection from the top of the image down to just below the horizon line (**Figure 10.31**).

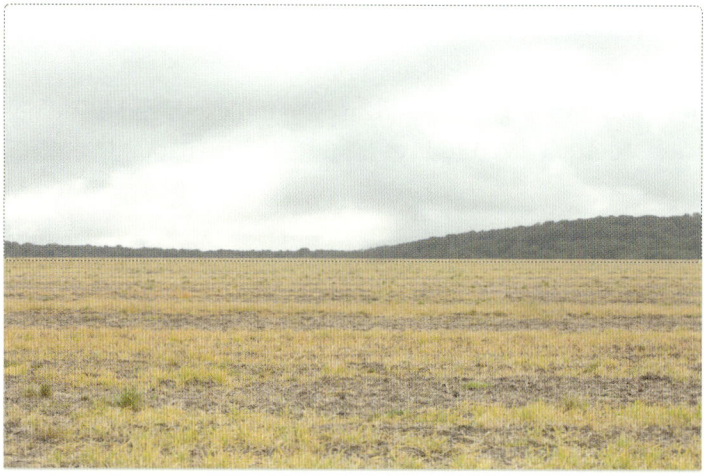

FIGURE 10.31

To blend the haze more convincingly across the horizon line, go to *Select > Modify > Feather,* enter a Feather Radius of around 25 pixels, and click OK. In the Layers panel, click on the icon to add a new Layer Mask. This leaves the haze effect visible in the selected area and conceals it elsewhere, which is exactly what we want.

Look at the differences between **Figures 10.32** and **10.33** and notice how the reduced contrast and haze layers make the trees on the horizon line appear farther away, just as in real life.

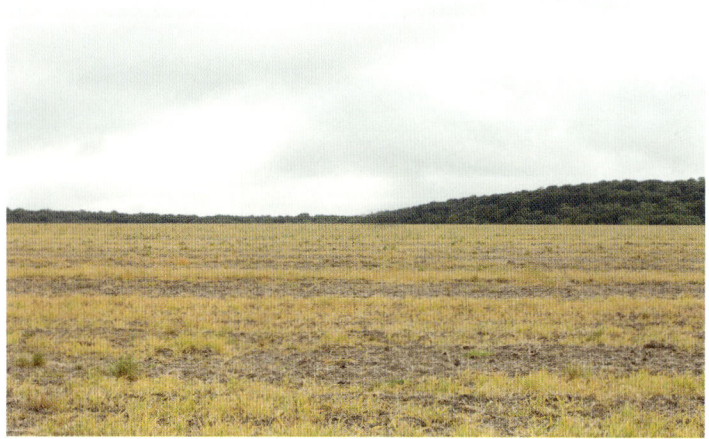

FIGURE 10.32 Before reducing contrast and adding haze layer

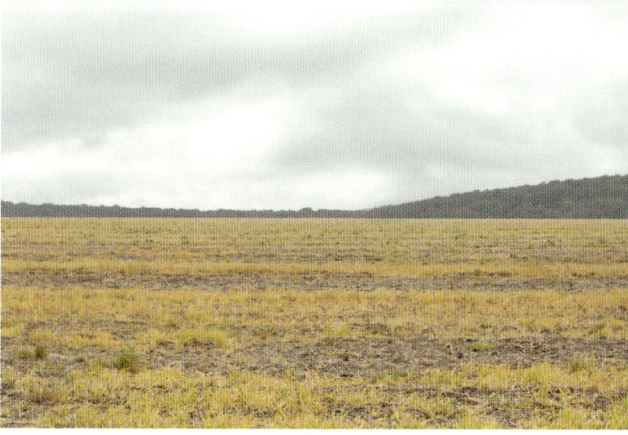

FIGURE 10.33 After reducing contrast and adding haze layer

12. Later on we'll be adding in shadows and sun flare, but doing so means that everything needs to look as real as possible. The current sky is way too cloudy for there to be any significant shadows in the image, so let's add a new one.

Grab the Quick Selection Tool (**W**), and in the options at the top of the screen, ensure that Sample All Layers is checked (**Figure 10.34**).

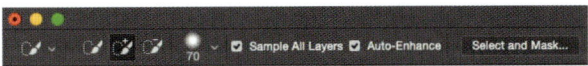

FIGURE 10.34

Click and drag across the sky to select it (**Figure 10.35**). To prevent a halo effect from appearing across the top of the trees when we add in the new sky, go to *Select > Modify > Expand,* enter an amount of 2 pixels, and click OK (**Figure 10.36**).

We need to feather the selection so that the sky blends into the trees in a realistic way. Go to *Select > Modify > Feather,* add a Feather Radius of 2 pixels, and click OK.

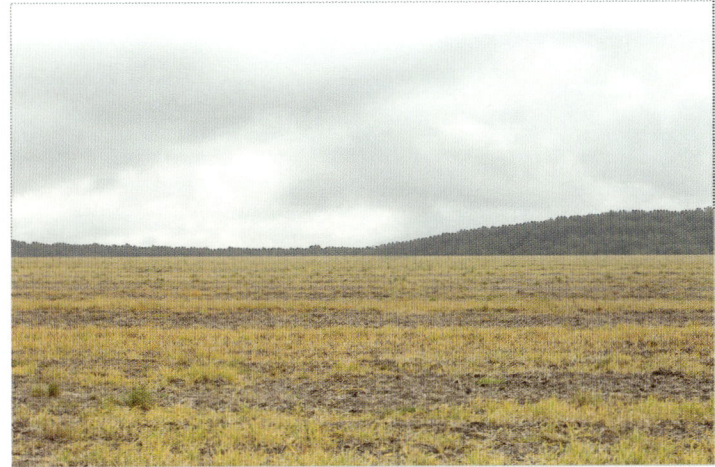

FIGURE 10.35

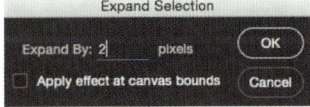

FIGURE 10.36

13. Open the clouds.dng file, and when it opens in Camera RAW, click Open Image to send it straight to Photoshop. In Photoshop, grab the Rectangular Maquee Tool (**M**) and drag out a selection of the sky from the top of the image down to the tops of the trees (**Figure 10.37**).

Go to *Edit > Copy,* click on the tab at the top of the screen to open our main image, and then go to *Edit > Paste Special > Paste Into* (**Figure 10.38**).

Once the clouds are in place, go to *Edit > Transform > Flip Horizontal,* and then to *Edit > Free Transform.* Hold down Option + Shift (Mac) or Alt + Shift (PC) and click and drag the upper-left or upper-right transform handle outward until this new sky fills the width of our image (**Figure 10.39**). Press Return (Mac) or Enter (PC).

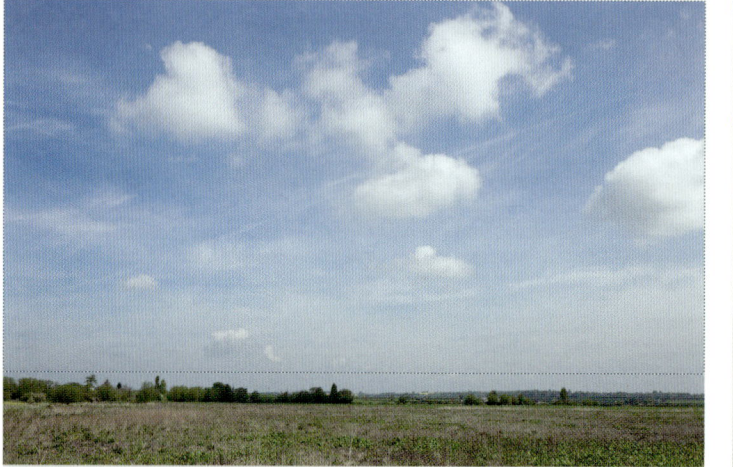

FIGURE 10.37

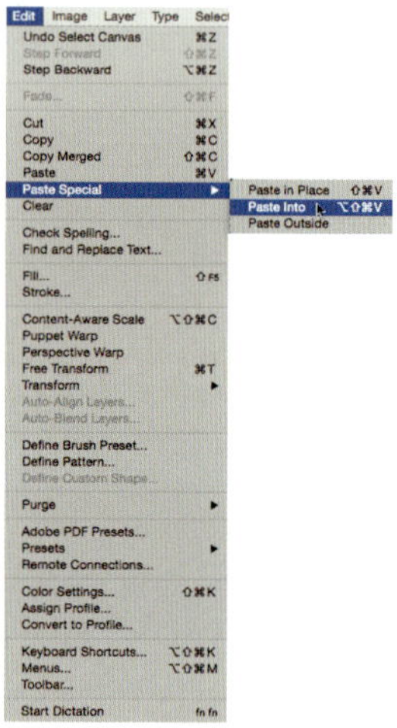

FIGURE 10.38

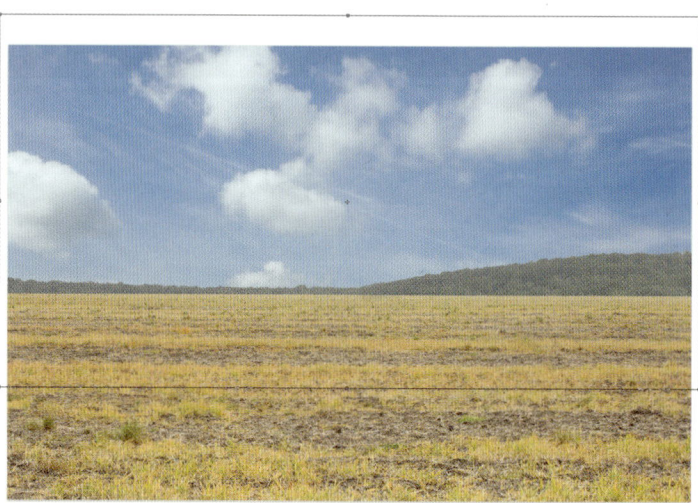

FIGURE 10.39

Select the Move Tool (**V**) and while holding down the Shift key, click on the sky and drag it upward until the smaller clouds at the bottom (the ones farthest away) are visible just above the tree line. Rename this layer "sky" and lower the Opacity to 80% (**Figures 10.40** and **10.41**).

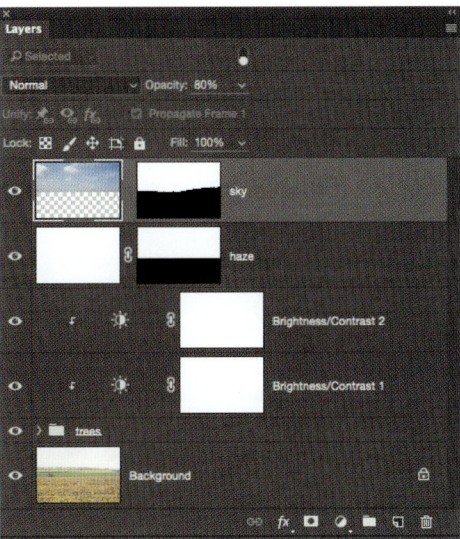

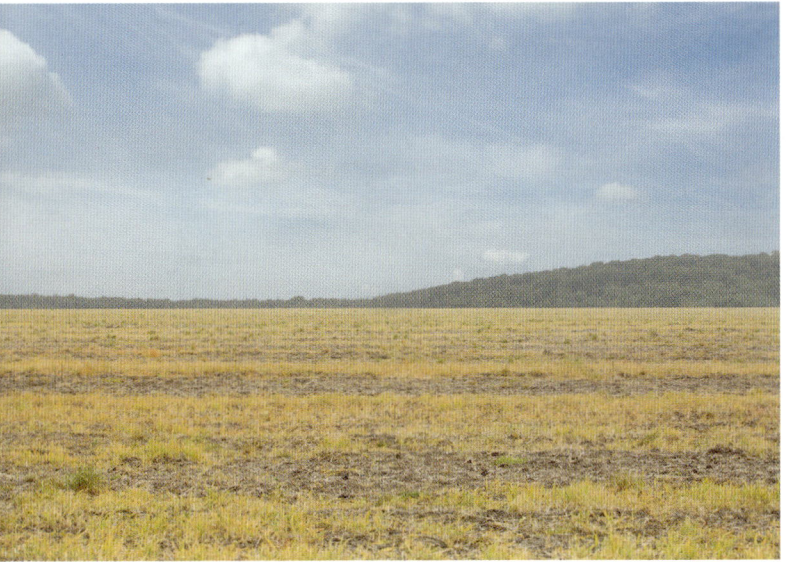

14. Now let's add in the watering hole. Go to *File > Open* and navigate to the water.dng file. There's nothing to do in Camera RAW, so click on Open Image in the bottom-right corner of the screen to send the file into to Photoshop.

    In Photoshop, grab the Lasso Tool (**L**) and draw a rough selection around the water. Make sure to include some of the mud around it, too (**Figure 10.42**).

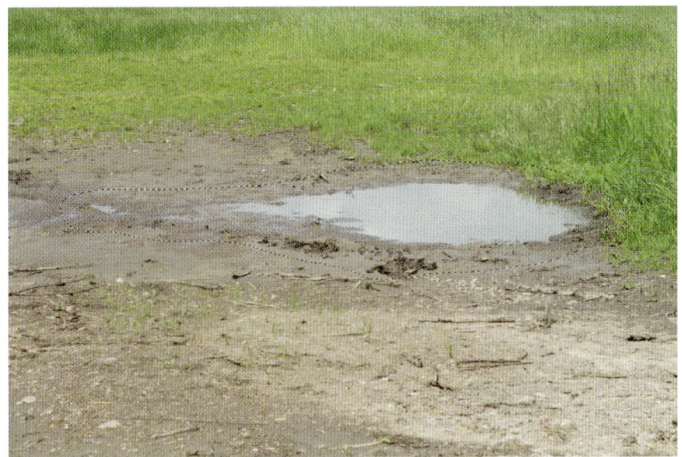

With the marching ant selection active, go to *Edit > Copy,* and then click on the tab to go back to the scene we have been creating. Go to *Edit > Paste* to drop this watering hole selection at the top of the layer stack. Rename this layer "watering hole" (**Figures 10.43** and **10.44**).

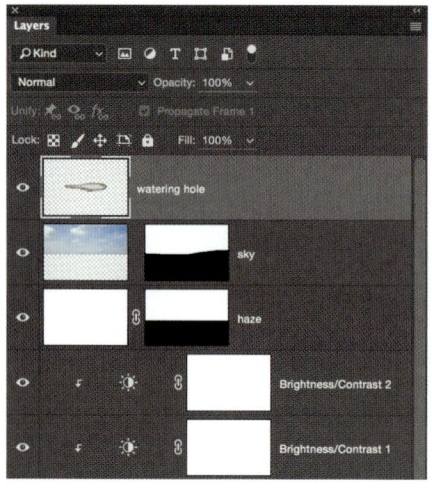

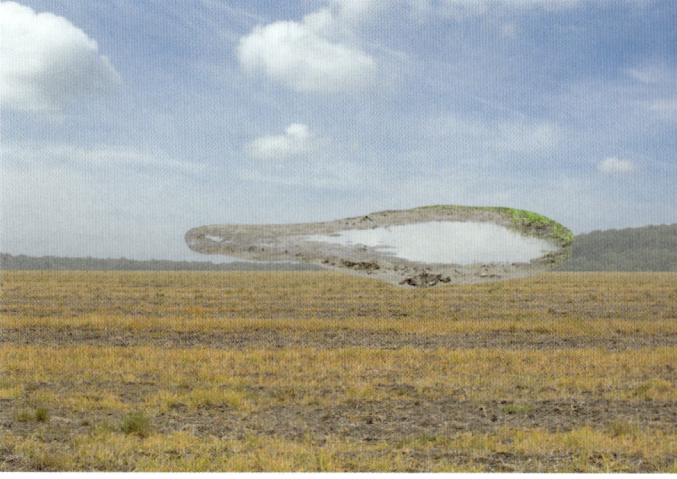

FIGURE 10.43

FIGURE 10.44

15. Before we position the watering hole exactly where we want it, go to *Edit > Transform > Flip Horizontal* to flip the layer so that the majority of the mud is on the right-hand side (**Figure 10.45**), which is where the adult elephant will be.

Grab the Move Tool (**V**) and click and drag the watering hole into position (**Figure 10.46**).

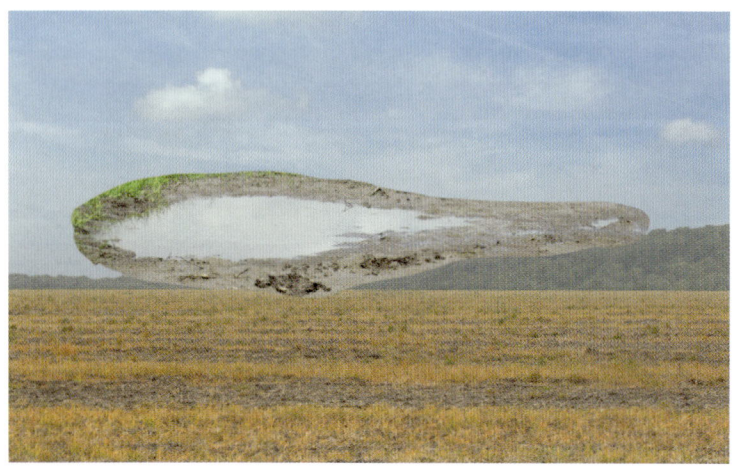

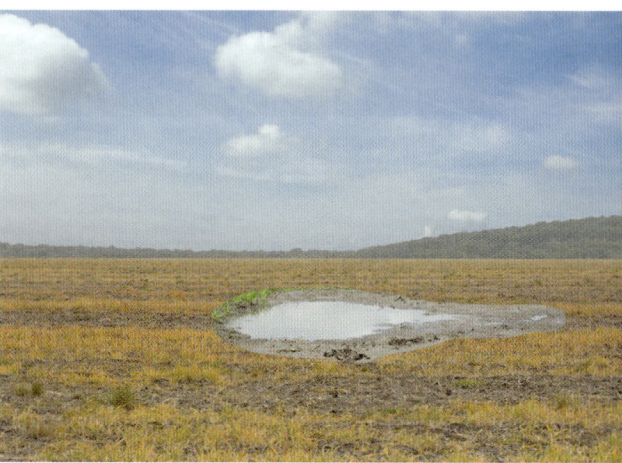

FIGURE 10.45

FIGURE 10.46

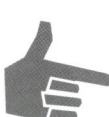

NOTE *When you're photographing different elements that will be added together to make a new scene, try to photograph them from the same angle. This will help you to blend everything together seamlessly so that the final image looks much more realistic.*

16. Let's reduce the size of the watering hole because at the moment it looks a little too big. Go to *Edit > Transform > Scale* (**Figure 10.47**), and in the options bar at the top of the screen, activate the chain icon so that the adjustment we make will affect both the height and width in equal amounts. Change the Height to 90% (**Figure 10.48**).

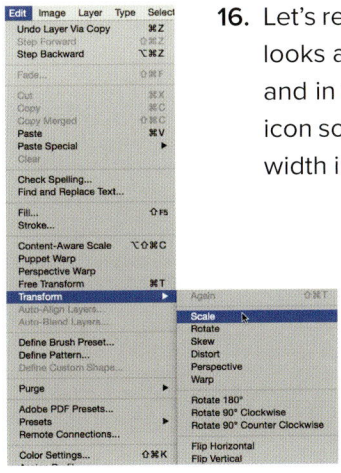

FIGURE 10.47

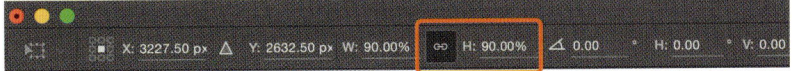

FIGURE 10.48

17. To blend the watering hole into the ground and also keep the reflective surface, change the Blend Mode of the watering hole layer to Luminosity (**Figure 10.49**).

Now we'll blend the outline of the watering hole in with the ground. Add a Layer Mask to the watering hole layer (**Figure 10.50**), and then use a round, soft-edged brush and a black foreground color to paint around the outside area of the watering hole (**Figure 10.51**).

With the watering hole now in place, it's time to cut out the elephants from their original backgrounds.

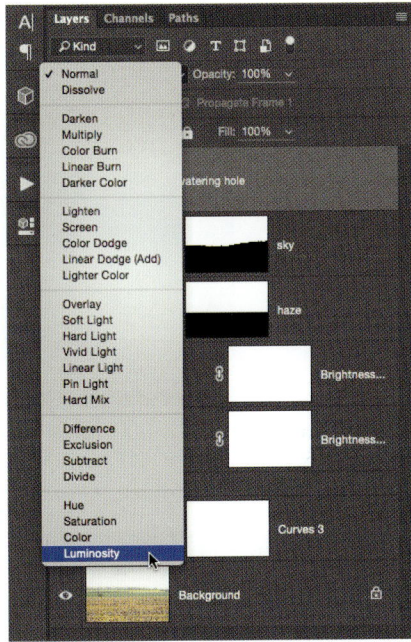

FIGURE 10.49

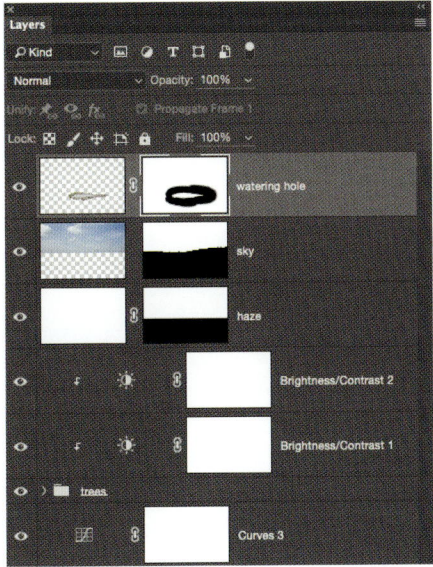

FIGURE 10.50

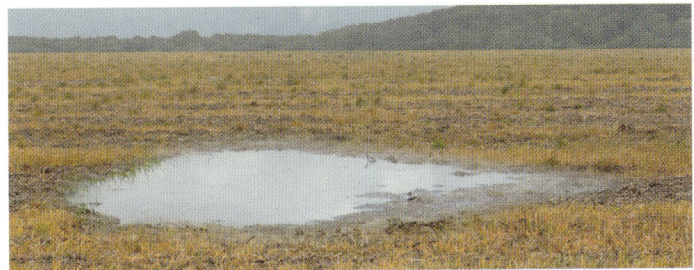

FIGURE 10.51

18. Open adult_elephant.dng in Camera RAW, increase the Shadows slider to +25 to add a bit of detail back into the shadow areas (**Figure 10.52**), and then click on Open Image to send the file over to Photoshop.

Choose the Quick Selection Tool (**W**) and click and drag around the elephant to start making a selection (**Figure 10.53**)

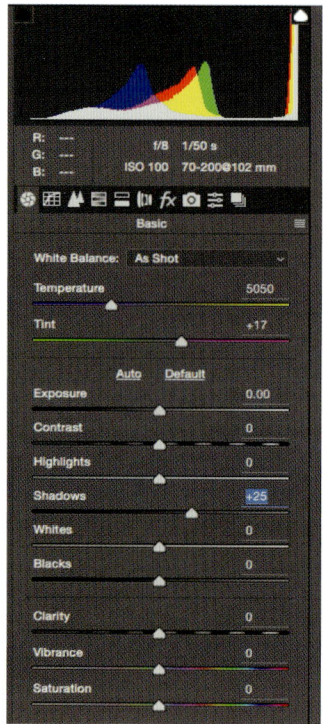

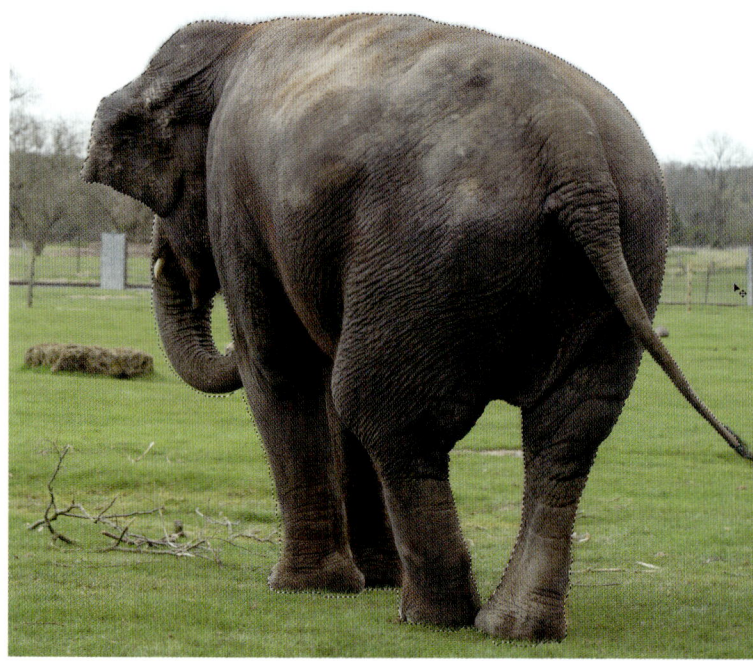

FIGURE 10.52   FIGURE 10.53

With the selection active, click on Select and Mask, and then use the Refine Edge Brush Tool (**Figure 10.54**) to paint over and select the little bit of hair on the elephant's tail (**Figure 10.55**).

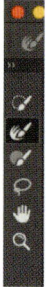   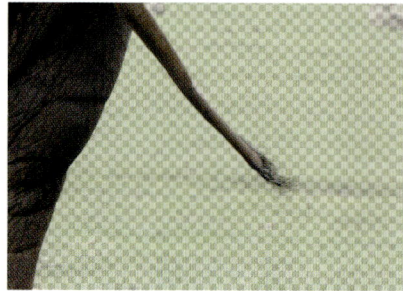

FIGURE 10.54   FIGURE 10.55

Click on Smart Radius to see if Photoshop can pick up any of the extra-fine hairs around the elephant's body. In the Output Settings section on the right side of the screen, choose New Layer with Layer Mask from the Output To menu (**Figure 10.56**) and click OK. Note that if you're working in a slightly earlier version of Photoshop and are using Refine Edge, this option is also available to you at the bottom right of the screen.

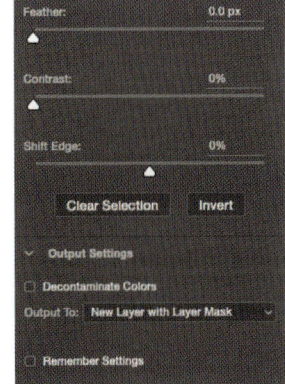

FIGURE 10.56

19. Now we have a new layer with a Layer Mask cutting the elephant from its original background. With the Move Tool (**V**), click and drag this layer on top of the tab that contains the scene we just created, and when it opens, drag the elephant into the center of the screen and position it on the right side of the watering hole (**Figure 10.57**).

There's a little bit of a halo around the elephant in my selection (**Figure 10.58**). To remove this, click on the Layer Mask in the Layers panel and use the Lasso Tool (**L**) to draw a rough selection around the elephant, but don't include the hair on it's tail (**Figure 10.59**).

Then go to *Filter > Blur > Gaussian Blur*, set Radius to 1 Pixel, and click OK (**Figure 10.60**).

NOTE *Adding a small amount of Gaussian Blur will help to soften and blend the next adjustment so that when the halo is removed, it looks natural as opposed to creating a very sharp and defined outline.*

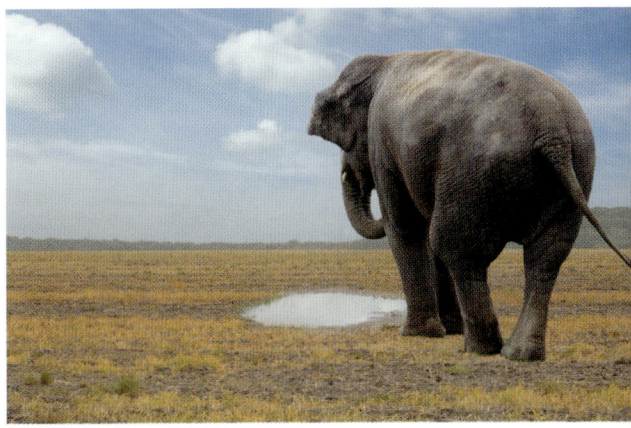

FIGURE 10.57

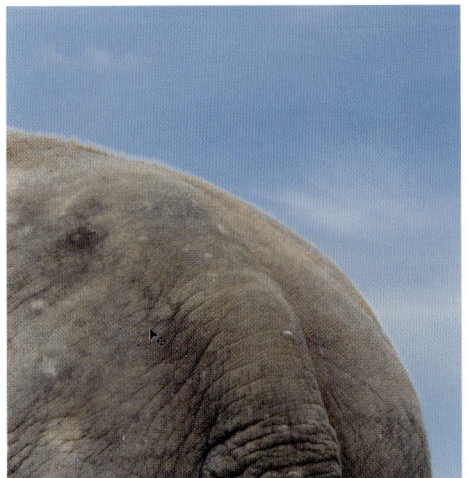

FIGURE 10.58 The halo around the elephant is actually part of its original background

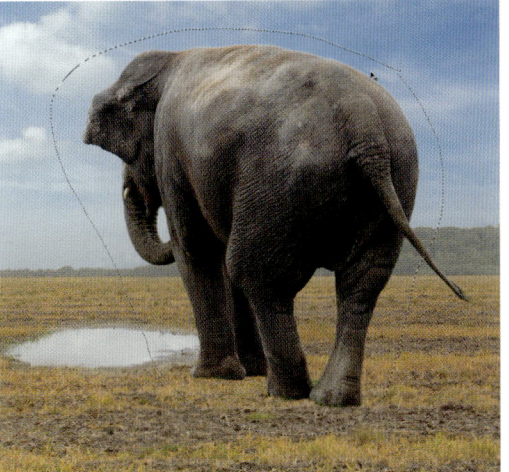

FIGURE 10.59

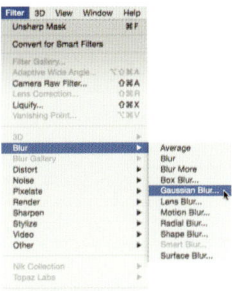

FIGURE 10.60

Finally, go to *Image > Adjustment > Levels* and drag the black Output Levels marker on the far left over to the right (**Figure 10.61**) until you see the halo disappear. Then go to *Select > Deselect* to remove the marching ants selection from around the elephant (**Figure 10.62**).

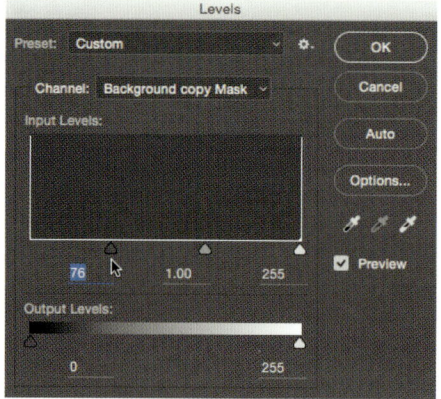

FIGURE 10.61

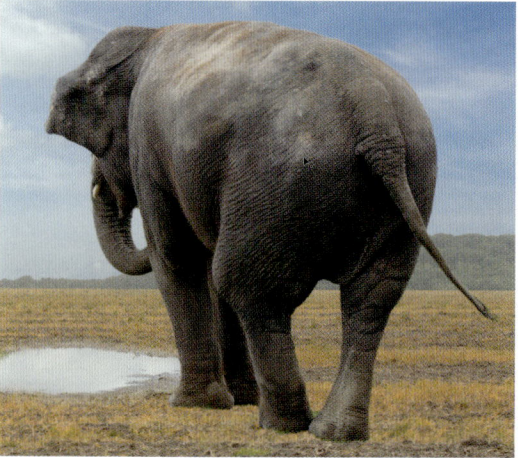

FIGURE 10.62 The halo around the elephant has been removed

20. The selection of the elephant contains a bit of grass from the original background, which we can actually use to our advantage. We can simply change the color of this grass to make the elephant look like it's standing on the ground in our new scene.

Click on the Hue/Saturation icon to add a Hue/Saturation adjustment layer to the top of the layer stack. In the Properties, click on the Clipping Mask icon at the bottom so that the adjustments we make only affect the layer directly below the Hue/Saturation adjustment layer; in this case, the elephant (**Figure 10.63**).

Choose Greens from the Master drop-down menu, and then click and drag on the outer markers on the color bar and bunch them together (**Figure 10.64**).

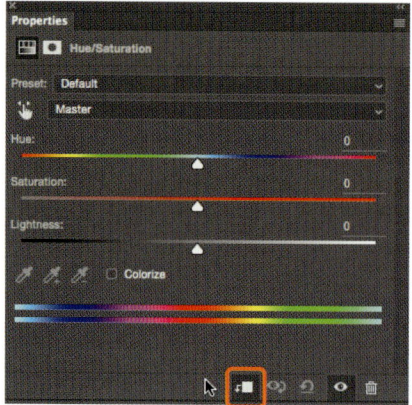

FIGURE 10.63

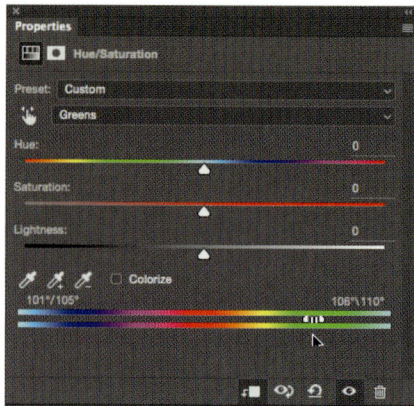

FIGURE 10.64

Click on the Add to Sample tool in the Hue/Saturation Properties (**Figure 10.65**), and then click and drag over the areas of green grass around the elephant's feet (**Figure 10.66**).

Finally, drag the Hue slider to around -33 to make the color of the grass around the elephant's feet match the rest of the grass in the scene (**Figure 10.67**).

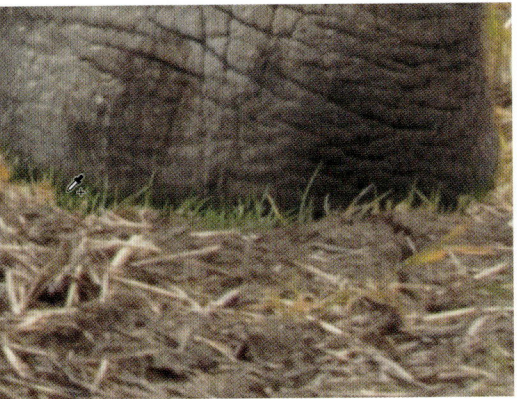

FIGURE 10.65 Click and drag over the green grass to sample the different shades of green

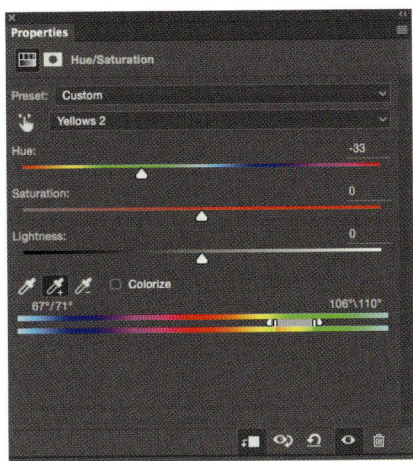

FIGURE 10.66

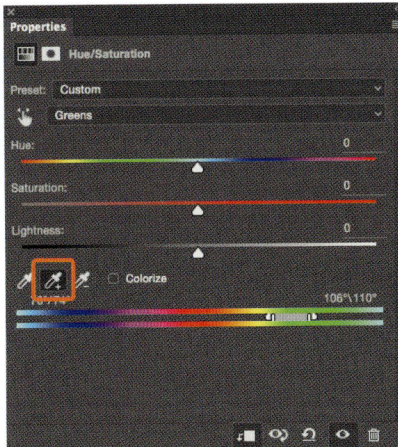

FIGURE 10.67

NOTE *Notice how the markers on the color bar in the Hue/Saturation Properties begin to separate and include more colors as we click and drag over the green grass. This means Photoshop is seeing more than just green, so that when we change the color of the grass, all of the grass will be affected, not just the green grass.*

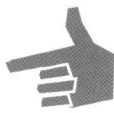

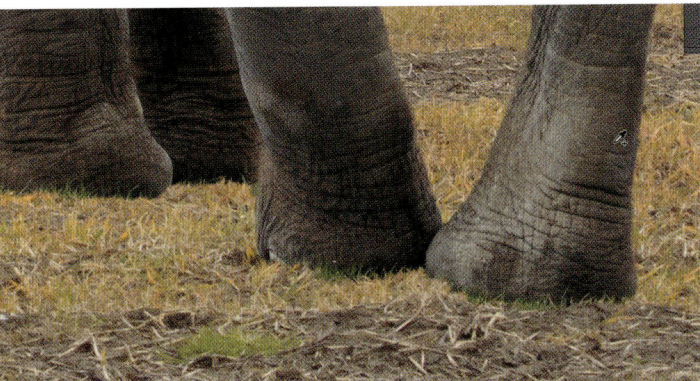

FIGURE 10.68 Before

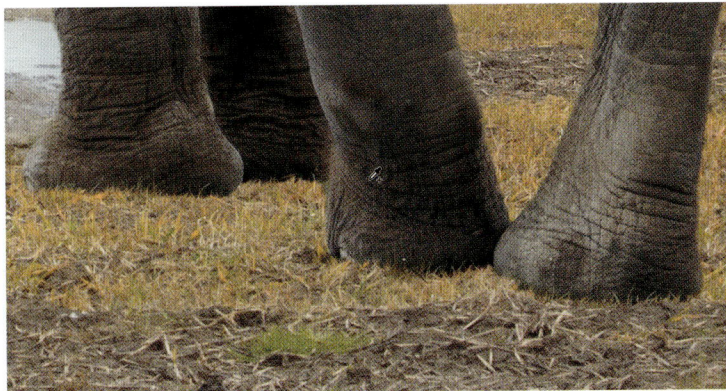

FIGURE 10.69 After

21. Now let's bring in the baby elephant. Open baby_elephant.dng in Camera RAW, increase the Shadows slider to +25, and click Open Image to send the file over into Photoshop. We'll use the Quick Selection Tool (**W**) again to make a selection of the baby elephant, but because it's so close to another elephant, you'll find that it's not quite as easy this time. Here we can use a combination of the Quick Selection Tool and the Quick Mask technique I covered in chapter 4 (page 73) to get as good of a selection as possible. We'll also use the grass technique for the elephant's hair, so allow for a bit of space around the elephant's back and head when you make the selection (**Figure 10.70**).

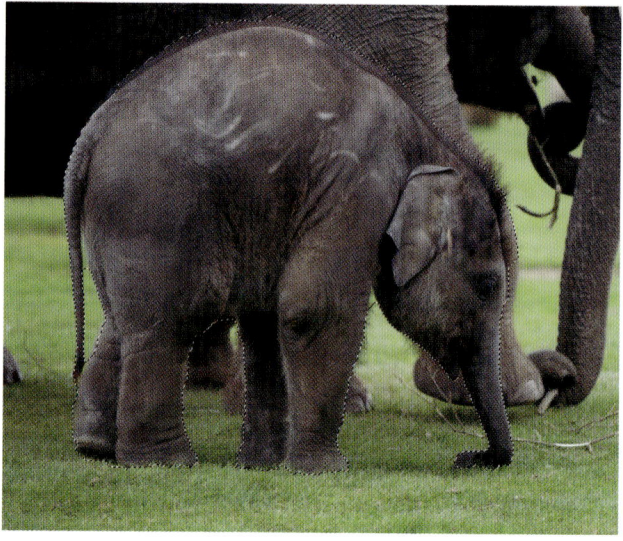

FIGURE 10.70

After making a selection of the Baby Elephant, we'll do the same thing we did with the selection of the adult elephant in step 18. In the Output Settings section on the right side of the screen, choose New Layer with Layer Mask from the Output To menu and click. Back in Photoshop, click on this new layer and drag it into our scene like we did with the adult elephant in step 19 (**Figure 10.71**).

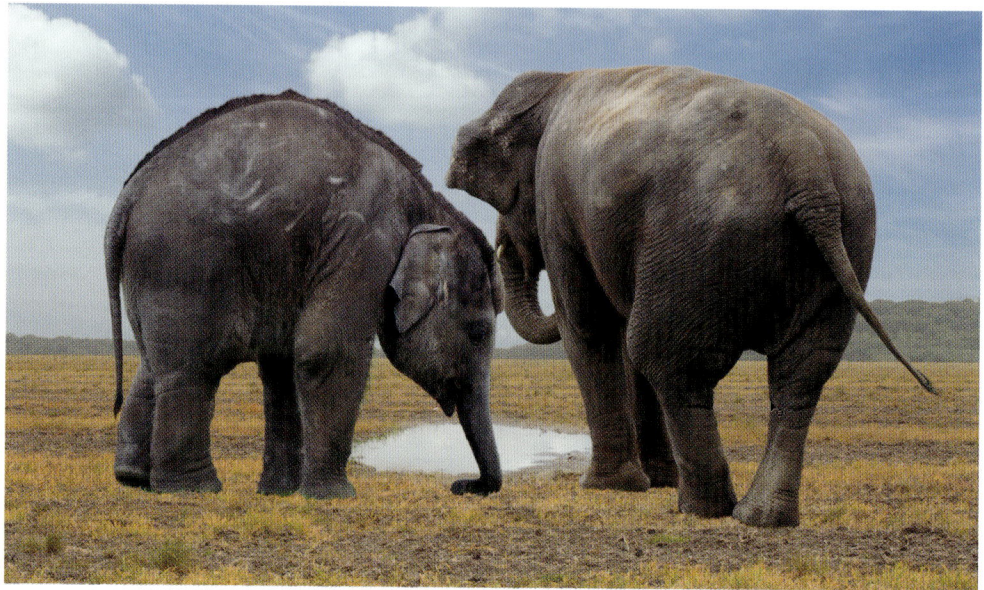

FIGURE 10.71

22. Go to *Edit > Free Transform,* and while holding down Shift + Option (Mac) or Shift + Alt (PC), click on one of the corner transform handles and drag it inward to make the baby elephant smaller. Use the Move Tool (**V**) to reposition the elephant (**Figure 10.72**).

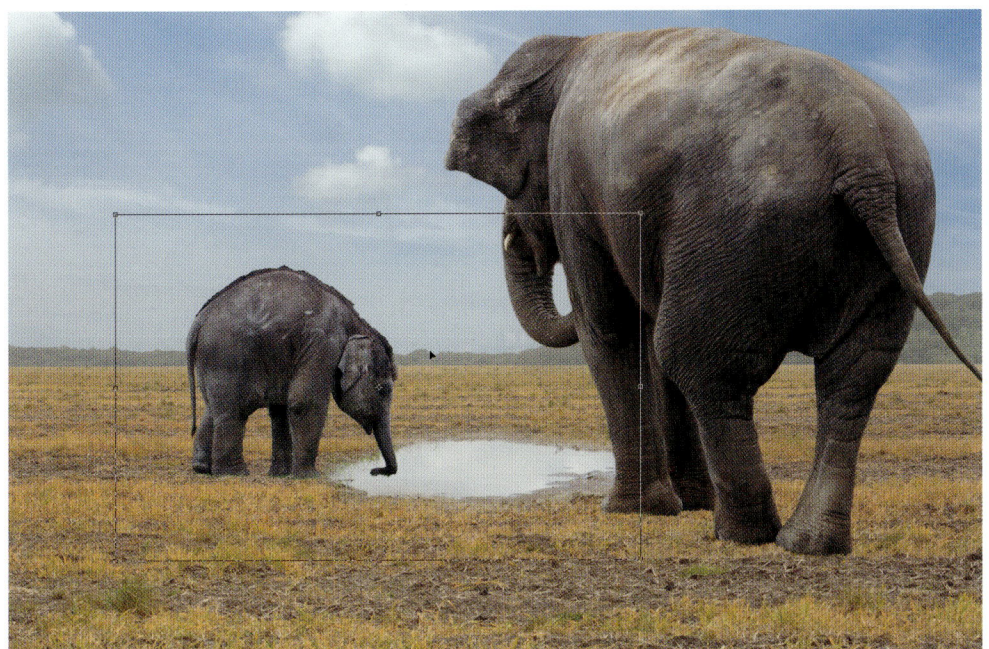

FIGURE 10.72

23. Now we'll fix the hair on the baby elephant's back and head using the technique I covered in chapter 4 (page 76). Choose the Brush Tool (**B**), and with the baby elephant Layer Mask active, use a round, hard-edged brush and black foreground color to paint over the hair on the baby elephant (**Figure 10.73**).

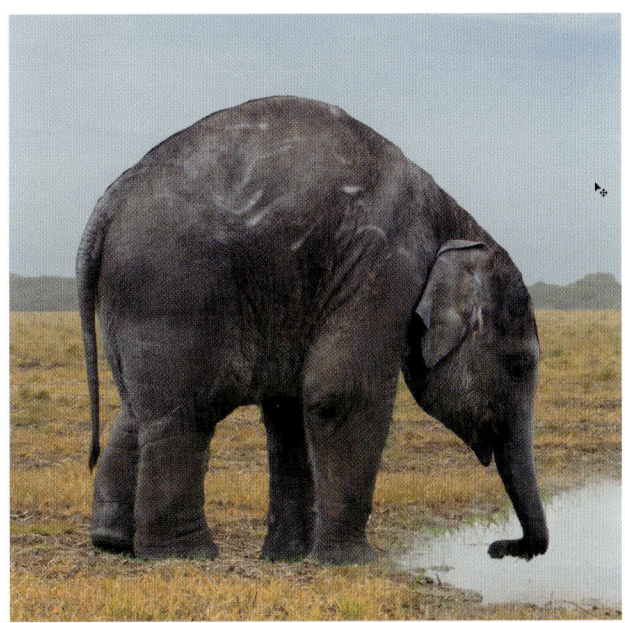

FIGURE 10.73

Next, choose Brush 112 from the Brush Presets (**Figure 10.74**) and set the foreground color in the toolbar to white.

Click on the Brush panel, and in the Brush Tip Shape tab, click on Flip X (**Figure 10.75**). In the Shape Dynamics tab, set Size Jitter to 10% and Angle Jitter to 7% (**Figure 10.76**).

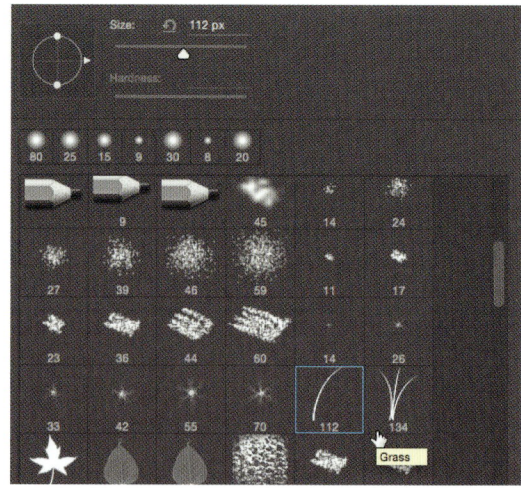

FIGURE 10.74

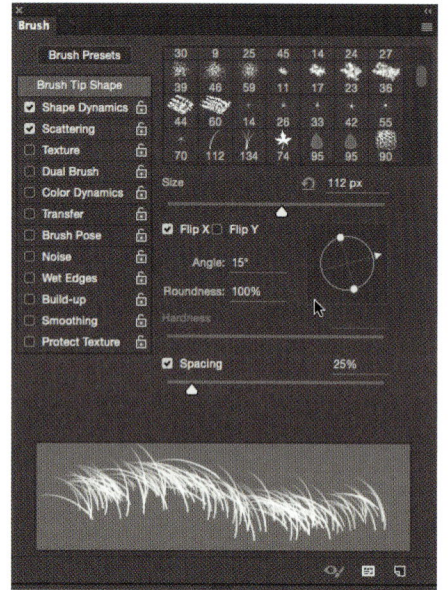

FIGURE 10.75

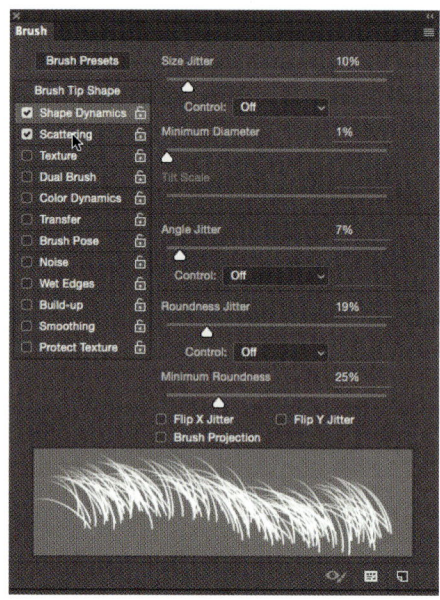

FIGURE 10.76

Finally, in the Scattering tab, set Scatter to around 56% (**Figure 10.77**).

Now paint across the elephant's back and head to bring back the hair. The shape of the brush makes it look as though we actually captured the hair in our original selection (**Figure 10.78**). Note: As you paint along the Elephant's back and head, make regular adjustments to the Angle amount in the Brush Tip Shape tab to follow the line of the body.

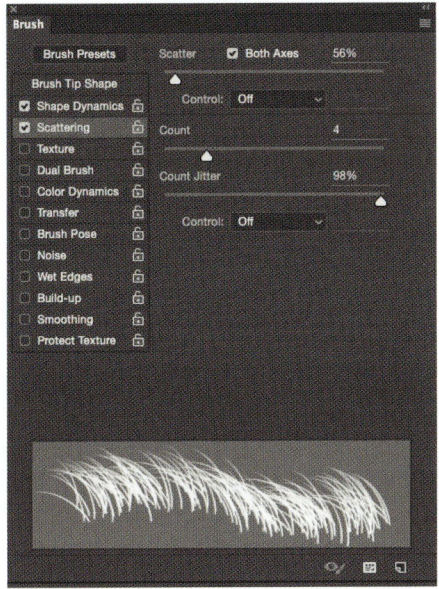

FIGURE 10.77

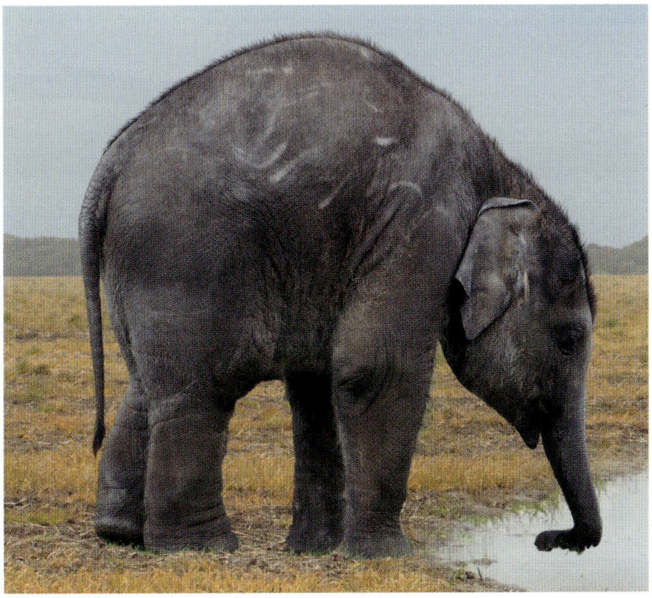

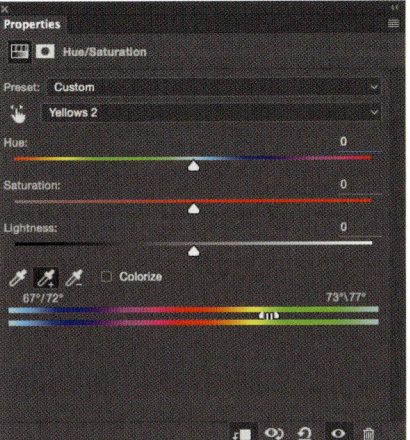

FIGURE 10.78

24. Add a Hue/Saturation adjustment layer and click the Clipping Mask icon so that the adjustment only affects the layer below; in this case, the baby elephant. Then, as we did with the adult elephant, choose Greens from the Master drop-down menu and bunch the markers together on the color bar (**Figure 10.79**). Select the Add to Sample Tool and click and drag over the grass around the baby elephant's feet.

Drag the Hue slider to around -42 so that the grass around the baby elephant's feet matches the grass in the rest of the scene.

FIGURE 10.79

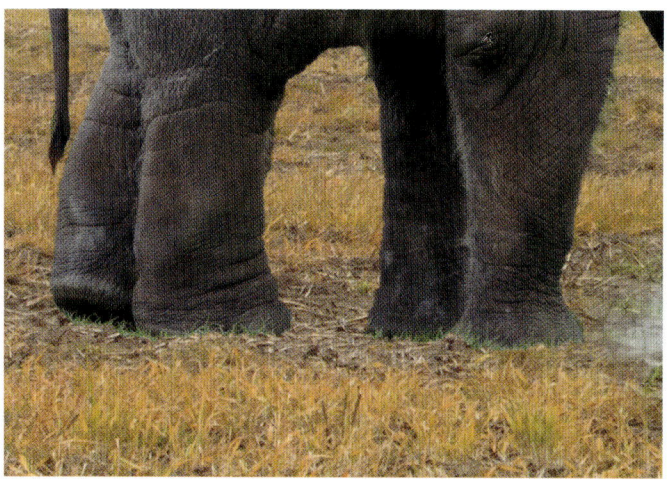

FIGURE 10.80 Before

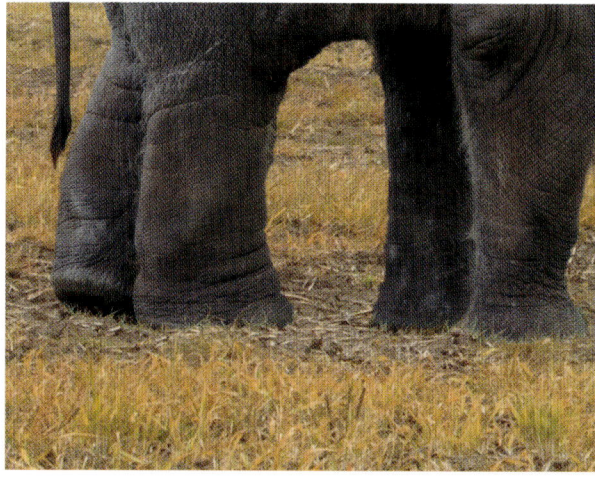

FIGURE 10.81 After

While we're doing this, you may notice that there is a reflection of green grass in the watering hole (**Figure 10.82**). We can use the Hue/Saturation adjustment layer technique to make this more yellow as well. Click on the watering hole layer in the Layers panel, add a Hue/Saturation adjustment layer, and follow the steps we used to change the color of the grass around the elephants' feet.

25. Eventually, we're going to add some sunlight coming in from the right side of the picture, which will make it look like sunset. This would also cause the elephants to cast shadows, so we need to add those in as well. Let's start with the adult elephant.

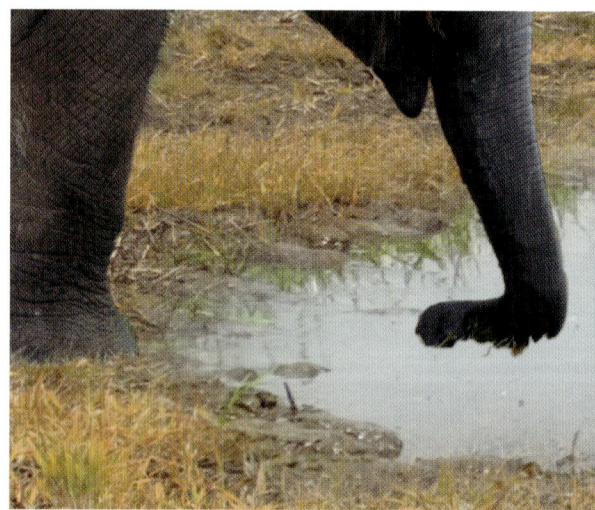

FIGURE 10.82

Click on the adult elephant layer in the Layers panel and press Command + J (Mac) or Ctrl + J (PC) to create a duplicate layer called "adult elephant copy." Click on the Layer Mask for the layer below (the original adult elephant layer), and then right-click on this layer in the Layers panel and choose Apply Layer Mask from the pop-up menu (**Figure 10.83**).

Rename this layer "adult shadow." Hold down the Command key (Mac) or Ctrl key (PC) and click once on the thumbnail of the adult shadow layer in the Layers panel to load it as a selection (**Figure 10.84**). Go to *Edit > Fill,* choose Black from the Contents menu, and click OK (**Figure 10.85**).

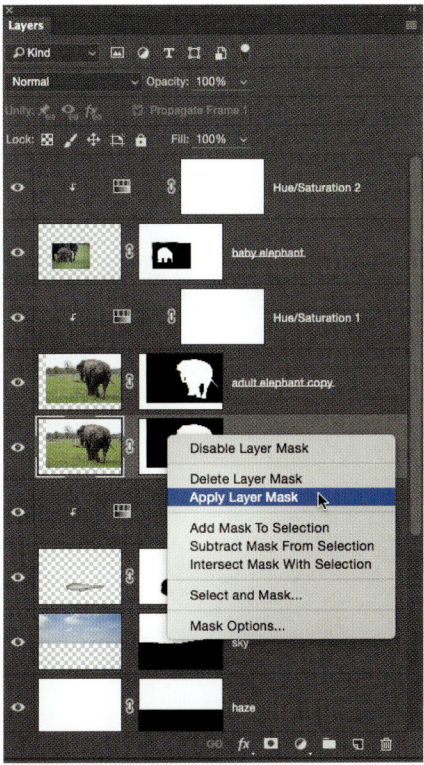

FIGURE 10.83

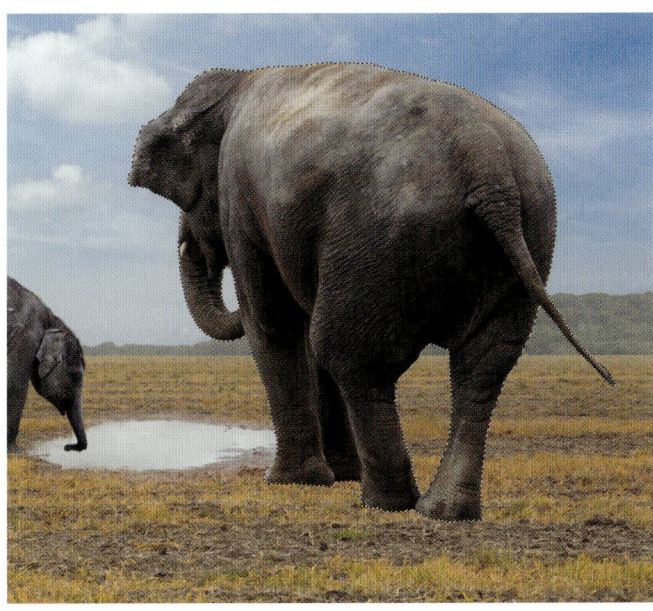

FIGURE 10.84

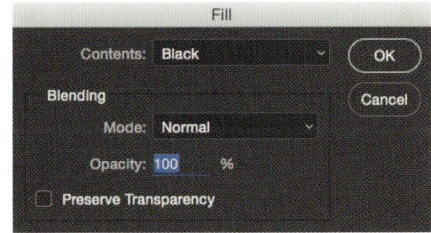

FIGURE 10.85

26. Go to *Edit > Transform > Distort* (**Figure 10.86**) and drag out the adult shadow so that it extends down to the bottom-left of the scene (**Figure 10.87**), and then press Return (Mac) or Enter (PC). Next, grab the Brush Tool (**B**), and with a brush set to 100% Hardness and a black foreground color, paint to join the adult shadow to the elephant's feet. Fill in areas and paint however you feel the shadow would be cast, but don't worry about being too accurate here because we're only looking to "sell the fake," as photographer and digital artist Joel Grimes would say (**Figure 10.88**).

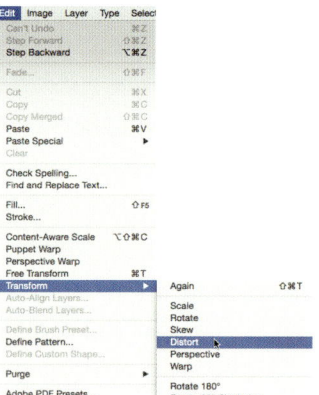

FIGURE 10.86

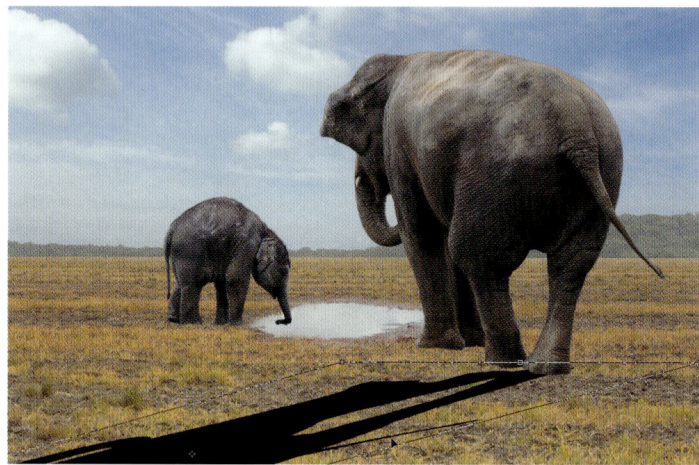

FIGURE 10.87

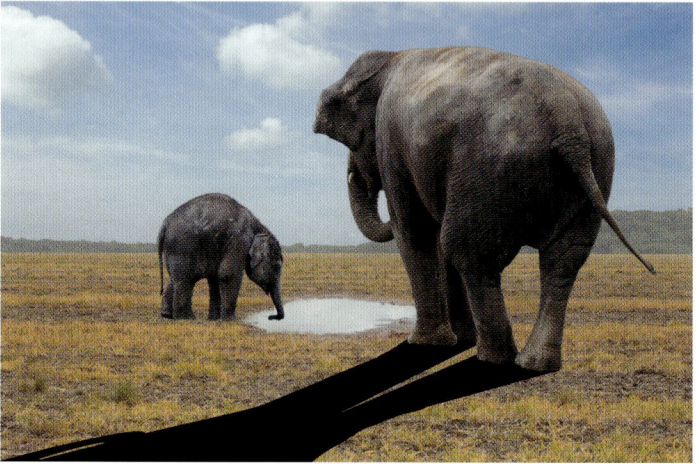

FIGURE 10.88

With the adult shadow layer still selected, go to *Filter > Convert for Smart Filters,* and then to *Filter > Blur > Gaussian Blur.* Set Radius to 6 Pixels and click OK. Lower the opacity of the layer to around 50% (**Figure 10.89**).

NOTE *Converting the layer to a Smart Object will allow us to make changes to the blur later on without having to redo any steps if we decide it's too much or not enough.*

27. Now we need to create the baby elephant's shadow (**Figure 10.90**), which is simply a case of repeating steps 25 and 26 with the baby elephant layer.

28. There are a few marks on the baby elephant's body, which were caused by him rubbing against an object in the enclosure where he was originally photographed, so we'll remove those. Click on the thumbnail of the baby elephant copy layer in the Layers panel. Select the Patch Tool and drag around a mark on the elephant's body (**Figure 10.91**). Drag the selection to a clean part of the body, and information from the clean area will be blended into the area with the mark to replace it. Continue working with the Patch Tool to remove all of the marks (**Figure 10.92**).

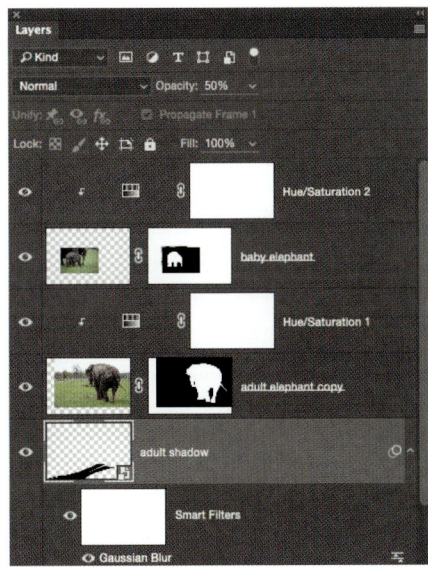

FIGURE 10.89

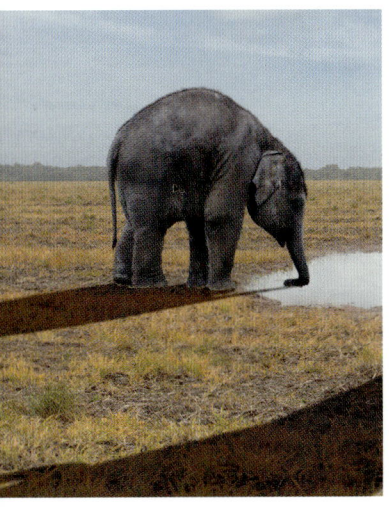

FIGURE 10.90

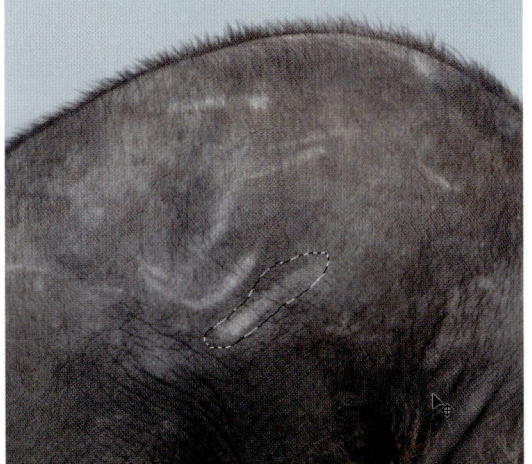

FIGURE 10.91

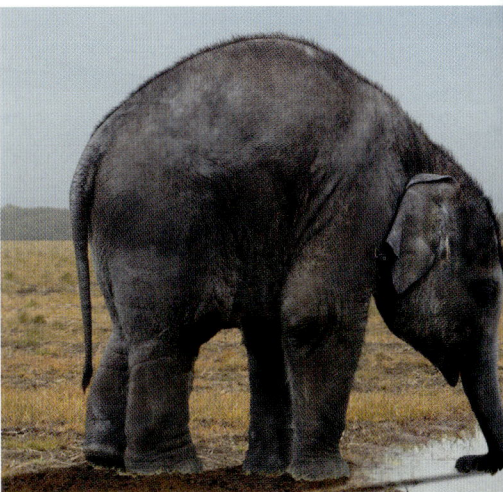

FIGURE 10.92

29. Now that we have added in the cast shadows, we need to darken the parts of the elephants that the sun does not reach (i.e., the sides on which we have created the cast shadows). Let's start with the adult elephant.

Click on the adult elephant copy layer, and then click to add a Levels adjustment layer. In the Levels Properties, drag the white Output Levels marker in toward the middle to around 170 (**Figure 10.93**). This has the desired result of darkening the elephant (**Figure 10.94**).

The Levels adjustment layer comes with its own Layer Mask, so we'll paint on this with a

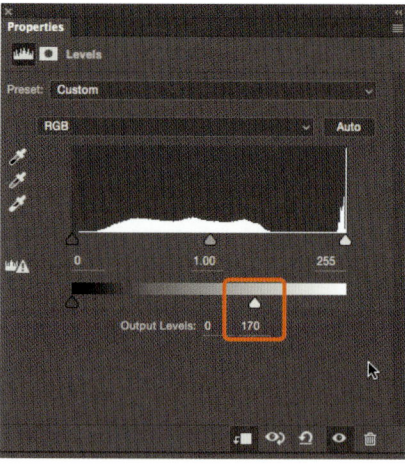

FIGURE 10.93

round, medium-soft brush (around 25% Hardness) across the top of the elephant's back, part of its trunk, and parts of its legs, in areas where the sunlight would catch if it was coming in from the right side (**Figure 10.95**).

Repeat these steps to darken the baby elephant.

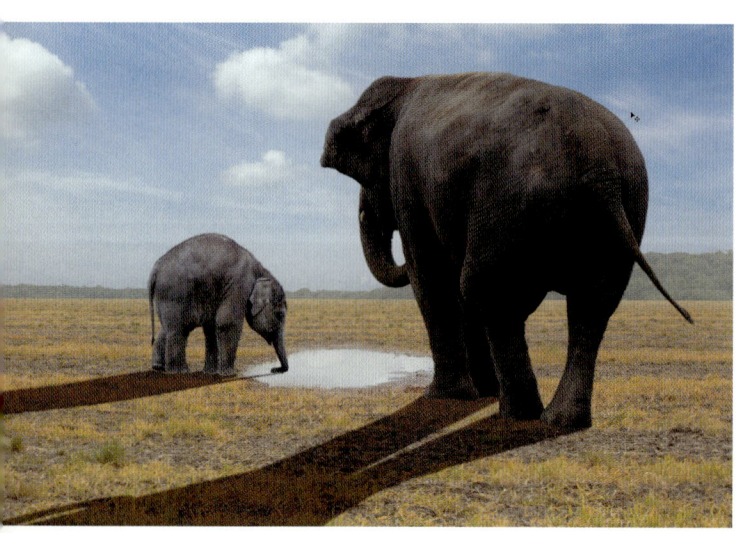

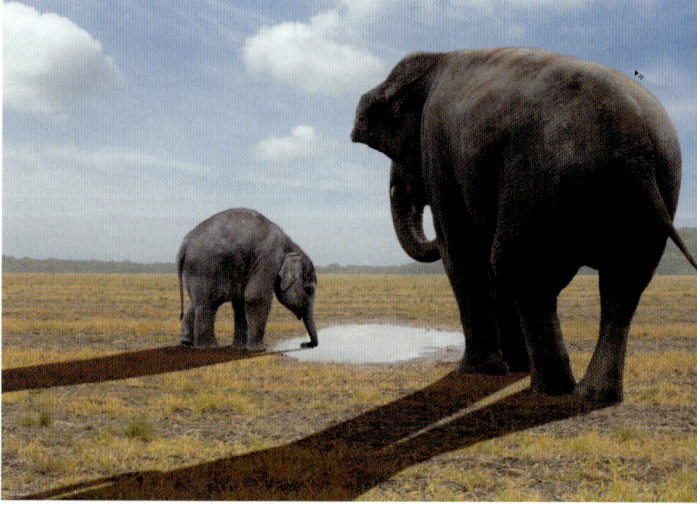

FIGURE 10.94 The elephant has been darkened using a Levels adjustment layer

FIGURE 10.95

30. Now let's make it look as though the baby elephant has its trunk in the water and is drinking from the watering hole. Click on the Layer Mask for the baby elephant copy layer (**Figure 10.96**). With the Layer Mask active, use a round brush at around 70% Hardness and a black foreground color to paint over and remove the curled part of the baby elephant's trunk (**Figure 10.97**).

Go to *File > New,* and in the settings, create a document that measures 800 × 600 pixels and has a White Background. The ripples we're creating are going to be very small, so I'm not concerned about the bit depth or resolution (**Figure 10.98**).

Choose the Gradient Tool (**G**) and select a preset that has three colors. It doesn't matter which one because we'll be making changes in the next step. I chose the Gradient labeled Blue, Yellow, Blue (**Figure 10.99**).

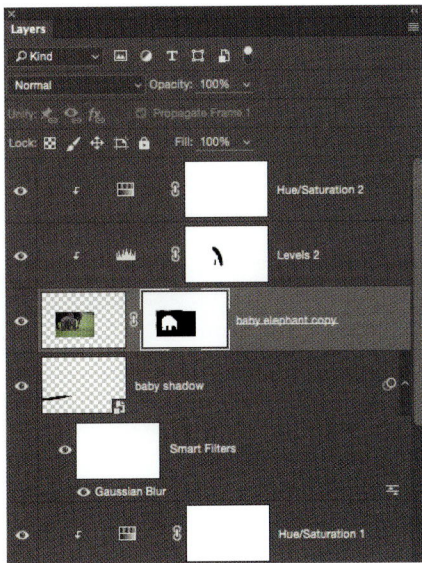

FIGURE 10.96

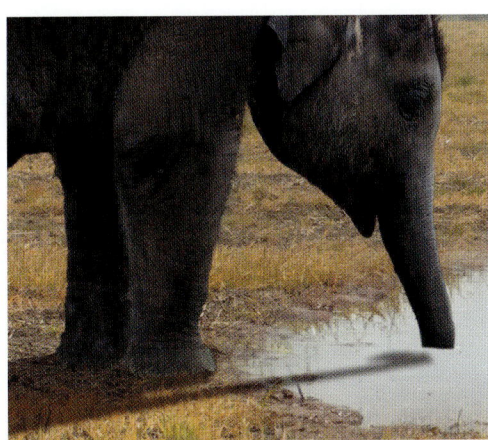

FIGURE 10.97

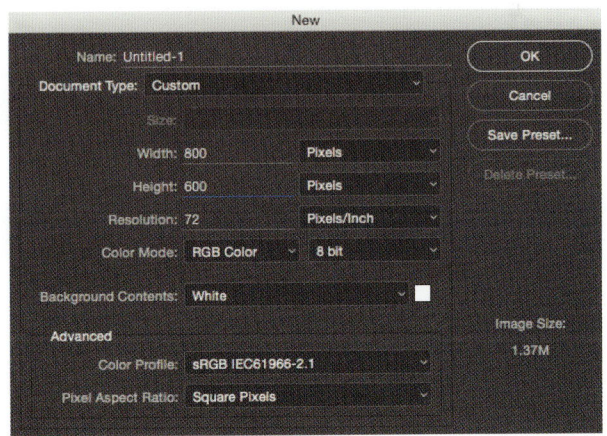

FIGURE 10.98

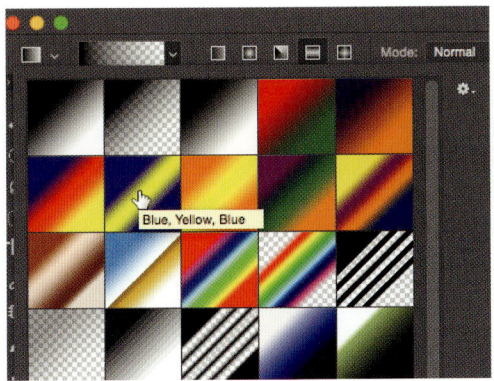

FIGURE 10.99

31. With the Blue, Yellow, Blue gradient selected, click directly on the gradient in the options bar (**Figure 10.100**) to bring up the Gradient Editor (**Figure 10.101**).

Drag the outer gradient color stops to the far left and far right (**Figure 10.102**), and then click on the blue stop on the far left. This puts the color in the Color Swatch at the bottom-left of the dialog. Click on this blue Color to bring up the Color Picker, and then choose a mid-gray (**Figure 10.103**). I chose H:243, S:0, and b:67. Click OK.

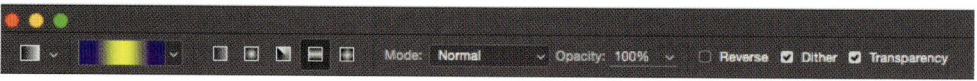

FIGURE 10.100

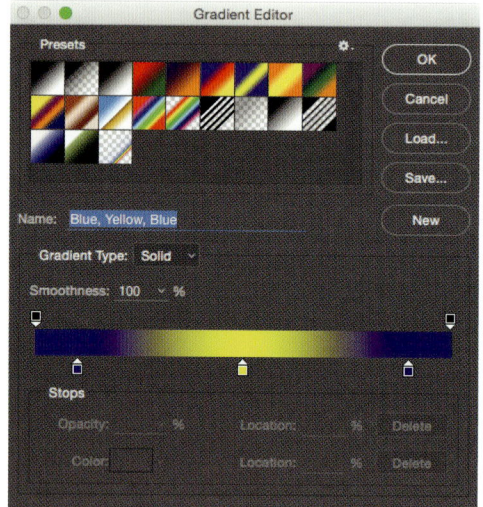

FIGURE 10.101

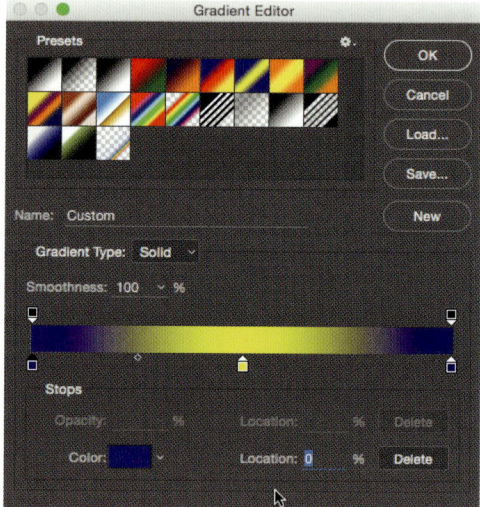

FIGURE 10.102

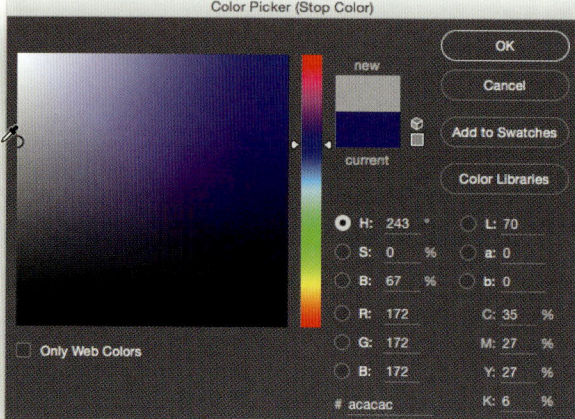

FIGURE 10.103

32. Click on the middle color stop (yellow) in the Gradient Editor, and then click on the Color Swatch to enter the Color Picker properties (**Figure 10.104**). Choose a darker gray (I chose H: 59, S:0, and B: 43) and click OK.

Finally, click on the far right color stop (blue) in the Gradient Editor, and then click on the Color Swatch to bring up the Color Picker (**Figure 10.105**). This time choose a much brighter gray (not quite white; I chose H: 243, S:0, and B:93), and click OK.

NOTE *The different shades of gray we just dialed in will be the shadow, midtone, and highlight areas of our water ripple.*

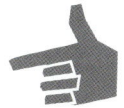

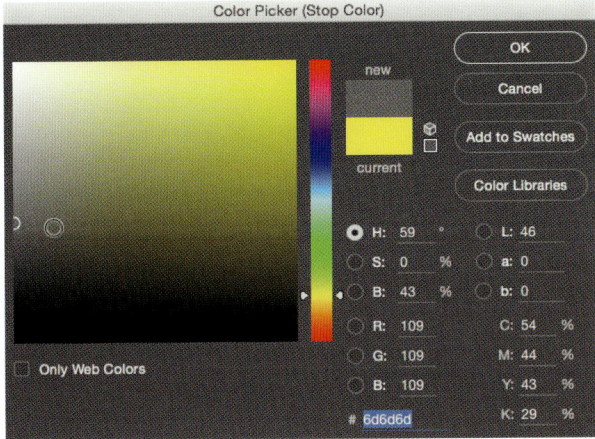

FIGURE 10.104

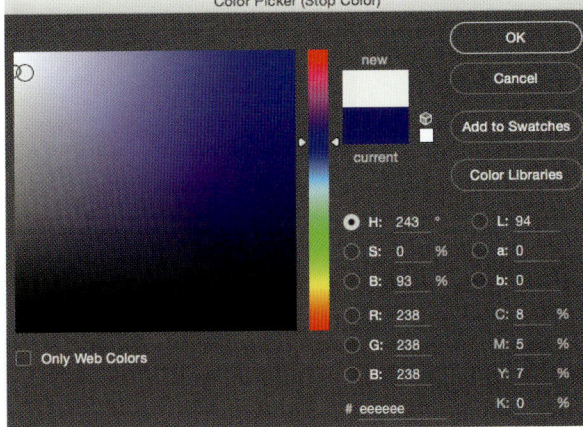

FIGURE 10.105

33. Click OK to close the Gradient Editor, and from the options bar at the top of the screen, choose the Radial Gradient (**Figure 10.106**).

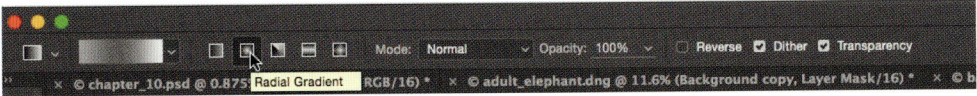

FIGURE 10.106

Click in the bottom-left corner of the new document and drag upward and across to the upper-right corner, then release (**Figure 10.107**).

FIGURE 10.107

34. Go to *Filter > Distort > Twirl,* and in the Twirl properties, move the Angle slider all the way to 999°. Click on the minus sign to zoom out in the preview and see the result (**Figure 10.108**). Click OK.

Go to *Filter > Distort > ZigZag,* select Pond Ripples from the Style menu, set Amount to around 54, and set Ridges to 17 (**Figure 10.109**). Click OK.

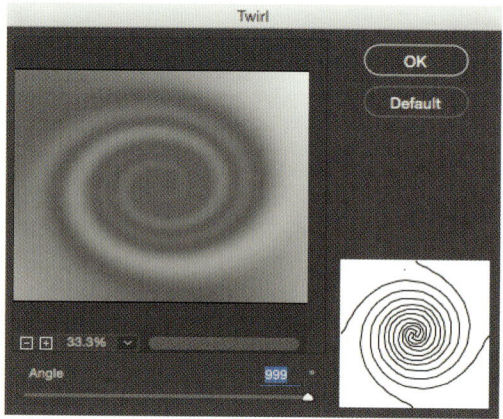

FIGURE 10.108

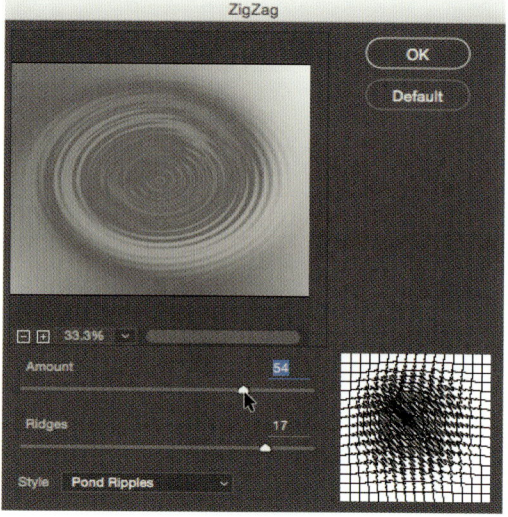

FIGURE 10.109

35. Go to *Select > All* and then to *Edit > Copy.* Click on the tab to reveal the scene into which we have added our elephants, and then click on the uppermost layer in the layer stack (**Figure 10.110**). Go to *Edit > Paste* to add the water ripple layer to the top of the layer stack (**Figure 10.111**). Rename this layer "water ripples."

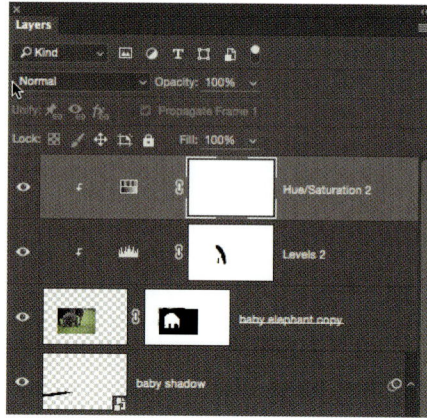

FIGURE 10.110

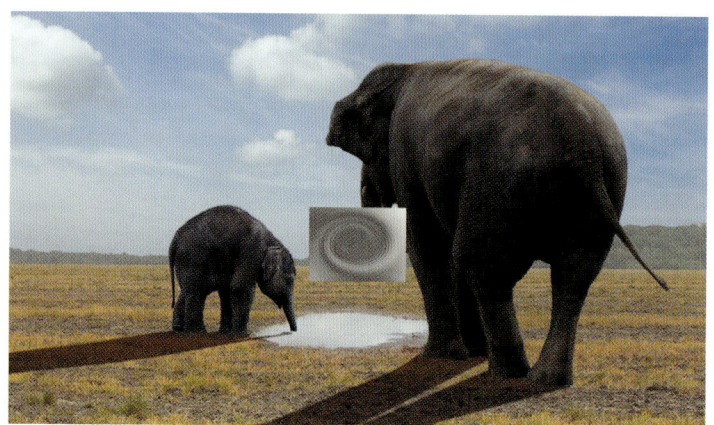

FIGURE 10.111

36. Use the Move Tool (**V**) to position the water ripples layer over the watering hole. Go to *Edit > Free Transform* and drag the bottom-middle transform handle upward to squash the ripples together and adjust the perspective so that the ripples look as though they are at the same angle as the watering hole (**Figure 10.112**).

Hold down Shift + Option (Mac) or Shift + Alt (PC:) and click and drag a corner transform handle inward to resize the water ripples. Use the Move Tool to reposition the middle of the ripples at the base of the baby elephant's trunk (**Figure 10.113**). Press Return (Mac) or Enter (PC).

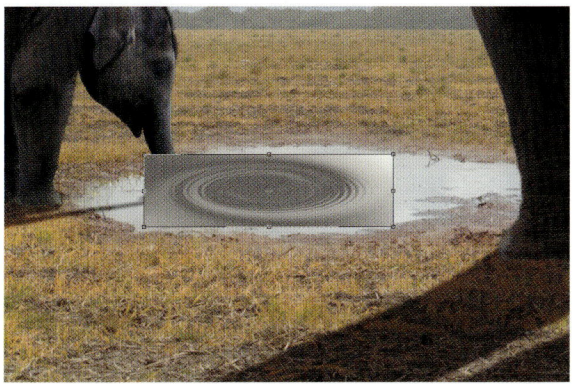

FIGURE 10.112

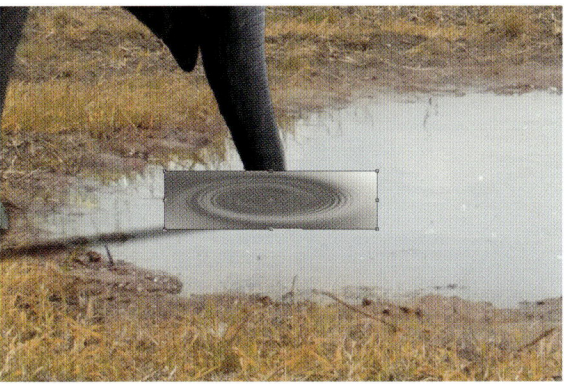

FIGURE 10.113

37. Change the Blend Mode of the water ripples layer to Hard Light. Add a Layer Mask and use a round, soft-edged brush and a black foreground color to paint away some parts of the water ripples layer so that the ripples blend naturally.

Select the Layer Mask for the baby elephant copy layer and use the same brush at 80% Opacity to paint over the bottom of the trunk so that it is just barely visible under the water.

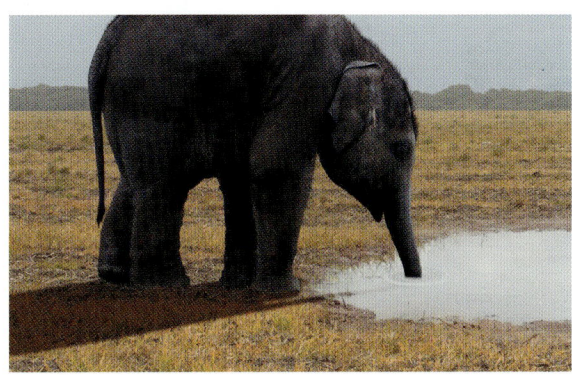

Finally, add a Layer Mask to the baby shadow layer and use the same brush to paint over the parts of the shadow that are no longer needed. Then set the brush to 60% Opacity and paint over the shadow of the trunk on the water to reduce its visibility (**Figure 10.114**).

FIGURE 10.114

38. Now let's add in the sunlight. Add a new blank layer to the top of the layer stack and rename it "sun." Choose a round, soft-edged brush and a white foreground color and press once with the brush on the back of the adult elephant (**Figure 10.115**).

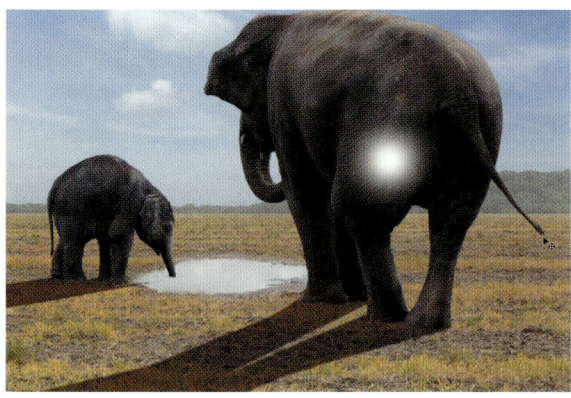

FIGURE 10.115

Change the Blend Mode of the sun layer to Linear Dodge and add a Hue/Saturation adjustment layer with the Clipping Mask icon activated. Dial in a Hue of 40, a Saturation of up to 100, and a Lightness of around -60 (**Figure 10.116**). Go to *Edit > Free Transform,* press and hold Shift + Option (Mac) or Shift + Alt (PC), and click and drag a corner transform handle outward to enlarge the sun flare. Use the Move Tool (**V**) to position it at the far-right side of the image with the center outside the canvas area (**Figure 10.117**). Since we used an adjustment layer to do this, we can change it at any stage.

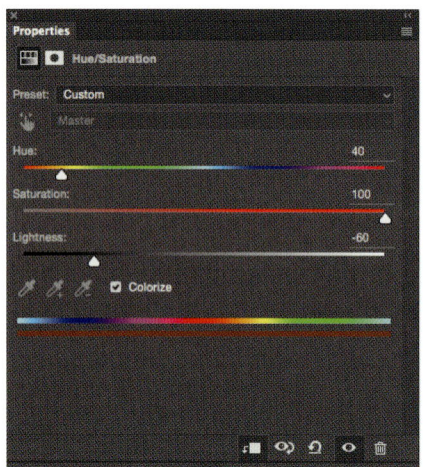

FIGURE 10.116

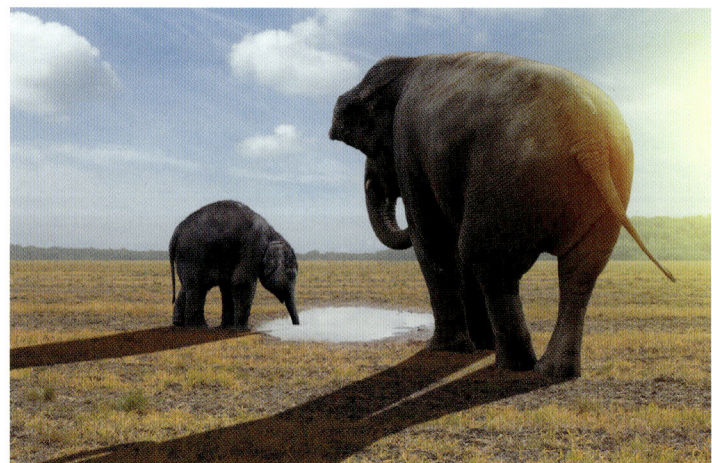

FIGURE 10.117

39. Now we'll do the black-and-white conversion. There is a seemingly unlimited number ways to do this, but for this image we'll start with a Gradient Map. Press **D** to set the foreground and background colors to their defaults of black and white, and then click on the Gradient Map icon in the Adjustments panel to add a Gradient Map adjustment layer.

Straight away I think that the ground is too light and the sky doesn't pack enough punch

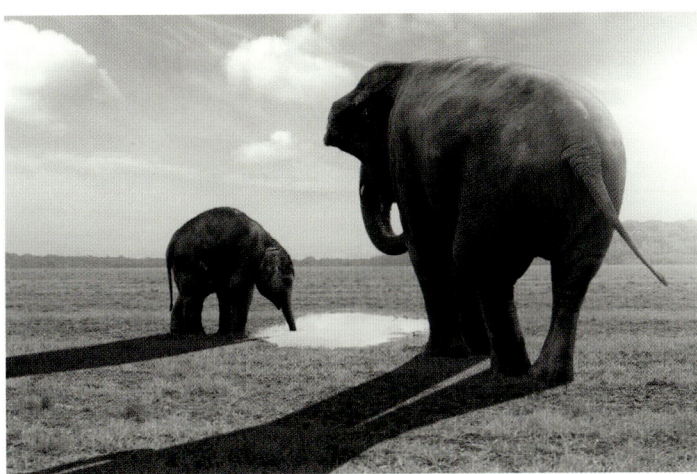

FIGURE 10.118

(**Figure 10.118**), so we'll make some changes there. Thankfully, because we've been working nondestructively, we can make these changes without having to redo lots of work.

Click on the very bottom layer (Background) and go to *Filter > Convert for Smart Filters*. Then go to *Filter > Camera RAW filter* and grab the Graduated Filter Tool. Click in the center of the grass and drag upward (**Figure 10.119**), and then reduce the Exposure to around -1.05 and click OK (**Figure 10.120**).

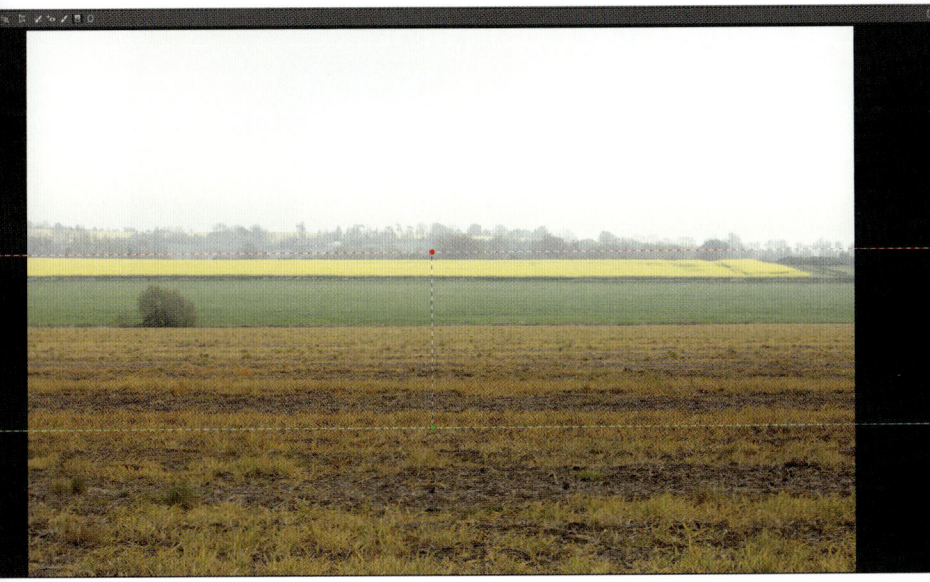

FIGURE 10.119

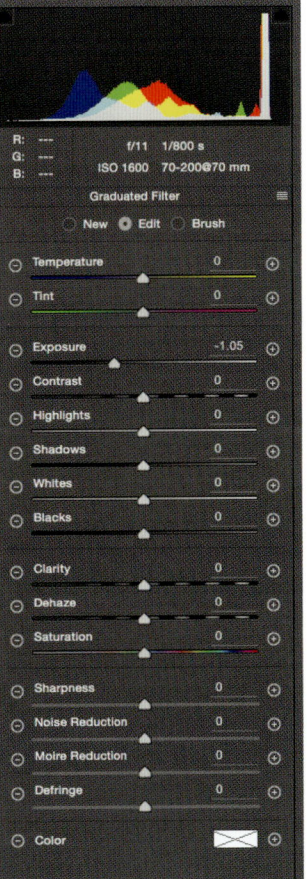

FIGURE 10.120

40. Click on the sky layer and press Command + J (Mac) or Ctrl + J (PC) to create a duplicate layer. Click on the Layer Mask for this sky copy layer, then right-click and choose Apply Layer Mask from the context menu (**Figure 10.121**).

Go to *Filter > Convert for Smart Filters,* and then to *Filter > Camera RAW filter.* Choose the Graduated Filter Tool and drag out a gradient from the top of the sky to just about the tree line (**Figure 10.122**).

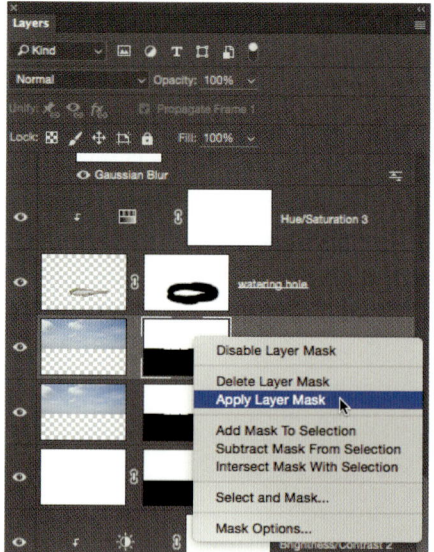

FIGURE 10.121

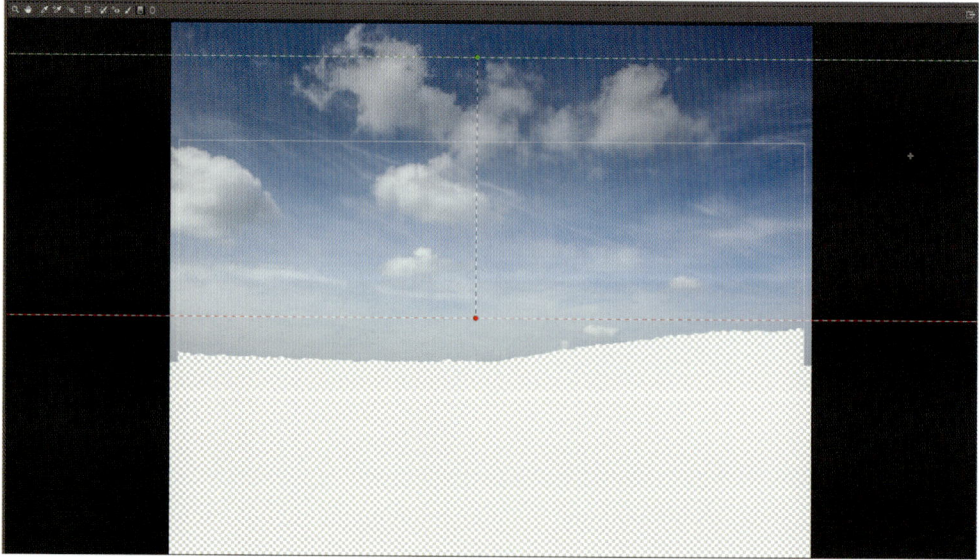

FIGURE 10.122

Change the Exposure to -1.05 and the Clarity to +100 (**Figure 10.123**). Click on the HSL/Grayscale tab, and in the Luminance section, adjust the Blues to -40 (**Figure 10.124**).

Figures 10.125 and **10.126** show the changes made to the ground and the sky. This was all possible because we worked nondestructively.

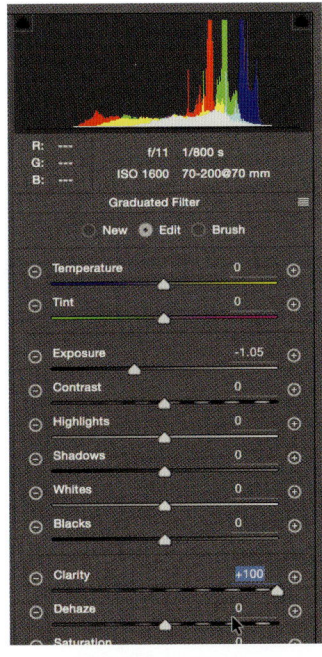

FIGURE 10.123

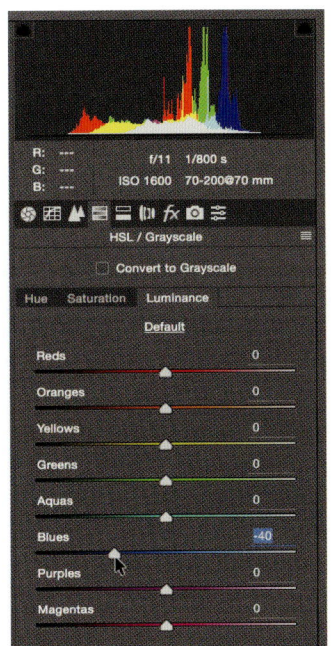

FIGURE 10.124

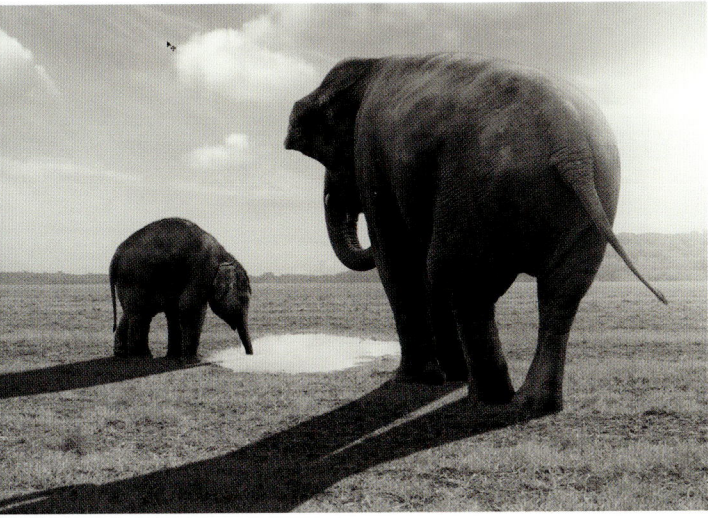

FIGURE 10.125 Before

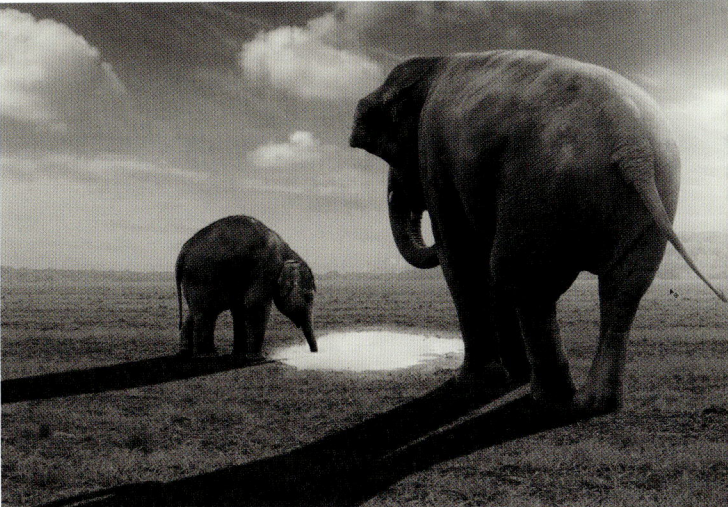

FIGURE 10.126 After

41. Looking at the image, I see a few more things I want to do. First, I think we should darken the adult elephant a touch more on the side that is nearest the viewer. To do this, click on the Levels adjustment layer attached to the adult elephant copy layer (**Figure 10.127**), and in the Levels Properties, drag the white Output Levels pointer left until it reaches around 128 (**Figure 10.128**).

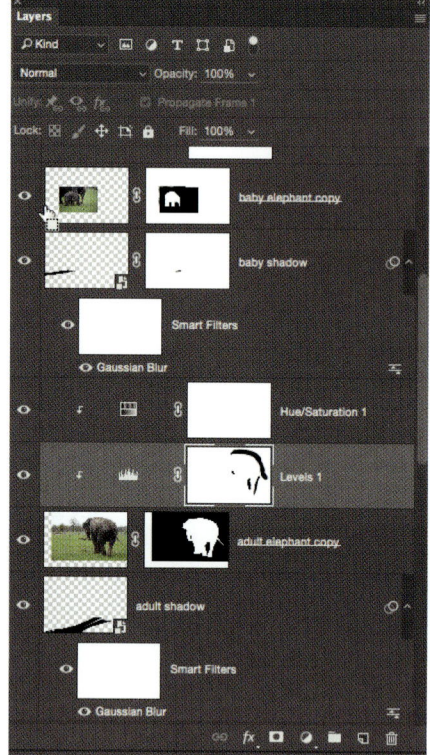

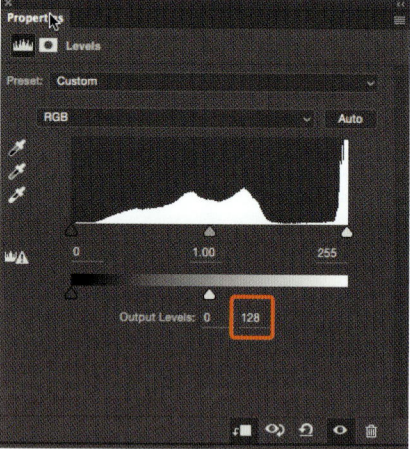

FIGURE 10.127

FIGURE 10.128

42. Click on the uppermost layer in the layer stack and create a merged layer (which is a combination of every layer beneath the selected layer) by pressing Shift + Option + Command + E (Mac) or Shift + Alt + Ctrl + E (PC). Rename this layer "FT" for finishing touches (**Figure 10.129**).

Now go to *Filter > Camera RAW filter* and click on the Split Toning tab. Under Highlights, dial in Hue: 42 and Saturation: 8, and under Shadows, dial in Hue: 50 and Saturation: 17 (**Figure 10.130**).

Next, select the Gradient Filter and drag out a gradient from the bottom of the image up to and including the elephants' feet (**Figure 10.131**). Dial in an Exposure of -0.70 and click OK (**Figure 10.132**).

Let's also add some overall contrast. I'll use the Topaz Clarity plugin, but of course, you can use any other method you prefer. I'll increase Micro Contrast to 0.27 and Low Contrast to 0.14, then click OK (**Figure 10.133**).

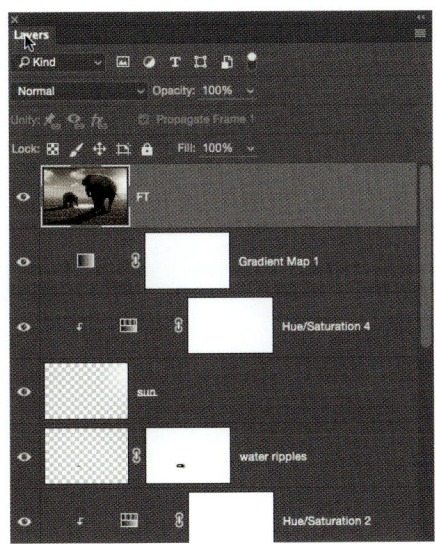

FIGURE 10.129

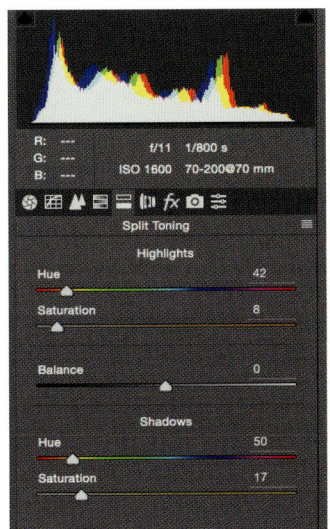

FIGURE 10.130

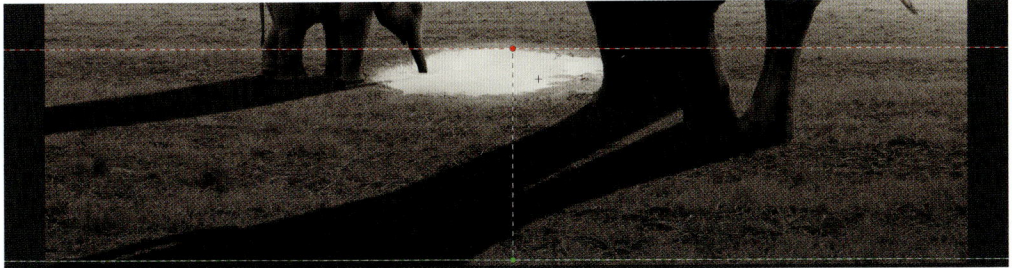

FIGURE 10.131

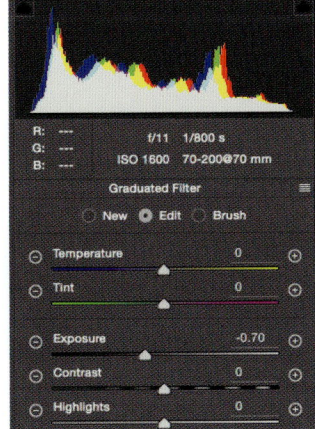

FIGURE 10.132

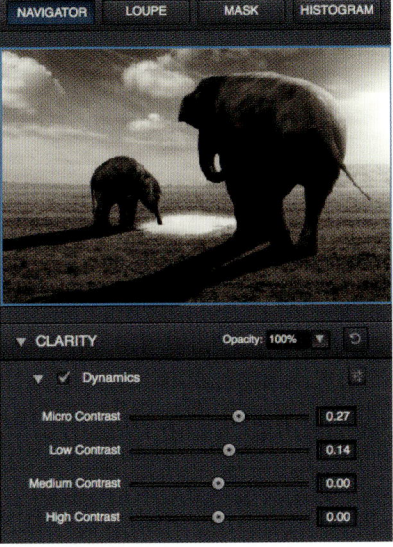

FIGURE 10.133

43. At this point in the post-processing, I saved my work and returned to the image some time later to look at it with fresh eyes and determine whether I felt it was complete. We've gone through a lot of steps so far, and spending so much time at the computer can make us what I call "pixel blind," where we lose the ability to see exactly what we've done and whether we've done a bit too much or not enough. As I've mentioned before, looking at an image with fresh eyes lets us see what we need to do to really finish the picture off.

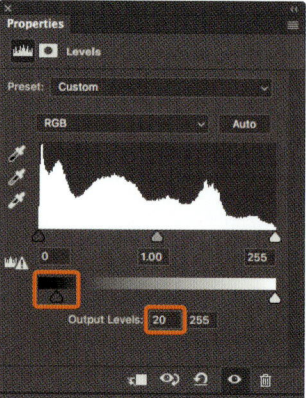

One of the extra things we can do is flatten the image out. We've just added some contrast, but I want to lift the shadow areas. To do this, add a Levels adjustment layer and in the Properties, drag the black Output Levels marker to the right to around 20 (**Figure 10.134**).

FIGURE 10.134

44. To make the image look even more realistic, let's add some water dripping from the adult elephant's trunk. Go to *File > Place Embedded* (**Figure 10.135**; or *File > Place* if you're using an earlier version of Photoshop), navigate to the splash.jpg file that you downloaded from the book's webpage, and click Place (**Figure 10.136**).

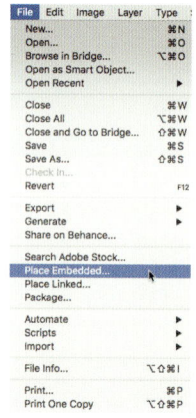

FIGURE 10.135

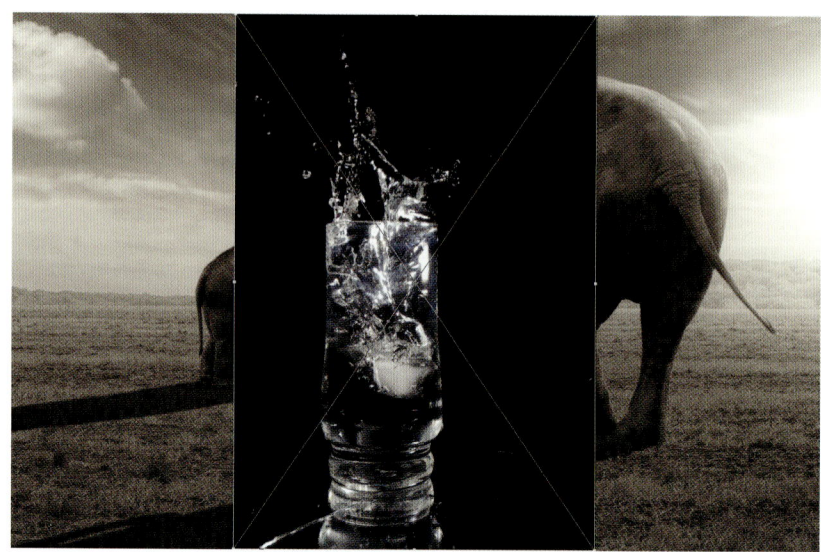

FIGURE 10.136

Now go to *Edit > Transform > Rotate 180°* (**Figure 10.137**). Hold down Shift + Option (Mac) or Shift + Alt (PC), then click on a corner transform handle and drag it inward to make the glass and splash image much smaller (**Figure 10.138**). Press Return (Mac) or Enter (PC).

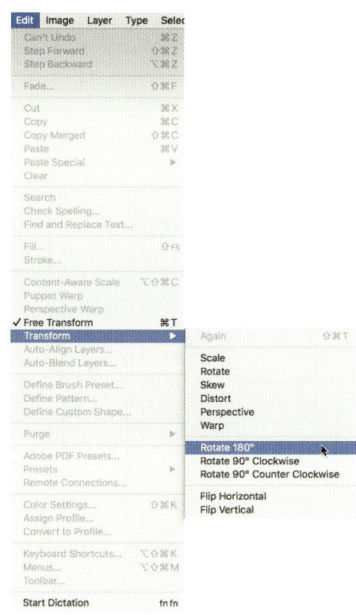

FIGURE 10.137

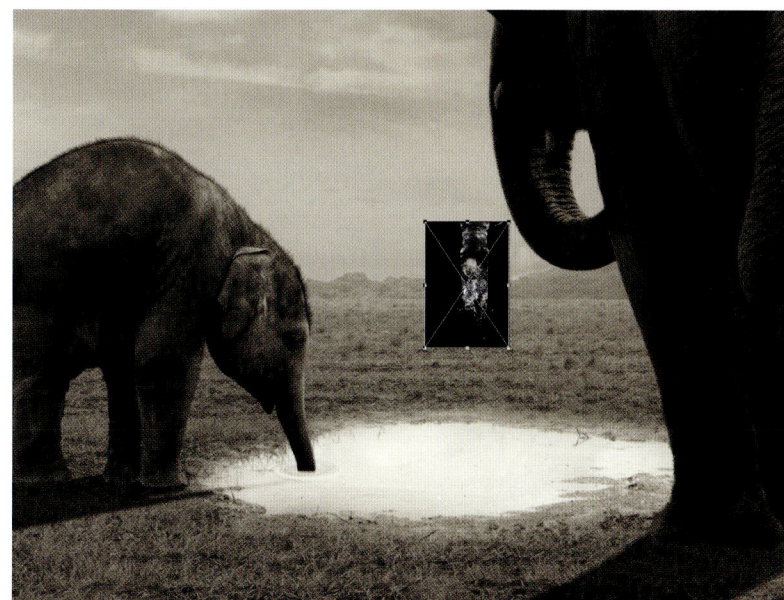

FIGURE 10.138

To remove the black but keep the glass and water, change the Blend Mode of the splash layer to Screen (**Figure 10.139**).

Now use the Move Tool to drag the splash into position. Add a Layer Mask to the splash layer, and then use a round, soft-edged brush and black foreground color to paint over the glass and conceal it, leaving just the water (**Figure 10.140**).

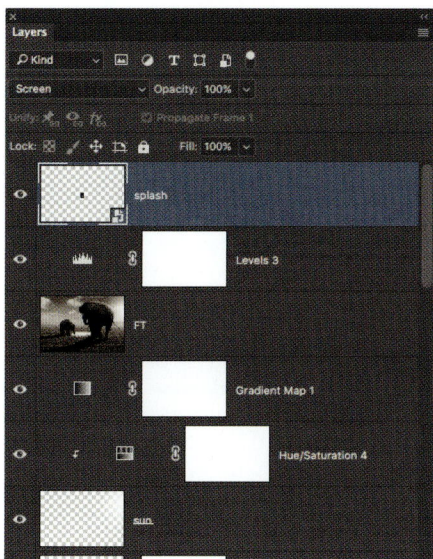

FIGURE 10.139

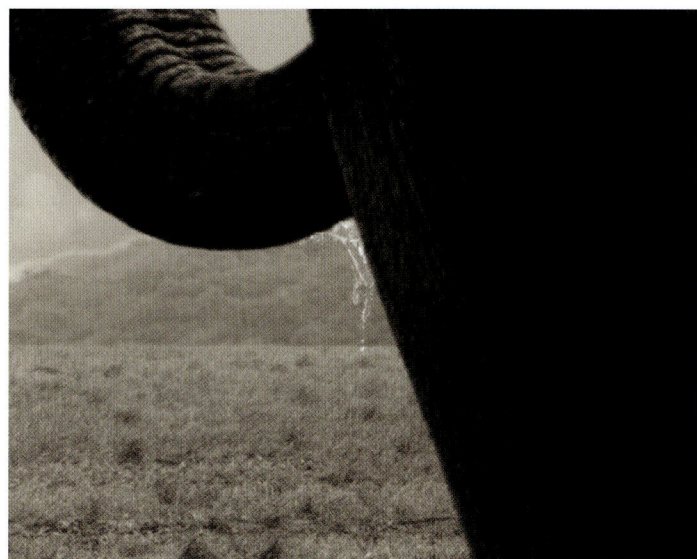

FIGURE 10.140

45. The last thing I'd like to do is add a few birds in the background. This is something I tend to do to most of the pictures I make for my Animals project. You can find pictures of birds on stock websites or on Adobe Stock.

Once you have a picture of a bird (I've gone for a vulture against a plain blue sky), go to *File > Open*, and with the Quick Selection Tool, drag around the sky to select it. With the sky area selected, go to *Select > Inverse* so that the selection is now surrounding the bird (**Figure 10.141**).

Press Command + J (Mac) or Ctrl + J (PC) to copy this selection onto its own layer (**Figure 10.142**).

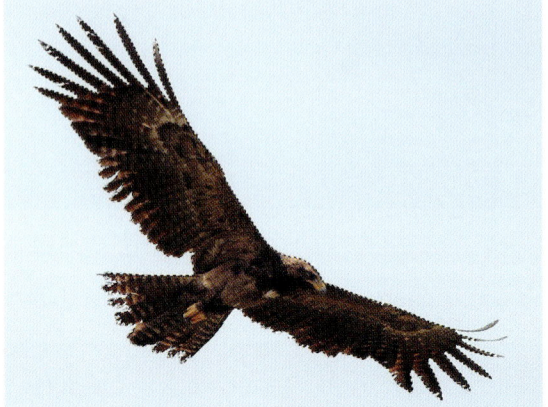

FIGURE 10.141

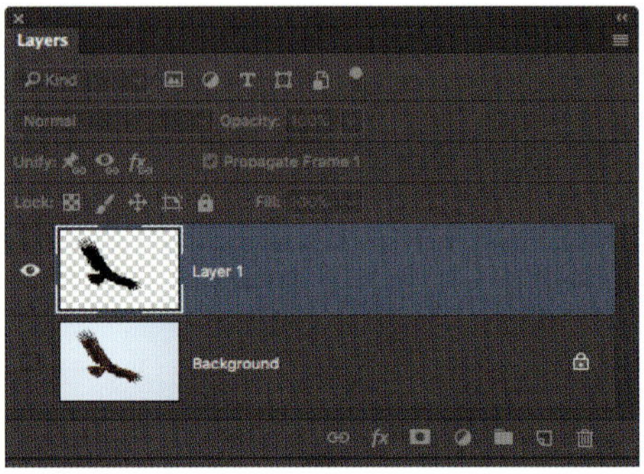

FIGURE 10.142

Go to *Image > Adjustments > Levels*, and in the properties, drag the white Output Levels marker to the left to 70 (**Figure 10.143**). This will make the vulture darker, but it will retain a little bit of the color. Click OK.

46. Choose the Move Tool (**V**) and drag the bird on top of the elephant tab. Once the elephant image is open, continue to drag the bird into place and then release (**Figure 10.144**).

Go to *Edit > Free Transform,* and while holding down Shift + Option (Mac) or Shift + Alt (PC), drag a corner handle inward to make

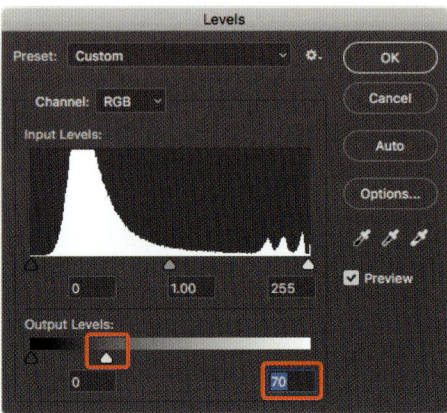

FIGURE 10.143

the vulture much smaller (we want it to appear way in the distance). Press Return (Mac) or Enter (PC).

Finally, go to *Filter > Blur > Gaussian Blur,* add in 1 Pixel of blur, and click OK. Then lower the Opacity of the vulture layer to around 60% (**Figure 10.145**).

These final additions are purely based on my personal taste and add to the style that I like for these particular images. You may notice that the working file is slightly different than the final image shown here—the tree line looks a little different, there are more birds and clouds, and so on—but the idea here is to show you the techniques I used should you wish to do the same.

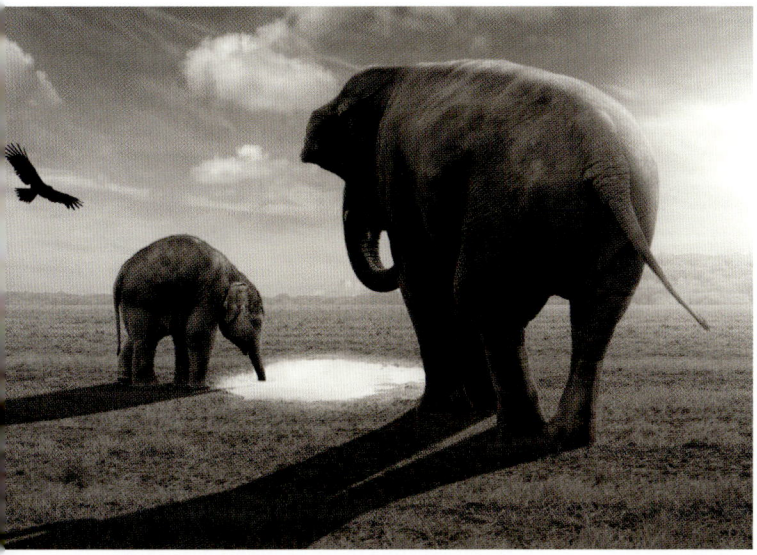

FIGURE 10.144

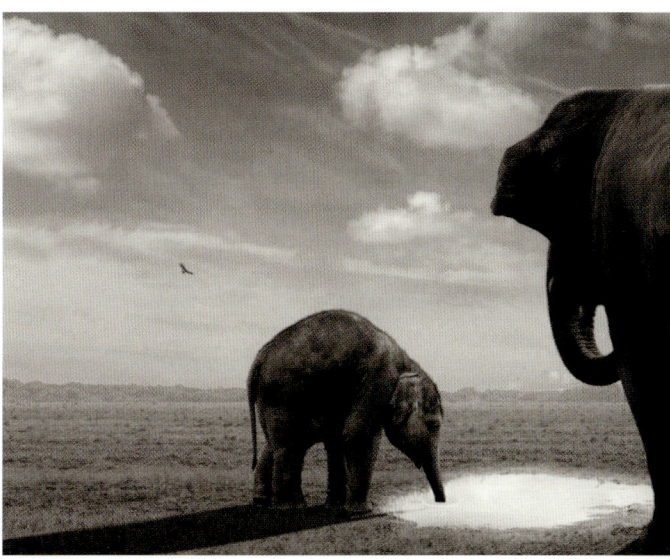

FIGURE 10.145

FIGURE 10.146   Final image

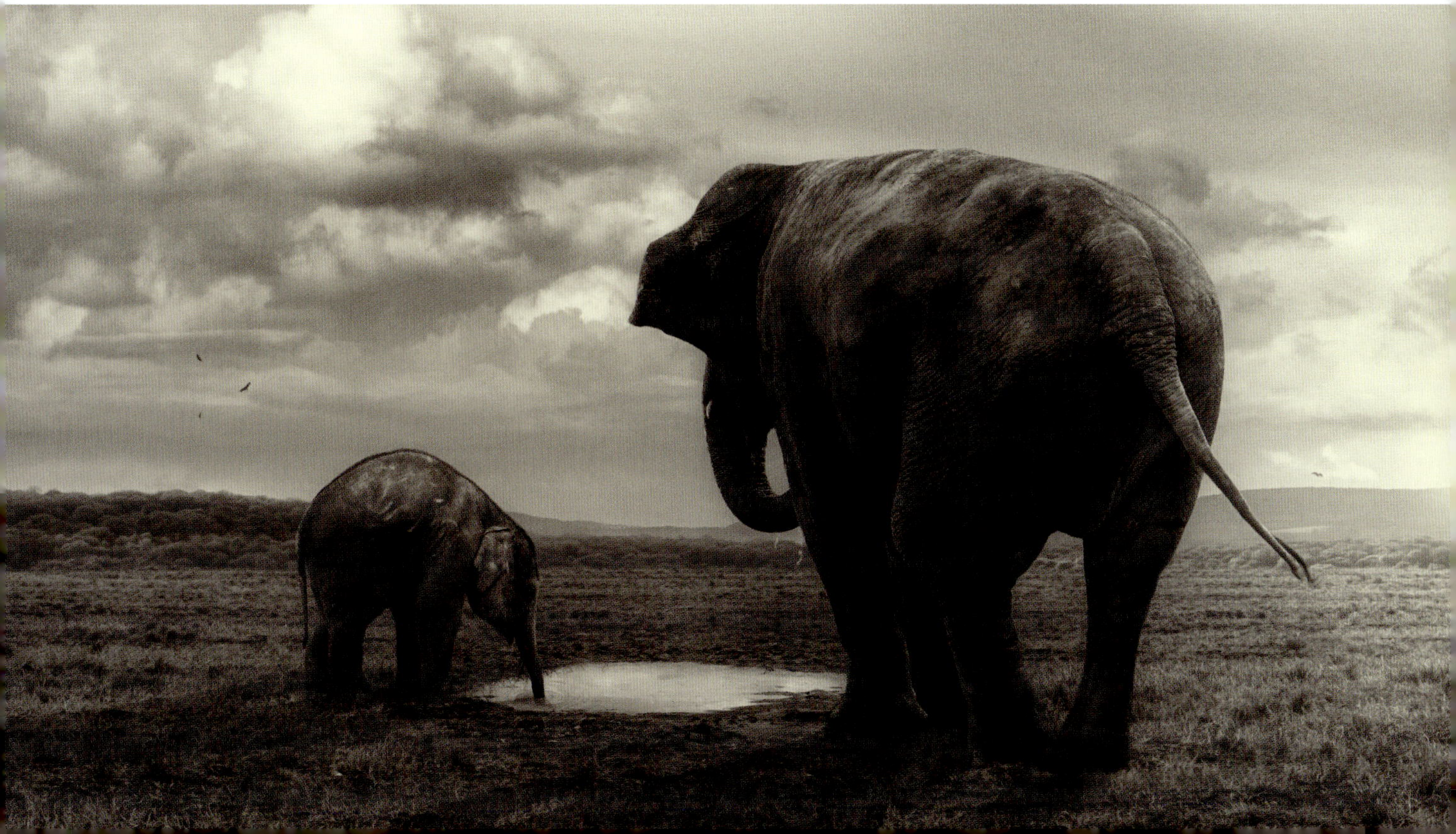

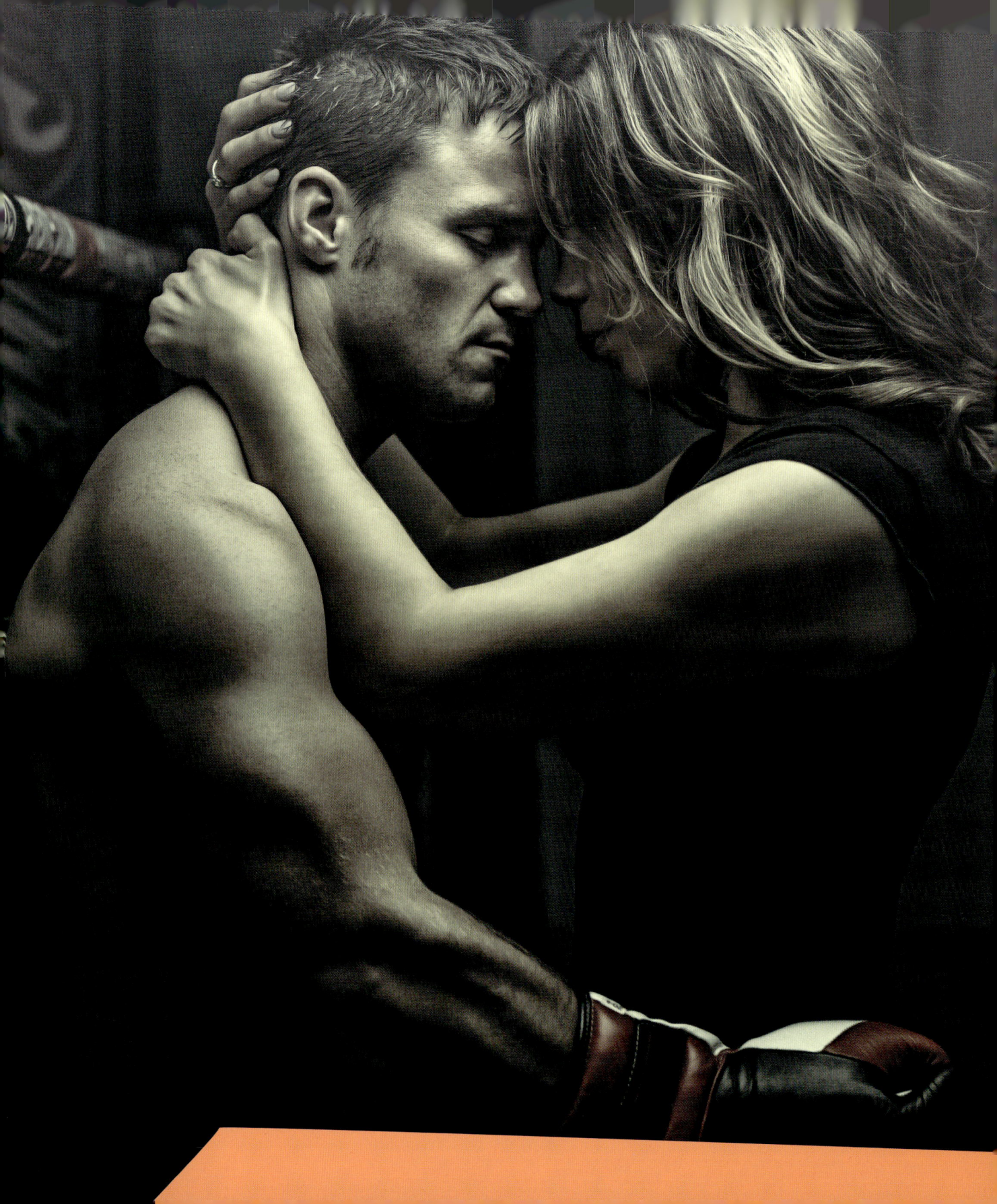

11 MOVIE POSTER INSPIRED

Without question, one of the biggest benefits of being involved in this industry is the people I've met and the friends I've made along the way. To this day, I have to pinch myself when I think about how I get to share the stage with folks whose books and DVDs I've bought, whose seminars I've attended, and whose online classes I've watched (and still do, I hasten to add). But more than that, I can call so many of them my friends. I've met people who are so open, genuine, and honest. Even when they're at the top of their game, they are constantly looking to improve their craft and help others improve, too.

Being a photographer has introduced me to worlds I knew very little about, and likely never would have encountered. A perfect example of this is my friend, World Champion kickboxer turned professional boxer Steven Cook, aka Pocket Rocket, who introduced me to the world of boxing.

I first met Steven through our mutual friend Brian Worley, and from then on we started putting together regular photo shoots—personal projects for me and pictures for Steven to keep. There were times when we'd meet once a week to try out a new idea, and I'll be forever thankful to Steven for his time and willingness to try out some of the crazy ideas I come up with, some that work and some that don't and will never grace a webpage.

The picture we'll be working on in this chapter actually came about after Steven recommended I see the movie *Southpaw,* which had just been released. I'd seen trailers online, but after our chat I went and searched on Google and the impawards.com website that I mentioned in chapter 1 to see what posters had been made for the movie. One of the posters jumped out at me and I knew straight away that I wanted to create something similar for Steven and his beautiful partner, Sofie. I took a screen grab, messaged it to Steven, and the date was set.

REVERSE ENGINEERING

When I first looked at the original movie poster for Southpaw (**Figure 11.1**), I immediately concluded that just one main light was used, positioned directly above the subjects pointing down at them.

We can see that the tops of the subjects' heads are lit, but the main clue to the lighting is on their arms. The tops of their arms are lit but the undersides are in shadow, and the light along the arms is even.

The light itself is neither hard nor soft; it's kind of in between. The shadows and highlights sort of blend in with each other where they meet. There is no hard line between the two, rather there is a very slight gradient, albeit a short one. You can see this particularly on the female character's shoulder.

It's possible that a reflector was used to bounce a bit of light into the shadow areas, which aren't completely black and do show detail. Of course, this could have been altered in post-processing, but we'll go with getting it in-camera.

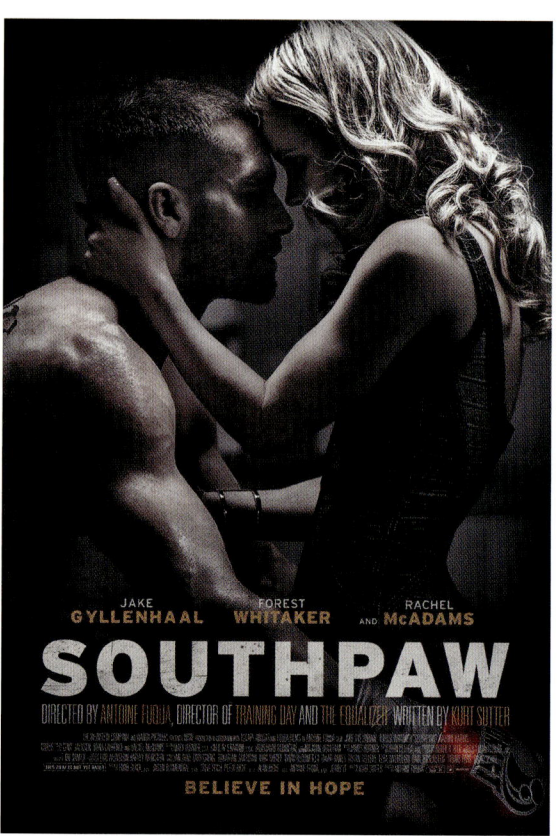

FIGURE 11.1

We can see also that the photograph was taken with a wide aperture (maybe around f/4.0) because the background is out of focus, even though it looks to be fairly close to the characters.

THE SETUP

I went with my feeling that the original picture was lit from above and set up my lighting accordingly. Steven and Sofie were positioned on the outside of the boxing ring where, as luck would have it, the walls in the gym were very similar to the walls in the original poster. Sofie sat in with her arms outstretched while I got the light into position. In **Figure 11.2** you can see how the lighting is already similar to that of the original poster, with the tops of Sofie's arms lit and the underside in shadow.

I positioned a light stand and boom inside the boxing ring, with the boom reaching out directly across the top of Sofie and pointing straight down (**Figure 11.3**). Once I set the exposure, I had to get both Steven and Sofie into the scene and pose them.

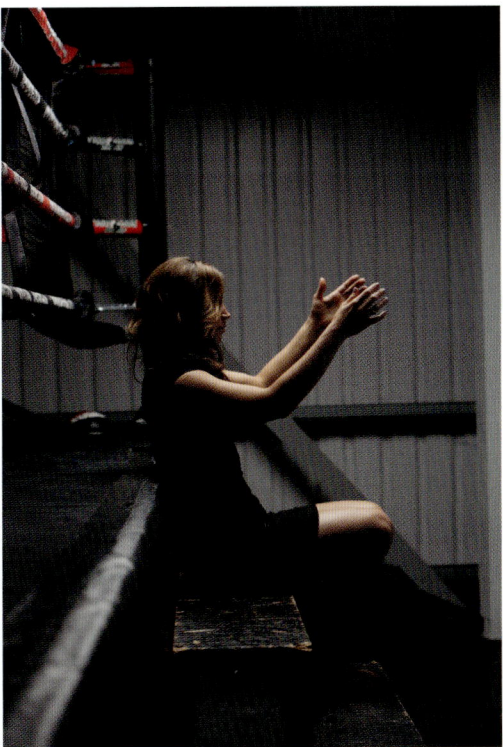

FIGURE 11.2

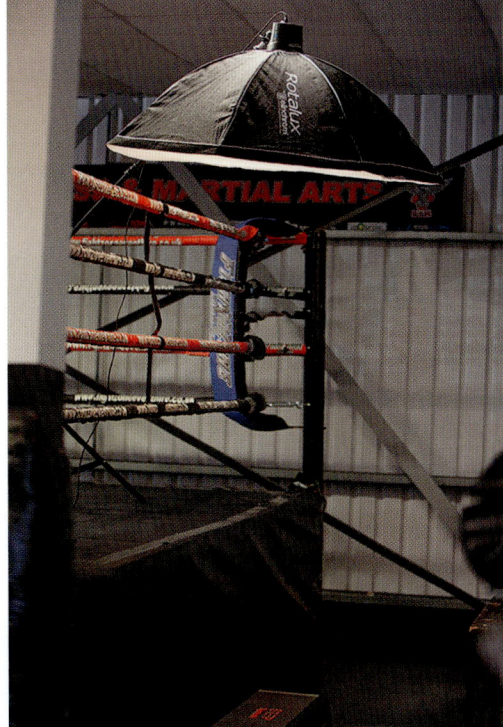

FIGURE 11.3

With the light positioned directly above Steven and Sofie, the highlights were exactly how I wanted them, but the shadow areas were a little too dark (**Figure 11.4**). To fix this, I positioned a reflector near them so that I was able to bounce a little bit of light. **Figure 11.5** is a diagram of the setup to give you an idea of how everything was positioned.

You can see in **Figure 11.6** that the light bounced off of the reflector allowed me to get more detail in the shadows. This is the image that I ended up working on.

My camera was mounted on a tripod and tethered to my MacBook Pro. Although you can't see it in Figure 11.4, the light modifier I used above Steven and Sofie (an Elinchrom Rotalux 135cm Octa Softbox) was fitted with just the outer diffusion panel as opposed to both the inner and outer panels. This created a light that was neither hard nor soft, but was somewhere in between.

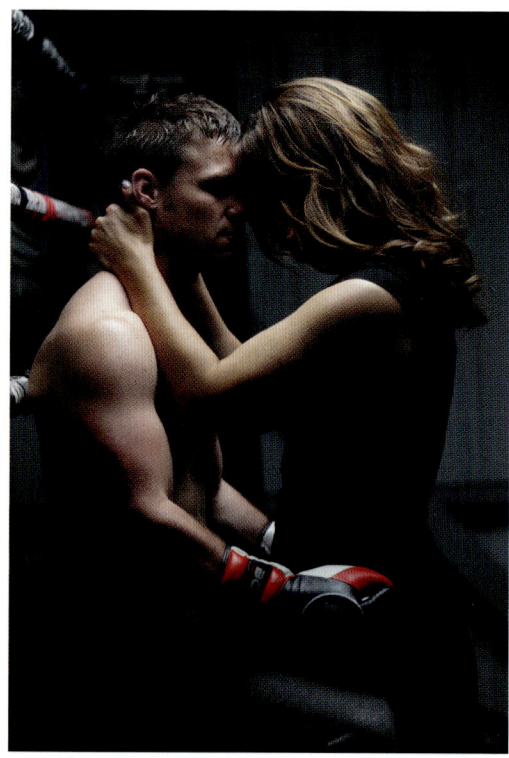

FIGURE 11.4 The highlights look great but the shadows are too dark

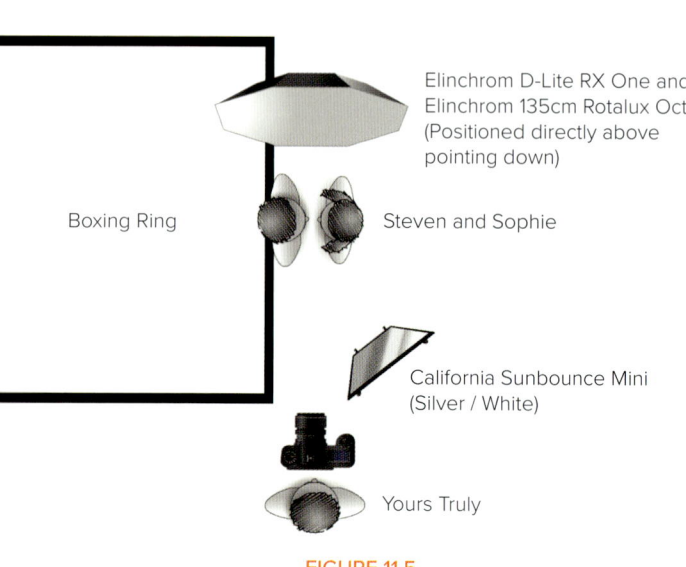

Elinchrom D-Lite RX One and Elinchrom 135cm Rotalux Octa (Positioned directly above pointing down)

Boxing Ring

Steven and Sophie

California Sunbounce Mini (Silver / White)

Yours Truly

FIGURE 11.5

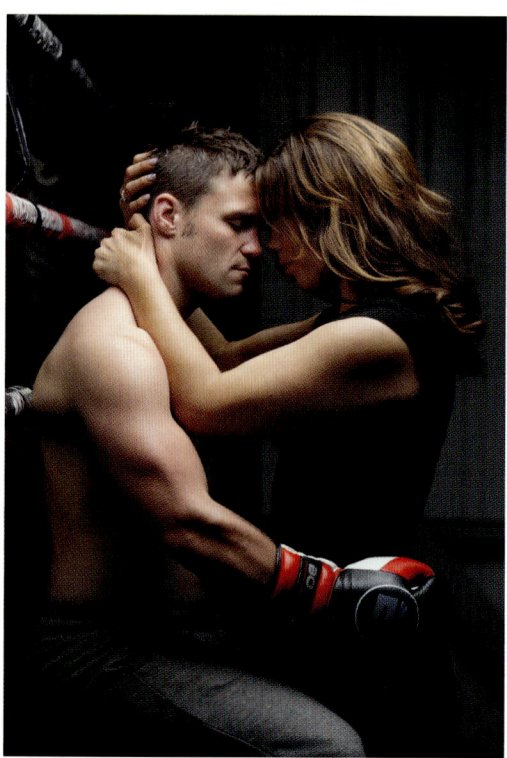

FIGURE 11.6

CAMERA SETTINGS

I chose to shoot with an aperture of f/4.0 so that the gym wall was out of focus and both Steven and Sofie were sharp. Therefore, the light above (the Octa) was metered to give a reading of f/4.0 with the ISO at 100 for the cleanest possible file. A shutter speed of 1/100sec was enough to allow sufficient ambient light into the scene.

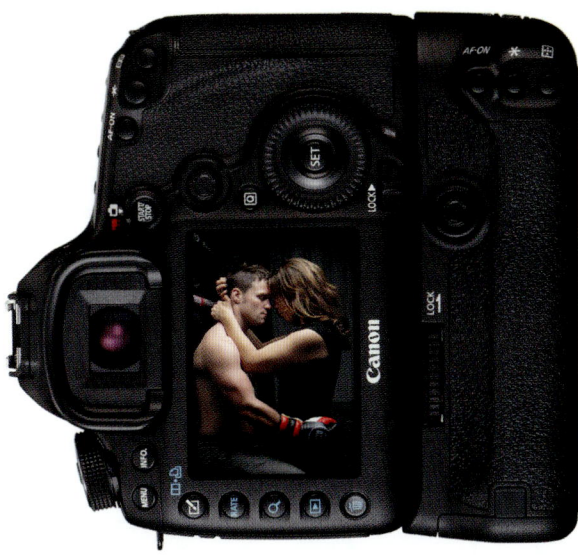

FIGURE 11.7

MODE Manual

ISO 100

APERTURE f/4.0

SHUTTER SPEED 1/100 sec.

LENS Canon 70-200mm f/2.8 L IS II USM

GEAR GUIDE

Because I was using a boom with a light directly above Steven and Sofie, I used my Elinchrom D-Lite RX One flash (**Figure 11.8**). Although it's considered to be an entry-level light, this is a great addition to every photographer's kit because it's small, incredibly light, and comes with built-in fan and wireless receiver.

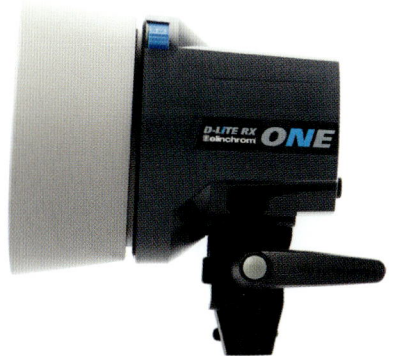

FIGURE 11.8

I also used an Elinchrom Rotalux 135cm Octa Softbox (**Figure 11.9**), a Sunbounce Mini silver/white reflector (**Figure 11.10**), and an Avenger A4041B boom (**Figure 11.11**).

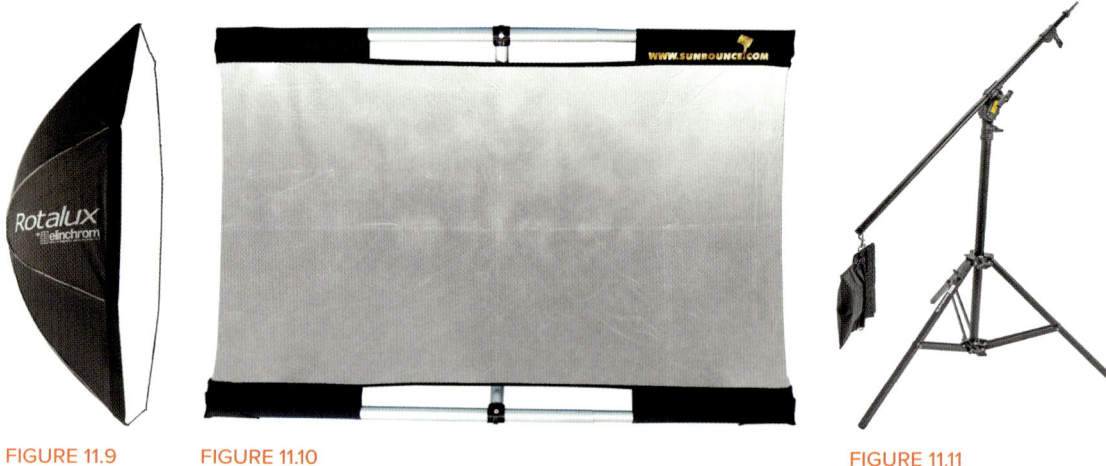

FIGURE 11.9   FIGURE 11.10   FIGURE 11.11

SMALL FLASH GEAR GUIDE

If you are a small flash user, you could replace the Elinchrom light and modifier (or any other studio lighting for that matter) with a Phottix Mitros+ TTL Transceiver Flash (**Figure 11.12**) and a Lastolite 90cm Hotrod Octa Softbox (**Figure 11.13**).

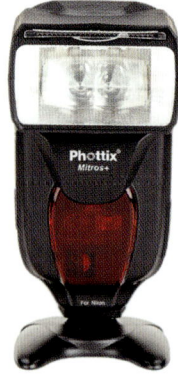

FIGURE 11.12

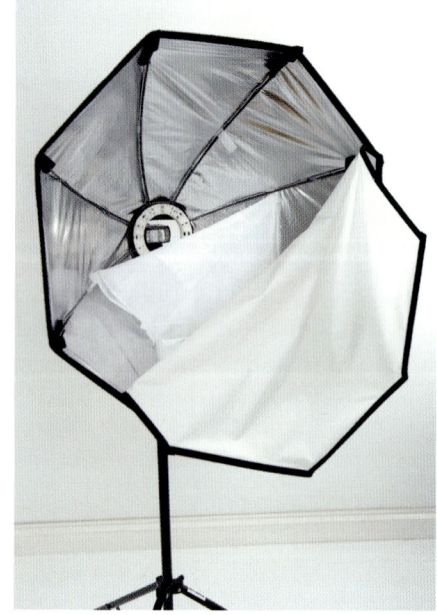

POST-PROCESSING

In all honesty, there's not that much that needs to be done to this picture. We'll do a little body reshaping (because of the positions Steven and Sofie were in) and some dodging and burning. Then we'll add in a fake light source, and finally, we'll colorize the image to make sure we capture the right mood and atmosphere.

FIGURE 11.13

NOTE *Download the file you need to follow along step-by-step at: http://www.rockynook.com/ photograph-like-a-thief-reference/*

1. Let's kick things off in the Develop Module in Lightroom (or Camera RAW) and work our way down the adjustments. First, we need to bring down the exposure just a touch. In the Basics tab, drag the Exposure slider left until you hit -0.80 (**Figure 11.14**). Because I lit Steven and Sofie from above, and even though I used a reflector, we need to bring a bit more detail back into the shadow areas by moving the Shadows slider over to the right to around +80.

2. To start giving the picture a bit more punch (no pun intended), increase the Clarity slider to +65, and then reduce the overall saturation by dragging the Saturation slider to around -40.

3. Now we'll move to the Detail section to add in some Sharpening. Increase the Amount slider to 30 (**Figure 11.15**), and then hold down the Option key (Mac) or Alt key (PC) as you increase the Masking slider to 80 so that the sharpening is mainly restricted to Steven and Sofie. The white areas in **Figure 11.16** indicate the areas in the picture that are being sharpened.

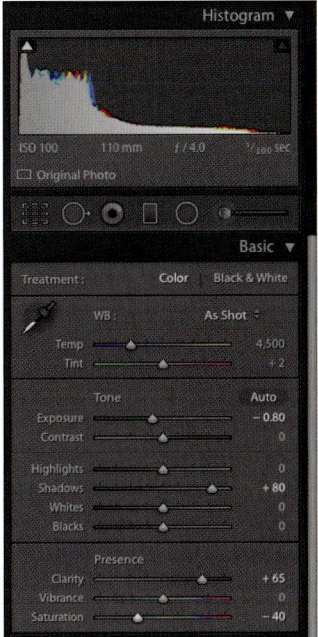

FIGURE 11.14

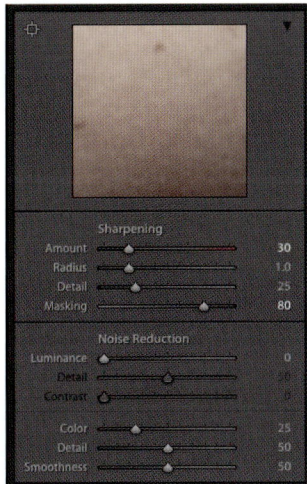

FIGURE 11.15

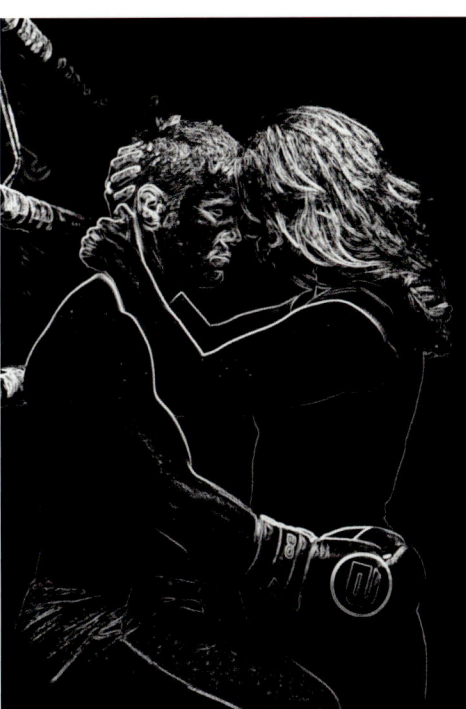

FIGURE 11.16 Holding down the Option key (Mac) or Alt key (PC) while dragging the Masking slider reveals a mask indicating areas that are being sharpened in white and areas not being sharpened in black

4. The last thing we'll do before opening the picture in Photoshop is add an overall vignette. In the Effects tab, drag the Amount slider to the left to around -20, and leave Style at its default of Highlight Priority (**Figure 11.17**).

Figures **11.18** and **11.19** show our image before and after the adjustments we've made so far.

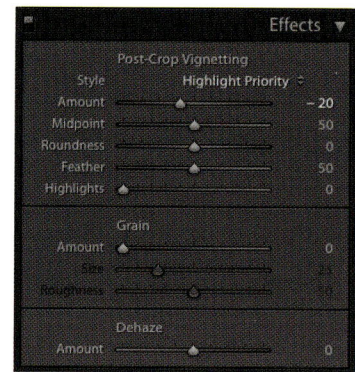

FIGURE 11.17

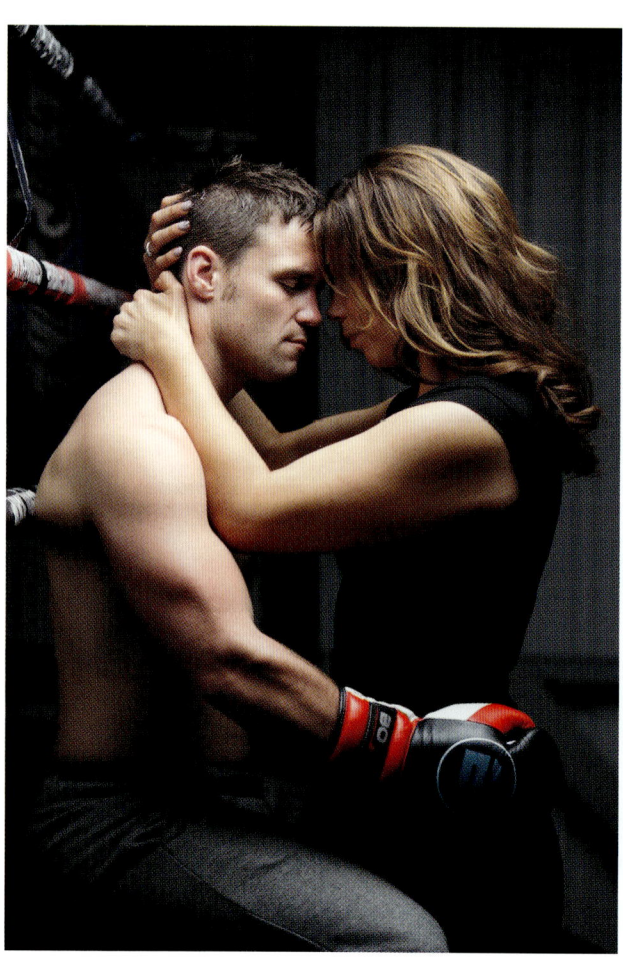

FIGURE 11.18 Before

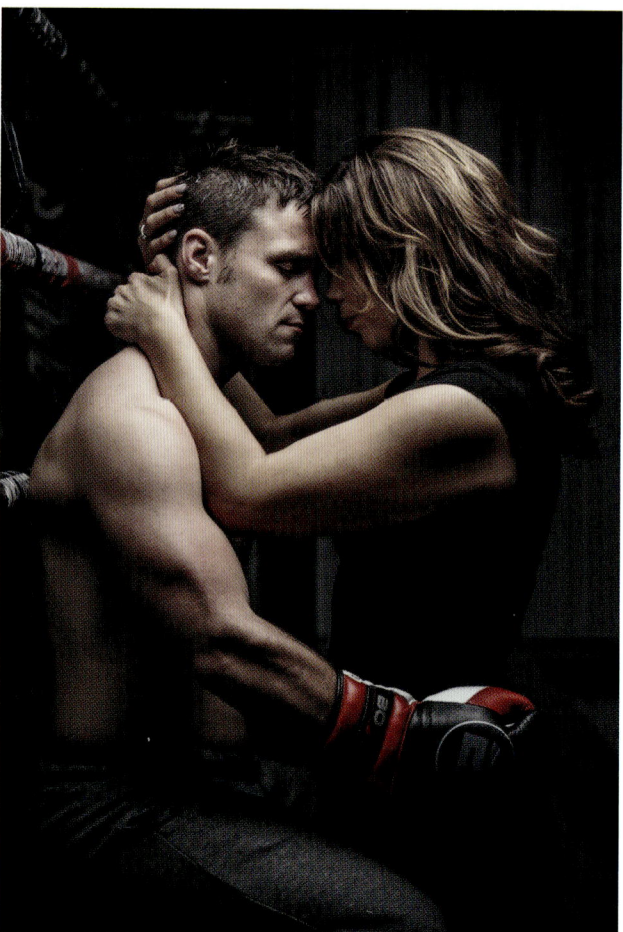

FIGURE 11.19 After

5. Now let's open the image in Photoshop so we can continue with the retouching. If you're using Lightroom, go to *Photo > Edit In > Adobe Photoshop...* If you're using Camera RAW, simply click on Open Image in the bottom-right hand of the screen.

6. In the setup for this picture, Steven was sitting down on the side of the boxing ring and Sofie was standing on a wooden box so that her head was at roughly the same height as Steven's, which meant she had to push her hips forward to get close enough to him. Neither of these positions are the most flattering, so we'll do a little bit of body shaping to get them back to looking their best.

Create a duplicate of the Background layer by pressing Command + J (Mac) or Ctrl + J (PC). Rename this layer to "Body Shaping."

We're going to the use the Liquify Filter to make some changes here and this is a filter that can very easily be overdone. Thankfully, we can use it as a Smart Filter, meaning we can always make changes at a later stage without having to redo lots of retouching steps.

Go to *Filter > Convert for Smart Filters* (**Figure 11.20**) to change the Body Shaping layer into a Smart Object (**Figure 11.21**).

7. Go to *Filter > Liquify,* and then choose the Freeze Mask Tool from the toolbar on the right side of the screen (**Figure 1.22**).

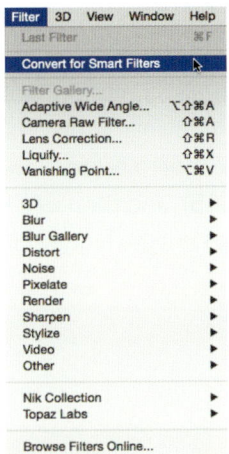

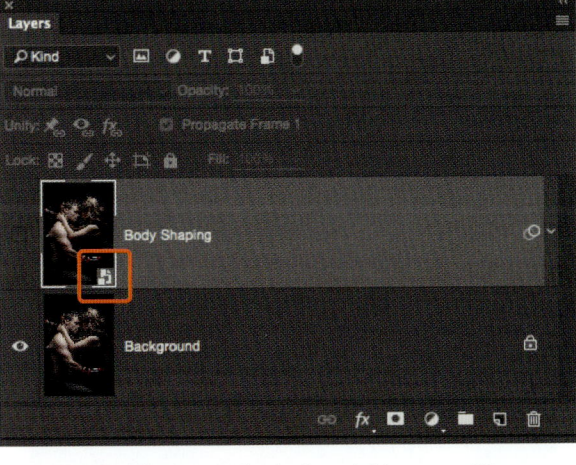

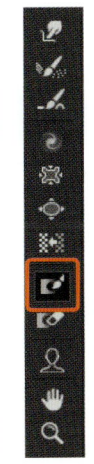

FIGURE 11.20

FIGURE 11.21 The icon in the bottom-right corner of the image thumbnail indicates that the layer is a Smart Object

FIGURE 11.22

NOTE *Freeze Mask allows us to paint over areas to protect them from being affected by any adjustments we make with the Liquify Filter.*

Use the Freeze Mask Tool to paint over areas of Steven and Sofie near where we're going to make some adjustments (**Figure 11.23**).

Choose the Forward Warp Tool (**W**) and push left on Steven's waist to bring it inward a touch since he is sitting down. You can adjust the size of the Forward Warp Tool using the left and right bracket keys on your keyboard.

Reshape Steven's trapezius muscle a touch by dragging upward with the Forward Warp Tool, and drag to the left on his triceps muscle to increase its size.

Keeping with the Forward Warp Tool, push upward on the underside of Sofie's left arm (closest to the camera), and then push downward a touch on the top part of her upper arm. Then bring in her waist between Steven's leg and boxing glove.

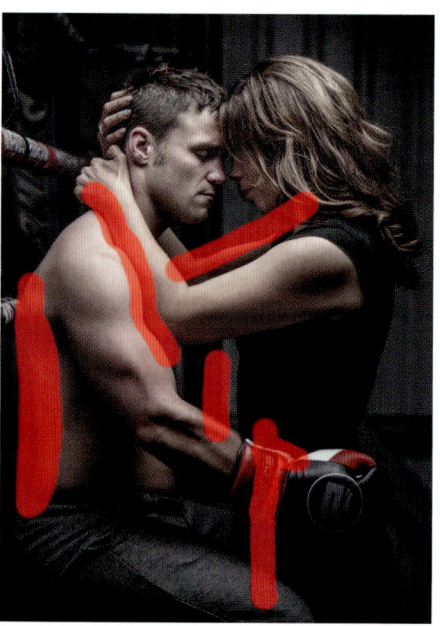

FIGURE 11.23

 TIP *Try to use the Forward Warp Tool at a size that is as large as possible. This makes the adjustments look more realistic and prevents lots of uneven bumps that you have to attempt to flatten out.*

As you're working around the image making adjustments, you can also unfreeze areas so that you can adjust them. In this case, we can use the Thaw Mask Tool (**Figure 11.24**) to remove the protection on Sofie's right arm. Use the Freeze Mask Tool to protect areas like both Steven's and Sofie's faces and the nearest arm (**Figure 11.25**), and then use the Forward Warp Tool to reduce the curve on Sofie's right arm. Click OK to exit the Liquify Filter.

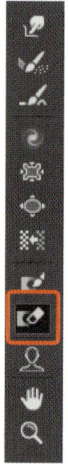 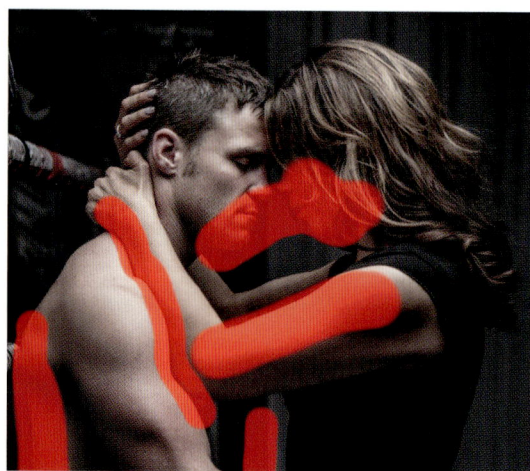

FIGURE 11.24   FIGURE 11.25

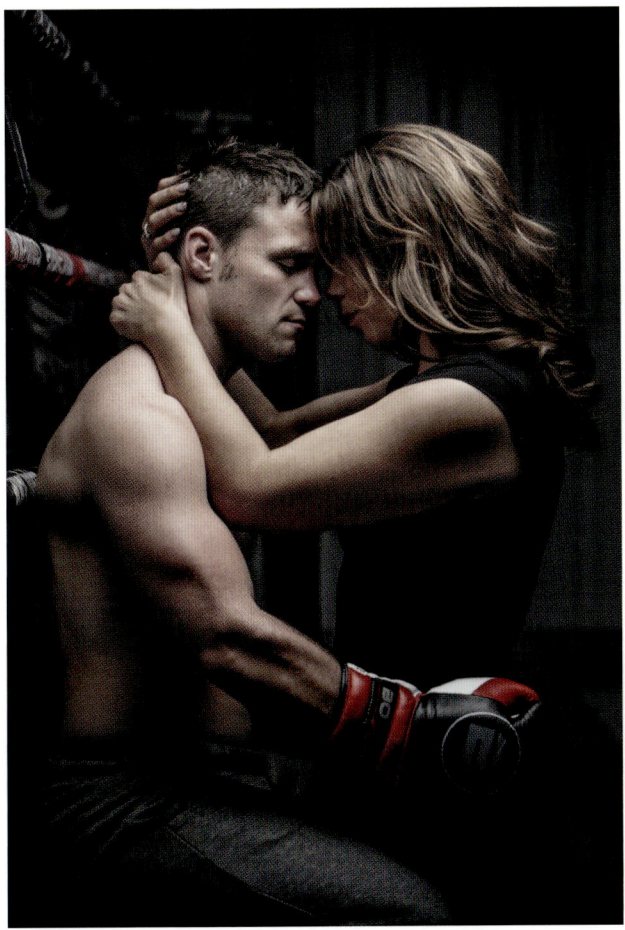

FIGURE 11.26 Before Liquify Filter

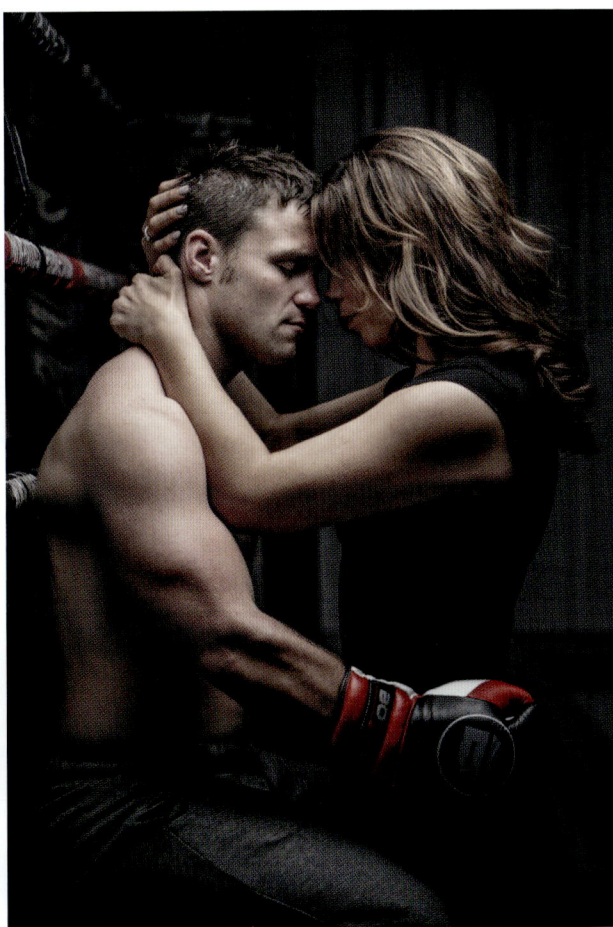

FIGURE 11.27 After Liquify Filter

8. Add a new blank layer to the top of the layer stack and rename it "Blemishes." Choose the Spot Healing Brush from the toolbar (**Figure 11.28**), and in the options at the top of the screen, ensure that Mode is set to Normal, Type is set to Content-Aware, and the Sample All Layers checkbox is checked (**Figure 11.29**).

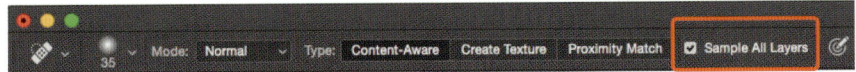

FIGURE 11.28   FIGURE 11.29

Work around the picture clicking over some of the blemishes you want to remove (or that your model wants you to remove; **Figure 11.30**).

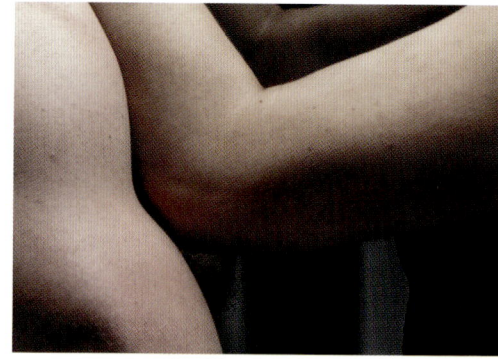

TIP *For best results, use the left and right bracket keys to resize the Spot Healing Brush so that it is slightly bigger than the blemishes you are removing.*

In some areas, such as under Sofie's arm, you may find that the Spot Healing Brush

FIGURE 11.30

struggles to remove the scarring (**Figure 11.31**). In areas like this where the blemishes are close together and Photoshop doesn't have clean areas nearby to work with, try changing the options at the top of the screen from Content Aware to Proximity Match (**Figure 11.32**).

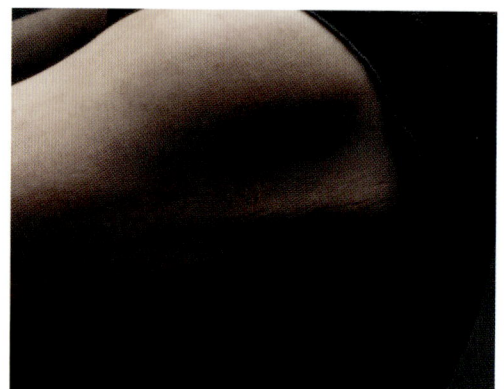

FIGURE 11.31

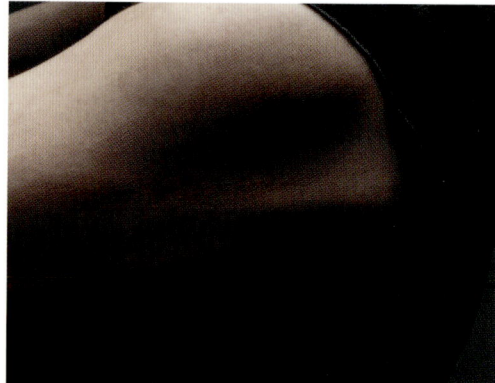

FIGURE 11.32

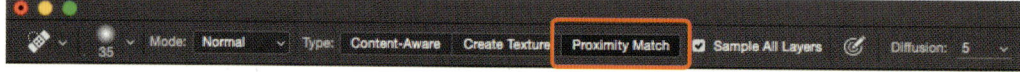

FIGURE 11.33 Changing the Spot Healing Brush Type to Proximity Match gives us a much better result

9. Click on the Levels icon in the Adjustments panel (**Figure 11.34**) to add a Levels adjustment layer to the top of the layer stack. Change its Blend Mode to Screen (**Figure 11.35**).

This brightens the entire image (**Figure 11.36**), but we're just going to use this to increase the highlights in Sofie's hair. So to hide the effect we need to invert the Layer Mask attached to the Levels adjustment layer by pressing Command + I (Mac) or Ctrl + I (PC), or by going to *Image > Adjustments > Invert* (**Figure 11.37**).

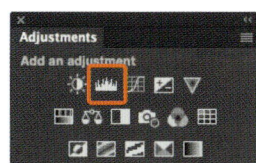

FIGURE 11.34

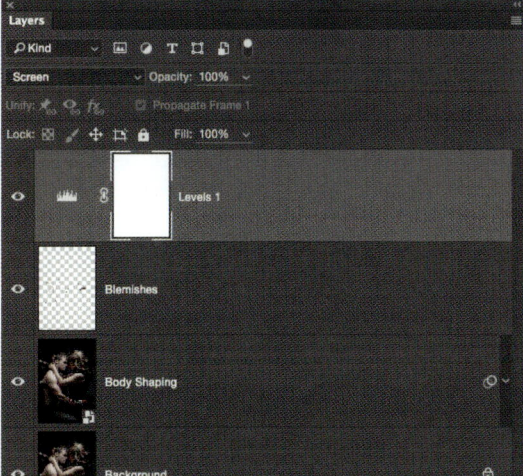

FIGURE 11.35

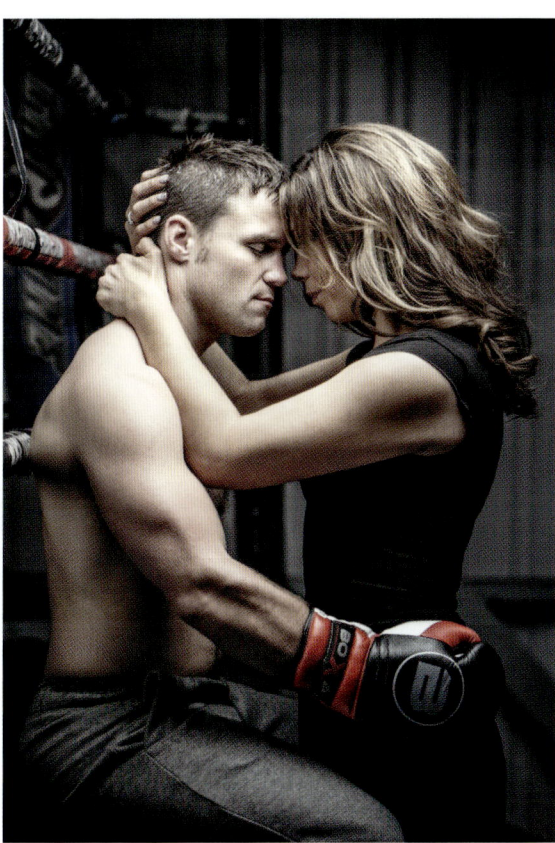

FIGURE 11.36

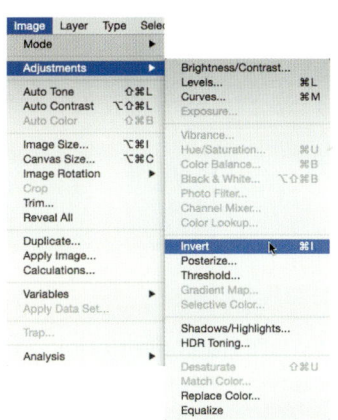

FIGURE 11.37

10. From the toolbar, choose a round, soft-edged brush (**Figure 11.38**) and a white foreground color and paint over the highlight areas of Sofie's hair. This will reveal the brightening effect only in those areas (**Figure 11.39**).

To help these brightened areas blend more naturally, hold down the Option key (Mac) or Alt key (PC) and click on the Layer Mask attached to the Levels adjustment. This gives us a view of the layer mask (**Figure 11.40**).

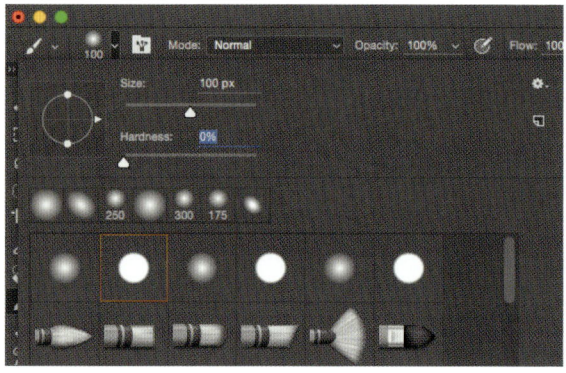

FIGURE 11.38

Go to *Filter > Blur > Gaussian Blur,* set the Radius to 20 Pixels (**Figure 11.41**), and click OK. This softens the brushstrokes we made so now the blend of the highlights is much more realistic. To return to the normal view, hold down the Option key (Mac) or Alt key (PC) and click on the Layer Mask again. Rename this Levels adjustment layer "Sophie Hair."

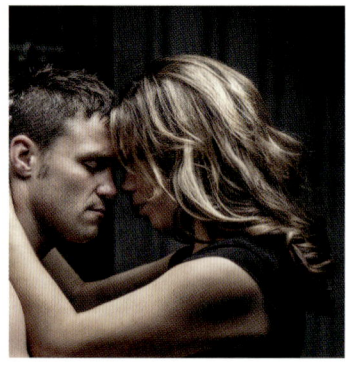

FIGURE 11.39

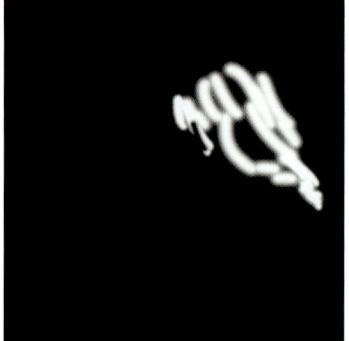

FIGURE 11.40

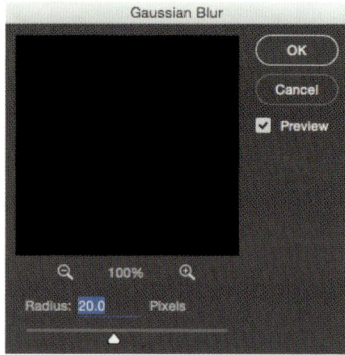

FIGURE 11.41

11. Now let's do some dodging and burning to give the picture a little more depth and dimension. Go to *Layer > New > Layer* (**Figure 11.42**), and in the New Layer properties, name the layer Dodge & Burn, change the Mode to Soft Light, and put a check in the Fill with Soft-Light-neutral color (50% gray) checkbox (**Figure 11.43**). Click OK.

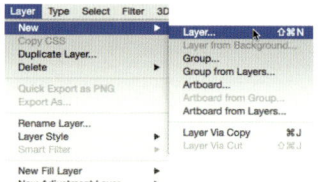

FIGURE 11.42

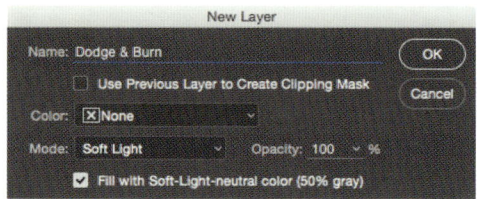

FIGURE 11.43

12. Choose the Dodge Tool from the toolbar (**Figure 11.44**), and in the options at the top of the screen, leave Range set to Midtones, set the Exposure to 5%, and tick the Protect Tones checkbox (**Figure 11.45**).

Start adding brushstrokes over the highlight areas and other areas of the picture you want to brighten. Wherever you add brushstrokes to the highlights, hold down the Option key (Mac) or Alt key (PC) to switch over to the Burn Tool with the same settings and add some brushstrokes to the shadow areas. The more you brush over an area, the more the effect builds up, which is why it's always best to start with a low Exposure settings.

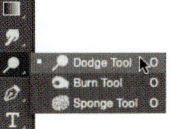

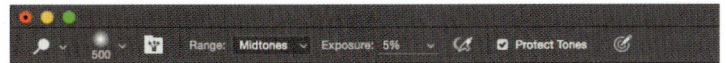

FIGURE 11.44   FIGURE 11.45

To view the gray Dodging and Burning layer (**Figure 11.46**) so that you can see the areas you've worked on, hold down the Option key (Mac) or Alt key (PC) and click on the eye icon next to the layer thumbnail. This turns off every other layer, leaving only the gray one visible. To return to normal view, hold down the Option key (Mac) or Alt key (PC) and click to turn on the visibility.

Compare **Figures 11.47** and **11.48** (on the following page) to see the subtle difference that the dodging and burning has made.

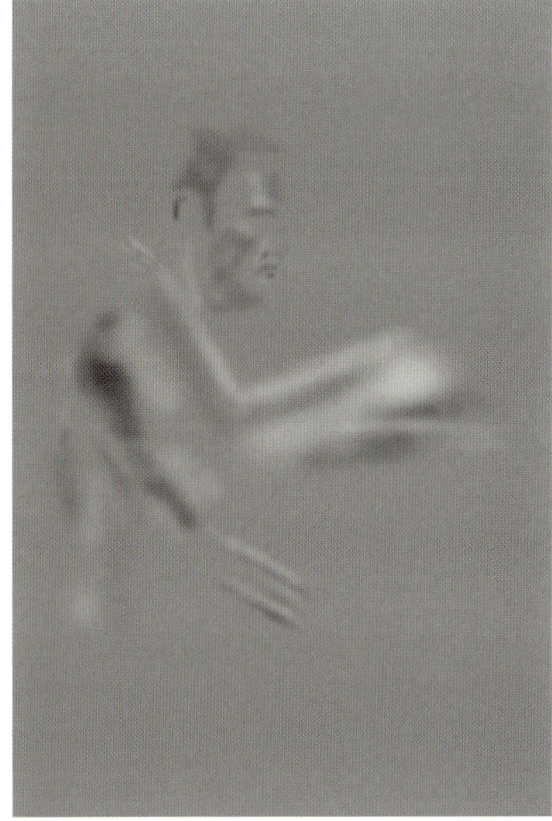

FIGURE 11.46

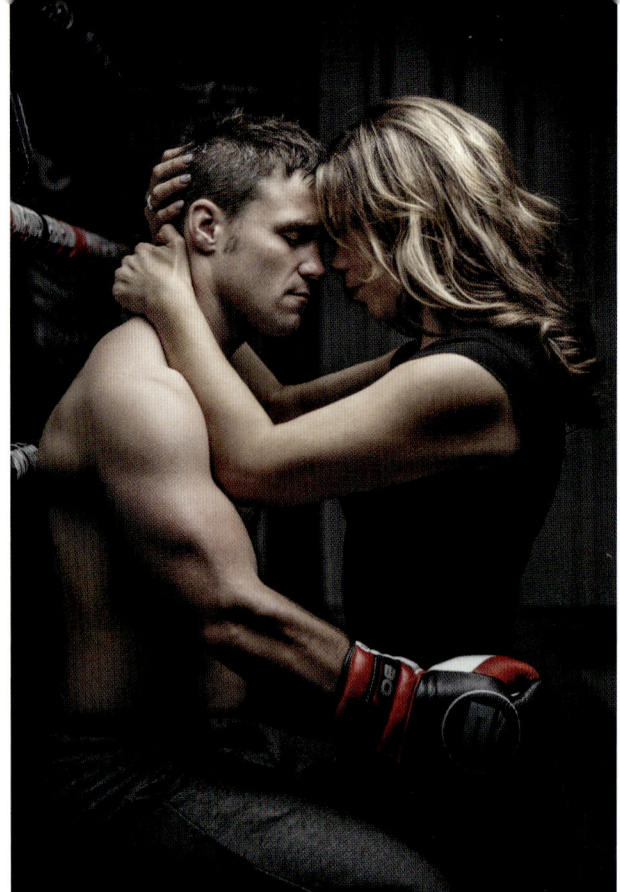

FIGURE 11.47 Before dodging and burning

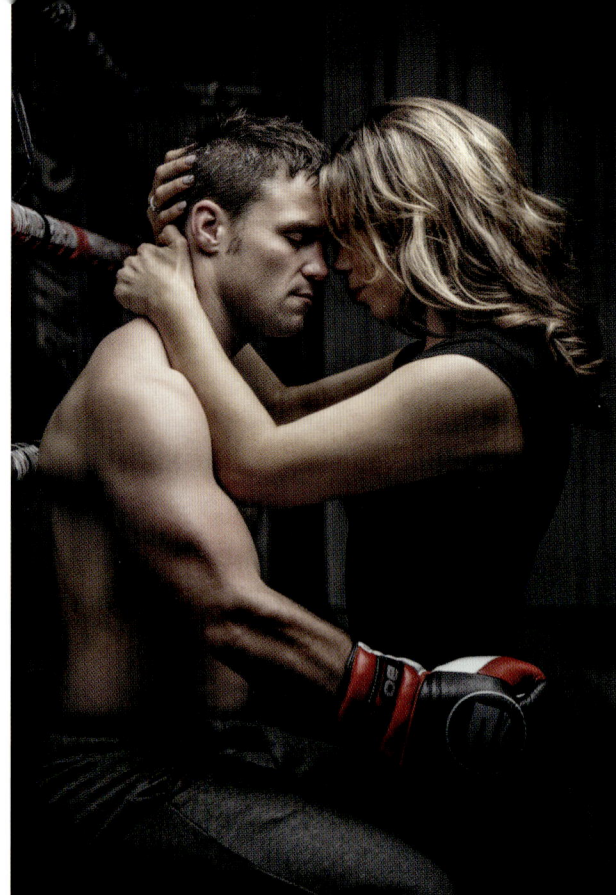

FIGURE 11.48 After dodging and burning

13. Now we'll use a technique I call the Never Ending Lighting Rig to add in a fake light source coming from above. This isn't an essential addition, but it's one that I tend to do quite a bit so that viewers can make sense of the lighting in the scene.

Add a new layer to the top of the layer stack and rename it "Spotlight" (**Figure 11.49**).

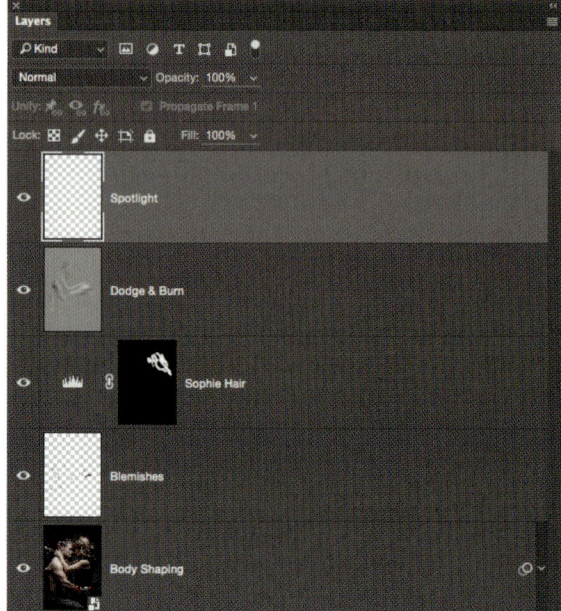

FIGURE 11.49

Grab a round, soft-edged brush from the toolbar and choose a white foreground color. Press down once with the brush in the center of the picture to add a soft, round spot (**Figure 11.50**). Then go to *Edit > Free Transform,* and while holding down Shift + Option (Mac) or Shift + Alt (PC), click and drag outward beyond the frame to increase the size of the soft, round spot (**Figure 11.51**). Press Return (Mac) or Enter (PC).

Use the Move Tool (**V**) to drag the spotlight upward so that just the softest bottom area is visible (**Figure 11.52**).

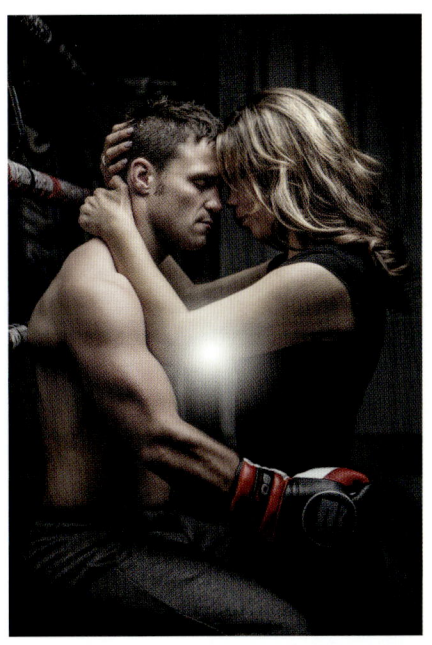

FIGURE 11.50

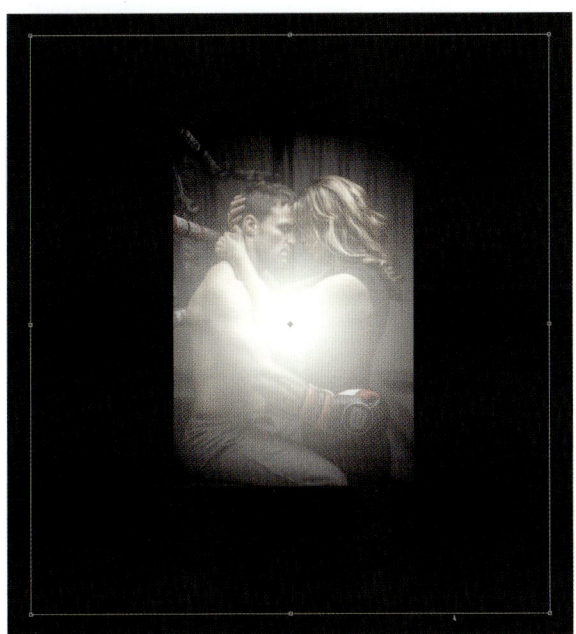

FIGURE 11.51

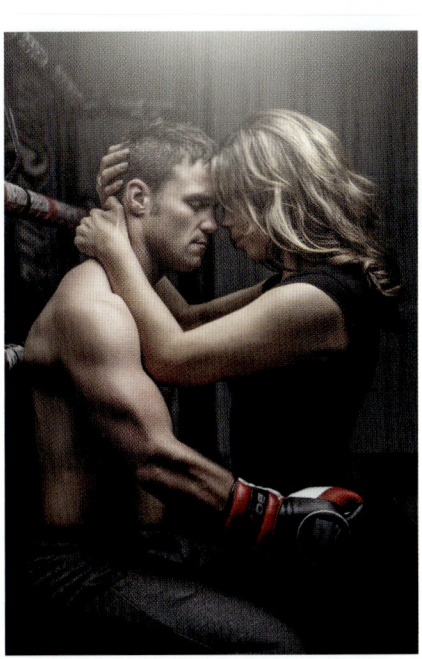

FIGURE 11.52

14. After the photo shoot, Steven requested that I remove the branding from the boxing glove, so let's address that before we add our finishing touches.

Add a merged layer to the top of the layer stack by going to *Edit > Select All*, then to *Edit > Copy Merged*, and then to *Edit > Paste*. Rename this layer "Boxing Glove" (**Figure 11.53**).

Use the Lasso Tool (**L**) to make a loose selection around the logo

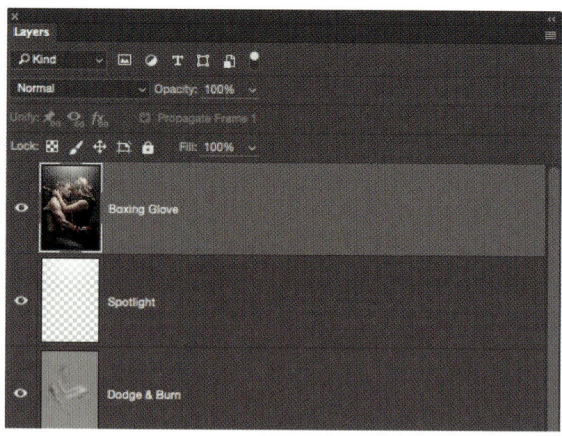

FIGURE 11.53

on the boxing glove (**Figure 11.54**). Go to *Edit > Fill*, choose Content-Aware from the Contents menu (**Figure 11.55**), and click OK (**Figure 11.56**).

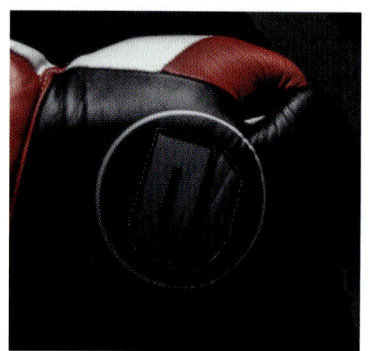

FIGURE 11.54

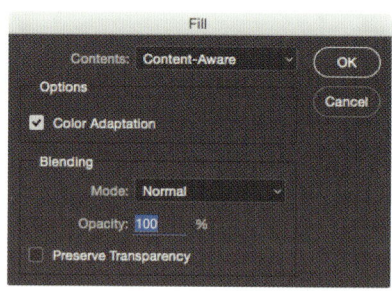

FIGURE 11.55

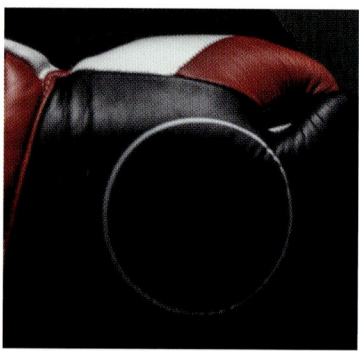

FIGURE 11.56

15. Use the Lasso Tool again to draw out a rough selection around the circular print on the boxing glove, leaving a section unselected (**Figure 11.57**).

Go to *Edit > Fill*, select Content-Aware from the Contents Menu (**Figure 11.58**), and click OK.

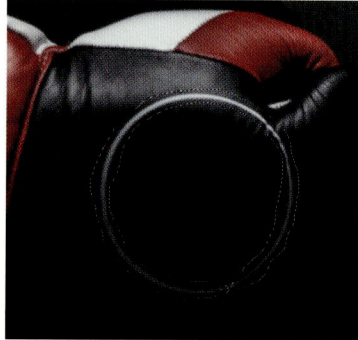

FIGURE 11.57

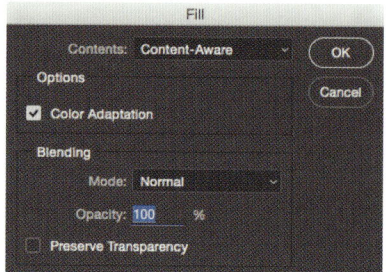

FIGURE 11.58

Turn off the visible selection by going *Select > Deselect*. Choose the Clone Stamp Tool, and while holding down the Option key (Mac) or Alt key (PC), click to sample an area next to the remaining bit of the circle, and then apply a brushstroke to cover it (**Figure 11.59**).

Use the Clone Stamp Tool and this Option-clicking (Mac) or Alt-clicking (PC) method to sample areas of the glove and cover the logo on the wrist section as well (**Figure 11.60**).

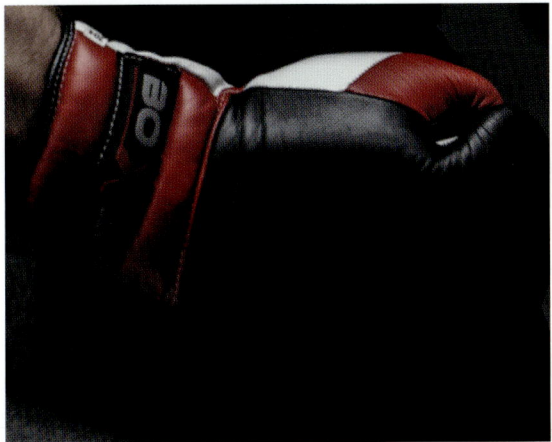

FIGURE 11.59

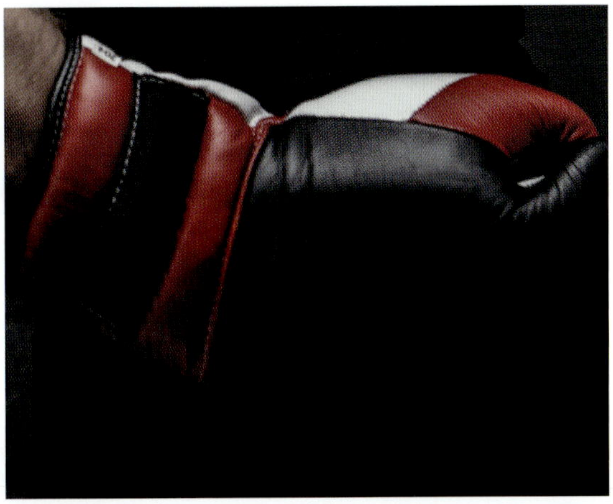

FIGURE 11.60

16. Duplicate the Boxing Glove layer by pressing Command + J (Mac) or Ctrl + J (PC). Rename this layer "FT" for Finishing Touches (**Figure 11.61**).

Now we're going to colorize the picture. For this one, I'm going to use the Nik Colleciton Color Efex Pro 4 plugin; however, you can use any method you prefer, including the Color Lookup adjustment layer that I covered in chapter 4 (page 56).

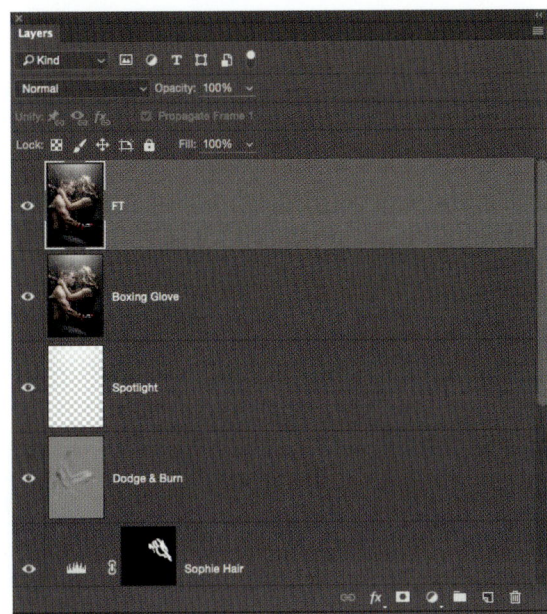

FIGURE 11.61

Go to *Filter > Nik Collection > Color Efex Pro 4* (**Figure 11.62**) and start by choosing Cross Processing (**Figure 11.63**). In the Cross Processing menu on the right side of the window, choose Y06 from the Method menu and set Strength to 80%, then click on Add Filter (**Figure 11.64**).

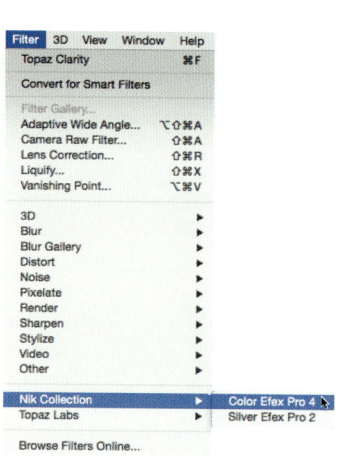

FIGURE 11.62

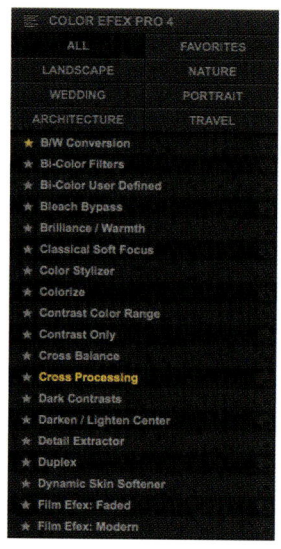

FIGURE 11.63

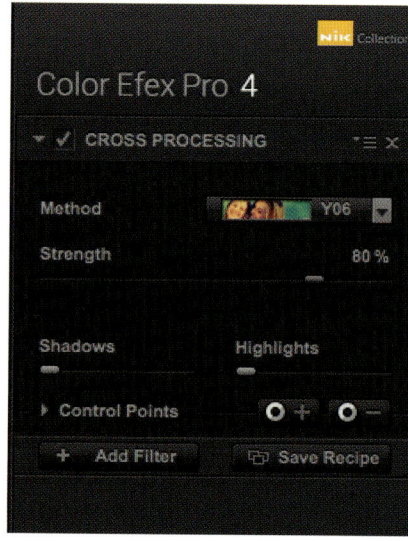

FIGURE 11.64

17. Click to add the Cross Balance preset (**Figure 11.65**), choose the Tungsten To Daylight (2) preset from the drop-down menu, set the Strength to 40%, and click on Add Filter (**Figure 11.66**).

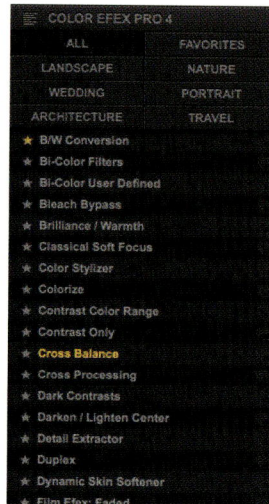

FIGURE 11.65

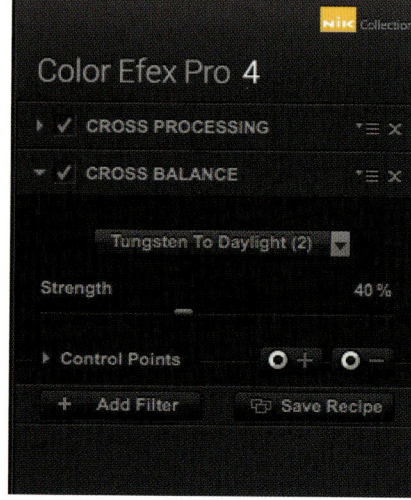

FIGURE 11.66

Next, click to add the Colorize preset (**Figure 11.67**), choose 2 from the Method menu, set the Strength to 20% (**Figure 11.68**), and click OK (which is located in the bottom-right corner of the Color Efex Pro 4 plugin screen) to apply this entire effect and send the image back into Photoshop.

18. Finally, I want to add a little more contrast to the whole image. I'm going to do that with the Topaz Clarity plugin, but again, you can use one of the other methods I covered in chapter 4 (page 62) or any other method you prefer.

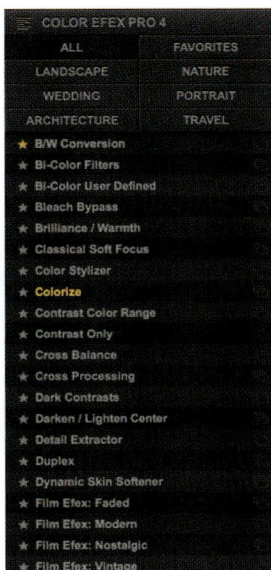

FIGURE 11.67

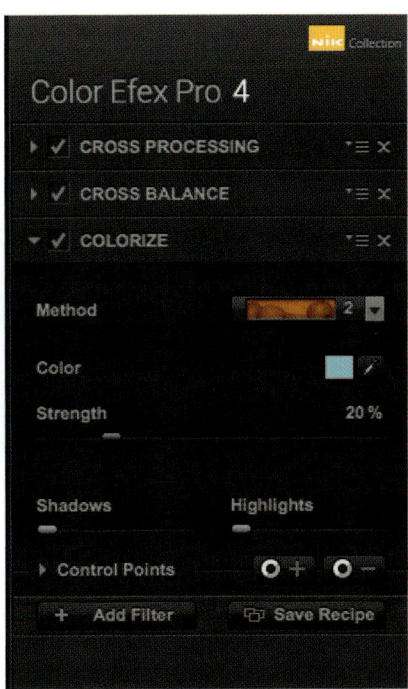

FIGURE 11.68

Go to *Filter > Topaz Labs > Topaz Clarity,* and in the settings on the right side of the window, increase Micro Contrast to 0.20 and Low Contrast to 0.10 (**Figure 11.69**). Click OK.

Press **D** to set the foreground and background colors to their defaults of black and white, and then click to add a Gradient Map adjustment layer (**Figure 11.70**). Lower the Opacity of the layer to 20% (**Figure 11.71**) to desaturate the image a little.

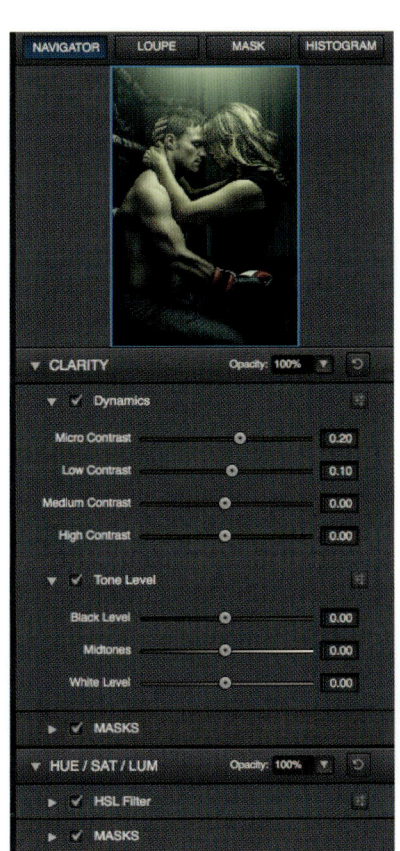

FIGURE 11.69

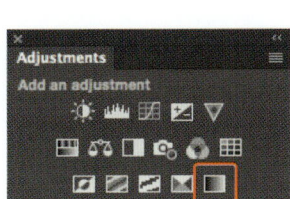

FIGURE 11.70

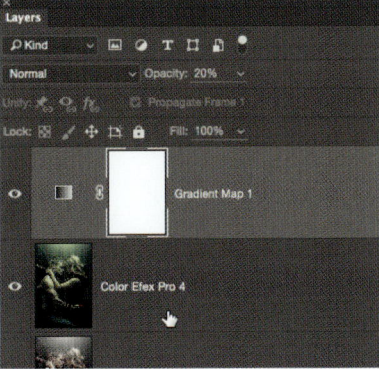

FIGURE 11.71

Figure 11.72 shows the original RAW image, straight out of the camera, and **Figure 11.73** shows the final retouched image. You can see that I also cropped a little off the bottom of the picture.

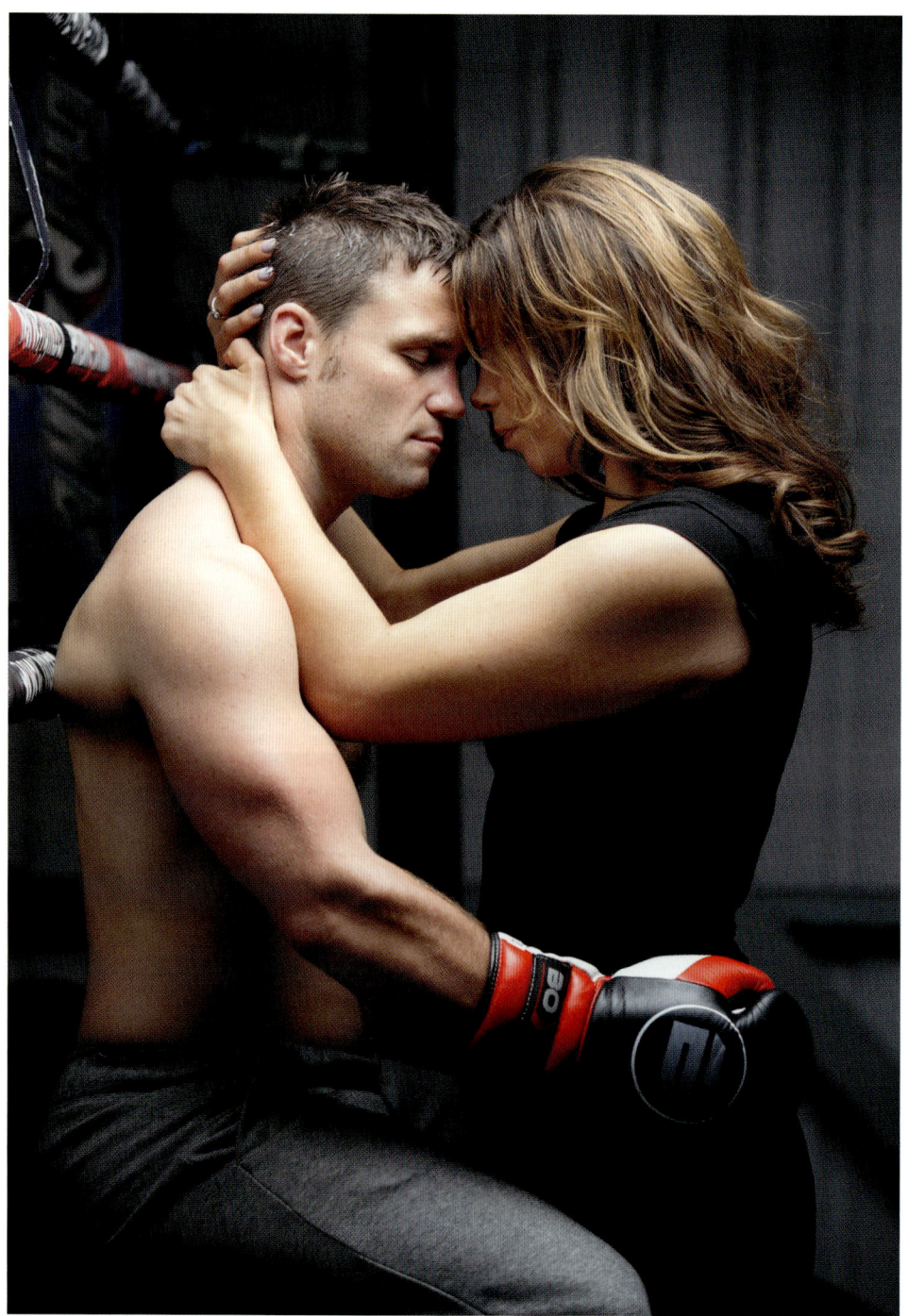

FIGURE 11.72 Original RAW image

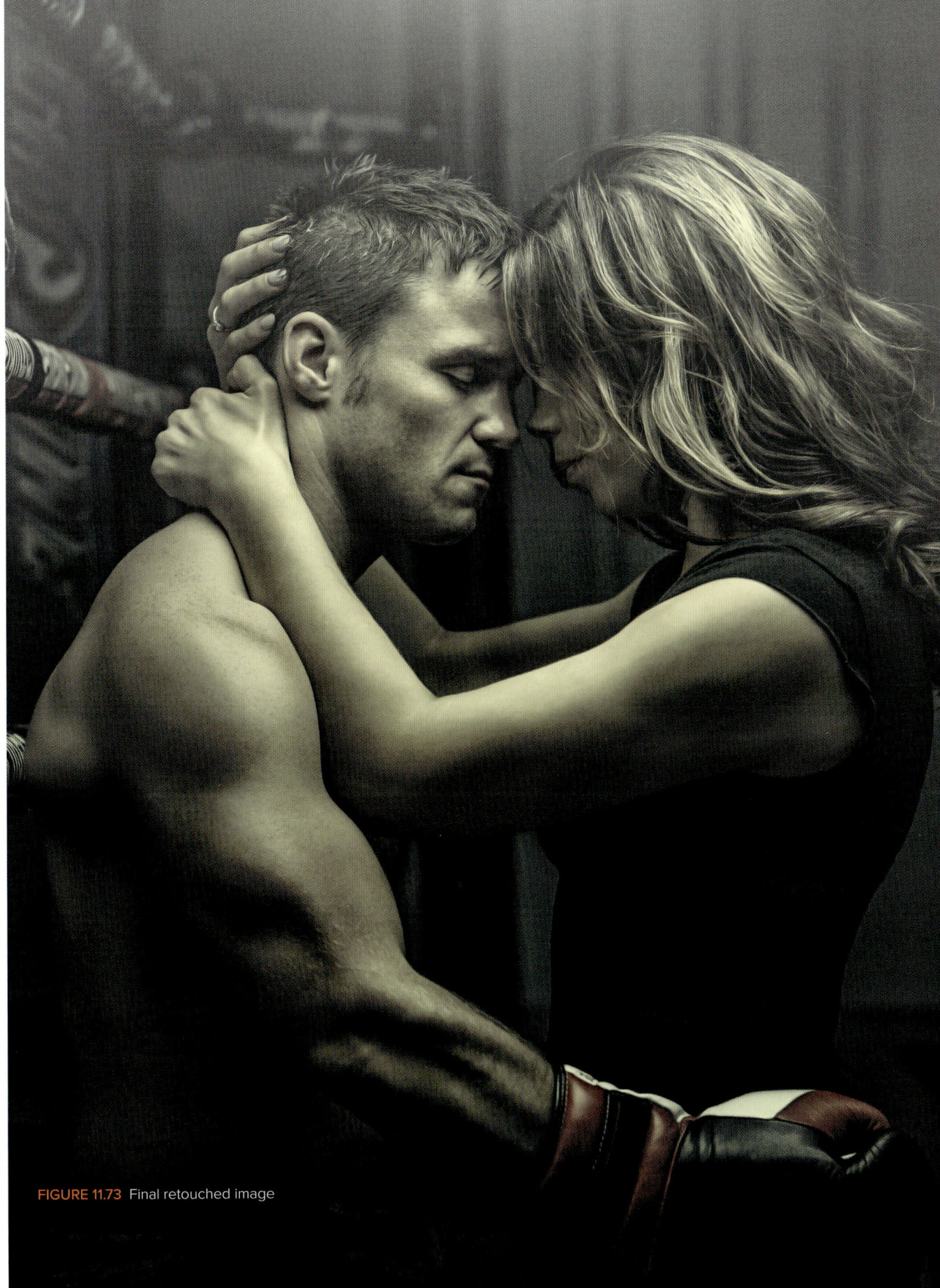

FIGURE 11.73 Final retouched image

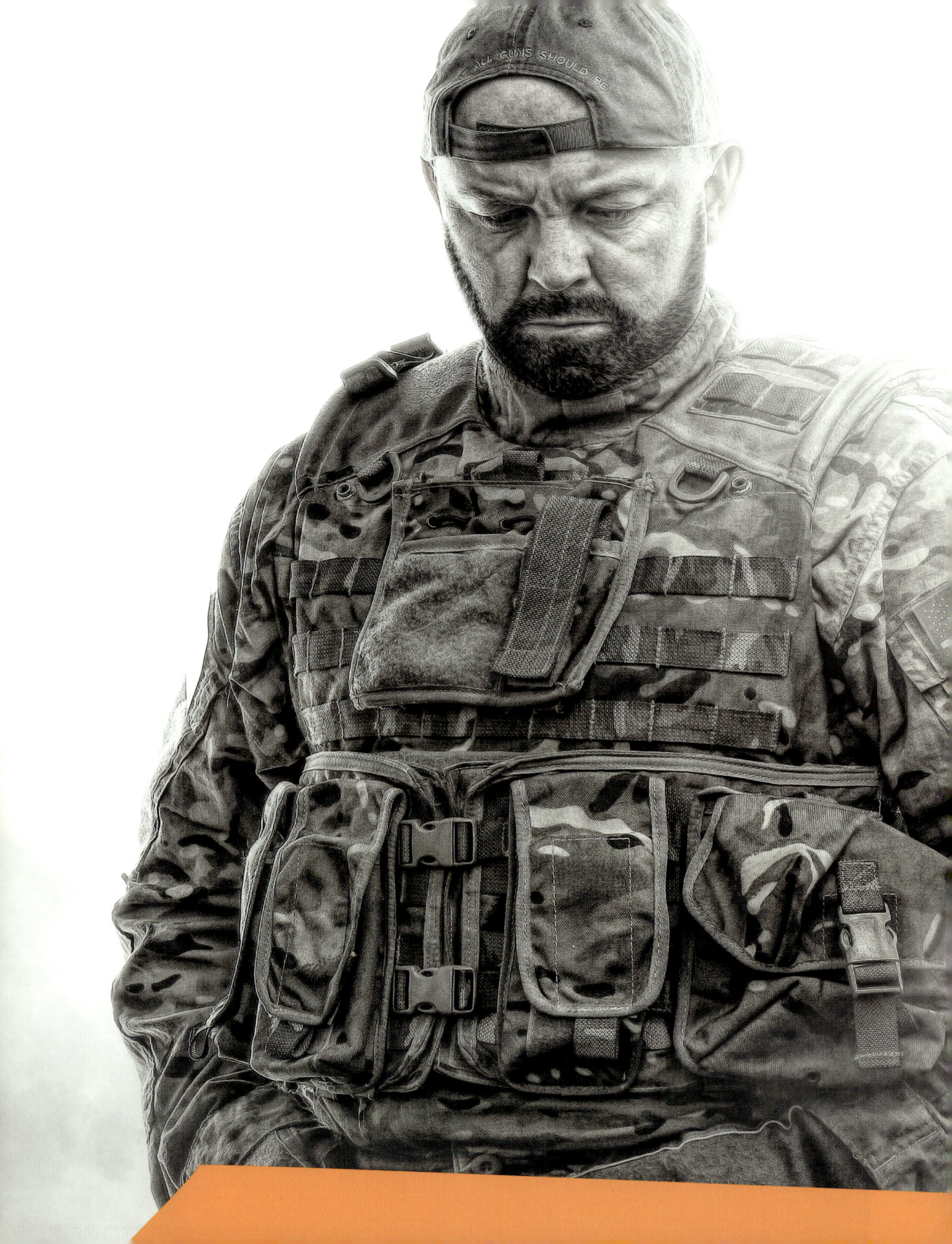

12 BOOK COVER INSPIRED

Creating this picture was very much one of those spur of the moment ideas that came to me on a day when I (unusually) had some down time. My wife had given me a copy of *American Sniper* (**Figure 12.1**), the autobiography of Chris Kyle. The book had since been made into a movie and I just happened to look at the cover image and thought it would be kind of cool to create my own version, just as a one off. I wanted give myself a challenge to see how I would shoot the photograph and then retouch it.

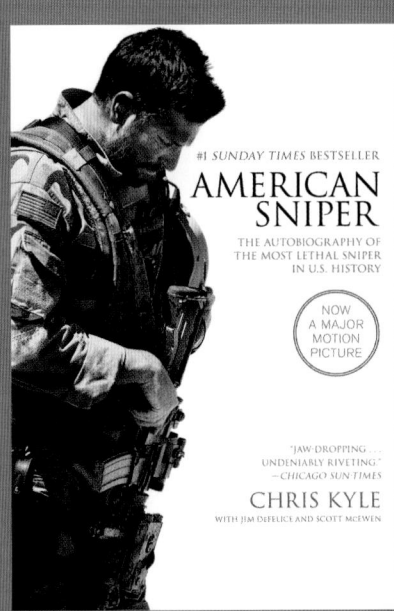

FIGURE 12.1

First things first, though, who would I photograph and where could I get access to authentic-looking military kit?

As luck would have it, my dear friend Barry (**Figure 12.2**)—who incidentally was the first person I ever photographed when I became interested in photography and lighting—happens to have connections with the United States military and lives not too far from me in the UK.

Rather than trying to explain what kind of picture I wanted to work on, I texted Barry the cover of the book to see if he'd like to be my model. After what must have been a nanosecond, he replied, "OH YES," in uppercase letters. Barry was free right then, so I packed the car with some kit and headed off through the lanes to his house.

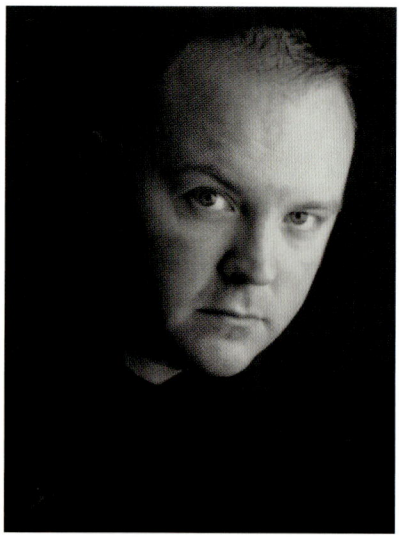

FIGURE 12.2 Barry, my first model

We took the photograph out in Barry's back garden, and you'll see a little later on how we set it up to get that pure-white background without the use of an artificial background and supports. We used a technique I stumbled across during one of my projects with kickboxer Steven Cook that I mentioned in chapter 1. Basically, it's a two-light setup that can give you a background, rim lighting, and light your subject from the front. Oh, and in the post-processing section I'll also show you a really cool way to use brushes in Photoshop to create fake facial hair (i.e., Barry's beard).

Right, we've got lots to cover over the next few pages so let's get started.

REVERSE ENGINEERING

I would hazard a guess that the picture on the cover of the book was actually taken outside, possibly on location during filming, or maybe it's a still from the movie itself. The dominant light is coming from behind the subject, so I would suggest that he has his back to the sun. His front (his face, chest, etc.) is definitely in shadow.

We can see very defined lines where the highlight and shadow areas meet, especially on his neck around his ear and on his arm that is nearest the camera. Notice how the patch on his shoulder casts a shadow onto his arm. This shadow is angled from across, which would suggest the light source is coming in from behind and high above. Again, this suggests that he is being lit by the sun, which is a hard light source due to its distance from the subject.

THE SETUP

As it happens, the lighting in my image of Barry is slightly different than that of the image on the book cover, which I used more for inspiration rather than "stealing" the lighting style.

I wanted this picture to have the same white background, as if it had been shot in a studio in front of a seamless, white roll of paper. Since we shot the photograph in Barry's backyard, I set up my Elinchrom Rotalux 175cm Octa Softbox and positioned him in front of it, and I used my Elinchrom Rotalux 135cm Octa Softbox to light him from the front (**Figure 12.3**).

I often use a softbox as a white background because it's much more portable than background stands with paper rolls and it takes up less space. Naturally, it has it's limitations in that it doesn't work for full-length portraits, but for anything at around knee height and up, this large Octa works perfectly (**Figure 12.4**).

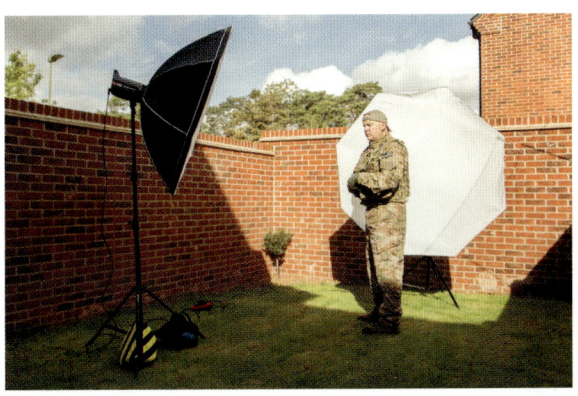

FIGURE 12.3

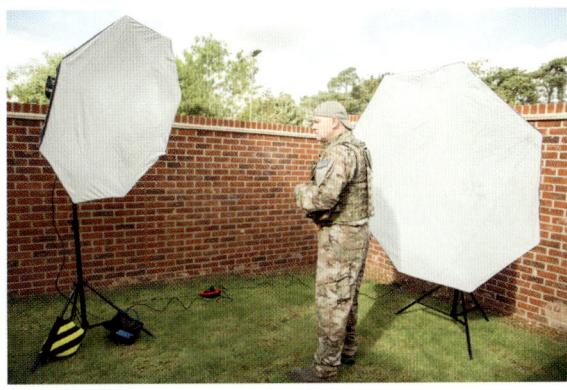

FIGURE 12.4

The technique for getting a clean, bright-white background is to meter the background light (Octa) at no more than two stops brighter than what would normally be a perfect exposure. For example, I photographed Barry at f/11 to ensure that he was entirely in focus. I metered the rear light at f/11, and then I increased the power of the light by two stops to give me approximately f/22.

I metered the front light at f/11 and then lowered the power by about half a stop. As you can see, I tend to use my light meter to get me to a good starting point, and then I make adjustments to suit exactly what I'm after.

In the behind-the-scenes pictures and lighting diagram (**Figure 12.5**) you can see how I positioned the lights. As I mentioned, I positioned one Octa behind Barry to create the white background and one to the side, but with Barry turned toward it so that the light on his face and body was even.

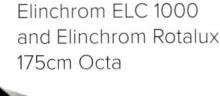

Elinchrom ELC 1000 and Elinchrom Rotalux 175cm Octa

Barry

Elinchrom ELC 1000 and Elinchrom Rotalux 135cm Octa

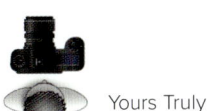

Yours Truly

FIGURE 12.5

Positioning the Octa behind and quite close to Barry also adds rim lighting to either side (**Figure 12.6**). The further he steps away from the Octa, the less of a rim light there is, until eventually it disappears.

CAMERA SETTINGS

I shot in Manual mode and I chose to use an aperture of f/11 so that Barry would be sharp and in focus from the tip of his nose to the back of his head and beyond.

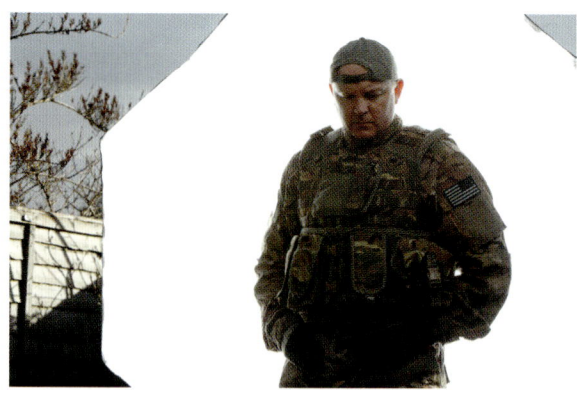

FIGURE 12.6

As mentioned in the setup section, I metered both the front and rear lights at f/11, and then increased the power of the rear light by around two stops to f/22 to ensure a clean, bright-white background. I lowered the power of the front light by around half a stop.

I kept the ISO as low as possible at ISO 100 and used a shutter speed of 1/125sec, which allowed just enough ambient light into the scene.

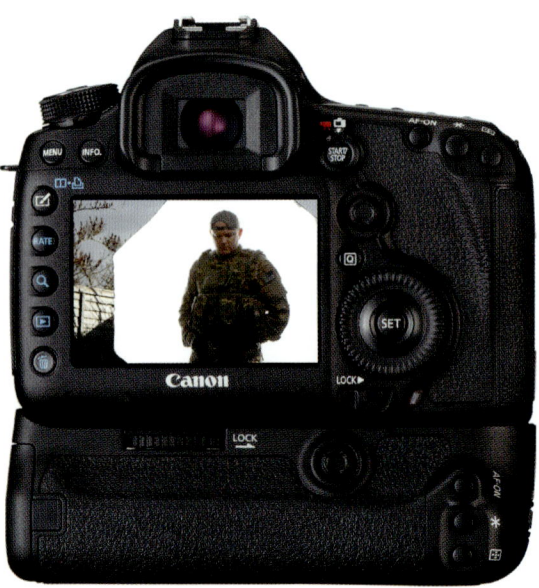

FIGURE 12.7

MODE Aperture Priority

ISO 100

APERTURE f/11.0

SHUTTER SPEED 1/125 sec.

LENS Canon 70–200mm f/2.8L IS II USM

GEAR GUIDE

For this shoot, I used an Elinchrom Rotalux 175cm Octa Softbox (**Figure 12.8**) and an Elinchrom Rotalux 135cm Octa Softbox (**Figure 12.9**).

The 175cm Octa is great for using as a background when you're photographing anything from a head shot to around three-quarter length. You can extend the canvas in Photoshop with the Crop Tool and simply fill it with white (which we'll do during the post-processing section in this chapter) to make it as big as you like.

SMALL FLASH GEAR GUIDE

For those of you who are using small, battery-powered flashes such as Speedlights, I've put together an example of a kit you could use to create the same or similar look.

A large 60" shoot-through umbrella (**Figure 12.10**) would work great behind your subject.

However, you may find that you'll need to do a little extra post-processing to remove the umbrella framework (**Figure 12.11**). You can fix this easily by simply adding a new blank layer in Photoshop and painting over the framework with a round brush and a white foreground color.

For the front light you could use another 60" umbrella or maybe even the Lastolite Ezybox II Octa Large 1.2m (**Figure 12.12**).

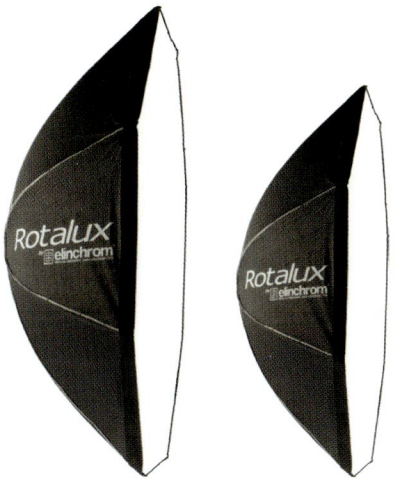
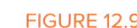

FIGURE 12.8   FIGURE 12.9

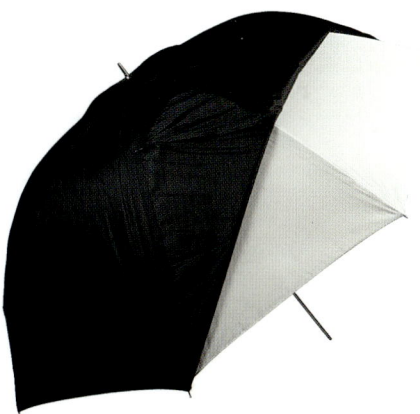

FIGURE 12.10

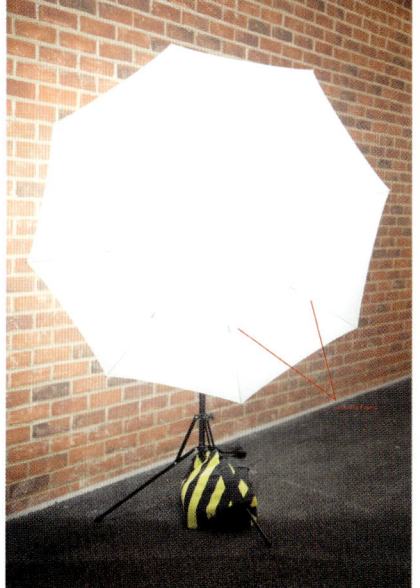

FIGURE 12.11

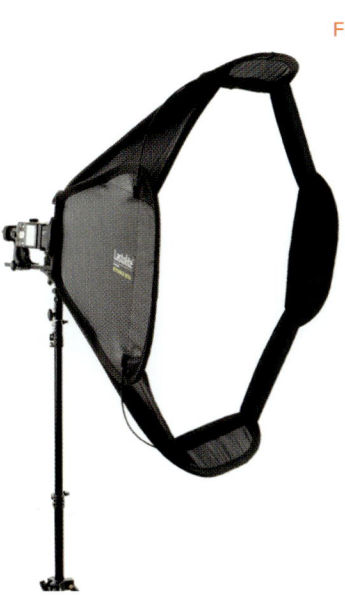

FIGURE 12.12

POST-PROCESSING

The post-processing for this picture is actually quite straightforward. The main part of the retouch involves enhancing the details and giving the picture a grungy, gritty look that is so fitting for the subject.

We'll be using brushes in Photoshop to add a beard onto Barry's face and to create some smoke and dust. Brushes in Photoshop are an incredibly powerful tool, so I'd highly recommend that you start experimenting with them, if you haven't already. As photographers, there are so many ways we can use them to refine our images.

We'll also use the little trick I shared in chapter 7 for enhancing male physiques. It's just one step, but it really does make a big difference.

So, although you may never end up making a picture exactly like this one, you'll certainly learn some techniques that will come in handy for other pictures you may find yourself working on in the future.

Right, let's get cracking.

 **NOTE** *Download the file you need to follow along step-by-step at: http://www.rockynook.com/ photograph-like-a-thief-reference/*

1. With the file open in Camera RAW, we'll start by bringing back a bit of detail in the shadow areas. In the Basic tab, increase the Shadows slider to around +55 (**Figure 12.13**).

   Next, we'll add some sharpening. In the Detail tab under Sharpening, increase the Amount to 40 (**Figure 12.14**). Then hold down the Option key (Mac) or Alt key (PC) and drag the Masking slider to around 60. This determines where the sharpening is mainly applied, which is indicated by the white areas in **Figure 12.15**.

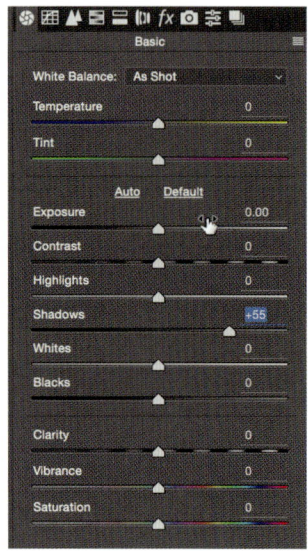

FIGURE 12.13

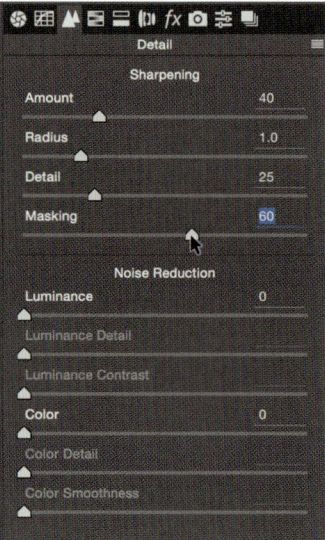

FIGURE 12.14

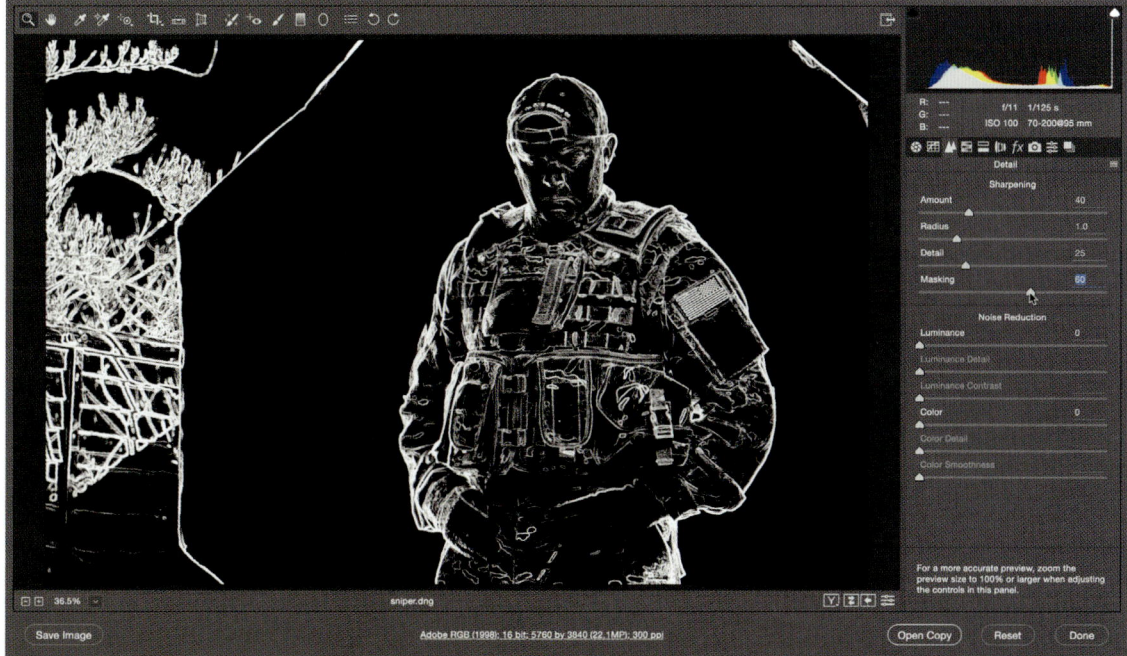

FIGURE 12.15

Release the Option key (Mac) or Alt key (PC) and click on Open Image at the bottom-right corner of the screen to send the image into Photoshop.

2. Go to *Window > Info,* and then without clicking down on the image, drag your cursor around the white area surrounding Barry, which in this case is our 175cm Octa. As you do so, look in the Info Properties and you'll see that the RGB values are all 255, which is pure white (**Figure 12.16**).

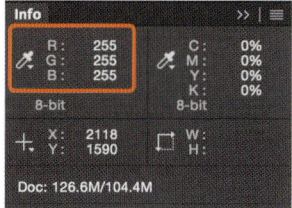

FIGURE 12.16

Close the Info Properties and use the Lasso Tool to make a selection of the upper-right corner of the image (**Figure 12.17**). Hold down the Shift key and use the Lasso Tool to drag out a selection that encompasses the left side of the image (**Figure 12.18**). Make sure to overlap a little onto the Octa.

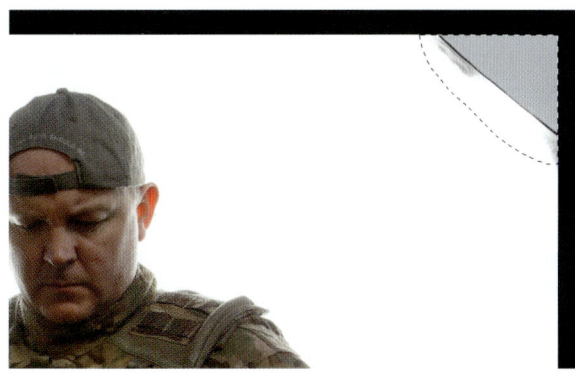

FIGURE 12.17

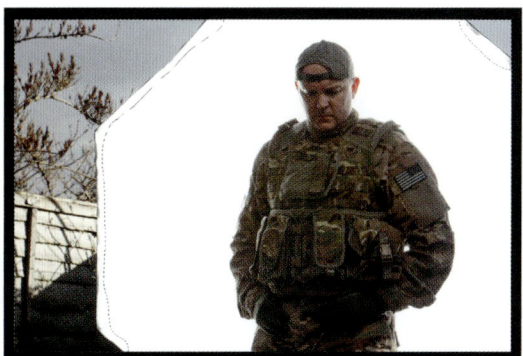

FIGURE 12.18

Now go to *Edit > Fill,* choose White from the Contents Menu (**Figure 12.19**), and click OK. This fills the selected areas, extending the background behind Barry (**Figure 12.20**).

Turn off the active selection by going to *Select > Deselect,* or by pressing Command + D (Mac) or Ctrl + D (PC).

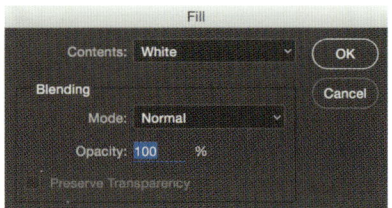

FIGURE 12.19

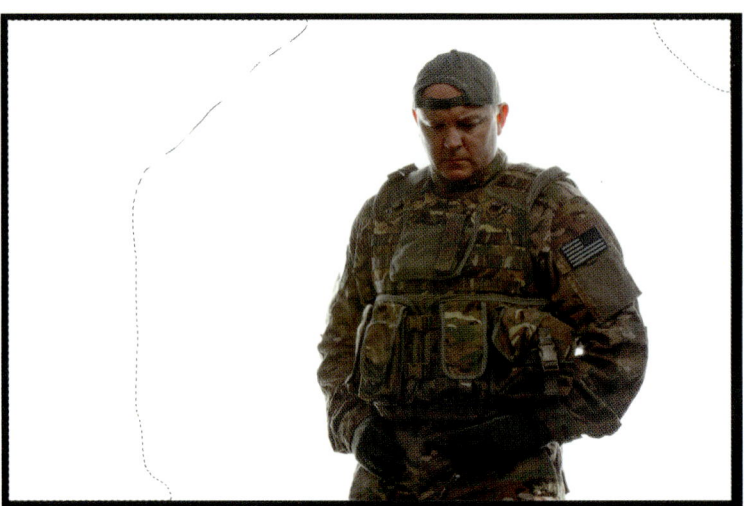

FIGURE 12.20

3. This next step is something I do when I'm working on pictures of males and looking to enhance their power and impact. It's especially good for physique pictures.

Create a duplicate of the Background layer by pressing Command + J (Mac) or Ctrl + J (PC). Rename this layer "width" (**Figure 12.21**).

Then go to *Edit > Free Transform,* or press Command + T (Mac) or Ctrl + T (PC). In the options at the top of the screen, ensure that the chain icon linking the width (W) and the height (H) is not active, and then increase the width to 105% (**Figure 12.22**) and press Return (Mac) or Enter (PC).

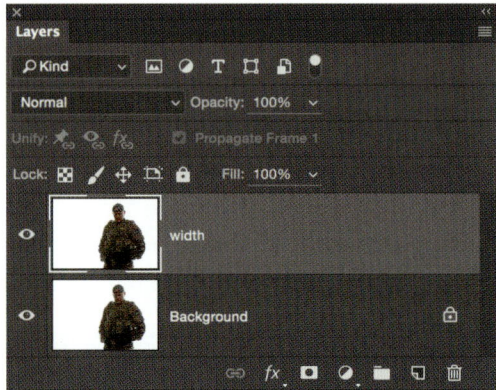

FIGURE 12.21

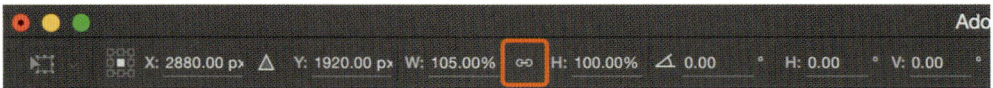

FIGURE 12.22

TIP *When you add extra width, use an increase of no more than 5%; otherwise, you risk stretching your subject, making it look both obvious and a little, ermmm, strange.*

If you turn the visibility of the width layer on and off by clicking on it's eye icon in the Layers panel, you can see that we've increased the width of Barry, but not to the point that it looks fake.

4. We're going to be using a couple of brushes while retouching this picture, but neither are included in Photoshop. However, one of them is free and the other is incredibly inexpensive and comes with a bunch of additional brushes from my buddy Aaron Blaise.

Aaron is an artist in the true sense of the word, having worked at Disney for around 20 years on movies such as *The Lion King, Pocahontas,* and *Beauty and the Beast,* to name just a few. He also directed the movie *Brother Bear.* He's an insanely talented guy who is incredibly open and willing to share his techniques and teach others. He has created all manner of brushes—ranging from special effects brushes to create snow and debris to brushes that mimic hair and fur—that you can purchase and download from his website (creatureartteacher.com) for use in Photoshop (**Figure 12.23**).

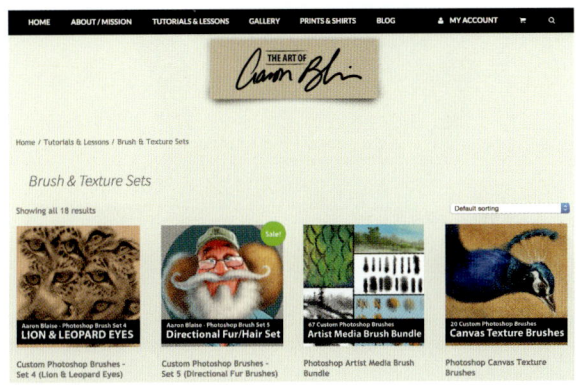

FIGURE 12.23

First, we're going to use brush 344 from Aaron's Directional Hair/Fur set (**Figure 12.24**) to give Barry a beard.

Without making any changes to the brush, press **D** on the keyboard to set the foreground and background colors to their defaults of black and white. Then create a new layer in the layer stack and rename it "beard" (**Figure 12.25**).

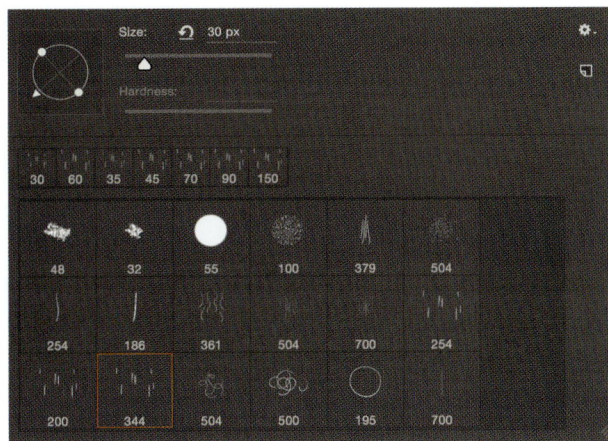

FIGURE 12.24

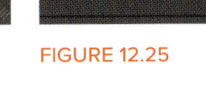

FIGURE 12.25

Using the right and left bracket keys to increase and decrease the size of the brush, paint a beard on Barry's face (**Figure 12.26**).

If you go over the edges, simply use the Eraser Tool (**E**) to remove the mistake. Rather than using the default round eraser, you can go to the options at the top of the screen and change the shape of the eraser to match the brush you're using. This way when you erase the parts you don't want, the eraser will remove them in the shape of hair (**Figure 12.27**).

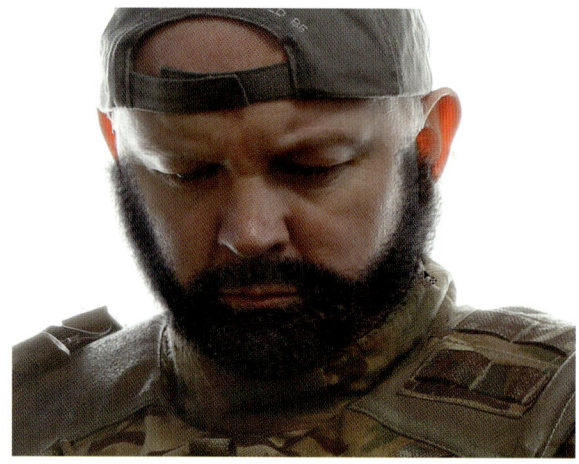

FIGURE 12.26

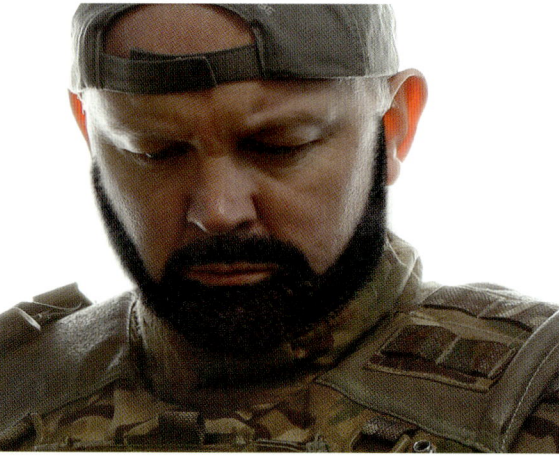

FIGURE 12.27

5. Add a Hue/Saturation adjustment layer to the top of the layer stack (above the beard layer). In the properties, ensure that the Clipping Mask is active so that the adjustments we make will only affect the beard layer below. Put a check in the Colorize checkbox, and then change Hue to 39, Saturation to 18, and Lightness to -20 to give Barry's new beard a brownish color (**Figure 12.28**).

6. The beard looks like it's been painted on and is very flat and two-dimensional, so we'll do a little bit of dodging and burning so that it takes on the shape of Barry's face.

Go to *Layer > New > Layer,* and in the New Layer properties, rename the layer "db beard" for dodge and burn beard. Select Soft Light from the Mode menu, check the box for Fill with Soft-Light-neutral color (50% gray), and click OK (**Figure 12.29**).

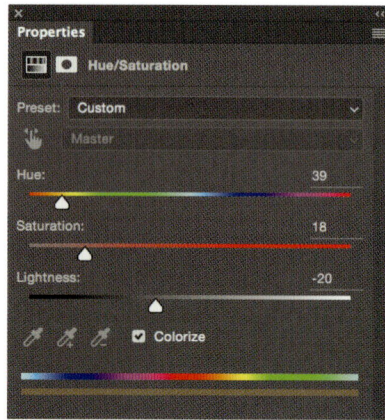

FIGURE 12.28

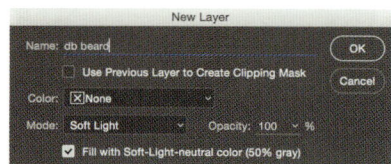

FIGURE 12.29

Now use the Dodge and Burn Tools as I showed in chapter 4 (page 66) to brighten and darken areas around the beard to add some depth and dimension. Remember, you can toggle between the Dodge Tool and Burn Tool by simply holding down the Option key (Mac) or Alt key (PC). This allows you to maintain the same settings for both tools.

In Figure **12.30** you can see where I added some dodging and burning. To see only the gray layer you're working on, hold down the Option key (Mac) or Alt key (PC) and

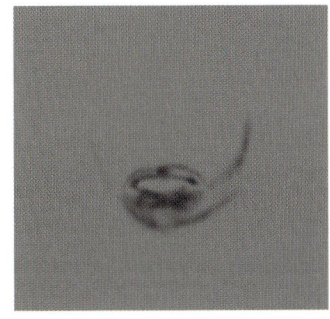

FIGURE 12.30

click on the eye icon next to the gray (db beard) layer in the Layers panel. This will turn every other layer off. To go back to normal view, hold down the Option key (Mac) or Alt key (PC) again and click where the eye icon for the gray (db beard) layer would be.

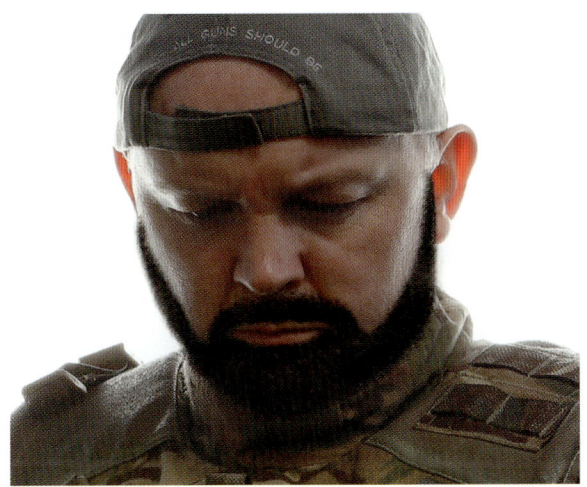

FIGURE 12.31 Before dodging and burning

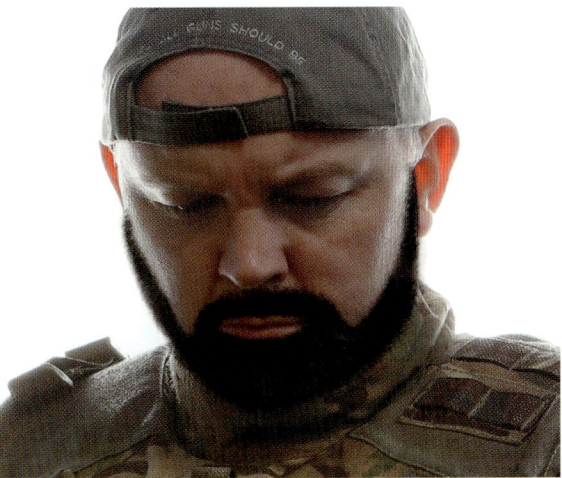

FIGURE 12.32 After dodging and burning

7. Click on the width layer in the Layers panel (**Figure 12.33**) and use the Lasso Tool to draw a selection around the American Flag (**Figure 12.34**).

Press the **Q** key to enter Quick Mask mode, and then go to *Filter > Blur > Gaussian Blur.* Add in a Radius of 2 pixels and click OK (**Figure 12.35**). Press **Q** to exit Quick Mask mode.

TIP *When you have an active selection and then enter Quick Mask mode, this is a great way to feather your selection by simply adding blur. This technique takes the guesswork out of determining how much to feather your selection because you can see it.*

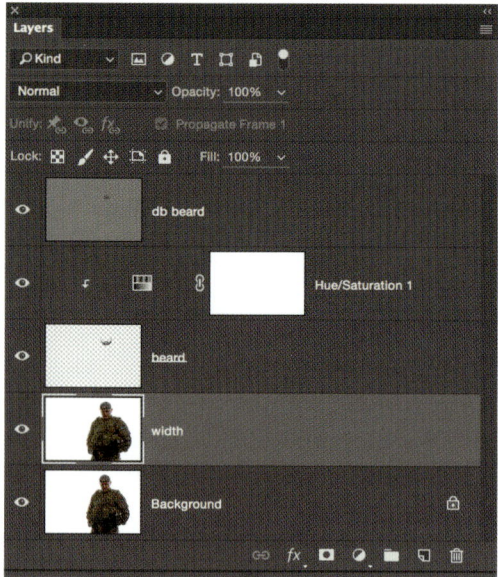

FIGURE 12.33

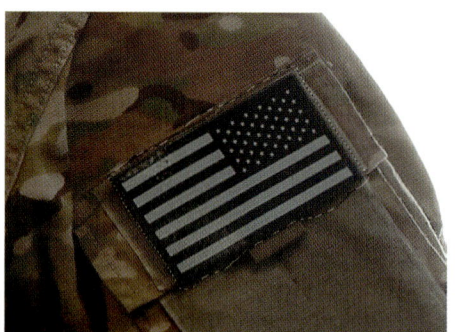

FIGURE 12.34

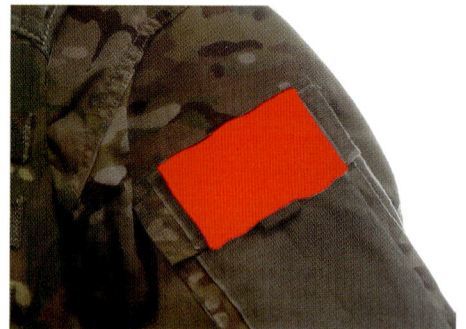

FIGURE 12.35

Press Command + J (Mac) or Ctrl + J (PC) to add a new layer containing this selection of the arm badge, and then rename the layer "arm badge." Hold down the Command key (Mac) or Ctrl key (PC) and press the right bracket key three times to put the arm badge layer at the top of the layer stack (**Figure 12.36**).

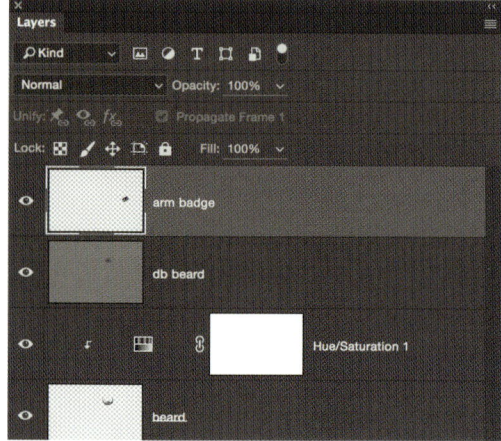

FIGURE 12.36

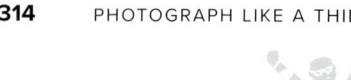

8. Go to *Edit > Transform > Flip Horizontal* (**Figure 12.37**), and then to *Edit > Free Transform* to bring up the transform handles. Position your cursor outside of the handles and click and drag to rotate the patch into place (**Figure 12.38**). Press Return (Mac) or Enter (PC).

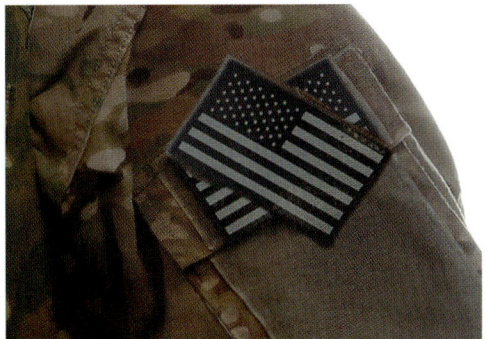

FIGURE 12.37

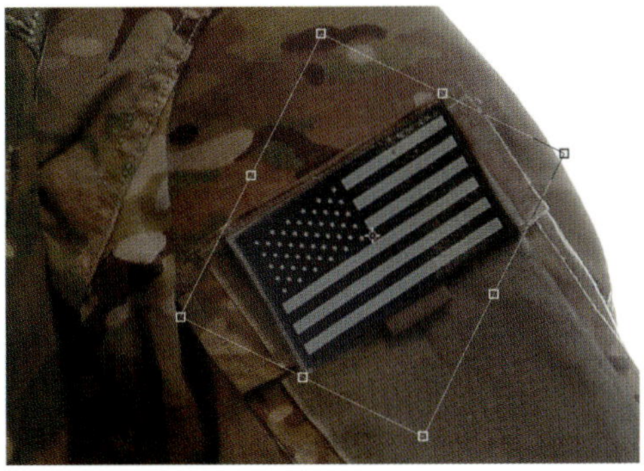

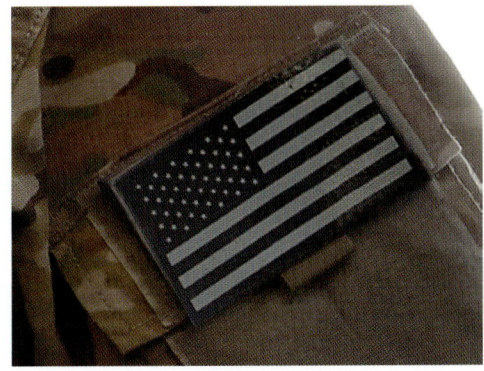

FIGURE 12.38

Now add a Layer Mask to the arm badge layer. With a black foreground color and a round, soft-edged brush, paint around the arm badge to blend it in by revealing original shadows that may now be underneath it and maybe even some stitching (**Figure 12.39**).

9. Let's look at increasing the details to add a bit of drama and grunge to our picture. Up until fairly recently, I used a plugin from Topaz Labs called Topaz Details that is great for this, but there's also a technique we can use in Photoshop that is very good. I'll go through the Photoshop technique, which I first saw being demonstrated by German photographer Calvin Hollywood. I don't tend to use it much now, but if you want to add a gritty look to your pictures this works great.

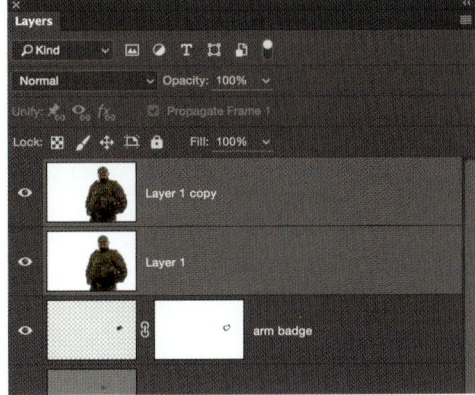

FIGURE 12.39

Start off by adding a merged layer to the top of the layer stack. To do this, go to *Select > All,* then *Edit > Copy Merged,* and then *Edit > Paste.* Next, create a duplicate of this layer by pressing Command + J (Mac) or Ctrl + J (PC). Finally, hold down the Shift key and click on the first merged layer (**Figure 12.40**) so that both layers are selected.

FIGURE 12.40

Press Command + G (Mac) or Ctrl + G (PC) to put the layers into a group. Rename the group "details" (**Figure 12.41**).

Change the Blend Mode of the group from Pass Through to Overlay (**Figure 12.42**), and then click on the uppermost layer in the group and change its Blend Mode to Vivid Light (**Figure 12.43**).

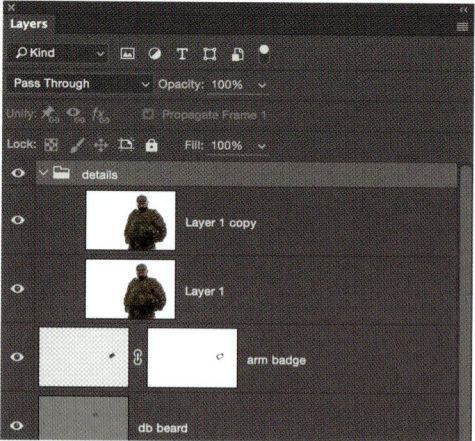

FIGURE 12.41

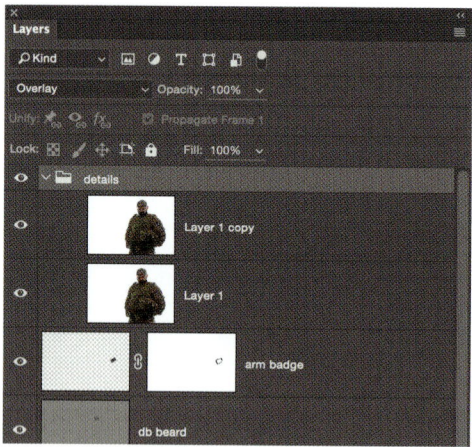

FIGURE 12.42

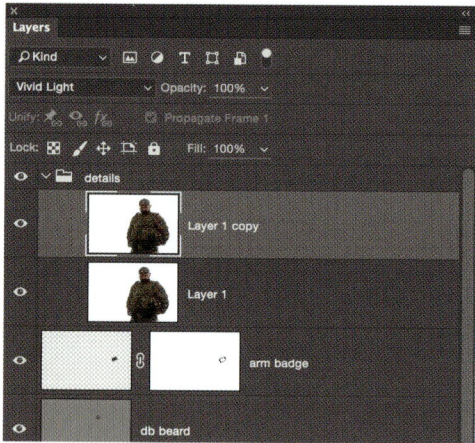

FIGURE 12.43

10. With the uppermost layer still selected, go to *Image > Adjustments > Invert*. We are going to use a filter to increase the details in the image, so we'll convert this layer to a Smart Object so that we can change the settings at a later stage, if necessary. Go to *Filter > Convert for Smart Filters* (**Figure 12.44**).

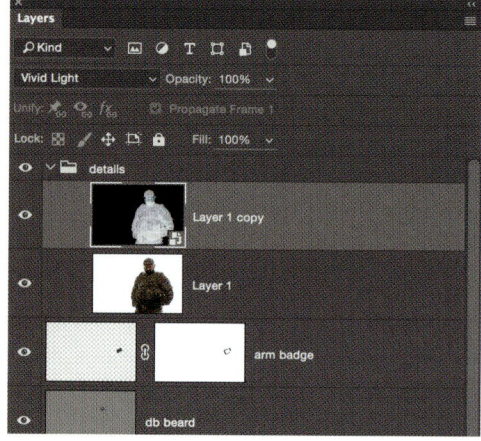

FIGURE 12.44

11. Go to *Filter > Blur > Surface Blur* (**Figure 12.45**), and in the properties, add in a Radius of 40 pixels and a Threshold of 15 levels and click OK (**Figure 12.46**).

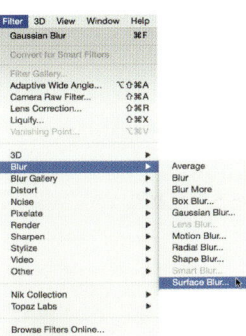

FIGURE 12.45

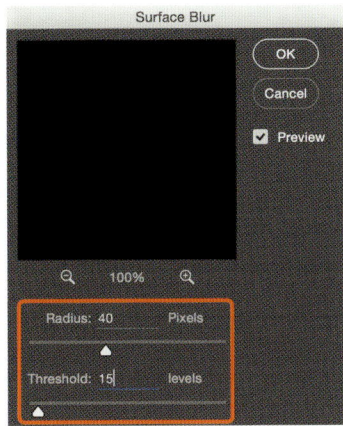

FIGURE 12.46

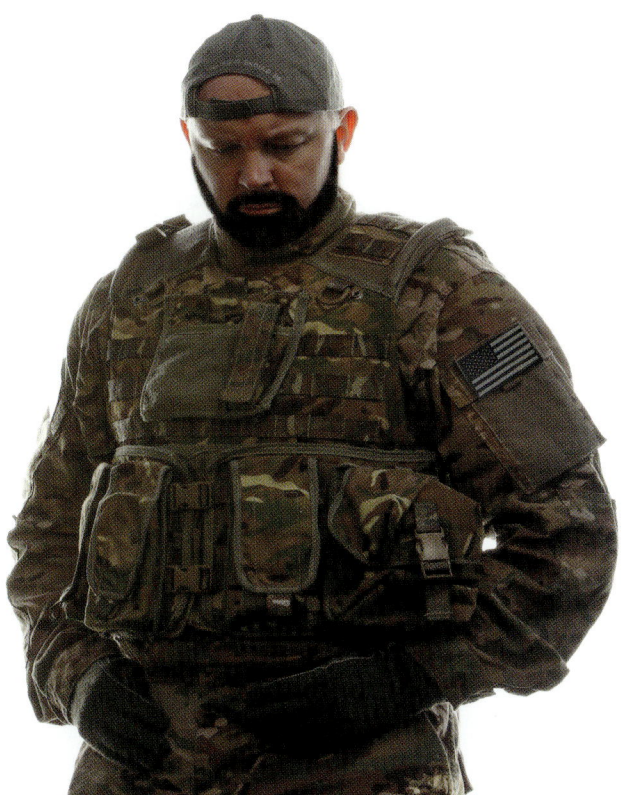

FIGURE 12.47 Before adding the Surface Blur filter

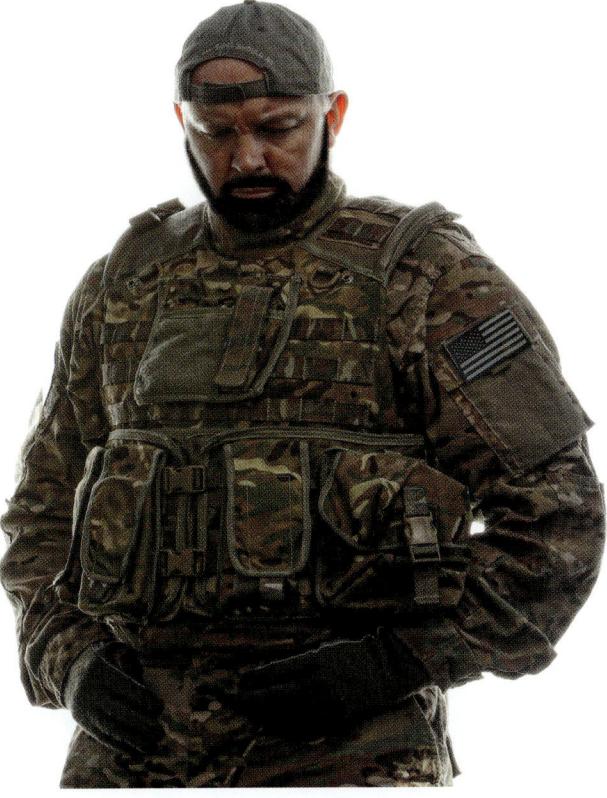

FIGURE 12.48 After adding the Surface Blur filter

12. I want to add even more grit to this picture, which I'll do by increasing the contrast with the Topaz Clarity plugin.

Add a merged layer to the top of the layer stack and rename it "contrast." Then go to *Filter > Topaz Labs > Topaz Clarity* (**Figure 12.49**).

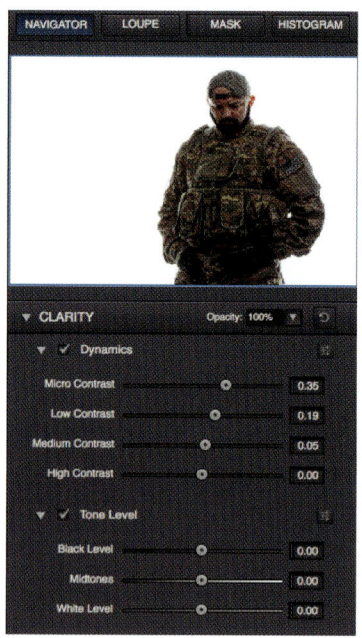

In the Topaz Clarity window on the right side of the screen, make the following adjustments: Micro Contrast 0.35, Low Contrast 0.19, and Medium Contrast 0.05 (**Figure 12.50**). Click OK.

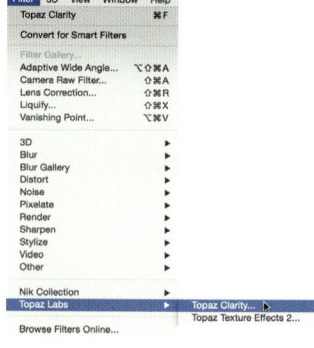

FIGURE 12.49

FIGURE 12.50

13. Once you're back in Photoshop, hold down the Option key (Mac) or Alt key (PC) and click to add a Layer Mask. This adds a black Layer Mask, which hides the contrast that was added to the entire picture. Since we only want it on Barry's face and hat, choose a white foreground color and then use a round, soft-edged brush to paint over Barry's face and reveal the contrast.

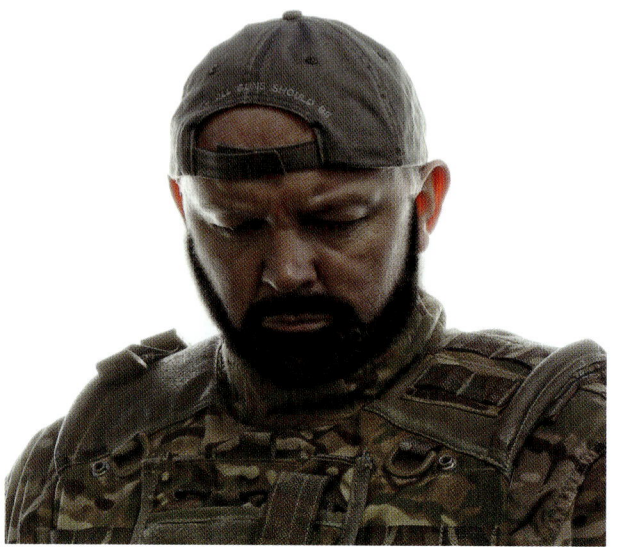

FIGURE 12.51 Before increasing contrast with Topaz Clarity

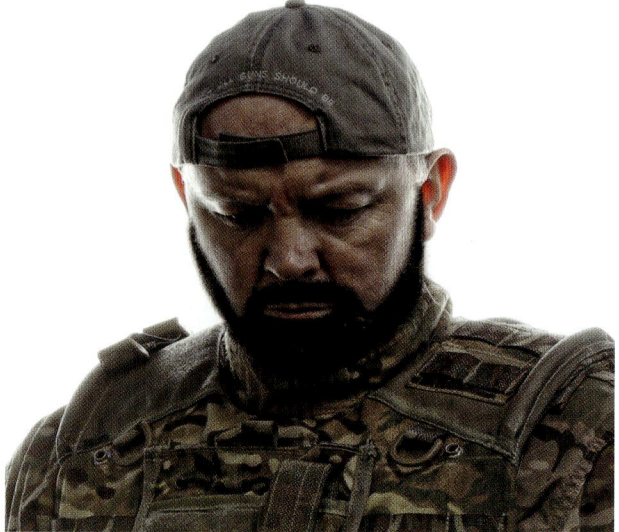

FIGURE 12.52 After increasing contrast with Topaz Clarity

14. Add a blank layer to the top of the layer stack and rename it "flare." With a white foreground color and a round, soft-edged brush, press once on Barry's left shoulder (**Figure 12.53**).

Go to *Edit > Free Transform,* and then hold down Shift + Option (Mac) or Shift + Alt (PC) and drag outward on a corner transform handle to increase the size of the flare. Press Return (Mac) or Enter (PC). Use the Move Tool (**V**) to click and drag the flare into position so that it's mainly over Barry's shoulder and just touching his face (**Figure 12.54**).

15. After taking a short break from the screen and coming back to the image with fresh eyes, I think we need to add a little more contrast. Add a merged layer to the top of the layer stack and rename it "contrast 2."

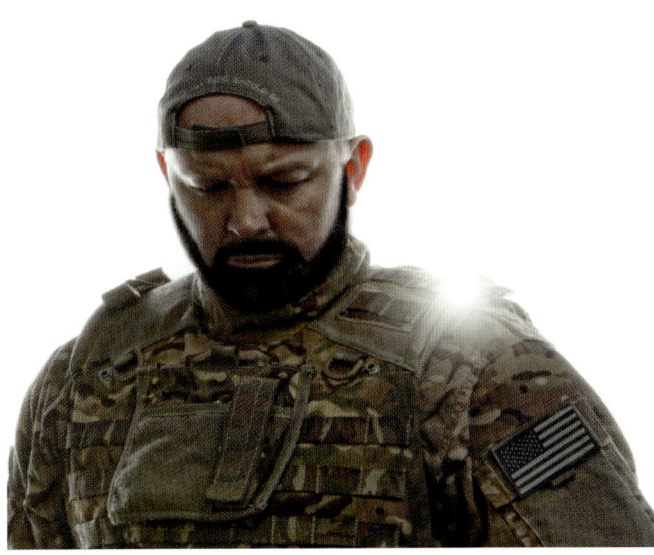

FIGURE 12.53

Then use whatever technique you like to add some contrast to the image (see chapter 4, page 60). I'll use Topaz Clarity and increase Micro Contrast to 0.38, Low Contrast to 0.13, and Medium Contrast to 0.03 (**Figure 12.55**).

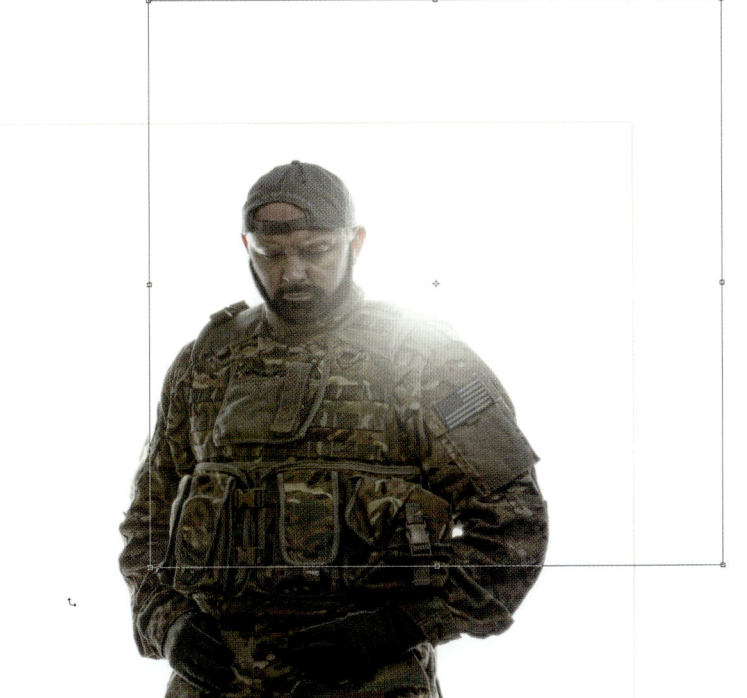

FIGURE 12.54

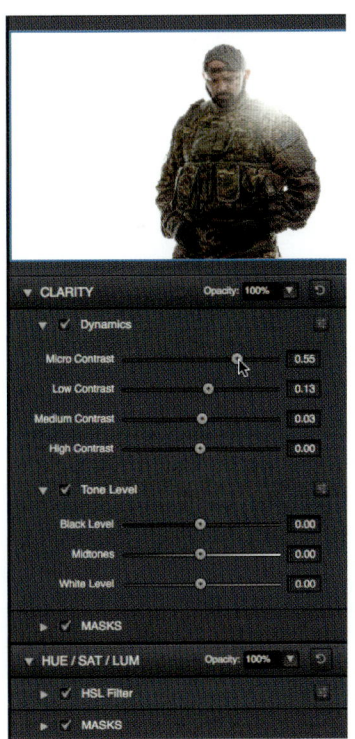

FIGURE 12.55

16. Now we'll do the black-and-white conversion. There is a seemingly unlimited number of ways to do this in Photoshop and with third-party plugins. We'll use Photoshop this time, so press **D** to set the foreground and background colors to their defaults of black and white, and then click to add a Gradient Map adjustment layer (**Figure 12.56**).

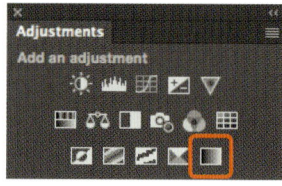

FIGURE 12.56

This does a pretty good job straight out the gate, but we'll bring back just a little of the color by lowering the Opacity of the Gradient Map adjustment layer to 80% (**Figure 12.57**).

17. With all the contrast that's been added, I think the shadow areas have gone a little too far toward the dark side. To fix this, click to add a Levels adjustment layer (**Figure 12.58**), in the Levels adjustment properties, drag the black Output Levels marker to the right until it reads 40 (**Figure 12.59**).

With the Levels adjustment layer mask active, use a black foreground color and a round, soft-edged brush set to 100% Opacity to paint over Barry's face and remove the effect of the Levels adjustment layer (**Figure 12.60**).

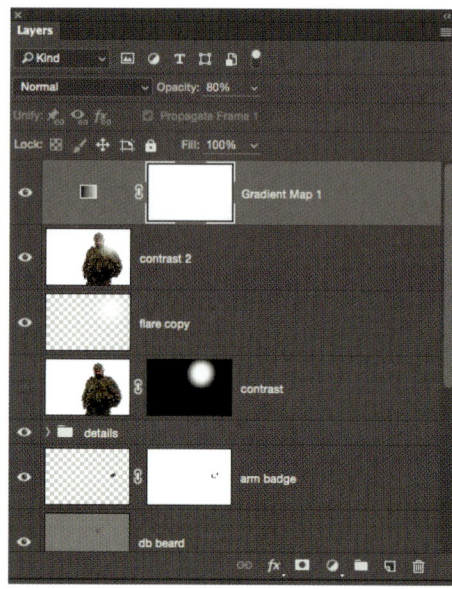

FIGURE 12.57

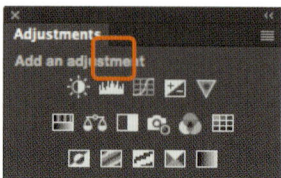

FIGURE 12.58

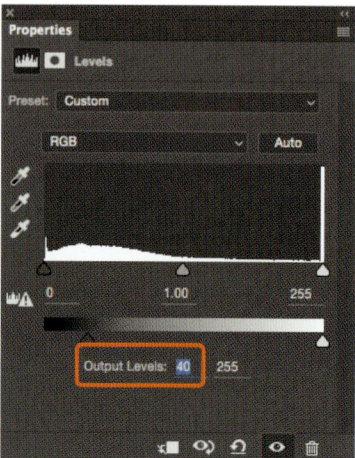

FIGURE 12.59

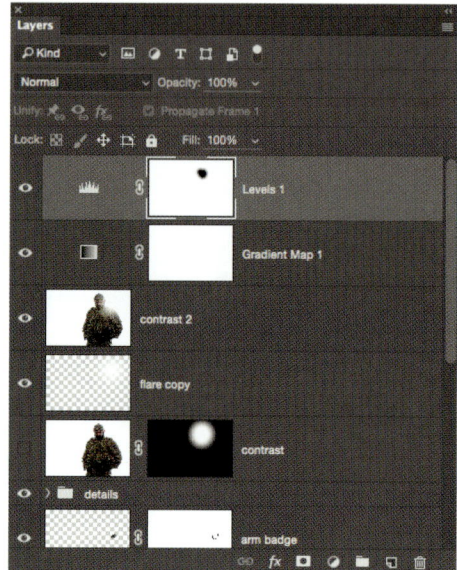

FIGURE 12.60

18. The last thing we'll do is add in some smoke and dust. Again, there are lots of ways to do this, but one of the most effective and flexible ways is by using Photoshop brushes. The very best brushes (by far) for this kind of effect were recommended to me by my friend Uli Staiger, a digital artist based in Germany. What makes them even better is that they are completely free. You can download the xplosion brush set at: http://bit.ly/PLAT_brushes.

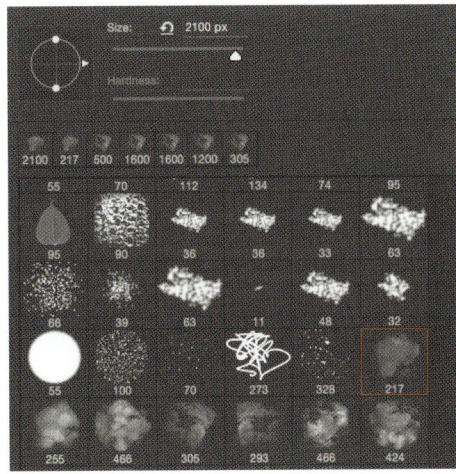

FIGURE 12.61

Once you've installed the xplosion brush set, add a new layer to the top of the layer stack and rename it "smoke." Choose brush 217 from the Brush Preset Picker (**Figure 12.61**), and then click to open the Brush panel. In the Brush Tip Shape section, increase Spacing to 33% (**Figure 12.62**). In the Shape Dynamics section, set Size Jitter to 100% and Angle Jitter to 100% (**Figure 12.63**). In the Transfer section, set Opacity Jitter to 100% and Flow Jitter to 30% (**Figure 12.64**).

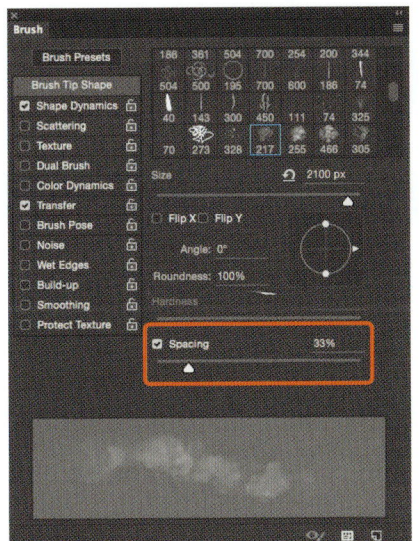

FIGURE 12.62

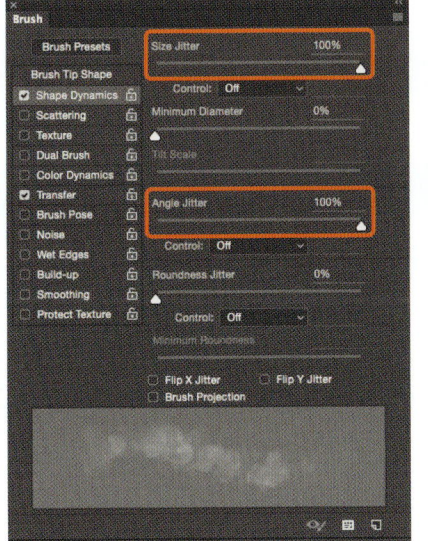

FIGURE 12.63

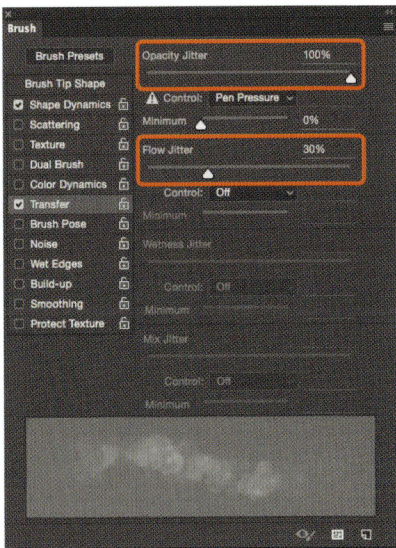

FIGURE 12.64

19. Finally, with a black foreground color, start painting around the lower portion of the picture to lay down some smoke. Because the smoke is on its own layer, we can lower the Opacity of the layer to get the exact look we're after (**Figure 12.65**).

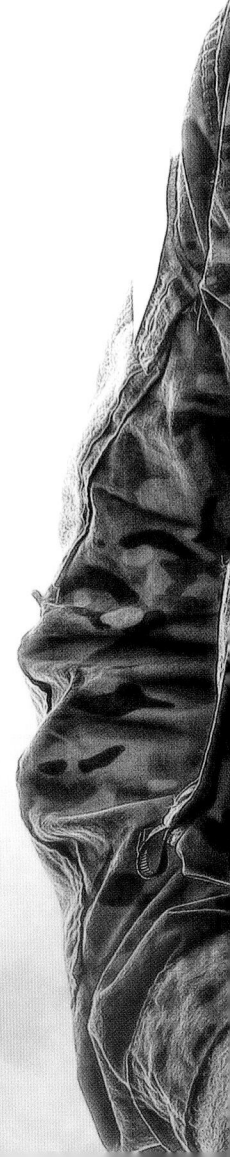

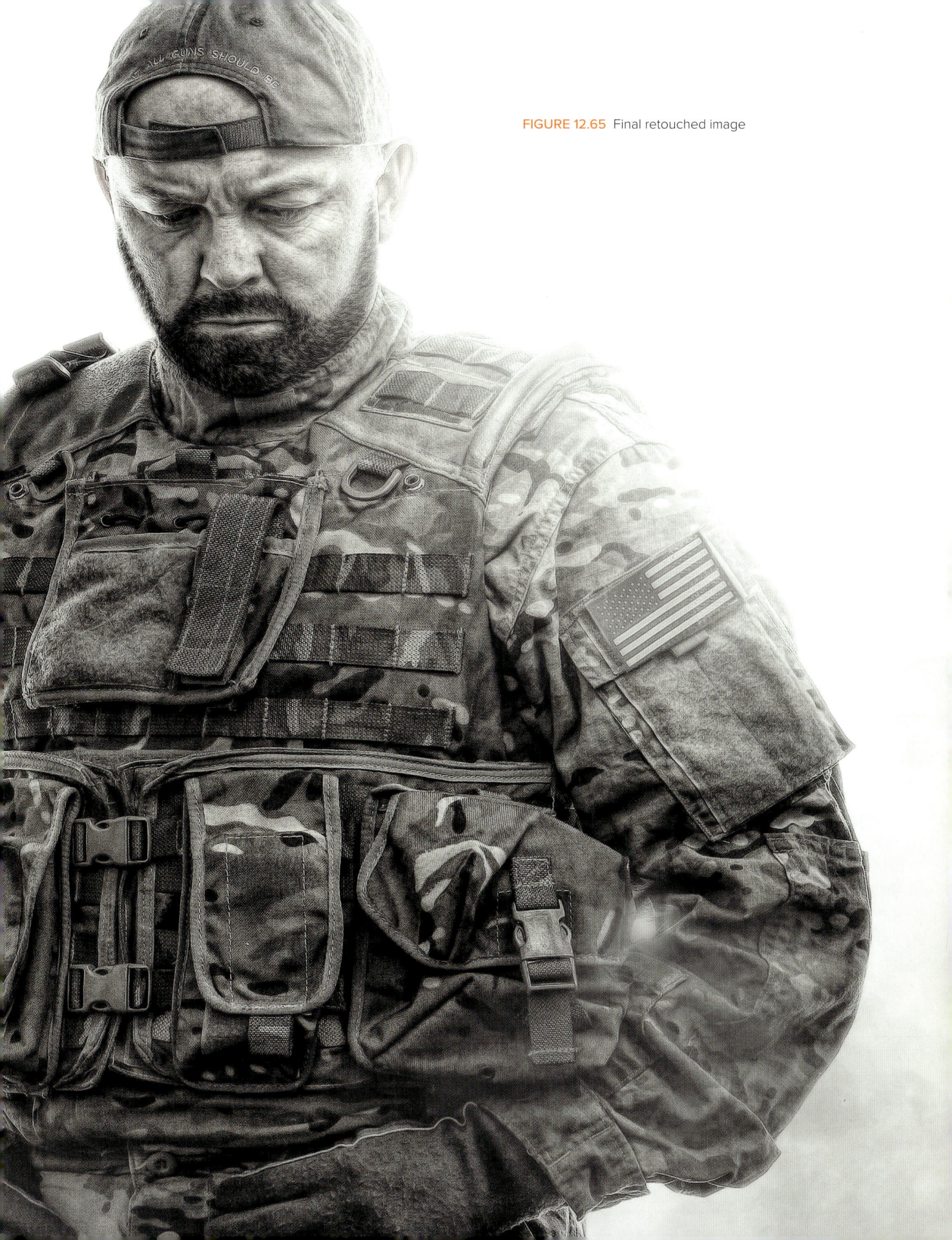

FIGURE 12.65 Final retouched image

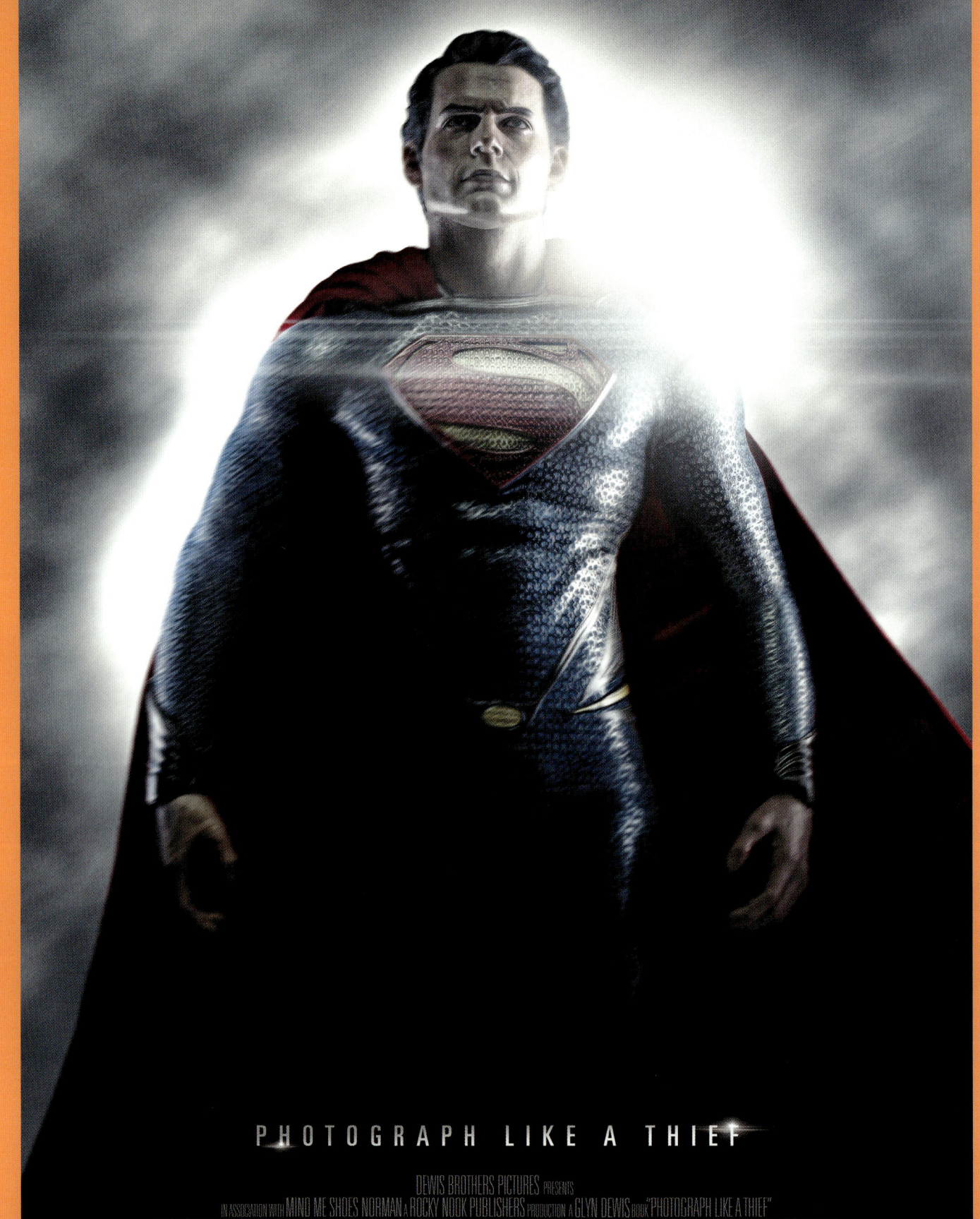

PHOTOGRAPH LIKE A THIEF

DEWIS BROTHERS PICTURES PRESENTS

IN ASSOCIATION WITH MIND ME SHOES NORMAN A ROCKY NOOK PUBLISHERS PRODUCTION A GLYN DEWIS BOOK "PHOTOGRAPH LIKE A THIEF"
MAC MCBRIDE SAM J WALKER STEVEN 'POCKET ROCKET' COOK MICHAEL GRAHAM ROGER GLEDHILL ARNOLD SCHWARZENEGGER (KIND OF) BARRY PAYNE
SUPERMAN DAVID LEE ELINCHROM PHOTTIX SEKONIC BENQ 3 LEGGED THING TETHERTOOLS WACOM ROGUE
DAVE CLAYTON SCOTT COWLIN TED WAITT JOCELYN HOWELL JESSICA TIERNAN

13 MOVIE POSTER INSPIRED II

I had so much fun working on this picture—getting in the zone with my headphones on, blasting out the movie soundtrack—that by the time I was finished I was pretty much convinced a man really could fly.

I was originally inspired to create this picture by a photographer friend of mine from Norway, Glenn Meling, who was creating some truly incredible images with model action figures, such as the Joker from Batman and, one of my favorites, Popeye.

The first action figure I purchased (I mean, invested in) was the Arnold Schwarzenegger *Terminator Genisys: Guardian* figure that's in chapter 9. Rather than create an action scene with that figure, I wanted to see if I could make a realistic portrait, and that was where I intended to stop. However, Glenn did warn me that one action figure inevitably leads to another, and well...

One day I happened to be browsing the Hot Toys action figure collection (again) and when I saw the Man of Steel, an overriding force came over me. Before I knew it, the mailman was at the door with another delivery. Glenn was right!

Seriously though, I had the most fun working on this picture, recreating a version of one of the original movie posters I'd spotted on impawards.com.

Trying to copy something like a movie poster is such a great way to push yourself and test your retouching skills. It forces you to be a problem solver and experiment with recreating effects. You'll inevitably discover things you never knew about Photoshop along the way.

REVERSE ENGINEERING

Trying to reverse engineer a movie poster can be quite confusing at times because inevitably, lighting has been manipulated and added in during post-production.

However, I think the highlights in the original movie poster are pretty much as they would have been during the photo shoot, despite the lens flares (**Figure 13.1**). Obviously, we're going to create a composite by adding in the sky and ground, but the main character is quite simple to break down.

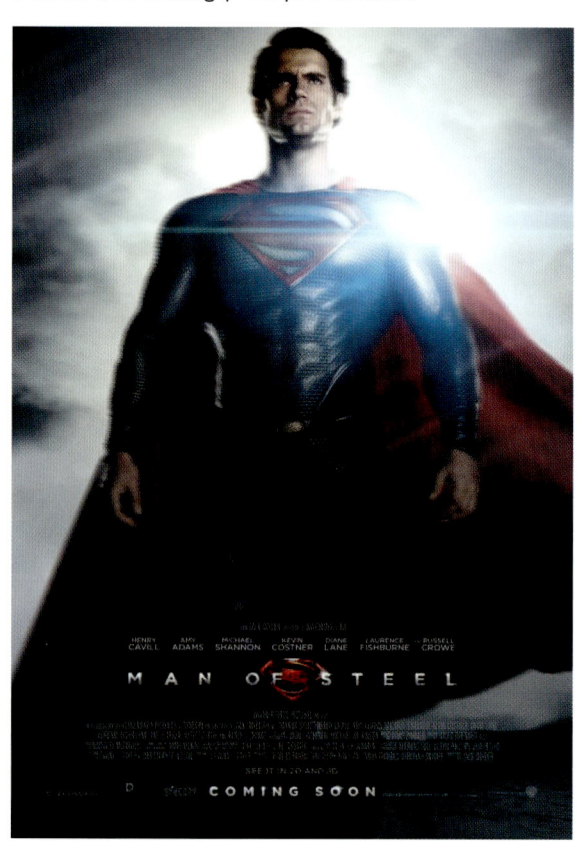

That being said, I'm not a hundred percent sure if the red cape was worn at the time of the shoot. I say this because of the highlight going down the right side of the character's body (camera left). This particular area looks as though it would be shielded from the light by the position of the cape, but there could have been a small gap for the light to get through.

We can tell that the lighting is hard because the highlights are very defined and they don't blend gradually into the shadows. There is a definite point where the highlights and shadows meet.

FIGURE 13.1

In terms of the lighting setup, this very well could have been shot with three lights. We can see that the character's right jawline is illuminated (**Figure 13.2**), and there's also a highlight on the back of his right hand and on the side of his torso.

The light for his jaw appears to be coming from the side and slightly behind him, and was likely positioned parallel to the ground. If the light had been angled down toward him, I don't think the highlight on his jaw would be quite as even along the back of his jawbone and toward his mouth. The light is also even all along the underside of his jaw and is not angled in any way.

The light on this side was probably something like a gridded reflector because the light is very direct and there is no spill on the top of his shoulder.

There also could have been a gridded light positioned directly to the right of the character (camera left), aimed at the side of his waist. This would explain the highlight, which separates his dark clothing from the shadow caused by the cape (**Figure 13.3**).

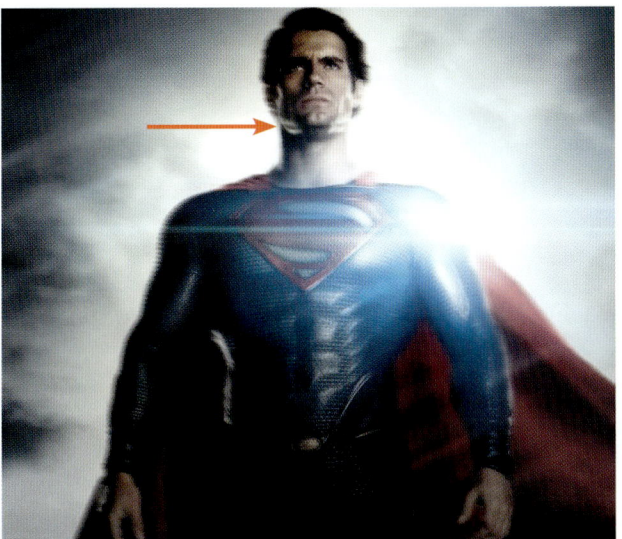

FIGURE 13.2

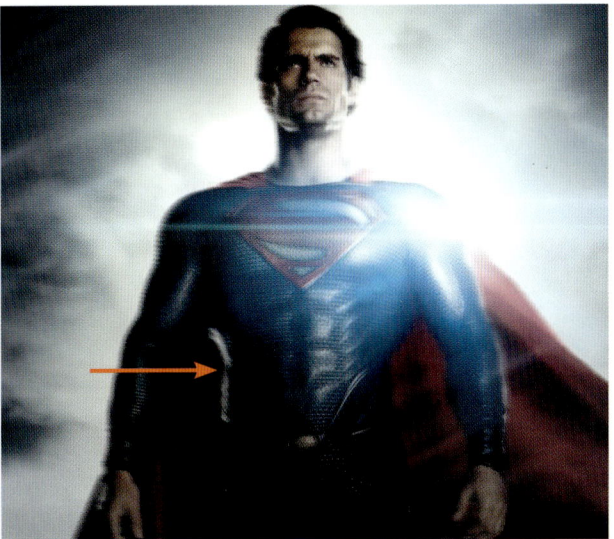

FIGURE 13.3

I would assume that the position of the light at camera right was very similar to the setups we've used in earlier chapters to create a cross-lighting effect—to the side and slightly in front of the character. The left side of his face is lit while the right side is in shadow, except for the triangular pattern of light under his right eye (**Figure 13.4**).

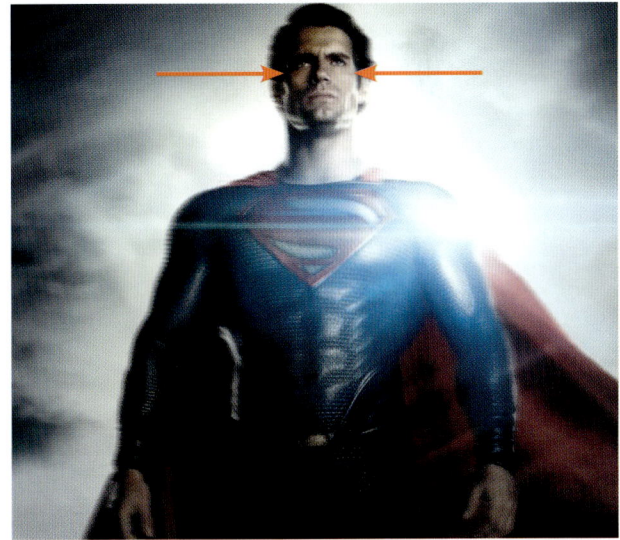

FIGURE 13.4

This light could have been something like a gridded beauty dish or even a softbox, such as the Elinchrom Rotalux 135cm Octa Softbox, with just one diffusion panel fitted so that the light wasn't soft. Based on the shape of the shadow under his eye and the angle of the shadow that goes across the front of his neck, we can assume that this light was angled down slightly. It could also be responsible for the highlights along the character's left arm (camera right), and the highlights on his chest and waist are clearly brighter on this side (**Figure 13.5**).

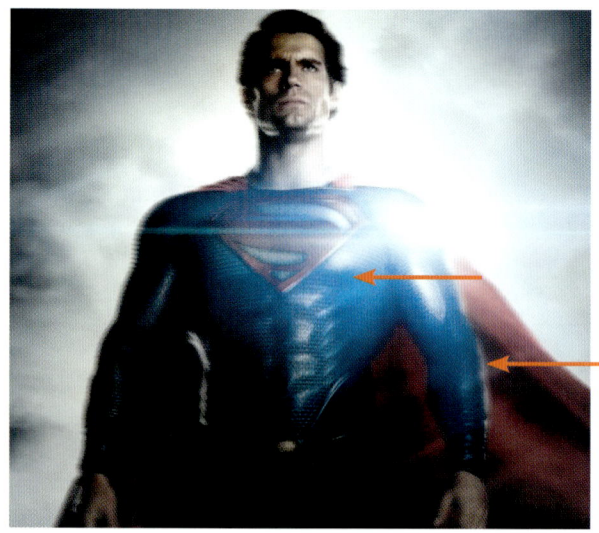

FIGURE 13.5

Figure 13.6 shows a diagram of what I think the three-light setup could have looked like.

However, if the highlights across his chest aren't from the one light positioned at camera right, it's possible that there was an additional light positioned at camera right horizontal to the ground, meaning the setup could have looked like the diagram in **Figure 13.7**.

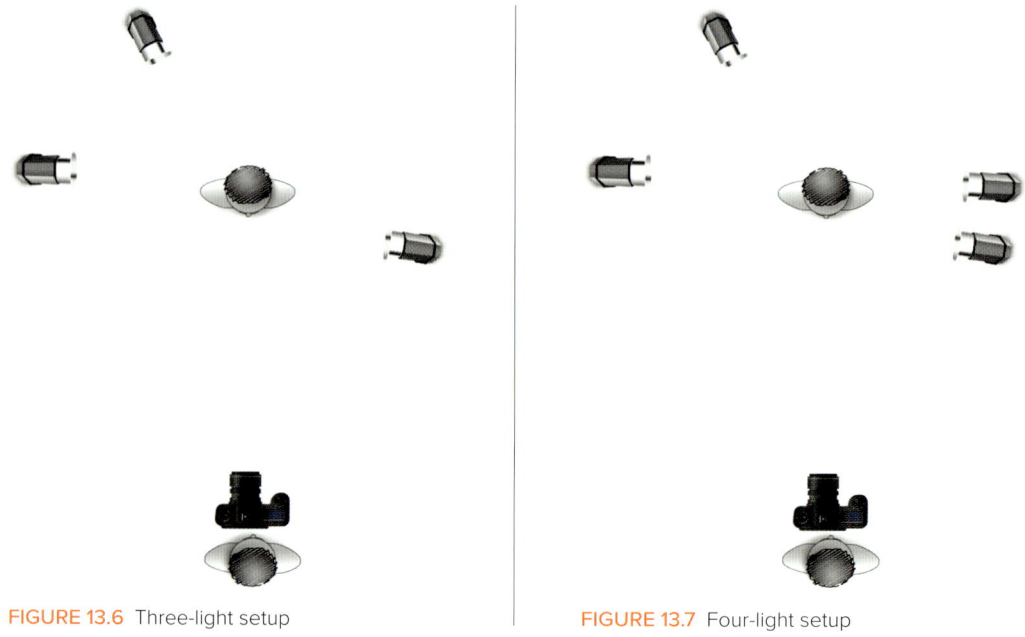

FIGURE 13.6 Three-light setup

FIGURE 13.7 Four-light setup

Of course, any time we reverse engineer a picture, the best we can do is suggest what could have been used. We don't know for certain what works until we try it ourselves. All we can see is the flat, two-dimensional scene, whereas if we were actually there at the time, we'd see all the gaps, distances, and so on.

THE SETUP

With all that being said, I went for a simplified version of the lighting. I used small flash (speedlight-type) units and instead of a three-light setup (or possibly four lights), I opted to use a two-light setup to create something of my own (**Figure 13.8**). I was also swayed by the fact that I was doing this on the desk in my office and space was limited.

The Rogue FlashBenders with the grids gave me a directional light that I could control. In **Figure 13.9** you can see that I used tape to hold the cape in position.

Because I was photographing a small object with an incredible amount of detail, I shot with a macro lens. My camera was mounted on a tripod and tethered to my MacBook Pro with a TetherTools cable. I also used a cable release to avoid causing any movement in the camera.

For the background, I attached gray paper to my monitor with some tape, making it easy to cut out the figure during post-production or, if need be, use a Blend Mode to add in a new background scene.

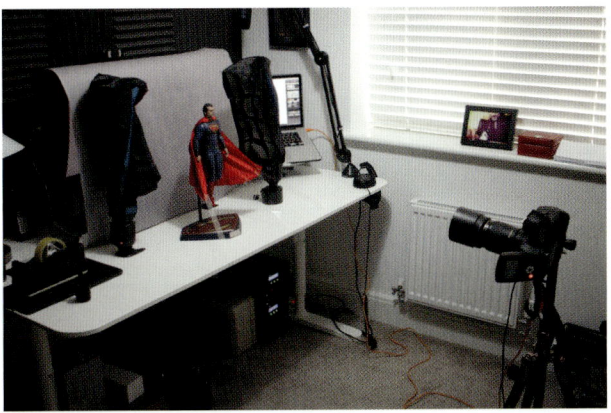

FIGURE 13.8

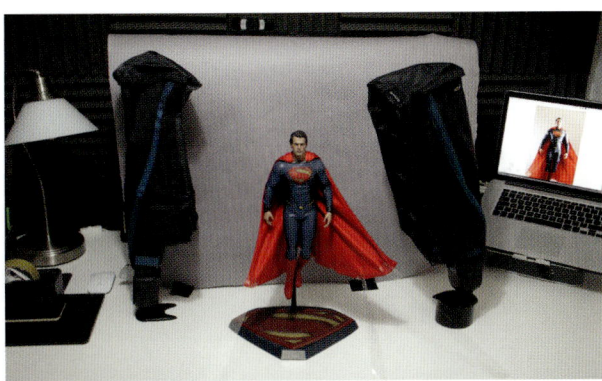

FIGURE 13.9

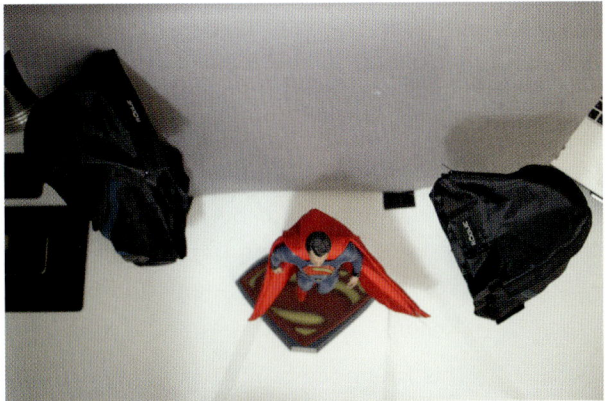

FIGURE 13.10

CAMERA SETTINGS

I chose an aperture of f/5.6 to give me plenty of depth of field to work with. I kept the ISO as low as possible at ISO 100 for the cleanest possible image.

I set my camera to Aperture Priority, which consistently resulted in a shutter speed of around 1/5 sec. This was just fine since the camera was mounted on a tripod and I was using a cable release.

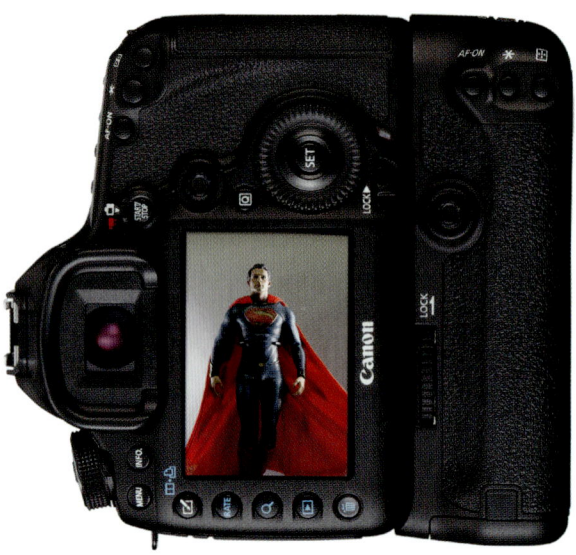

FIGURE 13.11

MODE Manual

ISO 100

APERTURE f/4.0

SHUTTER SPEED 1/100 sec.

LENS Canon 70–200mm f/2.8 L IS II USM

GEAR GUIDE

For this particular setup I used two Phottix Mitros + TTL Transceiver flashes (**Figure 13.12**) and two Rogue FlashBender 2 XL Pro modifiers (**Figure 13.13**).

POST-PROCESSING

What I really loved about working on this picture was the problem-solving it forced me to go through as I tried to recreate the look and feel of the original poster.

This isn't necessarily a picture I would use as part of my portfolio that I share with clients, but being forced to work out how to recreate an effect is a great exercise and a good way to learn more about Photoshop by simply experimenting. It's also a heck of a lot of fun, which is the number one reason I got involved in this industry in the first place.

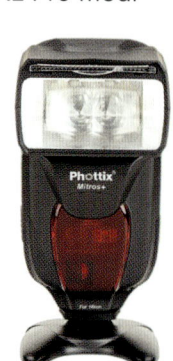
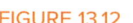
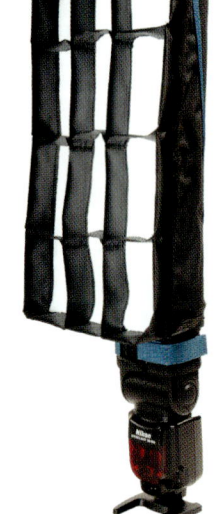

FIGURE 13.12　　　**FIGURE 13.13**

Photoshop is vast and something I'm constantly learning more about each and every time I use it. By stretching ourselves, we're keeping ourselves in the learning zone, and as a result, we're continually improving.

There's a lot to go through here, so let's get started.

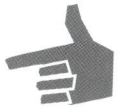

NOTE *Download all the files you need to follow along step-by-step at: http://www.rockynook.com/ photograph-like-a-thief-reference/*

1. We'll start off in Lightroom (or Camera RAW) and crop the out-of-camera image to improve the composition. Select the Crop Tool (**Figure 13.14**) and drag in the top and bottom corner handles to crop the image just below the top of the figure's boots and just above his head. Pull in the right and left sides until the figure is in the center of the frame (**Figure 13.15**). Press Return (Mac) or Enter (PC) to commit the crop.

2. In the Basics tab, increase the Shadows slider to around +77 and bring the Highlights slider down to around -89 (**Figure 13.16**).

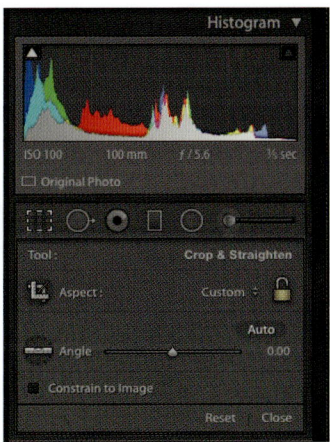

FIGURE 13.14

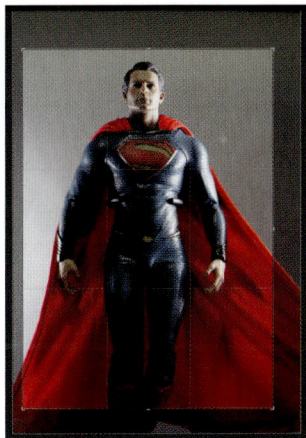

FIGURE 13.15

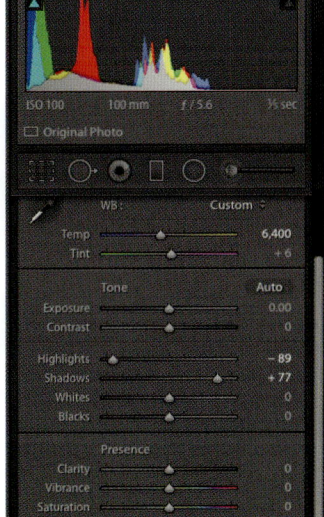

FIGURE 13.16

3. In the movie poster, Superman's outfit is quite dark, so we'll start to darken our action figure's cape and bodysuit. Click to open the HSL tab, and in the Luminance section, set Red to -100, Orange to -20, Aqua to -8, and Blue to -69 (**Figure 13.17**).

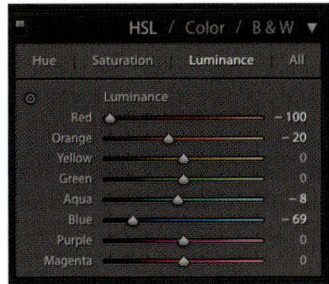

FIGURE 13.17

4. Go to the Detail section and under Sharpening, increase the Amount to 40 (**Figure 13.18**). Hold down the Option key (Mac) or Alt key (PC) and drag the Masking slider to the right until the sharpening (indicated by the white areas) is mainly visible on the figure (**Figure 13.19**). A setting of 76 is just about right.

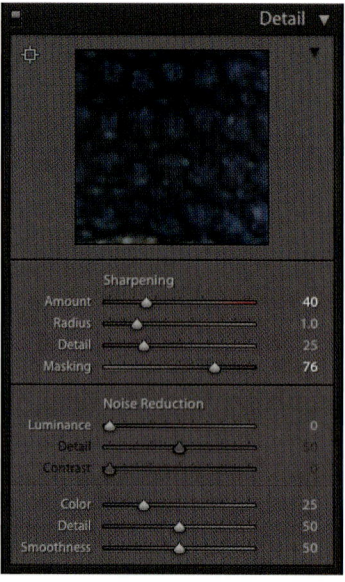

FIGURE 13.18

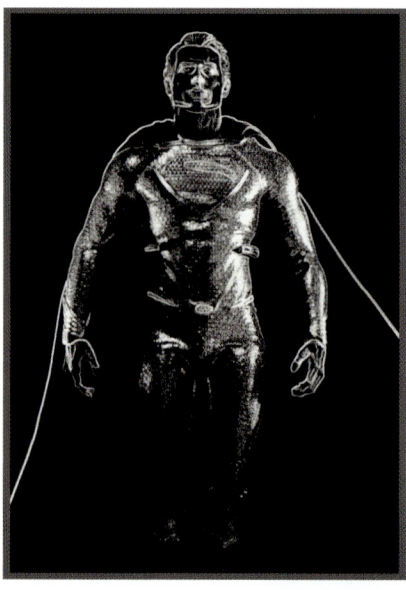

FIGURE 13.19

5. At this stage, the gray background seems to be holding a bit of color and we want this to be completely gray. Grab the Adjustment Brush (**Figure 13.20**) and double-click on the word Effect to reset all the adjustment sliders to their defaults of 0. Drag the Saturation slider to -100 and tick the Auto Mask checkbox (**Figure 13.21**).

Now paint around the gray background area to remove any color. You can use the left and right bracket keys on your keyboard to adjust the size of the Adjustment Brush.

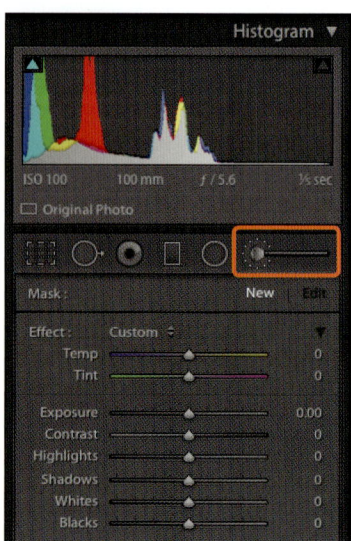

FIGURE 13.20

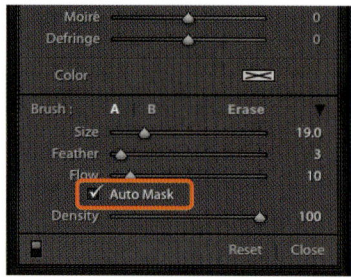

FIGURE 13.21

6. Choose the Spot Removal Tool (**Figure 13.22**) and set it to Heal. Then clean up the gray background by brushing over any marks (**Figure 13.23**). When you're done, click on the Spot Removal Tool icon to exit.

We're done in Lightroom for now, so we'll send the image over to Photoshop by going *Photo > Edit In > Adobe Photoshop…* (If you're using Camera RAW, click on Open Image.)

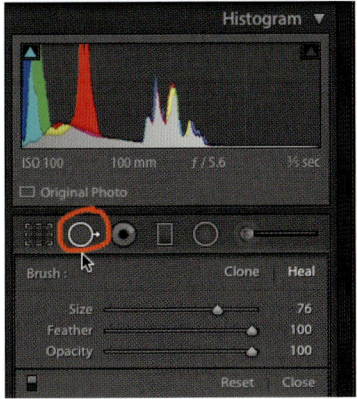

FIGURE 13.22

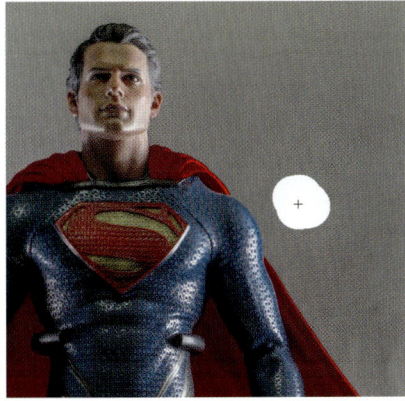

FIGURE 13.23

7. Now that we're in Photoshop, before we do anything else, we'll make a decent selection of our superhero so that we can use it later when we add in the new background and lighting effects, and for anything else we do.

Grab the Quick Selection Tool (**W**) and drag around the gray background area. Once you've selected the background area, go to *Select > Inverse* (**Figure 13.24**) so that the selection is now around our superhero (**Figure 13.25**).

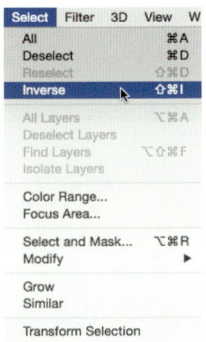

FIGURE 13.24

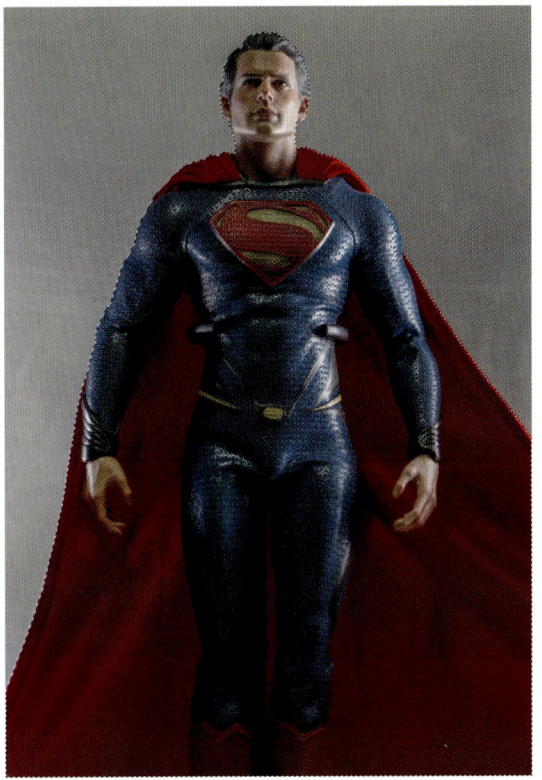

FIGURE 13.25

8. We'll use the Quick Mask Tool to check the selection, but first we need to ensure that it's set up in such a way that makes it easy to see what is selected and what is not. Double-click on the Quick Mask icon in the toolbar (**Figure 13.26**), and in the Quick Mask Options dialog, ensure that Selected Areas is checked (**Figure 13.27**). Then click OK.

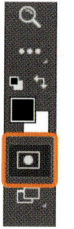

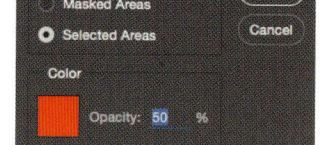

FIGURE 13.26   FIGURE 13.27

Press **Q** to enter Quick Mask mode, and you'll see the figure covered in a red overlay. This indicates what is currently selected. Zoom in and move around the image by holding down the space bar and clicking and dragging to see if there are any areas that need to be added to the selection (**Figure 13.28**). If you spot any of these areas, choose a black foreground color and round, soft-edged brush (about 30% hardness) and paint over the areas to add them to the selection (**Figure 13.29**).

When you're done, Press **Q** to edit Quick Mask mode.

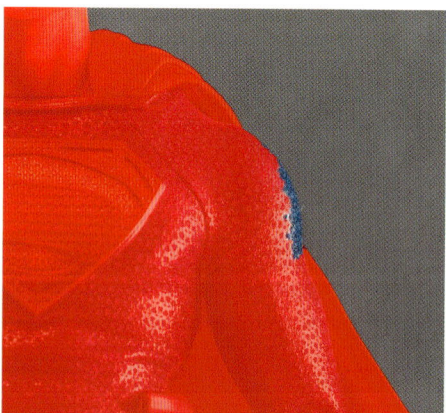

FIGURE 13.28 Before   FIGURE 13.29 After

9. Go to *Select > Modify > Feather* and add in a very small amount of feathering (0.5 pixels; **Figure 13.30**) so that the outline of the figure isn't razor-sharp and obvious when we add in the background. Click OK.

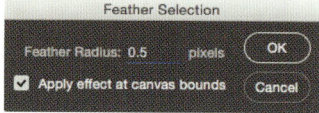

FIGURE 13.30

Now go to *Select > Save Selection* (**Figure 13.31**), name the selection "cut out" (**Figure 13.32**), and click OK. Then go to *Select > Deselect*, or simply hold press Command + D (Mac) or Ctrl + D (PC).

10. The side of the figure's chest seems to be protruding a bit more than normal, making it look like a toy (which it is, but that's not what we're going for here). To fix this, first create a duplicate of the Background layer by pressing Command + J (Mac) or Ctrl + J (PC) (**Figure 13.33**). Then go to *Filter > Liquify*, and use the Freeze Mask Tool (**Figure 13.34**) to brush over the upper area of the figure's left arm (**Figure 13.35**). This protects the area from the following adjustment. Select the Forward Warp Tool (**Figure 13.36**) and push the bit on the side of the figure's chest inward (**Figure 13.37**). Click OK to exit the Liquify Filter.

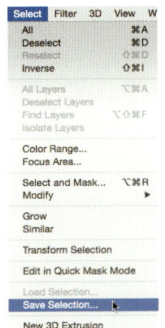

FIGURE 13.31

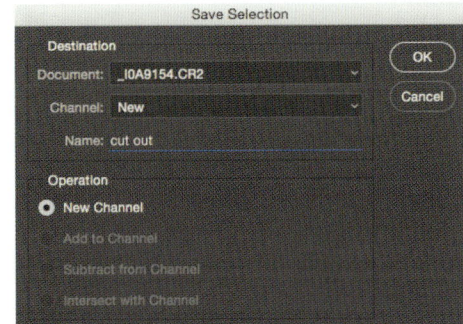

FIGURE 13.32

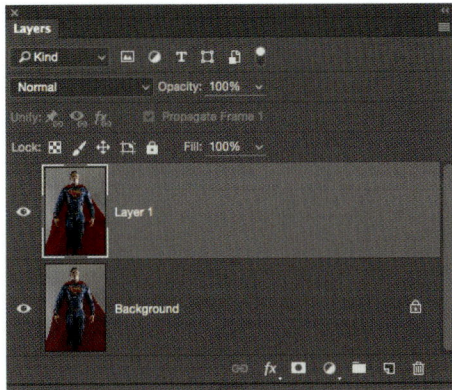

FIGURE 13.33

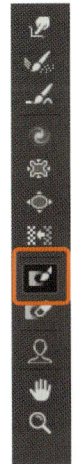
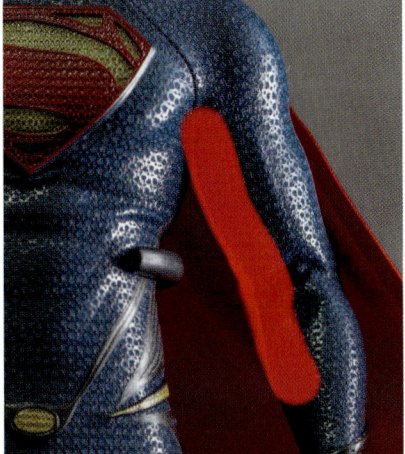

FIGURE 13.34   FIGURE 13.35

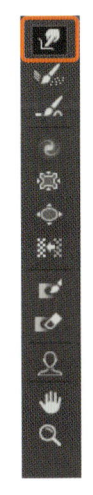
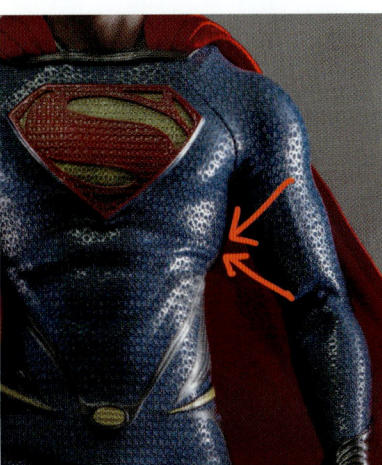

FIGURE 13.36   FIGURE 13.37

11. Now select the Clone Stamp Tool (**S**) (**Figure 13.38**), and then hold down the Option key (Mac) or Alt key (PC) and click to sample areas of the figure's body with which to cover the plastic support arms holding him in position (**Figure 13.39**). Release the Option or Alt key and brush over the plastic support arms to cover them with information from the sampled areas. Click and sample areas of the cape nearby as well, following the line of the body up and down.

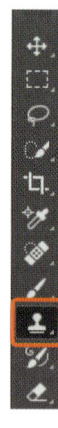

FIGURE 13.38

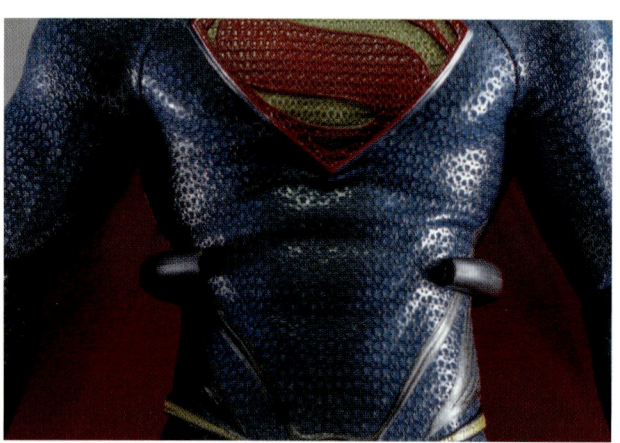

FIGURE 13.39 Before

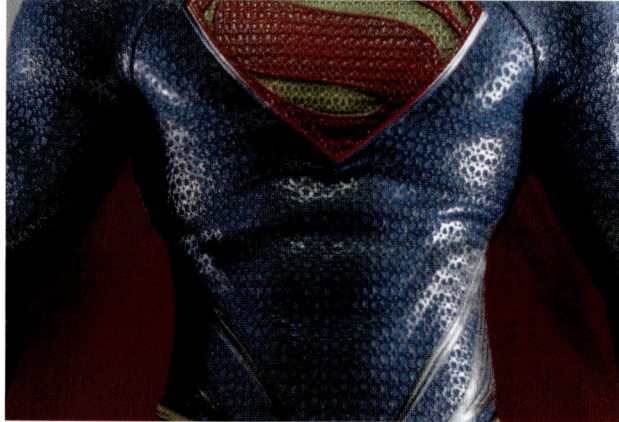

FIGURE 13.40 After

12. Flatten the layers by pressing Command + E (Mac) or Ctrl + E (PC). Add a new blank layer to the top of the layer stack, press **D** to set the foreground and background colors to their defaults of black and white, and then go to *Filter > Render > Clouds* (**Figure 13.41**).

Choose the Rectangular Marquee Tool (**Figure 13.42**) and draw out a small marquee selection in the middle of the layer (**Figure 13.43**). Press Command + J (Mac) or Ctrl + J (PC) to copy this selected area onto its own layer. Rename this layer "clouds" and delete the layer that we originally applied the Clouds filter to (**Figure 13.44**).

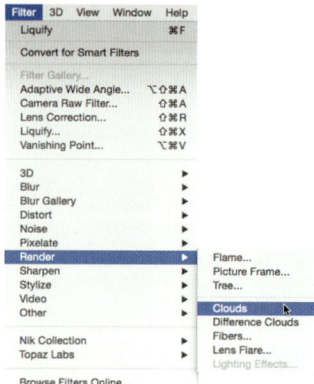

FIGURE 13.41

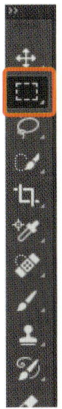
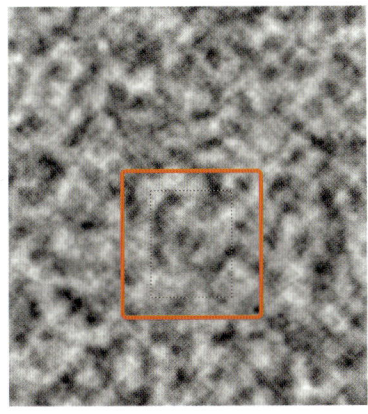
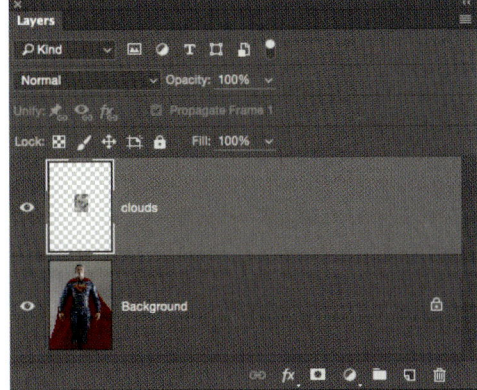

FIGURE 13.42   FIGURE 13.43   FIGURE 13.44

13. Click on the clouds layer, and then go to *Filter > Free Transform* (**Figure 13.45**). While holding down Shift + Option (Mac) or Shift + Alt (PC), click and drag outward to enlarge the clouds layer beyond the boundaries of the image (**Figure 13.46**). Then press Return (Mac) or Enter (PC).

14. Next we're going to use a Blur Filter, but first, go to *Filter > Convert for Smart Filters* (**Figure 13.47**) to turn the clouds layer into a Smart Object. This will allow us to quickly make changes to the blur amount later on if we need to.

    Go to *Filter > Blur > Motion Blur*, and in the Motion Blur properties, set the Angle to 30° and the Distance to 65 Pixels (**Figure 13.48**). Click OK.

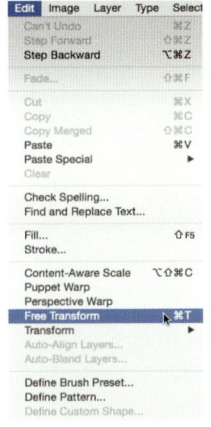
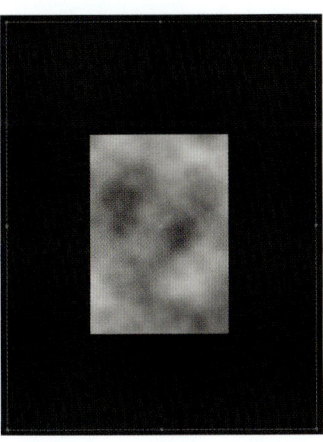
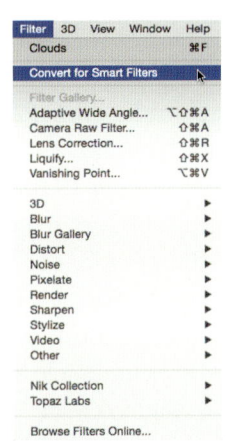
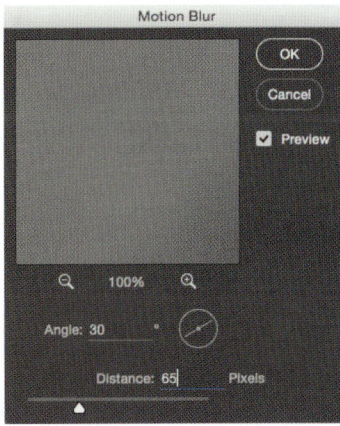

FIGURE 13.45   FIGURE 13.46   FIGURE 13.47   FIGURE 13.48

15. Now we'll place the clouds behind our figure. Go to *Select > Load Selection* (**Figure 13.49**), choose cut out from the Channel menu (**Figure 13.50**), and click OK. This adds the selection we saved in step 9 to the clouds layer. Hold down the Option key (Mac) or Alt key (PC) and click to add a Layer Mask (**Figure 13.51**).

NOTE *When you hold down the Option key (Mac) or Alt key (PC) and click to add a Layer Mask, the selected area will automatically be filled with black.*

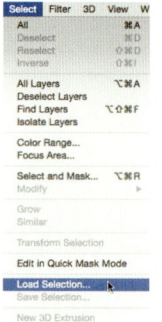

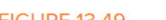

FIGURE 13.49

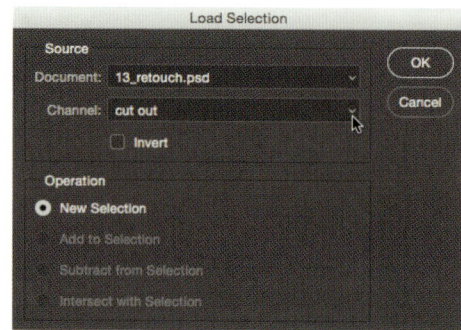

FIGURE 13.50

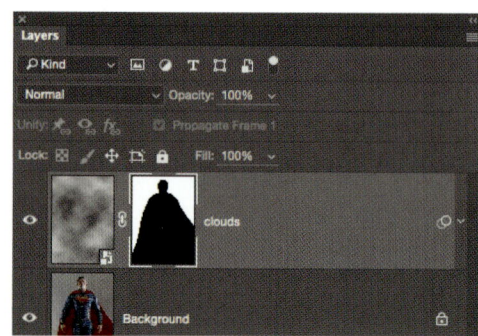

FIGURE 13.51

16. Before we go any further, there's a few areas I've noticed that I want to tidy up, namely the seams that join the suit together around the figure's chest (**Figure 13.52**) and on his legs. Also, I can see the black plastic support pole between the figure's legs.

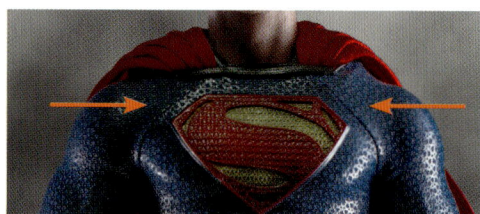

FIGURE 13.52

To clean up these areas, click on the Background layer and add a new blank layer above it (**Figure 13.53**). Select the Clone Stamp Tool, and in the options at the top of the screen, set the Sample menu to Current & Below (**Figure 13.54**). Hold down the Option key (Mac) or Alt key (PC) and click to sample areas around the parts we want to cover. Then release the Option or Alt key and brush over the problem areas to cover them with the sampled areas. Rename this layer "Clean Up."

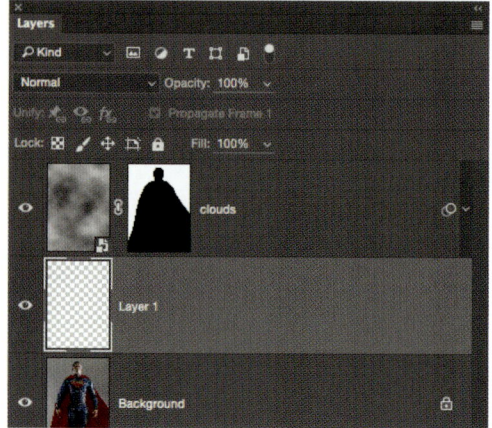

FIGURE 13.53

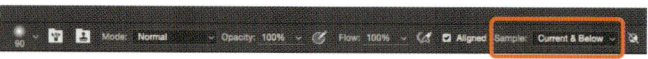

FIGURE 13.54

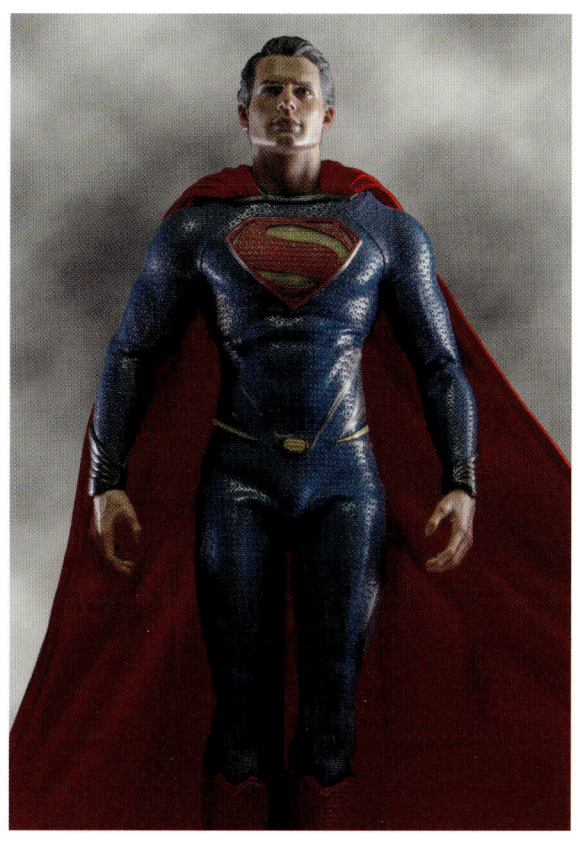

FIGURE 13.55 Before

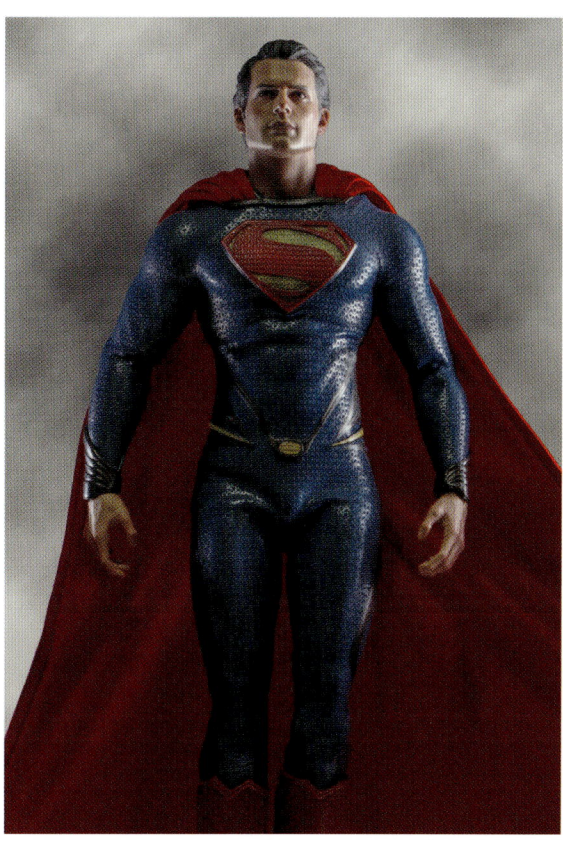

FIGURE 13.56 After

17. Add a new layer to the top of the layer stack and rename it "Bright" (**Figure 13.57**). Choose a round, soft-edged brush with a white foreground color and add a few brush-strokes around the top part of the figure by his shoulders and head (**Figure 13.58**).

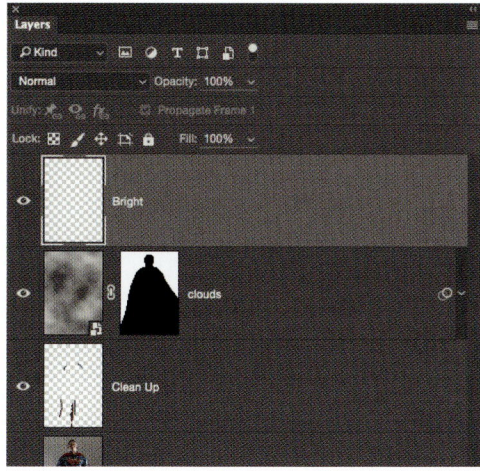

FIGURE 13.57

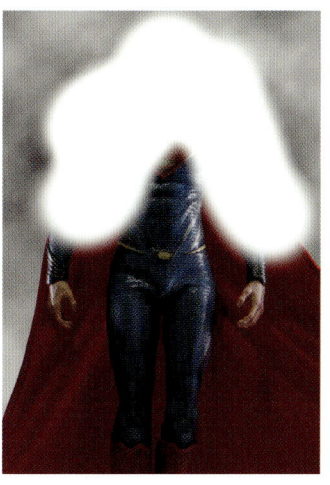

FIGURE 13.58

Go to *Layer > Create Clipping Mask* (**Figure 13.59**) so that the brushstrokes do not appear on top of our figure and are hidden behind the black areas of the mask below. Then go to *Filter > Gaussian Blur*, add in a Radius of 140 Pixels (**Figure 13.60**), and click OK.

Change the Blend Mode of the Bright layer to Overlay (**Figure 13.61**).

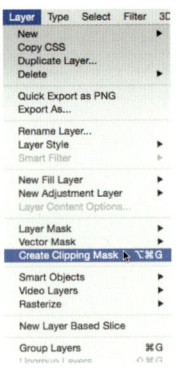
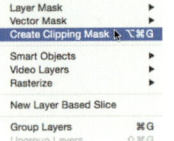

FIGURE 13.59

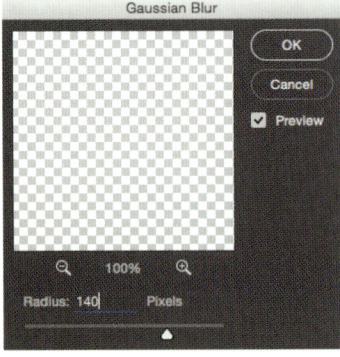

FIGURE 13.60

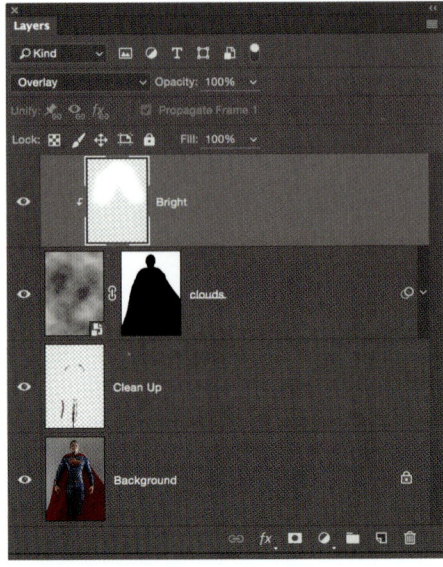

FIGURE 13.61

18. Add a blank layer to the top of the layer stack and create another clipping mask by going to *Layer > Create Clipping Mask*. With the same white brush, paint a few more brushstrokes over the areas you want to brighten further. In my case, I needed more on the right side of the picture. Go to *Blur > Gaussian Blur*, dial in a Radius of around 140 Pixels, and click OK. Rename this layer Bright 2 and change the Blend Mode to Overlay (**Figure 13.62**).

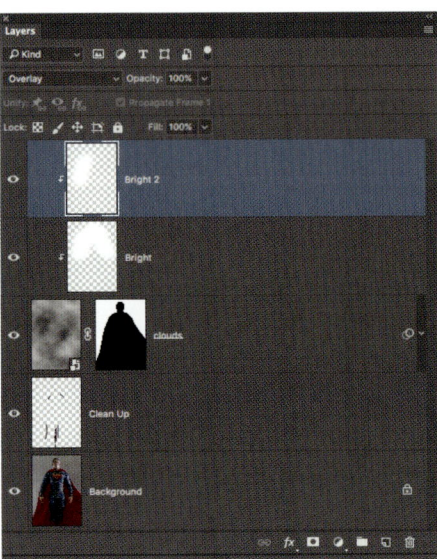

FIGURE 13.62

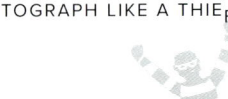

19. Add a merged layer to the top of the layer stack by going to *Select > All*, then *Edit > Copy Merged*, and then *Edit > Paste* (**Figure 13.63**).

Now we'll add some contrast. I'm going to use the Topaz Clarity plugin for this, but you can use whatever method you prefer (see chapter 4 for other suggestions). Go to *Filter > Topaz Labs > Topaz Clarity*, and in the settings on the right side of the window, increase Micro Contrast to 0.30, Low Contrast to 0.14, and Medium Contrast to 0.03 (**Figure 13.64**). Click OK, and then rename this layer "Topaz Clarity."

20. Duplicate the Topaz Clarity layer by pressing Command + J (Mac) or Ctrl + J (PC), and then rename the new layer "Camera RAW." Go to *Filter > Convert for Smart Filters*, followed by *Filter > Camera RAW filter*.

Choose the Adjustment Brush (**Figure 13.65**), and in the Adjustment Brush settings, reduce the Temperature to -8 and the Tint to -2 (**Figure 13.66**). Brush over the figure's face and hands to improve the skin tone.

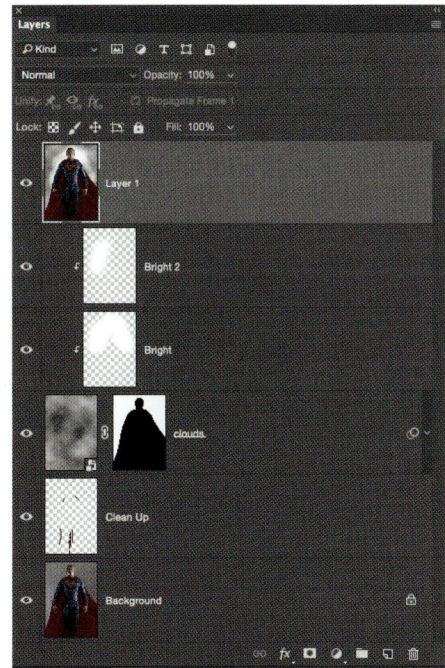

FIGURE 13.63

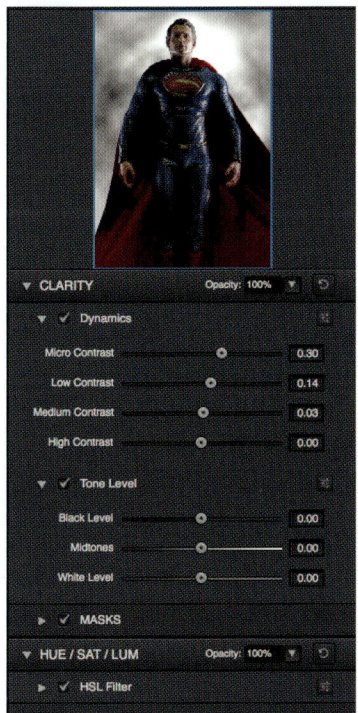

FIGURE 13.64

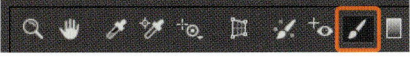

FIGURE 13.65

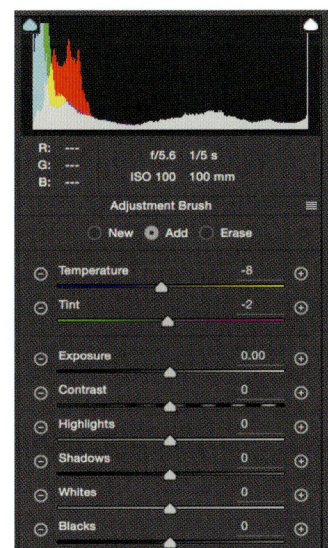

FIGURE 13.66

21. Click New to add another Adjustment Brush (**Figure 13.67**), and then reset all the sliders to their defaults of zero by double-clicking on each marker. Increase the Exposure to +0.60 and brush over the left side of the figure's face to brighten it further.

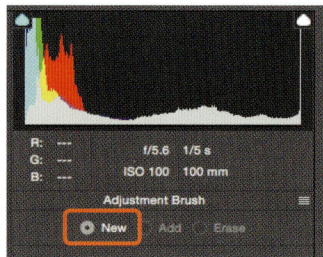

FIGURE 13.67

22. Click New to add another Adjustment Brush and reset all the sliders to zero. Increase the Clarity slider to +27 (**Figure 13.68**) and brush over the top half of the figure's body, including his arms, chest, and the areas with obvious highlights.

23. Choose the Graduated Filter (**Figure 13.69**) and reset all the adjustment sliders. Decrease the Exposure to -2.60 and drag out a gradient from around the bottom right of the image upward and across to the left, stopping just under the figure's chest (**Figure 13.70**).

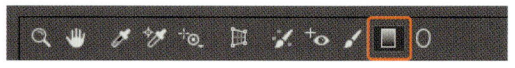

FIGURE 13.69

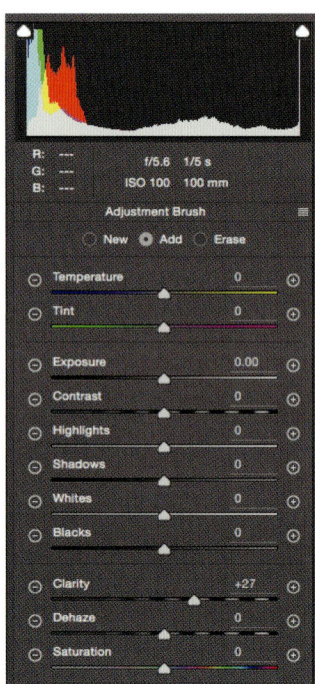

FIGURE 13.68

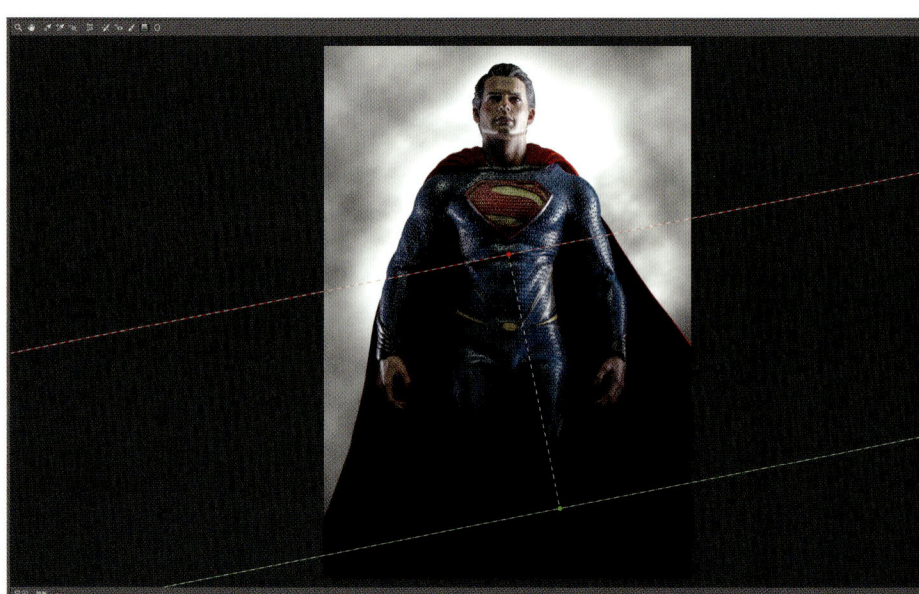

FIGURE 13.70

24. Grab the Adjustment Brush and reduce the Exposure to -2.15. Brush around the left side of the figure and over the legs a little more to darken this area further.

Click to add a New Adjustment Brush and reset all the sliders to zero. Decrease the Exposure to -0.60 and increase Clarity to +46, and then brush over the clouds around the figure to give them more impact. Click OK.

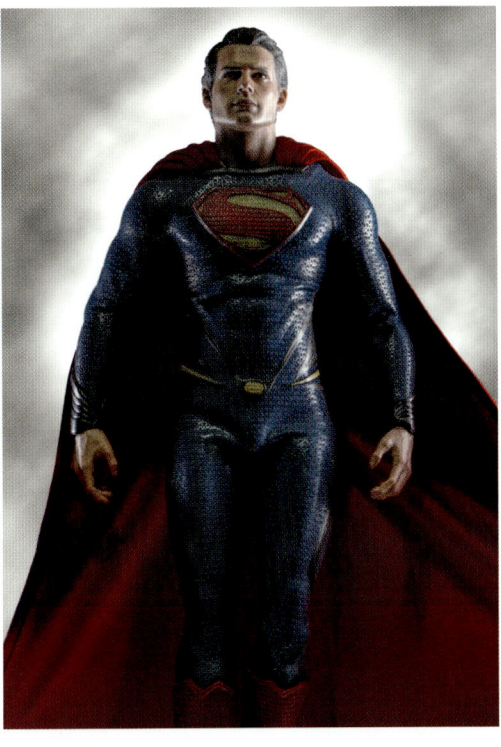

FIGURE 13.71 Before Camera RAW adjustments

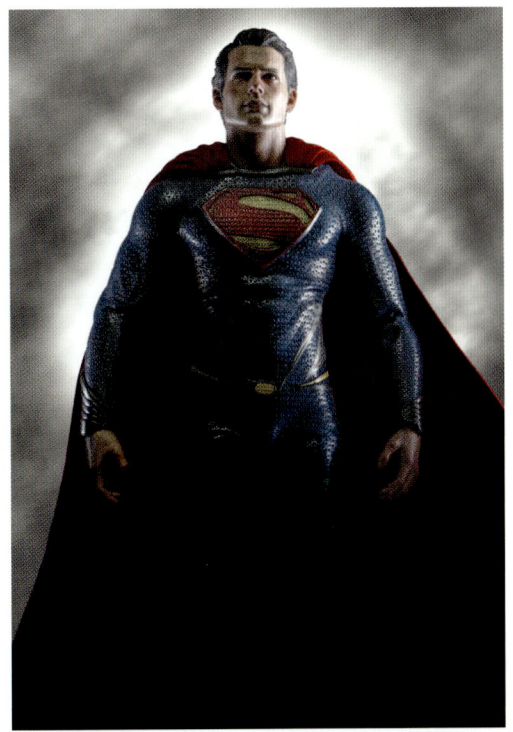

FIGURE 13.72 After Camera RAW adjustments

25. Go to *Filter > Liquify* and zoom in on the face. These Hot Toys action figures are incredible and the detail blows me away, but I think the face on this one needs some work to harden it up a little. The lips look a little too pronounced, so use the Freeze Mask Tool (**Figure 13.73**) to brush across the middle of the lips to protect that area (**Figure 13.74**), and then use the Forward Warp Tool to push down the middle of the upper lip (**Figure 13.75**).

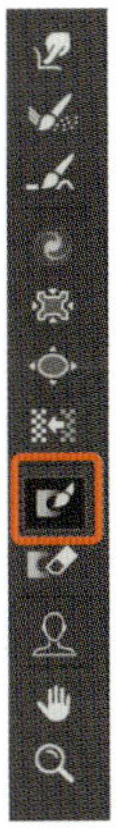

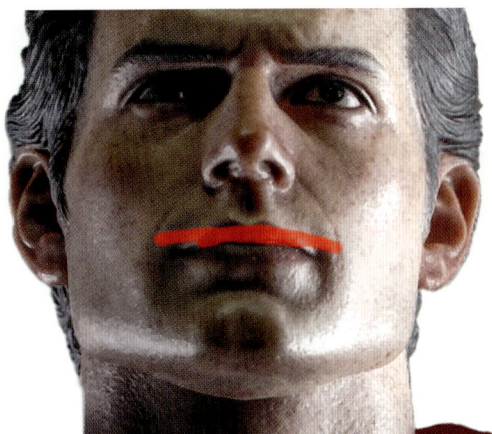

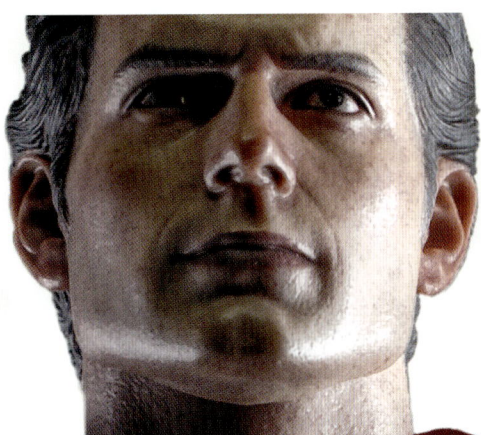

FIGURE 13.73

FIGURE 13.74

FIGURE 13.75 The upper lip has been pushed down to make it a little less pronounced

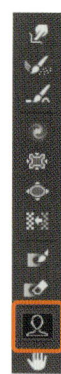

Grab the Face Tool (**Figure 13.76**) and drag the Smile slider to -100 (**Figure 13.77**). Click OK.

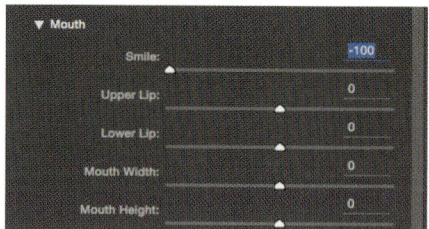

FIGURE 13.76   FIGURE 13.77

26. Navigate to the eyes.jpg file that you downloaded from the book's webpage (http://www.rockynook.com/photograph-like-a-thief-reference/) and open it in Photoshop. Use the Lasso Tool to drag out a selection of the eye on the left (**Figure 13.78**). Go to *Edit > Copy*, and then click on the tab to go back to our action figure and select *Edit > Paste*. Rename this layer "eye-left."

Use the Move Tool (**V**) to position the eye, and then go *Edit > Free Transform*. Hold down Shift + Option (Mac) or Shift + Alt (PC) and drag inward to resize the eye so it fits in place (**Figure 13.79**).

 TIP *When positioning and resizing the eye, lower the opacity of the eye layer so you can match it perfectly with the layer beneath.*

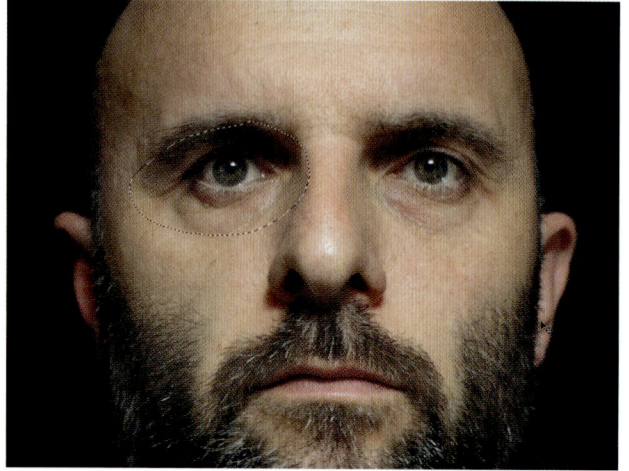

FIGURE 13.78

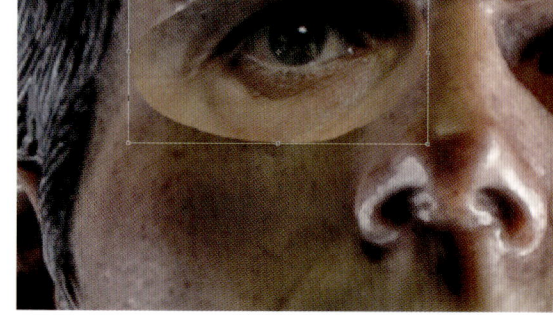

FIGURE 13.79

27. Add a Layer Mask to the eye-left layer and use a round, soft-edged brush with a black foreground color to blend the eye in place (**Figure 13.80**).

Repeat steps 26 and 27 for the other eye and rename the layer "eye-right."

28. Select the eye-left layer and add a Levels adjustment layer. Click on the Clipping Mask icon so the adjustment only affects the layer directly below, and then darken the eye by dragging the white Output Levels marker inward to 130 (**Figure 13.81**).

Repeat this process for the eye-right layer, but this time drag the white Output Levels marker to around 160.

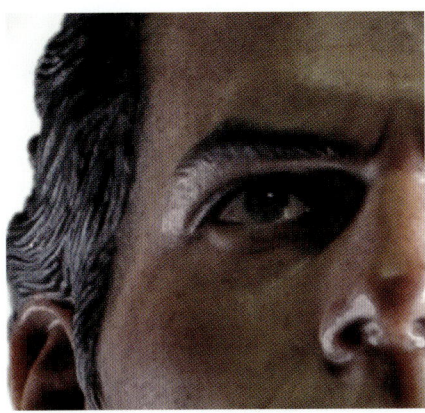

FIGURE 13.80

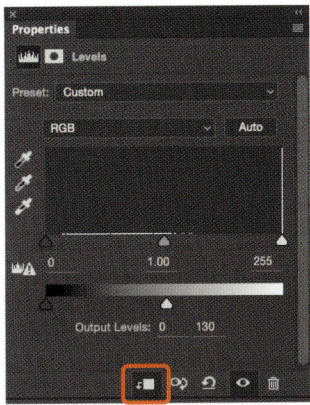

FIGURE 13.81

Now let's group the eye layers together to keep things organized. With the eye-right Levels adjustment layer still active, hold down the Shift key and click on the eye-left layer so that both eye layers and their Levels adjustment layers are highlighted in the Layers panel. Then go to *Layer > New > Group from Layers*, rename the group "eyes," and click OK.

29. Go to *Layer > New*, and in the properties, rename the layer dodge & burn, choose Overlay from the Mode menu, and tick the Fill with Overlay-neutral color (50% gray) checkbox (**Figure 13.82**). Click OK.

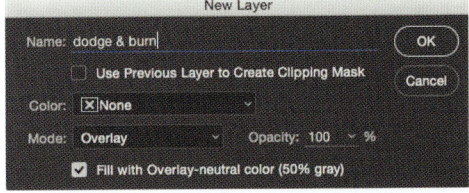

FIGURE 13.82

Grab the Dodge Tool and use it to enhance the highlights in the image. Then use the Burn Tool to enhance the shadow areas (body and face) and darken the figure's hair. Remember, you can toggle from the Dodge Tool to the Burn Tool by simply holding down the Option key (Mac) or Alt key (PC). This allows you to maintain the same settings for both tools. I cover dodging and burning in more detail in chapter 4 (page 66).

You can see where I applied dodging and burning in **Figure 13.83**.

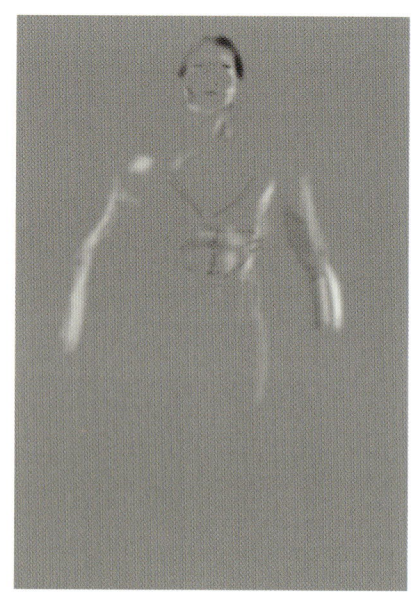

FIGURE 13.83

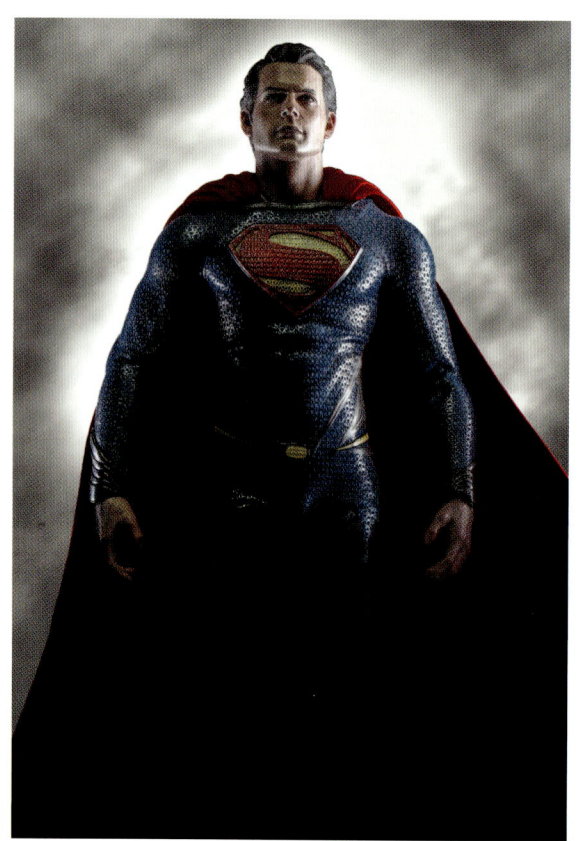

FIGURE 13.84 Before dodging and burning

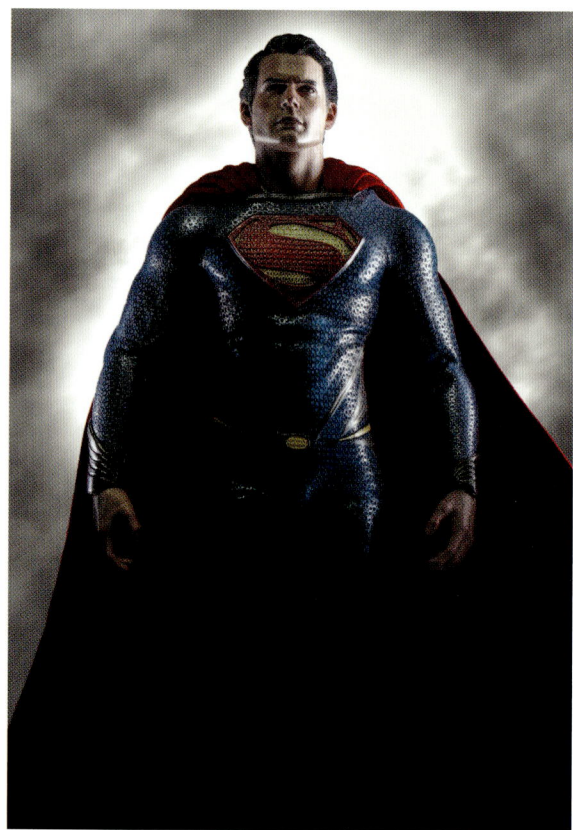

FIGURE 13.85 After dodging and burning

30. Add a new blank layer to the top of the layer stack and rename it "Clean Up." Select the Clone Stamp Tool, and in the options bar at the top of the screen, set Mode to Current & Below. Then clone out the bright area just below the figure's waistline (**Figure 13.86**).

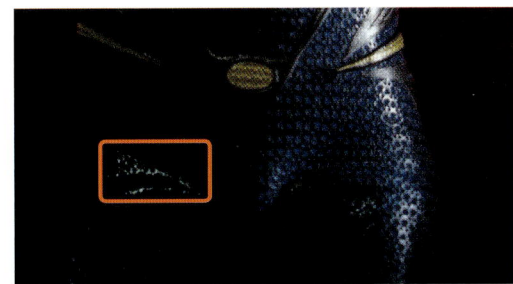

FIGURE 13.86

31. Add a merged layer to the top of the layer stack and rename it "width." Go to Free Transform by pressing Command + T (Mac) or Ctrl + T (PC), and in the options bar at the top of the screen, increase the width (W) to 103% (**Figure 13.87**), then press Return (Mac) or Enter (PC). This widens our figure slightly, giving it some additional power. This is something I do on most male pictures.

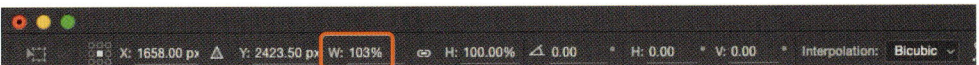

FIGURE 13.87

32. Add a new blank layer to the top of the layer stack and rename it "Light." Grab a round, soft-edged brush with a brush size of around 9 pixels and select a white foreground color. Then press once to apply a brushstroke to the right side of the figure's neck (**Figure 13.88**).

33. Add a merged layer to the top of the layer stack, rename it "Motion Blur," and then go to *Filter > Convert for Smart Filters* (**Figure 13.89**).

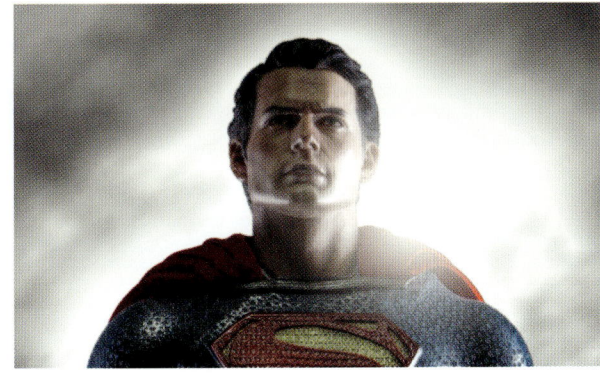

FIGURE 13.88

Now go to *Filter > Blur > Motion Blur*, add in an Angle of 30° and a Distance of 20 Pixels (**Figure 13.90**), and click OK.

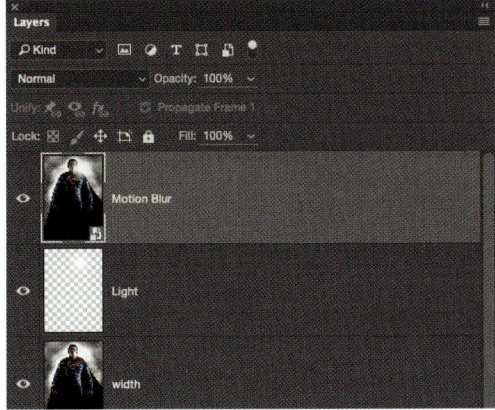

FIGURE 13.89

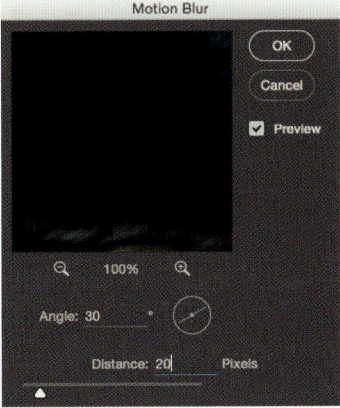

FIGURE 13.90

With a black foreground color and a round, soft-edged brush at 100% opacity, paint onto the Layer Mask attached to the Smart Object (**Figure 13.91**) to remove the blur from the figure's face and the logo on his chest. Then reduce the Opacity of the brush to around 60% and paint around the arm on the right to reduce the blur there as well, but not remove it completely (**Figure 13.92**).

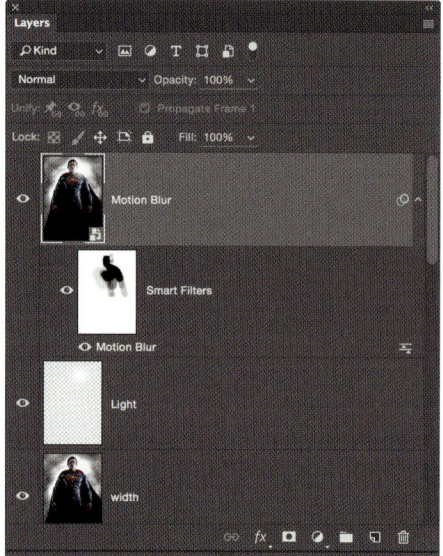

FIGURE 13.91

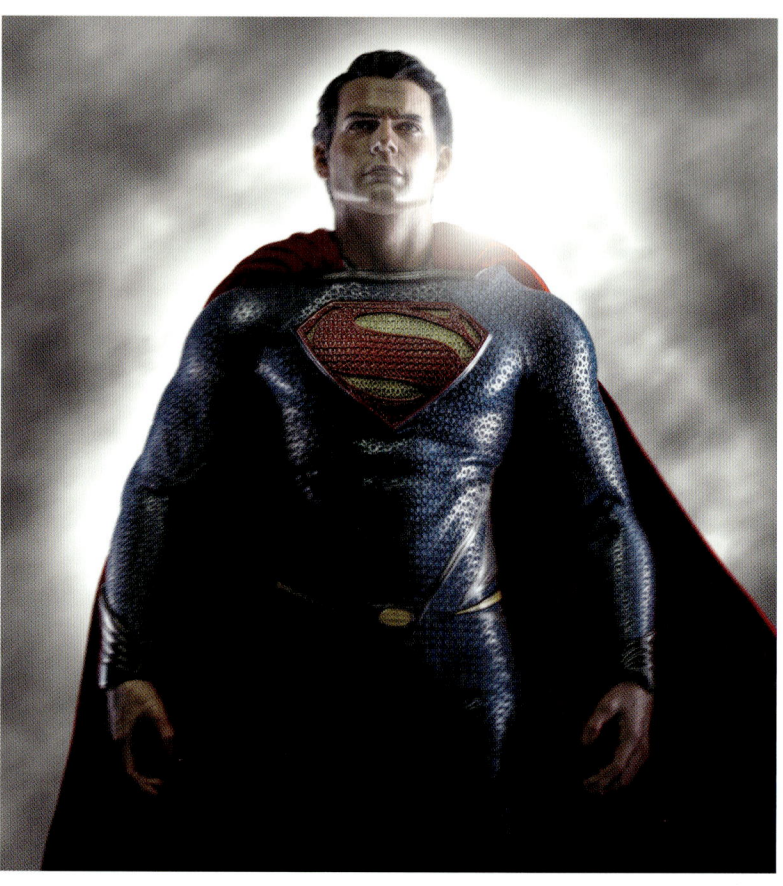

FIGURE 13.92 Motion Blur added

34. Now we'll add what I call a cartoon or painterly look to the picture. I don't know if that's the right name to give this technique, but I couldn't think of anything else. You'll see that it adds a very specific look to the image, and I use this a lot give the skin an almost waxy feel.

Add a merged layer to the top of the layer stack and rename it "Look." Duplicate this layer by pressing Command + J (Mac) or Ctrl + J (PC), and rename the copy "Sharpness."

Turn off the visibility of the Sharpness layer by clicking on its eye icon, and then click on the Look layer (**Figure 13.93**). Go to *Filter > Noise > Reduce Noise*, dial in a Strength of 10, and leave all the other sliders set to zero (**Figure 13.94**). Click OK.

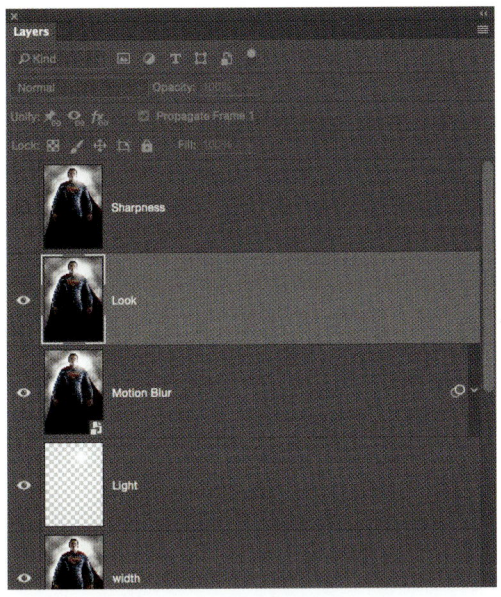

FIGURE 13.93

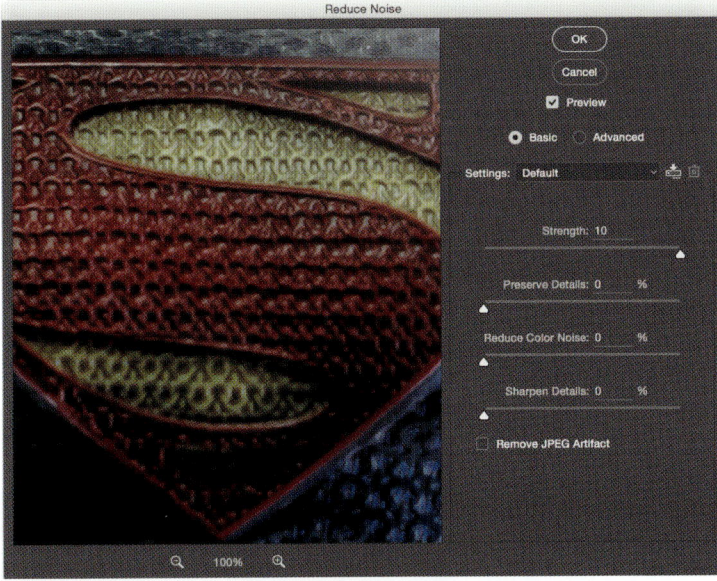

FIGURE 13.94

Click on the Sharpness layer and turn on its visibility. Go to *Filter > Other > High Pass*, dial in a Radius of 1 Pixel, and click OK (**Figure 13.95**). Change the Blend Mode of the Sharpness layer to Hard Light (**Figure 13.96**). This High Pass layer brings back sharpness in the main areas of the picture.

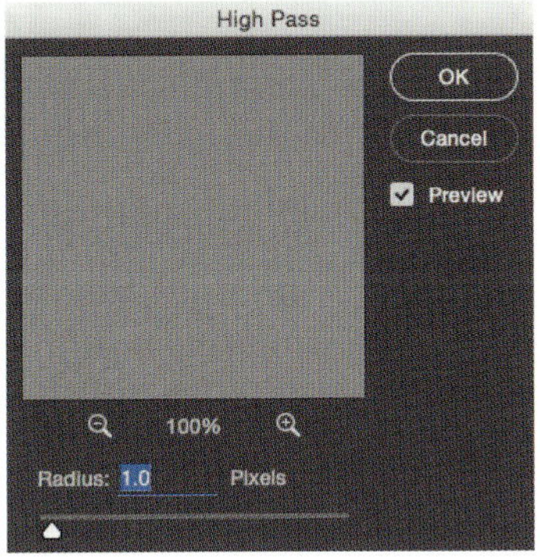

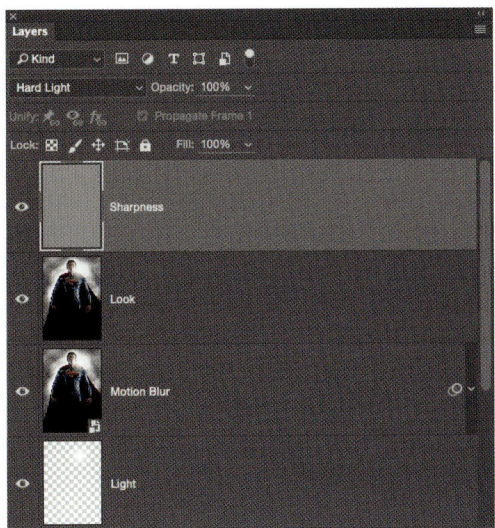

FIGURE 13.96

FIGURE 13.95

35. I always add in some contrast after applying this effect, so add another merged layer to the top of the layer stack and rename it "Contrast – USM" for Unsharp Mask. Then go to *Filter > Sharpen > Unsharp Mask* and dial in an Amount of 20% and a Radius of 20 Pixels (**Figure 13.97**). Click OK.

36. Next we'll add in some lens flare. As you'd expect, there are lots of ways to do this. You could, of course, make a lens flare in Photoshop, but I turned to Adobe Stock for the one I used in this picture.

Once the image is downloaded into Photoshop (**Figure 13.98**), hold down Shift + Command (Mac) or Shift + Ctrl (PC) and press U to desaturate it (**Figure 13.99**).

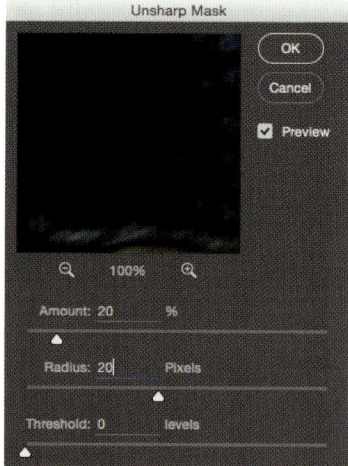

FIGURE 13.97

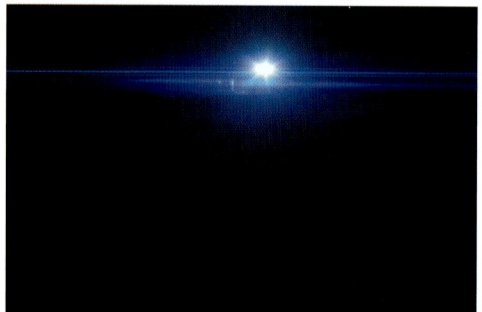

FIGURE 13.98

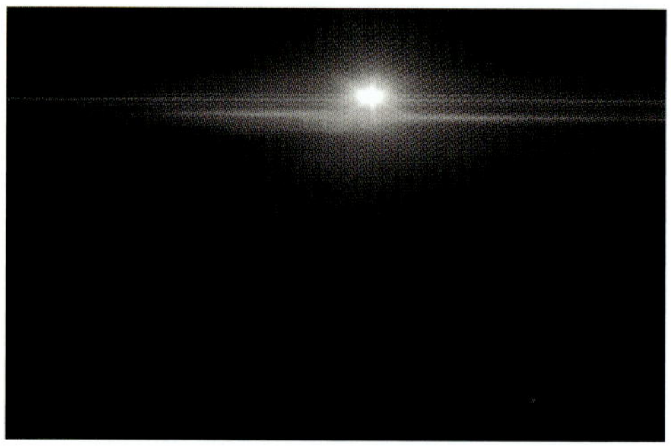

FIGURE 13.99

Then open the Levels adjustment by pressing Command + L (Mac) or Ctrl + L (PC), select the Black Sample Point (**Figure 13.100**), and click on the image just underneath the flare (**Figure 13.101**). Click OK.

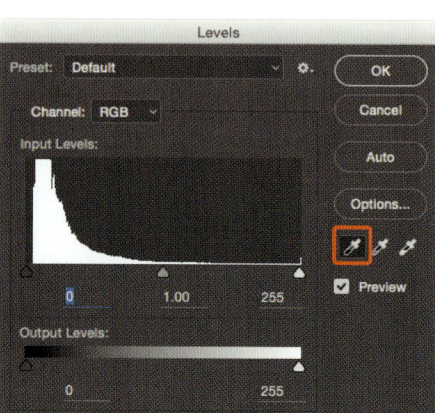

FIGURE 13.101

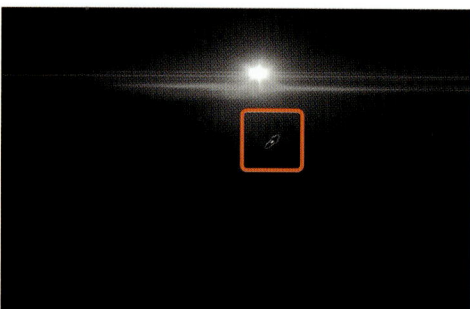

FIGURE 13.100

37. Grab the Crop Tool (**C**) and move the bottom crop line upward (**Figure 13.102**), then press Return (Mac) or Enter (PC).

Go to *Select > All*, followed by *Edit > Copy*, and then click the tab to open up the action figure picture. Then go to *Edit > Paste*, rename the new layer "Lens Flare," and change it's Blend Mode to Screen. Use the Move Tool (**V**) to drag it into place on the figure's shoulder (**Figure 13.103**).

Add a Layer Mask and grab a large, round, soft-edged brush with a black foreground color. Press once with the brush just outside of the canvas area so that the soft, feathered area of the brush gently removes part of the lens flare (**Figure 13.104**).

Using the same brush, press once just outside of the canvas area on the other side of the picture to gently remove part of the lens flare from that side as well.

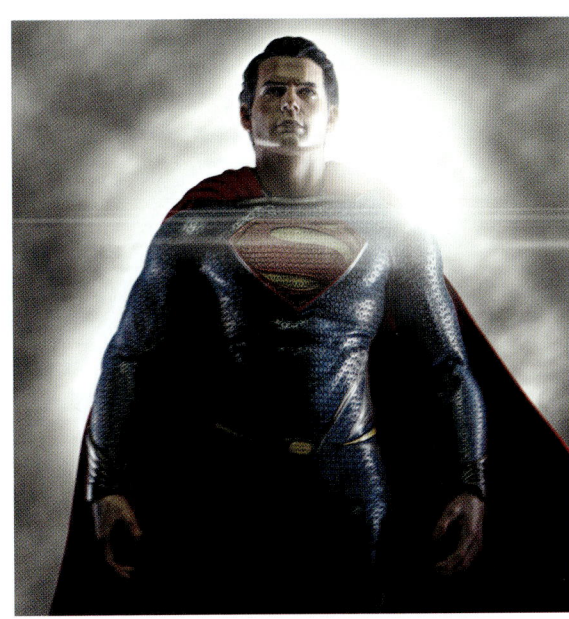

FIGURE 13.102

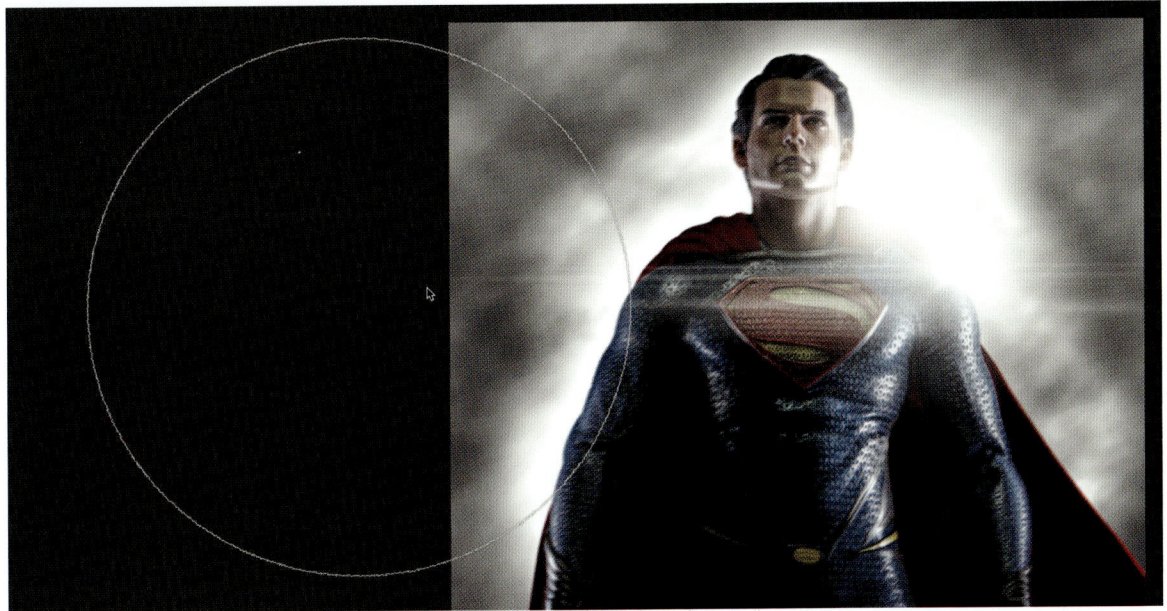

FIGURE 13.103

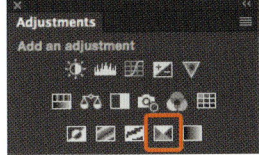

FIGURE 13.104

38. Now let's colorize the picture. Add a Selective Color adjustment layer (**Figure 13.105**), and in the properties, choose Neutrals from the Colors menu and make the following adjustments: Cyan +2%, Magenta -3%, Yellow -15% (**Figure 13.106**).

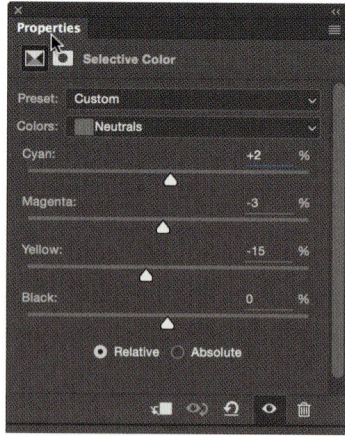

FIGURE 13.105

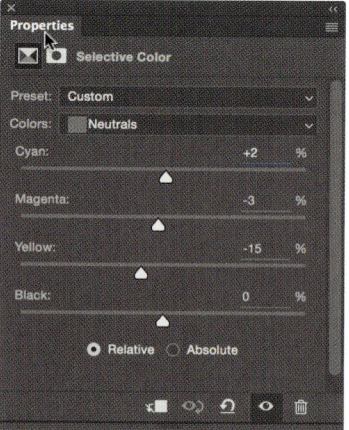

FIGURE 13.106

39. Now we'll add what I call thingys (download the jpg file at: http://www.rockynook.com/photograph-like-a-thief-reference/). This is just a picture of rain photographed at night using a flash, which was given to me by my friend, digital artist Olaf Giermann. I guarantee that after using this layer, you'll see very similar thingys on almost every action movie poster from now on.

Go to *File > Place Embedded* (*File > Place* in earlier versions of Photoshop), navigate to the thingys.jpg file, and click OK. Use the transform handles to stretch it out to fit the image area (**Figure 13.107**) and press Return (Mac) or Enter (PC).

Go to *Layer > Rasterize > Smart Object* (**Figure 13.108**), and then to *Image > Adjustments > Levels*. Grab the Black Point Sampler (**Figure 13.109**) and click once in a dark area of the layer (**Figure 13.110**). Click OK.

FIGURE 13.107

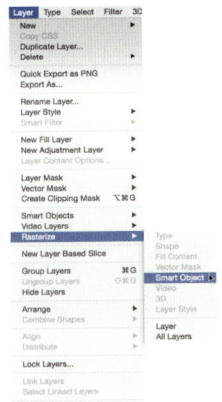

FIGURE 13.108

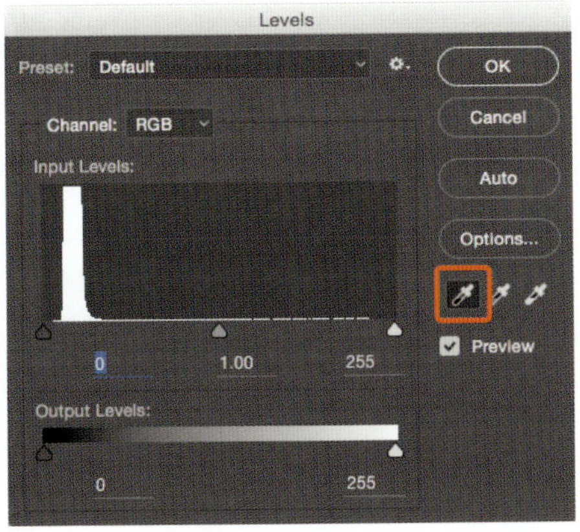

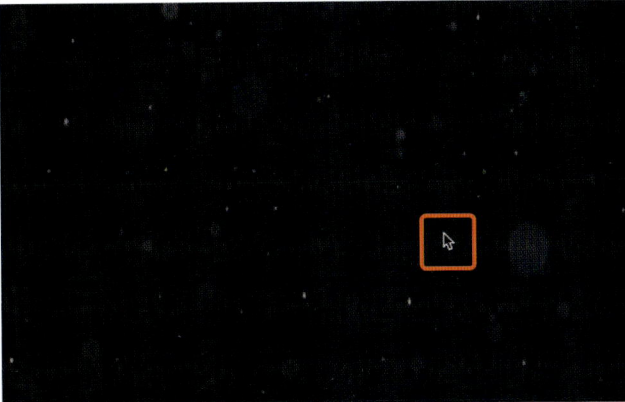

FIGURE 13.109

FIGURE 13.110

40. Go to *Filter > Blur > Motion Blur*, add an Angle of 30° and a Distance of 100 Pixels (**Figure 13.111**), and click OK.

Press Command + J (Mac) or Ctrl + J (PC) to duplicate the thingys layer, and then use the Move Tool (**V**) to drag it to another area of the picture to add more of the effect elsewhere. Hold down the Shift key and click on the bottom thingys layer in the Layers panel so that both thingys layers are selected. Go to *Layer > New > Group from Layers*. In the properties, name the group "thingys" (**Figure 13.112**) and click OK.

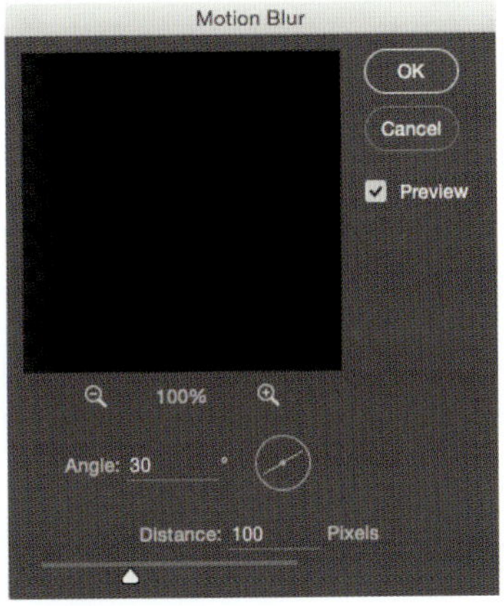

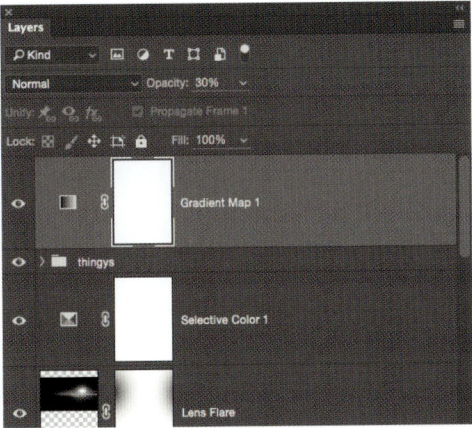

FIGURE 13.111

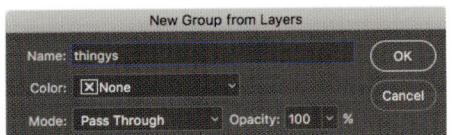

FIGURE 13.112

41. We've got just a few finishing touches to add, I reckon. We'll start by desaturating the image a little. Press **D** to set the foreground and background colors to their defaults of black and white, and then click to add a Gradient Map adjustment layer (**Figure 13.113**). Lower the Opacity of this layer to 30% (**Figure 13.114**).

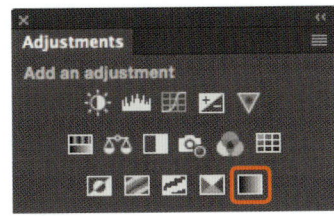

FIGURE 13.113

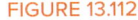

FIGURE 13.114

42. Create one final merged layer at the top of the layer stack and rename it "FT" for Finishing Touches. Go to *Filter > Camera RAW Filter* and use the Adjustment Brush to enhance the highlights on the shoulder with the lens flare and paint some Clarity (contrast) onto the figure's face. Then go to the FX tab and add in some Grain with an Amount of 30 and click OK.

Finally, back in Photoshop, grab the Clone Stamp Tool and clone out the creases in the elbow joints that kind of give away the fact that the character is a toy, or rather an action figure.

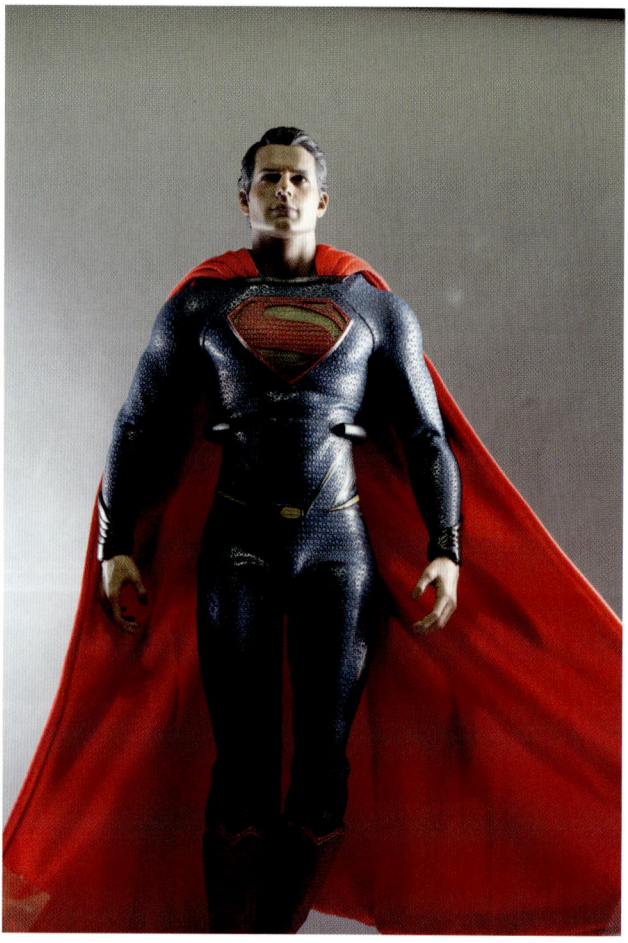

FIGURE 13.115 Original RAW image

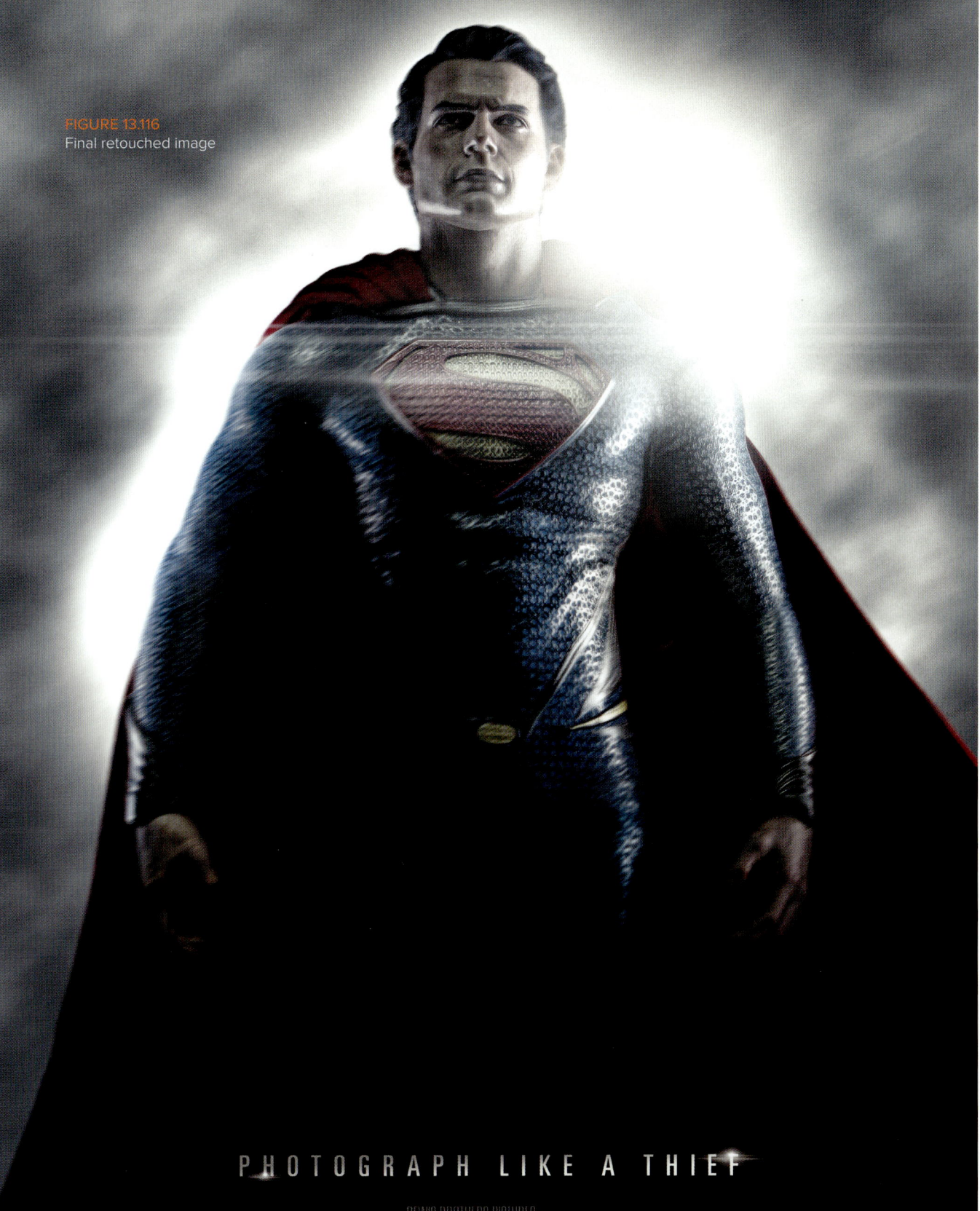

PHOTOGRAPH LIKE A THIEF

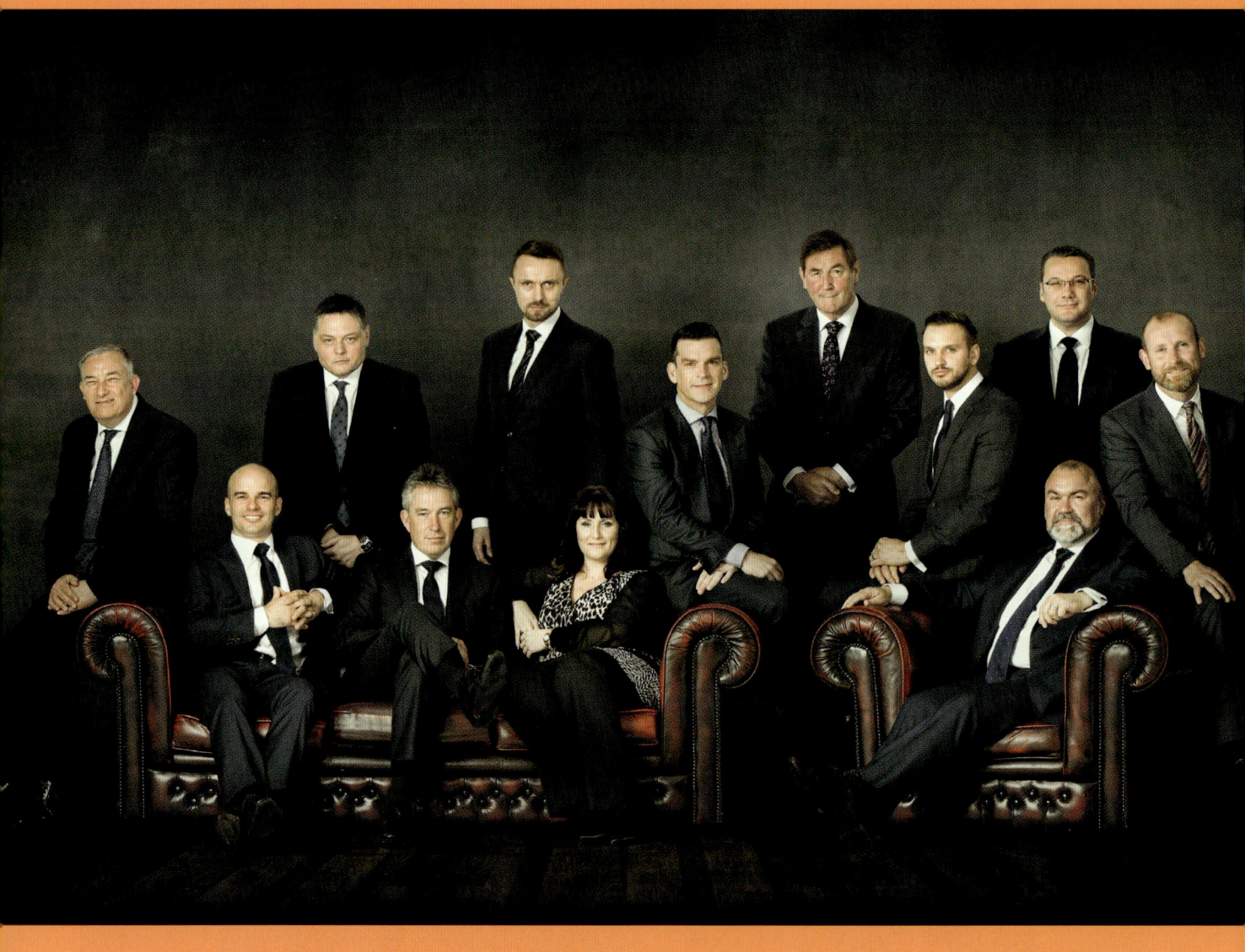

14 GROUP SHOT
K.I.S.S. INSPIRED

(K.I.S.S. = KEEP IT SIMPLE, STUPID)

This group shot was part of a commissioned project for a financial management company called Eight Wealth Management. On the first day of the shoot we took head shots at their office complex, and on the second day we moved to a studio to photograph the whole group together.

In the months leading up to the photo shoot, we had a number of meetings and conference calls via Skype to discuss what the group shot was going to look like. The client asked what I would like to do that was different, so I gathered a whole mix of group photographs from the likes of Annie Leibovitz and Mark Seliger and sent them over to the company to give them an idea of what I wanted to do. It's so much easier to explain a photo concept in pictures rather than words.

We finally came up with the idea of arranging the group on and around a large Chesterfield sofa and chair. Because we were unable to shoot the photograph in a stately home, we set everything up in a studio. I used a gray, seamless-paper backdrop and covered the floor so that I could create a new wall and floor in Photoshop, similar to what I did in chapter 5.

However, you'll see as we go through the post-processing for this image that it wasn't quite that straightforward. Knowing how to make selections in Photoshop certainly saved the day.

THE SETUP

Photographing a 12-person group shot certainly comes with its challenges, but for this particular photo shoot the lighting was actually quite simple in the end.

As you've probably gathered from reading this book, I'm a huge fan of Annie Leibovitz's work and I love how she keeps the lighting simple. So with that in mind—and due to the fact that organizing 12 people can be quite a challenge, especially when there is limited time available—I decided to go with my version of Annie's "Keep It Simple" lighting.

Prior to the photo shoot, we discussed at length the style of shots we wanted, which resulted in us renting a studio space and hiring a furniture rental company to bring in various items of furniture so that we could arrange a set.

The studio that we rented was great. It had all white walls and an infinity cove, and because the space was primarily used to photograph cars, it also had a turn table. At first, it appeared to be an ideal blank canvas that we could make into whatever we wanted, but it turned out that the white walls did cause issues.

I was going for cross lighting, and due to the number of people in the group, I accomplished this with two Elinchrom Rotalux Octa Softboxes: the 175cm and 135cm. I positioned them next to each other to create a very large light source (**Figure 14.1**).

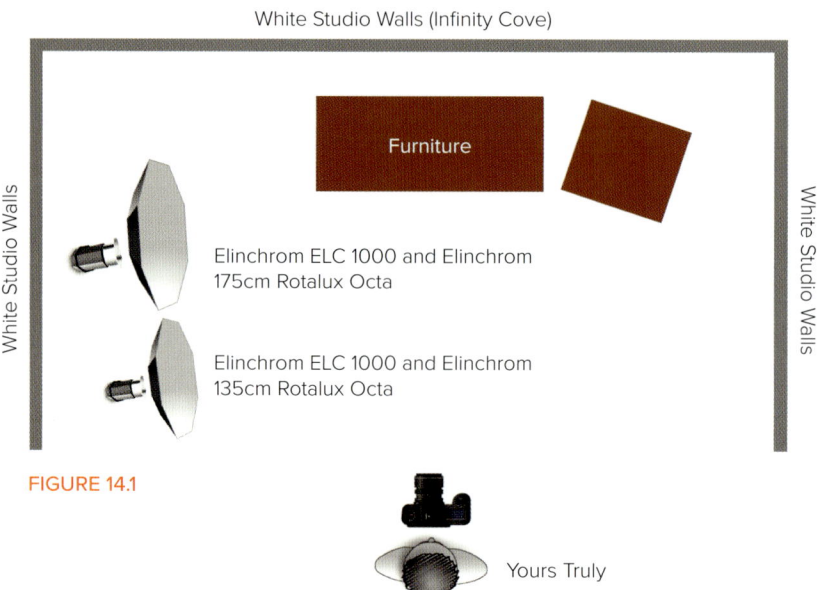

FIGURE 14.1

I placed the lights far enough away from the subjects being photographed that I could take advantage of the Inverse Square Law, which meant that when metering the light, there was just a one-stop difference from the left side of the frame to the right side.

What I love about cross lighting is the shadow and light patterns it creates on your subject. This gives an image depth and dimension and makes it much more interesting. However, it turned out that no matter where we positioned the light sources and subjects, light would reflect off the white walls and fill in the shadows created by the octas, making everything look very flat and uninteresting.

As luck would have it, there were two white poly boards in the corner of the studio, which we covered with lengths of black, seamless paper (which I'd brought along just in case) that was held in place with gaffer tape (**Figure 14.2**).

These two boards were eventually propped up against the studio wall on the opposite side of the octas, just outside of the frame (**Figure 14.3**).

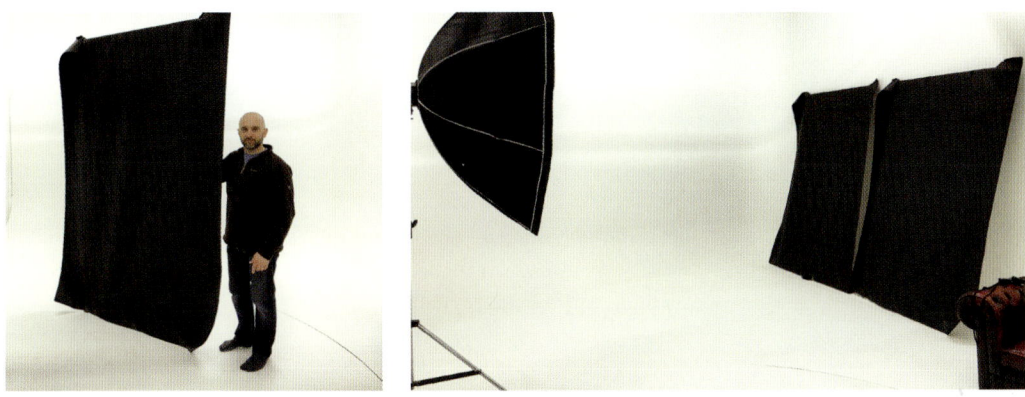

FIGURE 14.2

FIGURE 14.3

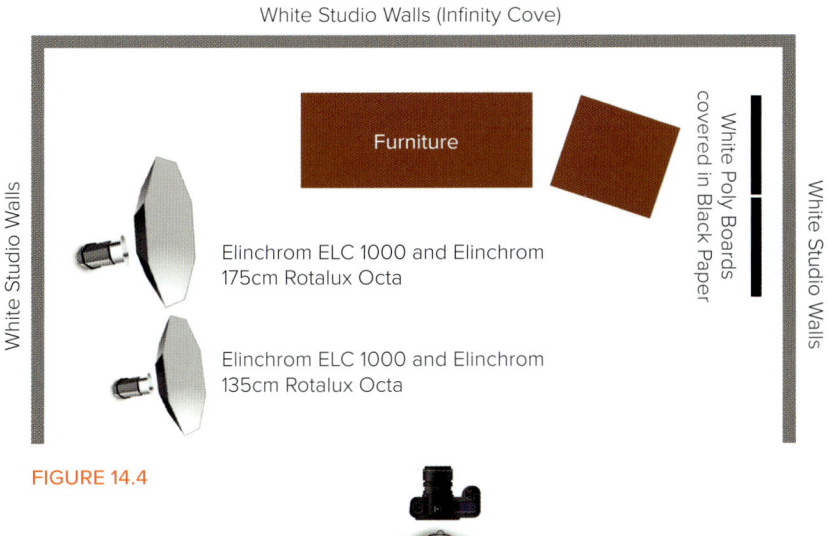

White Studio Walls (Infinity Cove)

Furniture

White Poly Boards covered in Black Paper

White Studio Walls

White Studio Walls

Elinchrom ELC 1000 and Elinchrom 175cm Rotalux Octa

Elinchrom ELC 1000 and Elinchrom 135cm Rotalux Octa

FIGURE 14.4

Yours Truly

The light from the octas (**Figure 14.5**) was stopped dead in its tracks as it hit the black boards, so it didn't bounce back onto our subjects. This resulted in visible shadows (**Figure 14.6**).

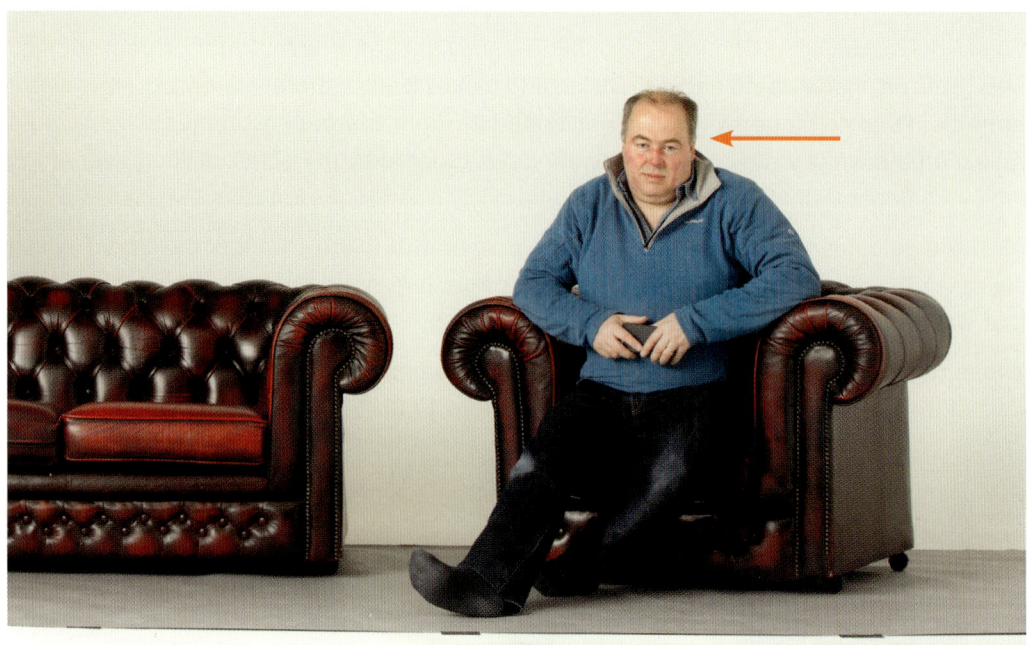

FIGURE 14.5 Before: The reflected light completely removes any shadow on the camera-right side of my buddy Brian Worley's face

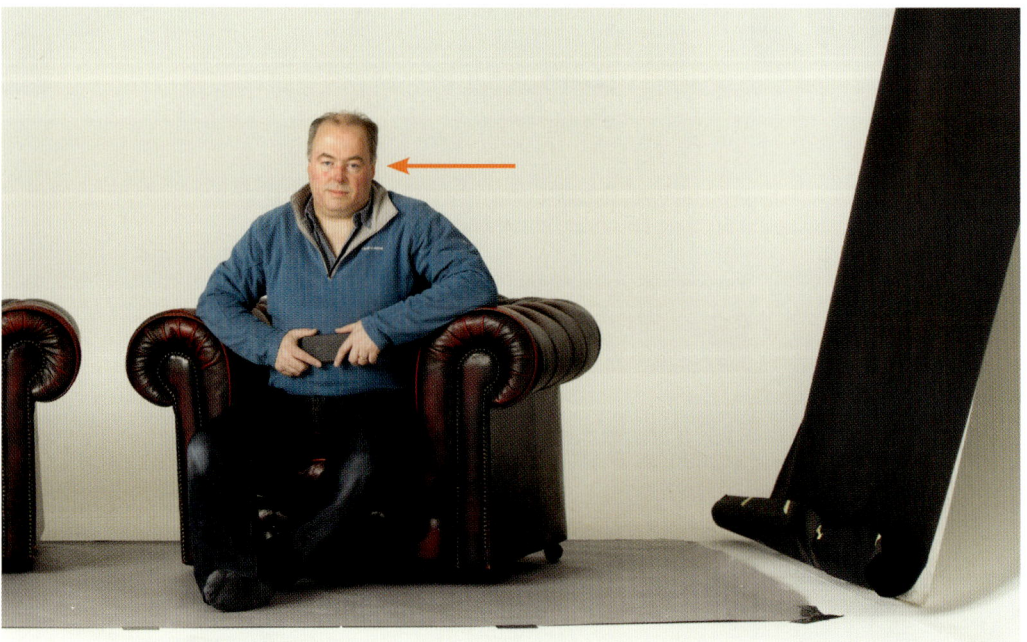

FIGURE 14.6 After: With the black boards in place, the light reflecting back onto the camera-right side of Brian's face is drastically reduced and you can see some shadows

CAMERA SETTINGS

As I mentioned earlier, the original plan was to place a sheet of gray, seamless paper behind the subjects and on the floor, but this just wasn't possible. Our next idea was to see if we could position the lights far enough away from the background to make the wall behind the subjects darker (think Inverse Square Law), but unfortunately, we didn't have enough space in the studio to allow this.

At that point, I had to do the unthinkable and concede, "I'll do that later in Photoshop."

All joking aside, it's times like this when Photoshop enters into a league of its own because it certainly saved the day on this occasion, as you'll see in the post-production later on in this chapter.

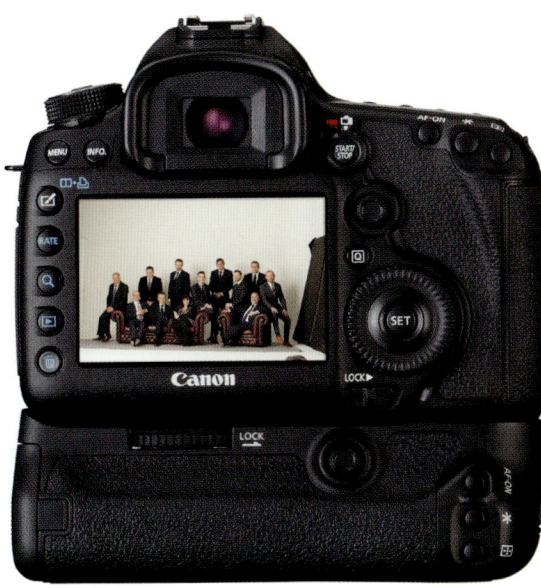

FIGURE 14.7

MODE Manual

ISO 125

APERTURE f/11

SHUTTER SPEED 1/125 sec.

LENS Canon 70–200mm f/2.8 IS II USM

GEAR GUIDE

I kept the lighting really simple for this shoot by creating what was, in effect, a single light source made up of two lights positioned closely together. I used two Elinchrom ELC Pro HD 1000 flash heads (**Figure 14.8**), an Elinchrom Rotalux 175mm Octa Softbox (**Figure 14.9**), and an Elinchrom Rotalux 135cm Octa Softbox (**Figure 14.10**). If I had brought two 175cm octas with me, I would have used those instead.

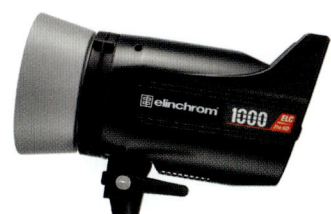

FIGURE 14.8

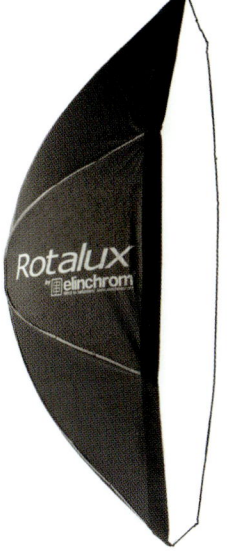

FIGURE 14.9

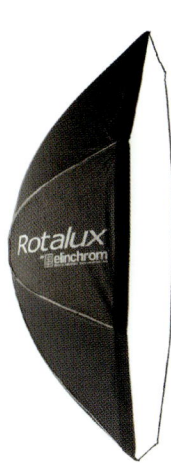

FIGURE 14.10

SMALL FLASH GEAR GUIDE

If I were to do this same photo shoot, but was only able to use small, speedlight-type flashes, I'd more than likely try hanging a large white bed sheet or shower curtain over a background support (pole and light stands), positioning it in the same area as the octas, and firing the speedlights through it (**Figure 14.11**).

The only challenge here would be to get enough light from the speedlights to expose for all 12 people, so this setup may require more flashes.

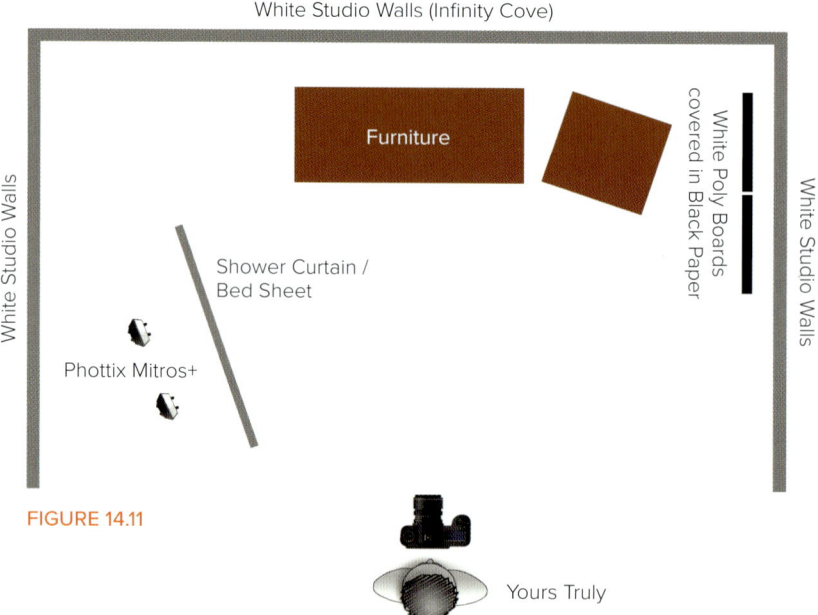

FIGURE 14.11

POST-PROCESSING

I don't think there's ever been a time when I've been more thankful for Photoshop than I was during this photo shoot. Without it, there's no way we would have produced what we did with what we had.

I've already mentioned that the initial plan was to have gray, seamless paper behind the subjects and on the floor so that adding in a new wall and floor would be a breeze in Photoshop. However, because it wasn't possible to use the paper, I started to play around in Photoshop to see what I could do. Purely by accident, I discovered that I could get the same result by faking the look of the paper. I know this sounds kind of weird, but you'll see what I mean later on.

More than ever, I believe that knowledge of Photoshop (in particular, how to make good selections and cutouts) is a vital skill for today's photographer because as this photo shoot proved, it can seriously help you out. Sure, getting the very best possible picture is the priority, and hopefully you've seen the effort we put in to ensure that, but it was the post-production that brought it all together.

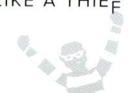

There are quite a few steps ahead, but in these steps there are lots of little techniques that I'm sure will come in handy when you're working on other images as well. So without further delay, let's get going.

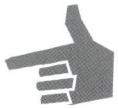

NOTE *Download all the files you need to follow along step-by-step at: http://www.rockynook.com/ photograph-like-a-thief-reference/*

1. Let's kick things off in Lightroom (or Camera RAW) by cropping the image. Then in the Develop module, open the Basics tab and drag the Shadows slider to +20 to open up a bit of detail in the shadow areas (**Figure 14.12**).

2. Now we'll add in some Sharpening. In the Detail tab, increase the Sharpening Amount to +50 and the Masking to +90 (**Figure 14.13**).

TIP *To see the mask view with the areas being sharpened in white, hold down the Option key (Mac) or Alt key (PC) while dragging the Masking slider.*

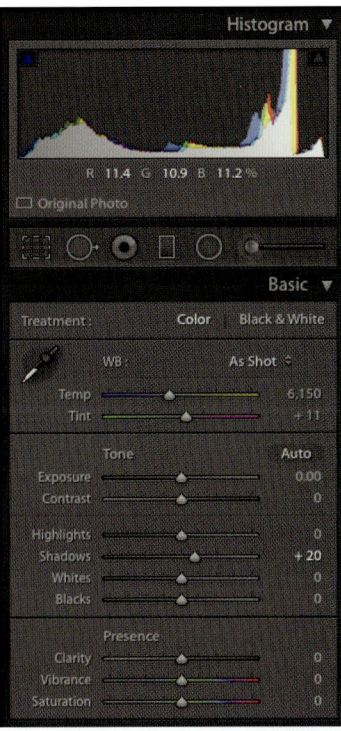

FIGURE 14.12

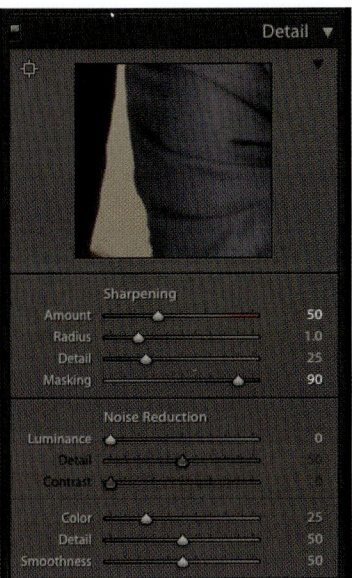

FIGURE 14.13

Now we'll send the image over into Photoshop. In Lightroom, go to *Photo > Edit In > Adobe Photoshop...* If you're using Camera RAW, click on Open Image.

3. Ideally, we would have had gray paper behind the subjects and covering the floor, but at the time of the shoot, this wasn't possible for a number of reasons. So this is where we need to make the scene look as though we did have all that gray paper.

With the image file open in Photoshop, press Command + J (Mac) or Ctrl + J (PC) to duplicate the Background layer. Rename this layer "Clean Up."

Select the Rectangular Marquee Tool (**M**) and drag out a selection across the entire width of the picture, from the bottom up to just underneath the subjects' shoes. Make sure you don't include any of their shadows in the selection (**Figure 14.14**).

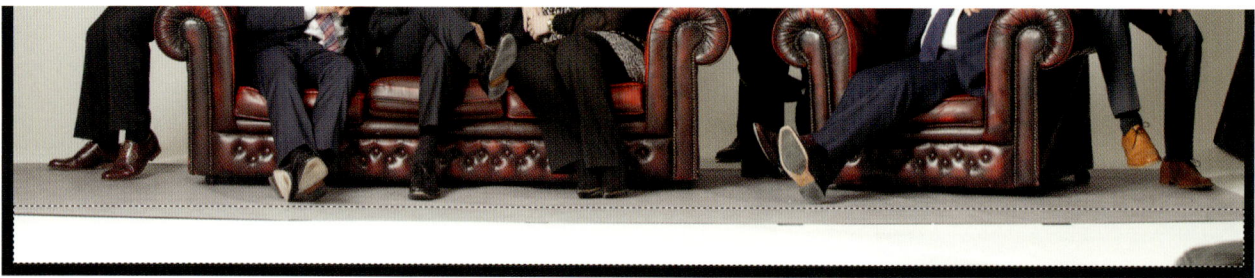

Go to *Edit > Free Transform* and drag the bottom-middle transform handle downward until the gray paper stretches out enough to cover the floor (**Figure 14.15**). Press Return (Mac) or Enter (PC).

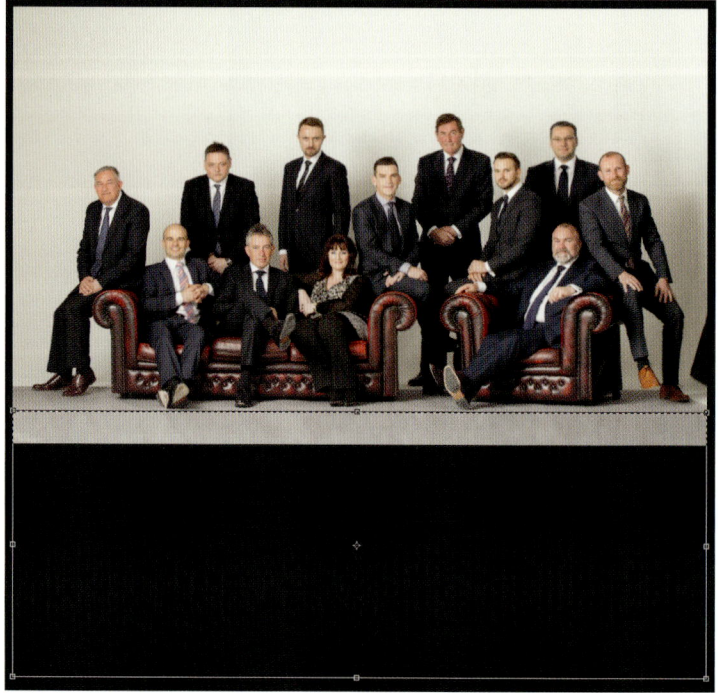

FIGURE 14.15

Go to *Select* > *Deselect* or press Command + D (Mac) or Ctrl + D (PC) to turn off the active selection (**Figure 14.16**).

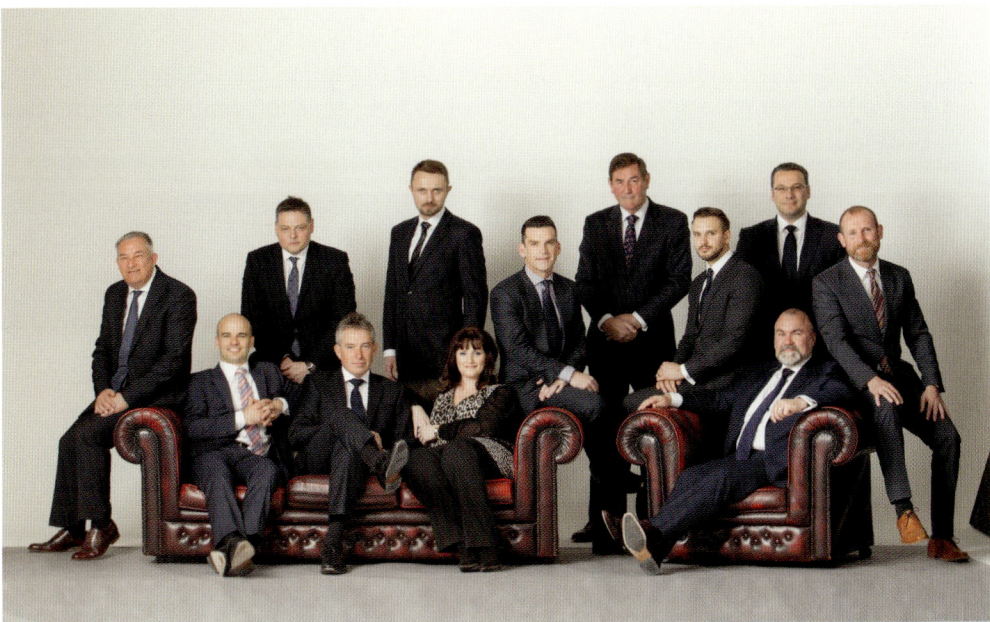

FIGURE 14.16

4. Use the Lasso Tool (**L**) to draw a selection around the object over on the far right side of the picture (**Figure 14.17**), which is actually one of the boards with the black paper. With the selection active, go to *Edit* > *Fill*, choose Content-Aware from the Contents menu (**Figure 14.18**), and click OK. Press Command + D (Mac) or Ctrl + D (PC) to turn off the selection.

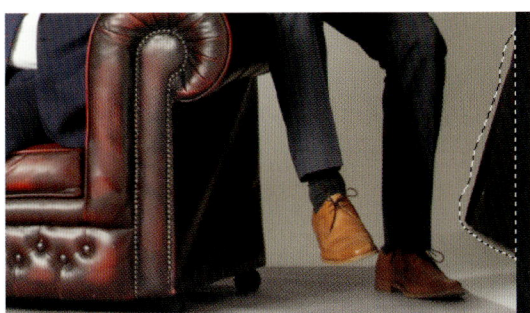

FIGURE 14.17

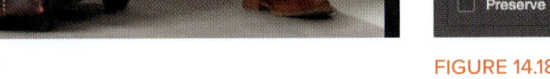

FIGURE 14.18

5. With the Quick Selection Tool (**W**), drag out a selection that includes the area of the floor where the paper is still missing on the far right side of the picture, but don't include the subject's shoe (**Figure 14.19**). Select the Rectangular Marquee Tool (**M**) and hold down the Option key (Mac) (PC) as you drag out a rectangle that continues from the line of the gray paper upward. This removes the portion of the original selection that is above the floor area and leaves us with an active selection where the paper needs to be (**Figure 14.20**).

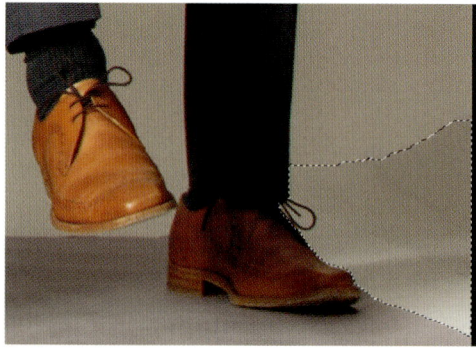
FIGURE 14.19

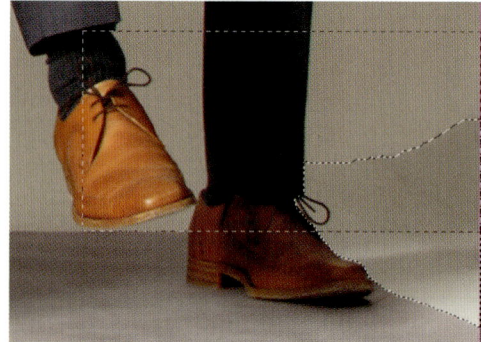
FIGURE 14.20

6. Now we'll feather this selection. Go to *Select > Modify > Feather*, dial in a Feather Radius of 1 pixel, and click OK (**Figure 14.21**).

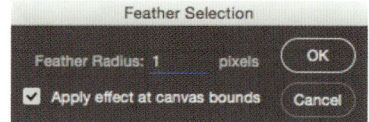
FIGURE 14.21

Select the Clone Stamp Tool (**S**), hold down the Option key (Mac) or Alt key (PC), and click to sample areas of the paper floor nearby, then clone the selected areas into the space within the selection (**Figure 14.22**). Having a selection like this means that when we clone, it remains within the selected area and doesn't spill onto other parts of the picture, such as the subject's shoes or the back wall.

Go to *Select > Deselect* to turn off the active selection. Set the Opacity of the Clone Stamp Tool to 50% and clone over the obvious line dividing the original floor and this added part so that the areas blend together (**Figure 14.23**).

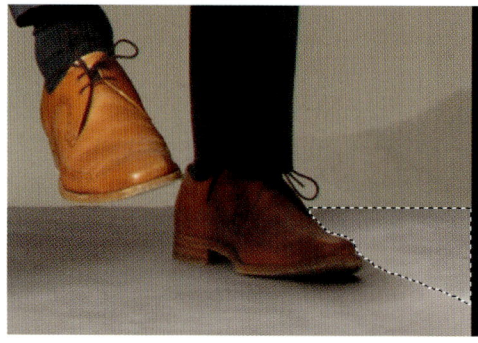
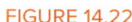
FIGURE 14.22

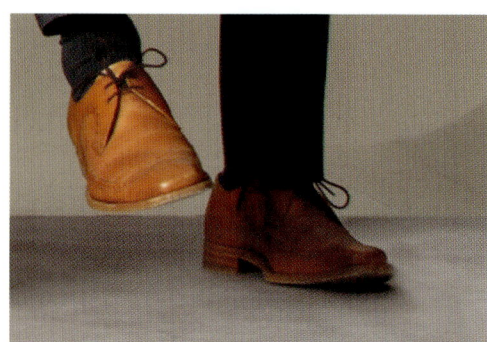
FIGURE 14.23

7. With the Quick Selection Tool (**W**), click and drag across the back wall to select it. Hold down the Option key (Mac) or Alt key (PC) and drag over areas you want to remove from the selection, but make sure to include all the bits of the back wall in the gaps by the subjects' legs, arms, etc. (**Figure 14.24**).

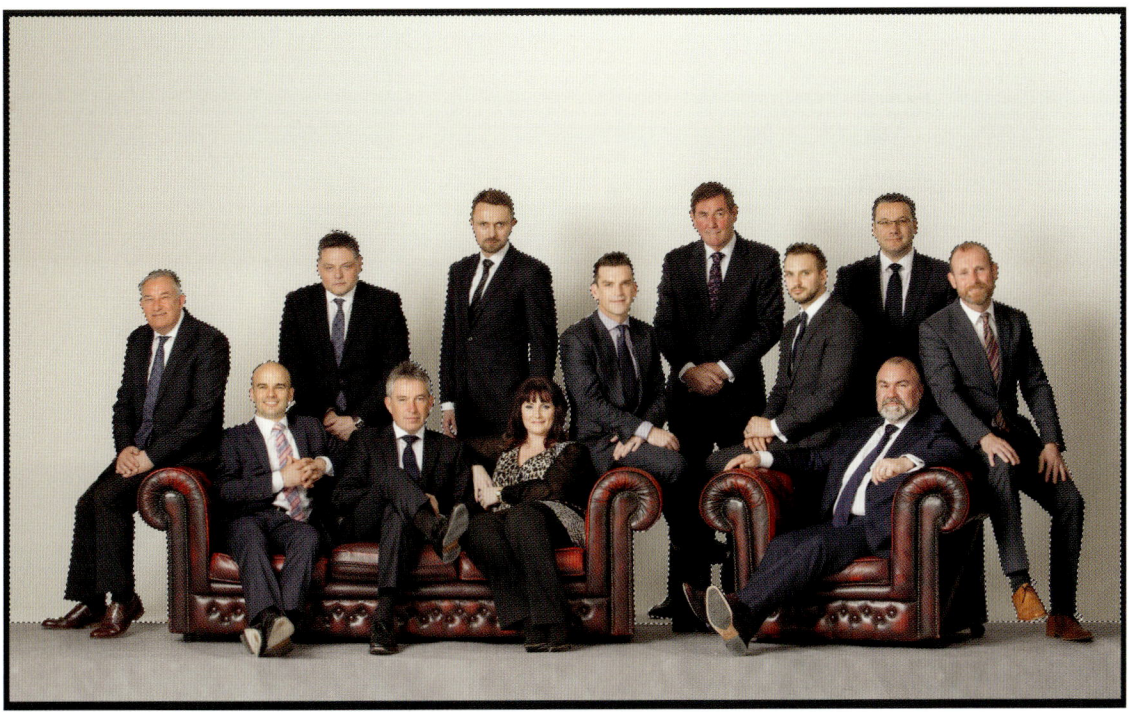

FIGURE 14.24

8. Go to *Select > Inverse* so that the group of people is now selected, and then click on Select and Mask at the top of the screen (**Figure 14.25**).

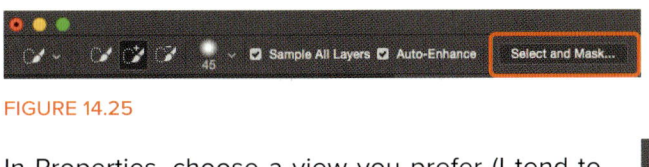

FIGURE 14.25

In Properties, choose a view you prefer (I tend to choose On White; **Figure 14.26**), and then use the Refine Edge Brush Tool (**Figure 14.27**) to brush along the subjects' hair so that Photoshop can pick up any of the fine hairs missed by the Quick Selection Tool.

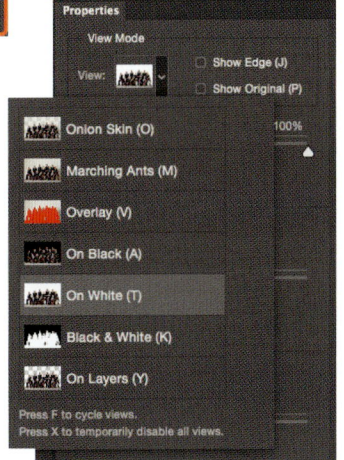

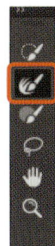

FIGURE 14.26   FIGURE 14.27

In the Output options, choose Selection and then click OK to go back to Photoshop. Go to *Select > Modify > Feather* (**Figure 14.28**), add in a Feather Radius of 1 pixel (**Figure 14.29**), and click OK.

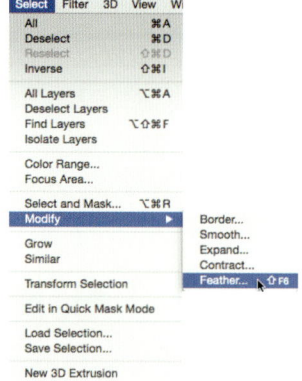

FIGURE 14.28

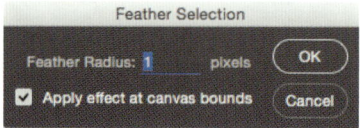

FIGURE 14.29

9. Making the selection has taken quite a bit of effort and we'll also need to use it in a bit, so we'll save it. Go to *Select > Save Selection*, and in the Save Selection properties, name the selection "Group Selection" (**Figure 14.30**) and click OK.

10. With the selection active, go to *Select > Inverse* so that the back wall is selected again, and then click to add a Levels adjustment layer. In the Levels adjustment Properties, click and drag the white Output Levels marker to the left until it reads 125 (**Figure 14.31**). Rename this Levels adjustment layer "Gray Wall."

This has turned the back wall gray (**Figure 14.32**), which is kind of what it would have looked like if we had been able to put up gray, seamless paper behind the subjects.

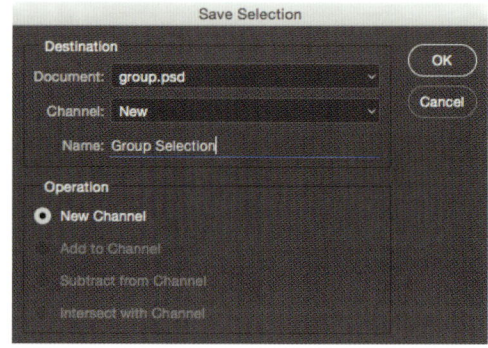

FIGURE 14.30

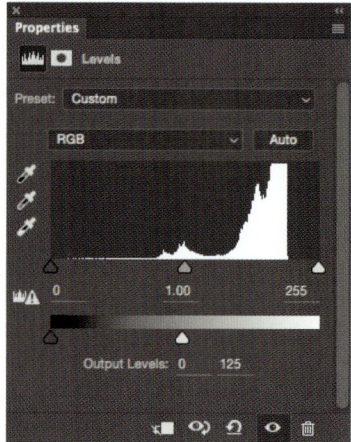

FIGURE 14.31

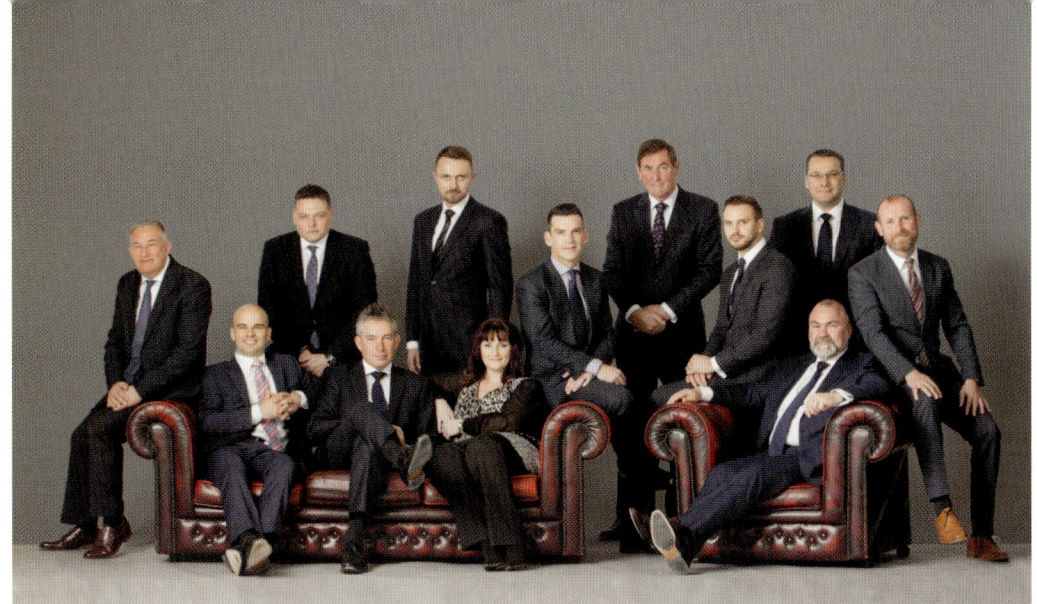

FIGURE 14.32

11. Now we need to darken the floor. Click on the "Clean Up" layer in the Layers panel and use the Quick Selection Tool (**W**) to drag out a selection of the floor area (**Figure 14.33**).

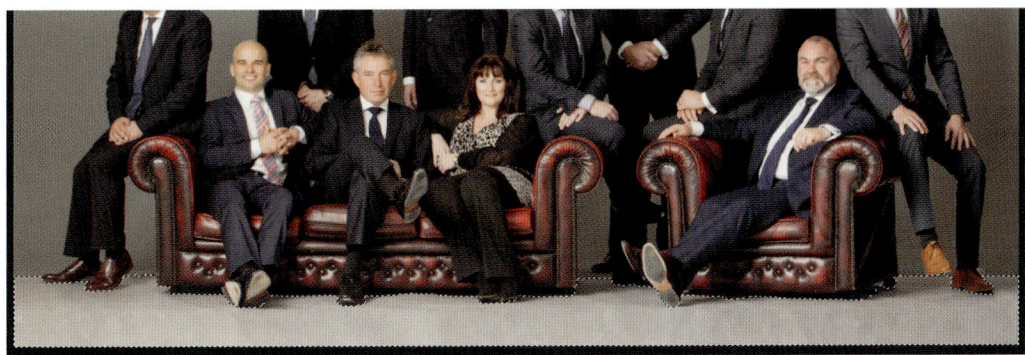

FIGURE 14.33

With the selection active, click to add a Levels adjustment layer. In Properties, click and drag the white Output Levels marker to 160 (**Figure 14.34**). Rename this Levels adjustment layer "Gray Floor."

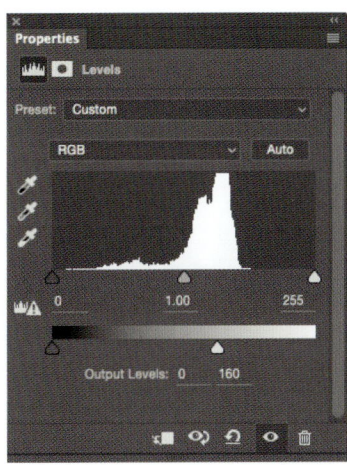

FIGURE 14.34

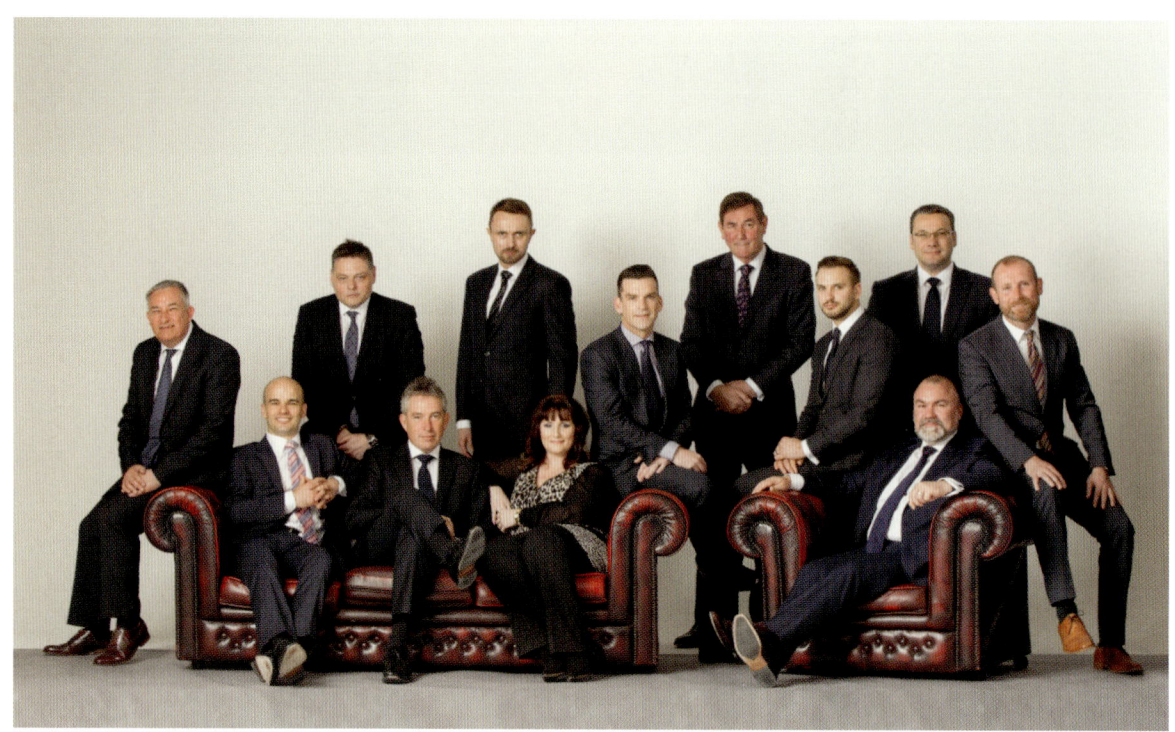

FIGURE 14.35 Before

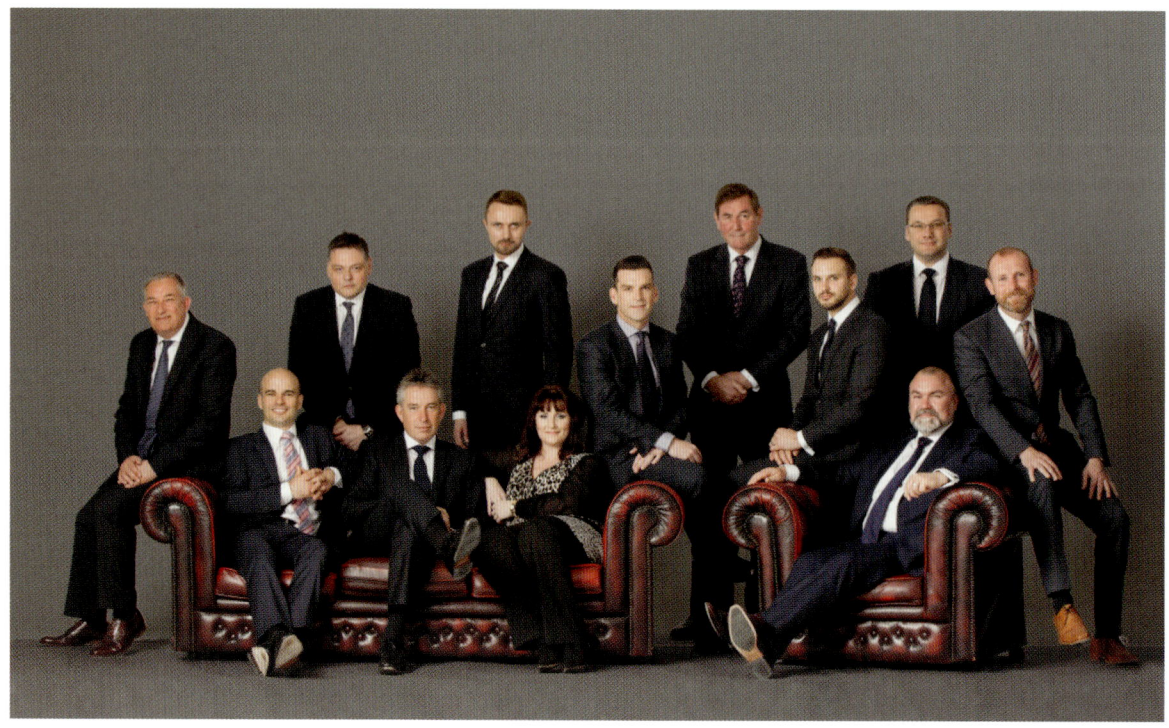

FIGURE 14.36 After

12. Click on the "Gray Wall" layer in the Layers panel, then go to *File > Place Embedded* (*File > Place* in earlier versions of Photoshop), navigate to the texture.jpg file you downloaded from the book's website, and click OK. This places the texture directly into our working document (**Figure 14.37**). Press Return (Mac) or Enter (PC) to set it into place and remove the transform handles.

Next we need to remove the color from the texture, but to do so we need to turn the texture layer into a regular layer. Go to *Layer > Rasterize > Smart Object* (**Figure 14.38**), and then to *Image > Adjustments > Desaturate* (**Figure 14.39**).

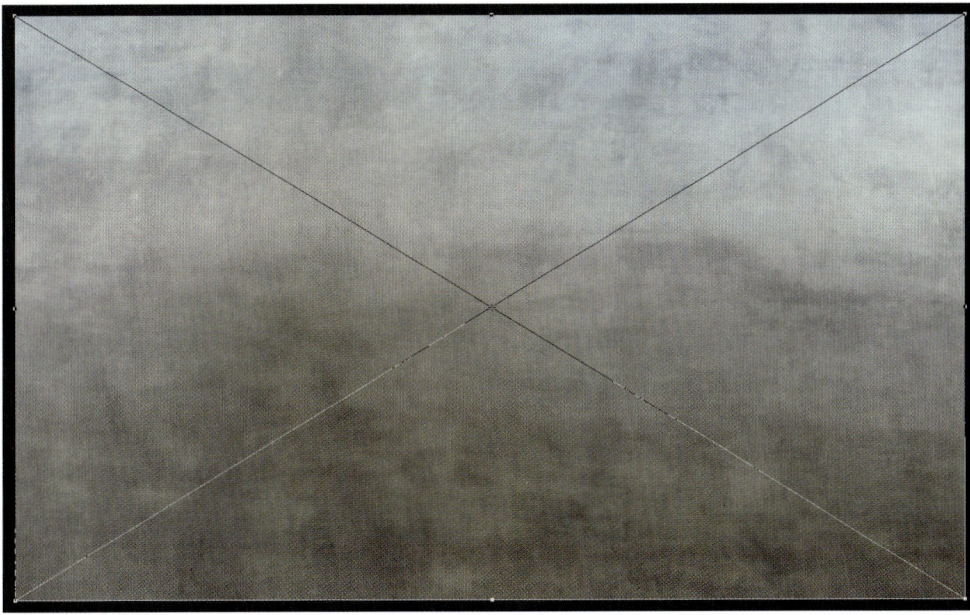

FIGURE 14.37

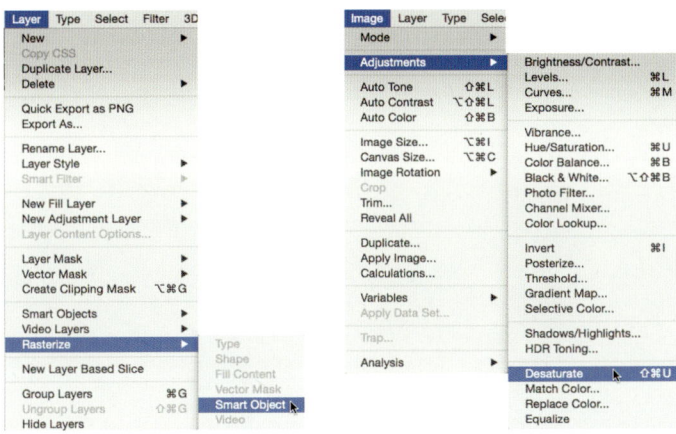

FIGURE 14.38   FIGURE 14.39

13. Now change the Blend Mode of the texture layer to Overlay (**Figure 14.40**). Then go to *Select > Load Selection*, and in the Load Selection dialog, choose Group Selection (which we created earlier) from the Channel drop-down menu (**Figure 14.41**) and click OK.

With the Group Selection active, hold down the Option key (Mac) or Alt key (PC) and click to add a Layer Mask. This automatically adds a black layer mask (**Figure 14.42**) that hides the texture effect on the people, furniture, and floor and leaves it visible on the back wall (**Figure 14.43**).

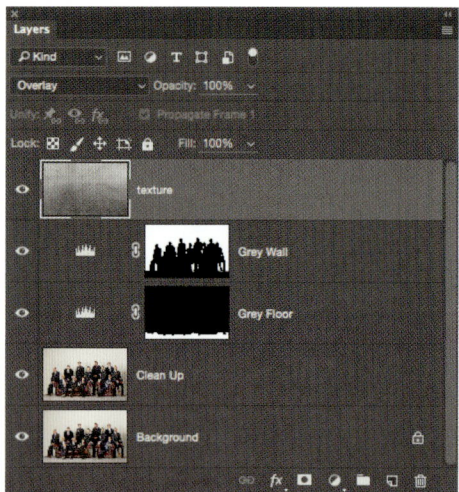

FIGURE 14.40

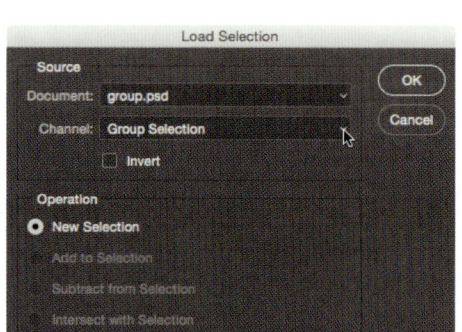

FIGURE 14.41

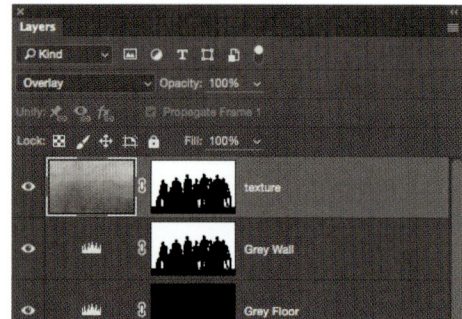

FIGURE 14.42

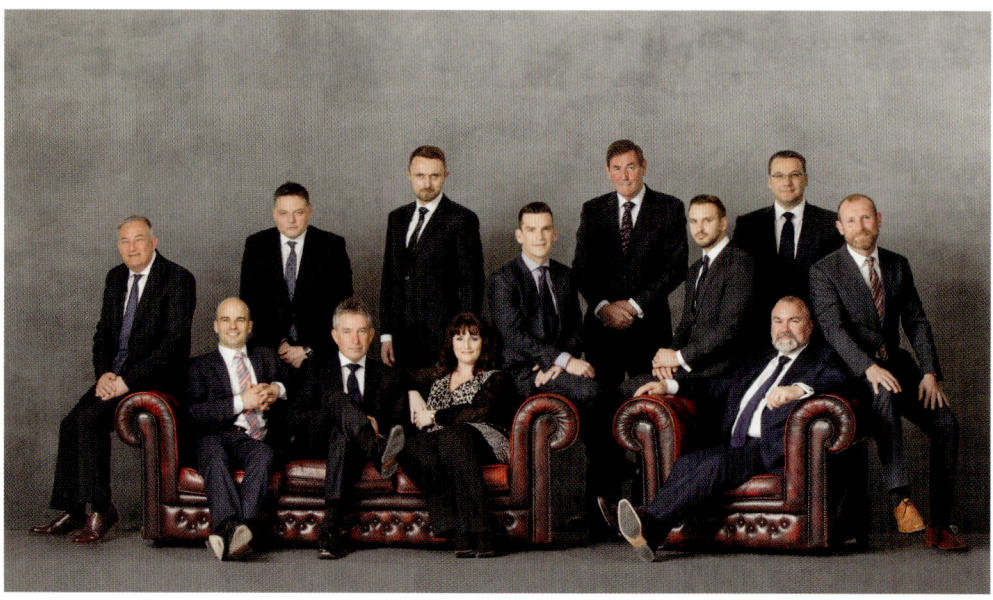

FIGURE 14.43

14. Next we'll add in the wooden floor. Go to *File > Place Embedded* (*File > Place* in earlier versions of Photoshop), navigate to the wooden_floor.jpg file (downloaded from the book's website), and click OK. Hold down the Shift key and use the Move Tool (**V**) to drag the wooden floor down so that the top of it lines up with the bottom of the back wall (**Figure 14.44**).

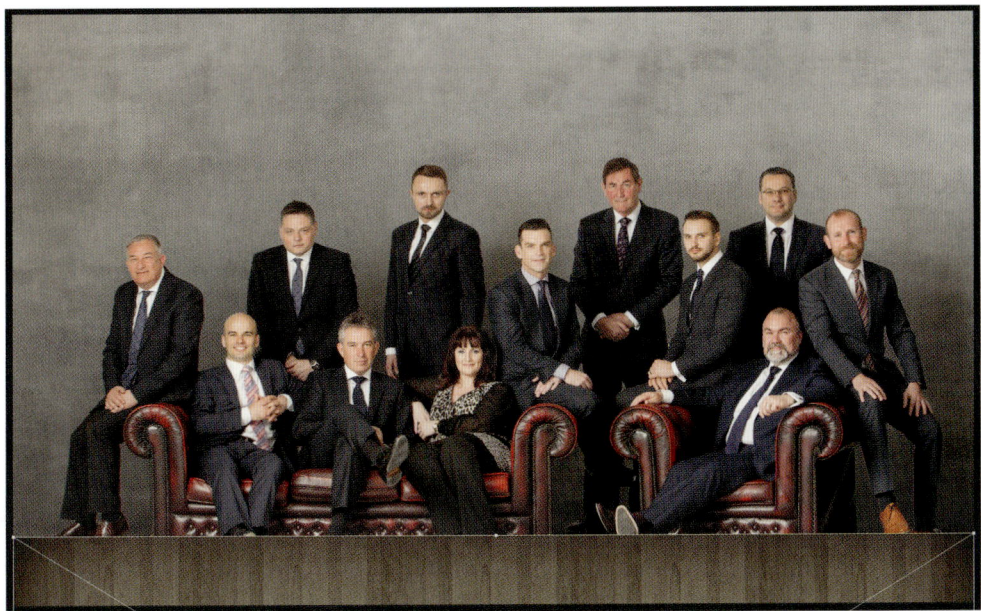

FIGURE 14.44

Press Return (Mac) or Enter (PC), then go to *Edit > Transform > Perspective*. Click on the bottom-left transform handle and drag out to the left to give the wooden floor the correct perspective (**Figure 14.45**).

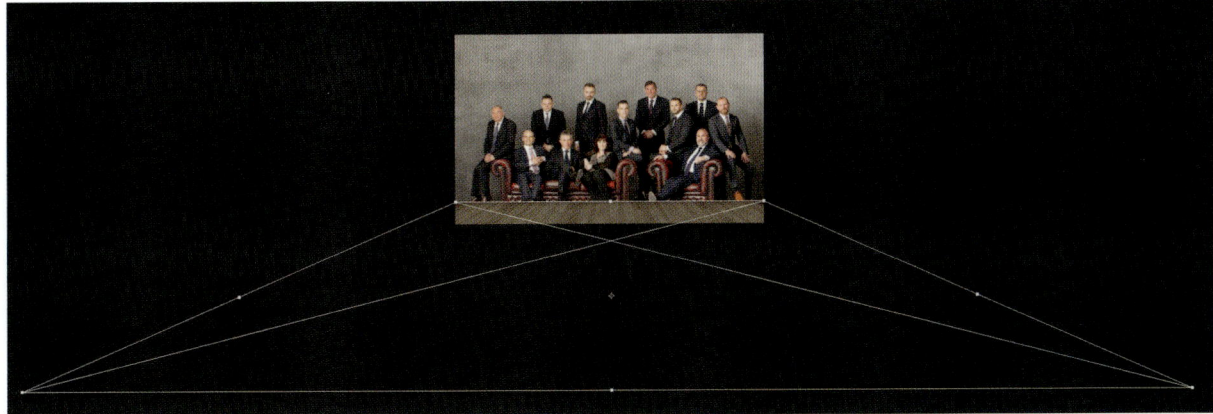

FIGURE 14.45

Go to *Edit > Transform > Scale*, click on the bottom-middle transform handle, and drag up toward the bottom of the picture (**Figure 14.46**). Press Return (Mac) or Enter (PC).

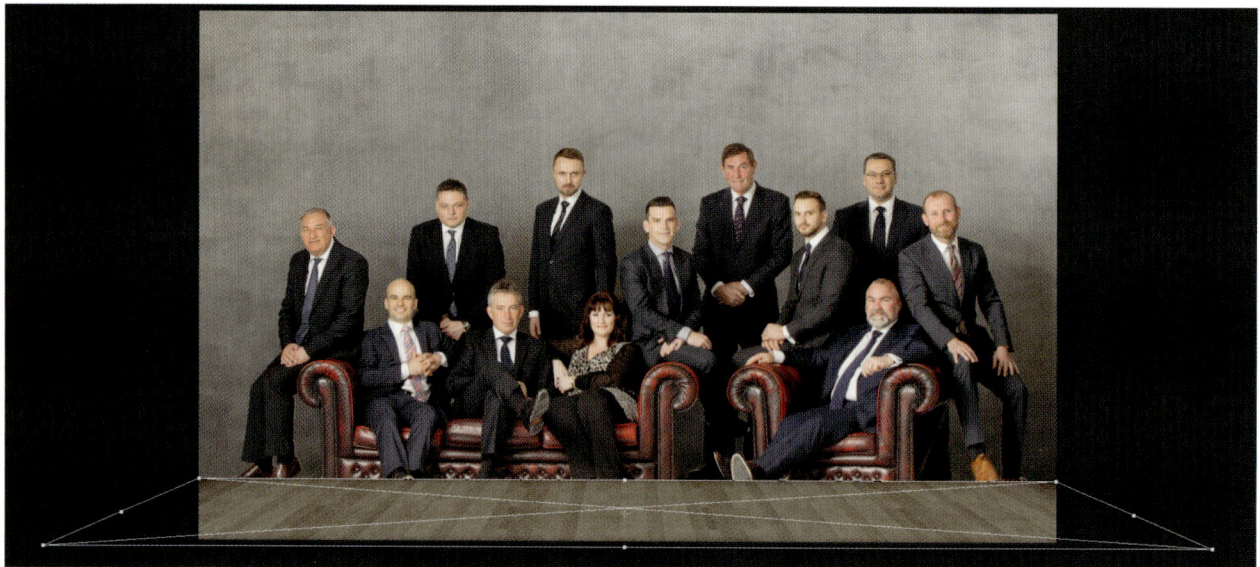

FIGURE 14.46

15. Change the Blend Mode of the wooden floor layer to Overlay, and then click to add a Layer Mask. With a round, soft-edged brush (about 30% Hardness) and a black foreground color, paint to remove the floor from the subjects' shoes, clothing, and the furniture (**Figure 14.47**).

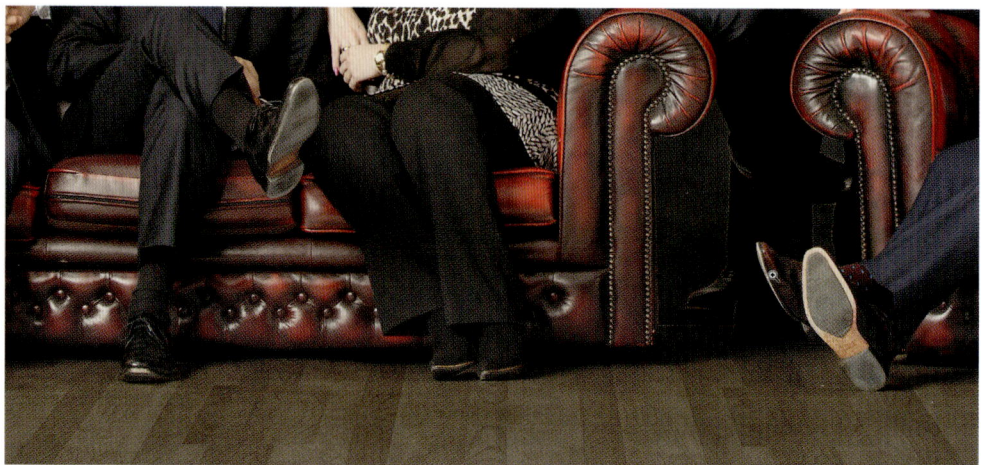

FIGURE 14.47

16. Click on the Gray Wall layer and double-click on the Levels adjustment thumbnail to open the Properties. Drag the white Output Levels marker over to the left until it reads 100 (**Figure 14.48**) to darken the back wall.

17. The clients made a few requests after they initially received their pictures, which is what we'll work on now.

The first was to change the multicolored tie (**Figure 14.49**) to a plain black and blue. Click on the "Clean Up" layer and use the Lasso Tool (**L**) to draw a rough selection around the tie of the man to his right (**Figure 14.50**).

Press Command + J (Mac) or Ctrl + J (PC) to put this selection on its own layer. Rename the new layer "Tie," and then use the Move Tool (**V**) to drag it on top of the multicolored tie (**Figure 14.51**).

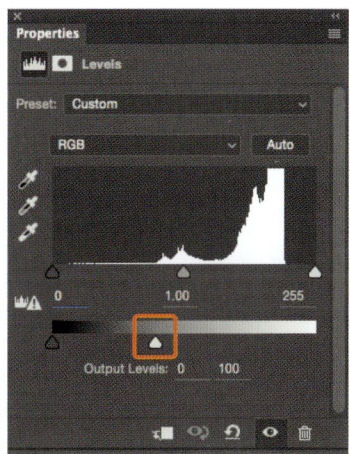

FIGURE 14.48

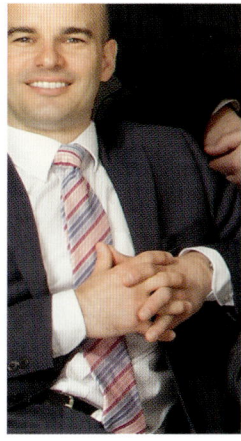

FIGURE 14.49

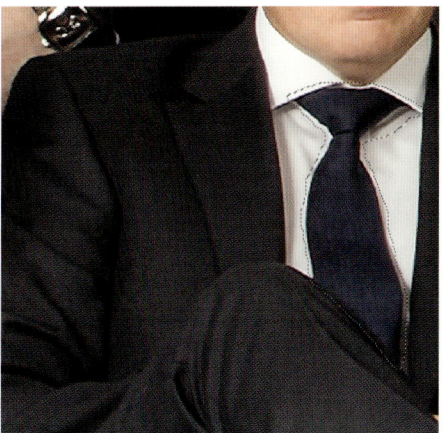

FIGURE 14.50

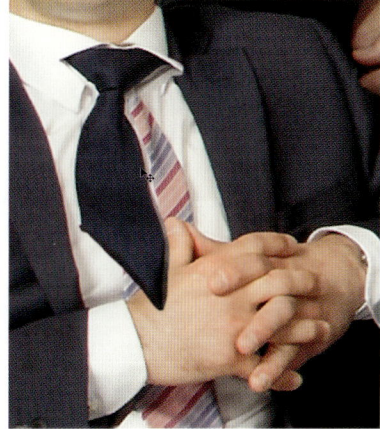

FIGURE 14.51

18. Go to *Edit > Free Transform*, and then click and drag outside of the transform handles to rotate the tie into position. Then go to *Edit > Transform > Warp*, and click and drag within the warp grid to stretch the tie out so that it pretty much covers the original multicolored tie (**Figure 14.52**).

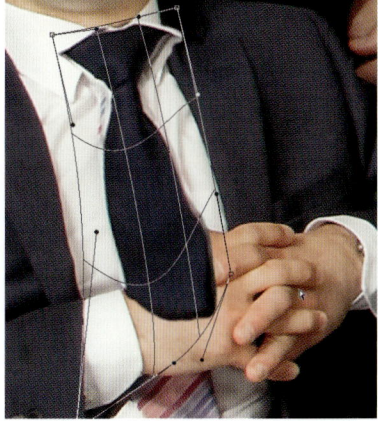

FIGURE 14.52

Click to add a Layer Mask to the Tie layer, and then use a round, soft-edged brush and black foreground color to paint around the tie and blend it into place. If there are areas of the colored tie still showing, add a layer below the Tie layer, name it "Tie Clean Up," (**Figure 14.53**) and select the Clone Stamp Tool. In the options bar at the top of the screen, set the Sample menu to Current & Below (**Figure 14.54**), and then sample areas of the white shirt and clone over the tie.

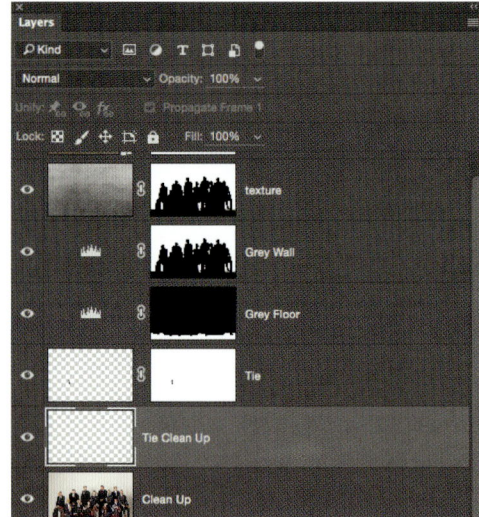

FIGURE 14.53

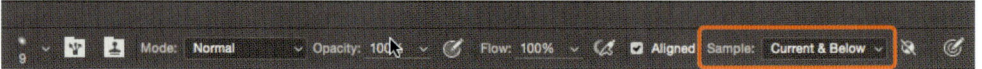

FIGURE 14.54

19. Click on the Clean Up layer and use the Lasso Tool (**L**) to drag out another selection of the dark tie (**Figure 14.55**). Press Command + J (Mac) or Ctrl + J (PC) to put this selection on a new layer. Rename the layer "Tie 2." Use the Move Tool (**V**) to position the Tie 2 layer over the lower portion of the multicolored tie, and then use *Edit > Warp* to stretch it out so that it covers that portion of the tie (**Figure 14.56**).

Add a Layer Mask to the Tie 2 layer and use a round, soft-edged brush and black foreground color to paint around the tie and blend it into place (**Figure 14.57**).

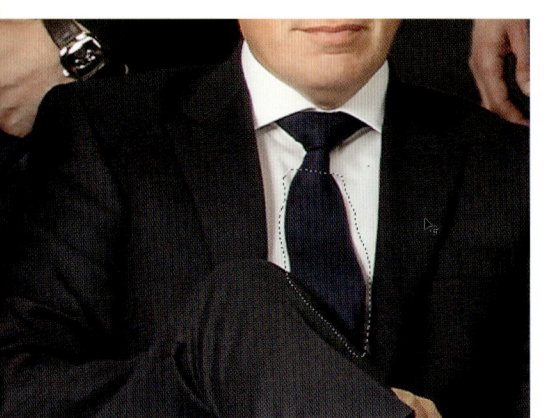

FIGURE 14.55

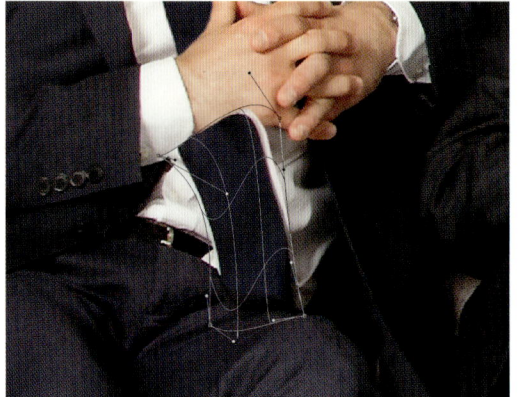

FIGURE 14.56

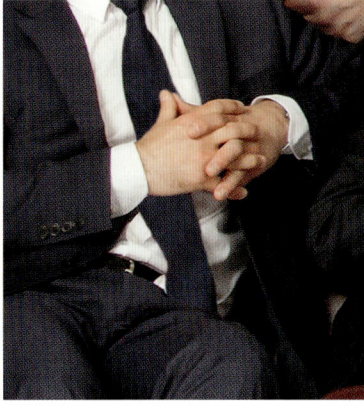

FIGURE 14.57

20. Double-click on the Quick Mask icon in the toolbar (**Figure 14.58**), and in the Quick Mask Options, make sure that Selected Areas is chosen (**Figure 14.59**).

Press **Q** to turn on Quick Mask mode, and then use a round, soft-edged brush and black foreground color to paint over the light brown shoes (**Figure 14.610**).

Press **Q** to exit Quick Mask mode and show the active selection (**Figure 14.61**).

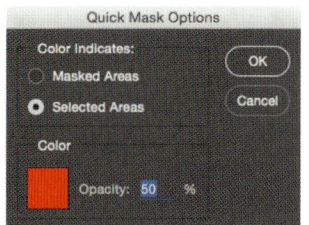
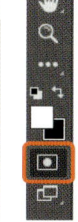

FIGURE 14.58

FIGURE 14.59

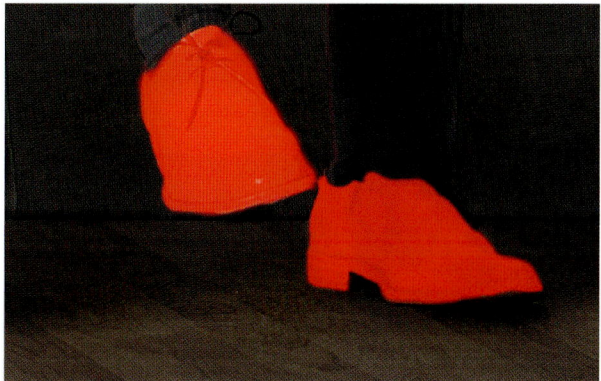

FIGURE 14.60

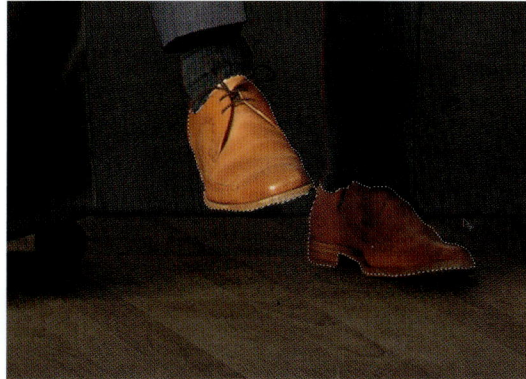

FIGURE 14.61

21. Click on the Selective Color icon in the Adjustments panel to add a Selective Color adjustment layer (**Figure 14.62**). In the properties, choose Neutrals from the Colors menu and drag the Black slider all the way to the right to 100% (**Figure 14.63**).

Add a Hue/Saturation adjustment layer, and in the properties, click on the Clipping Mask icon so that the adjustment is restricted to the layer directly below. Then drag the Saturation slider to -100 and the Lightness slider to -44 (**Figure 14.64**).

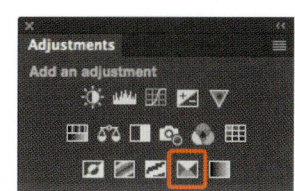

FIGURE 14.62

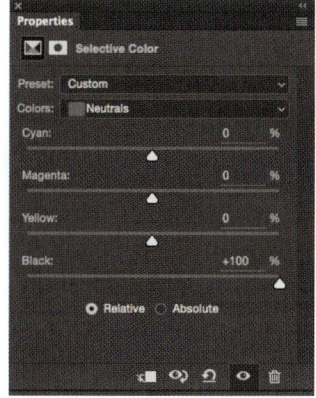

FIGURE 14.63   FIGURE 14.64

22. Click on the Clean Up layer and use the Lasso Tool (**L**) to drag out a selection of the dark rubber area on the shoes of the man sitting in the chair (**Figure 14.65**).

Press Command + J (Mac) or Ctrl + J (PC) to put this selection on its own layer and rename the layer "Shoe." Then go to *Edit > Free Transform*, and while holding down Shift + Option (Mac) or Shift + Alt (PC), click on the upper-left transform handle and drag it outward until the transform frame is bigger than the sole of the shoe (**Figure 14.66**).

Press Return (Mac) or Enter (PC), and then add a Layer Mask to the Shoe layer. With a round, soft-edged brush and black foreground color, paint away areas of this layer so that it appears to cover only the sole of the shoe (**Figure 14.67**).

TIP *When you're painting away excess areas, try lowering the Opacity of the layer with the Layer Mask so you can see where you need to paint (**Figure 14.68**).*

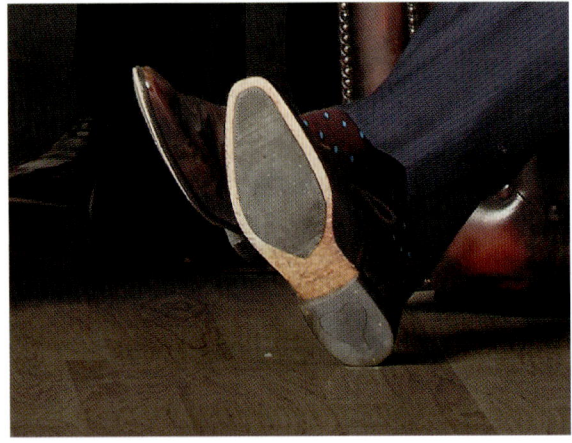

FIGURE 14.65

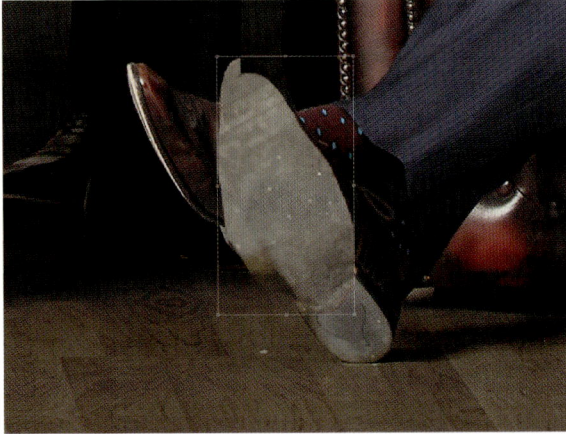

FIGURE 14.66

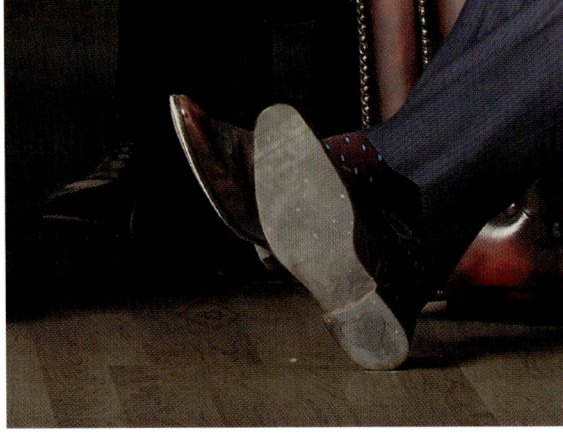

FIGURE 14.67

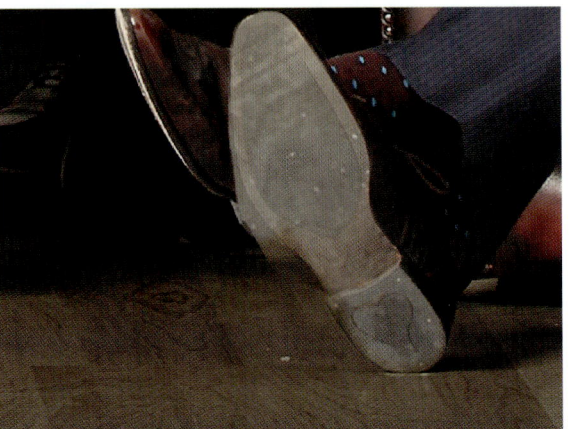

FIGURE 14.68

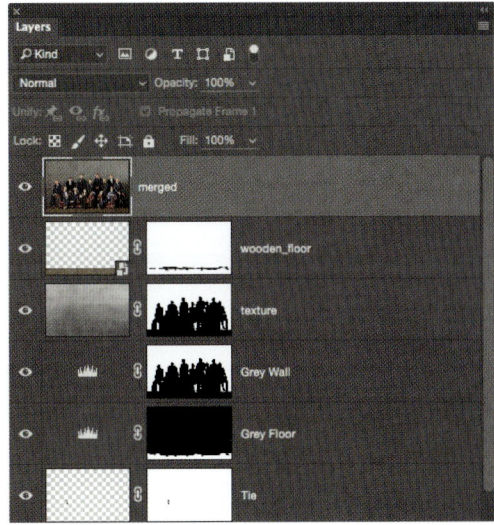

FIGURE 14.69

23. Click on the uppermost layer in the layer stack (wooden_floor) and add a merged layer to the top of the stack by going to *Select > All*, then *Edit > Copy Merged*, and then *Edit > Paste* [or use the keyboard shortcut Shift + Option + Command + E (Mac) or Shift + Alt + Ctrl+ E (PC)]. Rename this layer "merged" (**Figure 14.69**).

24. Go to *Filter > Camera RAW Filter*, choose the Graduated Filter (**Figure 14.70**), and drag a gradient from the bottom of the picture up to just above the subjects' shoes (**Figure 14.71**).

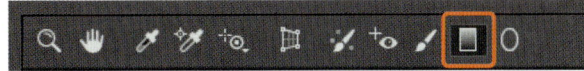

FIGURE 14.70

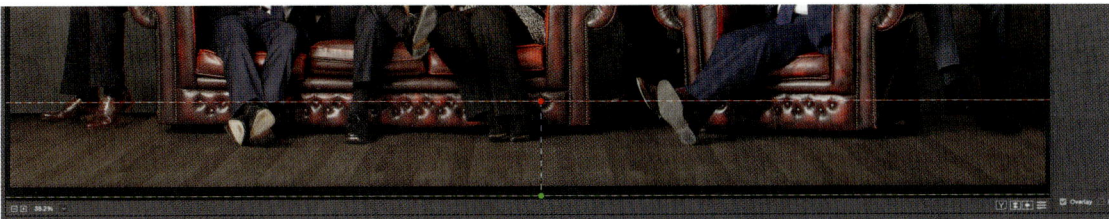

FIGURE 14.71

FIGURE 14.72

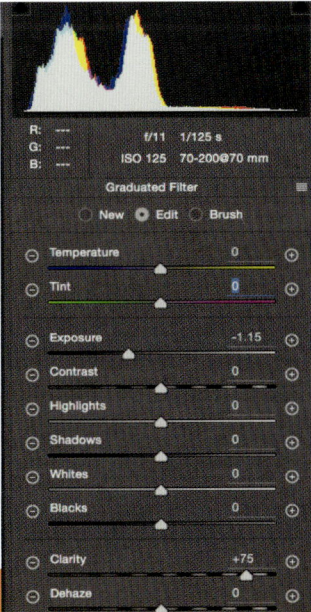

In the settings over on the right side of the window, reduce the Exposure to -1.15 and increase the Clarity to +75 (**Figure 14.72**).

25. Click New (**Figure 14.73**) and drag a gradient from the top of the picture down to the top of the standing subjects' heads (**Figure 14.74**). In the settings on the right side of the window, keep the Exposure as before (-1.15) and set the Clarity to 0 (**Figure 14.75**).

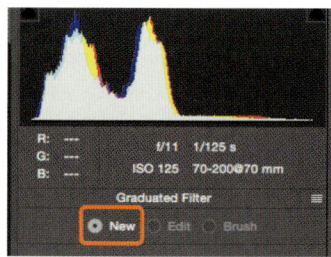

FIGURE 14.73

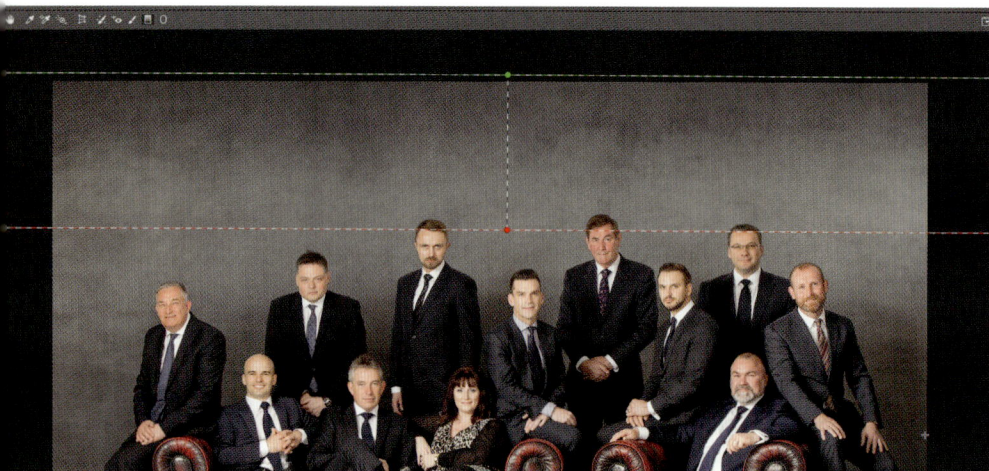

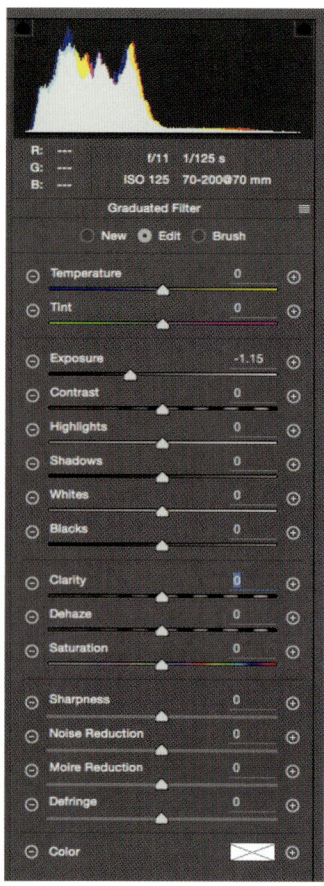

FIGURE 14.75

26. Choose the Radial Filter (**Figure 14.76**) and drag out a vignette from the center of the image (**Figure 14.77**). Set the Exposure to -1.15 once again.

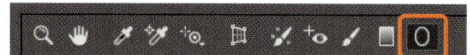

FIGURE 14.76

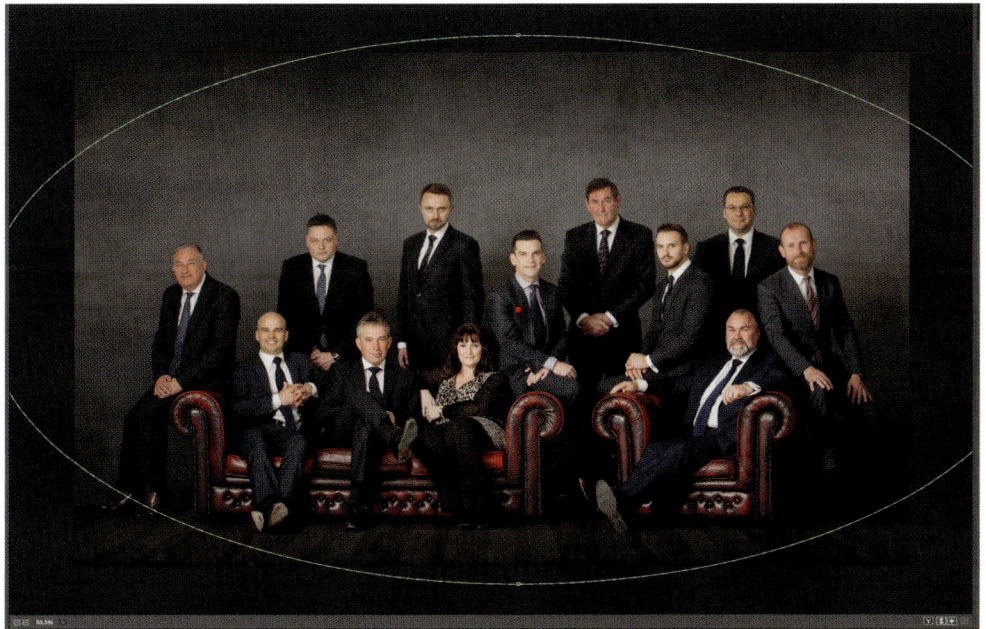

FIGURE 14.77

27. Choose the Adjustment Brush (**Figure 14.78**) and brush over the soles of the shoes on the far left of the picture, then reduce the Exposure to -1.60 to darken them further (**Figure 14.79**).

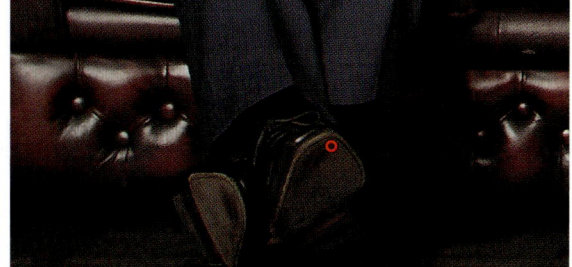

FIGURE 14.79

FIGURE 14.78

28. Now we'll alter the subjects' skin tones with the Adjustment Brush. Click on New under Adjustment Brush (**Figure 14.80**), and then brush over the male subject whose face is a bit more red than the others (**Figure 14.81**). In the settings on the right side of the window, move the tint slider to around -14 and the Temperature slider to around -9 to reduce the redness. Then increase the Exposure to +0.05 (**Figure 14.82**).

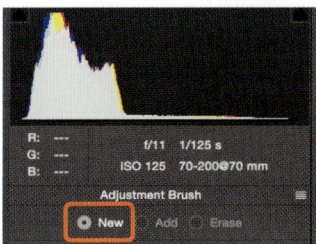

FIGURE 14.80

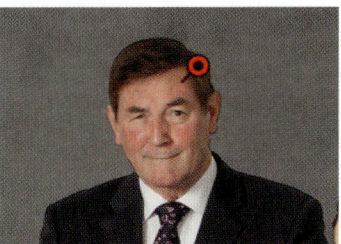

FIGURE 14.81

FIGURE 14.82

Repeat these steps, adding a New Adjustment Brush to brush over each subject's face and using the settings on the right to adjust their skin tone (e.g., reduce the yellow, increase exposure, etc.).

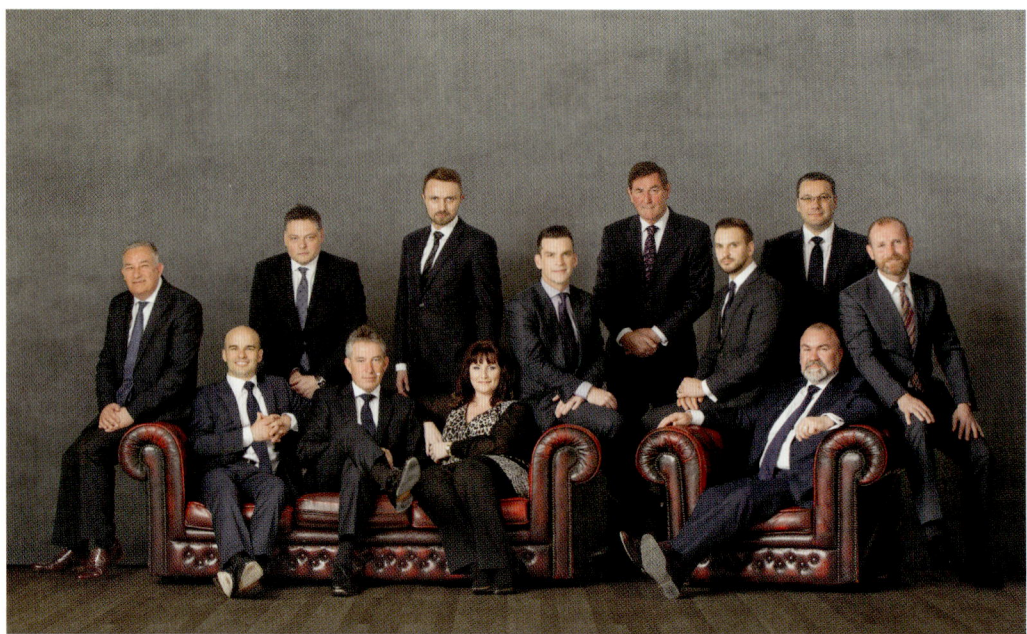

FIGURE 14.83 Before

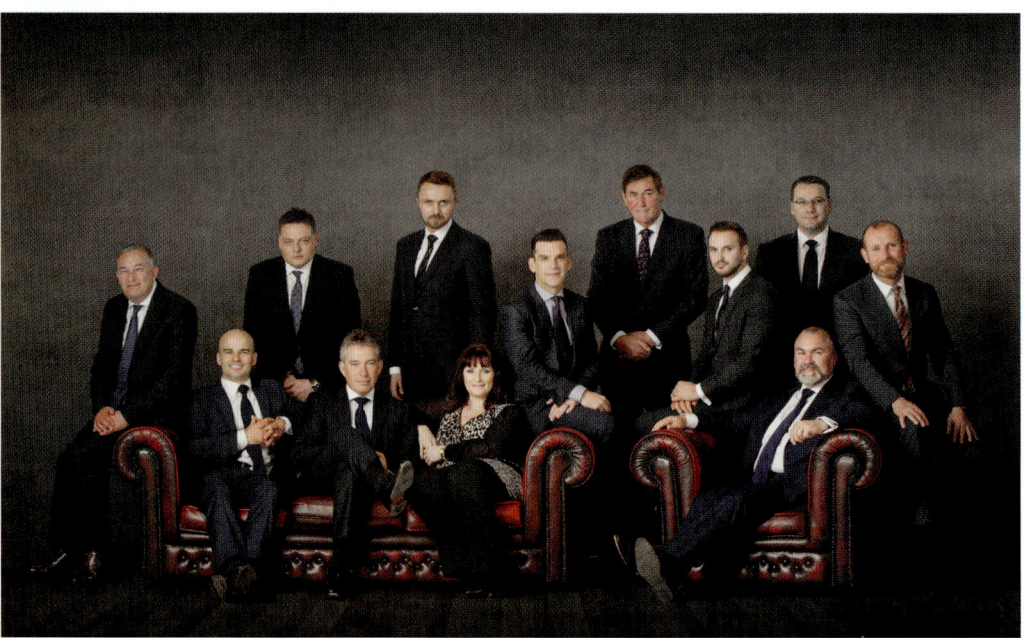

FIGURE 14.84 After

29. Click OK to return to Photoshop. Now it's time for some finishing touches, such as colorizing and contrast. First, press Command + J (Mac) or Ctrl + J (PC) to duplicate the merged layer and rename it "FT" for Finishing Touches.

Let's start off by colorizing the picture. This time, I'm going to use the free Nik Color Efex Pro 4 plugin. Go to *Filter > Nik Collection > Color Efex Pro 4*. Choose Cross Processing (**Figure 14.85**), and in the presets, choose Y06 from the Method menu and set Strength to 22% (**Figure 14.86**). Then click Add Filter.

Choose Cross Balance (**Figure 14.87**), and in the presets, choose Tungsten to Daylight (1) from the drop-down menu and set Strength to 70% (**Figure 14.88**). Then click Add Filter.

Click on Colorize (**Figure 14.89**), and in the presets, select 2 from the Method menu and set Strength to 15% (**Figure 14.90**). Click OK to apply the overall effect and return to Photoshop.

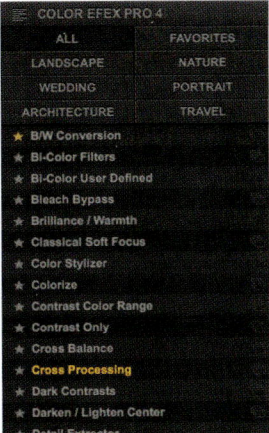

FIGURE 14.85

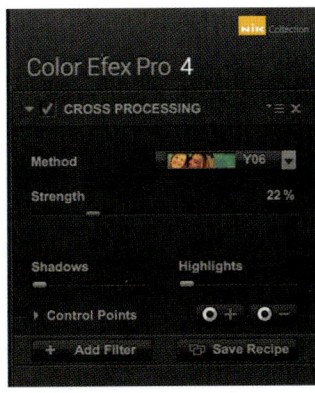

FIGURE 14.86

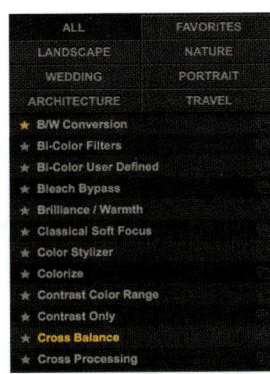

FIGURE 14.87

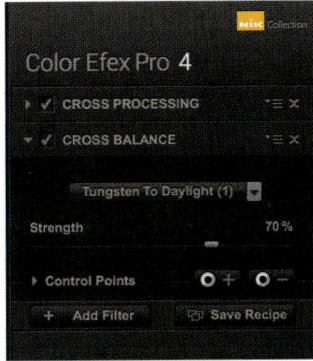

FIGURE 14.88

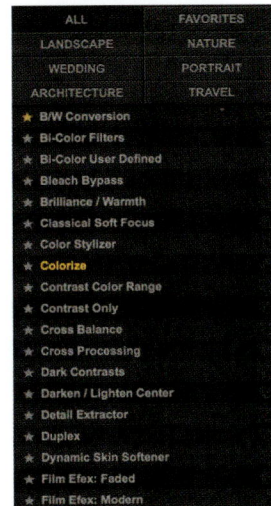

FIGURE 14.89

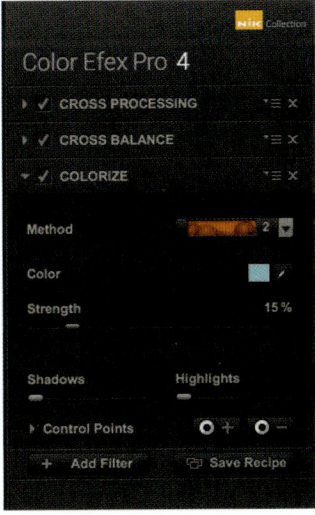

FIGURE 14.90

30. Now we'll add in some contrast. I'm going to use the Topaz Clarity plugin. Go to *Filter > Topaz Labs > Topaz Clarity*, and in the settings, increase Micro Contrast to 0.25 and Low Contrast to 0.10 (**Figure 14.91**), and then click OK.

31. Press **D** to set the foreground and background colors to their defaults of black and white. Click on the Gradient Map icon in the Adjustments panel to add a Gradient Map adjustment layer (**Figure 14.92**), and then lower the Opacity of this layer to 25% to slightly desaturate the image.

Press Command + E (Mac) or Ctrl + E (PC) to merge the Gradient Map adjustment layer with the layer directly beneath it. Then go to *Filter > Camera RAW Filter* and finish by increasing the Temperature slider to +12 (**Figure 14.93**).

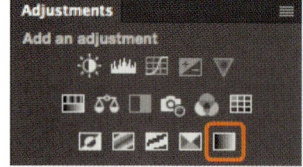

FIGURE 14.91

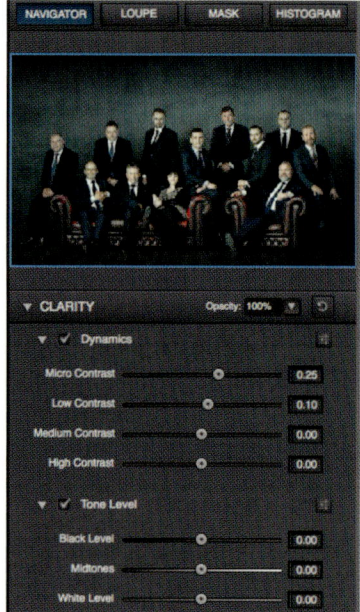

FIGURE 14.92

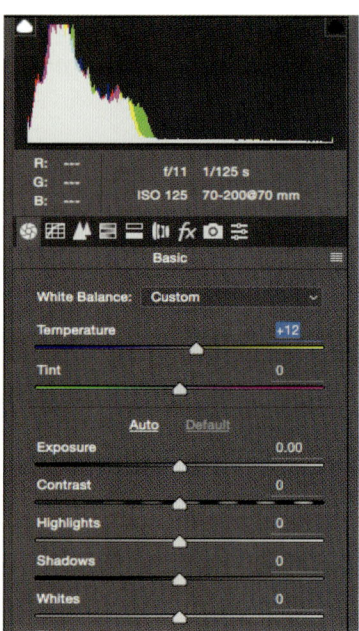

FIGURE 14.93

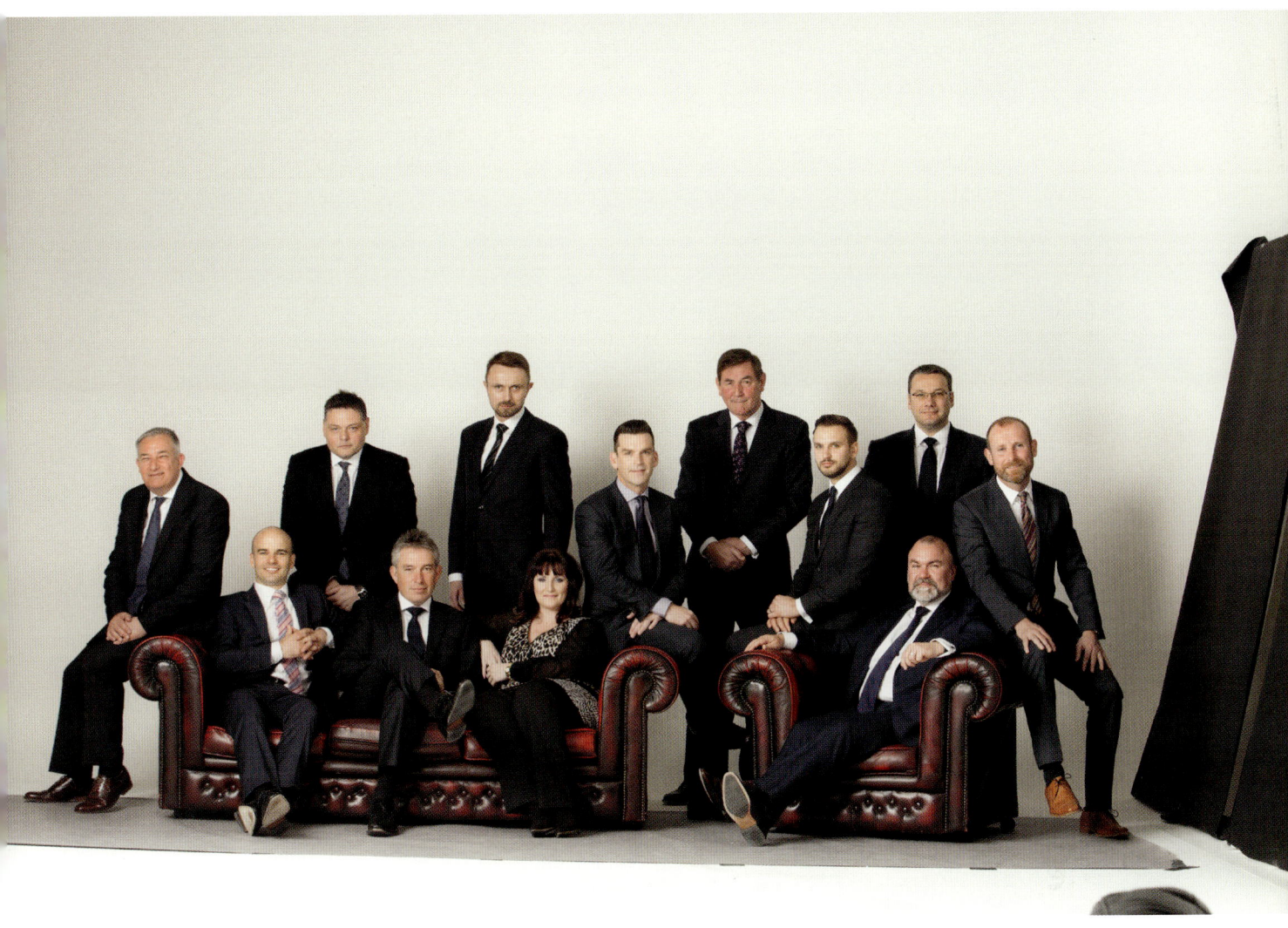

FIGURE 14.94 Original RAW image

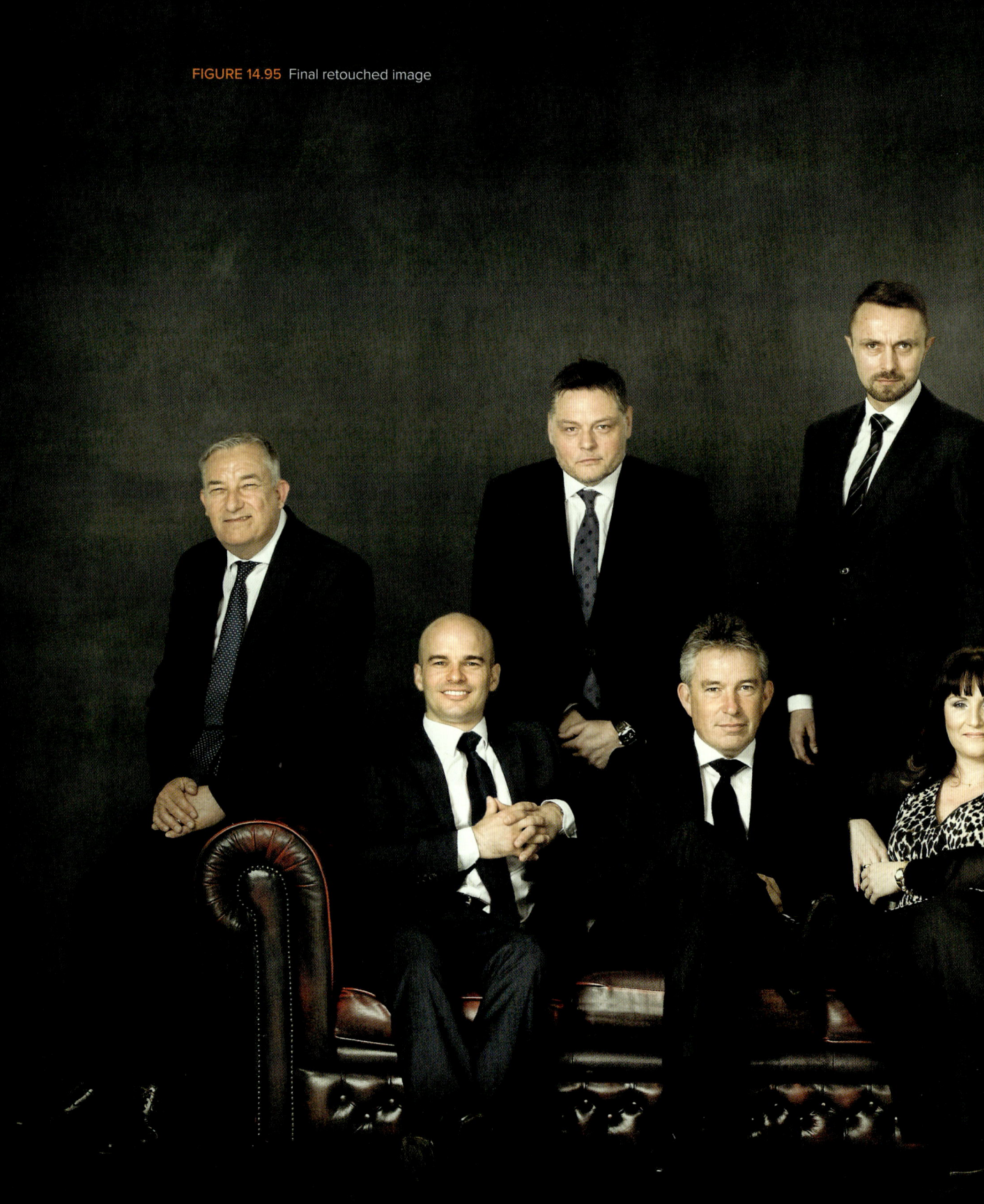

FIGURE 14.95 Final retouched image

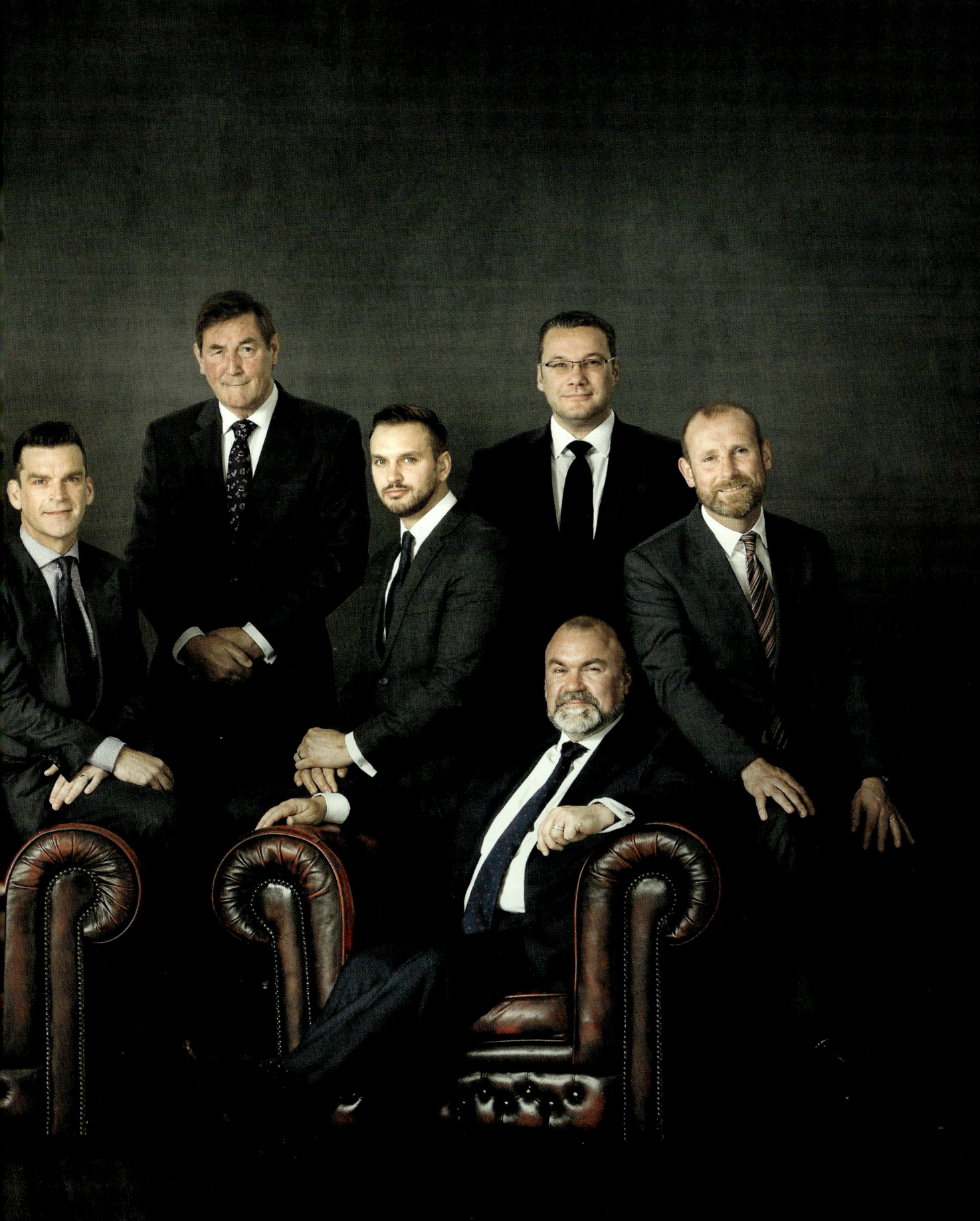

INDEX

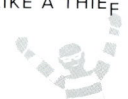

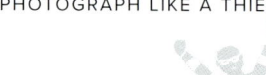